Lecture Notes in Computer Scie

Francesco Logozzo Doron A. Peled
Lenore D. Zuck (Eds.)

Verification, Model Checking, and Abstract Interpretation

9th International Conference, VMCAI 2008
San Francisco, USA, January 7-9, 2008
Proceedings

Springer

Volume Editors

Francesco Logozzo
One Microsoft Way, Redmond, WA, 8052, USA
E-mail: logozzo@microsoft.com

Doron A. Peled
Bar-Ilan University
Department of Computer Science
Ramat Gan, 52900, Israel
E-mail: doron.peled@gmail.com

Lenore D. Zuck
University of Illinois at Chicago
Department of Computer Science
SEO-1125, 851 S. Morgan St Chicago, IL 60607
E-mail: lenorezuck@gmail.com

Library of Congress Control Number: 2008921735

CR Subject Classification (1998): F.3.1-2, D.3.1, D.2.4

LNCS Sublibrary: SL 1 – Theoretical Computer Science and General Issues

ISSN 0302-9743
ISBN-10 3-540-78162-5 Springer Berlin Heidelberg New York
ISBN-13 978-3-540-78162-2 Springer Berlin Heidelberg New York

Springer is a part of Springer Science+Business Media

springer.com

Printed in Germany

Typesetting: Camera-ready by author, data conversion by Scientific Publishing Services, Chennai, India
Printed on acid-free paper SPIN: 12228195 06/3180 5 4 3 2 1 0

Preface

This volume contains the proceedings of the 9th international conference on Verification, Model Checking, and Abstract Interpretation (VMCAI 2008), held in San Francisco, January 7–9, 2008. The purpose of VMCAI is to provide a forum for researchers from three communities—Verification, Model Checking, and Abstract Interpretation— that will facilitate interaction, cross-fertilization, and the advance of hybrid methods that combine the three areas. With the growing need for formal tools to reason about complex, infinite-state, and embedded systems, such hybrid methods are bound to be of great importance.

Topics covered by VMCAI include program verification, program certification, model checking, debugging techniques, abstract interpretation, abstract domains, static analysis, type systems, deductive methods, and optimization.

VMCAI 2008 was the 9th VMCAI meeting. Previous meetings were held in Port Jefferson 1997, Pisa 1998, Venice 2002, New York 2003, Venice 2004, Paris 2005, Charleston 2006, and Nice 2007.

The program committee selected 21 papers out of over 60 on the basis of at least three reviews. The principal criteria were relevance and quality. The program of VMCAI 2008 included, in addition to the research papers, three invited talks, by Radhia Cousot, Maurice Herlihy and Neil Jones, and three tutorials, by Orna Kupferman, Jens Palsberg, and Marco Pistoia.

We would like to thank the Program Committee members and the reviewers, without whose dedicated effort the conference would not have been possible. Our thanks also to the Steering Committee members for their helpful advice. Thanks to Radu Grosu, the local arrangement chair. Special thanks are due to Venkat Vishwanath for handling the Web site. Alfred Hofmann and his team at Springer-Verlag were very helpful in preparing the proceedings.

Special thanks are due to the institutions that helped sponsor this event: the University of Illinois at Chicago and Microsoft.

January 2008

Francesco Logozzo
Doron A. Peled
Lenore D. Zuck

Organization

Program Chairs

Francesco Logozzo	Microsoft Research, Redmond, USA
Doron A. Peled	The University of Warwick, UK
Lenore D. Zuck	University of Illinois at Chicago, USA

Program Committee

Roberto Bagnara	University of Parma, Italy
Christel Baier	Technische Universität Dresden, Germany
Clark Barrett	New York University, USA
Agostino Cortesi	Università Ca' Foscari, Venice, Italy
Radhia Cousot	CNRS, Paris, France
Nicolas Halbwachs	Vérimag, Grenoble, France
Thomas Henzinger	École Polytechnique Fédérale de Lausanne, Switzerland
Michael Huth	Imperial College, London, UK
Orna Kupferman	Hebrew University, Jerusalem, Israel
K. Rustan M. Leino	Microsoft Research, Redmond, USA
Alan Mycroft	Cambridge University, UK
Catuscia Palamidessi	INRIA, Paris, France
Frank Pfenning	Carnegie Mellon University, Pittsburgh, USA
Andreas Podelski	University of Freiburg, Germany
Tayssir Touili	CNRS, Paris, France
Andrei Voronkov	The University of Manchester, UK

Steering Committee

Agostino Cortesi	Università Ca' Foscari, Venice, Italy
Patrick Cousot	École Normale Supérieure, Paris, France
Allen E. Emerson	University of Texas at Austin, USA
Giorgio Levi	University of Pisa, Italy
Andreas Podelski	University of Freiburg, Germany
Thomas W. Reps	University of Wisconsin-Madison, USA
David A. Schmidt	Kansas State University, USA
Lenore D. Zuck	University of Illinois at Chicago, USA

External Reviewers

Hasan Amjad
Jesus Aranda
Stephan Arlt
Eugene Asarin
Sebastien Bardin
Julien Bertrane
Thierry Cachat
Krischnendu Chatterjee
Kostas Chatzikokolakis
Adam Chlipala
Nicoletta Cocco
Christopher Conway
Silvia Crafa
Alessandro Dal Palú
Florent de Dinechin
Dino Distefano
Laurent Doyen
Jérôme Feret
Jean-Claude Fernandez
Pietro Ferrara
Dana Fisman
Enrico Franchi
Blaise Genest
Alexey Gotsman
Nevin Heintze
Patricia Hill
Himanshu Jain
Ranjit Jhala
Barbara Jobstmann
Jerome Leroux
Etienne Lozes
Denis Lugiez
Yoad Lustig
Stephen Magill
Damien Massé
Maria Mateescu
Laurent Mauborgne
Sean McLaughlin
Antoine Miné
David Monniaux
Arjan Mooij
Matthieu Moy
Nicholas Nethercote
Carlos Olarte
Mathias Peron
Nir Piterman
Claudia Pons
Francesco Ranzato
Jean-Francois Raskin
Pascal Raymond
Xavier Rival
Adam Rogalewicz
Marco Roveri
Andrey Rybalchenko
Arnaud Sangnier
Sriram Sankaranarayanan
Sven Schewe
Russell Schwartz
Olivier Serre
Mihaela Sighireanu
Fausto Spoto
Tobe Toben
Claus Traulsen
Angelo Troina
Viktor Vafeiadis
Frank Valencia
Tomas Vojnar
Peng Wu
Farn Wang
Thomas Wies
Greta Yorsh
Laurent Van Begin
Enea Zaffanella

Table of Contents

Abstract Interpretation of Non-monotone Bi-inductive Semantic Definitions*,**

Radhia Cousot

CNRS, Paris, France
radhia.cousot@ens.fr

Divergence/nonterminating behaviors definitely need to be considered in static program analysis [13][1], in particular for typing [2,11].

Divergence information is part of the classical order-theoretic fixpoint denotational semantics [12] but not explicit in small-step/abstract-machine-based operational semantics [14,15,16] and absent of big-step/natural operational semantics [8]. A standard approach is therefore to generate an execution trace semantics from a (labelled) transition system/small-step operational semantics, using either an order-theoretic [3] or metric [19] fixpoint definition or else a categorical definition as a final coalgebra for a behavior functor (modeling the transition relation) up to a weak bisimulation [7,10,18] or using an equational definition for recursion in an order-enriched category [9].

However, the description of execution traces by small steps may be impractical as compared to a compositional definition using big steps. Moreover, execution traces are not always at an appropriate level of abstraction and relational semantics often look more natural.

We introduce *bi-inductive structural definitions*, a simple order-theoretic generalization of structural set-theoretic inductive definitions [14,15,16]. This generalization covers inductive, co-inductive and bi-inductive definitions which allows simultaneous inductive and co-inductive definitions, possibly non-monotone, a case extending [6]. These bi-inductive structural definitions can be presented in several equivalent forms including fixpoints and rule-based definitions. The notion of bi-inductive structural definitions unifies the various presentations of semantics and static analyzes in apparently different styles.

Bi-inductive structural definitions can be used in *bi-finite structural semantics* since it allows the simultaneous definition of finite/terminating and infinite/diverging behaviors — in both big-step and small-step styles. Using induction only would exclude infinite behaviors while using co-induction only might introduce spurious finite behaviors (for example in big-step relational semantics).

---

* Joint work with Patrick Cousot, École normale supérieure, Paris, France.

** This work was done in the project team Abstraction common to the CNRS, INRIA and the École normale supérieure.

[1] For example, the authors of [17] state that their "work is the first provably correct strictness analysis and call-by-name to call-by-value transformation for an untyped higher-order language" but since the considered big-step semantics does not account for divergence, the considered analysis is not *strictness* [13] but a weaker *needness* analysis.

F. Logozzo et al. (Eds.): VMCAI 2008, LNCS 4905, pp. 1–3, 2008.

The bi-inductive structural definitions are illustrated on the structural bi-finitary semantics of the call-by-value λ-calculus [14,15,16] (for which co-induction is shown to be inadequate). The finite and infinite behaviors are specified both in small/big-step style and at various levels of abstractions thus generalizing and completing [3] in which only transition-based — that is small step — semantics are considered.

The bi-inductive structural definitions are preserved by abstraction. This allows to prove the soundness and completeness of semantics at various levels of abstraction by abstract interpretation [1,4,5].

This is illustrated on the eager λ-calculus by abstraction of a trace semantics into a relational semantics and a reduction operational semantics. We get the following hierarchy of semantics

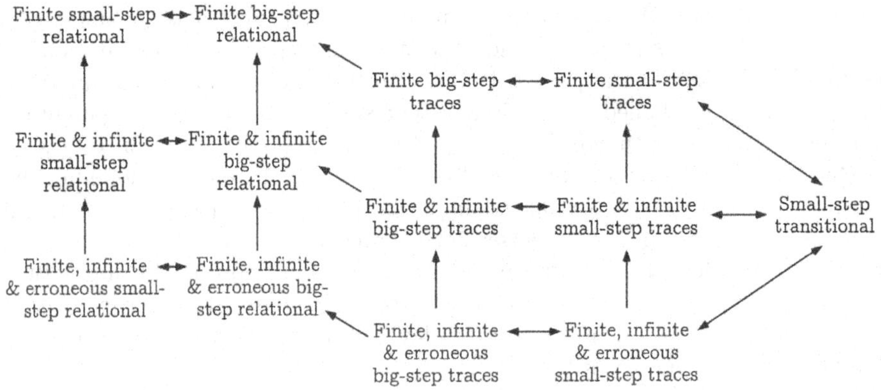

This proves that all the semantics are well-behaved in the sense that they abstract the intuitive small-step trace semantics.

In conclusion bi-inductive definitions should satisfy the need for formal semantics describing both finite and infinite behaviors, at various levels of abstraction, and in different styles, despite the possible absence of monotony. Static analysis algorithms can also be presented using bi-inductive definitions thus unifying the fixpoint and rule-based approaches.

References

1. Cousot, P.: Méthodes itératives de construction et d'approximation de points fixes d'opérateurs monotones sur un treillis, analyse sémantique de programmes (in French). In: Thèse d'État ès sciences mathématiques, Université scientifique et médicale de Grenoble, Grenoble, France (March 21, 1978)
2. Cousot, P.: Types as abstract interpretations, invited paper. In: Conference Record of the Twentyfourth Annual ACM SIGPLAN-SIGACT Symposium on Principles of Programming Languages, January 1997, pp. 316–331. ACM Press, New York (1997)
3. Cousot, P.: Constructive design of a hierarchy of semantics of a transition system by abstract interpretation. Theoretical Computer Science 277(1—2), 47–103 (2002)

4. Cousot, P., Cousot, R.: Abstract interpretation: A unified lattice model for static analysis of programs by construction or approximation of fixpoints. In: Conference Record of the Fourth Annual ACM SIGPLAN-SIGACT Symposium on Principles of Programming Languages, Los Angeles, California, pp. 238–252. ACM Press, New York (1977)
5. Cousot, P., Cousot, R.: Systematic design of program analysis frameworks. In: Conference Record of the Sixth Annual ACM SIGPLAN-SIGACT Symposium on Principles of Programming Languages, pp. 269–282. ACM Press, New York (1979)
6. Cousot, P., Cousot, R.: Inductive definitions, semantics and abstract interpretation. In: Conference Record of the Nineteenth Annual ACM SIGPLAN-SIGACT Symposium on Principles of Programming Languages, pp. 83–94. ACM Press, New York (1992)
7. Jacobs, B., Rutten, J.: A tutorial on (co)algebras and (co)induction. EATCS Bulletin 62, 222–269 (1997)
8. Kahn, G.: Natural semantics. In: Fuchi, K., Nivat, M. (eds.) Programming of Future Generation Computers, pp. 237–258. Elsevier Science Publishers, B.V., Amsterdam, The Netherlands (1988)
9. Klin, B.: Adding recursive constructs to bialgebraic semantics. Journal of Logic and Algebraic Programming 60-61, 259–286 (2004)
10. Klin, B.: Bialgebraic methods in structural operational semantics. Electronic Notes in Theoretical Computer Science 175(1), 33–43 (2007)
11. Leroy, X.: Coinductive big-step operational semantics. In: Sestoft, P. (ed.) ESOP 2006 and ETAPS 2006. LNCS, vol. 3924, pp. 54–68. Springer, Heidelberg (2006)
12. Mosses, P.D.: Denotational semantics. In: van Leeuwen, J. (ed.) Formal Models and Semantics, volume B of Handbook of Theoretical Computer Science, vol. 11, pp. 575–631. Elsevier Science Publishers, B.V., Amsterdam, The Netherlands (1990)
13. Mycroft, A.: The theory and practice of transforming call-by-need into call-by-value. In: Robinet, B. (ed.) Programming 1980. LNCS, vol. 83, pp. 270–281. Springer, Berlin, Germany (1980)
14. Plotkin, G.D.: A structural approach to operational semantics. Technical Report DAIMI FN-19, Aarhus University, Denmark (September 1981)
15. Plotkin, G.D.: The origins of structural operational semantics. Journal of Logic and Algebraic Programming 60–61, 3–15 (2004)
16. Plotkin, G.D.: A structural approach to operational semantics. Journal of Logic and Algebraic Programming 60–61, 17–139 (2004)
17. Steckler, P., Wand, M.: Selective thunkification. In: Le Charlier, B. (ed.) SAS 1994. LNCS, vol. 864, pp. 162–178. Springer, Heidelberg (1994)
18. Turi, D., Plotkin, G.D.: Towards a mathematical operational semantics. In: Proceedings of the Twelfth LICS 1997, Warsaw, Poland,, California, United States, June 29 – July 2, 1997, pp. 280–291. IEEE Computer Society Press, Los Alamitos (1997)
19. van Breugel, F.: An introduction to metric semantics: operational and denotational models for programming and specification languages. Theoretical Computer Science 258, 1–98 (2001)

CTL as an Intermediate Language

Neil D. Jones[1] and René Rydhof Hansen[2]

[1] DIKU, University of Copenhagen (retired)
neil@diku.dk
[2] Department of Computer Science, Aalborg University
rrh@cs.aau.dk

Abstract. The Coccinelle system is a program transformer used to automate and document collateral evolutions in Linux device drivers. Semantics are developed for the its underlying *semantic patch language* (SmPL). A richer and more efficient version is defined, implemented by compiling to the temporal logic CTL-V as an intermediate language.

This invited talk overviews [1], and describes as well a semantics example, a correctness proof, and sketches a model checker [2]. Two semantics are developed for the core of Coccinelle [3,4]: one a traditional continuation semantics, and an alternative that uses a temporal logic as intermediate compiling language.

The first semantics is denotational – in essence a higher-order functional program and so executable, but inefficient and limited to straight-line source programs. The alternative of compiling into CTL-V (as in [3]) ameliorates both problems. The compilation is proven correct and a model check algorithm is outlined. CTL-V is CTL extended with existentially quantified variables ranging over source code parameters and program points. Quantification is defined using the staging concept from partial evaluation. Related work includes [5,6,7].

References

1. Jones, N.D., Hansen, R.R.: The semantics of semantic patches in Coccinelle: Program transformation for the working programmer. In: Shao, Z. (ed.) APLAS 2007. LNCS, vol. 4807, pp. 303–318. N.D. Jones, R.R. Hansen, Heidelberg (2007)
2. Jones, N.D., Hansen, R.R.: Technical appendix to [1]. (unpublished) (2007), `http://www.diku.dk//hjemmesider/ansatte/neil/sempatch.pdf`
3. Padioleau, Y., et al.: Semantic patches for documenting and automating collateral evolutions in Linux device drivers. In: PLOS 2006: Proc. of workshop on Programming languages and operating systems, p. 10 (2006)
4. Coccinelle project home page, `http://www.emn.fr/x-info/coccinelle/`
5. De Moor, O., Lacey, D., Van Wyk, E.: Universal regular path queries. Higher-order and Symbolic Computation 16(1-2), 15–35 (2003)
6. Liu, Y.A., et al.: Parametric regular path queries. In: PLDI 2004: Proceedings of the ACM SIGPLAN 2004 conf. on Programming language design and implementation, pp. 219–230. ACM Press, New York (2004)
7. Lacey, D., et al.: Compiler optimization correctness by temporal logic. Higher Order and Symbolic Computation 17(3), 173–206 (2004)

F. Logozzo et al. (Eds.): VMCAI 2008, LNCS 4905, p. 4, 2008.

Multi-valued Logics, Automata, Simulations, and Games

Orna Kupferman and Yoad Lustig

Hebrew University, School of Engineering and Computer Science, Jerusalem 91904, Israel
{orna,yoadl}@cs.huji.ac.il

Multi-valued systems are systems in which the atomic propositions and the transitions are not Boolean and can take values from some set. *Latticed systems*, in which the elements in the set are partially ordered, are useful in abstraction, query checking, and reasoning about multiple view-points. For example, abstraction involves systems in which an atomic proposition can take values from $\{true, unknown, false\}$, and these values can be partially ordered according to a "being more true" order ($true \geq unknown \geq false$) or according to a "being more informative" order ($true \geq unknown$ and $false \geq unknown$). For Boolean temporal logics, researchers have developed a rich and beautiful theory that is based on viewing formulas as descriptors of languages of infinite words or trees. This includes a relation between temporal-logic formulas and automata on infinite objects, a theory of simulation relation between systems, a theory of two-player games, and a study of the relations among these notions. The theory is very useful in practice, and is the key to almost all algorithms and tools we see today in verification.

Since traditional temporal logics are Boolean, the automata, simulation relations, and games are Boolean too: An automaton may accept or reject its input, a system may or may not simulate another system, and a player either wins or loses a game. When we interpret temporal-logic formulas over latticed systems, the truth value of a formula is a lattice element, and it essentially denotes the truth value of the statement "the system satisfies the formula". We study an extension of automata, simulation relations, and games to such a setting. We start by introducing *latticed automata*. A lattice automaton $\mathcal{A}$ associates with an input word w a lattice element that denotes the truth value of the statement "w is in the language of $\mathcal{A}$". Our study of lattice automata includes their expressive power, closure properties, the blow-up involved in related constructions (in terms of the size of both the automaton and the underlying lattice), and decision problems for them. We continue to *latticed simulation relations*, which associate with two systems $\mathcal{S}_1$ and $\mathcal{S}_2$ a lattice element that denotes the truth value of the statement "every behavior of $\mathcal{S}_1$ is also a behavior of $\mathcal{S}_2$". We show that latticed simulation is logically characterized by the universal fragment of latticed μ-calculus, and can be calculated in polynomial time. We then proceed to defining *latticed two-player games*. As you may guess by now, the value of the game denotes the truth value of the statement "Player 1 can force the game to computations that satisfy the winning condition".[1] We prove a min-max property for latticed games, and show that they can be solved by decomposition to Boolean games. Finally, we relate the three latticed notions, and conclude that most of the properties that these notions enjoy in the Boolean setting are maintained in the latticed setting.

[1] Well, this is not obvious; you may have also guessed that the value of the game is a lattice element l such that Player 1 can force the game to computations that satisfy the winning condition with truth value at least l. Do these definitions coincide?

F. Logozzo et al. (Eds.): VMCAI 2008, LNCS 4905, p. 5, 2008.

Verification of Register Allocators

Jens Palsberg

UCLA Computer Science Department
University of California, Los Angeles, USA
palsberg@ucla.edu
http://www.cs.ucla.edu/~palsberg

A register allocator is difficult to write and debug. The task is to assign hardware registers to as many program variables as possible, assign memory locations to the rest, and avoid memory traffic to the extent possible. A good register allocator can produce code that is 2.5 times faster than code generated by a naive register allocator.

I will survey recent approaches to verification of register allocators. The goal is to answer three questions: What is correctness of a register allocator and how can we specify it? How can we specify a register allocator such that we can reason about it? Which proof techniques can we use?

I will cover four rather different approaches. One approach uses a type system to check the output of a register allocator [1]. We have implemented the type system in LLVM and found it to be highly useful for finding bugs in register allocators. A second approach is to prove the correctness of a constraint-based specification of a register allocator. We have carried out such a proof for Appel and George's ILP-based register allocator [2]. A third approach is to prove the correctness of a step-by-step specification of a register allocator. The proof amounts to proving a preservation theorem that establishes an invariant for the register allocator; we have carried out such a proof for a register allocator based on puzzle solving [3]. A fourth approach is to prove the correctness of the original program and then specify register allocation as proof transformation [4].

Jens Palsberg is a Professor of Computer Science at UCLA. He is an associate editor of ACM Transactions of Programming Languages and Systems, a member of the editorial board of Information and Computation, and a former member of the editorial board of IEEE Transactions on Software Engineering.

References

1. Nandivada, V.K., Pereira, F.M.Q., Palsberg, J.: A Framework for End-to-End Verification and Evaluation of Register Allocators. In: Riis Nielson, H., Filé, G. (eds.) SAS 2007. LNCS, vol. 4634, pp. 153–169. Springer, Heidelberg (2007)
2. Naik, M., Palsberg, J.: Correctness of ILP-based register allocation (2004)
3. Pereira, F.M.Q., Palsberg, J.: Register allocation by puzzle solving (2007), http://compilers.cs.ucla.edu/fernando/projects/puzzles
4. Ohori, A.: Register allocation by proof transformation. Science of Computer Programming 50(1–3), 161–187 (2004)

F. Logozzo et al. (Eds.): VMCAI 2008, LNCS 4905, p. 6, 2008.

Program Analysis and Programming Languages for Security

Marco Pistoia

IBM T.J. Watson Research Center, Hawthorne, New York, USA
pistoia@us.ibm.com

Abstract. The security of a software system is almost always retrofitted to an afterthought. When security problems arise, understanding and correcting them can be very challenging. On the one hand, the program-analysis and programming-languages research community has created numerous static and dynamic analysis tools for performance optimization and bug detection in object-oriented programs. On the other hand, the security and privacy research community has been looking for solutions to automatically detect security problems, information-flow violations, and access-control requirements in object-oriented programs. This tutorial discusses advantages and disadvantages of static and dynamic analysis for automated detection of security problems such as access-control violations and information-flow vulnerabilities.

Contents

Security has progressively become more interesting to the program analysis community. Both static and dynamic program analysis have been extensively applied to security issues, such as access control and information flow. However, there is still high potential for more research on how to apply analysis, testing, and verification to security problems, including:

- Evaluation of security and privacy policies
- Identification of vulnerabilities that could lead to denial of service attacks
- Verification of access control
- Computation of access control requirements
- Identification of mutability, accessibility, and isolation policy violations
- Verification of complete authorization
- Intrusion detection
- Secure programming
- Detection of integrity and confidentiality violations

This tutorial describes the state of the art in program analysis and verification for security, and discusses advantages and disadvantages of different techniques currently used.

F. Logozzo et al. (Eds.): VMCAI 2008, LNCS 4905, p. 7, 2008.

An Improved Tight Closure Algorithm for Integer Octagonal Constraints*

Roberto Bagnara[1], Patricia M. Hill[2], and Enea Zaffanella[1]

[1] Department of Mathematics, University of Parma, Italy
{bagnara,zaffanella}@cs.unipr.it
[2] School of Computing, University of Leeds, UK
hill@comp.leeds.ac.uk

Abstract. Integer octagonal constraints (a.k.a. *Unit Two Variables Per Inequality* or *UTVPI integer constraints*) constitute an interesting class of constraints for the representation and solution of integer problems in the fields of constraint programming and formal analysis and verification of software and hardware systems, since they couple algorithms having polynomial complexity with a relatively good expressive power. The main algorithms required for the manipulation of such constraints are the satisfiability check and the computation of the inferential closure of a set of constraints. The latter is called *tight* closure to mark the difference with the (incomplete) closure algorithm that does not exploit the integrality of the variables. In this paper we present and fully justify an $O(n^3)$ algorithm to compute the tight closure of a set of UTVPI integer constraints.

1 Introduction

Integer octagonal constraints, also called *Unit Two Variables Per Inequality (UTVPI) integer constraints* —that is, constraints of the form $ax + by \leq d$ where $a, b \in \{-1, 0, +1\}$, $d \in \mathbb{Z}$ and the variables x and y range over the integers—, constitute an interesting subclass of linear integer constraints admitting polynomial solvability. The place which these constraints occupy in the complexity/expressivity spectrum is, in fact, peculiar. Concerning complexity, relaxing the restriction of (at most) two variables per constraint and/or relaxing the restriction on coefficient make the satisfiability problem NP-complete [13,14]. Concerning expressivity, integer octagonal constraints can be used for representing and solving many integer problems in the field of constraint programming, such as temporal reasoning and scheduling [13]. In the field of formal analysis and verification of software and hardware systems, these constraints have been successfully used in a number of applications [5,6,9,18].

* This work has been partly supported by MURST project "AIDA — Abstract Interpretation: Design and Applications," and by a Royal Society (UK) International Joint Project (ESEP) award.

F. Logozzo et al. (Eds.): VMCAI 2008, LNCS 4905, pp. 8–21, 2008.

When (integer or rational) octagonal constraints are used to build abstract domains[1] —such as the *Octagon Abstract Domain* implemented in the library with the same name [19] or the domain of *octagonal shapes* defined in [2] and implemented in the *Parma Polyhedra Library* [4]— the most critical operation is not the satisfiability check (although very important in constraint programming) but *closure by entailment*. This is the procedure whereby a set of octagonal constraints is augmented with (a finite representation of) all the octagonal constraints that can be inferred from it. The closure algorithms for rational octagonal constraints are sound but not complete for integer octagonal constraints. The latter require so-called *tight* closure algorithms that fully exploit the integrality of the variables.

In 2005, Lahiri and Musuvathi proposed an $O(n^3)$ algorithm for the satisfiability check of a (non trivially redundant) system of UTVPI integer constraints [15]. They also sketched (without formal definitions and proofs) a tight closure algorithm with the same worst-case complexity bound. Still in 2005, Miné proposed a modification of the strong (i.e., non-tight) closure algorithm for *rational* octagonal constraints and argued that this would provide a good and efficient approximation of tight closure [18,19]. In the same year we showed that the algorithm for computing the strong closure of rational octagonal constraints as described in [16,18,19] could be simplified with a consequential improvement in its efficiency [2,3]. In this paper we show that our result can be extended so as to apply to integer octagonal constraints. This enables us to present and fully justify an $O(n^3)$ algorithm to compute the tight closure of a set of UTVPI integer constraints. In particular, this is the first time that an algorithm achieving such a complexity bound is provided with a proof of correctness.

In Section 2 we briefly introduce the terminology and notation adopted throughout the paper and we recall a few standard results on weighted graphs. In Section 3, we give the definition of rational-weighted octagonal graphs and recall some of the results that were established in [2,3]. In Section 4, we extend these results to the case of integer-weighted octagonal graphs. Finally, in Section 5 we conclude and briefly discuss future work.

2 Preliminaries

Let $\mathbb{Q}_\infty := \mathbb{Q} \cup \{+\infty\}$ be totally ordered by the extension of '$<$' such that $d < +\infty$ for each $d \in \mathbb{Q}$. Let $\mathcal{N}$ be a finite set of *nodes*. A *rational-weighted directed graph* (graph, for short) G in $\mathcal{N}$ is a pair $(\mathcal{N}, w)$, where $w \colon \mathcal{N} \times \mathcal{N} \to \mathbb{Q}_\infty$ is the weight function for G.

Let $G = (\mathcal{N}, w)$ be a graph. A pair $(n_i, n_j) \in \mathcal{N} \times \mathcal{N}$ is an *arc* of G if $w(n_i, n_j) < +\infty$; the arc is *proper* if $n_i \neq n_j$. A *path* $\pi = n_0 \cdots n_p$ in G is a non-empty and finite sequence of nodes such that (n_{i-1}, n_i) is an arc of G, for

[1] In *abstract interpretation* theory [8], an *abstract domain* is an algebraic structure formalizing a set of assertions endowed with an approximation relation, plus various operations that correctly approximate the operations of some *concrete domain*, i.e., the domain being abstracted/approximated.

all $i = 1, \ldots, p$. Each node n_i where $i = 0, \ldots, p$ and each arc (n_{i-1}, n_i) where $i = 1, \ldots, p$ is said to be *in* the path π. The *length* of the path π is the number p of occurrences of arcs in π and denoted by $\|\pi\|$; the *weight* of the path π is $\sum_{i=1}^{p} w(n_{i-1}, n_i)$ and denoted by $w(\pi)$. The path π is *simple* if each node occurs at most once in π. The path π is *proper* if all the arcs in it are proper. The path π is a *proper cycle* if it is a proper path, $n_0 = n_p$ and $p \geq 2$. If $\pi_1 = n_0 \cdots n_h$ and $\pi_2 = n_h \cdots n_p$ are paths, where $0 \leq h \leq p$, then the path concatenation $\pi = n_0 \cdots n_h \cdots n_p$ of π_1 and π_2 is denoted by $\pi_1 :: \pi_2$; if $\pi_1 = n_0 n_1$ (so that $h = 1$), then $\pi_1 :: \pi_2$ will also be denoted by $n_0 \cdot \pi_2$. Note that path concatenation is not the same as sequence concatenation.

A graph $(\mathcal{N}, w)$ can be interpreted as the system of *potential constraints*

$$\mathcal{C} := \bigl\{\, n_i - n_j \leq w(n_i, n_j) \bigm| n_i, n_j \in \mathcal{N} \,\bigr\}.$$

Hence, the graph $(\mathcal{N}, w)$ is *consistent* if and only if the system of constraints it represents is satisfiable in $\mathbb{Q}$, i.e., there exists a rational valuation $\rho \colon \mathcal{N} \to \mathbb{Q}$ such that, for each constraint $(n_i - n_j \leq d) \in \mathcal{C}$, the relation $\rho(n_i) - \rho(n_j) \leq d$ holds. It is well-known that a graph is consistent if and only if it has no negative weight cycles (see [7, Section 25.5] and [22]).

The set of consistent graphs in $\mathcal{N}$ is denoted by $\mathbb{G}$. This set is partially ordered by the relation '$\trianglelefteq$' defined, for all $G_1 = (\mathcal{N}, w_1)$ and $G_2 = (\mathcal{N}, w_2)$, by

$$G_1 \trianglelefteq G_2 \quad\iff\quad \forall i, j \in \mathcal{N} : w_1(i, j) \leq w_2(i, j).$$

We write $G \triangleleft G'$ when $G \trianglelefteq G'$ and $G \neq G'$. When augmented with a bottom element $\bot$ representing inconsistency, this partially ordered set becomes a non-complete lattice $\mathbb{G}_\bot = \langle \mathbb{G} \cup \{\bot\}, \trianglelefteq, \sqcap, \sqcup \rangle$, where '$\sqcap$' and '$\sqcup$' denote the finitary greatest lower bound and least upper bound operators, respectively.

Definition 1 (Closed graph). *A consistent graph $G = (\mathcal{N}, w)$ is* closed *if the following properties hold:*

$$\forall i \in \mathcal{N} : w(i, i) = 0; \tag{1}$$

$$\forall i, j, k \in \mathcal{N} : w(i, j) \leq w(i, k) + w(k, j). \tag{2}$$

The (shortest-path) closure *of a consistent graph G in $\mathcal{N}$ is*

$$\mathrm{closure}(G) := \bigsqcup \bigl\{\, G' \in \mathbb{G} \bigm| G' \trianglelefteq G \text{ and } G' \text{ is closed} \,\bigr\}.$$

Although the lattice of rational graphs is not complete, it will include the infinite least upper bound defining the closure of a rational graph G. Informally, this must hold since the weights of the least upper bound graph must be linear combinations of the rational weights of G and hence are also rational.

When trivially extended so as to behave as the identity function on the bottom element $\bot$, shortest-path closure is a kernel operator (monotonic, idempotent and reductive) on the lattice $\mathbb{G}_\bot$, therefore providing a canonical form.

The following lemma recalls a well-known result for closed graphs (for a proof, see Lemma 5 in [3]).

Lemma 1. *Let $G = (\mathcal{N}, w) \in \mathbb{G}$ be a closed graph. Then, for any path $\pi = i \cdots j$ in G, it holds that $w(i, j) \leq w(\pi)$.*

3 Rational Octagonal Graphs

We assume in the following that there is a fixed set $\mathcal{V} = \{v_0, \ldots, v_{n-1}\}$ of n variables. The octagon abstract domain allows for the manipulation of *octagonal constraints* of the form $av_i + bv_j \leq d$, where $a, b \in \{-1, 0, +1\}$, $a \neq 0$, $v_i, v_j \in \mathcal{V}$, $v_i \neq v_j$ and $d \in \mathbb{Q}$. Octagonal constraints can be encoded using potential constraints by splitting each variable v_i into two forms: a positive form v_i^+, interpreted as $+v_i$; and a negative form v_i^-, interpreted as $-v_i$. Then any octagonal constraint $av_i + bv_j \leq d$ can be written as a potential constraint $v - v' \leq d_0$ where $v, v' \in \{v_i^+, v_i^-, v_j^+, v_j^-\}$ and $d_0 \in \mathbb{Q}$. Namely, an octagonal constraint such as $v_i + v_j \leq d$ can be translated into the potential constraint $v_i^+ - v_j^- \leq d$; alternatively, the same octagonal constraint can be translated into $v_j^+ - v_i^- \leq d$. Furthermore, unary (octagonal) constraints such as $v_i \leq d$ and $-v_i \leq d$ can be encoded as $v_i^+ - v_i^- \leq 2d$ and $v_i^- - v_i^+ \leq 2d$, respectively.

From now on, we assume that the set of nodes is $\mathcal{N} := \{0, \ldots, 2n-1\}$. These will denote the positive and negative forms of the variables in $\mathcal{V}$: for all $i \in \mathcal{N}$, if $i = 2k$, then i represents the positive form v_k^+ and, if $i = 2k+1$, then i represents the negative form v_k^- of the variable v_k. To simplify the presentation, for each $i \in \mathcal{N}$, we let $\bar{\imath}$ denote $i+1$, if i is even, and $i-1$, if i is odd, so that, for all $i \in \mathcal{N}$, we also have $\bar{\imath} \in \mathcal{N}$ and $\bar{\bar{\imath}} = i$. Then we can rewrite a potential constraint $v - v' \leq d$ where $v \in \{v_k^+, v_k^-\}$ and $v' \in \{v_l^+, v_l^-\}$ as the potential constraint $i - j \leq d$ in $\mathcal{N}$ where, if $v = v_k^+$, $i = 2k$ and if $v = v_k^-$, $i = 2k+1$; similarly, if $v' = v_l^+$, $j = 2l$ and if $v' = v_l^-$, $j = 2l+1$.

It follows from the above translations that any finite system of octagonal constraints, translated into a set of potential constraints in $\mathcal{N}$ as above, can be encoded by a graph G in $\mathcal{N}$. In particular, any finite *satisfiable* system of octagonal constraints can be encoded by a *consistent* graph in $\mathcal{N}$. However, the converse does not hold since in any valuation ρ of an encoding of a set of octagonal constraints we must also have $\rho(i) = -\rho(\bar{\imath})$, so that the arcs (i, j) and $(\bar{\jmath}, \bar{\imath})$ should have the same weight. Therefore, to encode rational octagonal constraints, we restrict attention to consistent graphs over $\mathcal{N}$ where the arcs in all such pairs are *coherent*.

Definition 2 (Octagonal graph). *A (rational)* octagonal graph *is any consistent graph $G = (\mathcal{N}, w)$ that satisfies the coherence assumption:*

$$\forall i, j \in \mathcal{N} : w(i, j) = w(\bar{\jmath}, \bar{\imath}). \tag{3}$$

The set $\mathbb{O}$ of all octagonal graphs (with the usual addition of the bottom element, representing an unsatisfiable system of constraints) is a sub-lattice of $\mathbb{G}_\perp$, sharing the same least upper bound and greatest lower bound operators. Note that, at the implementation level, coherence can be automatically and efficiently enforced by letting arc (i, j) and arc $(\bar{\jmath}, \bar{\imath})$ share the same representation. This also implies that an octagonal constraint such as $v_i + v_j \leq d$ will always be translated into both $v_i^+ - v_j^- \leq d$ and $v_j^+ - v_i^- \leq d$.

When dealing with octagonal graphs, observe that the coherence assumption links the positive and negative forms of variables. A closure by entailment procedure should consider, besides transitivity, the following inference rule:

$$\frac{i - \bar{\imath} \leq d_1 \qquad \bar{\jmath} - j \leq d_2}{i - j \leq \dfrac{d_1 + d_2}{2}} \tag{4}$$

Thus, the standard shortest-path closure algorithm is not enough to obtain a canonical form for octagonal graphs.

Definition 3 (Strongly closed graph). *An octagonal graph $G = (\mathcal{N}, w)$ is* strongly closed *if it is closed and the following property holds:*

$$\forall i, j \in \mathcal{N} : 2w(i, j) \leq w(i, \bar{\imath}) + w(\bar{\jmath}, j). \tag{5}$$

The strong closure *of an octagonal graph G in $\mathcal{N}$ is*

$$\text{S-closure}(G) := \bigsqcup \bigl\{ G' \in \mathbb{O} \bigm| G' \trianglelefteq G \text{ and } G' \text{ is strongly closed} \bigr\}.$$

When trivially extended with a bottom element, strong closure is a kernel operator on the lattice of octagonal graphs.

A modified closure procedure is defined in [16], yielding strongly closed octagonal graphs. A significant efficiency improvement can be obtained thanks to the following theorem (for a proof, see Theorem 2 in [3]).

Theorem 1. *Let $G = (\mathcal{N}, w)$ be a closed octagonal graph. Consider the graph $G_S = (\mathcal{N}, w_S)$, where w_S is defined, for each $i, j \in \mathcal{N}$, by*

$$w_S(i, j) := \min\left\{ w(i, j), \frac{w(i, \bar{\imath})}{2} + \frac{w(\bar{\jmath}, j)}{2} \right\}.$$

Then $G_S = \text{S-closure}(G)$.

Intuitively, the theorem states that strong closure can be obtained by application of any shortest-path closure algorithm followed by a *single* local propagation step using the constraint inference rule (4). In contrast, in the strong closure algorithm of [16], the outermost iterations of (a variant of) the Floyd-Warshall shortest-path algorithm are interleaved with n applications of the inference rule (4), leading to a more complex and less efficient implementation.

4 Integer Octagonal Graphs

We now consider the case of integer octagonal constraints, i.e., octagonal constraints where the bounds are all integral and the variables are only allowed to take integral values. These can be encoded by suitably restricting the codomain of the weight function of octagonal graphs.

Definition 4 (Integer octagonal graph). *An* integer octagonal graph *is an octagonal graph $G = (\mathcal{N}, w)$ having an integral weight function:*

$$\forall i, j \in \mathcal{N} : w(i, j) \in \mathbb{Z} \cup \{+\infty\}.$$

As an integer octagonal graph is also a rational octagonal graph, the constraint system that it encodes will be satisfiable when interpreted to take values in $\mathbb{Q}$. However, when interpreted to take values in $\mathbb{Z}$, this system may be unsatisfiable since the arcs encoding unary constraints can have an odd weight; we say that an octagonal graph is $\mathbb{Z}$-*consistent* if its encoded integer constraint system is satisfiable. For the same reason, the strong closure of an integer octagonal graph does not provide a canonical form for the integer constraint system that it encodes and we need to consider the following *tightening* inference rule:

$$\frac{i - \bar{\imath} \leq d}{i - \bar{\imath} \leq 2\lfloor d/2 \rfloor}. \tag{6}$$

Definition 5 (Tightly closed graph). *An octagonal graph $G = (\mathcal{N}, w)$ is* tightly closed *if it is a strongly closed integer octagonal graph and the following property holds:*

$$\forall i \in \mathcal{N} : w(i, \bar{\imath}) \text{ is even.} \tag{7}$$

The tight closure *of an octagonal graph G in $\mathcal{N}$ is*

$$\text{T-closure}(G) := \bigsqcup \bigl\{\, G' \in \mathbb{O} \bigm| G' \trianglelefteq G \text{ and } G' \text{ is tightly closed} \,\bigr\}.$$

By property (7), any tightly closed integer octagonal graph will encode a satisfiable integer constraint system and is therefore $\mathbb{Z}$-consistent. Moreover, since the encoding of any satisfiable integer constraint system will result in a $\mathbb{Z}$-consistent integer octagonal graph G that satisfies property (7), its tight closure T-closure(G) will also be $\mathbb{Z}$-consistent. This means that, if G is *not* $\mathbb{Z}$-consistent, then T-closure(G) $= \bigsqcup \varnothing = \bot$; that is, the tight closure operator computes either a tightly closed graph or the bottom element. Therefore, tight closure is a kernel operator on the lattice of octagonal graphs, as was the case for strong closure.

An incremental closure procedure for obtaining the tight closure of an octagonal graph was defined in [13] and improved in [12]. The algorithm, which is also presented and discussed in [18, Section 4.3.5], maintains the tight closure of a system of octagonal constraints by performing at most $O(n^2)$ operations each time a new constraint is added: thus, for m constraints, the worst case complexity is $O(mn^2)$. In particular, for the case of a dense system of octagonal constraints where $m \in O(n^2)$, the worst case complexity is $O(n^4)$.

The following theorem shows that a more efficient tight closure algorithm can be obtained by a simple modification to the improved strong closure algorithm of Theorem 1. Basically, inference rule (6) must be applied to ensure property (7) holds before applying inference rule (4).

Theorem 2. *Let $G = (\mathcal{N}, w)$ be a closed integer octagonal graph. Consider the graph $G_{\mathrm{T}} = (\mathcal{N}, w_{\mathrm{T}})$, where w_{T} is defined, for each $i, j \in \mathcal{N}$, by*

$$w_{\mathrm{T}}(i,j) := \min\left\{ w(i,j), \left\lfloor \frac{w(i,\bar{\imath})}{2} \right\rfloor + \left\lfloor \frac{w(\bar{\jmath},j)}{2} \right\rfloor \right\}.$$

Then, if G_{T} is an octagonal graph, $G_{\mathrm{T}} = \mathrm{T\text{-}closure}(G)$.

```
procedure tight_closure_if_consistent(var w [0..2n − 1] [0..2n − 1])
    { Classical Floyd-Warshall: O(n^3) }
    for k := 0 to 2n − 1 do
        for i := 0 to 2n − 1 do
            for j := 0 to 2n − 1 do
                w[i, j] := min(w[i, j], w[i, k] + w[k, j]);
    { Tight coherence: O(n^2) }
    for i := 0 to 2n − 1 do
        for j := 0 to 2n − 1 do
            w[i, j] := min(w[i, j], floor(w[i, ī]/2) + floor(w[j̄, j]/2));
```

Fig. 1. A $O(n^3)$ tight closure algorithm for $\mathbb{Z}$-consistent integer octagonal graphs

Figure 1 shows the pseudo-code for a $O(n^3)$ tight closure algorithm based on Theorem 2 and on the classical Floyd-Warshall shortest-path closure algorithm. Note that the pseudo-code in Figure 1 assumes that the data structure recording the weight function w, here denoted to be similar to a two-dimensional array, automatically implements the coherence assumption for octagonal graphs (i.e., property (3) of Definition 2).

In the case of sparse graphs, a better complexity bound can be obtained by modifying the code in Figure 1 so as to compute the shortest path closure using Johnson's algorithm [7]: the worst case complexity of such an implementation will be $O(n^2 \log n + mn)$, which significantly improves upon the $O(mn^2)$ worst case complexity of [12,13] when, e.g., $m \in \Theta(n)$. However, as observed elsewhere [18,23], some of the targeted applications (e.g., static analysis) typically require the computation of graphs that are dense, so that the Floyd-Warshall algorithm is often a better choice from a practical perspective.

It is possible to define an incremental variant of the tight closure algorithm in Figure 1, which is simply based on the corresponding incremental version of the Floyd-Warshall shortest path closure algorithm. In such a case, we obtain the same worst case complexity of [12,13].

The proof of Theorem 2 relies on a few auxiliary lemmas. The first two were also used in [3] for the formal proof of Theorem 1 above (for their detailed proofs, see Lemmas 9 and 10 in [3]).

Lemma 2. *Let* $G = (\mathcal{N}, w)$ *be an octagonal graph,* $G^\star = (\mathcal{N}, w^\star) := \operatorname{closure}(G)$ *and* (z_1, z_2) *be an arc in* $G^\star$*. Then there exists a simple path* $\pi = z_1 \cdots z_2$ *in* G *such that* $w^\star(z_1, z_2) = w(\pi)$*.*

Lemma 3. *Let* $G = (\mathcal{N}, w)$ *be a closed octagonal graph and* $i, j \in \mathcal{N}$ *be such that* $i \neq \bar{\jmath}$ *and* $2w(i,j) \geq w(i, \bar{\imath}) + w(\bar{\jmath}, j)$*. Let* $G_\mathrm{s}^\star = (\mathcal{N}, w_\mathrm{s}^\star) := \operatorname{closure}(G_\mathrm{s})$ *where* $G_\mathrm{s} := (\mathcal{N}, w_\mathrm{s})$ *and, for each* $h_1, h_2 \in \mathcal{N}$*,*

$$w_\mathrm{s}(h_1, h_2) := \begin{cases} \bigl(w(i,\bar{\imath}) + w(\bar{\jmath}, j)\bigr)/2, & \text{if } (h_1, h_2) \in \bigl\{(i,j), (\bar{\jmath}, \bar{\imath})\bigr\}; \\ w(h_1, h_2), & \text{otherwise.} \end{cases}$$

Let also $z_1, z_2 \in \mathcal{N}$*. Then one or both of the following hold:*

$$w_\mathrm{s}^\star(z_1, z_2) = w(z_1, z_2);$$
$$2w_\mathrm{s}^\star(z_1, z_2) \geq w(z_1, \bar{z}_1) + w(\bar{z}_2, z_2).$$

Informally, Lemma 3 states that if inference rule (4) is applied to a closed octagonal graph, then the resulting graph can be closed just by making further applications of inference rule (4). Note that, if G is an integer octagonal graph and property (7) holds, then the derived graph G_s will also be an integer octagonal graph. We now state a new lemma for integer octagonal graphs showing that when inference rule (6) is applied we obtain a similar conclusion to that for Lemma 3.

Lemma 4. *Let* $G = (\mathcal{N}, w)$ *be a closed integer octagonal graph and* $i \in \mathcal{N}$*. Let* $G_\mathrm{t}^\star := \operatorname{closure}(G_\mathrm{t})$ *where* $G_\mathrm{t} := (\mathcal{N}, w_\mathrm{t})$ *is an octagonal graph and, for each* $h_1, h_2 \in \mathcal{N}$*,*

$$w_\mathrm{t}(h_1, h_2) := \begin{cases} w(i, \bar{\imath}) - 1, & \text{if } (h_1, h_2) = (i, \bar{\imath}); \\ w(h_1, h_2), & \text{otherwise.} \end{cases} \tag{8}$$

Let $G_\mathrm{t}^\star = (\mathcal{N}, w_\mathrm{t}^\star)$ *and* $z_1, z_2 \in \mathcal{N}$*. Then one or both of the following hold:*

$$w_\mathrm{t}^\star(z_1, z_2) = w(z_1, z_2), \tag{9}$$

$$w_\mathrm{t}^\star(z_1, z_2) \geq \left\lfloor \frac{w(z_1, \bar{z}_1)}{2} \right\rfloor + \left\lfloor \frac{w(\bar{z}_2, z_2)}{2} \right\rfloor. \tag{10}$$

Proof. By hypothesis and Definition 1, $G_\mathrm{t}^\star \trianglelefteq G_\mathrm{t} \trianglelefteq G$. If (z_1, z_2) is not an arc in $G_\mathrm{t}^\star$, then $w_\mathrm{t}^\star(z_1, z_2) = +\infty$; thus, as $G_\mathrm{t}^\star \trianglelefteq G$, we also have $w(z_1, z_2) = +\infty$ and hence property (9) holds. Suppose now that (z_1, z_2) is an arc in $G_\mathrm{t}^\star$. Then we can apply Lemma 2, so that there exists a simple path $\pi = z_1 \cdots z_2$ in G_t such that $w_\mathrm{t}^\star(z_1, z_2) = w_\mathrm{t}(\pi)$.

Suppose first that $w_\mathrm{t}(\pi) = w(\pi)$. Then, as G is closed, by Lemma 1 we obtain $w(\pi) \geq w(z_1, z_2)$ so that $w_\mathrm{t}^\star(z_1, z_2) \geq w(z_1, z_2)$. However $G_\mathrm{t}^\star \trianglelefteq G$ so that $w_\mathrm{t}^\star(z_1, z_2) \leq w(z_1, z_2)$ and therefore property (9) holds.

Secondly, suppose that $w_\mathrm{t}(\pi) \neq w(\pi)$. Then, by Equation (8), $(i, \bar{\imath})$ must be an arc in π, so that

$$\pi = \pi_1 :: (i\,\bar{\imath}) :: \pi_2, \tag{11}$$

where $\pi_1 = z_1 \cdots i$, $\pi_2 = \bar{\imath} \cdots z_2$ are simple paths in G_{t} that do not contain the arc $(i, \bar{\imath})$. Therefore, by Equation (8), we have $w_{\mathrm{t}}(\pi_1) = w(\pi_1)$, $w_{\mathrm{t}}(\pi_2) = w(\pi_2)$.

For $\pi = j_0 \cdots j_p$ any path in a graph in $\mathcal{N}$, let $\overline{\pi}$ denote the path $\bar{\jmath}_p \cdots \bar{\jmath}_0$. Consider (11) and let

$$\pi_1' = \pi_1 :: (i\,\bar{\imath}) :: \overline{\pi}_1, \qquad\qquad \pi_2' = \overline{\pi}_2 :: (i\,\bar{\imath}) :: \pi_2.$$

As G is an octagonal graph, we have $w(\pi_1) = w(\overline{\pi}_1)$ and $w(\pi_2) = w(\overline{\pi}_2)$ so that

$$w(\pi_1') = 2w(\pi_1) + w(i, \bar{\imath}), \qquad\qquad w(\pi_2') = 2w(\pi_2) + w(i, \bar{\imath}).$$

As G is closed, by Lemma 1,

$$w(\pi_1') \geq w(z_1, \bar{z}_1), \qquad\qquad w(\pi_2') \geq w(\bar{z}_2, z_2)$$

so that

$$w(\pi_1) + \frac{w(i, \bar{\imath})}{2} \geq \frac{w(z_1, \bar{z}_1)}{2}, \qquad\qquad w(\pi_2) + \frac{w(i, \bar{\imath})}{2} \geq \frac{w(\bar{z}_2, z_2)}{2}.$$

Therefore

$$\begin{aligned}
w_{\mathrm{t}}(\pi) &= w_{\mathrm{t}}(\pi_1) + w_{\mathrm{t}}(i, \bar{\imath}) + w_{\mathrm{t}}(\pi_2) \\
&= w(\pi_1) + \frac{w(i, \bar{\imath}) - 1}{2} + w(\pi_2) + \frac{w(i, \bar{\imath}) - 1}{2} \\
&\geq \frac{w(z_1, \bar{z}_1)}{2} - \frac{1}{2} + \frac{w(\bar{z}_2, z_2)}{2} - \frac{1}{2} \\
&\geq \left\lfloor \frac{w(z_1, \bar{z}_1)}{2} \right\rfloor + \left\lfloor \frac{w(\bar{z}_2, z_2)}{2} \right\rfloor.
\end{aligned}$$

Hence, as $w_{\mathrm{t}}^{\star}(z_1, z_2) = w_{\mathrm{t}}(\pi)$, we obtain property (10), as required. □

The next result uses Lemmas 3 and 4 to derive a property relating the weight functions for a closed integer octagonal graph and its tight closure.

Lemma 5. *Let $G = (\mathcal{N}, w)$ be a closed integer octagonal graph such that $G^{\mathrm{T}} = (\mathcal{N}, w^{\mathrm{T}}) :=$ T-closure(G) is an octagonal graph and let $z_1, z_2 \in \mathcal{N}$. Then one or both of the following hold:*

$$w^{\mathrm{T}}(z_1, z_2) = w(z_1, z_2); \tag{12}$$

$$w^{\mathrm{T}}(z_1, z_2) = \left\lfloor \frac{w(z_1, \bar{z}_1)}{2} \right\rfloor + \left\lfloor \frac{w(\bar{z}_2, z_2)}{2} \right\rfloor. \tag{13}$$

Proof. The proof is by contraposition; thus we assume that neither (12) nor (13) hold. Without loss of generality, let the graph G be $\trianglelefteq$-minimal in the set of all closed integer octagonal graphs such that T-closure$(G) = G^{\mathrm{T}}$ and for which neither (12) nor (13) hold. Clearly the negation of (12) implies that $G \neq G^{\mathrm{T}}$, so that $G^{\mathrm{T}} \triangleleft G$.

As G is closed but not tightly closed, by Definitions 3 and 5, it follows that there exist $i, j \in \mathcal{N}$ such that either

(i) $i = \overline{\jmath}$ and $w(i, \overline{\imath})$ is odd; or
(ii) property (7) holds and $2w(i, j) > w(i, \overline{\imath}) + w(\overline{\jmath}, j)$.

Consider graph $G_1 = (\mathcal{N}, w_1)$ where the weight function w_1 is defined, for all $h_1, h_2 \in \mathcal{N}$, by

$$w_1(h_1, h_2) := \begin{cases} \left\lfloor \frac{w(i,\overline{\imath})}{2} \right\rfloor + \left\lfloor \frac{w(\overline{\jmath},j)}{2} \right\rfloor, & \text{if } (h_1, h_2) \in \bigl\{(i, j), (\overline{\jmath}, \overline{\imath})\bigr\}; \\ w(h_1, h_2), & \text{otherwise.} \end{cases}$$

Let $G_1^\star = \text{closure}(G_1)$. By Definitions 1, 3 and 5,

$$G^{\mathrm{T}} \trianglelefteq G_1^\star \trianglelefteq G_1 \triangleleft G. \tag{14}$$

Thus T-closure$(G_1^\star) = G^{\mathrm{T}}$ so that, by the minimality assumption on G, one or both of the following hold:

$$w^{\mathrm{T}}(z_1, z_2) = w_1^\star(z_1, z_2); \tag{15}$$

$$w^{\mathrm{T}}(z_1, z_2) = \left\lfloor \frac{w_1^\star(z_1, \overline{z}_1)}{2} \right\rfloor + \left\lfloor \frac{w_1^\star(\overline{z}_2, z_2)}{2} \right\rfloor. \tag{16}$$

As $G^{\mathrm{T}} \neq \bot$, by (14), G_1 is consistent. Therefore, by construction, G_1 is an integer octagonal graph. If property (i) holds for i, j, then Lemma 4 can be applied and, if property (ii) holds for i, j, then Lemma 3 can be applied and also, since property (7) holds, both $w_1(z_1, \overline{z}_1)$ and $w(\overline{z}_2, z_2)$ are even. Hence, letting $G_1^\star := (\mathcal{N}, w_1^\star)$, one or both of the following hold:

$$w_1^\star(z_1, z_2) = w(z_1, z_2); \tag{17}$$

$$w_1^\star(z_1, z_2) \geq \left\lfloor \frac{w(z_1, \overline{z}_1)}{2} \right\rfloor + \left\lfloor \frac{w(\overline{z}_2, z_2)}{2} \right\rfloor. \tag{18}$$

Again by Lemmas 3 and 4,

$$w_1^\star(z_1, \overline{z}_1) \geq 2\left\lfloor \frac{w(z_1, \overline{z}_1)}{2} \right\rfloor,$$

$$w_1^\star(\overline{z}_2, z_2) \geq 2\left\lfloor \frac{w(\overline{z}_2, z_2)}{2} \right\rfloor;$$

since the lower bounds for $w_1^\star(z_1, \overline{z}_1)$ and $w_1^\star(\overline{z}_2, z_2)$ are even integers, we obtain

$$\left\lfloor \frac{w_1^\star(z_1, \overline{z}_1)}{2} \right\rfloor + \left\lfloor \frac{w_1^\star(\overline{z}_2, z_2)}{2} \right\rfloor \geq \left\lfloor \frac{w(z_1, \overline{z}_1)}{2} \right\rfloor + \left\lfloor \frac{w(\overline{z}_2, z_2)}{2} \right\rfloor. \tag{19}$$

Suppose first that (15) and (17) hold. Then by transitivity we obtain (12), contradicting the contrapositive assumption for G.

If (15) and (18) hold, then it follows

$$w^{\mathrm{T}}(z_1, z_2) \geq \left\lfloor \frac{w(z_1, \overline{z}_1)}{2} \right\rfloor + \left\lfloor \frac{w(\overline{z}_2, z_2)}{2} \right\rfloor. \tag{20}$$

On the other hand, if (16) holds, then, by (19), we obtain again property (20). However, by Definitions 3 and 5 we also have

$$w^{\mathrm{T}}(z_1, z_2) \leq \left\lfloor \frac{w(z_1, \overline{z}_1)}{2} \right\rfloor + \left\lfloor \frac{w(\overline{z}_2, z_2)}{2} \right\rfloor.$$

By combining this inequality with (20) we obtain (13), contradicting the contrapositive assumption for G. □

Proof (of Theorem 2). Let $G^{\mathrm{T}} :=$ T-closure(G). By definition of G_{T}, $G_{\mathrm{T}} \trianglelefteq G$ so that T-closure(G_{T}) $\trianglelefteq G^{\mathrm{T}}$. As G_{T} is an octagonal graph, G_{T} is consistent, and hence $G^{\mathrm{T}} \neq \bot$; let $G^{\mathrm{T}} = (\mathcal{N}, w^{\mathrm{T}})$. Letting $i, j \in \mathcal{N}$, to prove the result we need to show that $w^{\mathrm{T}}(i,j) = w_{\mathrm{T}}(i,j)$. Let $k_{ij} := \lfloor w(i,\overline{\imath})/2 \rfloor + \lfloor w(\overline{\jmath}, j)/2 \rfloor$.

By Definitions 1, 3 and 5, it follows that both properties $w^{\mathrm{T}}(i,j) \leq w(i,j)$ and $w^{\mathrm{T}}(i,j) \leq k_{ij}$ hold so that, by definition of w_{T}, we have $w^{\mathrm{T}}(i,j) \leq w_{\mathrm{T}}(i,j)$. By Lemma 5, $w^{\mathrm{T}}(i,j) = w(i,j)$ and/or $w^{\mathrm{T}}(i,j) = k_{ij}$. Therefore since, by definition, $w_{\mathrm{T}}(i,j) = \min\{w(i,j), k_{ij}\}$, we obtain $w_{\mathrm{T}}(i,j) \leq w^{\mathrm{T}}(i,j)$. □

It follows from the statement of Theorem 2 that an implementation based on it also needs to check the consistency of G_{T}. In principle, one could apply again a shortest-path closure procedure so as to check whether G_{T} contains some negative weight cycles. However, a much more efficient solution is obtained by the following result.

Theorem 3. *Let $G = (\mathcal{N}, w)$ be a closed integer octagonal graph. Consider the graphs $G_{\mathrm{t}} = (\mathcal{N}, w_{\mathrm{t}})$ and $G_{\mathrm{T}} = (\mathcal{N}, w_{\mathrm{T}})$ where, for each $i, j \in \mathcal{N}$,*

$$w_{\mathrm{t}}(i,j) := \begin{cases} 2\lfloor w(i,j)/2 \rfloor, & \text{if } j = \overline{\imath}; \\ w(i,j), & \text{otherwise}; \end{cases} \tag{21}$$

$$w_{\mathrm{T}}(i,j) := \min\left\{ w(i,j), \left\lfloor \frac{w(i,\overline{\imath})}{2} \right\rfloor + \left\lfloor \frac{w(\overline{\jmath},j)}{2} \right\rfloor \right\}. \tag{22}$$

Suppose that, for all $i \in \mathcal{N}$, $w_{\mathrm{t}}(i,\overline{\imath}) + w_{\mathrm{t}}(\overline{\imath}, i) \geq 0$. Then G_{T} is an octagonal graph.

This result is a corollary of the following result proved in [15, Lemma 4].

Lemma 6. *Let $G = (\mathcal{N}, w)$ be an integer octagonal graph with no negative weight cycles and $G_{\mathrm{t}} = (\mathcal{N}, w_{\mathrm{t}})$, where w_{t} satisfies (21), have a negative weight cycle. Then there exists $i, \overline{\imath} \in \mathcal{N}$ and a cycle $\pi = (i \cdot \pi_1 \cdot \overline{\imath}) :: (\overline{\imath} \cdot \pi_2 \cdot i)$ in G such that $w(\pi) = 0$ and the weight of the shortest path in G from i to $\overline{\imath}$ is odd.*

Proof (of Theorem 3). The proof is by contradiction; suppose G_{T} is not an octagonal graph; then by Definitions 1, 3 and 5, G_{T} is inconsistent. We show that G_{t} is also inconsistent. Again, we assume to the contrary that G_{t} is consistent and derive a contradiction. Let $i, j \in \mathcal{N}$. By (21), we have $w_{\mathrm{t}}(i,j) \leq w(i,j)$ and $w_{\mathrm{t}}(i,\overline{\imath})/2 + w_{\mathrm{t}}(\overline{\jmath}, j)/2 = k_{ij}$, where $k_{ij} := \lfloor w(i,\overline{\imath})/2 \rfloor + \lfloor w(\overline{\jmath}, j)/2 \rfloor$. Letting S-closure($G_{\mathrm{t}}$) $= (\mathcal{N}, w_{\mathrm{t}}^{\mathrm{S}})$, we have, by Definition 3, $w_{\mathrm{t}}^{\mathrm{S}}(i,j) \leq w_{\mathrm{t}}(i,j)$

and $w_t^S(i,j) \le w_t(i,\bar\imath)/2 + w_t(\bar\jmath,j)/2$. Thus $w_t^S(i,j) \le \min\bigl(w(i,j),k_{ij}\bigr)$. As this holds for all $i,j \in \mathcal{N}$, by (22), S-closure$(G_t) \trianglelefteq G_T$, contradicting the assumption that G_t was consistent. Hence G_t is inconsistent and therefore contains a negative weight cycle.

By Lemma 6, there exists $i,\bar\imath \in \mathcal{N}$ and a cycle $\pi = (i \cdot \pi_1 \cdot \bar\imath) :: (\bar\imath \cdot \pi_2 \cdot i)$ in G such that $w(\pi) = 0$ and the weight of the shortest path in G from i to $\bar\imath$ is odd. As G is closed, $w(i,\bar\imath) \le w(i \cdot \pi_1 \cdot \bar\imath)$ and $w(\bar\imath,i) \le w(\bar\imath \cdot \pi_2 \cdot i)$. Thus $w(i,\bar\imath) + w(\bar\imath,i) \le w(\pi) = 0$. Moreover, $(i\bar\imath)$ is a path and hence the shortest path from i to $\bar\imath$ so that $w(i\bar\imath)$ is odd; hence, by (21), $w(i,\bar\imath) = w_t(i,\bar\imath) + 1$ and $w(\bar\imath,i) \ge w_t(\bar\imath,i)$. Therefore $w_t(i,\bar\imath) + w_t(\bar\imath,i) < 0$. □

```
function tight_closure(var w[0..2n − 1][0..2n − 1]) : bool
    { Initialization: O(n) }
    for i := 0 to 2n − 1 do w[i, i] := 0;
    { Classical Floyd-Warshall: O(n^3) }
    for k := 0 to 2n − 1 do
        for i := 0 to 2n − 1 do
            for j := 0 to 2n − 1 do
                w[i, j] := min(w[i, j], w[i, k] + w[k, j]);
    { Check for Q-consistency: O(n) }
    for i := 0 to 2n − 2 step 2 do
        if w[i, i] < 0 return false;
    { Tightening: O(n) }
    for i := 0 to 2n − 1 do
        w[i, ī] := 2 · floor(w[i, ī]/2);
    { Check for Z-consistency: O(n) }
    for i := 0 to 2n − 2 step 2 do
        if w[i, ī] + w[ī, i] < 0 return false;
    { Strong coherence: O(n^2) }
    for i := 0 to 2n − 1 do
        for j := 0 to 2n − 1 do
            w[i, j] := min(w[i, j], w[i, ī]/2 + w[j̄, j]/2);
    return true;
```

Fig. 2. A $O(n^3)$ tight closure algorithm for integer coherent graphs

The combination of the results stated in Theorems 2 and 3 (together with the well known result for rational consistency) leads to an $O(n^3)$ tight closure algorithm, such as that given by the pseudo-code in Figure 2, that computes the tight closure of any (possibly inconsistent) coherent integer-weighted graph returning the Boolean value 'true' if and only if the input graph is $\mathbb{Z}$-consistent.

5 Conclusion and Future Work

We have presented and fully justified an $O(n^3)$ algorithm that computes the tight closure of a set of integer octagonal constraints. The algorithm —which is based on the extension to integer-weighted octagonal graphs of the one we proposed for rational-weighted octagonal graphs [2,3]— and its proof of correctness means the issue about the possibility of computing the tight closure at a computational cost that is asymptotically not worse than the cost of computing all-pairs shortest paths is finally closed.

In the field of hardware and software verification, the integrality constraint that distinguishes integer-weighted from rational-weighted octagonal graphs can be seen as an abstraction of the more general imposition of a set of congruence relations. Such a set can be encoded by an element of a suitable abstract domain such as the non-relational congruence domain of [10] (that is, of the form $x = a \pmod{b}$), the weakly relational *zone-congruence* domain of [17] (that is, also allowing the form $x - y = a \pmod{b}$), the linear congruence domain of [11], and the more general fully relational *rational grids* domain developed in [1]. The combination of such domains with the abstract domain proposed in [2,3] is likely to provide an interesting complexity-precision trade-off. Future work includes the investigation into such a combination, exploiting the ideas presented in this paper.

References

1. Bagnara, R., et al.: Grids: A Domain for Analyzing the Distribution of Numerical Values. In: Puebla, G. (ed.) LOPSTR 2006. LNCS, vol. 4407, pp. 219–235. Springer, Heidelberg (2007)
2. Hill, P.M., et al.: Widening Operators for Weakly-Relational Numeric Abstractions. In: Hankin, C., Siveroni, I. (eds.) SAS 2005. LNCS, vol. 3672, pp. 3–18. Springer, Heidelberg (2005)
3. Bagnara, R., et al.: Widening operators for weakly-relational numeric abstractions. Quaderno 399, Dipartimento di Matematica, Università di Parma, Italy (2005), `http://www.cs.unipr.it/Publications/`
4. Bagnara, R., Hill, P.M., Zaffanella, E.: The Parma Polyhedra Library: Toward a complete set of numerical abstractions for the analysis and verification of hardware and software systems. Quaderno 457, Dipartimento di Matematica, Università di Parma, Italy (2006), `http://www.cs.unipr.it/Publications/`, also pulished as arXiv:cs.MS/0612085, `http://arxiv.org/`
5. Balasundaram, V., Kennedy, K.: A technique for summarizing data access and its use in parallelism enhancing transformations. In: Knobe, B. (ed.) Proceedings of the ACM SIGPLAN 1989 Conference on Programming Language Design and Implementation (PLDI), Portland, Oregon, USA. ACM SIGPLAN Notices, vol. 24(7), pp. 41–53. ACM Press, New York (1989)
6. Ball, T., et al.: Zapato: Automatic theorem proving for predicate abstraction refinement. In: Alur, R., Peled, D. (eds.) CAV 2004. LNCS, vol. 3114, pp. 457–461. Springer, Heidelberg (2004)
7. Cormen, T.H., Leiserson, T.E., Rivest, R.L.: Introduction to Algorithms. The MIT Press, Cambridge, MA (1990)

8. Cousot, P., Cousot, R.: Abstract interpretation: A unified lattice model for static analysis of programs by construction or approximation of fixpoints. In: Proceedings of the Fourth Annual ACM Symposium on Principles of Programming Languages, pp. 238–252. ACM Press, New York (1977)
9. Cousot, P., et al.: The ASTREÉ Analyzer. In: Sagiv, M. (ed.) ESOP 2005. LNCS, vol. 3444, pp. 21–30. Springer, Heidelberg (2005)
10. Granger, P.: Static analysis of arithmetical congruences. International Journal of Computer Mathematics 30, 165–190 (1989)
11. Granger, P.: Static analysis of linear congruence equalities among variables of a program. In: Abramsky, S., Maibaum, T.S.E. (eds.) CAAP 1991 and TAPSOFT 1991. LNCS, vol. 493, pp. 169–192. Springer, Heidelberg (1991)
12. Harvey, W., Stuckey, P.J.: A unit two variable per inequality integer constraint solver for constraint logic programming. In: Patel, M. (ed.) ACSC 1997: Proceedings of the 20th Australasian Computer Science Conference. Australian Computer Science Communications, vol. 19, pp. 102–111 (1997)
13. Jaffar, J., et al.: Beyond finite domains. In: Borning, A. (ed.) PPCP 1994. LNCS, vol. 874, pp. 86–94. Springer, Heidelberg (1994)
14. Lagarias, J.C.: The computational complexity of simultaneous Diophantine approximation problems. SIAM Journal on Computing 14(1), 196–209 (1985)
15. Lahiri, S.K., Musuvathi, M.: An Efficient Decision Procedure for UTVPI Constraints. In: Gramlich, B. (ed.) FroCos 2005. LNCS (LNAI), vol. 3717, pp. 168–183. Springer, Heidelberg (2005)
16. Miné, A.: The octagon abstract domain. In: Proceedings of the Eighth Working Conference on Reverse Engineering (WCRE 2001), Stuttgart, Germany, 2001, pp. 310–319. IEEE Computer Society Press, Los Alamitos (2001)
17. Miné, A.: A Few Graph-Based Relational Numerical Abstract Domains. In: Hermenegildo, M.V., Puebla, G. (eds.) SAS 2002. LNCS, vol. 2477, Springer, Heidelberg (2002)
18. Miné, A.: Weakly Relational Numerical Abstract Domains. PhD thesis, École Polytechnique, Paris, France (March 2005)
19. Miné, A.: The octagon abstract domain. Higher-Order and Symbolic Computation 19(1), 31–100 (2006)
20. Nelson, G., Oppen, D.C.: Fast decision algorithms based on Union and Find. In: Proceedings of the 18th Annual Symposium on Foundations of Computer Science (FOCS 1977), Providence, RI, USA, pp. 114–119. IEEE Computer Society Press, Los Alamitos (1977), The journal version of this paper is [21]
21. Nelson, G., Oppen, D.C.: Fast decision procedures based on congruence closure. Journal of the ACM 27(2), 356–364 (1980), An earlier version of this paper is [20]
22. V. R. Pratt. Two easy theories whose combination is hard. Memo sent to Nelson and Oppen concerning a preprint of their paper [20] (September 1977)
23. Venet, A., Brat, G.: Precise and efficient static array bound checking for large embedded C programs. In: Proceedings of the ACM SIGPLAN 2004 Conference on Programming Language Design and Implementation (PLDI 2004), Washington, DC, USA, 2004, pp. 231–242. ACM Press, New York (2004)

Handling Parameterized Systems with Non-atomic Global Conditions

Parosh Aziz Abdulla[1], Noomene Ben Henda[1], Giorgio Delzanno[2], and Ahmed Rezine[1]

[1] Uppsala University, Sweden
parosh@it.uu.se, Noomene.BenHenda@it.uu.se, Rezine.Ahmed@it.uu.se
[2] Università di Genova, Italy
giorgio@disi.unige.it

Abstract. We consider verification of safety properties for parameterized systems with linear topologies. A process in the system is an extended automaton, where the transitions are guarded by both local and global conditions. The global conditions are non-atomic, i.e., a process allows arbitrary interleavings with other transitions while checking the states of all (or some) of the other processes. We translate the problem into model checking of infinite transition systems where each configuration is a labeled finite graph. We derive an over-approximation of the induced transition system, which leads to a symbolic scheme for analyzing safety properties. We have implemented a prototype and run it on several nontrivial case studies, namely non-atomic versions of Burn's protocol, Dijkstra's protocol, the Bakery algorithm, Lamport's distributed mutual exclusion protocol, and a two-phase commit protocol used for handling transactions in distributed systems. As far as we know, these protocols have not previously been verified in a fully automated framework.

1 Introduction

We consider verification of safety properties for *parameterized systems.* Typically, a parameterized system consists of an arbitrary number of processes organized in a linear array. The task is to verify correctness regardless of the number of processes. This amounts to the verification of an infinite family; namely one for each size of the system. An important feature in the behaviour of a parameterized system is the existence of *global conditions.* A global condition is either *universally* or *existentially* quantified. An example of a universal condition is that all processes to the left of a given process i should satisfy a property θ. Process i can perform the transition only if all processes with indices $j < i$ satisfy θ. In an existential condition we require that *some* (rather than *all*) processes satisfy θ. Together with global conditions, we allow features such as shared variables, broadcast communication, and processes operating on unbounded variables.

All existing approaches to automatic verification of parameterized systems (e.g., [13, 5, 7, 9]) make the unrealistic assumption that a global condition is performed atomically, i.e., the process which is about to make the transition

F. Logozzo et al. (Eds.): VMCAI 2008, LNCS 4905, pp. 22–36, 2008.

checks the states of all the other processes and changes its own state, all in one step. However, almost all protocols (modeled as parameterized systems with global conditions) are implemented in a distributed manner, and therefore it is not feasible to test global conditions atomically.

In this paper, we propose a method for automatic verification of parameterized systems where the global conditions are not assumed to be atomic. The main idea is to translate the verification problem into model checking of systems where each configuration is a labeled *finite graph.* The labels of the nodes encode the local states of the processes, while the labels of the edges carry information about the data flow between the processes. Our verification method consists of three ingredients each of which is implemented by a fully automatic procedure: (i) a preprocessing phase in which a *refinement protocol* is used to translate the behaviour of a parameterized system with global conditions into a system with graph configurations; (ii) a *model checking phase* based on symbolic backward reachability analysis of systems with graph configurations; and (iii) an *over-approximation scheme* inspired by the ones proposed for systems with *atomic* global conditions in [4] and [2]. The over-approximation scheme is extended here in a non-trivial manner in order to cope with configurations which have graph structures. The over-approximation enables us to work with efficient symbolic representations (upward closed sets of configurations) in the backward reachability procedure. Below, we describe the three ingredients in detail.

In order to simplify the presentation, we consider a basic model. Nevertheless, the method can be generalized to deal with a number of features which are added to enrich the basic model, such as broadcast communication and shared variables (see [3] for details). In the basic model, a process is a finite-state automaton which operates on a set of local variables ranging over the Booleans. The transitions of the automaton are conditioned by the local state of the process, values of the local variables, and by global conditions. Transitions involving global conditions are not assumed to be atomic. Instead, they are implemented using an underlying protocol, here referred to as the *refinement protocol.* Several different versions of the protocol are possible. The one in the basic model works as follows. Let us consider a process, called the *initiator*, which is about to perform a transition with a global condition. Suppose that the global condition requires that all processes to the left of the initiator satisfy θ. Then, the initiator sends a request asking the other processes whether they satisfy θ or not. A process sends an acknowledgment back to the initiator only if it satisfies θ. The initiator performs the transition when it has received acknowledgments from all processes to its left. The acknowledgments are sent by the different processes independently. This means that the initiator may receive the acknowledgments in any arbitrary order, and that a given process may have time to change its local state and its local variables before the initiator has received its acknowledgment.

The refinement protocol induces a system with an infinite set of configurations each of which is a finite graph. The nodes of the graph contain information about the local states and the values of the local variables of the processes, while the edges represent the flow of request and acknowledgment messages used to implement the refinement protocol. We observe that the graph representation defines a natural ordering on configurations, where a configuration is smaller than another configuration, if the graph of the former is contained in the graph of the latter (i.e., if there is a label-respecting injection from the smaller to the larger graph). To check safety properties, we perform backward reachability analysis on sets of configurations which are upward closed under the above mentioned ordering. Two attractive features of upward closed sets are (i) checking safety properties can almost always be reduced to the reachability of an upward closed set; and (ii) they are fully characterized by their minimal elements (which are finite graphs), and hence these graphs can be used as efficient symbolic representations of infinite sets of configurations. One problem is that upward closedness is not preserved in general when computing sets of predecessors. To solve the problem, we consider a transition relation which is an over-approximation of the one induced by the parameterized system. To do that, we modify the refinement protocols by eliminating the processes which have failed to acknowledge a universal global condition (either because they do not satisfy the condition or because they have not yet sent an acknowledgment). For instance in the above example, it is always the case that process i will eventually perform the transition. However, when performing the transition, we eliminate each process j (to the left of i) which has failed to acknowledge the request of i. The approximate transition system obtained in this manner is *monotonic* w. r. t. the ordering on configurations, in the sense that larger configurations can simulate smaller ones. The fact that the approximate transition relation is monotonic, means that upward closedness is maintained when computing predecessors. Therefore, all the sets which are generated during the backward reachability analysis procedure are upward closed, and can hence be represented by their minimal elements. Observe that if the approximate transition system satisfies a safety property then we can conclude that the original system satisfies the property too. The whole verification process is fully automatic since both the approximation and the reachability analysis are carried out without user intervention. Termination of the approximated backward reachability analysis is not guaranteed in general. However, the procedure terminates on all the examples we report in this paper.

In this paper, we will also describe how the method can be generalized to deal with the model where processes are infinite-state. More precisely, the processes may operate on variables which range over the natural numbers, and the transitions may be conditioned by *gap-order constraints*. Gap-order constraints [17] are a logical formalism in which one can express simple relations on variables such as lower and upper bounds on the values of individual variables; and equality, and gaps (minimal differences) between values of pairs of variables.

Another aspect of our method is that systems with graph configurations are interesting in their own right. The reason is that many protocols have inherently distributed designs, rather than having explicit references to global conditions. For instance, configurations in the Lamport distributed mutual exclusion protocol [15] or in the two-phase commit protocol of [12] are naturally modeled as graphs where the nodes represent the local states of the processes, and the edges describe the data traveling between the processes. In such a manner, we get a model identical to the one extracted through the refinement protocol, and hence it can be analyzed using our method.

We have implemented a prototype and used it for verifying a number of challenging case studies such as parameterized non-atomic versions of Burn's protocol, Dijkstra's protocol, the Bakery algorithm, Lamport's distributed mutual exclusion protocol [15] , and the two-phase commit protocol used for handling transactions in [12]. As far as we know, none of these examples has previously been verified in a fully automated framework.

Related Work. We believe that this is the first work which can handle automatic verification of parameterized systems where global conditions are tested non-atomically. All existing automatic verification methods (e.g., [13, 5, 7, 9, 10, 4, 2]) are defined for parameterized systems where universal and existential conditions are evaluated atomically. Non-atomic versions of parameterized mutual exclusion protocols such as the Bakery algorithm and two-phase commit protocol have been studied with heuristics to discover invariants, ad-hoc abstractions, or semi-automated methods in [6, 14, 16, 8]. In contrast to these methods, our verification procedure is fully automated and is based on a generic approximation scheme for quantified conditions.

The method presented in this paper is related to those in [4, 2] in the sense that they also rely on combining over-approximation with symbolic backward reachability analysis. However, the papers [4,2] assume *atomic* global conditions. As described above, the passage from the atomic to the non-atomic semantics is not trivial. In particular, the translation induces models whose configurations are graphs, and are therefore well beyond the capabilities of the methods described in [4, 2] which operate on configurations with linear structures. Furthermore, the underlying graph model can be used in its own to analyze a large class of distributed protocols. This means that we can handle examples none of which can be analyzed within the framework of [4, 2].

2 Preliminaries

In this section, we define a basic model of parameterized systems.

For a natural number n, let $\overline{n}$ denote the set $\{1, \ldots, n\}$. We use $\mathcal{B}$ to denote the set $\{true, false\}$ of Boolean values. For a finite set A, we let $\mathbb{B}(A)$ denote the set of formulas which have members of A as atomic formulas, and which are closed under the Boolean connectives $\neg, \wedge, \vee$. A *quantifier* is either *universal* or *existential*. A universal quantifier is of one of the forms $\forall_L$, $\forall_R$, $\forall_{LR}$. An existential quantifier is of one of the forms $\exists_L$, $\exists_R$, or $\exists_{LR}$. The subscripts L, R, and LR stand for *Left*, *Right*, and *Left-Right* respectively. A *global condition* over A is of the form $\Box\theta$ where $\Box$ is a quantifier and $\theta \in \mathbb{B}(A)$. A global condition is said to be *universal* (resp. *existential*) if its quantifier is *universal* (resp. *existential*). We use $\mathbb{G}(A)$ to denote the set of global conditions over A.

Parameterized Systems. A parameterized system consists of an arbitrary (but finite) number of identical processes, arranged in a linear array. Sometimes, we refer to processes by their indices, and say e.g., the process with index i (or simply process i) to refer to the process with position i in the array. Each process is a finite-state automaton which operates on a finite number of Boolean local variables. The transitions of the automaton are conditioned by the values of the local variables and by *global* conditions in which the process checks, for instance, the local states and variables of all processes to its left or to its right. The global transitions are not assumed to be atomic operations. A transition may change the value of any local variable inside the process. A parameterized system induces an infinite family of finite-state systems, namely one for each size of the array. The aim is to verify correctness of the systems for the whole family (regardless of the number of processes inside the system). A *parameterized system* $\mathcal{P}$ is a triple (Q, X, T), where Q is a set of *local states*, X is a set of *local Boolean variables*, and T is a set of *transition rules*. A transition rule t is of the form

$$t : \begin{bmatrix} q \\ grd \rightarrow stmt \\ q' \end{bmatrix} \tag{1}$$

where $q, q' \in Q$ and $grd \rightarrow stmt$ is a *guarded command*. Below we give the definition of a guarded command. Let Y denote the set $X \cup Q$. A *guard* is a formula $grd \in \mathbb{B}(X) \cup \mathbb{G}(Y)$. In other words, the guard grd constraints either the values of local variables inside the process (if $grd \in \mathbb{B}(X)$); or the local states and the values of local variables of other processes (if $grd \in \mathbb{G}(Y)$). A *statement* is a set of assignments of the form $x_1 = e_1; \ldots ; x_n = e_n$, where $x_i \in X$, $e_i \in \mathcal{B}$, and $x_i \neq x_j$ if $i \neq j$. A *guarded command* is of the form $grd \rightarrow stmt$, where grd is a guard and $stmt$ is a statement.

3 Transition System

In this section, we describe the induced transition system.

A *transition system* $\mathcal{T}$ is a pair $(D, \Longrightarrow)$, where D is an (infinite) set of *configurations* and $\Longrightarrow$ is a binary relation on D. We use $\stackrel{*}{\Longrightarrow}$ to denote the reflexive transitive closure of $\Longrightarrow$. For sets of configurations $D_1, D_2 \subseteq D$ we use $D_1 \Longrightarrow D_2$ to denote that there are $c_1 \in D_1$ and $c_2 \in D_2$ with $c_1 \Longrightarrow c_2$. We will consider several transition systems in this paper.

First, a parameterized system $\mathcal{P} = (Q, X, T)$ induces a transition system $\mathcal{T}(\mathcal{P}) = (C, \longrightarrow)$ as follows. In order to reflect non-atomicity of global conditions, we use a protocol, called the *refinement protocol*, to refine (implement) these conditions. The refinement protocol uses a sequence of request and acknowledgment messages between processes. Therefore, a configuration is defined by (i) the local states and the values of the local variables of the different processes; and by (ii) the flow of requests and acknowledgments which are used to implement the refinement protocol. Below, we describe these two components, and then use them to define the set of configurations and the transition relation.

Process States. A *local variable state* v is a mapping from X to $\mathcal{B}$. For a local variable state v, and a formula $\theta \in \mathbb{B}(X)$, we evaluate $v \models \theta$ using the standard interpretation of the Boolean connectives. Given a statement *stmt* and a variable state v, we denote by $stmt(v)$ the variable state obtained from v by mapping x to e if $(x = e) \in stmt$, $v(x)$ otherwise. We will also work with temporary states which we use to implement the refinement protocol. A *temporary* state is of the form q^t where $q \in Q$ and $t \in T$. The state q^t indicates that the process is waiting for acknowledgments from other processes while trying to perform transition t (which contains a global condition). We use Q^T to denote the set of temporary states, and define $Q^\bullet = Q \cup Q^T$. A *process state* u is a pair (q, v) where $q \in Q^\bullet$ and v is a local variable state. We say that u is *temporary* if $q \in Q^T$, i.e., if the local state is temporary. For a temporary process state $u = (q^t, v)$, we write u^* to denote the process state (q, v), i.e., we replace q^t by the corresponding state q. If u is not temporary then we define $u^* = u$.

Sometimes, abusing notation, we view a process state (q, v) as a mapping $u : X \cup Q^\bullet \mapsto \mathcal{B}$, where $u(x) = v(x)$ for each $x \in X$, $u(q) = true$, and $u(q') = false$ for each $q' \in Q^\bullet - \{q\}$. The process state thus agrees with v on the values of local variables, and maps all elements of $Q^\bullet$, except q, to *false*. For a formula $\theta \in \mathbb{B}(X \cup Q^\bullet)$ and a process state u, the relation $u \models \theta$ is then well-defined. This is true in particular if $\theta \in \mathbb{B}(X)$.

The Refinement Protocol. The refinement protocol is triggered by an *initiator* which is a process trying to perform a transition involving a global condition. The protocol consists of three phases described below. In the first phase, the initiator enters a temporary state and sends a request to the other processes asking whether they satisfy the global condition. In the second phase, the other processes are allowed to respond to the initiator. When a process receives the request, it sends an acknowledgment only if it satisfies the condition. The initiator remains in the temporary state until it receives acknowledgments from all relevant processes (e.g., all processes to its right if the quantifier is $\forall_R$, or some process to its left if the quantifier is $\exists_L$, etc). Then, the initiator performs the third phase which consists of leaving the temporary state, and changing its local state and variables according to the transition. The request of the initiator is received independently by the different processes. Also, the processes send their acknowledgments independently. In particular this means that the initiator may receive the acknowledgments in any arbitrary order. To model the status of the request and acknowledgments, we use *edges*. A *request edge* is of the form $i \xrightarrow{\texttt{req}}_t j$ where i and j are process indices and $t \in T$ is a transition. Such an edge indicates that process i is in a temporary state trying to perform transition t (which contains a global condition); and that it has issued a request which is yet to be acknowledged by process j. An *acknowledgment edge* is of the form $i \xleftarrow{\texttt{ack}}_t j$ with a similar interpretation, except that it indicates that the request of process i has been acknowledged by process j. Observe that if a process is in a temporary state, then it must be an initiator.

Configurations. A *configuration* $c \in C$ is a pair (U, E) where $U = u_1 \cdots u_n$ is a sequence of process states, and E is a set of edges. We use $|c|$ to denote the number of processes inside c, i.e., $|c| = n$. Intuitively, the above configuration corresponds to an instance of the system with n processes. Each pair $u_i = (q_i, v_i)$ gives the local state and the values of local variables of process i. We use $U[i]$ to denote u_i. The set E encodes the current status of requests and acknowledgments among the processes. A configuration must also satisfy the following two invariants:

1. If u_i is a temporary process state (for some transition t) then, for each $j : 1 \leq j \neq i \leq n$, the set E contains either an edge of the form $i \xrightarrow{\texttt{req}}_t j$ or an edge of the form $i \xleftarrow{\texttt{ack}}_t j$ (but not both). This is done to keep track of the processes which have acknowledged request of i.
2. If u_i is not a temporary process state then the set E does not contain any edge of the form $i \xrightarrow{\texttt{req}}_t j$ or $i \xleftarrow{\texttt{ack}}_t j$, for any $t \in T$ and for any $j : 1 \leq j \neq i \leq n$. That is, if process i is not in a temporary states, then it is not currently waiting for acknowledgments, and hence no edges of the above form need to be stored.

Transition Relation. Consider two configurations $c = (U, E)$ and $c' = (U', E')$ with $|c| = |c'| = n$. We describe how c can perform a transition to obtain c'. Such a transition is performed by some process with index i for some $i : 1 \leq i \leq n$. We write $c \xrightarrow{i} c'$ to denote that (i) $U[j] = U'[j]$ for each $j : 1 \leq j \neq i \leq n$ (i.e., only process i changes state during the transition); and (ii) that there is a $t \in T$ of the form (1) such that one the following four conditions is satisfied (each condition corresponds to one type of transitions):

- *Local Transitions:* $grd \in \mathbb{B}(X)$, $U[i] = (q, v)$, $U'[i] = (q', v')$, $v \models grd$, $v' = stmt(v)$, and $E' = E$. By $grd \in \mathbb{B}(X)$, we mean that t is a local transition. The values of the local variables of the process should satisfy the guard *grd*, and they are modified according to *stmt*. The local states and variables of other processes are not relevant during the transition. Since the transition does not involve global conditions, the edges remains unchanged.
- *Refinement Protocol – First Phase:* $grd = \Box\theta \in \mathbb{G}(Y)$, $U[i] = (q, v)$, $U'[i] = (q^t, v)$, and $E' = E \cup \{i \xrightarrow{\texttt{req}}_t j | \ 1 \leq j \neq i \leq n\}$. Since $grd \in \mathbb{G}(Y)$, the transition t contains a global condition. The initiator, which is process i, triggers the first phase of the refinement protocol. To do this, it moves to the temporary state q^t. It also sends a request to all other processes, which means that the new set of edges E' should be modified accordingly. The local variables of the initiator are not changed during this step.
- *Refinement Protocol – Second Phase:* $grd = \Box\theta \in \mathbb{G}(Y)$, $U[i]$ is a temporary process state, $U'[i] = U[i]$, and there is a $j : 1 \leq j \neq i \leq n$ such that $U[j]^* \models \theta$ and $E' = E - \{i \xrightarrow{\texttt{req}}_t j\} \cup \{i \xleftarrow{\texttt{ack}}_t j\}$. A process (with index j) which satisfies the condition θ sends an acknowledgment to the initiator (process i). To reflect this, the relevant request edge is replaced by the corresponding acknowledgment edge. No local states or variables of any processes

are changed. Notice that we use $U[j]^*$ in the interpretation of the guard. This means that a process which is in the middle of checking a global condition, is assumed to be in its original local state until all the phases of the refinement protocol have successfully been carried out.

– *Refinement Protocol – Third Phase:* $grd = \Box\theta \in \mathbb{G}(Y)$, $U[i] = (q^t, v)$, $U'[i] = (q', v')$, $v' = stmt(v)$, $E' = E - \{i \overset{\texttt{ack}}{\longleftarrow}_t j |\ 1 \leq j \neq i \leq n\} - \{i \overset{\texttt{req}}{\longrightarrow}_t j |\ 1 \leq j \neq i \leq n\}$, and one of the following conditions holds:
  - $\Box = \forall_L$ and $(i \overset{\texttt{ack}}{\longleftarrow}_t j) \in E$ for each $j : 1 \leq j < i$.
  - $\Box = \forall_R$ and $(i \overset{\texttt{ack}}{\longleftarrow}_t j) \in E$ for each $j : i < j \leq n$.
  - $\Box = \forall_{LR}$ and $(i \overset{\texttt{ack}}{\longleftarrow}_t j) \in E$ for each $j : 1 \leq j \neq i \leq n$.
  - $\Box = \exists_L$ and $(i \overset{\texttt{ack}}{\longleftarrow}_t j) \in E$ for some $j : 1 \leq j < i$.
  - $\Box = \exists_R$ and $(i \overset{\texttt{ack}}{\longleftarrow}_t j) \in E$ for some $j : i < j \leq n$.
  - $\Box = \exists_{LR}$ and $(i \overset{\texttt{ack}}{\longleftarrow}_t j) \in E$ for some $j : 1 \leq j \neq i \leq n$.

  The initiator has received acknowledgments from the relevant processes. The set of relevant processes depends on the type of the quantifier. For instance, in case the quantifier is $\forall_L$ then the initiator waits for acknowledgments from all processes to its left (with indices smaller than i). Similarly, if the quantifier is $\exists_R$ then the initiator waits for an acknowledgment from some process to its right (with index larger than i), and so on. The initiator leaves its temporary state and moves to a new local state (the state q') as required by the transition rule t. Also, the values of the local variables of the initiator are updated according to *stmt*. Since, process i is not in a temporary state any more, all the corresponding edges are removed from the configuration.

We use $c \longrightarrow c'$ to denote that $c \overset{i}{\longrightarrow} c'$ for some i.

Variants of Refinement Protocols. Our method can be modified to deal with several different variants of the refinement protocol described in Section 3. Observe that in the original version of the protocol, a process may either acknowledge a request or remain passive. One can consider a variant where we allow processes to explicitly refuse acknowledging of requests, by sending back a negative acknowledgment (a `nack`). We can also define different variants depending on the way a failure of a global condition is treated (in the third phase of the protocol). For instance, the initiator may be allowed to reset the protocol, by re-sending requests to all the processes (or only to the processes which have sent a negative acknowledgment).

4 Safety Properties

In order to analyze safety properties, we study the *coverability problem* defined below. Given a parameterized system $\mathcal{P} = (Q, X, T)$, we assume that, prior to starting the execution of the system, each process is in an (identical) *initial* process state $u_{init} = (q_{init}, v_{init})$. In the induced transition system $\mathcal{T}(\mathcal{P}) = (C, \longrightarrow)$, we use *Init* to denote the set of *initial* configurations, i.e., configurations of the form (U_{init}, E_{init}), where $U_{init} = u_{init} \cdots u_{init}$ and $E_{init} = \emptyset$. In other words, all processes are in their initial states, and there are no edges between the processes. Notice that the set of initial configurations is infinite.

We define an ordering on configurations as follows. Given two configurations, $c = (U, E)$ with $|c| = m$, and $c' = (U', E')$ with $|c'| = n$, we write $c \preceq c'$ to denote that there is a strictly monotonic[1] injection h from the set $\overline{m}$ to the set $\overline{n}$ such that the following conditions are satisfied for each $t \in T$ and $i, j : 1 \leq i \neq j \leq m$: (i) $u_i = u'_{h(i)}$, (ii) if $(i \xrightarrow{\texttt{req}}_t j) \in E$ then $(h(i) \xrightarrow{\texttt{req}}_t h(j)) \in E'$, and (iii) if $(i \xleftarrow{\texttt{ack}}_t j) \in E$ then $(h(i) \xleftarrow{\texttt{ack}}_t h(j)) \in E'$. In other words, for each process in c there is a corresponding process in c' with the same local state and with the same values of local variables. Furthermore, each request edge in c is matched by a request edge between the corresponding processes in c', while each acknowledgment edge in c is matched by an acknowledgment edge between the corresponding processes in c'.

A set of configurations $D \subseteq C$ is *upward closed* (with respect to $\preceq$) if $c \in D$ and $c \preceq c'$ implies $c' \in D$. The *coverability problem* for parameterized systems is defined as follows:

PAR-COV
Instance A parameterized system $\mathcal{P} = (Q, X, T)$ and an upward closed set C_F of configurations.
Question $Init \xrightarrow{*} C_F$?

It can be shown, using standard techniques (see e.g. [18,11]), that checking safety properties (expressed as regular languages) can be translated into instances of the coverability problem. Therefore, checking safety properties amounts to solving PAR-COV (i.e., to the reachability of upward closed sets). Intuitively, we use C_F to denote a set of bad states which we do not want to occur during the execution of the system. For instance, in a mutual exclusion protocol, if the local state q_{crit} corresponds to the process being in the critical section, then C_F can be defined to be the set of all configurations where at least two processes are in q_{crit}. In such a case, C_F is the set of bad configurations (those violating the mutual exclusion property). Notice that once a configuration has two processes in q_{crit} then it will belong to C_F regardless of the values of the local variables, the states of the rest of processes, and the edges between the processes. This implies that C_F is upward closed.

5 Approximation

In this section, we introduce an over-approximation of the transition relation of a parameterized system. The aim of the over-approximations is to derive a new transition system which is *monotonic* with respect to the ordering $\preceq$ defined on configurations in Section 4. Formally, a transition system is monotonic with respect to the ordering $\preceq$, if for any configurations c_1, c_2, c_3 such that $c_1 \rightarrow c_2$

[1] $h : \overline{m} \rightarrow \overline{n}$ strictly monotonic means: $i < j \Rightarrow h(i) < h(j)$ for all $i, j : 1 \leq i, j \leq m$.

and $c_1 \preceq c_3$; there exists a configuration c_4 such that $c_3 \rightarrow c_4$ and $c_2 \preceq c_4$. The only transitions which violate monotonicity are those corresponding to the third phase of the refinement protocol when the quantifier is universal. Therefore, the approximate transition system modifies the behavior of the third phase in such a manner that monotonicity is maintained. More precisely, in the new semantics, we remove all processes in the configuration which have failed to acknowledge the request of the initiator (the corresponding edge is a request rather than an acknowledgment). Below we describe formally how this is done.

In Section 3, we mentioned that each parameterized system $\mathcal{P} = (Q, X, T)$ induces a transition system $\mathcal{T}(\mathcal{P}) = (C, \longrightarrow)$. A parameterized system $\mathcal{P}$ also induces an *approximate* transition system $\mathcal{A}(\mathcal{P}) = (C, \rightsquigarrow)$; the set C of configurations is identical to the one in $\mathcal{T}(\mathcal{P})$. We define $\rightsquigarrow = (\longrightarrow \cup \rightsquigarrow_1)$, where $\longrightarrow$ is defined in Section 3, and $\rightsquigarrow_1$ (which reflects the approximation of universal quantifiers in third phase of the refinement protocol) is defined as follows.

Consider two configurations $c = (U, E)$ and $c' = (U', E')$ with $|c| = n$ and $|c'| = m$. Suppose that $U[i] = (q^t, v)$ for some $i : 1 \leq i \leq n$ and some transition of the form of (1) where $grd = \Box\theta \in \mathbb{G}(Y)$ with $\Box \in \{\forall_L, \forall_R, \forall_{LR}\}$. In other words, in c, process i is in a temporary state, performing the second phase of refinement protocol with respect to a universal quantifier. We write $c \overset{i}{\rightsquigarrow}_1 c'$ to denote that there is a strictly monotonic injection $h : \overline{m} \mapsto \overline{n}$ such that the following conditions are satisfied (the image of h represents the indices of the processes we keep in the configuration):

- j is in the image of h iff one of the following conditions is satisfied: (i) $j = i$, (ii) $\Box = \forall_L$ and either $j > i$ or $(i \overset{\mathtt{ack}}{\longleftarrow}_t j) \in E$, (iii) $\Box = \forall_R$ and either $j < i$ or $(i \overset{\mathtt{ack}}{\longleftarrow}_t j) \in E$, (iv) $\Box = \forall_{LR}$ and $(i \overset{\mathtt{ack}}{\longleftarrow}_t j) \in E$. That is we keep the initiator (process i) together with all the relevant processes who have acknowledged its request.
- $U'[h^{-1}(i)] = (q', \mathit{stmt}(v))$ and $U'[j] = U[h(j)]$ for $h(j) \neq i$, i.e., the local variables of process i are updated according to *stmt* while the states and local variables of other processes are not changed.
- E' is obtained from E as follows. For all $j, k \in \overline{m}$ and $t' \in T$, (i) $(j \overset{\mathtt{ack}}{\longleftarrow}_{t'} k) \in E'$ iff $(h(j) \overset{\mathtt{ack}}{\longleftarrow}_{t'} h(k)) \in E$, and (ii) $(j \overset{\mathtt{req}}{\longrightarrow}_{t'} k) \in E'$ iff $(h(j) \overset{\mathtt{req}}{\longrightarrow}_{t'} h(k)) \in E$. In other words, we remove all edges connected to processes which are removed from the configuration c.

We use $c \rightsquigarrow_1 c'$ to denote that $c \overset{i}{\rightsquigarrow}_1 c'$ for some i.

Lemma 1. *The approximate transition system* $(C, \rightsquigarrow)$ *is monotonic w.r.t.* $\preceq$.

We define the coverability problem for the approximate system as follows.

<u>APRX-PAR-COV</u>
Instance A parameterized system $\mathcal{P} = (Q, X, T)$ and an upward closed set C_F of configurations.
Question $\mathit{Init} \overset{*}{\rightsquigarrow} C_F$?

Since $\longrightarrow \subseteq \rightsquigarrow$, a negative answer to APRX-PAR-COV implies a negative answer to PAR-COV.

6 Backward Reachability Analysis

In this section, we present a scheme based on backward reachability analysis and we show how to instantiate it for solving APRX-PAR-COV. For the rest of this section, we assume a parameterized system $\mathcal{P} = (Q, X, T)$ and the induced approximate transition system $\mathcal{A}(\mathcal{P}) = (C, \rightsquigarrow)$.

Constraints. The scheme operates on *constraints* which we use as a symbolic representation for sets of configurations. A constraint ϕ denotes an upward closed set $[\![\phi]\!] \subseteq C$ of configurations. The constraint ϕ represents minimal conditions on configurations. More precisely, ϕ specifies a minimum number of processes which should be in the configuration, and then imposes certain conditions on these processes. The conditions are formulated as specifications of the states and local variables of the processes, and as restrictions on the set of edges. A configuration c which satisfies ϕ should have at least the number of processes specified by ϕ. The local states and the values of the local variables should satisfy the conditions imposed by ϕ. Furthermore, c should contain at least the set of edges required by ϕ. In such a case, c may have any number of additional edges and processes (whose local states and local variables are then irrelevant for the satisfiability of ϕ by c). This definition implies that the interpretation $[\![\phi]\!]$ of a constraint ϕ is upward closed (a fact proved in Lemma 2). Below, we define the notion of a constraint formally.

A constraint is a pair (Θ, E) where $\Theta = \theta_1 \cdots \theta_m$ is a sequence with $\theta_i \in \mathbb{B}(X \cup Q^\bullet)$, and E is a set of edges of the form $i \xrightarrow{\texttt{req}}_t j$ or $i \xleftarrow{\texttt{ack}}_t j$ with $t \in T$ and $1 \leq i, j \leq m$. We use $\Theta(i)$ to denote θ_i and $|\phi|$ to denote m. Intuitively, a configuration satisfying ϕ should contain at least m processes, where the local state and variables of the ith process satisfy θ_i. Furthermore the set E defines the minimal set of edges which should exist in the configuration. More precisely, for a constraint $\phi = (\Theta, E_1)$ with $|\phi| = m$, and a configuration $c = (U, E_2)$ with $|c| = n$, we write $c \models \phi$ to denote that there is a strictly monotonic injection h from the set $\overline{m}$ to the set $\overline{n}$ such that the following conditions are satisfied for each $t \in T$ and $i, j : 1 \leq i, j \leq m$: (i) $u_{h(i)} \models \theta_i$, (ii) if $(i \xrightarrow{\texttt{req}}_t j) \in E_1$ then $(h(i) \xrightarrow{\texttt{req}}_t h(j)) \in E_2$, and (iii) if $(i \xleftarrow{\texttt{ack}}_t j) \in E_1$ then $(h(i) \xleftarrow{\texttt{ack}}_t h(j)) \in E_2$. Given a constraint ϕ, we let $[\![\phi]\!] = \{c \in C |\ c \models \phi\}$. Notice that if some θ_i is unsatisfiable then $[\![\phi]\!]$ is empty. Such a constraint can therefore be safely discarded if it arises in the algorithm. For a (finite) set of constraints Φ, we define $[\![\Phi]\!] = \bigcup_{\phi \in \Phi} [\![\phi]\!]$. The following lemma follows from the definitions.

Lemma 2. *For each constraint ϕ, the set $[\![\phi]\!]$ is upward closed.*

In all the examples we consider, the set C_F in the definition of APRX-PAR-COV can be represented by a finite set Φ_F of constraints. The coverability question can then be answered by checking whether $Init \overset{*}{\rightsquigarrow} [\![\Phi_F]\!]$.

Entailment and Predecessors. To define our scheme we will use two operations on constraints; namely *entailment*, and *computing predecessors*, defined below. We define an *entailment relation* $\sqsubseteq$ on constraints, where $\phi_1 \sqsubseteq \phi_2$ iff $[\![\phi_2]\!] \subseteq [\![\phi_1]\!]$. For sets Φ_1, Φ_2 of constraints, abusing notation, we let $\Phi_1 \sqsubseteq \Phi_2$ denote that for each $\phi_2 \in \Phi_2$ there is a $\phi_1 \in \Phi_1$ with $\phi_1 \sqsubseteq \phi_2$. Observe that $\Phi_1 \sqsubseteq \Phi_2$ implies that $[\![\Phi_2]\!] \subseteq [\![\Phi_1]\!]$. The lemma below, which follows from the definitions, gives a syntactic characterization which allows computing of the entailment relation.

Lemma 3. *For constraints $\phi = (\Theta, E)$ and $\phi' = (\Theta', E')$ of size m and n respectively , we have $\phi \sqsubseteq \phi'$ iff there exists a strictly monotonic injection $h : \overline{m} \rightarrow \overline{n}$ such that:*

1. *$\Theta'(h(i)) \Rightarrow \Theta(i)$ for each $i \in \overline{m}$, and*
2. *$\forall i, j : 1 \leq i, j \leq m$ and $\forall t \in T$, the following conditions holds: (i) if $i \xrightarrow{\texttt{req}}_t j \in E$ then $h(i) \xrightarrow{\texttt{req}}_t h(j) \in E'$, and (ii) if $i \xleftarrow{\texttt{ack}}_t j \in E$ then $h(i) \xleftarrow{\texttt{ack}}_t h(j) \in E'$.*

For a constraint ϕ, we let $Pre(\phi)$ be a set of constraints, such that $[\![Pre(\phi)]\!] = \{c |\ \exists c' \in [\![\phi]\!] \,.\, c \rightsquigarrow c'\}$. In other words $Pre(\phi)$ characterizes the set of configurations from which we can reach a configuration in ϕ through the application of a single rule in the approximate transition relation. In the definition of *Pre* we rely on the fact that, in any monotonic transition system, upward-closedness is preserved under the computation of the set of predecessors (see e.g. [1]). From Lemma 2 we know that $[\![\phi]\!]$ is upward closed; by Lemma 1, $(C, \rightsquigarrow)$ is monotonic, we therefore know that $[\![Pre(\phi)]\!]$ is upward closed.

Lemma 4. *For any constraint ϕ, $Pre(\phi)$ is computable.*

For a set Φ of constraints, we let $Pre(\Phi) = \bigcup_{\phi \in \Phi} Pre(\phi)$.

Scheme. Given a finite set Φ_F of constraints, the scheme checks whether $Init \xrightarrow{*} [\![\Phi_F]\!]$. We perform a backward reachability analysis, generating a sequence $\Phi_0 \sqsupseteq \Phi_1 \sqsupseteq \Phi_2 \sqsupseteq \cdots$ of finite sets of constraints such that $\Phi_0 = \Phi_F$, and $\Phi_{j+1} = \Phi_j \cup Pre(\Phi_j)$. Since $[\![\Phi_0]\!] \subseteq [\![\Phi_1]\!] \subseteq [\![\Phi_2]\!] \subseteq \cdots$, the procedure terminates when we reach a point j where $\Phi_j \sqsubseteq \Phi_{j+1}$. Notice that the termination condition implies that $[\![\Phi_j]\!] = (\bigcup_{0 \leq i \leq j} [\![\Phi_i]\!])$. Consequently, Φ_j characterizes the set of all predecessors of $[\![\phi_F]\!]$. This means that $Init \overset{*}{\rightsquigarrow} [\![\Phi_F]\!]$ iff $(Init \bigcap [\![\Phi_j]\!]) \neq \emptyset$. In order to check emptiness of $(Init \bigcap [\![\Phi_j]\!])$, we rely on the result below which follows from the definitions. For a constraint $\phi = (\Theta, E)$, we have $(Init \bigcap [\![\phi]\!]) = \emptyset$ iff either $E \neq \emptyset$, or $u_{init} \not\models \Theta(i)$ for some $i \in \overline{n}$. Observe that, in order to implement the scheme we need to be able to (i) compute *Pre* (Lemma 4); (ii) check for entailment between constraints (Lemma 3); and (iii) check for emptiness of $(Init \bigcap [\![\phi]\!])$ for a constraint ϕ (as described above).

7 Unbounded Variables

In this section, we extend the basic model of Section 2 in two ways. First, we consider processes which operate on variables with unbounded domains. More precisely, we allow local variables to range over the integers, and use a simple set of formulas, called *gap-order formulas*, to constrain the numerical variables in the guards. Furthermore, we allow nondeterministic assignment, where a variable may be assigned any value satisfying a guard. The new value of a variable may also depend on the values of variables of the other processes. Due to shortage of space we will only give an overview of the main ideas.

Consider a set A, partitioned into a set $A_{\mathcal{B}}$ of Boolean variables, and a set $A_{\mathbb{N}}$ of numerical variables. The set of *gap-order formulas* over $A_{\mathbb{N}}$, denoted $\mathbb{GF}(A_{\mathbb{N}})$, is the set of formulas which are either of the form $x = y$, $x \leq y$ or $x <_k y$, where $k \in \mathbb{N}$. Here $x <_k y$ stands for $x + k < y$ and specifies a *gap* of k units between y and x. We use $\mathbb{F}(A)$ to denote the set of formulas which have members of $\mathbb{B}(A_{\mathcal{B}})$ and of $\mathbb{GF}(A_{\mathbb{N}})$ as atomic formulas, and which is closed under the Boolean connectives $\wedge, \vee$. For a set A, we use $A^{next} = \{x^{next} | \; x \in A\}$ to refer to the *next-value* versions of the variables in A.

Transitions. In our extended model, the set of local variables X is the union of a set $X_{\mathcal{B}}$ of Boolean variables and a set $X_{\mathbb{N}}$ of numerical variables. As mentioned above, variables may be assigned values which are derived from those of the other processes. To model this, we use the set $p{\cdot}Y = \{p{\cdot}x | x \in Y\}$ to refer to the local state and variables of process p. We consider a global condition to be of the form $\forall p : \theta$ where $\theta \in \mathbb{F}(X \cup p{\cdot}Y \cup X^{next})$. In other words, the formula checks the local variables of the initiator (through X), and the local states and variables of the other processes (through $p{\cdot}Y$). It also specifies how the local variables of the process in transition are updated (through X^{next}). Notice that the new values are defined in terms of the current values of variables and local states of all the other processes. Other types of transitions can be extended in an analogous manner. Values of next-variables not mentioned in θ remain unchanged.

Example 1. As an example, let the guard in the above transition rule be of the form $\forall p : p \cdot num < num^{next}$ where num is a numerical variable. Then, this means that the process assigns to its variable num, a new value which is strictly greater than the values of num in all other processes. Such a rule is used for instance in the Bakery algorithm to generate new tickets.

The Refinement Protocol. The first phase of the refinement protocol remains the same as in the basic model, i.e., the initiator sends requests to all other processes. The second phase is modified, so that an acknowledgment edge carries information about the responding process, i.e., the acknowledgment sent by process p has the form $ack_p(u_p)$ where u_p is the current local state of p. In the third phase, the initiator checks the global condition by looking at the values attached to the acknowledgments, and updates its own local variables accordingly. For instance, in the above example, the initiator receives the values of the variables num of all the other processes on the acknowledgment edges. Then, it chooses a new value which is larger than all received values.

Constraints. The constraint system is modified so that we add gap-order constraints on the local variables of the processes and also on the values carried by the acknowledgment edges. Performing operations such as checking entailment and computing predecessors on constraints with gap-orders can be carried out in a similar manner to [2].

8 Experimental Results

We have implemented our method in a prototype that we have run on several parameterized systems, including non-atomic refinements of Burn's protocol, Dijkstra's protocol and the Bakery's algorithm, as well as on the Lamport distributed Mutual exclusion protocol and the two-phase commit protocol. The Bakery and Lamport protocols have numerical local variables, while the rest have bounded local variables. The refinement $\mathcal{R}_1$ used for the first two algorithms corresponds to the refinement protocol introduced in Section 3. The refinements $\mathcal{R}_2$ and $\mathcal{R}_3$ are those introduced in the end of Section 3. More precisely, in $\mathcal{R}_2$, the initiator re-sends a request to all the processes whose values violate the global condition being tested. In $\mathcal{R}_3$, the initiator re-sends requests to all other processes.

The results, using a 2 GHZ computer with 1 GB of memory, are summarized in Table 1. We give for each case study, the number of iterations, the time, the number of constraints in the result, and an estimate of memory usage. Details of the case studies can be found in [3].

Table 1. Experimental results on several mutual exclusion algorithms

	refine	iterat.	time	final constr.	memory
Burns	$\mathcal{R}_1$	26	0.5 sec	44	1MB
Dijkstra	$\mathcal{R}_1$	93	0.5 sec	41	1MB
Bakery	$\mathcal{R}_2$	4	0.06 sec	12	1MB
Bakery	$\mathcal{R}_3$	4	0.06 sec	12	1MB
Two Phase Commit	-	6	0.03 sec	9	1MB
Lamport	-	29	30 mn	4676	222MB

9 Conclusions and Future Work

We have presented a method for automatic verification of parameterized systems. The main feature of the method is that it can handle global conditions which are not assumed to be atomic operations. We have built a prototype which we have successfully applied on a number of non-trivial mutual exclusion protocols. There are several interesting directions for future work. First, our algorithm operates essentially on infinite sets of graphs. Therefore, it seems feasible to extend the method to other classes of systems whose configurations can be modeled by graphs such as cache coherence protocols and dynamically allocated data structures. Furthermore, although the method works successfully on several examples, there is at least one protocol (namely the non-atomic version of Szymanski's protocol) where the method gives a false positive. We believe that this problem can be solved by introducing a scheme which allows refining the abstraction (the over-approximation). Therefore, we plan to define a CEGAR (Counter-Example Guided Abstraction Refinement) scheme on more exact representations of sets of configurations.

References

1. Abdulla, P., et al.: Algorithmic analysis of programs with well quasi-ordered domains. ICom 160, 109–127 (2000)
2. Abdulla, P., Delzanno, G., Rezine, A.: Parameterized Verification of Infinite-State Processes with Global Conditions. In: Damm, W., Hermanns, H. (eds.) CAV 2007. LNCS, vol. 4590, pp. 145–157. Springer, Heidelberg (2007)
3. Abdulla, P., et al.: Handling parameterized systems with non-atomic global conditions. Technical Report 2007-030, it (2007)
4. Abdulla, P., et al.: Regular Model Checking Without Transducers (On Efficient Verification of Parameterized Systems). In: Grumberg, O., Huth, M. (eds.) TACAS 2007. LNCS, vol. 4424, pp. 721–736. Springer, Heidelberg (2007)
5. Abdulla, P., et al.: Regular Model Checking Made Simple and Efficient. In: Brim, L., et al. (eds.) CONCUR 2002. LNCS, vol. 2421, pp. 116–130. Springer, Heidelberg (2002)
6. Pnueli, A., et al.: Parameterized Verification with Automatically Computed Inductive Assertions. In: Berry, G., Comon, H., Finkel, A. (eds.) CAV 2001. LNCS, vol. 2102, pp. 221–234. Springer, Heidelberg (2001)
7. Boigelot, B., Legay, A., Wolper, P.: Iterating Transducers in the Large. In: Hunt Jr., W.A., Somenzi, F. (eds.) CAV 2003. LNCS, vol. 2725, pp. 223–235. Springer, Heidelberg (2003)
8. Chkliaev, D., Hooman, J., van der Stok, P.: Mechanical verification of transaction processing systems. In: ICFEM 2000 (2000)
9. Clarke, E., Talupur, M., Veith, H.: Environment Abstraction for Parameterized Verification. In: Emerson, E.A., Namjoshi, K.S. (eds.) VMCAI 2006. LNCS, vol. 3855, pp. 126–141. Springer, Heidelberg (2005)
10. Delzanno, G.: Automatic verification of cache coherence protocols. In: Emerson, E.A., Sistla, A.P. (eds.) CAV 2000. LNCS, vol. 1855, pp. 53–68. Springer, Heidelberg (2000)
11. Godefroid, P., Wolper, P.: Using partial orders for the efficient verification of deadlock freedom and safety properties. FMSD 2(2), 149–164 (1993)
12. Gray, J., Reuter, A.: Transaction Processing: Concepts and Techniques. Morgan Kaufmann, San Francisco (1992)
13. Kesten, Y., et al.: Symbolic model checking with rich assertional languages. TCS 256, 93–112 (2001)
14. Lahiri, S.K., Bryant, R.E.: Indexed Predicate Discovery for Unbounded System Verification. In: Alur, R., Peled, D.A. (eds.) CAV 2004. LNCS, vol. 3114, pp. 135–147. Springer, Heidelberg (2004)
15. Lamport, L.: Time, clocks and the ordering of events in a distributed system. CACM 21(7), 558–565 (1978)
16. Manna, Z., et al.: STEP: the Stanford Temporal Prover. Draft Manuscript (1994)
17. Revesz, P.: A closed form evaluation for datalog queries with integer (gap)-order constraints. TCS 116, 117–149 (1993)
18. Vardi, M.Y., Wolper, P.: An automata-theoretic approach to automatic program verification. In: Proc. LICS 1986, pp. 332–344 (1986)

Abstract Interpretation of the Physical Inputs of Embedded Programs

Olivier Bouissou[1] and Matthieu Martel[2]

[1] CEA LIST
Laboratoire MeASI
F-91191 Gif-sur-Yvette Cedex, France
Olivier.Bouissou@cea.fr

[2] Laboratoire ELIAUS-DALI
Université de Perpignan Via Domitia
66860 Perpignan Cedex
Matthieu.Martel@univ-perp.fr

Abstract. We define an abstraction of the continuous variables that serve as inputs to embedded software. In existing static analyzers, these variables are most often abstracted by a constant interval, and this approach has shown its limits. We propose a different method that analyzes in a more precise way the continuous environment. This environment is first expressed as the semantics of a special continuous program, and we define a safe abstract semantics. We introduce the abstract domain of interval valued step functions and show that it safely over-approximates the set of continuous functions. The theory of guaranteed integration is then used to effectively compute an abstract semantics and we prove that this abstract semantics is safe.

1 Introduction

The behavior of an embedded system depends on both a discrete system (the program) and a continuous system (the physical environment). The program constantly interacts with the environment, picking up physical values by means of sensors and modifying them via actuators. Thus, static analyzers for critical embedded software [4,13] usually face the discrete part of a wider, hybrid system [17] but they often poorly abstract the physical environment in which, in practice, the embedded systems are run. To take an extreme example (more reasonable examples abound in articles dedicated to hybrid systems [1,23]), the static analysis of avionic codes should abstract the plane environment, that is, the engines, the wings, and the atmosphere itself.

In practice, the sensors correspond to volatile variables in C programs and, at analysis-time, the user must assign to these variables a range given by the minimal and maximal values the sensor can send. In this case, a static analyzer assumes that the value sent by the sensor may switch from its minimum to its maximum in an arbitrary short laps of time, while, in practice, it follows a continuous evolution. As a consequence, the results of the static analysis are

F. Logozzo et al. (Eds.): VMCAI 2008, LNCS 4905, pp. 37–51, 2008.

significantly over-approximated, and our experience with Fluctuat [13] has shown that this naive abstraction of the continuous variables is an important source of loss of precision. The abstraction of the physical environment is even more crucial for embedded systems that cannot be physically tested in their real environment, like space crafts whose safety only relies on verification tools.

In this article, we consider a special case of hybrid systems: the continuous environment serves as input for the discrete system which is represented by the embedded program. We present an analysis of the continuous part of the system using the abstract interpretation framework [8]. Our analysis permits a better over-approximation of the continuous variables than an abstraction with intervals and can be seen as the first step in the process of introducing hybrid components to existing static analyzers. A first approach to the abstraction of a continuous function could be done as follows: first partition the time line into (not necessarily regular) steps and then chose for each step an over- and under-approximation of the function on this step. This technique defines a family of Galois connections between various domains (one for each choice of the partitioning [22]), but is not compatible with efficient implementations. We indeed compute the over- and under-approximations using validated ODE solvers (see Section 4); modern algorithms [6,24] dynamically change the step size, and thus dynamically partition the time line, in order to reach a user defined precision. We must then consider an abstract domain for which the step sizes are not statically defined (see Section 3). This article is focused on the definition and correction of the abstract domain and we omit for the sake of conciseness the purely numerical aspects of the computation: the method briefly described in Section 5 is fully developped in [6]. In addition, a guaranteed extrapolation algorithm that safely bounds a function on an interval $[t, \infty[$ would be necessary to find a non naive widening. These purely numerical aspects are out of the scope of this article.

This article is organized as follows. In Section 2, we describe the continuous environment as the collecting semantics of a continuous program, described by an interval valued ODE. As most collecting semantics of usual programs, this semantics is neither representable in machine nor computable, so we present in Section 3 an abstract domain which can be effectively used for the over-approximation of continuous functions. We also give correctness criteria in order to build a safe abstraction of elements of the concrete domain. In Section 4, we show that guaranteed integration algorithms compute an abstract semantics of the ODE and we prove that this semantics is a safe over-approximation of the collecting one in Section 5. Finally, we show (Section 6) using a basic example that our approach gives better results than a naive abstraction of the environment using intervals.

To our knowledge, this is the first formalism that allows for the integration of the continuous environment in an abstract interpretation of embedded software. Edalat et al. defined a domain theoretic characterization of continuous functions [11,12] and showed that the solution to ODEs can be obtained by successive approximations. Their work is located at the concrete level, as they describe the continuous functions, and it does not provide an abstraction in the sense of the abstract interpretation theory, which is the main result of the present article. On the other hand, the analysis of non-linear hybrid automata using guaranteed ODE solvers was implemented in HyperTech [18], but the continuous dynamics is not defined by its own, which is necessary for the analysis of embedded software where the discrete and the continuous subsystems are clearly disjoint. Previous works on abstract interpretation strategies for hybrid systems mainly involved the analysis of hybrid automata [16].

1.1 Notation

The set of real numbers is $\mathbb{R}$, while the set of non negative real numbers is $\mathbb{R}_+$. The set of natural numbers is $\mathbb{N}$. We will also consider the set of floating point numbers $\mathbb{F}$ [25]. The domain of continuous functions defined on $\mathbb{R}_+$ with values in $\mathbb{R}$ is $\mathcal{C}^0_+$ and the set of differentiable functions from $\mathbb{R}_+$ to $\mathbb{R}$ is $\mathcal{C}^1_+$. For a function $f \in \mathcal{C}^1_+$, we note $\dot{f} \in \mathcal{C}^0_+$ its first derivative. We use bold symbols to represent intervals: given a domain $\mathcal{D}$ with an order $\leq_{\mathcal{D}}$, the set of *intervals* on $\mathcal{D}$ is $\boldsymbol{D}$. Elements of $\boldsymbol{D}$ are denoted $\boldsymbol{x}$; for an interval $\boldsymbol{x} \in \boldsymbol{D}$, we note its lower bound $\underline{\boldsymbol{x}}$ and its upper bound $\overline{\boldsymbol{x}}$, such that $\boldsymbol{x} = \{x \in \mathcal{D} \mid \underline{\boldsymbol{x}} \leq_{\mathcal{D}} x \leq_{\mathcal{D}} \overline{\boldsymbol{x}}\}$. In particular, we will consider the set of intervals on real numbers $\boldsymbol{R}$, intervals on non negative real numbers $\boldsymbol{R}_+$ and intervals on floating point numbers $\boldsymbol{F}$. Finally, we use arrows to represent vectors: given a domain $\mathcal{D}$, the set of vectors of dimension n is $\mathcal{D}^n$ and elements of $\mathcal{D}^n$ are denoted $\overrightarrow{x}$. Vectors of intervals are denoted $\overrightarrow{\boldsymbol{x}}$.

2 Syntax and Semantics of Continuous Processes

Hybrid systems are composed of two intrinsically different processes that run in parallel: a discrete program and a continuous environment. In order to deal with and to analyze the whole system, one needs to find a unified representation of both parts. As for computer programs, we define a syntax, a collecting and an abstract semantics of the continuous environment. This section is dedicated to the definition of the concrete part.

2.1 Syntax

The environment represents physical quantities such as the temperature of the air, the speed of the wind or the deceleration of a car. Such quantities evolve continuously with time (i.e. their value cannot instantaneously jump from a to b), and thus follow a function from $\mathcal{C}^0_+$. Most often, this function is not explicitly known, but is defined as the solution to an *ordinary differential equation* (ODE). An ODE can be seen as a relation between a function $y \in \mathcal{C}^1_+$ and its first derivative $\dot{y}$ via a continuous function F: $\dot{y} = F\big(y; \overrightarrow{p}\big)$. $\overrightarrow{p}$ is a set of constant parameters (e.g. the gravitational constant, the length of the plane, etc.). This representation as an autonomous ODE of order 1 (i.e. F only depends on the spatial value of y, and not on the time t) is expressive enough to capture other forms of ODE (non-autonomous and higher order ODEs are easily transformed into higher dimensional autonomous ODEs of order one). An ODE relates the value of the system at time $t + dt$ with the value of the system at time t, which is the continuous equivalent to any discrete dynamical system. It consequently forms the *syntax* of the continuous process. In order to achieve more expressiveness, we allow the parameters of the function F to be intervals, leading to the notion of *interval ODE.*

Definition 1. *Interval ODE.*
Let F be a continuous function with a set of parameters $\overrightarrow{p} \in \overrightarrow{\mathbb{R}}$. An interval ordinary differential equation *(interval ODE) is given by the relation:* $\dot{y} = F(y; \overrightarrow{\boldsymbol{p}}),\ \ \overrightarrow{\boldsymbol{p}} \subseteq \overrightarrow{\boldsymbol{R}}$.

This formalism is expressive enough to capture most dynamical systems and the introduction of interval parameters makes it suitable to express uncertainties on the system. We extend the uncertainty to the initial conditions of the ODE, and define the notion of interval initial value problems.

Definition 2. *Interval IVP.*
Let F be a continuous function with a set of parameters $\overrightarrow{p}$. An interval initial value problem *is given by an interval ODE and an interval initial condition:*

$$\dot{y} = F(y, \overrightarrow{\boldsymbol{p}}) \quad y(0) \in \boldsymbol{y_0} \tag{1}$$

An interval IVP gives a complete characterization of a set of continuous environments using only three terms: a continuous function, a set of parameters and an initial interval value. We will thus write the physical environment `P:=(F,p,y)`, where `F` is the function, `p` its parameters and `y` the initial value. Example 1 shows how this compact notation is used to define a set of functions.

Example 1. The continuous process `P=(F,p,y)` with `F(y)=p*y`, `p=[-2,-1]` and `y=[0.5,3]` corresponds to the IVP $\dot{y} = p.y,\ y(0) \in [0.5, 3],\ p \in [-2, -1]$. It defines the functions $y(x) = q.e^{p.x}$ with $q \in [0.5, 3]$, $p \in [-2, -1]$ (see Figure 1).

2.2 Collecting Semantics

Just like the collecting semantics of a discrete program is the set of all the (discrete) execution traces corresponding to a set of input parameters, the collecting semantics of the continuous process `(F,p,y)` is the solution to the corresponding interval IVP, that is, the set of all possible dynamics (i.e. continuous traces) of the system. The solution to a (real valued) ODE $\dot{y} = F(y; \overrightarrow{p})$ is a function $y \in C^1_+$ such that for every time t, it holds that $\dot{y}(t) = F(y(t); \overrightarrow{p})$. The solution to a real valued initial value problem is a solution to the ODE that additionally satisfies the initial condition. The existence and/or uniqueness of this solution depends mainly on the function F, and this question is not relevant for this article. On the contrary, we will always assume that F is smooth enough so that there exists a solution y defined on $\mathbb{R}_+$ for any initial condition and any parameter. The notion of solution to an IVP is then extended to interval IVP:

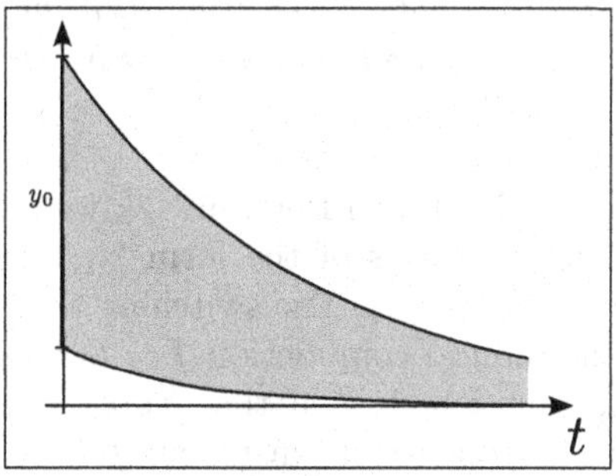

Fig. 1. Solutions to the interval ODE of Example 1

Definition 3. *Solution to an interval IVP.*
The solution to the interval IVP (1) is a set of functions $\mathcal{Y} \subseteq \mathcal{C}^1_+$ such that $y \in \mathcal{Y}$ if and only if there exists $p \in \boldsymbol{p}$ and $y_0 \in \boldsymbol{y_0}$ such that y is a solution to the (real valued) IVP $\dot{y} = F(y, p)$, $y(0) = y_0$.

The semantics $[\![\mathtt{P}]\!]$ of `P=(F,p,y)` is the solution to the interval initial value problem $\dot{y} = \mathtt{F}(y, \mathtt{p})$, $y(0) \in \mathtt{y}$. It is an element of the concrete domain $\mathcal{D} = \mathcal{P}(\mathcal{C}^1_+)$, the power set of $\mathcal{C}^1_+$. The inclusion $\subseteq$, union $\cup$ and intersection $\cap$ give a lattice structure to $\mathcal{D}$. Each element of $[\![\mathtt{P}]\!]$ is a continuous function which characterizes *one* particular evolution of the continuous system under *one* set of parameters and *one* input.

3 Abstract Domain

The concrete domain for the continuous processes is thus the powerset of the set of differentiable functions $\mathcal{C}^1_+$. In this section, we present an abstract domain that collects elements from $\mathcal{C}^1_+$.

3.1 Interval Valued Step Functions

Continuous functions are not enumerable in machine as they assign to an infinite, uncountable number of elements (every $t \in \mathbb{R}_+$) a value that is itself not representable (as a real number) in finite precision. Thus, an abstraction of a set of continuous functions must abstract the values reached by the functions as well as the instants at which these values are obtained. The former is done by using intervals instead of sets while the latter is done by considering step functions, i.e. functions that are almost always constant.

Definition 4. *Interval valued step functions.*
$\mathcal{D}^\sharp$ is the set of all step functions from $\mathbb{R}_+$ to $\boldsymbol{R}$. We recall that given a domain D, a function $f : \mathbb{R}_+ \to D$ is a step function if and only if either:

- *there exist an infinite sequence $t_0 = 0 < t_1 < \dots < t_n < t_{n+1} < \dots$ such that $\forall n \in \mathbb{N}$, f is constant between t_n and t_{n+1};*

– *there exist* $t_0 = 0 < t_1 < \cdots < t_n < \cdots < t_N$ *such that* $\forall n \in [0, N-1]$, f *is constant between* t_n *and* t_{n+1} *and* f *is constant between* t_N *and* ∞.

Representation of step functions
Following the notations used by Julien Bertrane [2], we represent the step functions as a conjunction of constraints of the form "$t_i : \boldsymbol{x_i}$", which means that the function switches to $\boldsymbol{x_i}$ at time t_i. The switching times t_i do not need to be ordered, nor different; the infinite conjunction $f = t_0 : \boldsymbol{x_0} \wedge t_1 : \boldsymbol{x_1} \wedge \cdots \wedge t_n : \boldsymbol{x_n} \wedge \ldots$ represents the function f such that $\forall t \in \mathbb{R}_+, f(t) = \boldsymbol{x_i}$ with $i = \max\{j \in \mathbb{N} | t_j \leq t\}$. A finite sequence of constraints $f = t_0 : \boldsymbol{x_0} \wedge t_1 : \boldsymbol{x_1} \wedge \cdots \wedge t_N : \boldsymbol{x_N}$ represents the step function f such that $\forall t \in \mathbb{R}_+,\ f(t) = \boldsymbol{x_i}$ with $i = \max\{j \in [0, N] | t_j \leq t\}$. We use the more compact notation $f = \bigwedge_{0 \leq i \leq N} t_i : \boldsymbol{x_i}$, with $N \in \mathbb{N} \cup \{\infty\}$. Let us remark that this notation is not unique. For example, the conjunctions $3 : [1,2] \wedge 0 : [1,2]$ and $0 : [1,2] \wedge 1 : [1,2]$ define the same constant function with value $[1,2]$. This makes the equality of functions difficult to define (we can say that $f = g \Leftrightarrow \forall t \in \mathbb{R}_+, f(t) = g(t)$ but this is not satisfying as it cannot be used for an implementation). To solve this problem, we define a normal form for the conjunctions of constraints characterized by:

1. The switching times are sorted increasingly and all different, i.e. if $f = \bigwedge_{0 \leq i \leq N} t_i : \boldsymbol{x_i}$, then $0 = t_0 < t_1 < \cdots < t_n < \ldots$
2. Consecutive constraints cannot have equal values: $\forall i \in [0, N],\ \boldsymbol{x_i} \neq \boldsymbol{x_{i+1}}$.

With these conditions, the representation is unique. It is moreover easy to compute the normalized form $Norm(f)$ of a given conjunction of constraints f. First we sort the constraints by ascending switching time, with the convention that if two constraints have the same time, then we only keep the one with the highest index. This makes the conjunction to fulfill the first normalization condition. Then, we remove any constraint $t_i : \boldsymbol{x_i}$ such that $\boldsymbol{x_{i-1}} = \boldsymbol{x_i}$. This way, we only keep the longest possible steps, which satisfies the second condition. It is easy to see that the normalization process does not change the meaning of the representation: for a conjunction f, then it holds that $\forall t \in \mathbb{R}_+,\ f(t) = Norm(f)(t)$. Given two normalized conjunctions, we define an equality test:

$$\bigwedge_{0 \leq i \leq N} t_i : \boldsymbol{x_i} = \bigwedge_{0 \leq j \leq M} u_j : \boldsymbol{y_j} \Longleftrightarrow N = M \text{ and } \forall i \in [0, N],\ t_i = u_i \text{ and } \boldsymbol{x_i} = \boldsymbol{y_i}. \quad (2)$$

The normalization process induces an equivalence relation ($f \equiv g \Leftrightarrow Norm(f) = Norm(g)$). Thus, from now on we work in the domain $\mathcal{D}^\sharp{}_{/\equiv}$, i.e. we always consider that the conjunctions are normalized. We will however keep the notation $D^\sharp$ for $D^\sharp{}_{/\equiv}$ whenever it is clear from the context.

Proposition 1. *Let* $f, g \in D^\sharp$. *Then it holds that:*

$$f = g \Longleftrightarrow \forall t \in \mathbb{R}_+,\ f(t) = g(t) \quad (3)$$

Proof. Clearly, we have $f = g \Rightarrow \forall t \in \mathbb{R}_+,\ f(t) = g(t)$. Let us prove the other direction. Let $f, g \in \mathcal{D}^\sharp$ such that $\forall t \in \mathbb{R}_+,\ f(t) = g(t)$, with $f = \bigwedge_{0 \leq i \leq N} t_i : \boldsymbol{x_i}$ and $g = \bigwedge_{0 \leq j \leq M} u_j : \boldsymbol{y_j}$. We have $N = M$: suppose that $N \neq M$, then we can suppose that $N < M$ and $N \neq \infty$, so $\forall t \geq t_N,\ f(t) = g(t) = \boldsymbol{x_N}$; however, g has at least a step in $[t_n, \infty]$, and thus its value changes at least once, hence the contradiction. Now, let us suppose that $A = \{i \in \mathbb{N} | t_i \neq u_i\} \neq \emptyset$, and let $k = \min A$, with $t_k < u_k$. Then we have $t_{k-1} = u_{k-1} < t_k < u_k$, so $f(t_{k-1}) = g(t_{k-1}) = \boldsymbol{x_{k-1}}$ and $f(t_k) = \boldsymbol{x_k}$, $g(t_k) = g(t_{k-1}) = \boldsymbol{x_{k-1}}$, so $\boldsymbol{x_k} = \boldsymbol{x_{k-1}}$, hence the contradiction. So, $\forall i \in [0, N],\ t_i = u_i$, and $\boldsymbol{x_i} = \boldsymbol{y_i}$. □

3.2 Concretisation and Abstraction

The function $f = \bigwedge_{0 \leq i \leq N} t_i : \boldsymbol{x_i}$ represents the set of continuous, differentiable functions that remain within $\boldsymbol{x_i}$ for any time $t \in [t_i, t_{i+1}]$. The concretisation function $\gamma : \mathcal{D}^\sharp \to \mathcal{D}$ is thus defined by:

$$\gamma(\bigwedge_{0 \leq i \leq N} t_i : \boldsymbol{x_i}) = \{y \in \mathcal{C}^1_+ \mid \forall i \leq N,\ \forall t \in [t_i, t_{i+1}],\ y(t) \in \boldsymbol{x_i}\} \tag{4}$$

If N is finite, the last constraint transforms into $\forall t \geq t_N,\ y(t) \in \boldsymbol{x_N}$.

For example, Figure 2(a) shows a step function (represented by the black bold steps) and a function within its concretisation (the dashed curve). Among others, the solutions of Example 1 are contained in the concretisation (gray surface).

The definition of an abstraction is not as direct as for the concretisation. As in the case of the polyhedra domain [9], we cannot define a best abstraction: it is always possible to increase the quality of the abstraction by selecting smaller steps. Thus, we only give a criteria for a function to be a safe abstraction. Let us first define the lower- ($\underline{\mathcal{Y}}$) and upper-functions ($\overline{\mathcal{Y}}$) of a set of continuous real functions $\mathcal{Y} \in \mathcal{D} : \underline{\mathcal{Y}} = \lambda t.inf\,\{y(t) \mid y \in \mathcal{Y}\}$ and $\overline{\mathcal{Y}} = \lambda t.sup\,\{y(t) \mid y \in \mathcal{Y}\}$. Equivalently, we define the lower- and upper-functions of an interval valued step function. Let $f \in \mathcal{D}^\sharp$, the real valued step functions $\underline{f}$ and $\overline{f}$ are: $\underline{f} = \lambda t.\underline{\boldsymbol{f(t)}}$ and $\overline{f} = \lambda t.\overline{\boldsymbol{f(t)}}$. These four functions are the basis of the *Validity condition*:

Definition 5. *A function $\alpha : \mathcal{D} \to \mathcal{D}^\sharp$ satisfy the* Validity condition *(V.C.) if and only if for all $\mathcal{Y} \in \mathcal{D}$, it holds that:*

$$\forall t \in \mathbb{R}_+,\ \underline{\alpha(\mathcal{Y})}(t) \leq \underline{\mathcal{Y}}(t) \leq \overline{\mathcal{Y}}(t) \leq \overline{\alpha(\mathcal{Y})}(t) \tag{5}$$

This property states that the computed interval valued step function indeed encloses the set $\{y(t) \mid y \in \mathcal{Y}\}$ for all $t \in \mathbb{R}_+$. The V.C. is a necessary and sufficient condition for the abstraction α to be sound (see Theorem 1).

3.3 Structure of the Abstract Domain

Let us now show that $\mathcal{D}^\sharp$ can be given a lattice structure and that, under the V.C., the abstraction $\alpha : \mathcal{D} \to \mathcal{D}^\sharp$ is sound. Intuitively, we want to define the order $\subseteq^\sharp$ pointwise (i.e. $f \subseteq^\sharp g \Leftrightarrow \forall t \in \mathbb{R}_+, f(t) \subseteq g(t)$). We give a condition (6) on the constraints that allows for the effective testing of whether $f \subseteq^\sharp g$. Let $f = \bigwedge_{0 \leq i \leq N} t_i : \boldsymbol{x_i}$ and $g = \bigwedge_{0 \leq j \leq M} u_j : \boldsymbol{y_j}$, then

$$f \subseteq^\sharp g \Longleftrightarrow \forall (i,j) \in [0,N] \times [0,M],\ [t_i, t_{i+1}] \cap [u_j, u_{j+1}] \neq \emptyset \Rightarrow \boldsymbol{x_i} \subseteq \boldsymbol{y_j} \tag{6}$$

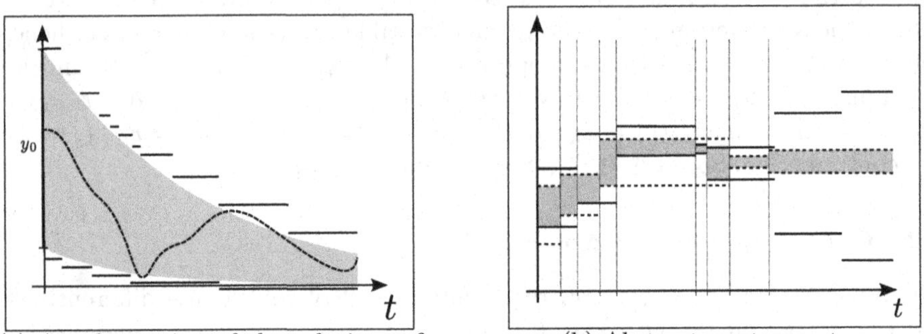

(a) An abstraction of the solutions of Example 1.

(b) Abstract meet operator.

Fig. 2. Abstract domain

Proposition 2. *If $f, g \in \mathcal{D}^\sharp$ are in a normalized form, then it holds that:*

$$f \subseteq^\sharp g \iff \forall t \in \mathbb{R}_+,\ f(t) \subseteq g(t) \tag{7}$$

Proof. Let $f = \bigwedge_{0 \le i \le N} t_i : \boldsymbol{x_i}$ and $g = \bigwedge_{0 \le j \le M} u_j : \boldsymbol{y_j}$ be such that $f \subseteq^\sharp g$, and let $t \in \mathbb{R}_+$. There exist $i \in [0, N]$ and $j \in [0, M]$ such that $t \in [t_i, t_{i+1}]$ and $t \in [u_j, u_{j+1}]$. Thus, $[t_i, t_{i+1}] \cap [u_j, u_{j+1}] \neq \emptyset$, so $f(t) = \boldsymbol{x_i} \subseteq \boldsymbol{y_j} = g(t)$.

Now, let $f, g \in \mathcal{D}^\sharp$ such that $\forall t \in \mathbb{R}_+,\ f(t) \subseteq g(t)$, f and g written as above. Let $i, j \in [0, N] \times [0, M]$ such that $[t_i, t_{i+1}] \cap [u_j, u_{j+1}] \neq \emptyset$, and let $t \in [t_i, t_{i+1}] \cap [u_j, u_{j+1}]$. Then, $f(t) = \boldsymbol{x_i}$ and $g(t) = \boldsymbol{y_j}$, so $\boldsymbol{x_i} \subseteq \boldsymbol{y_j}$. □

The equality (Equation (2)) and the partial order (Equation (6)) defined on $\mathcal{D}^\sharp$ are equivalent to the usual equality and order on functions, but the characterization we provide allows their efficient implementation (between normalized functions, the operations run in linear time and yield normalized functions).

The meet operator $\cap^\sharp$ on $\mathcal{D}^\sharp$ is defined as follows. If $f = \bigwedge_{0 \le i \le N} t_i : \boldsymbol{x_i}$ and $g = \bigwedge_{0 \le j \le M} u_j : \boldsymbol{y_j}$, then

$$f \cap^\sharp g = Norm\left(\bigwedge_{0 \le i \le N} t_i : \tilde{\boldsymbol{x_i}} \wedge \bigwedge_{0 \le j \le M} u_j : \tilde{\boldsymbol{y_j}} \right) \text{ where} \tag{8}$$

$$\tilde{\boldsymbol{x_i}} = \boldsymbol{x_i} \cap \boldsymbol{y_k},\quad k = \max\{j | u_j \le t_i\} \tag{9}$$

$$\tilde{\boldsymbol{y_j}} = \boldsymbol{y_j} \cap \boldsymbol{x_k},\quad k = \max\{i | t_i \le u_j\} \tag{10}$$

The intersection $f \cap^\sharp g$ creates a new step function whose value is at every time t the intersection $f(t) \cap g(t)$. If this intersection is empty (i.e. $\tilde{\boldsymbol{x_i}} = \emptyset$ for some i or $\tilde{\boldsymbol{y_j}} = \emptyset$ for some j), we define $f \cap^\sharp g$ as $\bot^\sharp$, the bottom element of $\mathcal{D}^\sharp$. A graphical representation of the effect of $\cap^\sharp$ is shown in Figure 2(b): the intersection of two step functions (bold and dashed steps) is computed. The result is the gray area, and the vertical dashed lines represent the switching times.

The abstract join operator $\sqcup^\sharp$ is defined in the same way. Let $h = f \sqcup^\sharp g$, h is given as for the meet $\sqcap^\sharp$, except that Equations (9) and (10) are changed into:

$$\tilde{\boldsymbol{x}}_i = \boldsymbol{x}_i \cup \boldsymbol{y}_k \text{ where } k = \max\{j|u_j \leq t_i\} \tag{11}$$
$$\tilde{\boldsymbol{y}}_j = \boldsymbol{y}_j \cup \boldsymbol{x}_k \text{ where } k = \max\{i|t_i \leq u_j\} \tag{12}$$

The only difference is that we set the value of h at any time t to be $f(t) \cup g(t)$.

Proposition 3. *Let $\top^\sharp = 0 : [-\infty, \infty]$ be the step function with only one step with value $\mathbb{R}$. We define a special element $\bot^\sharp$ such that $\gamma(\bot^\sharp) = \emptyset$ and $\forall f \in \mathcal{D}^\sharp$, $\bot^\sharp \sqsubseteq^\sharp f$. Then $\langle \mathcal{D}^\sharp, \top^\sharp, \bot^\sharp, \sqsubseteq^\sharp, \sqcap^\sharp, \sqcup^\sharp \rangle$ is a lattice.*

Proof. Clearly, $\forall f \in \mathcal{D}^\sharp$, $\bot^\sharp \sqsubseteq^\sharp f \sqsubseteq^\sharp \top^\sharp$. We still need to prove that:

1. $\sqcap^\sharp$ is a meet operator: let $f, g \in \mathcal{D}^\sharp$ and $h = f \sqcap^\sharp g$, with $f = \bigwedge_{0 \leq i \leq N} t_i : \boldsymbol{x}_i$ and $g = \bigwedge_{0 \leq j \leq M} u_j : \boldsymbol{y}_j$. We first show that $h \sqsubseteq^\sharp f$ by showing that $\forall t \in \mathbb{R}_+$, $h(t) \subseteq f(t)$. Let $t \in \mathbb{R}_+$, and $i, j \in [0, N] \times [0, M]$ be such that $t \in [t_i, t_{i+1}]$ and $t \in [u_j, u_{j+1}]$. Then, depending on the relative positions of t_i, t_{i+1}, u_j and u_{j+1}, the computation of h (Equation (8)) defines $h(t)$ to be $\tilde{\boldsymbol{x}}_i$ or $\tilde{\boldsymbol{y}}_j$, with $\tilde{\boldsymbol{x}}_i = \boldsymbol{x}_i \cap \boldsymbol{y}_j$ and $\tilde{\boldsymbol{y}}_j = \boldsymbol{y}_j \cap \boldsymbol{x}_i$. Thus, we have $h(t) \in \boldsymbol{x}_i = f(t)$. So, $h \sqsubseteq^\sharp f$. Equivalently, we have $h \sqsubseteq^\sharp g$. Now, let $H \in \mathcal{D}^\sharp$ such that $H \sqsubseteq^\sharp f$ and $H \sqsubseteq^\sharp g$. Let $t \in \mathbb{R}_+$ and i, j such that $t \in [t_i, t_{i+1}]$ and $t \in [u_j, u_{j+1}]$. Then, $H(t) \subseteq f(t) = \boldsymbol{x}_i$ and $H(t) \subseteq g(t) = \boldsymbol{y}_j$, so $H(t) \subseteq \boldsymbol{x}_i \cap \boldsymbol{y}_j$, i.e. $H(t) \subseteq h(t)$. So, $H \sqsubseteq^\sharp h$.
2. $\sqcup^\sharp$ is a join operator: the proof runs as for $\sqcap^\sharp$. □

We now formulate the main theorem of this section that guarantees the soundness of the abstraction.

Theorem 1. *If α satisfies the V.C., then for every $\mathcal{Y} \in \mathcal{D}$, $\mathcal{Y} \subseteq \gamma(\alpha(\mathcal{Y}))$.*

Proof. Let $\mathcal{Y} \in \mathcal{D}$ and $f = \alpha(\mathcal{Y}) \in \mathcal{D}^\sharp$. We want to prove that $\mathcal{Y} \subseteq \gamma(f)$. As α satisfies the V.C., we know that $\forall t \in \mathbb{R}_+$, $\forall y \in \mathcal{Y}$, $y(t) \in f(t)$. Let now $y \in \mathcal{Y}$; y is a continuous function that verifies $\forall t \in \mathbb{R}_+$, $y(t) \in f(t)$, thus $y \in \gamma(f)$. So, it holds that $\mathcal{Y} \subseteq \gamma(f)$. □

4 Guaranteed Integration

In this section, we present a technique called *guaranteed integration* of ODEs that, as shown in Section 5, enables one to compute the abstract semantics of the continuous processes. Guaranteed integration of ODEs tries to answer the following question: given an ODE (possibly with interval parameters), an initial value (possibly an interval) and a final time T, can we compute bounds on the value of the solution to the IVP at T? There are basically two kinds of methods for computing such bounds on the solution to the IVP. On the one side, classical methods use the Taylor series decomposition of the solution and then interval arithmetics. Advanced techniques are used in order to limit the wrapping effect inherent to the interval computations, and the first tools (e.g. VNODE [24] or AWA [20]) use such techniques. On the other side, new methods (e.g. GRKLib [6] or VALENCIA-IVP [26]) have recently been proposed that compute the bounds as the sum of a non-validated approximation point and a guaranteed error, i.e. an interval that is proved to contain the distance between the real solution and the approximation point. We give the main ideas of how the GRKLib [6] method works in the proof of Theorem 2. The reader can find more detailed explanations about GRKLib and a complete proof in [6].

Theorem 2. *Given an interval ODE $\dot{y} = F(y, \boldsymbol{p})$ and an interval initial value denoted $y(0) \in y_n + \boldsymbol{e_n}$, where $\boldsymbol{e_n}$ is the error and y_n the approximation point, it is possible to find a step size h, a global enclosure $\tilde{\boldsymbol{y}}$, an approximation point y_{n+1} and a local enclosure $\boldsymbol{e_{n+1}}$ of the error such that $\forall t \in [0, h],\ y(t) \subseteq \tilde{\boldsymbol{y}}$ and $y(h) \subseteq y_{n+1} + \boldsymbol{e_{n+1}}$, where y is any solution to the interval IVP.*

Proof sketch. Let us first assume that the step size h is given. The next point y_{n+1} is computed by the classical RK4 algorithm [15] that uses four evaluations of F to approximate the mean derivative between t and $t + h$. y_{n+1} is a function of y_n and h only. So, $y_{n+1} = \psi(y_n, h)$, where ψ is expressed using F only.

The computation of $\boldsymbol{e_{n+1}}$ requires a two steps process: first we compute the a priori bound $\tilde{\boldsymbol{y}}$ and then we use it to compute a tighter bound on the global error at $t + h$. The computation of $\tilde{\boldsymbol{y}}$ uses the Picard interval operator and a Banach fix-point argument as in [20]. Using results from [3,19], we compute $\boldsymbol{e_{n+1}}$ as $\boldsymbol{e_{n+1}} = \boldsymbol{\eta} + \boldsymbol{\chi} + \boldsymbol{\mu}$. The three terms are computed as follows:

- $\boldsymbol{\eta}$ represents the discretization error and is computed as the distance between the flows of the real valued solution to the IVP and the real valued function ψ. Both functions are equal at time t and so are their first 4 derivatives. As a consequence, $\boldsymbol{\eta}$ can be expressed as a function of their fifth derivative only (we use Taylor expansion to prove it).
- $\boldsymbol{\chi}$ represents the propagation of the error $\boldsymbol{e_n}$ into $\boldsymbol{e_{n+1}}$. In other words, it is the distance between the images by ψ of two points inside $y_n + \boldsymbol{e_n}$. This is computed using the Jacobian matrix of ψ and this is mainly where the wrapping effect occurs (if the matrix is a rotation matrix, then big over-approximations arise).
- $\boldsymbol{\mu}$ represents the implementation error, i.e. the distance between the computed floating point number y_{n+1} and the real value that would have been obtained on an infinite precision computer. We use the global error domain [21] to compute y_{n+1} so that we obtain both the floating point number and an over-approximation of its distance to the real number, i.e. an over-approximation of $\boldsymbol{\mu}$.

By combining these three computations, we obtain an over-approximation of the global error at time $t + h$ based on the error at time t. □

We leave the problem of finding an appropriate step size h open for now and show in Section 5 how to deal with it, and that it can be seen as some kind of dynamic partitioning [7] of the set of control points of the continuous semantics.

Input: P=(F,p,y)
Output: $[\![\mathtt{P}]\!]^\sharp$
$t = 0$; $h = \text{InitialGuess}(\mathtt{F})$;
$\boldsymbol{yn} = \mathtt{y}$;
while $(h, \tilde{\boldsymbol{y}}, \boldsymbol{y}) = GRK(F, p, \boldsymbol{yn})$ **do**
| $res = res \wedge t : \tilde{\boldsymbol{y}}$; $\boldsymbol{yn} = \boldsymbol{y}$;
end
return $res \wedge t : \mathbb{R}$

Algorithm 1. Abstract semantics computation

5 Abstract Semantics

In this section, we show that the guaranteed integration methods provide a safe abstract semantics for the continuous processes. An abstract semantics $[\![\mathtt{P}]\!]^\sharp$ of a continuous process P=(F,p,y) is an interval valued step functions (i.e. an element of $\mathcal{D}^\sharp$) that provides two things. On the one side, we have an abstraction of the values that represents as an interval the set $\{y(t)|y \in [\![\mathtt{P}]\!]\}$ at all time $t \in \mathbb{R}_+$. On the other side, we have an abstraction of the time line that collects the instants whose values are abstracted by the same interval. In Section 4, we showed that these abstractions are provided by the guaranteed integration algorithms: given an abstraction of the values at one time t ($y(t) \in \boldsymbol{y_n}$), a function $GRK(\mathtt{F}, \mathtt{P}, \boldsymbol{y_n})$ exists that computes h (i.e. the abstraction on the instants), $\tilde{\boldsymbol{y}}$ (i.e. the abstraction on the values) and a new interval $\boldsymbol{y}$ such that $\forall u \in [t, t+h]$, $y(u) \in \tilde{\boldsymbol{y}}$ and $y(t+h) \in \boldsymbol{y}$. Let us briefly explain how the step size h is chosen: first, during the computation of the a priori approximation $\tilde{y}$, we use a Banach fix-point argument, and thus compute $\tilde{y}$ as the limit of the iterates of a contracting function. On a computer, this can loop forever either due to rounding errors or because the fix-point is reached after an infinite iteration. Thus, we use a limit on the number of iterations and we use a smaller step size if this limit is reached. Secondly, after each step, the width of $\boldsymbol{y}$ is compared to the user specified tolerance and control theoretic techniques are used in order to adjust the next step-size and avoid the error to grow. Thus, the partitioning of the time line is dynamically computed at each step.

Definition 6. *Abstract semantics.*
Let P=(F,p,y) be a continuous process. The abstract semantics $[\![P]\!]^\sharp$ of P is the result of Algorithm 1.

The abstract semantics is computed by iterating the guaranteed integration process. Let us remark that the implementation of the GRK function can fail to find h, $\tilde{\boldsymbol{y}}$ and $\boldsymbol{y}$ if the selected step size becomes smaller than the machine precision. Whenever this happens, a sort of widening is performed as we end the constraint conjunction by the safe over-approximation $t : \mathbb{R}_+$.

Theorem 3. *Let P=(F,p,y) be a continuous process. Then the abstract semantics $[\![P]\!]^\sharp$ is a safe abstraction of the concrete semantics, i.e.:*

$$[\![P]\!] \subseteq \gamma([\![P]\!]^\sharp) \tag{13}$$

Proof. Let $\alpha : \mathcal{D} \rightarrow \mathcal{D}^\sharp$ be the abstraction function defined by $\alpha(\llbracket \mathtt{P} \rrbracket) = \llbracket \mathtt{P} \rrbracket^\sharp$ and $\forall \mathcal{Y} \in \mathcal{D},\ \mathcal{Y} \neq \llbracket \mathtt{P} \rrbracket,\ \alpha(\mathcal{Y}) = \top^\sharp$. If we show that α satisfies the V.C., then Equation (13) holds. Let $\mathcal{Y} \in \mathcal{D}$, we show that $\alpha(\mathcal{Y})$ satisfies Equation (5). This is clearly the case if $\mathcal{Y} \neq \llbracket \mathtt{P} \rrbracket$. Let us suppose that $\mathcal{Y} = \llbracket \mathtt{P} \rrbracket$, and let $\llbracket \mathtt{P} \rrbracket^\sharp = \bigwedge_{0 \leq i \leq N} t_i : \boldsymbol{x_i}$. We need to prove that $\forall i \in [0, N]$, $\forall t \in [t_i, t_{i+1}]$ and $\forall y \in \mathcal{Y}$, $y(t) \in \boldsymbol{x_i}$. We prove this by induction on i.

For $i = 0$, we have $\forall y \in \mathcal{Y}$, $y(0) \in \mathrm{y}$ and the *GRK* function gives h, $\tilde{y}$ and y_1 such that $\forall t \in [0, h]$, $\forall y \in \mathcal{Y}$, $y(t) \in \tilde{y}$. The algorithm 1 sets x_0 to $\tilde{y}$, which proves the case $i = 0$.

Let now $i \in [0, N]$ be such that $\forall y \in \mathcal{Y}$, $\forall t \in [t_i, t_{i+1}]$, $y(t) \in \boldsymbol{x_i}$. Clearly, the algorithm 1 also gives an interval $\boldsymbol{y_i}$ such that $\forall y \in \mathcal{Y}$, $y(t_{i+1}) \in \boldsymbol{y_i}$. Let $\mathtt{P'}$=$(\mathtt{F},\mathtt{p},\boldsymbol{y_i})$ be the interval IVP which differs from $\mathtt{P}$ only for the initial value. Then, for every $H > 0$, it holds that $\{y(t) | t \in [0, H],\ y \in \llbracket \mathtt{P'} \rrbracket\} = \{y(t) | t \in [t_{i+1}, t_{i+1} + H],\ y \in \llbracket \mathtt{P} \rrbracket\}$, i.e. the solutions to the initial IVP for time between t_{i+1} and $t_{i+1} + H$ are the same as the solutions to the IVP $\mathtt{P'}$ for time between 0 and H, as by hypothesis our systems are autonomous. The *GRK* function gives $\tilde{y}$ and h such that $\forall t \in [0, H]$, $\forall y \in \llbracket \mathtt{P'} \rrbracket$, $y(t) \in \tilde{y}$. The algorithm 1 sets $\boldsymbol{x_{i+1}}$ to be $\tilde{y}$ and t_{i+2} to $t_{i+1} + h$, so we have $\forall t \in [t_{i+1}, t_{i+2}]$, $\forall y \in \mathcal{Y}$, $y(t) \in \boldsymbol{x_{i+1}}$. □

6 Example

We present an example that illustrates how we intend to include our work into existing static analyzers. We consider a code that is often used in embedded programs: an integrator with thresholds. The program in Listing 1 (inspired from [14]) integrates using the rectangle method the input data. The integration is carried out up to some threshold defined by the interval `[INF,SUP]`. The input data are given by a sensor (the `volatile` variable `x`) at a frequency of 8KHz. The integrator is a well known difficult problem for the analysis of numerical precision [10]. Its behavior is extremely depending of the input data (i.e. the physical environment) of the frequency of the integration process (i.e. the sampling rate) and of the precision of the sensor.

```
1  #define SUP 4
2  #define INF -4
3  // assume x'=2*Pi*y and y'=-2*Pi*x
4  volatile float x;
5  static float intgrx=0.0,h=1.0/8;
6  void main() {
7     while (true) { // assume frequency = 8 KHz
8       xi = x; intgrx += xi*h;
9       if (intgrx > SUP)
10        intgrx = SUP;
11      if (intgrx < INF)
12        intgrx = INF;
13    }}
```

Listing 1. Simple integrator

The comments in the code in Listing 1 indicate how we could give the analyzers hints on the physical environment. The first one (Line 3) gives the differential

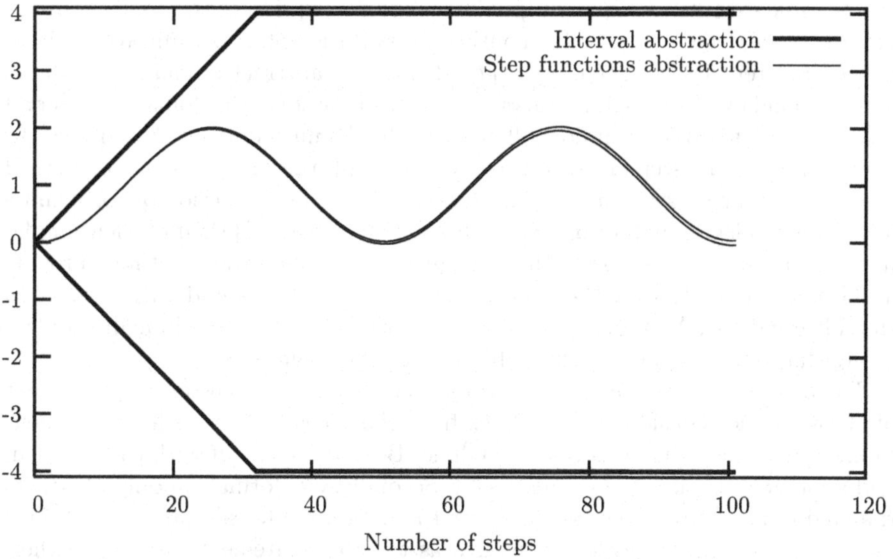

Fig. 3. Result of the analysis of the integrator

equation followed by x and y while the second one (Line 7) indicates the frequency of the main loop. Such comments could be understood by a static analyzer and are often already present (although not in this form) in embedded programs (it is very frequent to find a comment such as "this loop runs at 8KHz" in the code usually given to static analyzers). In this example, the input signal is $x(t) = sin(2\pi t)$. In theory (i.e. with a perfect knowledge of the environment and an infinite precision computer), the value of `intgrx` remains bounded by $[0, 2]$. As explained in the introduction, a naive abstraction of the continuous environment approximates x by the interval $[-1, 1]$. In this case, the analyzer binds the variable `intgrx` with the value $[-n \cdot h, n \cdot h]$ after unrolling the main loop n times. We implemented a prototype analyzer that uses the abstraction of the continuous environment of Section 5 to improve this result. The analyzer uses the GRKLib library [6] as guaranteed integration tool. The analyzer takes as input language a subset of C and the comments are changed into specific assertions that the analyzer understands. Figure 3 shows the results obtained by this analyzer and by an abstraction using intervals. After 100 iterations, the value of `intgrx` is $[-4, 4]$ with an interval based analyzer, because of the thresholds, and $[-4.353 \cdot 10^{-2}, 4.192 \cdot 10^{-2}]$ with our analyzer.

7 Conclusion

In this article, we provided a formalization and an abstraction of the physical environment of embedded software which is coherent with the analysis of the discrete program itself. Like the collecting semantics of a program describes all the possible executions for any input data, our description of the continuous environment describes all possible continuous evolutions for any initial condition and parameter of the system. We then defined an abstract domain that allows for the sound over-approximation of continuous functions: the domain of interval valued step functions. A major difficulty in the definition of this domain was to deal with dynamic step sizes in order to cope with the most efficient numerical algorithms. Our representation of such functions as a conjunction of constraints allows for an elegant definition of the abstract operators and their efficient implementation. Finally, we showed that the guaranteed integration methods provide an abstract semantics for the continuous process that is sound with respect to the collecting one. A simple example derived from a well known, difficult problem shows that our approach considerably improves the analysis.

The analysis of the complete hybrid system still needs some extensions. First of all, we do not consider yet feedback from the program, i.e. we have not mentionned actuators. Previous work by Olivier Bouissou [5] dealt with this problem and a merge of both results is necessary. Secondly, our formalism only abstracts the environment and does not consider the action of the sensors. These latter introduce some noise inside the system as their measurements as well as their sampling rate are imprecise. From a certain point of view, our model supposes that we have perfect sensors, i.e. that the values provided to the program are the exact values of the continuous environment. Clearly, a better modeling of sensors is necessary. For example, we can add comments and/or assertions in the program that describe the inaccuracy of the sensors. Thus, our abstraction of the environment remains valid, and it is only when the values are passed to the program that they are modified in order to match the specification of the sensor. Finally, the addition of an extrapolation method as a widening operator is needed to complete the abstract interpretation of continuous functions. This is a purely numerical problem that does not affect our domain.

References

1. Alur, R., et al.: The algorithmic analysis of hybrid systems. Theoretical Computer Science 138(1), 3–34 (1995)
2. Bertrane, J.: Static Analysis by Abstract Interpretation of the Quasi-synchronous Composition of Synchronous Programs. In: Cousot, R. (ed.) VMCAI 2005. LNCS, vol. 3385, pp. 97–112. Springer, Heidelberg (2005)
3. Bieberbach, L.: On the remainder of the runge-kutta formula. Z.A.M.P. 2, 233–248 (1951)
4. Cousot, P., et al.: Design and Implementation of a Special-Purpose Static Program Analyzer for Safety-Critical Real-Time Embedded Software. In: Mogensen, T.Æ., Schmidt, D.A., Sudborough, I.H. (eds.) The Essence of Computation. LNCS, vol. 2566, pp. 85–108. Springer, Heidelberg (2002)
5. Bouissou, O.: Analyse statique par interpretation abstraite de système hybrides discrets-continus. Technical Report 05-301, CEA-LIST (2005)
6. Bouissou, O., Martel, M.: GRKLib: A guaranteed runge-kutta library. In: International Symposium on Scientific Computing, Computer Arithmetic and Validated Numerics, IEEE, Los Alamitos (2006)

7. Bourdoncle, F.: Abstract interpretation by dynamic partitioning. Journal of Functional Programming 2(4), 407–423 (1992)
8. Cousot, P., Cousot, R.: Abstract interpretation: A unified lattice model for static analysis of programs by construction or approximation of fixpoints. In: POPL, pp. 238–252. ACM Press, New York (1977)
9. Cousot, P., Halbwachs, N.: Automatic discovery of linear restraints among variables of a program. In: POPL, pp. 84–97. ACM Press, New York (1978)
10. Daumas, M., Lester, D.: Stochastic formal methods: An application to accuracy of numeric software. In: Proceedings of the 40th IEEE Annual Hawaii International Conference on System Sciences (2007)
11. Lieutier, A., Edalat, A., Pattinson, D.: A Computational Model for Multi-variable Differential Calculus. In: Sassone, V. (ed.) FOSSACS 2005. LNCS, vol. 3441, pp. 505–519. Springer, Heidelberg (2005)
12. Edalat, A., Pattinson, D.: A Domain Theoretic Account of Picard's Theorem. In: Díaz, J., et al. (eds.) ICALP 2004. LNCS, vol. 3142, pp. 494–505. Springer, Heidelberg (2004)
13. Martel, M., Goubault, É., Putot, S.: Asserting the Precision of Floating-Point Computations: A Simple Abstract Interpreter. In: Le Métayer, D. (ed.) ESOP 2002 and ETAPS 2002. LNCS, vol. 2305, pp. 209–212. Springer, Heidelberg (2002)
14. Goubault, E., Martel, M., Putot, S.: Some future challenges in the validation of control systems. In: ERTS (2006)
15. Hairer, E., Norsett, S.P., Wanner, G.: Solving ordinary differential equations I: nonstiff problems, 2nd revised edn. Springer, Heidelberg (1993)
16. Halbwachs, N., Proy, Y., Raymond, P.: Verification of linear hybrid systems by means of convex approximations. In: LeCharlier, B. (ed.) SAS 1994. LNCS, vol. 864, pp. 223–237. Springer, Heidelberg (1994)
17. Henzinger, T.A.: The theory of hybrid automata. In: Symposium on Logic in Computer Science, pp. 278–292. IEEE Press, Los Alamitos (1996)
18. Henzinger, T.A., et al.: Beyond HYTECH: Hybrid Systems Analysis Using Interval Numerical Methods. In: Lynch, N.A., Krogh, B.H. (eds.) HSCC 2000. LNCS, vol. 1790, pp. 130–144. Springer, Heidelberg (2000)
19. Carr III., J.W.: Error bounds for the runge-kutta single-step integration process. JACM 5(1), 39–44 (1958)
20. Lohner, R.: Einschließung der Lösung gewöhnlicher Anfangs-und Randwertaufgaben und Anwendungen. PhD thesis, Universität Karlsruhe (1988)
21. Martel, M.: An overview of semantics for the validation of numerical programs. In *VMCAI*. In: Cousot, R. (ed.) VMCAI 2005. LNCS, vol. 3385, pp. 59–77. Springer, Heidelberg (2005)
22. Martel, M.: Towards an abstraction of the physical environment of embedded systems. In: NSAD (2005)
23. Mosterman, P.J.: An overview of hybrid simulation phenomena and their support by simulation packages. In: Vaandrager, F.W., van Schuppen, J.H. (eds.) HSCC 1999. LNCS, vol. 1569, pp. 165–177. Springer, Heidelberg (1999)
24. Nedialkov, N.S., Jackson, K.R.: An interval Hermite-Obreschkoff method for computing rigorous bounds on the solution of an initial value problem for an ordinary differential equation. In: Developments in Reliable Computing, pp. 289–310. Kluwer, Dordrecht (1999)
25. IEEE Task P754. ANSI/IEEE 754-1985, Standard for Binary Floating-Point Arithmetic. IEEE, New York, August 12 (1985).
26. Rauh, A., Auer, E., Hofer, E.: ValEncIA-IVP: A case study of validated solvers for initial value problems. In: SCAN (2006)

Diagnostic Information for Realizability

A. Cimatti[1], M. Roveri[1], V. Schuppan[2], and A. Tchaltsev[1]

[1] Fondazione Bruno Kessler — IRST, Via Sommarive 18, 38050 Povo (TN) – Italy
{cimatti,roveri,tchaltsev}@fbk.eu
[2] Verimag/CNRS, 2 Av. de Vignate, 38610 Gières – France
Viktor.Schuppan@imag.fr

Abstract. Realizability – checking whether a specification can be implemented by an open system – is a fundamental step in the design flow. However, if the specification turns out not to be realizable, there is no method to pinpoint the causes for unrealizability. In this paper, we address the open problem of providing diagnostic information for realizability: we formally define the notion of (minimal) explanation of (un)realizability, we propose algorithms to compute such explanations, and provide a preliminary experimental evaluation.

1 Introduction

The role of properties in the design flow is becoming increasingly important [19,2]. Properties are used to describe design intent and to document designs and components, and play a fundamental role both in dynamic and static verification. As a result, research has been devoted to the development of new algorithms and tools for requirements analysis, in order to guarantee that the starting point of the process is indeed free from flaws. Typical forms of analysis are consistency checking, and compatibility with scenarios [14,4]. However, most property verification algorithms and tools are currently lacking the ability to provide diagnostic information that can support the debugging. This is potentially a major shortcoming. In fact, the practical success of model checking is tightly related to the ability of producing counterexamples (e.g., [10]): when the system violates a requirement, model checking algorithms are able to provide a simulation trace witnessing the violation, which may help the designer to find suitable fixes.

In this paper, we address the problem of providing diagnostic information for the realizability of the specification of an open system (e.g., a component). In this setting, requirements are typically separated in *assumptions* (i.e., the admissible behaviors of the environment), and *guarantees* (i.e., the behaviors must be implemented by the system-to-be). Intuitively, realizability is the problem of checking the existence of a system implementing the required guarantees, given that the environment can do whatever allowed by the assumptions.

We make two contributions. First, we tackle the problem of precisely characterizing the idea of diagnostic information for realizability problems. We propose notions for explanation and minimal explanation of (un)realizability. This issue is in fact non trivial: realizability could be achieved by relaxing the assertions on the system, or strengthening the assumptions on the environment. These notions can be also used to provide

F. Logozzo et al. (Eds.): VMCAI 2008, LNCS 4905, pp. 52–67, 2008.

diagnostic information for realizable specifications, i.e., we allow pinpointing minimal subsets of the specification that might be covered by the remaining part.

Second, we propose two methods to extend a practical, symbolic algorithm for realizability, in order to extract explanations and minimal explanations in case of (un)realizability. One of the algorithms is based on a explicit search in the space of subsets of the specification, and is able to compute one explanation at a time. The other one is fully symbolic in nature, and relies on the idea of activation variables to extract all explanations. We implemented the methods within the NuSMV system, for the class of Generalized Reactivity(1) [15] specifications, and we tested them on some industrial cases. The symbolic computation of all the explanations of (un)realizability turns out to be computationally expensive. On the other hand, the explicit algorithm can produce, with moderate performance penalty, explanations that are significantly smaller - sometimes more than an order of magnitude - than the original specifications.

Related Work. To the best of our knowledge, the notion of explanation of realizability has never been defined in terms of requirements. Production of diagnostic information in case of unrealizability was addressed in [18,6,3] and in [20]. In [18,6,3] a counter-strategy is constructed showing how the environment can force the system to violate its guarantees. Yoshiura [20] developed heuristics to classify reasons for unrealizability based on notions that are harder to fulfil than temporal satisfiability but easier than realizability. In both cases, (i) the diagnostic information is "global", i.e., it takes into account all the input problem, and (ii) the link to the requirements in the original problem is lost. Our approach can complement both [18,6,3] and [20] by providing a smaller, yet unrealizable specification to work on. In particular, a counter-strategy might exploit more than one source of unrealizability. Our approach can help to obtain a more focused counter-strategy. In terms of techniques, the fully symbolic algorithm is inspired by the idea of activation variables for the case of Boolean satisfiability [13]. Closely related is also the extension to the case of unsatisfiable core for LTL specifications proposed in [9], for the less complex case of satisfiability. Finally, there is a large body of work on fault localization and explanation in a verification context, where both a program and a (potentially implicit) specification are given. We refer the reader to the section on related work in Groce's Ph.D. thesis [12] for a survey.

Document structure. In Sect. 2 we define some technical background. In Sect. 3, we informally discuss and formalize the notion of explanation. In Sect. 4, we present the explanation-extracting algorithm. In Sect. 5, we discuss the implementation and present some experimental evaluation. Finally, in Sect. 6, we draw some conclusions and outline directions for future work.

2 Preliminaries

2.1 Synthesis of Open Controllers

We are interested in the question of *realizability* of an LTL property [16,1]. [1] We start from two disjoint sets $\mathcal{E}$ and $\mathcal{S}$ of input and output signals respectively, and from a formula φ expressed in LTL over atomic propositions on $\mathcal{E} \cup \mathcal{S}$ (written $\varphi(\mathcal{E}, \mathcal{S})$).

[1] We assume the reader being familiar with LTL syntax and semantics.

$\mathcal{E}$ is the set of variables controlled by the environment, while $\mathcal{S}$ is the set of variables controlled by the system. The *realizability problem* for a property φ consists of checking whether there exists a *program* such that its behavior satisfies φ [16]. An LTL formula $\varphi(\mathcal{E}, \mathcal{S})$ is then *realizable* iff there exists such a program. Properties for which such a program exists are called *realizable* or *implementable*. Dually, properties for which such a program does not exist are called *not realizable* or *unrealizable*.

The realizability problem can be formalized as a two player game among the system we are going to realize and the environment: the system plays against the environment in such a way that at every step of the game the environment moves and then the system tries to move by producing behaviors compatible with the property. The system wins if it produces a correct behavior regardless of the behavior of the environment. In this framework, checking for realizability amounts to check for the existence of a winning strategy for the system in the corresponding game. This is tackled by generating from the property a deterministic Rabin automaton using the Safra construction [17]. This automaton is interpreted as a two player game among the system and environment and it is traversed as to find a witness of the non emptiness of the language of the automaton (which corresponds to a correct implementation of the given property) [16].

2.2 Assumptions and Guarantees

Practically a specification is often represented with two distinguished sets – a set of *assumptions* A and a set of *guarantees* G – plus a function f that turns such a set of constraints into an actual temporal formula φ using Boolean and temporal connectives. Under this assumption a specification is given as a tuple $\langle A, G\rangle$. Intuitively, assumptions are those constraints which the environment is supposed to obey to and guarantees are those constraints which the system has to satisfy. The function f has to have such a form that realizability is preserved by adding assumptions to or removing guarantees from an already realizable specification and, conversely, unrealizability is preserved by removing assumptions from or adding guarantees to an unrealizable specification. Similarly, adding a valid constraint to either assumptions or guarantees must not influence the realizability of a specification.[2] Note, that both A and G may be structured, such that f may not treat all elements of A and G in the same way. In the conceptual part of this work in Sect. 3 we are not concerned with the exact nature of the translation and view A and G as flat sets of atomic elements; only when we consider a concrete class of specifications (see below) for implementation we look into the structure of assumptions and guarantees. We denote the temporal formula resulting from $\langle A, G\rangle$ by applying f with $\phi_{\langle A,G\rangle} = f(\langle A, G\rangle)$. We say that $\langle A, G\rangle$ is realizable iff $\phi_{\langle A,G\rangle}$ is realizable.

2.3 Synthesis of GR(1) Properties

The high complexity established in [16] and the intricacy of Safra's determinization construction have caused the synthesis process to be identified as hopelessly intractable

[2] In this paper we need this property only in Sect. 4.2.

and discouraged many practitioners from ever attempting to implement it. However, there are several classes of properties restricted to particular subsets of LTL, which can be synthesized with more efficient algorithms. One of the most recent and advanced results is achieved in [15] where for the class of *Generalized Reactivity*(1) specifications (from now on referred to as GR(1) specification) is presented a (symbolic) algorithm for extracting a program from a GR(1) specification that runs in time polynomial in the size of the state space of the design. The class of GR(1) properties is sufficiently expressive to provide complete specifications of many designs [15].

A GR(1) specification has the form $\langle A, G\rangle = (\{\varphi_I^{\mathcal{E}}, \varphi_R^{\mathcal{E}}, \varphi_\psi^{\mathcal{E}}\}, \{\varphi_I^{\mathcal{S}}, \varphi_R^{\mathcal{S}}, \varphi_\psi^{\mathcal{S}}\})$. [3] For $\alpha \in \{\mathcal{E}, \mathcal{S}\}$, $\varphi_I^\alpha, \varphi_R^\alpha, \varphi_\psi^\alpha$ represent the *initial conditions*, the *transition relation* and the *liveness* or *fairness* conditions of the environment and system, respectively. They are such that:

- φ_I^α - a formula of the form $\bigwedge_i I_i$ where every I_i is a propositional formula over signals ($\varphi_I^{\mathcal{E}}$ is over $\mathcal{E}$ and $\varphi_I^{\mathcal{S}}$ is over $\mathcal{E} \cup \mathcal{S}$).
- φ_R^α - temporal formulas of the form $\bigwedge_i R_i$ where every R_i is a propositional formula over signals $\mathcal{E} \cup \mathcal{S}$ and expressions of the form $\mathbf{X}\, v$ where $v \in \mathcal{E}$ if $\alpha = \mathcal{E}$ and $v \in \mathcal{E} \cup \mathcal{S}$ if $\alpha \in \mathcal{S}$.
- φ_ψ^α - temporal formulas of the form $\bigwedge_i \mathbf{G}\,\mathbf{F}\, A_i$ where A_i is propositional formula over signals $\mathcal{E} \cup \mathcal{S}$.

Intuitively, the play is initialized in such a way that the environment chooses initial values for its signals as to satisfy $\varphi_I^{\mathcal{E}}$, and the system initializes its signals to satisfy $\varphi_I^{\mathcal{S}}$. At every consecutive step of the play at first the environment assigns its signals, trying to satisfy the environment transition relation $\varphi_R^{\mathcal{E}}$, and then the system does the same with its signals and its transition relation $\varphi_R^{\mathcal{S}}$. For an infinite behavior the environment and the system try to satisfy their liveness conditions $\varphi_\psi^{\mathcal{E}}$ and $\varphi_\psi^{\mathcal{S}}$, respectively. The player who first violates its constraints loses.

Realizability of a GR(1) specification can be reduced to the problem of computing the set of winning states W_S in a two-player game among the environment and the system and then checking W_S against initial conditions [15]. In the following we will use the algorithm of [15] to check for the realizability of a GR(1) specification $\langle A, G\rangle$.

3 Diagnosing (Un)Realizability

In this section we discuss what information can be returned to a developer in the case a given specification $\langle A, G\rangle$ turns out to be either unrealizable or realizable. We focus on "zooming into" the specification by pointing out fragments of the specification that are by themselves (un)realizable, in order to facilitate the understanding of the problem.

We therefore suggest to use a specification $\langle A', G'\rangle$ as an *explanation* for a specification $\langle A, G\rangle$ where A', G' are subsets of A, G. We first formalize minimality and maximality constraints on A' or G'. We then introduce a notion of unhelpfulness of assumptions or guarantees in an explanation, where unhelpful assumptions or guarantees can be removed from an explanation. We illustrate the concept with an example.

[3] We refer the reader to [15] for details on the corresponding LTL formula.

3.1 Explanations for (Un)Realizability

We first notice that assumptions and guarantees can be viewed as interacting, but opposing forces. As outlined in Sect. 2, adding assumptions or removing guarantees will "push" a specification towards realizability. Conversely, a realizable specification may become unrealizable when deleting assumptions or adding guarantees. These concepts are formalized as follows.

Definition 1 ((un-) fulfillable, (in-) sufficient). *Let $\mathcal{A}$ be a set of available assumptions, let $\mathcal{G}$ be a set of available guarantees, and let $A \subseteq \mathcal{A}$ and $G \subseteq \mathcal{G}$.*

If a specification $\langle A, G\rangle$ is realizable, we say that G is fulfillable *w.r.t. A, and, conversely, A is* sufficient *w.r.t. G. Otherwise, G is* unfulfillable *w.r.t. A, and A is* insufficient *w.r.t. G, respectively.*

G is minimally unfulfillable *w.r.t. A iff $\langle A, G\rangle$ is unrealizable and removal of any element of G leads to realizability: $\forall g \in G$. $\langle A, G \setminus \{g\}\rangle$ is realizable.*

G is maximally fulfillable *w.r.t. A in $\mathcal{G}$ iff $\langle A, G\rangle$ is realizable and addition of any element of $\mathcal{G} \setminus G$ leads to unrealizability: $\forall g \in \mathcal{G} \setminus G$. $\langle A, G \cup \{g\}\rangle$ is unrealizable.*

A is minimally sufficient *w.r.t. G iff $\langle A, G\rangle$ is realizable and removal of any element of A leads to unrealizability: $\forall a \in A$. $\langle A \setminus \{a\}, G\rangle$ is unrealizable.*

A is maximally insufficient *w.r.t. G in $\mathcal{A}$ iff $\langle A, G\rangle$ is unrealizable and addition of any element of $\mathcal{A} \setminus A$ leads to realizability: $\forall a \in \mathcal{A} \setminus A$. $\langle A \cup \{a\}, G\rangle$ is realizable.*

All above definitions are also transferable to a whole specification, i.e., a specification $\langle A, G\rangle$ is *maximally insufficient* iff A is maximally insufficient w.r.t. G, etc.

Why is separate terminology introduced for assumptions and guarantees? After all, if a specification $\langle A, G\rangle$ is unrealizable, then A is insufficient w.r.t. G and G is unfulfillable w.r.t. A (similarly for a realizable specification). However, while A is insufficient w.r.t. G iff G is unfulfillable w.r.t. A, A might, e.g., be maximally insufficient w.r.t. G although G is unfulfillable but not minimally unfulfillable w.r.t. A. In other words, minimality and maximality require introduction of separate terminology for both sides.

We now show how the above definitions can provide an explanation for an (un)realizable specification $\langle A, G\rangle$.

Minimally Unfulfillable Sets of Guarantees. First, assume that $\langle A, G\rangle$ is unrealizable. To understand the nature of the problem, the developer needs to see which sets of guarantees are not supported by sufficient assumptions or which sets of guarantees are conflicting. Hence, we suggest to return an explanation $\langle A, G'\rangle$ such that $G' \subseteq G$ is minimally unfulfillable. Each such G' is a minimal set of guarantees such that either A is not strong enough to realize G, or the elements of G are in conflict with each other. Clearly, there may be several such sets. The quest for minimality is based on the intuition that if a guarantee does not contribute to making a specification unrealizable then it can be omitted from the explanation.

Maximally Fulfillable Sets of Guarantees. While an explanation of the previous kind helps to find the cause of unrealizability, it does not immediately suggest a fix. Our second suggestion provides fixes in the restricted case that a fix is only allowed to remove guarantees. Obviously, such fix should remove as few guarantees as possible to achieve realizability. Hence, we suggest to provide the developer with a maximally fulfillable set of guarantees G' as an explanation. Notice that, addition of any $g \in G \setminus G'$

will make $\langle A, G' \cup \{g\}\rangle$ unrealizable. I.e., the complement of each such G' constitutes a minimal set of guarantees that, when removed from G, leads to realizability.

Note that, the distinction to minimally unfulfillable sets of guarantees as an explanation becomes particularly interesting when there is more than one set of unfulfillable guarantees. In that case a minimal fix is easier to see by providing the developer with a maximally fulfillable set of guarantees rather than with several minimally unfulfillable sets of guarantees as in the latter case the developer has to figure out herself which combinations of guarantees need to be removed to avoid all "unfulfillabilities".

A slightly different scenario where maximally fulfillable sets of guarantees can help is finding out the set of guarantees that may be realized with a given set of assumptions, i.e., strengthening the guarantees that the system under design will provide. In this case, given a set of available guarantees, $\mathcal{G} \supset G$, it is enough to compute the maximally fulfillable sets of guarantees for $\langle A, \mathcal{G}\rangle$.

Minimally Sufficient Sets of Assumptions. If $\langle A, G\rangle$ is realizable, the need for debugging information is less urgent. Still, the developer might benefit from additional information that helps her understanding. In particular, we suggest to point out minimal sets of assumptions A' that, on their own, are sufficient to realize a given set of guarantees G. If $\langle A, G\rangle$ is the original specification, A' may help to reduce the assumptions the environment has to fulfill. Another scenario is that G is only a subset of the guarantees under consideration. Here, the developer might want to understand which subset(s) of assumptions A' are responsible for realizability of this particular set of guarantees. It's easy to see that in both cases A' is a set of minimally sufficient assumptions.

If $\langle A, G\rangle$ turns out to be unrealizable and the set of available assumptions has not been exhausted (i.e., $A \subset \mathcal{A}$), minimally sufficient sets of assumptions for $\langle \mathcal{A}, G\rangle$ can help to find a minimal strengthening of A such that G can be realized.

Maximally Insufficient Sets of Assumptions We have not found a good intuition on how to use these as a debugging aid. We omit such sets from further consideration.

3.2 Criteria for Unhelpful Parts of an Explanation

Till now we proposed to remove constraints either only from assumptions or only from guarantees. We now proceed to remove constraints from the remaining side of an explanation. We first argue why constraints can be removed from both sides of a specification. We then formulate a criterion to identify *helpful* and *unhelpful* constraints.

Removing Constraints from the Remaining Side of an Explanation. As argued above, removing guarantees from an unrealizable specification or removing assumptions from a realizable specification is a natural approach to obtain a core of a specification that explains its (un)realizability. However, previously we have only modified one side of a specification to obtain an explanation. As mentioned, removing assumptions pushes towards unrealizability and removing guarantees pushes towards realizability. Hence, one might think that an explanation for unrealizability (in the form of a minimally unfulfillable specification) should contain the full set of assumptions A and, similarly, an explanation for realizability (in the form of a minimally sufficient specification) should contain the full set of guarantees G. Note, though, that an assumption or a guarantee might be redundant. In other words, it might be covered by the remaining set of assumptions or guarantees. Moreover, some assumptions or guarantees might be irrelevant w.r.t. a given explanation, i.e., they may have no influence on the behavior of a specification, we are interested in. We believe that the developer should be informed about such assumptions and guarantees. Below we expand that idea for the three types of explanations proposed in Sect. 3.1.

Minimally Unfulfillable Sets of Guarantees. The aim of a minimally unfulfillable explanation $\langle A, G\rangle$ is to show a conflict among the set of guarantees G or the lack of assumptions required for realizability of G. It is possible that some of the assumptions in A do not contribute to that aim, i.e., they do not influence the conflict among, or the realizability of, the guarantees G. Such assumptions may be removed from an explanation without losing valuable information, thereby making it simpler for understanding.

Maximally Fulfillable Sets of Guarantees. The purpose of a maximally fulfillable explanation $\langle A, G\rangle$ is to show which set(s) of guarantees can be realizable with a given set of assumptions or which set of guarantees are enough to remove to make the specification realizable. If removing an assumption a does not change realizability of an explanation, i.e., $\langle A \setminus \{a\}, G\rangle$ is realizable, then presence of such an assumption does not influence the property of the set G being maximally fulfillable. Indeed, since $\langle A, G \cup \{g\}\rangle$ is unrealizable for any $g \in \mathcal{G} \setminus G$ then $\langle A \setminus \{a\}, G \cup \{g\}\rangle$ is also unrealizable for any a because removing an assumption cannot make an unrealizable specification realizable. Therefore, if such an assumption is removed an explanation still fulfills its purpose and shows a maximal set of realizable guarantees.

Minimally Sufficient Sets of Assumptions. The purpose of a minimally sufficient explanation $\langle A, G\rangle$ is to point out a set of assumptions A that is enough to make a given set of guarantees G realizable such that each assumption $a \in A$ is essential for realizability. This case is symmetrical to the case of minimally unfulfillable set of guarantees, i.e., not every guarantee may be useful in such an explanation — some guarantees may be realizable independent of the assumptions, or one assumption may be essential for realizability of several guarantees therefore only one of such guarantees may be left in the explanation to show necessity of that assumption.

Formalization. We are now ready to formulate a criterion of when a constraint in an explanation should be considered unhelpful. Our intuition is as follows. Let $\langle A, G\rangle$ be an explanation, let $a \in A$ be an assumption. We say that a is *helpful* iff there is some subset of guarantees $G' \subseteq G$ s.t. $\langle A, G'\rangle$ is realizable, while $\langle A \setminus \{a\}, G'\rangle$ is not. In other words, there is a subset of guarantees G' s.t. a makes the difference between realizability and unrealizability for that subset (w.r.t. the given set of assumptions A). Similarly, a guarantee $g \in G$ is helpful iff there is at least one subset of assumptions $A' \subseteq A$ s.t. g make the difference between realizability and unrealizability: $\langle A', G \setminus \{g\}\rangle$ is realizable while $\langle A', G\rangle$ is not. We formalize that intuition below.

Definition 2 ((un-) helpful). *Let $\langle A, G\rangle$ be a specification.*

1. *An assumption $a \in A$ is* unhelpful *if*
   $$\forall G' \subseteq G \,.\, (\langle A, G'\rangle \textit{ is realizable} \Leftrightarrow \langle A \setminus \{a\}, G'\rangle \textit{ is realizable.})$$
2. *A guarantee $g \in G$ is* unhelpful *if*
   $$\forall A' \subseteq A \,.\, (\langle A', G\rangle \textit{ is realizable} \Leftrightarrow \langle A', G \setminus \{g\}\rangle \textit{ is realizable.})$$
3. *An assumption or a guarantee is* helpful *iff it is not unhelpful.*

The next proposition shows that Def. 2 is well-behaved in the following sense. If $\langle A, G\rangle$ is an explanation and $A' \subset A$ is obtained from A by a sequence of removals of unhelpful assumptions A'' (by a sequence of applications of Def. 2), then each of the removed assumptions in A'' is unhelpful also in A. Moreover, the assumptions in A'' could have been removed from A in any order. The case for guarantees is similar.

Proposition 1

1. *Let* $\langle A_0 = A, G\rangle, \langle A_1 = A_0 \setminus \{a_0\}, G\rangle, \langle A_2 = A_1 \setminus \{a_1\}, G\rangle, \ldots, \langle A' = A_k \setminus \{a_k\}, G\rangle$ *be a sequence of explanations s.t., for all* $0 \leq i \leq k$, *each* a_i *is unhelpful in* $\langle A_i, G\rangle$. *Let* $A'' \subseteq A \setminus A'$, *let* $a \in A''$. *Then* a *is unhelpful in* $\langle A' \cup A'', G\rangle$.
2. *Let* $\langle A, G_0 = G\rangle, \langle A, G_1 = G_0 \setminus \{g_0\}\rangle, \langle A, G_2 = G_1 \setminus \{g_1\}\rangle, \ldots, \langle A, G' = G_k \setminus \{g_k\}\rangle$ *be a sequence of explanations s.t., for all* $0 \leq i \leq k$, *each* g_i *is unhelpful in* $\langle A, G_i\rangle$. *Let* $G'' \subseteq G \setminus G'$, *let* $g \in G''$. *Then* g *is unhelpful in* $\langle A, G' \cup G''\rangle$.

The following proposition yields a practical way to remove unhelpful constraints from the remaining side of an explanation. Given $\langle A, G\rangle$ minimally unfulfillable, we suggest to remove assumptions from A until the result is not *minimally* unfulfillable any more (resp., if $\langle A, G\rangle$ is minimally sufficient, remove guarantees from G until the result is not *minimally* sufficient).

Proposition 2

1. *Let* $\langle A, G\rangle$ *be a minimally unfulfillable specification.* $a \in A$ *is unhelpful in* A *iff* $\langle A \setminus \{a\}, G\rangle$ *is minimally unfulfillable.*
2. *Let* $\langle A, G\rangle$ *be a minimally sufficient specification.* $g \in G$ *is unhelpful in* G *iff* $\langle A, G \setminus \{g\}\rangle$ *is minimally sufficient.*

Our next proposition shows the coincidence between Def.s 1 and 2. In particular, it shows that an unrealizable specification $\langle A, G\rangle$ contains no unhelpful guarantees iff it is minimally unfulfillable and a realizable specification $\langle A, G\rangle$ contains no unhelpful assumptions iff it is minimally sufficient.

Proposition 3

1. *Let* $\langle A, G\rangle$ *be unrealizable.* $g \in G$ *is unhelpful in* G *iff* $\langle A, G \setminus \{g\}\rangle$ *is unrealizable.*
2. *Let* $\langle A, G\rangle$ *be unrealizable.* G *is minimally unfulfillable iff all* $g \in G$ *are helpful.*
3. *Let* $\langle A, G\rangle$ *be realizable.* $a \in A$ *is unhelpful in* A *iff* $\langle A \setminus \{a\}, G\rangle$ *is realizable.*
4. *Let* $\langle A, G\rangle$ *be realizable.* A *is minimally sufficient iff all* $a \in A$ *are helpful.*

Thus Def. 2 can be used to obtain minimally unfulfillable explanations from unrealizable specifications (by removing unhelpful guarantees) and minimally sufficient explanations from realizable specifications (by removing unhelpful assumptions).

Putting the Pieces Together. In Fig. 1 we show the approach that applies the previous results according to the types of explanations suggested in Sect. 3.1.

3.3 Methodology

Unsatisfiable Assumptions and Guarantees. Sometimes subsets of assumptions or guarantees may be temporally unsatisfiable. Such situations should be pointed out to

Explaining Unrealizability — a Minimal Conflict

1. Assume $\langle A, G\rangle$ unrealizable.
2. Find some $G' \subseteq G$ s.t. $\langle A, G'\rangle$ is minimally unfulfillable.
3. Find a minimal $A' \subseteq A$ s.t. $\langle A', G'\rangle$ is minimally unfulfillable.
4. Return $\langle A', G'\rangle$.

Start with an unrealizable specification. First, remove unhelpful guarantees, then remove unhelpful assumptions. Now, every single guarantee in G' is required for a conflict; moreover, removing any assumption from A' leads to additional conflict(s), each involving fewer guarantees.

Explaining Unrealizability — a Minimal Fix

1. Assume $\langle A, G\rangle$ unrealizable.
2. Find some $G' \subseteq G$ s.t. $\langle A, G'\rangle$ is maximally fulfillable.
3. Find some $A' \subseteq A$ s.t. $\langle A', G'\rangle$ is minimally sufficient.
4. Return $\langle A', G'\rangle$.

Start with an unrealizable specification. First, remove just enough guarantees to make the specification realizable, then remove unhelpful assumptions. Now, adding any guarantee or removing any assumption leads to unrealizability. Moreover, $G \setminus G'$ is a minimal fix to make the original specification $\langle A, G\rangle$ realizable.

Explaining Realizability

1. Assume $\langle A, G\rangle$ realizable.
2. Find some $A' \subseteq A$ s.t. $\langle A', G\rangle$ is minimally sufficient.
3. Find a minimal $G' \subseteq G$ s.t. $\langle A', G'\rangle$ is minimally sufficient.
4. Return $\langle A', G'\rangle$.

Start with a realizable specification. First, remove unhelpful assumptions, then remove unhelpful guarantees. Now, every single assumption in A' is required for realizability; removing any guarantee in G' makes one or more assumptions unnecessary for realizability.

Fig. 1. A summary of our approach

the developer; however, as these situations may not be uniquely identifiable from the explanations suggested above, a separate check has to be performed. Satisfiability can be checked in various ways. A detailed treatment is out of the scope of this work. We therefore assume that the specification has been checked for satisfiability (in particular, the checks suggested in [20]) before applying our method.

Removing Unhelpful Constraints. When a specification is checked for unhelpful constraints, it is important to note that several constraints that have been found unhelpful cannot be removed at once. For example, if for a specification $\langle A, G\rangle$ the individual assumptions $a_1, a_2 \in A$ are found to be unhelpful, they should not be removed at once. Rather, it is necessary to remove one of them (e.g., a_1) and then recheck the second assumption a_2 for being unhelpful in $\langle A \setminus \{a_1\}, G\rangle$. Otherwise, the result can be incorrect. For example, if a_1 and a_2 are equivalent, they will always be unhelpful. Nevertheless, removing *both* of them can change realizability of the specification. Therefore, constraints can be checked and removed (if found unhelpful) only one by one.

3.4 Examples

Let us consider the following example with the assumptions on the left and guarantees on the right and e and s being an environment and a system variable (there may be other constraints that do not speak about e and s):

$$\begin{aligned} a_1 &\doteq e & g_1 &\doteq s \\ a_2 &\doteq \mathbf{G}((\mathbf{X}\, e) \leftrightarrow e) & g_2 &\doteq \mathbf{G}((\mathbf{X}\, s) \leftrightarrow e) \\ a_3 &\doteq \mathbf{G}\,\mathbf{F}\, e & g_3 &\doteq \mathbf{G}\,\mathbf{F}(\neg s \wedge e) \\ &\dots & &\dots \end{aligned}$$

The specification is unrealizable with a minimal conflict explanation $\langle A, G\rangle = \langle\{a_3\}, \{g_2, g_3\}\rangle$. A minimally unfulfillable guarantee set G shows the reason of unrealizability (i.e., the system cannot simultaneously make s equal to the previous value of e and at the same time reach $\neg s \wedge e$) and that the initial condition g_1 does not influence this conflict. The presence of the assumption a_3 is enough to show this conflict. By removing a_3 the explanation will not be minimally unfulfillable any more since it will remain unrealizable even without g_2 thereby losing the information about the original conflict among guarantees g_2 and g_3. Thus a_3 is required for the explanation.

4 Computing Explanations

In this section we describe our approach to computing explanations for specifications. First we explain explicit algorithms that are aimed to compute one explanation for a given specification, and we estimate their complexity. Then, we outline an alternative approach to computing explanations based on the use of activation variables [13,9].

4.1 Explicit Algorithms

In the most simplistic setting we assume that there is an external realizability checker considered as a black box and available for us as a function *Realizable*($\langle A, G\rangle$), which takes a specification $\langle A, G\rangle$ and returns $true$ iff the specification is realizable.

Among the possible kinds of explanations summarized in Fig. 1 let us begin with an unrealizable specification and its explanation in the form of a minimal conflict. The first step of the computation is to obtain a minimally unfulfillable set of guarantees. For that it is enough to identify which guarantees after removal keep the specification unrealizable. Propositions 1 and 3 establish that guarantees can be removed in any order.[4] In Sect. 3.3 we noticed that a check for realizability has to be done after each removal of any individual guarantee. As a result a simple algorithm to compute a minimally unfulfillable explanation for a given specification $\langle A, G\rangle$ is:

[4] Note, though, that while the order of removal of guarantees in a particular set of unhelpful guarantees $G' \subseteq G$ from G does not matter, it is still possible that there are different sets of unhelpful guarantees $G' \neq G''$ such that both $G \setminus G'$ and $G \setminus G''$ contain no unhelpful guarantees anymore (and similarly for assumptions). As a consequence, the algorithms presented here find minimal but not necessarily minimum explanations.

```
function ComputeMinUnfulfil(⟨A, G⟩)
  G' := G;
  foreach g ∈ G
    if ¬Realizable(⟨A, G' \ {g}⟩) then G' := G' \ {g};
  return ⟨A, G'⟩;
```

The second step of obtaining a "good" explanation is to remove unhelpful assumptions. Proposition 2 shows that it is enough to detect and remove assumptions whose removal keeps the specification minimally unfulfillable. Notice that, similarly to the previous algorithm it is necessary to check and remove only one assumption at every iteration. Thus the simplest algorithm is:

```
function ComputeGoodMinUnfulfil(⟨A, G⟩)
  A' := A;
  foreach a ∈ A
    if MinUnfulfil(⟨A' \ {a}, G⟩) then A' := A' \ {a};
  return ⟨A', G⟩;
```

where the predicate *MinUnfulfil*$(\langle A, G\rangle)$ returns $true$ iff the specification $\langle A, G\rangle$ is minimally unfulfillable:

$$\textit{MinUnfulfil}(\langle A, G\rangle) \doteq \forall g \in G \,.\, \textit{Realizable}(\langle A, G \setminus \{g\}\rangle)$$

Notice that, all above functions *ComputeMinUnfulfil*, *ComputeGoodMinUnfulfil* and *MinUnfulfil* expect as input an unrealizable specification.

In the case of computing explanations for realizable specifications (see Fig. 1) the corresponding algorithms are symmetric to the algorithms for unrealizable specifications explained above. Hence the functions *ComputeMinSuffic*, *ComputeGoodMinSuffic* and the predicate *MinSuffic* are defined similarly as *ComputeMinUnfulfil*, *Compute-GoodMinUnfulfil*, and *MinUnfulfil*, respectively, by switching realizability and unrealizability and the player whose constraints are minimized.

A minimal fix for an unrealizable specification according to Fig. 1 is also computed in two steps. The first step is to identify a maximal set of guarantees making the specification realizable. The simplest algorithm is very similar to *ComputeMinUnfulfil* with the exception that now the aim is to make the specification realizable and maximize the number of guarantees:

```
function ComputeMaxFulfil(⟨A, G⟩)
  G' := ∅;
  foreach g ∈ G
    if Realizable(⟨A, G' ∪ {g}⟩) then G' := G' ∪ {g};
  return ⟨A, G'⟩;
```

The second step is to find a minimally sufficient set of assumptions. For that the function *ComputeMinSuffic* defined above can be used.

To summarize, if a specification $\langle A, G\rangle$ is unrealizable and the cause of unrealizability is of interest, then an explanation is computed as

ComputeGoodMinUnfulfil(*ComputeMinUnfulfil*($\langle A, G\rangle$)). If a minimal fix is required, then *ComputeMinSuffic*(*ComputeMaxFulfil*($\langle A, G\rangle$)) is computed. Otherwise, if the specification $\langle A, G\rangle$ is realizable, the minimization of assumptions can be done and *ComputeGoodMinSuffic*(*ComputeMinSuffic*($\langle A, G\rangle$)) is returned.

Complexity. Let us assume that the upper bound on the time of checking the realizability of a specification $\langle A, G\rangle$ is denoted as $[\langle A, G\rangle]$, and that this upper bound cannot increase with the removal of some constraints from either A or G. Let $|A|$ and $|G|$ be the number of assumptions and guarantees, respectively. Then it is easy to see that the upper bound on the time of computing a minimal conflict for an unrealizable specification is $(|G| + |A| * |G|) * [\langle A, G\rangle]$, where $|G| * [\langle A, G\rangle]$ is the upper bound for the first step and $|A| * |G| * [\langle A, G\rangle]$ is for the second one. Similarly, the upper bound on computing an explanation for a realizable specification is $(|A| + |A| * |G|) * [\langle A, G\rangle]$, and $(|A| + |G|) * [\langle A, G\rangle]$ is the upper bound on computing a minimal fix for an unrealizable specification.

Notice that, for both, good minimally unfulfillable explanations and good minimally sufficient explanations, the number of realizability checks for computing a minimally unfulfillable set of guarantees (resp. a minimally sufficient set of assumptions), is linear in the number of constraints. While, for reducing the set of assumptions (resp. guarantees), the number of realizability checks may be quadratic.

4.2 Algorithms with Activation Variables

An alternative approach to computing explanations inspired by [13,9] works as follows. In a specification $\langle A, G\rangle$ for every constraint $c_i \in A \cup G$ a fresh activation variable av_i is created and then c_i is substituted by $av_i \rightarrow c_i$, obtaining in such a way the specification $\langle A^{AV}, G^{AV}\rangle$. Activation variables, differently from usual variables, cannot change their values after their initialization, and they belong neither to the system nor to the environment.

According to Sect. 2.2 the addition of the constraint *true* to assumptions or guarantees cannot change the realizability of a specification. Thus, setting an activation variable av_i to *false* disables the corresponding constraint c_i in the specification $\langle A^{AV}, G^{AV}\rangle$, whereas setting av_i to *true* makes the constraint $av_i \rightarrow c_i$ behave the same as the original one c_i. If a realizability checker is able to find assignments to activation variables that make a specification (un)realizable, then using these assignments we can directly identify which subsets of constraints cause (un)realizability of the specification. The algorithm for the class of GR(1) specifications mentioned in Sect. 2.3 is able to do that without any modifications. Given a modified specification $\langle A^{AV}, G^{AV}\rangle$ after finding winning states W_S and checking it against initial conditions the obtained result is not just a constant *true* or *false* but a formula over the activation variables. Each assignment that makes that formula *true* identifies a subset of the constraints that make the specification realizable.

The major difference from the previously described algorithms is that with activation variables one call to the realizability checker is enough to find all (un)realizable subsets of the constraints. Unfortunately, experimental results showed that introduction of new variables to the game slows down the realizability check considerably. As a result the computation of explanations with activation variables is often much slower than using the explicit algorithms described in Sect. 4.1.

5 Experimental Evaluation

We implemented all the algorithms described in Sect. 4 plus the algorithm for GR(1) synthesis [15] within the framework of the NuSMV system [7]. We applied several optimizations to the algorithm for checking realizability of [15] as to improve the performance. For instance, we compute the set of reachable states of the game structure and we use such set during the realizability check to restrict the search only to reachable states. The different explicit algorithms have been also optimized as to possibly re-use as much as possible results of previous checks. The implementation of activation variables takes into account that they remain constant after the initial state.

We evaluated our algorithms on two real-life specifications parametric on the number of components: the ARM AMBA AHB Arbiter [5] and the IBM GenBuf Controller[6]. We took these specifications from [5]: since that paper is about showing feasibility of synthesis, both specifications are realizable. We remark that, we were not able to find real-life unrealizable specifications in the literature. As we have pointed out before, we can make a GR(1) specification unrealizable by adding constraints to $\varphi_I^{\mathcal{S}}$, $\varphi_R^{\mathcal{S}}$, or $\phi_\psi^{\mathcal{S}}$, or by removing constraints from $\varphi_I^{\mathcal{E}}$, $\varphi_R^{\mathcal{E}}$, or $\varphi_\psi^{\mathcal{E}}$. We simulate the cases of adding to $\varphi_R^{\mathcal{S}}$ (referred to as W-GT), adding to $\varphi_\psi^{\mathcal{S}}$ (referred to as W-GF), and removing from $\varphi_\psi^{\mathcal{E}}$ (referred to as WO-AF).

We ran the experiments on an Intel Xeon 3GHz bi-processor equipped with 4GB of RAM running Linux. We fixed a memory limit to 1.5GB and a time-out to 1 hour. We report "T" and "M", respectively, when a time-out or a memory limit is reached. We used BDD dynamic variable ordering during the search since this resulted in better performances on average. All the experiments and an extended version of this paper [8] are available from `http://es.fbk.eu/people/roveri/tests/vmcai08`.

The table below shows the results of experiments with activation variables:

Specification Name	Assumptions/ Guarantees	Realizable	Time Realizability	Time Step 1	Time Step 1 and 2
AMBA-1	8/52	R	0.14	0.24	212
AMBA-W-GF-1	8/53	U	0.02	587	T

The first three columns show the name of a specification, its size, and its realizability, respectively. The fourth column gives the original realizability checking time (in seconds). The fifth column lists the checking time if only assumptions (for a realizable specification) or only guarantees (for an unrealizable one) are given activation variables — this corresponds to step 1 of the explicit algorithms. The last column shows realizability checking times if all constraints are given activation variables — this corresponds to both steps of the explicit algorithms.

The above results show how significantly activation variables may slow down the realizability check. This is the reason why only two specifications are in the table. We remark that (1) the algorithm using activation variables computes minimum rather than just minimal cores and (2) computing minimum cores by using activation variables has

[5] ARM Ltd. AMBA Specification (Rev. 2). Available from `www.arm.com`, 1999.

[6] `http://www.haifa.ibm.com/projects/verification/RB_Homepage/tutorial3/`

Table 1. Computation of explanations using explicit algorithms

Specification Name	Assumpt/ Guarant	Real- izable	Time Re- alizability	Time Step 1	Reduction Step 1	Time Step 2	Reduction Step 2
AMBA-1	8 / 52	R	0.14	0.25	**75.0%** (2 / 52)	1.93	**65.4%** (2 / 18)
AMBA-1-W-GF	8 / 53	U	0.02	0.24	**92.5%** (8 / 4)	0.02	**87.5%** (1 / 4)
AMBA-1-W-GT	8 / 53	U	0.02	0.21	**96.2%** (8 / 2)	0.01	**100%** (0 / 2)
AMBA-1-WO-AF	5 / 52	U	0.09	0.41	**76.9%** (5 / 12)	0.07	**100%** (0 / 12)
AMBA-2	11 / 80	R	1.22	2.97	**63.6%** (4 / 80)	64.1	**68.8%** (4 / 25)
AMBA-2-W-GF	11 / 81	U	0.19	1.06	**88.9%** (11 / 9)	0.12	**72.7%** (3 / 9)
AMBA-2-W-GT	11 / 81	U	0.17	0.97	**91.4%** (11 / 7)	0.06	**81.8%** (2 / 7)
AMBA-2-WO-AF	10 / 80	U	0.19	1.47	**87.5%** (10 / 10)	0.28	**100%** (0 / 10)
AMBA-3	14 / 108	R	14.3	35.2	**85.7%** (2 / 108)	26.7	**86.1%** (2 / 15)
AMBA-3-W-GF	14 / 109	U	0.51	4.31	**94.5%** (14 / 6)	0.09	**92.9%** (1 / 6)
AMBA-3-W-GT	14 / 109	U	0.39	2.92	**97.2%** (14 / 3)	0.04	**100%** (0 / 3)
AMBA-3-WO-AF	13 / 108	U	1.73	15.8	**90.7%** (13 / 10)	0.54	**100%** (0 / 10)
AMBA-4	17 / 136	R	74.9	292	**64.7%** (6 / 137)	T	-
AMBA-4-W-GF	17 / 137	U	1.17	23.9	**89.8%** (17 / 14)	0.71	**82.4%** (3 / 14)
AMBA-4-W-GT	17 / 137	U	0.86	12.5	**92.0%** (17 / 11)	0.29	**88.2%** (2 / 11)
AMBA-4-WO-AF	16 / 136	U	5.03	163	**92.6%** (16 / 10)	0.75	**100%** (0 / 10)
AMBA-5	20 / 164	R	525	T	-	-	-
AMBA-5-W-GF	20 / 165	U	19.7	188	**92.7%** (20 / 12)	0.50	**85.0%** (3 / 12)
AMBA-5-W-GT	20 / 165	U	11.6	70.1	**93.9%** (20 / 10)	0.26	**90.0%** (2 / 10)
AMBA-5-WO-AF	19 / 164	U	14.9	126	**93.9%** (19 / 10)	0.80	**100%** (0 / 10)
GENBUF-5	28 / 81	R	0.15	1.23	**46.4%** (15 / 81)	39.2	**54.3%** (15 / 37)
GENBUF-5-W-GF	28 / 82	U	0.15	2.38	**87.8%** (28 / 10)	0.60	**88.3%** (3 / 10)
GENBUF-5-W-GT	28 / 82	U	0.22	3.25	**86.6%** (28 / 11)	0.75	**82.1%** (5 / 11)
GENBUF-5-WO-AF	27 / 81	U	0.12	1.48	**87.7%** (27 / 10)	0.63	**96.3%** (1 / 10)
GENBUF-10	43 / 152	R	1.22	12.3	**53.5%** (20 / 152)	522	**62.5%** (20 / 57)
GENBUF-10-W-GF	43 / 153	U	1.26	29.3	**90.2%** (43 / 15)	3.34	**93.0%** (3 / 15)
GENBUF-10-W-GT	43 / 153	U	4.53	56.1	**89.5%** (43 / 16)	3.81	**88.4%** (5 / 16)
GENBUF-10-WO-AF	42 / 152	U	0.44	9.60	**93.4%** (42 / 10)	1.74	**97.6%** (1 / 10)
GENBUF-20	73 / 368	R	3.65	90.7	**58.9%** (30 / 368)	M	-
GENBUF-20-W-GF	73 / 369	U	3.51	470	**93.2%** (73 / 25)	35.5	**95.9%** (3 / 25)
GENBUF-20-W-GT	73 / 369	U	1328	T	-	-	-
GENBUF-20-WO-AF	72 / 368	U	2.21	115	**97.3%** (72 / 10)	7.78	**98.6%** (1 / 10)
GENBUF-30	103 / 683	R	24.4	920	**61.2%** (40 / 683)	M	-
GENBUF-30-W-GF	103 / 684	U	23.9	T	-	-	-
GENBUF-30-W-GT	103 / 684	U	T	T	-	-	-
GENBUF-30-WO-AF	102 / 683	U	7.61	842	**98.5%** (102 / 10)	22.7	**99.0%** (1 / 10)

incurred a significant performance penalty in [13,9], too. For the explicit algorithms the execution time results are considerably better. Table 1 reports all the results obtained with explicit algorithms.

The first column of Table 1 indicates the name of the specification. The original specifications have names AMBA-n and GENBUF-n, where n is the number of components of the described system. The modified ones have suffixes W-GF, W-GT, and WO-AF as explained above. The following three columns list the size (the number of assumptions and guarantees), the realizability and the time in seconds of checking the realizability of a specification. The fifth column is the time required to remove unhelpful guarantees from an unrealizable specification or unhelpful assumptions from a realizable one.

The sixth column shows the percentage of corresponding player's constraints that have been removed and the new size of the specification. The last two columns are similar to the previous two columns but dedicated to the removal of unhelpful constraints of the remaining player.

The experiments show that a considerable number of constraints can be removed from the explanations. For example, for unrealizable specifications the cause of unrealizability is found to be among only 9% (on average) of guarantees. Moreover, removing 92% (on average) of assumptions does not change the realizability of the obtained guarantees or any of their subsets. Thus before trying to understand and fix the problem a designer can decrease the size of a specification more than 10 times thereby decreasing the effort required to detect and comprehend a bug.

For the real-life realizable specifications ARM AMBA AHB Arbiter and IBM GenBuf Controller we found that about 64% of the assumptions are not required for the realizability of the guarantees. This may indicate that the designers over-constrained the environment in fear that the specification may become unrealizable at some state of the design development. Another possible reason is that not all intended guarantees have been added to the specification. In any case showing unnecessary assumptions can be a valuable debugging information for designers. In fact, our approach unexpectedly shows that going from AMBA-2 to AMBA-3 the number of required assumptions decreases from 4 to 2. The analysis of the generated core allowed us to detect a missing constraint in the AMBA-3 aiming to forbid one assignment to the two Boolean signals used to encode a three value variable. (See [8] for additional details.)

In our experiments the first step of explanation computation is on average 20 times slower than the realizability checking of the original specification. The second step is about 25 times slower than the original realizability checking. Though the time required for computation is relatively large, it is not exceedingly large and is very likely to be a good trade-off by potentially decreasing the time required for debugging a specification.

6 Conclusions and Future Works

In this paper we addressed the problem of providing diagnostic information in presence of formal analysis of requirements, and in particular in the case of realizability. We showed that the problem is nontrivial, formally characterized it, and proposed methods to automatically extract explanations, i.e., descriptions of the reasons for (un)realizability. The experimental evaluation shows the potential of the approach.

It is worth noticing that, most of the concepts and algorithms developed in this paper easily extend beyond realizability: given any computable Boolean-valued function r on a couple of finite sets $\langle A, G\rangle$ such that r has the monotonicity properties stated in Sect. 2.2, the definitions, theorems, and algorithms developed in Sect. 3 and 4.1 apply.

In the future, we plan to evaluate the integration of the explicit and the symbolic methods. We will investigate the use of heuristic search in the space subsets of the specification. We will also investigate the integration within a practical framework (e.g., contract-based design) where realizability comes into play (e.g., by composition of contracts). Finally, given that the use of activation variables has proved to be both a powerful and expensive means to extract minimum cores for several problem classes involving temporal logic, a separate investigation of how to improve this technique (e.g., by carrying over results from the Boolean domain) seems worthwhile to us.

References

1. Abadi, M., Lamport, L., Wolper, P.: Realizable and unrealizable specifications of reactive systems. In: Ronchi Della Rocca, S., Ausiello, G., Dezani-Ciancaglini, M. (eds.) ICALP 1989. LNCS, vol. 372, pp. 1–17. Springer, Heidelberg (1989)
2. European Railway Agency. Feasibility study for the formal specification of ETCS functions. Sep, Invitation to tender (2007), `http://www.era.europa.eu`
3. Behrmann, G., et al.: UPPAAL-Tiga: Time for playing games! In: Damm and Hermanns [11], pp. 121–125.
4. Bloem, R., et al.: RAT: Formal analysis of requirements. In: Damm and Hermanns [11], pp. 263–267.
5. Bloem, R., et al.: Interactive presentation: Automatic hardware synthesis from specifications: A case study. In: Lauwereins, R., Madsen, J. (eds.) DATE, pp. 1188–1193. ACM Press, New York (2007)
6. Bontemps, Y., Schobbens, P., Löding, C.: Synthesis of open reactive systems from scenario-based specifications. Fundam. Inform. 62(2), 139–169 (2004)
7. Clarke, E., et al.: NuSMV: A new symbolic model verifier. In: Halbwachs, N., Peled, D.A. (eds.) CAV 1999. LNCS, vol. 1633, pp. 495–499. Springer, Heidelberg (1999)
8. Cimatti, A., et al.: Diagnostic information for realizability. Technical Report FBK-092007-01, Fondazione Bruno Kessler (2007), `http://es.fbk.eu/people/roveri/tests/vmcai08`
9. Cimatti, A., et al.: Boolean abstraction for temporal logic satisfiability. In: Damm and Hermanns [11], pp. 532–546
10. Clarke, E., Veith, H.: Counterexamples Revisited: Principles, Algorithms, Applications. In: Dershowitz, N. (ed.) Verification: Theory and Practice. LNCS, vol. 2772, pp. 208–224. Springer, Heidelberg (2004)
11. Damm, W., Hermanns, H. (eds.): CAV 2007. LNCS, vol. 4590. Springer, Heidelberg (2007)
12. Groce, A.: Error Explanation and Fault Localization with Distance Metrics. PhD thesis, Carnegie Mellon University (2005)
13. Lynce, I., Marques Silva, J.: On computing minimum unsatisfiable cores. In: SAT (2004)
14. Pill, I., et al.: Formal analysis of hardware requirements. In: Sentovich, E. (ed.) DAC, pp. 821–826. ACM Press, New York (2006)
15. Pnueli, A., Piterman, N., Sa'ar, Y.: Synthesis of Reactive(1) Designs. In: Emerson, E.A., Namjoshi, K.S. (eds.) VMCAI 2006. LNCS, vol. 3855, pp. 364–380. Springer, Heidelberg (2005)
16. Pnueli, A., Rosner, R.: On the synthesis of a reactive module. In: 16th Annual ACM Symposium on Principles of Programming Languages, pp. 179–190 (1989)
17. Safra, S.: On the complexity of omega-automata. In: FOCS, pp. 319–327. IEEE, Los Alamitos (1988)
18. Tripakis, S., Altisen, K.: On-the-Fly Controller Synthesis for Discrete and Dense-Time Systems. In: Wing, J.M., Woodcock, J.C.P., Davies, J. (eds.) FM 1999. LNCS, vol. 1708, Springer, Heidelberg (1999)
19. `http://www.prosyd.org`
20. Yoshiura, N.: Finding the causes of unrealizability of reactive system formal specifications. In: SEFM, pp. 34–43. IEEE Computer Society Press, Los Alamitos (2004)

Approximation Refinement for Interpolation-Based Model Checking*

Vijay D'Silva[1], Mitra Purandare[1], and Daniel Kroening[2]

[1] Computer Systems Institute, ETH Zurich, Switzerland
{firstname.lastname}@inf.ethz.ch
[2] Computing Laboratory, Oxford University, UK
kroening@comlab.ox.ac.uk

Abstract. Model checking using Craig interpolants provides an effective method for computing an over-approximation of the set of reachable states using a SAT solver. This method requires proofs of unsatisfiability from the SAT solver to progress. If an over-approximation leads to a satisfiable formula, the computation restarts using more constraints and the previously computed approximation is not reused. Though the new formula eliminates spurious counterexamples of a certain length, there is no guarantee that the subsequent approximation is better than the one previously computed. We take an abstract, approximation-oriented view of interpolation based model checking. We study counterexample-free approximations, which are neither over- nor under-approximations of the set of reachable states but still contain enough information to conclude if counterexamples exist. Using such approximations, we devise a model checking algorithm for approximation refinement and discuss a preliminary implementation of this technique on some hardware benchmarks.

1 Introduction

Model Checking is an algorithmic technique for establishing that a transition system satisfies certain mathematically specified correctness requirements [1]. Symbolic model checking techniques employ implicit representations of set of states such as Binary Decision Diagrams (BDDs) or propositional logic formulae. Formulating stages in model checking as a Boolean satisfiability (SAT) problem allows model checking tools to harness the capabilities of propositional SAT solvers, thereby greatly enhancing their scalability. However, image computation and fixed point detection, two essential steps in model checking, both involve the expensive operation of quantifier elimination.

A Craig interpolant is a formula, which can be extracted from a resolution proof generated by a SAT-solver in linear time [2,3]. For a suitably constructed Boolean formula, the interpolant provides a conservative approximation of the image, obviating the need for precise image computation [4]. Interpolants also

* This research is supported by SRC contract 2006-TJ-1539 and a DAC graduate fellowship.

F. Logozzo et al. (Eds.): VMCAI 2008, LNCS 4905, pp. 68–82, 2008.

provide a means for detecting fixed points detection without quantifier elimination. On the other hand, the approximate image may contain spurious counterexamples, necessitating quality guarantees for the approximation.

The progress and efficiency of an interpolation-based model checking algorithm is contingent on its ability to (a) avoid and eliminate spurious counterexamples, and (b) to rapidly reach a fixed point. If the original algorithm encounters a spurious counterexample, the computation is begun afresh using a more constrained formula. Though techniques have been suggested for reusing interpolants [5], there is a significant loss of information between computations using different constraints. In particular, the approximation is guaranteed to exclude spurious counterexamples shorter than a specified bound. Increasing the bound from k to k' only guarantees that spurious counterexamples shorter than k' are eliminated. The new approximation may contain spurious counterexamples longer than k', which were previously absent, and may omit states that were previously known to be safe. Thus, both the spurious counterexamples and the number of iterations may differ vastly between subsequent runs of the interpolation-based algorithm.

Contribution. The motivation for our work is to devise a method to reuse and refine approximations after each restart. To this end, our contributions are:

1. Modeling interpolation-based model checking with approximate image and pre-image operators that provide *counterexample guarantees.* This abstract view allows us to employ standard tools from fixed point approximation.
2. *Counterexample-free approximations.* These neither over- nor under-approximate the set of reachable states but contain sufficient information to conclude if counterexamples exist. Such approximations do not result in satisfiability and can be reused.
3. A new algorithm for interpolation-based model checking. We combine approximate forward and backward analysis to successively refine counterexample-free approximations until a result is obtained.

Related Work. Model checking using interpolants was first proposed in [4]. Marques-Silva [6,5] identifies optimizations and conditions for interpolant reuse, but no guarantee about the approximation is provided. In fact, Jhala and McMillan [7] report that the interpolants are "*often unnecessarily weak,*" and introduce an interpolant strengthening method. Their observation concurs with our experience that the interpolant is often too weak to admit reusable approximations.

Approximate techniques combining forward and backward reachability are well known in symbolic model checking with BDDs [8,9,10] and abstract interpretation [11,12], and have been analyzed theoretically [13,14]. The work of Cabodi et al. [15] is closest to ours, combining forward and backward analyzes with interpolants. Their focus is eliminating redundancy in the interpolants, but reuse or refinement are not considered. Refinement techniques using interpolation focus on *abstractions* of the transition relation [16] rather than approximations, as we do. Our algorithm for refining counterexample-free approximations is inspired by that of [12] for refining abstract domains. The differences are that our approximation operators are not monotone and our algorithm is based on our fixed point characterization of counterexample-free approximations.

2 Background

We begin with a review of finite state model checking, followed by a description of symbolic model checking using Craig interpolants.

2.1 Finite State Model Checking

A transition system $M = (S, T)$ consists of a finite set of states S, and a transition relation $T \subseteq S \times S$. We fix M as the transition system for the rest of the paper. A path is a sequence of states $s_0 \to \cdots \to s_n$ such that for $0 \leq i < n$, the pair $(s_i, s_{i+1}) \in T$. The image of a set of states $Q \subseteq S$ is the set of successor states with respect to T, given by the operator $post(Q) = \{s' \in S | \exists s \in Q \text{ and } (s, s') \in T\}$. Let $post^0(Q) = Q$ and $post^{i+1}(Q) = post(post^i(Q))$. Given a set $I \subseteq S$ of initial states, the set of states reachable from I and a fixed point characterization thereof are given by the equation:

$$R_I = \bigcup_{i \geq 0} post^i(I) = \mu Q.(I \cup post(Q))$$

The pre-image of a set $Q \subseteq S$ is the set of states with a successor in Q, described by the operator $pre(Q) = \{s \in S | \exists s' \in Q \text{ and } (s, s') \in T\}$. The set of backward reachable states from a set $F \subseteq S$ of *failure states* and a fixed point characterization thereof are given by the equation:

$$B_F = \bigcup_{i \geq 0} pre^i(F) = \mu Q.(F \cup pre(Q)) .$$

A set of states P is *inductive* if for any $Q \subseteq P$, it holds that $post(Q) \subseteq P$. The set P is an *inductive invariant* of a system M with initial states I if P is inductive and $I \subseteq P$. Observe that R_I is the smallest inductive invariant of M, and that $\overline{B_F}$, the complement of B_F, is inductive.

Given sets I of initial and F of failure states, with $I \cap F = \emptyset$, let $\langle I, F \rangle$ denote the assertion that the states in F are unreachable from those in I. The *verification problem* requires deciding if $\langle I, F \rangle$ holds for M. We write $M \models \langle I, F \rangle$ if the assertion holds. A *counterexample* to $\langle I, F \rangle$ is a path $s_0 \to \cdots s_n$ with $s_0 \in I$ and $s_n \in F$. A *possible counterexample* is a path with $s_0 \in I$ or $s_n \in F$. A *spurious counterexample* is a path with $s_n \in F$ and $s_0 \notin R_I$ or $s_0 \in I$ and $s_n \notin B_F$. If $R_I \cap B_F = \emptyset$, we can conclude that $M \models \langle I, F \rangle$.

The length of a path is the number of transitions on it. Consider the set of shortest paths between pairs of states in S. The *diameter* of M is the length of the longest path in this set. The *reachability diameter* of $I \subseteq S$, denoted $rd(I)$, is the length of the longest path in this set emanating from a state in I. The *backward diameter* of $F \subseteq S$, denoted $bd(F)$, is the length of the longest path in this set terminating in a state in F.

2.2 Symbolic Model Checking Using Interpolants

In SAT-based symbolic model checking, sets and relations are represented using propositional logic formulae. In the sequel, we use sets and relations, and their propositional encoding by their characteristic Boolean functions interchangeably.

In 1957, Craig showed that for each inconsistent pair of formulae A, B in first order logic, there exists a formula φ – the *Craig interpolant* [17] – such that

- A implies φ,
- φ is inconsistent with B, and
- φ refers only to non-logical symbols common to A and B.

Intuitively, the interpolant φ can be understood as an abstraction of A. Computing precise images and pre-images using SAT is an expensive operation. McMillan proposed using Craig interpolation for effective, over-approximate image computation [4]. Given a depth k, one starts with an *unwinding* of the transition relation as in Bounded Model Checking (BMC):

$$I(x_0) \wedge T(x_0, x_1) \wedge \ldots \wedge T(x_{k-1}, x_k) \wedge (F(x_1) \vee \cdots \vee F(x_k)) \qquad (1)$$

A SAT solver is used to determine if the formula above is satisfiable. If so, there exists a counterexample to $\langle I, F\rangle$ of length at most k and the procedure terminates reporting an error. Otherwise, the formula is partitioned into two parts denoted by A and B as below.

$$\begin{aligned} A &\equiv I(x_0) \wedge T(x_0, x_1) \\ B &\equiv T(x_1, x_2) \wedge \ldots \wedge T(x_{k-1}, x_k) \wedge (F(x_1) \vee \cdots \vee F(x_k)) \end{aligned} \qquad (2)$$

The formulae A and B are inconsistent, so there exists an interpolant, say φ. The interpolant represents a set that contains $post(I)$, i.e., over-approximates the image of I. In addition, no failure state can be reached from φ in up to $k - 1$ steps because φ and B are inconsistent. The algorithm proceeds to the next iteration by checking $\langle \varphi, F\rangle$, which may yield a new interpolant φ'. If an interpolant implies the disjunction of all previously computed interpolants, a fixed point is reached, and one may conclude that F is unreachable from I.

However, as φ over-approximates the image, it may represent states that are not reachable, and thus, Eq. 1 with $\varphi(x_0)$ in place of $I(x_0)$ may become satisfiable even though no counterexample exists. In this case, McMillan's technique restarts the approximation with a higher value of k. The previously computed interpolants are abandoned, and the only information retained after a restart is the new value of k.

3 Approximate Analysis Using Counterexample Guarantees

3.1 Approximations in Model Checking

Interpolation-based model checking relies on computing approximations. In general, model checking methods that use approximations face two challenges:

1. **Counterexamples.** Let $s_0 \to \cdots \to s_n$ with $s_n \in F$ be a possible counterexample. Deciding if s_0 is reachable is as hard as model checking, hence other approaches are required to deal with counterexamples.
2. **Progress.** If the approximation computed does not lead to a conclusive answer, a better approximation has to be found, either by refining the existing one or repeating the computation using a better approximation operator.

Interpolation-based methods provide a *counterexample guarantee*, i.e., a formal statement about the counterexamples in the approximation. If a possible counterexample is encountered, the fixed point computation is repeated using a stronger guarantee. Though a stronger guarantee eliminates spurious counterexamples of a given length, the approximation computed need not be comparable to the previous one. In particular, the new approximation may contain spurious counterexamples that were previously absent and omit states previously known not to lead to counterexamples of a certain length.

We model the image computation step in interpolation-based model checking using approximate image operators and formalize the notion of counterexample guarantees. The goal of this formalization is to obtain an abstract, approximation-oriented view of interpolation-based model checking. This view allows us to utilize ideas from approximate model checking [8] and abstract interpretation [18] to derive a new algorithm incorporating approximation reuse and refinement.

3.2 Approximation Operators

We briefly recall standard results from fixed point approximation about combining forward and backward analyzes (See [19] for the related background).

An approximate image operator $\hat{post}$ satisfies $post(Q) \subseteq \hat{post}(Q)$ for all Q. An approximate pre-image operator $\hat{pre}$ satisfies $pre(Q) \subseteq \hat{pre}(Q)$ for all Q. The approximate sets of forward- and backward-reachable states are

$$\hat{R}_I = \bigcup_{i \geq 0} \hat{post}^i(I) \qquad \hat{B}_F = \bigcup_{i \geq 0} \hat{pre}^i(F) \; .$$

It is a standard fixed point approximation result that $R_I \subseteq \hat{R}_I$ and $B_F \subseteq \hat{B}_F$. We say *approximate operator* to refer to an approximate post- or pre-image operator. An operator $F : S \to S$ is *additive* if $F(Q \cup Q') = F(Q) \cup F(Q')$. F is *monotone* if for $Q \subseteq Q'$, it holds that $F(Q) \subseteq F(Q')$. An additive operator on a lattice is necessarily monotone. The operators *post* and *pre* are additive, hence monotone. We consider operators $\hat{post}$ and $\hat{pre}$ that are *not* additive or monotone. The approximate image obtained depends on a resolution proof generated by a SAT solver, which in turn depends on the SAT solver's heuristics, thus we cannot make conclusions about monotonicity or additivity. This is a significant difference from several approximate operators in the literature. Widening operators [18] may also not be additive or monotone.

Recall that $\langle I, F\rangle$ is the assertion that F is unreachable from I. Our aim is to determine if $\langle I, F\rangle$ holds by combining forward and backward analysis to successively refine approximations of R_I and B_F.

Definition 1. *Consider the assertions $\langle I, F\rangle$ and $\langle I', F'\rangle$. The assertion $\langle I', F'\rangle$* refines *$\langle I, F\rangle$ if $I' \subseteq I$ and $F' \subseteq F$. The assertion $\langle I', F'\rangle$* is sufficient for *$\langle I, F\rangle$ if it holds that if $M \models \langle I', F'\rangle$ then $M \models \langle I, F\rangle$.*

If $\langle I', F'\rangle$ refines $\langle I, F\rangle$, then $\langle I, F\rangle$ is sufficient for $\langle I', F'\rangle$. This is the core idea behind conservative approximation and abstraction techniques. Another approach, which we adopt, is to use conservative methods to refine a verification problem to a sufficient one. Lemma 1 illustrates one such well known refinement.

Lemma 1. *$M \models \langle I, F\rangle$ if and only if $M \models \langle I \cap B_F, F \cap R_I\rangle$.*

If approximate sets are used, $\langle I \cap \hat{B}_F, F \cap \hat{R}_I\rangle$ is sufficient for $\langle I, F\rangle$, but if $M \not\models \langle I \cap \hat{B}_F, F \cap \hat{R}_I\rangle$, the analysis is inconclusive. In this situation, we refine the approximations $\hat{R}_I$ and $\hat{B}_F$, which in turn may lead to a refinement of $\langle I \cap \hat{B}_F, F \cap \hat{R}_I\rangle$ sufficient for $\langle I, F\rangle$. Lemma 2 provides a fixed point characterization of this iterative refinement process (See [14] for a detailed discussion). The fixed point characterization does not affect the precise result computed. In contrast, if approximate operators are used, fixed point iteration may lead to a more precise result than just $\langle I \cap \hat{B}_F, F \cap \hat{R}_I\rangle$.

Lemma 2. *Let R_I and B_F be the forward- and backward-reachable states for the verification problem $\langle I, F\rangle$. Let $\hat{R}_I$ and $\hat{B}_F$ be corresponding approximate sets computed with $\hat{post}$ and $\hat{pre}$.*

1. *Let $G(\langle X, Y\rangle) = \langle I \cap X \cap B_Y, F \cap Y \cap R_X\rangle$ be a mapping between verification problems. Then, $\langle I \cap B_F, F \cap R_I\rangle$ is the greatest fixed point of G.*
2. *Let $\hat{post}$ and $\hat{pre}$ be monotone. Define $\hat{G}(\langle X, Y\rangle) = \langle I \cap X \cap \hat{B}_Y, F \cap Y \cap \hat{R}_X\rangle$. Let $\langle I_G, F_G\rangle$ be the greatest fixed point of G and $\langle I_{\hat{G}}, F_{\hat{G}}\rangle$ be the greatest fixed point of $\hat{G}$. Then, $I_G \subseteq I_{\hat{G}}$ and $F_G \subseteq F_{\hat{G}}$.*

Such a characterization forms the basis of our algorithm. Though the approximate operators we consider are not monotone, we can define an iterative computation to obtain a similar result. The main obstacle to realizing such an iteration is that $\hat{R}_I$ or $\hat{B}_F$ cannot be computed if the approximation introduces possible counterexamples. Interpolants are computed from proofs of unsatisfiability and counterexamples result in a satisfiable formula. Therefore, we need to study counterexamples in the approximation and design methods to avoid them.

3.3 Counterexample Guarantees

Approximate images computed by interpolation do not contain spurious counterexamples shorter than the specified bound. We formalize this notion as a *counterexample guarantee* and study its properties.

Definition 2. *A counterexample guarantee (P, k) is a set of states $P \subseteq S$ and a natural number k. An approximate image operator $\hat{post}$ provides the counterexample guarantee (P, k) if for all sets $Q \subseteq S$, states $s \in \hat{post}(Q)$ and paths $s = s_0 \rightarrow \cdots \rightarrow s_j$ with $j < k$, if $s_j \in P$, then $s \in post(Q)$. A counterexample guarantee for an approximate pre-image operator $\hat{pre}$ is similarly defined.*

We can be certain that a state in the approximate image, leading to a counterexample shorter than k is not introduced by the approximation. Similarly, a state in the approximate pre-image, reachable from a state in P by a path shorter than k is also contained in the precise pre-image. For example, the counterexample guarantee $(F, 0)$ provides no information about the spurious states in an approximate image. If $(F, 1)$ is the guarantee, the approximation does not introduce any states in F, but may introduce states on a path to F. Thus, if the approximate image of Q contains a state in F, we know that a state in Q leads to F.

Let $\textsc{Int}(A, B)$ be a procedure that returns the interpolant for an unsatisfiable pair A and B. An approximate image providing the counterexample guarantee (F, k) can be derived by computing $\textsc{Int}(A, B)$, where A and B are as follows [4]:

$$\begin{aligned} A &\equiv Q(x_0) \wedge T(x_0, x_1) \\ B &\equiv T(x_1, x_2) \wedge \ldots \wedge T(x_{k-1}, x_k) \wedge (F(x_1) \vee \cdots \vee F(x_k)) \end{aligned} \tag{3}$$

Similarly, we obtain an approximate pre-image operator providing the counterexample guarantee (I, k) by computing $\textsc{Int}(A, B)$, where A and B are:

$$\begin{aligned} A &\equiv T(x_{k-1}, x_k) \wedge Q(x_k) \\ B &\equiv (I(x_0) \vee \cdots \vee I(x_{k-1})) \wedge T(x_0, x_1) \wedge \ldots \wedge T(x_{k-2}, x_{k-1}) \end{aligned} \tag{4}$$

We refer to Eq. 3 and 4 as *interpolation formulae*. If the counterexample guarantee an operator provides is insufficient to reach a conclusion about a possible counterexample, we can generate an operator providing a stronger guarantee.

Definition 3. *A counterexample guarantee (P', k') is stronger than (P, k) if $P \subseteq P'$ and $k \leq k'$.*

McMillan's original algorithm increases k if a possible counterexample is discovered [4], and Marques-Silva [6] suggests heuristics for choosing the increment. This processes can be viewed as iterative strengthening of a counterexample guarantee until it is, intuitively speaking, strong enough. Another possibility is to add states to P. Let $\hat{R}_I$ and $\hat{B}_F$ be computed with $\hat{post}$ and $\hat{pre}$. A counterexample guarantee (P, k) is *image-adequate* if $\hat{R}_I$ contains no spurious counterexamples. (P, k) is *pre-image-adequate* if $\hat{B}_F$ contains no spurious counterexamples.

Theorem 1. *Let $\langle I, F \rangle$ be a verification problem. The counterexample guarantee $(F, bd(F) + 1)$ is image-adequate and $(I, rd(I) + 1)$ is pre-image-adequate.*

Adequate guarantees are worst-case requirements. In practice, properties can be proved using approximate operators that provide weaker guarantees [4]. Corollary 1 indicates the bounds for the special cases of inductive sets and Corollary 2 recalls different adequate guarantees.

Corollary 1. *The counterexample guarantee* $(F, 1)$ *is image-adequate if* $\overline{F}$ *is inductive.* $(I, 1)$ *is pre-image-adequate if* I *is inductive.*

Corollary 2. *For* $k > 1$, *if* (F, k) *is image-adequate, then so is* $(F \cup pre(F), k - 1)$. *If* (I, k) *is pre-image-adequate, then so is* $(I \cup post(I), k - 1)$.

To see Corollary 2, observe that if I and F are not inductive, then $rd(I) = rd(I \cup post(I)) + 1$ and $bd(F) = bd(F \cup pre(F)) + 1$. Thus, if, when feasible, the counterexample guarantee is strengthened by taking the union with an image or pre-image in addition to increasing k, fewer operators may have to be tried before the adequacy bound is reached.

3.4 Counterexample-Free Approximations

Strengthening a counterexample guarantee eliminates spurious counterexamples shorter than the specified bound, but need not result in a better approximation. We want to design an approximate image operator that also guarantees an improvement in the approximation. One possibility is to constrain subsequent approximations using previous ones.

A sequence of approximations cannot directly be reused after a restart because they may lead to satisfiability. The approximation cannot be used to constrain the next one because it may not include the reachable states. Marques-Silva [5] identifies conditions for interpolant reuse, but there is no guarantee that the new approximation computed is an improvement.

If the states leading to satisfiability can be eliminated, the formula will again be unsatisfiable and the method can progress. In particular, we want a *counterexample-free approximation*, an approximate set of states, which excludes violations but retains enough information to conclude if violations exist [12]. Figure 1 illustrates the relationship precise and approximate counterexample-free forward approximations. We define the set of counterexample-free reachable states, $S_{I,F}$, to contain all states reachable from I by a path that never visits F. Define $C_{I,F}$ to be the states backward-reachable from F by a path that never visits I.

$$S_{I,F} = \mu Q.[(I \cup post(Q)) \cap \overline{F}] \qquad\qquad C_{I,F} = \mu Q.[(F \cup pre(Q)) \cap \overline{I}]$$

The counterexample-free approximations of $S_{I,F}$ and $C_{I,F}$ in terms of the operators $\hat{post}_F(Q) = [\hat{post}(Q) \cap \overline{F}]$ and $\hat{pre}_I(Q) = [\hat{pre}(Q) \cap \overline{I}]$ and are as below.

$$\hat{S}_{I,F} = \bigcup_{i \geq 0} \hat{post}^{\,i}_F(I) \qquad\qquad \hat{C}_{I,F} = \bigcup_{i \geq 0} \hat{pre}^{\,i}_I(F)$$

The approximation computed using an $\hat{post}_P$, for a set of states P, is contained in $\overline{P}$. Therefore, we obtain a new approximation, which is not worse than the previous one as desired. If there is a counterexample, the sets $post(S_{I,F}) \cap F$ and $pre(C_{I,F}) \cap I$ are not empty. If $M \models \langle I, F \rangle$, then $R_I = S_{I,F}$ and $B_F = C_{I,F}$. The sets $\hat{S}_{I,F}$ and $\hat{C}_{I,F}$ are approximations which do not contain violations but may have states leading to a violation.

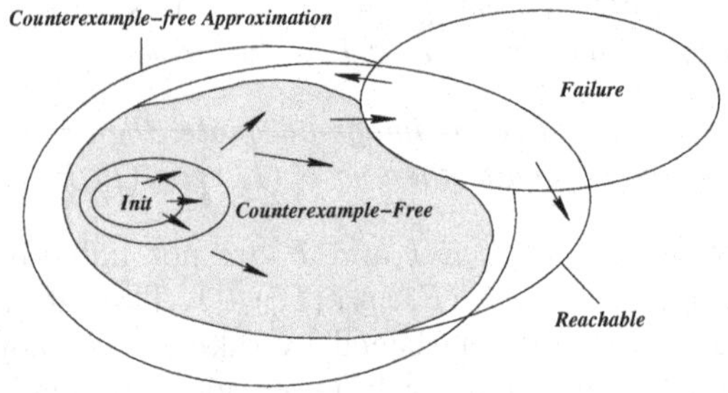

Fig. 1. Counterexample-free forward approximation

Lemma 3. *Let $\langle I, F\rangle$ be an assertion, R_I and B_F be forward- and backward-reachable states, and $S_{I,F}$, $C_{I,F}$, $\hat{S}_{I,F}$ and $\hat{C}_{I,F}$ be as above.*

1. $R_I \cap F = \emptyset$ *if and only if* $R_I = S_{I,F}$
2. $B_F \cap I = \emptyset$ *if and only if* $B_F = C_{I,F}$
3. $S_{I,F} \subseteq \hat{S}_{I,F}$ *and* $C_{I,F} \subseteq \hat{C}_{I,F}$

Assume, for now, that we can compute $\hat{S}_{I,F}$ and $\hat{C}_{I,F}$ using an interpolation-based method. If $post(\hat{S}_{I,F}) \subseteq \hat{S}_{I,F}$, we have an inductive invariant, which contains R_I and can conclude that the property holds. This can be determined using a SAT solver to see if $[\hat{S}_{I,F}(x_0) \wedge T(x_0, x_1) \wedge F(x_1)]$ is unsatisfiable. A similar check applies for $\hat{C}_{I,F}$ and fails if $pre(\hat{C}_{I,F}) \cap I$ is not empty.

Further, if $M \models \langle I, F\rangle$, then $\hat{S}_{I,F}$ and $\hat{C}_{I,F}$ contain R_I and B_F, respectively. If $M \not\models \langle I, F\rangle$, then $\hat{S}_{I,F}$ and $\hat{C}_{I,F}$ must contain a state on a path to and from a violation, respectively. The sets $\hat{S}_{I,F}$ and $\hat{C}_{I,F}$ lose no information about whether $M \models \langle I, F\rangle$ and we can refine the verification problem to $\langle I \cap pre(\hat{C}_{I,F})), F \cap post(\hat{S}_{I,F})\rangle$. Theorem 2 formalizes these intuitive arguments.

Theorem 2. *Let $S_{I,F}$ and $C_{I,F}$ be counterexample-free sets of forward- and backward-reachable states.*

1. *The problem $\langle I \cap pre(C_{I,F}), F \cap post(S_{I,F})\rangle$ is sufficient for $\langle I, F\rangle$.*
2. *Let $G(\langle X, Y\rangle) = \langle I \cap X \cap pre(C_{X,Y}), F \cap Y \cap post(S_{X,Y})\rangle$. Then, $\langle I \cap pre(C_{I,F}), F \cap post(S_{I,F})\rangle$ is the greatest fixed point of G.*

The proof is available in an electronic version of the paper. We can now use approximate operators and define an iterative sequence to compute refinements of $\langle I, F\rangle$, which over-approximate the greatest fixed point of G (the design and soundness of such an iteration follow from fixed point approximation [18]). We still need a method to improve subsequent approximations because $\hat{post}$ and $\hat{pre}$ are not monotone. The approximations $\hat{S}_{X,Y}$ and $\hat{C}_{X,Y}$ contain sufficient information to decide $M \models \langle I, F\rangle$ and can thus be used to soundly constrain new approximations.

4 Approximation Refinement with Interpolation

We present an interpolation-based model checking algorithm. Novel aspects of this algorithm are that:

1. It computes counterexample-free approximations, thus avoiding satisfiability until a fixed point is reached.
2. If an approximation leads to an inconclusive answer, a new approximation is computed, which is guaranteed to refine the previous approximation.
3. The approximation is improved using previously computed approximations, ensuring that computed information is not lost.

An additional feature is that we combine forward and backward analysis. Such combinations are by now standard in the model checking literature and have the benefits of both analyzes such as faster convergence to a result.

4.1 Interpolant-Based Approximation Refinement

Our algorithm is shown in Figure 2. It is provided a verification problem $\langle I, F\rangle$ as input. We assume that $I \cap F$ is the empty set. The pair $\langle I_j, F_j\rangle$ is a sufficient refinement of $\langle I, F\rangle$ obtained after j iterations. $\tilde{S}_j$ and $\tilde{C}_j$ are counterexample-free approximations of the reachable and backward reachable states from I_j and F_j, respectively. On Line 3, if a counterexample of length k_j exists, an error is returned. If not, two counterexample-free approximations are computed.

Recall that $\hat{post}_F$ is an approximate operator returning $[\hat{post}(Q) \cap \overline{F}]$ for any Q. The approximate operator $\hat{pre}_I$ similarly returns $[\hat{pre}(Q) \cap \overline{I}]$ for any Q. We can compute counterexample-free approximations using $\hat{post}_{F_j}$ and $\hat{pre}_{I_j}$, but they are not guaranteed to refine $\tilde{S}_{j-1}$ and $\tilde{C}_{j-1}$ because $\hat{post}$ and $\hat{pre}$ are not monotone. Instead, on Line 8, we use the function $[\hat{post}_{F_j}(Q) \cap \tilde{S}_{j-1}]$, to obtain a counterexample-free approximation which does refine $\tilde{S}_{j-1}$. On Line 9, we compute a similar approximation, $\tilde{C}_j$, which refines $\tilde{C}_{j-1}$.

We then check, on Line 10, if either set leads to counterexample. If not, we know that the approximation is an inductive set with no counterexamples, containing the reachable states, and we return NO COUNTEREXAMPLE. If this check fails, there are states in $\tilde{S}_j$ and $\tilde{C}_j$, which lead to counterexamples. These states may be introduced by the approximation. We progress by refining the verification problem and incrementing the bound k_j.

We need to implement all computations and checks in the algorithm using a SAT solver as shown on Line 3. To determine if $\tilde{S}_j$ and $\tilde{C}_j$ lead to counterexamples on Line 10, we check if either $[\tilde{S}_j(x_0) \wedge T(x_0, x_1) \wedge F_j(x_1)]$ or $[I_j(x_0) \wedge T(x_0, x_1) \wedge \tilde{C}_j(x_1)]$ is unsatisfiable. The main challenge is to compute the sets $\tilde{S}_j$ and $\tilde{C}_j$. We propose two methods, each making a trade-off between efficiency and accuracy. Given sets $Q, F, \tilde{S}$, we need to compute $\hat{post}(Q) \cap \overline{F} \cap \tilde{S}$. We recall the interpolation formula.

$$A \equiv Q(x_0) \wedge T(x_0, x_1)$$
$$B \equiv T(x_1, x_2) \wedge \ldots \wedge T(x_{k-1}, x_k) \wedge (F(x_1) \vee \cdots \vee F(x_k))$$

VERIFY$(M, \langle I, F\rangle)$

Input: Transition system M, Verification problem $\langle I, F\rangle$

$I_1 = I, F_1 := F, \tilde{S}_0 := \overline{F}, \tilde{C}_0 := \overline{I}, k_1 = 1$
for $j = 1, 2, 3 \ldots$ **do**
  if SAT$(I_j \wedge T(x_0, x_1) \cdots T(x_{k_j-1}, x_{k_j}) \wedge F_j)$ **then**
    return COUNTEREXAMPLE
  end if
  Let $\widehat{post}$ provide the guarantee (I_j, k_j).
  Let $\widehat{pre}$ provide the guarantee (F_j, k_j).
  $\tilde{S}_j := \bigcup_{i \geq 0}[\widehat{post}_{F_j}(I_j) \cap \tilde{S}_{j-1}]$
  $\tilde{C}_j := \bigcup_{i \geq 0}[\widehat{pre}_{I_j}(F_j) \cap \tilde{C}_{j-1}]$
  if $post(\tilde{S}_j) \cap F_j = \emptyset$ or $pre(\tilde{C}_j) \cap I_j = \emptyset$ **then**
    return NO COUNTEREXAMPLE
  else
    $I_{j+1} := I_j \cap pre(\tilde{C}_j)$
    $F_{j+1} := F_j \cap post(\tilde{S}_j)$
    $k_{j+1} := k_j + 1$
  end if
end for

Fig. 2. Interpolation-based Approximation Refinement

A possible counterexample exists if this formula is satisfiable. One possibility is to compute all satisfying assignments to identify the states $P \subseteq Q$, which lead to failures. If $Q(x_0)$ is replaced by $Q(x_0) \wedge \neg P(x_0)$, the formula becomes unsatisfiable and we can proceed. This process is repeated to obtain a sequence of sets $P_1, P_2, \ldots$ of states leading to counterexamples. This method amounts to computing pre-images of F contained in Q. If the approximation introduced by the interpolant is small, the number of satisfying instances is small and this procedure is feasible. We emphasize that this is *not* the same as computing images using a SAT-solver. We compute states in the approximation leading to satisfiability, rather than states in an image. If the set of reachable states is large, but the spurious counterexamples introduced by the approximation are small, this method is still feasible, whereas computing images this way is not.

Our second method uses the counterexample guarantee provided with Q. Any spurious counterexample must be of length at least k. Thus, if we constrain the formula above to be $B \wedge \neg F(x_k)$, the formula again becomes unsatisfiable. We can compute $Q'(x_1) = \text{INT}(A, B \wedge \neg F(x_k))$, a set of states satisfying that every path of length $k - 1$ from s either (a) never visits a failure state, or (b) visits a failure state exactly after $k - 1$ steps. The possibilities are mutually exclusive. If in the next iteration, the formula is unsatisfiable, we can compute the interpolant and proceed as before. If the formula is satisfiable, the counterexample may be of length k or $k-1$. We first add the constraint $\neg F(x_{k-1})$ to the formula B above. If it is unsatisfiable, we can proceed. Otherwise, we also add the constraint $\neg F(x_k)$. The formula must now be unsatisfiable and we can compute the interpolant.

With each constraint that is added, we obtain an approximate image which provides us weaker counterexample guarantees.

Forcing unsatisfiability by adding constraints can be adopted every time the formula becomes satisfiable. In the worst case, we may have to add $\neg F(x_i)$ for all $2 \leq i \leq k$. If the formula is still satisfiable, we can add the constraint $\neg F(x_1)$ to the formula A of the pair. In this case, the interpolant is just $\neg F(x_1)$, which is also the largest counterexample-free approximation we can obtain. A formal statement of correctness follows.

Theorem 3. *If the algorithm returns* COUNTEREXAMPLE, *then* $M \not\models \langle I, F\rangle$. *If the algorithm returns* NO COUNTEREXAMPLE, *then* $M \models \langle I, F\rangle$.

Proof. The proof of the negative case is straightforward, because an unwinding of the transition relation is used to detect the counterexample.

To prove the positive case, consider the sets $\tilde{S}_j$ and $\tilde{C}_j$. We have established in Theorem 2 that $\langle I \cap pre(C_{I,F}), F \cap post(S_{I,F})\rangle$ is sufficient for $\langle I, F\rangle$. It is enough to show that $\langle I_j, F_j\rangle$ in the algorithm is an over-approximation of this pair. Let $\langle X_j, Y_j\rangle$ be the sequence generated by the fixed point iteration in Theorem 2. The sequence is decreasing, so $S_{X_j,Y_j} \subseteq S_{X_{j+1},Y_{j+1}}$. The pair $\langle X_{j+1}, Y_{j+1}\rangle$ is computed using $post_{Y_j}$ and pre_{X_j}. The corresponding sets computed using $\hat{post}_{Y_j}$ and $\hat{pre}_{X_j}$ must therefore be over-approximations. Further, each set $\tilde{S}_j$ is only constrained using $\tilde{S}_{j-1}$, which is an over-approximation of S_{I_j,F_j}, therefore $\tilde{S}_j$ over-approximates S_{I_j,F_j}. The same applies for $\tilde{C}_j$. The pair $\langle I_j, F_j\rangle$ computed from this pair of sets is sufficient for $\langle I \cap pre(C_{I,F}), F \cap post(S_{I,F})\rangle$. Correctness follows. □

To complete the formal analysis, we have a statement about termination.

Theorem 4. *The algorithm always terminates with a positive or negative result.*

Proof. If $M \not\models \langle I, F\rangle$, then, because the sequence $\langle I_j, F_j\rangle$ computed by the algorithm is sufficient for $\langle I, F\rangle$, the pair I_j and F_j never becomes empty. In each iteration, the bound k_j is increased until it reaches the length of the counterexample, when the failure is reported.

If $M \models \langle I, F\rangle$, the bound k_j is eventually increased to either $rd(M) + 1$ or $bd(M) + 1$. Recall from Theorem 1 that such a counterexample guarantee is adequate, meaning that it does not introduce any spurious counterexamples. Thus, in the next iteration, either I_{j+1} or F_{j+1} computed by the algorithm is the empty set and the algorithm terminates. □

Optimizations. The algorithm as presented admits several optimizations. These include standard methods such as frontier set simplification and logic minimization. A standard check to make after Line 3 is to see if the new bound is k-inductive [20]. Recent developments which may enhance our method are dynamic abstraction and redundancy elimination for interpolants [15] and interpolant strengthening [7]. Our current implementation is naïve and is based on the blocking clauses algorithm for ALLSAT. Minimal inductive sub-clauses extracted from counterexamples [21] may reduce the effort required to obtain an unsatisfiable formula.

4.2 Experience

We have implemented a preliminary version of this algorithm and experimented with some hardware benchmarks. We have proposed obtaining an unsatisfiable formula by either constraining the satisfiable formula using either blocking clauses or the set of failure states. The second method being symbolic showed more promise, but we are unable to present an evaluation due to technical problems (which we are rectifying). Thus, we can only present results for our algorithm where the approximations are computed using ALLSAT.

Given the preliminary nature of our implementation, our conclusions are, for the moment, primarily qualitative.[1] If the interpolation formula never becomes satisfiable, our method essentially reduces to doing standard interpolation-based model checking. The hardware benchmarks we considered can be divided into three categories:

1. *Small.* Such circuits either have a small depth or result in approximations which preserve unsatisfiability. Examples include the ITC '99 benchmarks [22]. The basic interpolation algorithm is able to prove properties of these circuits using a small unwinding, so our method was never invoked.
2. *Medium.* These circuits compute arithmetic and Boolean functions. The over-approximation introduced does lead to satisfiability and our technique does help to reach a fixed point.
3. *Large.* These include processor benchmarks and satisfiable instances occur often. The enumerative procedure usually exhausts the memory or time limits set. Our experience with such circuits is that the approximation introduced by interpolation is extremely coarse, yielding no useful information.

It appears that our method is superfluous for small circuits, but may yield useful invariants for intermediate circuits, though it is unclear if there will be a performance improvement. With large circuits, the interpolants appear to be too coarse and computing a fixed point provides no benefits. It is an open question if methods for interpolant strengthening will help [7].

5 Conclusion

To summarize, we initiated a study of interpolation-based model checking using fixed point approximation. We introduced counterexample-free approximations to reduce the number of restarts and to enable the reuse of approximations during model checking. Our verification algorithm progresses by iteratively strengthening counterexample guarantees and refining approximations.

[1] The implementation is available at: `http://www.verify.ethz.ch/ebmc/`

The new method yields useful invariants and reduces the restarts required when model checking medium sized circuits but is unnecessary for small circuits. On large circuits, it is inconclusive, as it appears that the interpolants are extremely coarse, so computing a fixed point does not yield much information. This highlights the need for computing tighter interpolants, and other techniques to force unsatisfiability, the focus of our current research.

References

1. Clarke, E.M., Emerson, E.A.: Design and synthesis of synchronization skeletons using branching-time temporal logic. In: Kozen, D. (ed.) Logic of Programs 1981. LNCS, vol. 131, pp. 52–71. Springer, Heidelberg (1982)
2. Krajícek, J.: Interpolation theorems, lower bounds for proof systems, and independence results for bounded arithmetic. Journal of Symbolic Logic 62, 457–486 (1997)
3. Pudlák, P.: Lower bounds for resolution and cutting plane proofs and monotone computations. Journal of Symbolic Logic 62, 981–998 (1997)
4. McMillan, K.L.: Interpolation and SAT-Based Model Checking. In: Hunt Jr., W.A., Somenzi, F. (eds.) CAV 2003. LNCS, vol. 2725, pp. 1–13. Springer, Heidelberg (2003)
5. Marques-Silva, J.: Interpolant learning and reuse in SAT-based model checking. Electron. Notes Theor. Comput. Sci. 174, 31–43 (2007)
6. Marques-Silva, J.: Improvements to the Implementation of Interpolant-Based Model Checking. In: Borrione, D., Paul, W. (eds.) CHARME 2005. LNCS, vol. 3725, pp. 367–370. Springer, Heidelberg (2005)
7. Jhala, R., McMillan, K.L.: Interpolant-based transition relation approximation (2007)
8. Govindaraju, S.G., Dill, D.L.: Verification by approximate forward and backward reachability. In: International Conference on Computer-Aided Design (ICCAD), pp. 366–370. ACM Press, New York (1998)
9. Cabodi, G., Nocco, S., Quer, S.: Mixing forward and backward traversals in guided-prioritized BDD-based verification. In: Computer Aided Verification (CAV), Springer, pp. 471–484. Springer, Heidelberg (2002)
10. Stangier, C., Sidle, T.: Invariant Checking Combining Forward and Backward Traversal. In: Hu, A.J., Martin, A.K. (eds.) FMCAD 2004. LNCS, vol. 3312, pp. 414–429. Springer, Heidelberg (2004)
11. Cousot, P., Cousot, R.: Refining model checking by abstract interpretation. Automated Software Engineering 6, 69–95 (1999)
12. Cousot, P., Ganty, P., Raskin, J.F.: Fixpoint-guided abstraction refinements. In: Symposium on Static Analysis (SAS), pp. 333–348. Springer, Heidelberg (2007)
13. Henzinger, T.A., Kupferman, O., Qadeer, S.: From *Pre*-historic to *Post*-modern symbolic model checking. Formal Methods in System Design 23, 303–327 (2003)
14. Massé, D.: Combining Forward and Backward Analyses of Temporal Properties. In: Danvy, O., Filinski, A. (eds.) PADO 2001. LNCS, vol. 2053, pp. 155–172. Springer, Heidelberg (2001)
15. Cabodi, G., et al.: Stepping forward with interpolants in unbounded model checking. In: International conference on Computer-aided design (ICCAD), pp. 772–778. ACM Press, New York (2006)

16. Somenzi, F., Li, B.: Efficient Abstraction Refinement in Interpolation-Based Unbounded Model Checking. In: Hermanns, H., Palsberg, J. (eds.) TACAS 2006 and ETAPS 2006. LNCS, vol. 3920, pp. 227–241. Springer, Heidelberg (2006)
17. Craig, W.: Linear reasoning. A new form of the Herbrand-Gentzen theorem 22, 250–268 (1957)
18. Cousot, P., Cousot, R.: Abstract interpretation: a unified lattice model for static analysis of programs by construction or approximation of fixpoints. In: Principles of Programming Languages (POPL), pp. 238–252. ACM Press, New York (1977)
19. Cousot, P.: Semantic foundations of program analysis. In: Program Flow Analysis: Theory and Applications, pp. 303–342. Prentice-Hall, Englewood Cliffs (1981)
20. Sheeran, M., Singh, S., Stalmarck, G.: Checking safety properties using induction and a SAT-solver. In: Formal Methods in Computer-Aided Design (FMCAD), pp. 108–125. Springer, Heidelberg (2000)
21. Bradley, A., Manna, Z.: Checking safety by inductive generalization of counterexamples to induction. In: Formal Methods in Computer-Aided Design (FMCAD), IEEE, Los Alamitos (to appear, 2007)
22. Corno, F., Reorda, M.S., Squillero, G.: RT-level ITC'99 benchmarks and first ATPG results. IEEE Design and Test 17, 44–53 (2000)

Abstract Interpretation of Cellular Signalling Networks

Vincent Danos[1,4], Jérôme Feret[2,3], Walter Fontana[1,2], and Jean Krivine[5]

[1] Plectix Biosystems
[2] Harvard Medical School
[3] École Normale Supérieure*
[4] CNRS, Université Paris Diderot
[5] École Polytechnique

Abstract. Cellular signalling pathways, where proteins can form complexes and undergo a large array of post translational modifications are highly combinatorial systems sending and receiving extra-cellular signals and triggering appropriate responses. Process-centric languages seem apt to their representation and simulation [1,2,3]. Rule-centric languages such as κ [4,5,6,7,8] and BNG [9,10] bring in additional ease of expression.

We propose in this paper a method to enumerate a superset of the reachable complexes that a κ rule set can generate. This is done via the construction of a finite abstract interpretation. We find a simple criterion for this superset to be the exact set of reachable complexes, namely that the superset is closed under swap, an operation whereby pairs of edges of the same type can permute their ends.

We also show that a simple syntactic restriction on rules is sufficient to ensure the generation of a swap-closed set of complexes. We conclude by showing that a substantial rule set (presented in Ref. [4]) modelling the EGF receptor pathway verifies that syntactic condition (up to suitable transformations), and therefore despite its apparent complexity has a rather simple set of reachables.

1 Introduction

Biological signalling pathways are large, natural, quantitative concurrent systems in charge of sending and receiving extra-cellular signals and triggering appropriate responses in the cell —eg differentiation, migration, or growth. They involve multiple proteins, from membrane bound receptors to adapters and relays to transcription factors. As thorough a description as possible of these pathways is key to their understanding and control. Such a task is difficult for a variety of reasons, one being of a purely representational nature. Those networks are highly combinatorial, meaning that their agents can assemble and be modified in a huge number of ways —about 10^{19} unique complexes for the EGF receptor pathway model we consider later. Usual representations based on reactions

* Abstraction Project (INRIA, CNRS, and École Normale Supérieure).

F. Logozzo et al. (Eds.): VMCAI 2008, LNCS 4905, pp. 83–97, 2008.

between structureless entities must inevitably sample down this combinatorial complexity, and obtain models which stand in no clear relation to biological facts and are hard to keep abreast of new developments. Regev *et al.* have proposed using π-calculus [11] to avoid the combinatorial explosion besetting differential equations [1,2]. Other process-based languages have been proposed [3,12,13,14]. The rule-based languages κ [4,5,6,7] and BNG [9,10] bring additional ease in the building and modification of models [8].

The object of this paper is to explain and illustrate on a sizable example a method to explore the set of complexes that can be generated by a κ rule set, aka the system's *reachable complexes.* Although κ models can be run with no prior enumeration of reachable complexes [5], a convenient method for describing those can be used to:

- detect dead rules (which is useful when developing large models)
- coarsen rules (ie get rid of superfluous conditions while preserving the underlying qualitative transition system)
- refine rules (eg for kinetic reasons)
- determine whether a rule may activate another (which brings down the cost of stochastic simulations [5])
- generate the underlying ground system (or a truncated version thereof if too large), and equip it with a differential equation semantics for the purpose of fast calibration of a model on available data (not implemented yet).

The very combinatorial nature of signalling systems manifests itself in that computing reachables by transitive closure is unfeasible for any but the simplest networks. Our method works around this problem by defining a finite interpretation of rule sets. This finitisation is based on an approximation of complexes as sets of radius 1 neighbourhoods, which we call *views*, and a pair of adjoint maps to break down complexes into views, and recombine views into complexes. Thus one can generate efficiently a superset of the reachable views, and decide whether the corresponding set of complexes is infinite by detecting repeatable patterns (section 3). This begs the question when the reachable views recombine to form exactly the reachable complexes, not just a super-set. This happens when the set of reachables is closed under swap, an operation whereby pairs of edges of the same type can permute their ends (section 4). We call such sets *local*, and by extension say a model is local if its set of reachables is. The definition of locality for a model is not syntactical, since it is a condition on the set of associated reachables, but one can guarantee locality by placing syntactical restrictions on the model's rule set (section 5). Our EGF receptor network example satisfies that syntactical condition —up to some reachables-preserving transformations— and is local despite its apparent complexity (section 6).

This touches on an interesting and more speculative question. Situations can be expressed in κ which have little to do with biological signalling (eg it is straightforward to represent Turing machines). One would like to think, as the EGF example model indicates, that we have delineated a fragment of κ —that of local rule sets— where natural signalling pathways predominantly fall. What that may mean biologically is briefly discussed in the conclusion together with leads for future work.

$E ::= \emptyset \mid a, E$	(expression)		$s ::= n_\iota^\lambda$	(site)
$a ::= N(\sigma)$	(agent)		$n ::= x \in \mathcal{S}$	(site name)
$N ::= A \in \mathcal{A}$	(agent name)		$\iota ::= \epsilon \mid m \in \mathbb{V}$	(internal state)
$\sigma ::= \emptyset \mid s, \sigma$	(interface)		$\lambda ::= \epsilon \mid i \in \mathbb{N}$	(binding state)

Fig. 1. *Syntax*

$$E, A(\sigma, s, s', \sigma'), E' \equiv E, A(\sigma, s', s, \sigma'), E' \qquad E, a, a', E' \equiv E, a', a, E'$$

$$\frac{i, j \in \mathbb{N} \text{ and } i \text{ does not occur in } E}{E[i/j] \equiv E}$$

Fig. 2. *Structural equivalence*

2 κ

We first briefly present a simplified core κ using a process-like notation which facilitates the reachability analysis of the next section. This is in contrast with the equivalent graph-theoretical presentation chosen in Ref. [5] for the definition of the quantitative (stochastic) semantics.

We suppose given a finite set of agent names $\mathcal{A}$, representing different kinds of proteins; a finite set of sites $\mathcal{S}$, corresponding to protein domains and modifiable residues; a finite set of values $\mathbb{V}$, representing the modified states. The syntax of agents and expressions is given in Fig. 1.

An *interface* is a sequence of sites with internal and binding states; specifically one writes x_ι^λ for a site x with internal state ι, and binding state λ. If the binding state is ϵ, the site is *free*; otherwise it is *bound*. On the other hand, if the internal state is ϵ, this means the internal state is left unspecified. In the concrete notation both ϵs are omitted.

An *agent* is given by a name in $\mathcal{A}$ and an interface.

A well-formed *expression* is a sequence of agents such that:

- a site name can occur only once in an interface,
- a binding state occurs exactly twice if it does at all.

We suppose hereafter all expressions to be well-formed.

Sites sharing a same binding state are said to be bound.

The structural equivalence $\equiv$ defined as the smallest binary equivalence between expressions that satisfies the rules given in Fig. 2 stipulates that: neither the order of sites in interfaces, nor the order of agents in expressions matters, and that bindings states can be injectively renamed.

Equivalence classes of $\equiv$ are called *solutions* and one writes $[E]$ for the class of expression E. One says a solution $[E]$ is *reducible* whenever $E \equiv E', E''$ for some non empty expressions E', E''. A *complex* is an irreducible solution.

Complexes and solutions can equivalently be presented graphically. Fig. 3 shows an example for the following expression:

$$\mathit{EGF}(r^1), \mathit{EGF}(r^2), \mathit{EGFR}(l^1, r^3, \mathit{Y1048}_p^4, \mathit{Y1148}_p), \mathit{EGFR}(l^2, r^3, \mathit{Y1048}_u, \mathit{Y1148}_p^5),$$
$$\mathit{GRB2}(\mathit{SH2}^4, \mathit{SH3}^6), \mathit{SOS}(a^6), \mathit{SHC}(\mathit{PTB}^5, \mathit{Y317}_p^7), \mathit{GRB2}(\mathit{SH2}^7, \mathit{SH3})$$

A *rule* is a pair of expressions E_l, E_r.

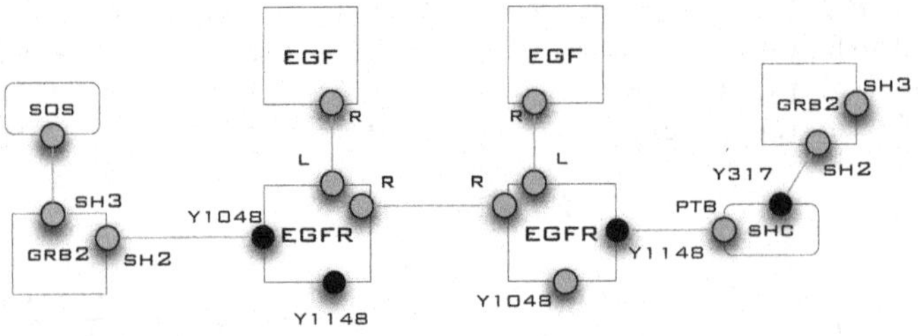

Fig. 3. A complex from the EGF receptor pathway: sites correspond to protein domains SH2, SH3, ... and modifiable amino-acid residues Y317, Y1048, ... edges correspond to bindings, solid black stands for phosphorylated tyrosine residues

$$
\begin{array}{cc}
n_\iota^\lambda \models n_\iota^\lambda & n_\iota^\lambda[n_{\iota_r}^{\lambda_r}] = n_{\iota_r}^{\lambda_r} \\
n_\iota^\lambda \models n^\lambda & n_\iota^\lambda[n^{\lambda_r}] = n_\iota^{\lambda_r} \\
\sigma \models \emptyset & \sigma[\emptyset] = \sigma \\
\dfrac{s \models s_l \quad \sigma \models \sigma_l}{s, \sigma \models s_l, \sigma_l} & s, \sigma[s_r, \sigma_r] = s[s_r], \sigma[\sigma_r] \\
\dfrac{\sigma \models \sigma_l}{N(\sigma) \models N(\sigma_l)} & N(\sigma)[N(\sigma_r)] = N(\sigma[\sigma_r]) \\
E \models \emptyset & E[\emptyset] = E \\
\dfrac{a \models a_l \quad E \models E_l}{a, E \models a_l, E_l} & (a, E)[a_r, E_r] = a[a_r], E[E_r]
\end{array}
$$

Fig. 4. Definition of matching $\models$ (left), and replacement (right)

The *left hand side* E_l describes the agents taking part in the event and various conditions on their internal and binding states for the event to actually happen. The *right hand side* E_r describes the rule's effect which is either:

- a *binding* (*unbinding*):E_r (E_l) is obtained by binding two free sites in E_l (E_r),
- or a *modification*: E_r is obtained by modifying some internal state in E_l.

Note that bindings and unbindings are symmetric, while modifications are self-symmetric.

In order to apply a rule E_l, E_r to a solution $[E]$, one uses structural equivalence (Fig. 2) to bring the participating agents at the beginning of the expression, with their sites in the same order as in E_l, and renames bindings to obtain an equivalent expression E' that matches E_l (Fig. 4, left). One then replaces E' with $E'[E_r]$ (Fig. 4, right).

This yields a *transition system* between solutions defined as $[E] \rightarrow_{E_l,E_r} [E[E_r]]$ whenever $E \models E_l$.

Note that sites not occurring in E_l are not constrained in any way, and that matching only uses structural equivalence on E, not E_l.

Our implementation also allows rules for agent creation and deletion. The methods and results presented here can be readily extended to this richer setting.

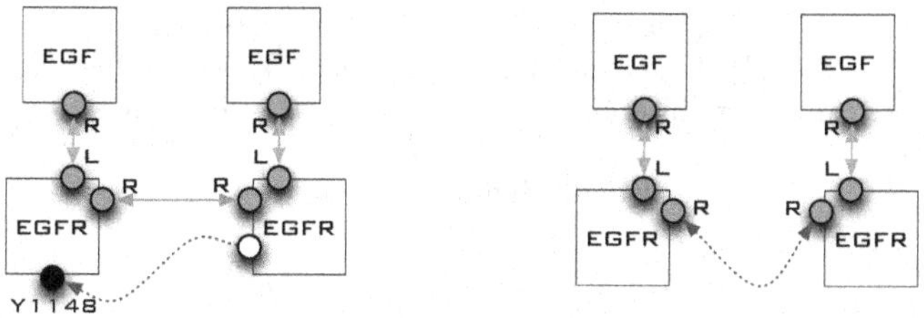

Fig. 5. Receptor 'cross-phosphorylation' (left): site *Y1148* is modified (phosphorylation induced by the receptor kinase domain represented as a solid white circle, and inducing a state change represented as a solid black circle); and receptor 'dimerisation' (right): the dotted edge represent binding, both ends of the link are modified

Here is an example of a modification, and a binding (see also Fig. 5):

$$\begin{array}{l} EGF(r^1), EGFR(l^1, r^2, Y1148_u), EGFR(r^2, l^3), EGF(r^3) \rightarrow \\ EGF(r^1), EGFR(l^1, r^2, Y1148_p), EGFR(r^2, l^3), EGF(r^3) \\ EGF(r^1), EGFR(l^1, r), EGFR(r, l^2), EGF(r^2) \rightarrow \\ EGF(r^1), EGFR(l^1, r^3), EGFR(r^3, l^2), EGF(r^2) \end{array}$$

3 Reachability

Let Σ denotes the set of all solutions, and Γ be the set of all complexes. Given R a set of rules and S_0 an initial solution, the set of reachable solutions is given as the least fixpoint in $\wp(\Sigma)$ greater than S_0, written $\mathit{lfp}_{S_0}\mathrm{POST}$, of the map $\mathrm{POST}(X) := X \cup \{S' \mid \exists S \in X,\ \exists r \in R,\ S \rightarrow_r S'\}$.

Write $[F] \in [E]$ if there is an expression E' such that $E \equiv F, E'$.

Define the maps $\alpha_c : \wp(\Sigma) \rightarrow \wp(\Gamma)$, $\gamma_c : \wp(\Gamma) \rightarrow \wp(\Sigma)$ as:

$$\begin{array}{l} \alpha_c(X) := \{c \in \Gamma \mid \exists S \in X : c \in S\} \\ \gamma_c(Y) := \{S \in \Sigma \mid c \in S \Rightarrow c \in Y\} \end{array}$$

The pair α_c, γ_c form a Galois connection and the set Γ^* of reachable complexes is $\alpha_c(\mathit{lfp}_{S_0}\mathrm{POST})$. The most precise counterpart to POST, $\mathrm{POST}_c := \alpha_c \,\mathrm{POST}\, \gamma_c$ can be written $\mathrm{POST}_c(X) = X \cup \{c \in \Gamma \mid \exists [c_1], \ldots, [c_m] \in X\, \exists r \in R\, \exists S \in \Sigma : [c_1, \ldots, c_m] \rightarrow_r S \wedge c \in S\}$. Clearly $\Gamma^* \subseteq \mathit{lfp}_{\alpha_c(S_0)}\mathrm{POST}_c$.

This abstraction is not always exact since it does not take into account the number of occurences of a complex in a solution. In practice rules are rarely asking for many occurrences of a same agent or complex, and it is safe to consider that each kind of agent occurs an unbounded number of time in S_0.

One thing that does matter in the application is that Γ^* may be large (even infinite in case of polymerisation) and this is why we set up now a finite approximation of this set. The idea is to only retain from a solution the information which is local to the agents and which we call agents *views* (as in Ref. [15]). Specifically, we replace each binding state in an expression with its associated

$$
\begin{array}{llll}
v ::= N(\sigma) & \text{(View)} & n ::= x \in \mathcal{S} & \text{(site name)} \\
N ::= A \in \mathcal{A} & \text{(Agent name)} & \iota ::= \epsilon \mid m \in \mathbb{V} & \text{(Internal state)} \\
\sigma ::= \emptyset \mid n_\iota^\lambda, \sigma & \text{(Interface)} & \lambda ::= \epsilon \mid n.N & \text{(Binding state)}
\end{array}
$$

Fig. 6. Syntax for views

$$A(\sigma, s, s', \sigma') \equiv A(\sigma, s', s, \sigma')$$

Fig. 7. Structural congruence

typed link, ie the site and agent names of the opposite end of the link, and call β the obtained transformation.

An example is:

$$
\begin{array}{l}
\beta(EGF(r^1), EGFR(l^1, r^2), EGFR(r^2, l^3), EGF(r^3)) = \\
EGF(r^{l.EGFR}), EGFR(l^{r.EGF}, r^{r.EGFR}), EGFR(l^{r.EGF}, r^{r.EGFR}), EGF(r^{l.EGFR})
\end{array}
$$

The syntax of views is given in Fig. 6, and the structural congruence which allows to reorder sites in a view is given in Fig. 7.

Operations on solutions transfer naturally to sequences of views. In particular one can define an abstract transition step between sequences of views (Fig. 8) that tests some conditions over the view relation $\models^\sharp$, and either changes the internal state of a site, or adds/removes the appropriate typed links in the binding state of two modified views.

Fig. 9 shows the graphical representation (repetitions are omitted) of the phosphorylation and dimerisation abstract rules (Fig. 5).

Thus one may now define the abstraction that collects the set of views that can be built during a computation sequence.

Define Δ to be the set of views and the map $\alpha : \wp(\Gamma) \to \wp(\Delta)$ as $\alpha(X) := \{[v_i] \mid \exists [c] \in X,\ \beta(c) = v_1, \ldots, v_n\}$. By construction α is a $\cup$-complete morphism of complete lattices, and has therefore an adjoint *concretization* $\gamma : \wp(\Delta) \to \wp(\Gamma)$, defined as $\gamma(Z) = \cup\{X \in \wp(\Gamma) \mid \alpha(X) \subseteq Z\}$, which maps a set of views

$$
\begin{array}{cc}
n_\iota^\lambda \models^\sharp n_\iota^\lambda & n_\iota^\lambda[n_{\iota_r}^{\lambda_r}]^\sharp = n_{\iota_r}^{\lambda^r} \\
n_\iota^\lambda \models^\sharp n^\lambda & n_\iota^\lambda[n^{\lambda_r}]^\sharp = n_\iota^{\lambda_r} \\
\sigma \models^\sharp \emptyset & \sigma[\emptyset]^\sharp = \sigma \\
\dfrac{s \models^\sharp s_l \quad \sigma \models^\sharp \sigma_l}{s, \sigma \models^\sharp s_l, \sigma_l} & s, \sigma[s_r, \sigma_r]^\sharp = s[s_r]^\sharp, \sigma[\sigma_r]^\sharp \\
\dfrac{\sigma \models^\sharp \sigma_l}{N(\sigma) \models^\sharp N(\sigma_l)} & N(\sigma)[N(\sigma_r)]^\sharp = N(\sigma[\sigma_r]^\sharp)
\end{array}
$$

$$
\frac{r = E_l \to E_r \quad \beta(E_l) = v_l^1, \ldots, v_l^n \quad \beta(E_r) = v_r^1, \ldots, v_r^n \quad v^i \models^\sharp v_l^i}{[v^1], \ldots, [v^n] \to_r^\sharp [v^1[v_r^1]^\sharp], \ldots [v^n[v_r^n]^\sharp]}
$$

Fig. 8. Abstract semantics

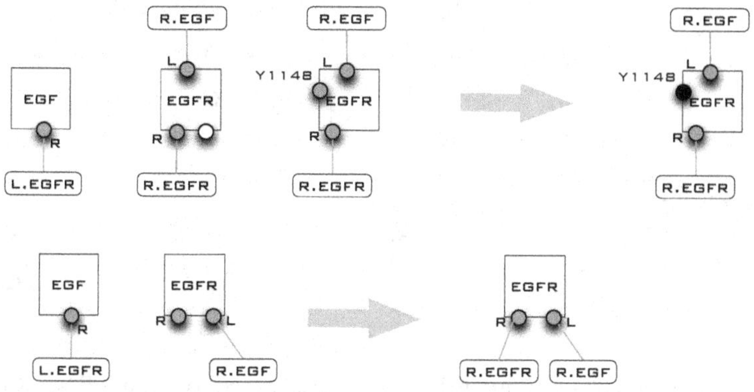

Fig. 9. The partial views associated to the 'cross-phosphorylation' and 'dimerisation' patterns (multiplicities are not shown); arrows represent the result of the rule action on views (only modified views are shown)

to the set of complexes that can be built from these, and verifies $\alpha(X) \subseteq Z$ iff $X \subseteq \gamma(Z)$. It is easy to see that α, γ are monotonic, $\alpha\gamma$ is a lower closure operator (anti-extensive, monotonic, and idempotent), and $\gamma\alpha$ an upper closure operator (extensive, monotonic, and idempotent) [16].

Let us consider a couple of examples of upper and lower closure:

$$\gamma\alpha(\{[A(a^1, b^1)]\}) = \{[A(a^n, b^1), \dots, A(a^{n-1}, b^n)];\ n \in \mathbb{N}\}$$
$$\alpha\gamma(\{[A(a^{b.A}, b^{a.A})], [B(a^{b.A}, b^{a.A})]\}) = \{[A(a^{b.A}, b^{a.A})]\}$$

In the first example the upper operator constructs rings of all lengths; in the second one the typed link $B(b^{a.A})$ has no corresponding *dual* typed link $A(a^{b.B})$ in the view set, so its view cannot be combined with an other one.[1]

Define $\text{POST}_v(Z) := Z \cup \{u_i \in \Delta \mid \exists v_1, \dots, v_n \in Z\, \exists r \in R : v_1, \dots, v_n \rightarrow_r^\sharp u_1, \dots, u_n\}$. This map is a $\cup$-complete endomorphism and it satisfies $\text{POST}_c\gamma \leq \gamma\,\text{POST}_v$ for the pointwise ordering. As a consequence, $\mathit{lfp}_{\alpha(\Gamma_0)}\text{POST}_v$ the least fixpoint of POST_v containing $\alpha(\Gamma_0)$ exists and we can state the soundness of our abstraction as follows: $\mathit{lfp}_{\Gamma_0}\text{POST}_c \subseteq \gamma(\mathit{lfp}_{\alpha(\Gamma_0)}\text{POST}_v)$. Thus the views generated by the abstract system reconstruct, via γ, a superset of the generated complexes. Note that while $\mathit{lfp}_{\alpha(\Gamma_0)}\text{POST}_v$ is certainly finite, its image under γ may not be.

One may wonder how efficient that finite computation is, and how precise. Regarding efficiency, we use decision diagrams [17] to manipulate view sets. To avoid an exponential blow up (the number of views of an agent is exponential in its number of sites), we use 'packing' techniques [18], splitting the interface of agents into smaller subinterfaces, and then considering only relations between states of sites belonging to a common subset. Our syntactic analysis ensures that the result is unchanged. The next section answers accuracy concerns.

---

[1] A trickier example is $\alpha\gamma(\{[A(a, b^{a.A})], [A(a^{b.A}, b^{a.A})]\}) = \{[A(a^{b.A}, b^{a.A})]\}$, since a finite chain with a free a must have a free b at the other end.

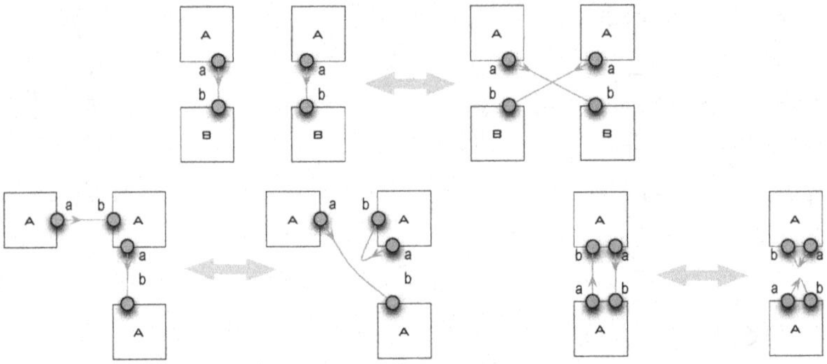

Fig. 10. The main swap involution (top row); if the names A and B are the same, some agents can be identified (bottom row); orientations are shown for clarity

4 Local Sets

Say $X \subseteq \Gamma$ is *local* if $X \in Im(\gamma)$, or equivalently $\gamma\alpha(X) = X$. We prove first that for such local sets, the finite interpretation is exact.

Theorem 1. *Consider* $Inv \in \wp(\Gamma)$*, a set of complexes such that:* $\Gamma_0 \subseteq Inv$*,* $\text{POST}_c(Inv) \subseteq Inv$*, and* $Inv = \gamma\alpha(Inv)$*, then* $\gamma(lfp_{\alpha(\Gamma_0)}\text{POST}_v) \subseteq Inv$*.*

The map POST_v is not the most precise counterpart of POST_c, because the relation $\models^\sharp$ does not require views to be embeddable in complexes. However we shall see below that $\text{POST}_v\alpha = \alpha\text{POST}_c\gamma\alpha$ which means that POST_v is the most precise counterpart of POST_c when applied to abstract elements that are closed with respect to $\alpha\gamma$. Assuming this for the moment we can prove Th. 1.

Proof. We first prove $\text{POST}_v^n\alpha(\Gamma_0) \in \alpha(\wp(\Gamma))$ and $\text{POST}_v^n\alpha(\Gamma_0) \subseteq \alpha(Inv)$:
- $\alpha(\Gamma_0) \in \alpha(\wp(\Gamma))$, and $\Gamma_0 \subseteq Inv$, so $\alpha(\Gamma_0) \subseteq \alpha(Inv)$;
- If $Z \in \alpha(\wp(\Gamma))$ and $Z \subseteq \alpha(Inv)$, then $Z = \alpha\gamma(Z)$, so $\text{POST}_v(Z) = \text{POST}_v\alpha\gamma(Z)$, and since $\text{POST}_v\alpha = \alpha\text{POST}_c\gamma\alpha$, $\text{POST}_v(Z) = \alpha\text{POST}_c\gamma(Z) \subseteq \alpha\text{POST}_c\gamma\alpha(Inv) = \alpha\text{POST}_c(Inv) \subseteq \alpha(Inv)$. Because $\wp(\Delta)$ is finite, $lfp_{\alpha(\Gamma_0)}\text{POST}_v = \text{POST}_v^n\alpha(\Gamma_0)$ for some n, so $lfp_{\alpha(\Gamma_0)}\text{POST}_v \subseteq \alpha(Inv)$, hence $\gamma(lfp_{\alpha(\Gamma_0)}\text{POST}_v) \subseteq \gamma\alpha(Inv) = Inv$. □

By setting $Inv = lfp_{\Gamma_0}\text{POST}_c$, one gets the immediate corollary:

Corollary 1. *If* $lfp_{\Gamma_0}\text{POST}_c \in \gamma(\wp(\Gamma))$*, then* $lfp_{\Gamma_0}\text{POST}_c = \gamma(lfp_{\alpha(\Gamma_0)}\text{POST}_v)$*.*

In words, if $lfp_{\Gamma_0}\text{POST}_c$ is local, the finite interpretation is exact. Likewise, taking *Inv* to be the local closure of $lfp_{\Gamma_0}\text{POST}_c$, one obtains the slightly more general result that $\gamma(lfp_{\alpha(\Gamma_0)}\text{POST}_v)$ is the smallest local set containing $lfp_{\Gamma_0}\text{POST}_c$, supposing that closure is itself closed under POST_c (it does not have to be).

We proceed now to the characterisation of local sets.

We call a *swap* any of the three transformations over solutions given Fig. 10. Note that swapped links have to be of the same A, a, B, b type.

Theorem 2. *$X \in$ is local iff the set of solutions over X is closed under swaps.*

Clearly views are invariant under swaps, which gives the left to right implication. To prove the other implication we introduce an 'assembly grammar' to describe $\gamma(Z)$ for $Z \subseteq \Delta$. This grammar also allows the enumeration (and the counting) of the elements of $\gamma(Z)$. It will also help in proving that $\text{POST}_v\alpha = \alpha\text{POST}_c\gamma\alpha$ by taking $Z \in Im(\alpha)$.

The assembly grammar $\Rightarrow_Z$ where E, E' stand for hybrid expressions (ie expressions mixing ordinary binding states and typed links), σ, σ' for hybrid interfaces, and x is a fresh binding, is given as:

- $E \Rightarrow_Z E'$ if $E \equiv E'$
- $\Rightarrow_Z v$ for $v \in Z$
- $A(a_\iota^{b.B}, \sigma), E \Rightarrow_Z A(a_\iota^x, \sigma), B(b_{\iota'}^x, \sigma'), E$ for $B(b^{a.A}, \sigma') \in Z$
- $A(a_\iota^{b.B}, \sigma), B(b_{\iota'}^{a.A}, \sigma'), E \Rightarrow_Z A(a_\iota^x, \sigma), B(b_{\iota'}^x, \sigma'), E$
- $A(a_\iota^{b.A}, b_{\iota'}^{a.A}, \sigma), E \Rightarrow_Z A(a_\iota^x, b_{\iota'}^x, \sigma), E$

The third clause states that a typed link in a view can be connected to any view taken from Z showing the dual typed link. Similarly, the last two clauses show how dual typed links may be connected to form a link.

We write $\Rightarrow_Z^*$ for the transitive closure of $\Rightarrow_Z$.

Say a hybrid expression c embeds in a complex $[c^*]$ if c is the prefix of a hybrid expression E' obtained from an expression $E \equiv c^*$ by replacing some bindings with their corresponding typed links.

Clearly $\Rightarrow_Z^* c$ implies that c is connected, and $\gamma(Z)$ is the set of all classes $[c]$ such that $\Rightarrow_Z^* c$ and c has no typed links.

Proof (Th. 2, continued). We want $\gamma\alpha(X) \subseteq X$, supposing X is closed under swap. It is enough to prove that whenever $\Rightarrow_{\alpha(X)}^* c$, c embeds in some $[c^*] \in X$. Indeed if $c \in \gamma\alpha(X)$ embeds in some $[c^*] \in X$, then $c \equiv c^*$, since c has no typed links. We prove this by induction on $\Rightarrow_{\alpha(X)}$:

- The base case is by definition of α.
- Suppose c is obtained from c_1 by replacing a typed link $b.B$ with a binding to a view v of type B; by induction we have $[c_1^*]$, and $[v^*] \in X$ containing respectively c_1 and v; we can assume that expressions c_1 and v do not share bindings; therein A, a and B, b must be connected to say B', b, and A', a. One can therefore swap the bindings in the expression c_1^*, v^*, and connect A, a and B, b; since c_1 is connected, it is contained in the post-swap connected component of A which is in X (because X is closed under swap), and so is c.
- Suppose c is obtained from c_1 by fusing two typed links $b.B$ and $a.A$ in two distinct agents; by induction there is $[c_1^*]$ which embeds c_1, if A, a, B, b are connected in $[c_1^*]$ we are done, else consider B', and A' as above (those may be the same agent). Again one can swap the bindings in $[c_1^*]$, and connect A, a and B, b, and their common component after the swap contains c and is in X.
- Suppose c is obtained from c_1 by fusing two typed links $b.B$ and $a.A$ within the same agents; by induction there is $[c_1^*]$ which embeds c_1, if A, a is connected to A, b we are done, else A, a, A, b are connected in $[c_1^*]$ to say A', b,

A'', a (which may belong to the same agent), so one can swap the bindings, and the resulting connected component of A contains c and is in X. □

Using the proof above for the local set $\gamma\alpha(X)$ obtains a stronger statement:

Theorem 3. *If* $\Rightarrow^*_{\alpha(X)} c$, *then* c *embeds in some* $c^* \in \gamma\alpha(X)$.

One may use the grammar $\Rightarrow_Z$ to obtain either an enumeration or a counting of $\gamma(Z)$, when $Z \in Im(\alpha)$ (which is the one case we are interested in in the application). In general, $\Rightarrow_Z$ has either finitely many rewrite sequences or, by a simple combinatorial argument, there must be a sequence of derivations that form a hybrid expression with a path connecting two instances of a typed link $b.B$. By Theorem 3, any such sequence can be completed so as to produce a complex (with no typed links), so one can effectively decide whether $\gamma(Z)$ is infinite (and practically stop the enumeration on derivations showing a repeatable pattern). Note that one may also infer from the same theorem that $\text{POST}_v(Z) = \alpha\text{POST}_c\gamma(Z)$ when $Z \in Im(\alpha)$ (the equation does not hold in general).

5 Local Rule Sets

At this stage, we know that local sets can be exactly counted or enumerated via the abstraction if they are finite, and neatly described if they are not.

Say a rule set R *is local* if given any set of disconnected agents, R generates a local set of complexes.

Proposition 1. *A rule set R is local if the following holds:*
- *(acyclicity) complexes in $\gamma\alpha(\Gamma^*)$ are acyclic;*
- *(local tests) rules only test the views of the agents they modify;*
- *(non interference) binding rules do not interfere, that is to say:*
- *whenever* $A(a_{\iota_1}, \sigma_1), B(b_{\iota_2}, \sigma_2) \to A(a^1_{\iota_1}, \sigma_1), B(b^1_{\iota_2}, \sigma_2)$
- *and* $A(a_{\iota_3}, \sigma_3), B(b_{\iota_4}, \sigma_4) \to A(a^1_{\iota_3}, \sigma_3), B(b^1_{\iota_4}, \sigma_4)$
- *then* $A(a_{\iota_1}, \sigma_1), B(b_{\iota_4}, \sigma_4) \to A(a^1_{\iota_1}, \sigma_1), B(b^1_{\iota_4}, \sigma_4)$

Before we sketch the proof, let us comment on the acyclicity condition which is the only non syntactical one.

Define the *contact map* of a rule set R, written $\chi(R)$, and defined as: a graph with nodes the agent names used in R, with sites those occurring in R, and where sites are connected iff they are bound by some $r \in R$. Note that $\chi(R)$ is not a (graphical) solution, since sites can be connected more than once; rather it is a constraint on generated complexes.

Say a complex is *compatible* with $\chi(R)$ if it projects to it.

Fig. 11 shows the contact map of an early EGF model, and the complex shown Fig. 3 does project to it.

One can test whether a rule set R is acyclic by inspecting $\chi(R)$.

Proposition 2. *Given R, and Γ_0 compatible with $\chi(R)$, if Γ^* contains a cyclic complex, then there exists $s : \mathbb{Z}_{2n} \to S$ such that for all $p \in \mathbb{Z}_n$: $s(2p), s(2p+1)$ belong to the same agent in $\chi(R)$, $s(2p) \neq s(2p+1)$, and $s(2p-1), s(2p)$ is an edge in $\chi(R)$.*

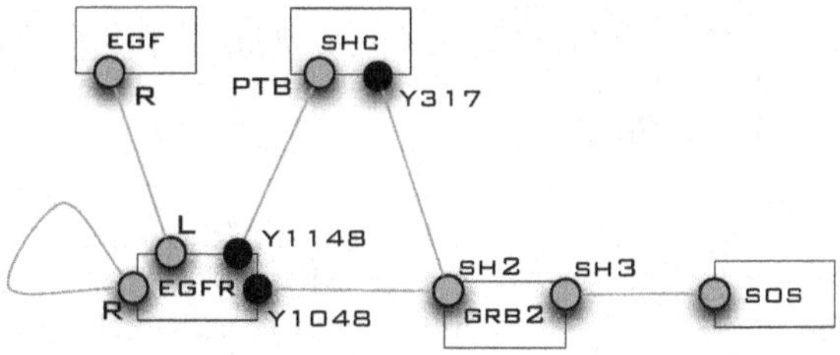

Fig. 11. The early EGF receptor cascade model contact map; some sites can change their internal states (solid black)

In Fig. 11, one sees that the contact map may be cyclic, but every cycle has to use twice the same site, so no complex in this model can be cyclic, provided one picks a compatible initial set of complexes.

Note also that the non-interference condition is only concerning binding operations and there is no comparable constraint on unbinding rules. The intuition is that both agents that want to connect have to do it on the sole basis of their views and are not allowed to communicate prior to context. This is reminiscent of synchronisation in CCS [19].

Proof (Prop. 1 sketch). Given $[E]$ a solution of complexes in Γ^*, and a swap s between links l_1, l_2 in $[E]$, one wants to prove that the obtained $[E^s]$ is still a solution of complexes in Γ^*. Call $[c_1]$, $[c_2]$ the connected components of l_1, l_2 in $[E]$; clearly, it is enough to prove it in the cases when $E \equiv c_1, c_2$ or when $E \equiv c_1 \equiv c_2$.

Suppose that $E \equiv c_1 \equiv c_2$, then l_1, l_2 are connected via a unique path in c_1 (by acyclicity). Suppose they have the same orientation along this path, then $[c_1^s]$ splits in two components, one of them, call it $[d_1]$, containing a cycle; on the other hand, $[d_1] \in \gamma\alpha(\Gamma^*)$, which contradicts acyclicity. So l_1, l_2 must have opposite orientations. Pick a copy of $[c_1]$, say $[c_1']$, with links l_1', l_2'; it is easy to see that swapping (l_1, l_2'), and (l_1', l_2) obtains two copies of $[c_1^s]$, so one can reduce that case to the other one where $E \equiv c_1, c_2$.

So suppose that $E \equiv c_1, c_2$ and pick separate traces leading to solutions which contains respectively $[c_1]$, and $[c_2]$ (there must be some, by definition of Γ^*). Because initial complexes are single agents, both l_1, l_2 have to be created along those traces; consider the last such event in both traces, say $[T_1] \rightarrow_{r_1} [S_1]$, and $[T_2] \rightarrow_{r_2} [S_2]$ creating respectively l_1, and l_2. By atomicity the views of the agents involved in l_1, say $[A_1]$, $[B_1]$, are the same before and after r_1, except of course for the typed links associated to l_1; the same thing holds of $[A_2]$, $[B_2]$, therefore in $[T_1, T_2]$, one can permute the bindings and apply r_1 to $[A_1]$, $[B_2]$, and r_2 to $[A_2]$, $[B_1]$ (by non interference). Using the final condition namely that tests are local, it is easy to see that all computation steps onward commute to that permutation. □

We illustrate now each condition of Prop. 1 in turn.

$$A(a_u), B(a_u) \to A(a_u^1), B(a_u^1)$$
$$A(a_u^1), B(a_u^1) \to A(a_p^1), B(a_u^1)$$
$$A(a_u^1), B(a_u^1) \to A(a_u^1), B(a_p^1)$$

(a)

$$R(a,b), R(a) \to R(a,b^1), R(a^1)$$

(b)

$$A(a_u) \leftrightarrow A(a_p)$$
$$A(a_u), A(a_p) \to A(a_u^1), A(a_p^1)$$

(c)

$$A(l, x_u, r) \to A(l, x_p, r)$$
$$A(x_p, r), A(l, x_u) \to A(x_p, r^1), A(l^1, x_u)$$
$$A(x_p, r^1), A(l^1, x_u) \to A(x_u, r^1), A(l^1, x_p)$$
$$A(x_u, r^1), A(l^1, x_p) \to A(x_p, r^1), A(l^1, x_u)$$

(d)

Fig. 12. Rule systems

Local tests: consider the initial complexes $A(a_u)$ and $B(a_u)$ and the rules in Fig. 12.(a), $A(a_p^1), B(a_p^1)$ is in $\gamma\alpha(\Gamma^*) \setminus \Gamma^*$; indeed the last two rules include non local tests.

Acyclicity: take as an initial complex $R(a, b)$ with the rule in Fig. 12.(b), all R-rings, eg $R(a^1, b^1)$, are in $\gamma\alpha(\Gamma^*) \setminus \Gamma^*$.

Non-interference: consider the initial complex $A(a_u)$ and the rules in Fig. 12.(c), $A(a_u^1), A(a_u^1)$ is in $\gamma\alpha(\Gamma^*) \setminus \Gamma^*$; indeed the rule set does not verify non-interference, since $A(a_u)$ should also be allowed to bind with $A(a_u)$.

In any of the above examples, the finite interpretation could be made exact by suitably extending the agent view radii. In Fig. 12.(d) gives an example which no finite radius approximation can interpret exactly. Indeed it is easy to see that, with $A(l, x_u, r)$ as the only initial complex, all generated chains of length > 1 have exactly one $A(x_p)$; whereas any $< n$ radius abstraction α will have A-chains with no $A(x_p)$, and length $\geq 2n$ in $\gamma\alpha(\Gamma^*)$. We shall refer to this model as the GLO model in the next section.

6 Examples

We have considered three examples:

- the early EGF receptor pathway model [20],
- the early FGF (fibroblast growth factor) receptor pathway model [21],
- and the EGF model of Ref. [4].

Those are referred to hereafter as the EGF, FGF, and SBF models.[2]

Proposition 3. *The sets of reachable complexes in the EGF, FGF and SBF models are local.*

All the above models can be shown to be acyclic using their contact maps as shown above for the EGF case. Furthermore the rule sets in these models can

[2] The models and relevant outputs of the analysis used in this proof are available at `www.di.ens.fr/~feret/proplx`.

	EGF	FGF	SBF	GLO
Number of rules	39	42	66	4
Abstraction time	0.08 s	0.06 s	0.08 s	0.01 s
Number of complexes	356	79 080	$\simeq 10^{19}$	∞
Complex counting time	<0.01 s	0.09 s	0.04 s	<0.01 s
Enumeration time	0.06 s	85 s	*	*
Number of complexes (non relational analysis)	14 374	709698	$\simeq 10^{25}$	∞
Decontextualization time	0.17 s	0.25 s	0.88 s	0.01
Local (by conjugation)	*true*	*true*	*true*	*false*

Fig. 13. Times refer to a run on a 2GHz Intel Centrino Duo, 2G RAM. We also give the number of complexes obtained by using a non-relational analysis to show the loss of precision. We skip the enumeration step when the set of complexes is too large. Recall the GLO model is explicitly designed to be non local.

be made to verify the other assumptions of Prop. 1. This is done by using two transformations on the rule set.

The first transformation is *decontextualization*. One groups rules that perform the same action. Then, for each group, one computes a Boolean encoding of the set of solutions that 1) may match the left hand side of rules and 2) may be reachable –according to the view-based analysis (Section 3). In good cases redundant conditions in left hand side expressions are revealed and one can simplify the rules. This operation of decontextualization is fully automatic and does not modify the transition system (it does change the kinetics of the system when merged rules have different rates but that is not of concern here).

The second transformation of *conjugation* comes into play to deal with the few non local rules that may remain. One adds rules that are in the transitive closure of the transition system (so that the set of reachable complexes remains the same) and invoke decontextualization again. More precisely, whenever an action can only be applied in a specific context, one looks for sequences of rules that allows to simulate the same action in any other reachable context. This second stage is not automated at the moment.

As noted in the introduction, the use of the view-based abstraction is not limited to proving that complex sets are local. The inverse operation of *contextualization* where one enumerates extensions of complexes in a rule is also useful to get rid of non-contextual rule involving agent deletions, or to extract ground rules from a rule set. Another noteworthy application is the approximation of causations and conflict relations between events as static relations between rules; that is useful for simulation [5], and abstracting those at the level of views accelerates greatly their computation.

7 Conclusion

Biological signalling networks are large and generate combinatorial and high-dimensional transition systems which are computationally unwieldy. We have presented in this paper an abstraction of such systems, as represented as κ rule sets, which is a prerequisite for a certain number of tasks to become feasible. Perhaps the most intriguing finding is that this leads naturally to the definition of a class of *local* networks, a rather weak fragment of the set of all κ systems, where one would not *a priori* expect real models to sit. We could prove that previously and independently constructed models actually fall into that class.

Obviously, more examples need to be studied, before one can claim this is the class of natural signalling networks. Suppose however, for the sake of the argument, that biological networks are indeed predominantly local, one wonders why. Our favourite speculation is that a local network can be brought to process signals reasonably well in a variety of circumstances, placing only low demand on the accuracy of the setup (eg kinetic rates), or the reliability of the signal.

One can unfold the hierarchy of classes which has been left implicit in this paper, by investigating larger radii approximations, which would cover a larger class of networks, although we know that no finite radius approximation can cover all cases (see the GLO example). One has to see if a nice characterisation of say 2-local complex sets can be obtained.

Note that there is no need for our views to be of uniform radii, and one could even refine this classification of dimension sets, using collections of non uniform views. Such a theory, which still needs to be developed, would likely characterize the closure and covering properties one needs for soundness. Our present local views would be just one particularly simple instance that is a good computation trade-off between too poor an abstraction (eg that based on discrete coverings) which is fast but retains little information, and the richer ones we just suggested.

Another tempting avenue for future research is to articulate quantitative extensions of those ideas. Specifically, one can use the multiset version of the abstraction map, and derive an approximate differential or stochastic operational model, to be compared with concrete exact simulations. One is looking for a manifestation of locality at the level of quantitative dynamics.

References

1. Priami, C., et al.: Application of a stochastic name-passing calculus to representation and simulation of molecular processes. In: Information Processing Letters (2001)
2. Regev, A., Shapiro, E.: Cells as computation. Nature 419 (September 2002)
3. Regev, A., et al.: BioAmbients: An abstraction for biological compartments. Theoretical Computer Science 325(1), 141–167 (2004)
4. Danos, V., et al.: Rule-Based Modelling of Cellular Signalling. In: Caires, L., Vasconcelos, V.T. (eds.) CONCUR 2007. LNCS, vol. 4703, pp. 17–41. Springer, Heidelberg (2007)
5. Danos, V., et al.: Scalable modelling of biological pathways. In: Shao, Z. (ed.) APLAS 2007. LNCS, vol. 4807, pp. 139–157. Springer, Heidelberg (2007)
6. Danos, V., Laneve, C.: Formal molecular biology. Theoretical Computer Science 325(1), 69–110 (2004)
7. Laneve, C., Danos, V.: Core Formal Molecular Biology. In: Degano, P. (ed.) ESOP 2003 and ETAPS 2003. LNCS, vol. 2618, pp. 302–318. Springer, Heidelberg (2003)

8. Danos, V.: Agile modelling of cellular signalling. In: Proceedings of ICCMSE 2007 (2007)
9. Blinov, M., et al.: Graph Theory for Rule-Based Modeling of Biochemical Networks. In: Priami, C., Ingólfsdóttir, A., Mishra, B., Riis Nielson, H. (eds.) Transactions on Computational Systems Biology VII. LNCS (LNBI), vol. 4230, pp. 89–106. Springer, Heidelberg (2006)
10. Hlavacek, W., et al.: Rules for Modeling Signal-Transduction Systems. Science's STKE 344 (2006)
11. Milner, R.: Communicating and mobile systems: the π-calculus. Cambridge University Press, Cambridge (1999)
12. Cardelli, L.: Brane calculi. In: Proceedings of BIO-CONCUR 2003, Marseille, France. Electronic Notes in Theoretical Computer Science, vol. 180, Elsevier, Amsterdam (2003)
13. Priami, C., Quaglia, P.: Beta binders for biological interactions. Proceedings of CMSB 3082, 20–33 (2004)
14. Danos, V., Krivine, J.: Formal molecular biology done in CCS. In: Proceedings of BIO-CONCUR 2003, Marseille, France. Electronic Notes in Theoretical Computer Science, vol. 180, pp. 31–49. Elsevier, Amsterdam (2003)
15. Feret, J.: Dependency Analysis of Mobile Systems. In: Le Métayer, D. (ed.) ESOP 2002 and ETAPS 2002. LNCS, vol. 2305, pp. 314–329. Springer, Heidelberg (2002)
16. Cousot, P., Cousot, R.: Abstract interpretation and application to logic programs. Journal of Logic Programming 13(2–3), 103–179 (1992)
17. Lee, C.Y.: Representation of switching circuits by binary-decision programs. Bell Systems Technical Journal 38, 985–999 (1959)
18. Blanchet, B., et al.: A static analyzer for large safety-critical software. In: Proceedings of the ACM SIGPLAN 2003 Conference on Programming Language Design and Implementation (PLDI 2003), San Diego, California, USA, June 7–14, 2003, pp. 196–207. ACM Press, New York (2003)
19. Milner, R.: Communication and Concurrency. In: International Series on Computer Science, Prentice-Hall, Englewood Cliffs (1989)
20. Blinov, M.L., et al.: A network model of early events in epidermal growth factor receptor signaling that accounts for combinatorial complexity. BioSystems 83, 136–151 (2006)
21. Kwiatkowska, M., et al.: Simulation and verification for computational modelling of signalling pathways. In: Proceedings of the 37th conference on Winter simulation, pp. 1666–1674 (2006)

Is Lazy Abstraction a Decision Procedure for Broadcast Protocols?

Rayna Dimitrova[1] and Andreas Podelski[2]

[1] Universität des Saarlandes
[2] University of Freiburg

Abstract. Lazy abstraction builds up an abstract reachability tree by locally refining abstractions in order to eliminate spurious counterexamples in smaller and smaller subtrees. The method has proven useful to verify systems code. It is still open how good the method is as a decision procedure, i.e., whether the method terminates for already known decidable verification problems. In this paper, we answer the question positively for broadcast protocols and other infinite-state models in the class of so-called well-structured systems. This extends an existing result on systems with a finite bisimulation quotient.

1 Introduction

Lazy abstraction [1] is an interesting verification method that deserves a study on its own right. It defines the de-facto standard for verification based on the scheme coined *counterexample-guided abstraction refinement* (CEGAR) in [2]. While lazy abstraction has demonstrated its practical usefulness [3,4], it is still open whether its practical performance is matched by its theoretical qualities.

In this paper, we investigate the suitability of lazy abstraction as a decision procedure. The general question is for what (already known) decidable verification problems the method is guaranteed to terminate. We give a positive answer for the case of so-called *well-structured systems*. This class, which contains broadcast protocols and other interesting infinite-state models, is well-investigated [5,6,7,8,9]. The corresponding verification problem (called *coverability*) is known to be decidable [10]. We prove that lazy abstraction is guaranteed to terminate for every well-structured system; i.e., lazy abstraction is a decision procedure for coverability.

The high-level formulation of lazy abstraction given in [1] specifies no control for building up the abstract reachability tree. Strictly speaking, our positive answer refers to a version of lazy abstraction with *control*. The control (for building up the abstract reachability tree) implements a breadth-first strategy. This corresponds to the default choice in the implementation of lazy abstraction, e.g., in the tool BLAST [1,3].

We also give a negative answer. If the lazy abstraction is implemented by a non-deterministic algorithm (the control for choosing the branches for building up the abstract reachability tree is non-deterministic choice), then there exists

F. Logozzo et al. (Eds.): VMCAI 2008, LNCS 4905, pp. 98–111, 2008.

an example of a well-structured system, an instance of the coverability problem and a sequence of non-deterministic choices that results in non-termination.

In summary, the contribution of the paper is the comprehensive answer to the question whether lazy abstraction is a decision procedure for broadcast protocols.

Related Work. Our result relates to two lines of work: the investigation of various notions of completeness for lazy abstraction and other CEGAR methods, and, respectively, the design of specific CEGAR methods as complete tests for well-structured systems.

Completeness of CEGAR for finite-state systems is established in [2]. Systems with finite trace equivalence include finite-state systems but also timed automata; lazy abstraction was shown complete for this class in [1]. The completeness proof exploits the termination guarantee of the finite-quotient construction in [11]. Weaker notions of completeness are investigated in [12] (for general CEGAR schemes) and in [13] (for lazy abstraction). The proofs employ combinatorial arguments which, again, are unrelated to the proof methods employed in this paper.

The design of two specific CEGAR methods as complete tests for well-structured systems is presented in [6]. The two methods differ from lazy abstraction. They lack its main characteristics, the incremental construction of an abstract reachability tree with localized abstraction refinement for subtrees. The proofs of the termination guarantee given in [6] and, respectively, in this paper, both rely on the property defining well-structured systems. In [6], the proofs are based on the saturation of the set of possible refinements. This is not sufficient here, already because refinements refer to the (a priori unbounded) number of subtrees in the abstract reachability tree.

To our knowledge, we are the first to investigate the logical intersection of the two lines of work described above: the question of whether lazy abstraction is already a complete test for well-structured systems.

2 Preliminaries

2.1 Well-Structured Systems and Coverability

Here we introduce the class of *well-structured transition systems*(WSS) following the conceptual frameworks from [5] and [10]. The preorder $\preceq$ on a set S is called a *well-quasi order* if for every infinite sequence $s_0, s_1, s_2, \ldots$ of elements of S, there exist indices i and j such that i is strictly less than j and $s_i \preceq s_j$. Let $(S, \preceq)$ be a well-quasi ordered set. A subset A of S is *upward-closed* if for every element s of A and for every element t of S such that $s \preceq t$, it holds that t is an element of A. The existence of such an order on the set of states of an infinite-state system, combined with some compatibility property of the transition relation with respect to this order, guarantees the termination of certain fixpoint computations.

A *labeled transition system* $\mathcal{S}$ is a tuple $\langle S, I, C, \delta \rangle$ where S is a possibly infinite set of states, $I \subseteq S$ is a set of initial states, C is a finite set of labels and

$\delta \subseteq S \times C \times S$ is a labeled transition relation. Transition systems are usually represented symbolically using formulas over some set of atoms. Let $\mathcal{V} = \mathcal{X} \cup \mathcal{X}'$ be a set of variables. The set $\mathcal{X}'$ consists of the primed versions of the variables in $\mathcal{X}$. Let $\mathcal{AP}$ be a fixed infinite set of atomic formulas over the variables from $\mathcal{V}$. The language $\mathcal{L}$ is the closure of $\mathcal{AP}$ under Boolean connectives. For a finite subset P of $\mathcal{AP}$, we write $\mathcal{L}(P)$ for the closure of P under Boolean connectives. The set of atomic formulas that appear in a formula φ we denote with $\mathsf{atoms}(\varphi)$. A program is specified by a tuple $\langle X, \mathsf{init}, D\rangle$ where $X = \{x_1, \ldots, x_n\} \subseteq \mathcal{X}$ is a finite set of program variables (including program counters), each of which is associated with a domain, $\mathsf{init}(X)$ is a formula that denotes the set of initial states, and D is a set of guarded commands that describes the transition relation. Each guarded command is of the form $c_i : g_i(X) \wedge x_1' = e_1^i(X) \wedge \ldots \wedge x_n' = e_n^i(X)$ where c_i is the label of the command, g_i is the guard and the other conjuncts are the updates of the variables (the primed variables stand for the next-state program variables). With each program $\mathcal{S} = \langle X, \mathsf{init}, D\rangle$ we associate a transition system $\mathcal{S} = \langle S, I, C, \delta\rangle$, which describes its semantics, in the usual way. Each formula φ over the variables in X denotes a set of states: the states in which φ evaluates to true. From now on, we identify formulas over the variables in X and the sets of states denoted by them. The symbolic operators post and pre that map a label of a guarded command and a set of states to a set of states are defined in the usual way.

Consider a transition system $\mathcal{S}$ equipped with some well-quasi order $\preceq$ on the set of states S. Let the transition relation satisfy the following notion of *strong compatibility w.r.t. the labeled transitions*, which is the *strong compatibility* notion from [5]. That is: for every three states s_1, s_2 and t_1 such that $s_1 \preceq t_1$ and $(s_1, c, s_2) \in \delta$ for some label $c \in C$, there exists a state t_2 such that $s_2 \preceq t_2$ and $(t_1, c, t_2) \in \delta$. Such labeled transition systems we call *well-structured systems.*

Let $\mathcal{S}$ be a WSS and the formula unsafe denote a set of error states which is upward-closed w.r.t. the corresponding order $\preceq$. The *coverability problem* is to check whether the upward-closed set of error states is reachable in $\mathcal{S}$. This problem is known to be decidable for WSS [10].

2.2 Predicate Abstraction

We define abstraction and concretization functions w.r.t. some finite set of predicates P in the usual way. Let $\models$ denote entailment modulo some fixed theory. The abstraction function α_P is parameterized by the finite set of predicates P. It maps a formula φ to the smallest w.r.t. $\models$ formula over P that is greater than φ w.r.t. $\models$, formally, $\alpha_P(\varphi) = \mu_{\models}\psi \in \mathcal{L}(P).\varphi \models \psi$. The concretization function γ_P is defined to be the identity. The functions α_P and γ_P form a Galois connection. Hence, they are monotone and $\varphi \models \gamma_P(\alpha_P(\varphi))$. If $\mathcal{L}(P)$ contains a formula that is equivalent to a formula φ, then the abstraction of φ is equivalent to φ. If P is a subset of the finite set of predicates Q then for every formula φ it holds that $\gamma_Q(\alpha_Q(\varphi)) \models \gamma_P(\alpha_P(\varphi))$.

2.3 Lazy Abstraction

We recall the *lazy abstraction* algorithm(LA) from [1]. The algorithm iteratively explores the abstract state space by constructing an abstract reachability tree. If it terminates, it returns either a *genuine counterexample* (a path in the concrete system from an initial to an error state) or an overapproximation of the set of reachable states whose intersection with the set of error states is empty. In order to simplify the presentation, in this section we present the general scheme of lazy abstraction. In the next section we present in more detail a particular instantiation of that scheme and then state our contribution.

We describe an algorithm scheme LA[$\star$] parameterized by: (1) the strategy for exploring the abstract state space, namely the operator $\mathsf{choose\text{-}element}$ used to select the node of the abstract reachability tree that is going to be processed, (2) the predicate $\mathsf{covered}$ that determines whether the subtree below a node can be discarded, (3) the abstract operator $\widehat{\mathsf{post}}$ used to compute the regions of the nodes in the tree and (4) the operator Φ that is used to select the refinement predicates.

Each edge in the abstract reachability tree is labeled by a label of a guarded command. The finite sequences of labels of guarded commands we call *traces*. We characterize a node $\mathbf{n}$ by the trace σ that labels the path from the root to $\mathbf{n}$. Each node $\mathbf{n}$ in the tree is labeled by a pair (φ, P) called *region*, written $\mathbf{n}$:(φ, P). P is a finite set of predicates over the variables in X and φ is a Boolean formula over P. The formula φ, which we call the *reachable region* of $\mathbf{n}$, denotes an overapproximation of the set of states reachable via the corresponding trace σ. If the conjunction of φ and the formula unsafe is satisfiable then $\mathbf{n}$ is an *error node*, otherwise we call it a *safe node*.

The procedure constructs a sequence of trees. We denote the current tree at iteration k with T_k. The initial tree T_0 consists of a single node $\mathbf{r}$ labeled with the region (init, P_0), where P_0 consists of the atoms that appear in the formula init and the atoms that appear in the formula unsafe. Each node in the current tree has a mark that can be one of the following: *unprocessed*, *covered* or *uncovered*. The list L consists of all nodes in the current tree that are marked as unprocessed. These are nodes that have been added to the tree but have not been processed yet. At each step the algorithm chooses a node $\mathbf{n}$ from L, unless L is empty, and deletes it from the list. Then it processes the node $\mathbf{n}$ and constructs the next tree T_{k+1} as explained below or returns a counterexample. If L is empty, the algorithm terminates with the formula *Reach* as a result, where the formula *Reach* is defined to be the disjunction of the reachable regions of all nodes in the current tree that are marked as uncovered.

When $\mathbf{n}$ is a safe node, the algorithm LA[$\star$] proceeds as follows. If $\mathbf{n}$ should be marked as covered, i.e., $\mathsf{covered}(\varphi)$ is true for the reachable region φ of $\mathbf{n}$ (this holds if φ is contained in the disjunction of the reachable regions of some of the nodes in the current tree that are marked as uncovered), then $\mathbf{n}$ is marked as covered and its children are not generated. Otherwise, it is marked as uncovered and for each command c, the algorithm does the following. If $\mathsf{post}(c, \varphi)$ is not empty, it adds a new node as a child of $\mathbf{n}$ and labels it with the region $\widehat{\mathsf{post}}(c, (\varphi, P))$.

Algorithm 1. LA[$\star$]

```
Input: a program S , a formula unsafe
Output: either "CORRECT" and a formula θ or
"NOT CORRECT" and counterexample σ
P0 := atoms(init) ∪ atoms(unsafe);
T consists of a single node r:(init, P0);
L := {r}; Reach = false;
repeat
    n:(φ, P) :=choose–element(L);
    remove n:(φ, P) from L;
    if φ ⊨ ¬unsafe then
        if covered(φ) then
            mark n as covered
        else
            mark n as uncovered;
            Reach := Reach ∨ φ;
            forall c ∈ C do
                if post(c, φ) ≠ ∅ then
                    add m:post^(c, (φ, P)) as a child of n in T;
                    label the edge from n to m with c;
                    mark m as unprocessed and add m to L
                end
            end
        end
    else
        m:(ψ, Q) is the pivot node for n;
        if m= ⊥ then
            return ("NOT CORRECT",the trace from the root to n)
        else
            τ is the trace from m to n;
            relabel m with (ψ, Q ∪ Φ(ψ, τ, unsafe));
            mark m as unprocessed and add it to L;
            delete the subtrees that start from the children of m;
            all nodes that were marked as covered after the last time m was
            processed are marked as unprocessed and added to L;
            Reach := ⋁_{n':(φ',P'):uncovered} φ'
        end
    end
until L = ∅ ;
return ("CORRECT", Reach)
```

The edge from $\mathbf{n}$ to the new node is labeled with c. All the children of $\mathbf{n}$ are marked as unprocessed and added to the list L.

When the processed node $\mathbf{n}{:}(\varphi, P)$ is an error node, the procedure analyzes the abstract counterexample backwards. The *error region* for a trace τ is defined as $\mathsf{pre}(\tau, \mathsf{unsafe})$. For each node $\mathbf{n}'$ on the path, LA[$\star$] computes the error region for the trace from $\mathbf{n}'$ to $\mathbf{n}$ until it finds the first (in backward direction) node on the path, for which the conjunction of the corresponding reachable and error regions is unsatisfiable. This is the *pivot node* $\mathbf{m}{:}(\psi, Q)$. Then, $\mathbf{m}$ *is refined w.r.t. the trace* τ, where τ is the *error trace* – the sequence of the labels of the edges on the path from $\mathbf{m}$ to $\mathbf{n}$. The set of predicates of the pivot node is enhanced with the predicates in $\Phi(\psi, \tau, \mathsf{unsafe})$. The subtrees that start at the children of the pivot node $\mathbf{m}$ are deleted, $\mathbf{m}$ is marked as unprocessed and so are all nodes marked as covered after $\mathbf{m}$ was last processed.

Provided that the operator $\widehat{\mathsf{post}}$ fulfills the requirement: if $\widehat{\mathsf{post}}(c, (\varphi, P)) = (\varphi', P')$, then $P' = P$ and $\mathsf{post}(c, \varphi) \models \varphi'$, the following two properties of the labels of the nodes are direct consequences of the construction of the sequence of trees.

Property 1. Let $\mathbf{n}{:}(\varphi, P)$ be a node in the tree T_i. Let j be an index greater or equal to i such that for every $i \leq k \leq j$, the node $\mathbf{n}$ is not deleted from the tree T_k. Let $\mathbf{m}{:}(\psi, Q)$ be a node in T_j that is in the subtree rooted at $\mathbf{n}$. Then, it holds that $P \subseteq Q$.

Property 2. Let $\mathbf{n}{:}(\varphi, P)$ and $\mathbf{m}{:}(\psi, Q)$ be two nodes in some tree T_i such that $\mathbf{m}$ is in the subtree rooted at $\mathbf{n}$. Let σ be the sequence of labels on the path from $\mathbf{n}$ to $\mathbf{m}$. The set denoted by ψ is an overapproximation of the set of states that can be reached from a state in φ by executing the sequence of commands σ, formally, $\mathsf{post}(\sigma, \varphi) \models \psi$.

3 Lazy Abstraction with Breadth-First Strategy: LA[BF]

We obtain the procedure LA[BF] by instantiating the algorithm scheme LA[$\star$]. In particular, we impose more control on the abstract state-space exploration by fixing the search strategy. We restrict the non-deterministic choice, which node to be processed at the current iteration, to the set $\mathsf{min\text{-}depth}(L)$ of unprocessed nodes with minimal depth. We instantiate choose-element with the operator pick-min-element, which selects non-deterministically an element of $\mathsf{min\text{-}depth}(L)$. This amounts to a breadth-first exploration of the abstract reachability tree. We mark a safe node $\mathbf{n}$ with reachable region φ as covered, i.e., $\mathsf{covered}(\varphi)$ is true, exactly when $\varphi \models \mathit{Reach}_{\mathbf{n}}$, where the formula $\mathit{Reach}_{\mathbf{n}}$ is defined to be the disjunction of the reachable regions of the nodes in the current tree with depth less than the depth of $\mathbf{n}$ that are marked as uncovered. The parameter $\widehat{\mathsf{post}}$ is instantiated with the abstract post operator $\mathsf{post}^{\#}$, which is defined as $\mathsf{post}^{\#}(c, (\varphi, P)) = (\alpha_P(\mathsf{post}(c, \varphi)), P)$.

Let $\mathbf{m}{:}(\psi, Q)$ be the pivot node that is to be refined by the procedure and τ be the corresponding error trace. We define the focus operator Φ, which determines the refinement predicates for the error trace τ, as follows. For a trace τ and indices $1 \leq i \leq j \leq |\tau| + 1$, we denote with $\tau[i, j)$ the subword of τ that starts at position i and ends at position $j - 1$ (including the $j - 1$-th element). Then $\Phi(\psi, \tau, \mathsf{unsafe}) = \bigcup_{i=1}^{|\tau|+1} \mathsf{atoms}(\mathsf{pre}(\tau[i, |\tau| + 1), \mathsf{unsafe}))$. The refinement consists in enhancing the set of predicates of the pivot node $\mathbf{m}$ and deleting the subtrees that originate from its children.

At each iteration LA[BF] processes an unprocessed node with minimal depth. Therefore, the refinement satisfies the following property.

Lemma 1. *Let* $\mathbf{n}$ *be the node that is processed by the procedure in the tree* T_i *at some iteration* i. *Let* σ *be a trace and* $\mathbf{m}$:(φ, P) *be a node in* T_i *such that the sum of the length of* σ *and the depth of* $\mathbf{m}$ *is strictly less than the depth of the node* $\mathbf{n}$. *Then,* $\varphi \wedge \mathsf{pre}(\sigma, \mathsf{unsafe})$ *is not satisfiable.*

Proof. The proof goes by induction on the length of σ.

Base case. The length of σ is 0. If we assume that for some node $\mathbf{m}$:(φ, P) with the stated property, the formula $\varphi \wedge \mathsf{pre}(\sigma, \mathsf{unsafe})$ is satisfiable, then $\mathbf{m}$ is an error node. Hence, it cannot be marked as covered or uncovered. Therefore, it is marked as unprocessed. Hence, in T_i there is an unprocessed node with depth strictly less than the depth of the node $\mathbf{n}$. This is a contradiction to the fact that $\mathbf{n}$ is a node of minimal depth marked as unprocessed.

Induction step. Let σ be of the form $c \cdot \sigma'$. By the induction hypothesis, for every node $\mathbf{r}$, such that the sum of the depth of $\mathbf{r}$ and the length of σ' is strictly less than the depth of $\mathbf{n}$, the conjunction of the reachable region of $\mathbf{r}$ and the error region for σ' is not satisfiable. Assume for contradiction that for a node $\mathbf{m}$:(φ, P), the conjunction $\varphi \wedge \mathsf{pre}(\sigma, \mathsf{unsafe})$ is satisfiable and the sum of the depth of $\mathbf{m}$ and the length of σ is strictly less than the depth of $\mathbf{n}$. Then, there is a state s that satisfies this conjunction. Hence, there is a state t, such that there is a transition labeled by c from s to t and t is an element of $\mathsf{pre}(\sigma', \mathsf{unsafe})$.

Since the depth of the node $\mathbf{m}$ is strictly less than the depth of the node $\mathbf{n}$, which the procedure processes in the current iteration, $\mathbf{m}$ should be marked either as covered or as uncovered. If we assume that $\mathbf{m}$ is marked as covered, then there exists a node $\mathbf{m}'$ with reachable region ψ' in T_i that is marked as uncovered, has depth less than the depth of the node $\mathbf{m}$ and is such that the state s satisfies ψ'. As t satisfies $\mathsf{post}(c, \psi')$, there is a node $\mathbf{m}''$ in T_i that is a child of $\mathbf{m}'$ and the edge between $\mathbf{m}'$ and $\mathbf{m}''$ is labeled by c. Let the reachable region of $\mathbf{m}''$ be ψ''. It contains the state t. If, on the other hand, we assume that $\mathbf{m}$ is marked as uncovered, there is a node $\mathbf{m}''$ in T_i that is a child of $\mathbf{m}$ and the edge between $\mathbf{m}$ and $\mathbf{m}''$ is labeled by c. If ψ'' is the reachable region of $\mathbf{m}''$, then the state t satisfies ψ''.

Hence, in both cases there is a node $\mathbf{m}''$ such that the state t belongs to its reachable region ψ'' and the sum of the depth of $\mathbf{m}''$ and the length of σ' is less than or equal to the sum of the depth of $\mathbf{m}$ and the length of σ which is strictly less than the depth of $\mathbf{n}$. Therefore, we can apply the induction hypothesis, which yields that the intersection of ψ'' and $\mathsf{pre}(\sigma', \mathsf{unsafe})$ is empty. This contradicts to the fact that the state t is an element of both of them. This concludes the proof. □

Algorithm 2. LA[BF]

```
Input: a program S , a formula unsafe
Output: either "CORRECT" and a formula θ or
"NOT CORRECT" and counterexample σ
P0 := atoms(init) ∪ atoms(unsafe);
T consists of a single node r:(init, P0);
L := {r}; Reach = false;
repeat
    n:(φ, P) :=pick-min-element(L);
    remove n:(φ, P) from L;
    if φ ⊨ ¬unsafe then
        if φ ⊨ Reach_n then
            mark n as covered
        else
            mark n as uncovered;
            Reach := Reach ∨ φ;
            forall c ∈ C do
                if post(c, φ) ≠ ∅ then
                    add m:post#(c, (φ, P)) as a child of n in T;
                    label the edge from n to m with c;
                    mark m as unprocessed and add m to L;
                end
            end
        end
    else
        m:(ψ, Q) is the pivot node for n;
        if m= ⊥ then
            return ("NOT CORRECT",the trace from the root to n)
        else
            τ is the trace from m to n;
            Q' := ⋃_{i=1}^{|τ|+1} atoms(pre(τ[i, |τ| + 1), unsafe));
            relabel m with (ψ, Q ∪ Q');
            mark m as unprocessed and add it to L;
            delete the subtrees that start from the children of m;
            all nodes that were marked as covered after the last time m was
            processed are marked as unprocessed and added to L;
            Reach := ⋁_{n':(φ',P'):uncovered} φ'
        end
    end
until L = ∅ ;
return ("CORRECT", Reach)
```

4 LA[BF] is a Decision Procedure

From now on, we assume that the program that is given as input to the procedure LA[BF] denotes a WSS $\mathcal{S}$ with a well-quasi order $\preceq$ and that the set of error states unsafe is upward-closed with respect to this order. We show that in this case the procedure LA[BF] is guaranteed to terminate.

It is easy to see that if the number of performed refinement operations is finite, then the procedure terminates. This is because with finitely many predicates we can generate only finitely many non-equivalent regions. To show that the number of iterations, at which the procedure performs a refinement, is finite, we prove that the following two properties hold. First, we prove that each particular node cannot be refined as a pivot node infinitely often. Then, we show that it is also impossible that the procedure refines infinitely many distinct pivot nodes. In both cases the proof is by contradiction. We assume that the property under consideration does not hold and show the existence of an infinite sequence of states that are pairwise incomparable with respect to the order $\preceq$. This can not be true because $\preceq$ is a well-quasi order. To show the existence of such a sequence, we make use of the fact that for each trace σ the set $\mathsf{pre}(\sigma, \mathsf{unsafe})$ is upward-closed when unsafe is upward-closed. We first show several lemmas that we use for proving the two main properties of LA[BF]. We begin with a lemma that states the progress property of the refinement. Recall that if at the i-th iteration, $\mathbf{n}$ is the pivot node and σ is the sequence of labels on the path from $\mathbf{n}$ to the corresponding error node that is processed in the current tree T_i, we say that $\mathbf{n}$ is refined w.r.t. σ in T_i.

Lemma 2. *Let the node $\mathbf{n}$:(φ, P) be refined in the tree T_i w.r.t. the trace σ. Let j be an index greater than i such that for every index k with $i \leq k \leq j$, the node $\mathbf{n}$ is not deleted from the tree T_k. Assume that the node $\mathbf{m}$:(ψ, Q) is in the subtree rooted at $\mathbf{n}$ in T_j, $\psi \models \neg\mathsf{pre}(\sigma, \mathsf{unsafe})$, the node $\mathbf{m}'$:(ψ', Q') is in the subtree rooted at $\mathbf{m}$ and the path from $\mathbf{m}$ to $\mathbf{m}'$ is labeled by $\sigma[1, l)$ for some l, i.e., with a prefix of σ. Then, $\psi' \models \neg\mathsf{pre}(\sigma[l, |\sigma| + 1), \mathsf{unsafe})$.*

Proof. The proof goes by induction. For l such that $1 \leq l \leq |\sigma|+1$, let $\mathbf{m}_l$:(ψ_l, Q_l) be the node in T_j such that the path from $\mathbf{m}$ to $\mathbf{m}_l$ is labeled by $\sigma[1, l)$, if such nodes exists in T_j. For every l we show that if $1 \leq l \leq |\sigma| + 1$ then $\psi_l \models \neg\mathsf{pre}(\sigma[l, |\sigma|+1), \mathsf{unsafe})$. For $l = 1$ we have $\psi_l = \psi$ and $\psi \models \neg\mathsf{pre}(\sigma[1, |\sigma|+1), \mathsf{unsafe})$. Let $l + 1 \leq |\sigma| + 1$. By induction hypothesis we have that $\psi_l \models \neg\mathsf{pre}(\sigma[l, |\sigma|+1), \mathsf{unsafe})$. This yields $\mathsf{post}(\sigma[l], \psi_l) \models \neg\mathsf{pre}(\sigma[l+1, |\sigma|+1), \mathsf{unsafe})$. Since by Property 1 $\mathsf{atoms}(\mathsf{pre}(\sigma[l + 1, |\sigma| + 1), \mathsf{unsafe})) \subseteq Q_l$, we have that $\alpha_{Q_l}(\mathsf{post}(\sigma[l], \psi_l)) \models \neg\mathsf{pre}(\sigma[l + 1, |\sigma| + 1), \mathsf{unsafe})$. Thus, $\psi_{l+1} \models \neg\mathsf{pre}(\sigma[l + 1, |\sigma| + 1), \mathsf{unsafe})$. □

This lemma implies that once a node $\mathbf{n}$ is refined w.r.t. a trace σ, no node in the subtree rooted at $\mathbf{n}$ will be refined w.r.t. the same trace at the next iterations, provided that $\mathbf{n}$ is not deleted meanwhile.

Lemma 3. *Let the node $\mathbf{n}$ be refined in the tree T_i w.r.t. the trace σ. Assume that for some index j strictly greater than i, it holds that for every index k with $i \leq k \leq j$, the node $\mathbf{n}$ is not deleted from the tree T_k. Then, for every node $\mathbf{m}$ that is in the subtree of $\mathbf{n}$ in the tree T_j, it holds that $\mathbf{m}$ cannot be refined in the tree T_j w.r.t. the trace σ.*

Proof. Let the label of the node $\mathbf{m}$ in T_j be (ψ, Q). Assume that $\mathbf{m}$ is refined in T_j w.r.t. the trace σ. Therefore, $\psi \models \neg\mathsf{pre}(\sigma, \mathsf{unsafe})$. Also, an error node

$\mathbf{m}'$:(ψ', Q') is processed in T_j and the path from $\mathbf{m}$ to $\mathbf{m}'$ is labeled with σ. According to Lemma 2, $\psi' \models \neg\mathsf{pre}(\sigma[|\sigma|+1, |\sigma|+1), \mathsf{unsafe})$, i.e. $\psi' \models \neg\mathsf{unsafe}$. This contradicts to the fact that $\mathbf{m}'$ is an error node. □

Now we are ready to prove that every node can be the refined as pivot node at only finitely many iterations.

Proposition 1. *A node $\mathbf{n}$ cannot be refined by LA[BF] infinitely often.*

Proof. We first show that if some node is not deleted infinitely often from the tree, then it cannot be refined infinitely often. Assume that the node $\mathbf{n}$ is refined infinitely often and deleted only finitely often. Thus, there is an infinite sequence of trees $T_{k_0}, T_{k_1}, \ldots$ such that the node $\mathbf{n}$ is refined in each tree T_{k_i} w.r.t. some trace σ_i and for every index k greater or equal to k_0, the node $\mathbf{n}$ is not deleted from the tree T_k. According to Lemma 3, all traces in the sequence $\sigma_0, \sigma_1, \ldots$ must be pairwise different. Since the set of labels C is finite, w.l.o.g. we can assume that for some label c, for each index i, the first element of the trace σ_i is exactly c. Let τ_i be the trace obtained from the trace σ_i by removing its first element, and the node $\mathbf{m}$ be the child of $\mathbf{n}$ with edge from $\mathbf{n}$ to $\mathbf{m}$ labeled with c. Let the sequence of formulas $\psi_0, \psi_1, \ldots$ consist of the reachable regions of the node $\mathbf{m}$ in the trees $T_{k_0}, T_{k_1}, \ldots$ respectively. For every index i, the conjunction $\psi_i \wedge \mathsf{pre}(\tau_i, \mathsf{unsafe})$ is satisfiable because the node $\mathbf{n}$ is refined in the tree T_{k_i} w.r.t. the trace σ_i. So, for each index i we can choose a state s_i that satisfies $\psi_i \wedge \mathsf{pre}(\tau_i, \mathsf{unsafe})$. Since $\preceq$ is a well-quasi order, for the sequence of states $s_0, s_1, \ldots$, there exist indices i and j such that i is strictly smaller than j and $s_i \preceq s_j$. The set of states $\mathsf{pre}(\tau_i, \mathsf{unsafe})$ is upward-closed. Therefore, the state s_j is an element of the set $\mathsf{pre}(\tau_i, \mathsf{unsafe})$. According to Lemma 2, the intersection of the sets ψ_j and $\mathsf{pre}(\tau_i, \mathsf{unsafe})$ is empty. This contradicts to the fact that the state s_j is an element of both sets.

It now remains to show that a node cannot be deleted infinitely often. The proof is by induction on the depth of the node. The root node is never deleted. Consider a node $\mathbf{n}$ different from the root. By the induction hypothesis we have that each of the nodes on the path from the root to the node $\mathbf{n}$ is deleted only finitely many times. Hence, as we showed already, each of these nodes can be refined only a finite number of times. Since a node is deleted only when some node on the path from the root to this node is refined, $\mathbf{n}$ can be deleted only finitely many times. □

To show that it is not possible that the procedure refines infinitely many different pivot nodes we need the next lemma, which states that if this is the case then we can construct an infinite sequence of different nodes that are refined by the procedure with the property that they belong to the same branch.

Lemma 4. *If the procedure refines infinitely many pivot nodes, then there is an infinite sequence $T_{k_0}, T_{k_1}, \ldots$ of trees and an infinite sequence $\mathbf{n}_0, \mathbf{n}_1, \ldots$ of corresponding nodes in those trees, such that the following two conditions hold. In the tree $T_{k_{i+1}}$ the node $\mathbf{n}_{i+1}$ is in the subtree rooted at $\mathbf{n}_i$. Each node $\mathbf{n}_i$ is* *refined in the tree T_{k_i} and for each index k strictly greater than k_i, $\mathbf{n}_i$ is not deleted from or refined in T_k.*

Proof. Assume that the procedure refines infinitely many different pivot nodes. Since the number of children of each node is bounded by $|C|$ and no node is deleted infinitely often, there exists a sequence $T_{l_0}, T_{l_1}, \ldots$ of trees and a sequence $\mathbf{m}_0, \mathbf{m}_1, \ldots$ of corresponding nodes such that $\mathbf{m}_{i+1}$ is a child of the node $\mathbf{m}_i$ in the tree $T_{l_{i+1}}$. As we showed, each of these nodes is refined as a pivot node at only finitely many iterations. If we assume that only finitely many of them are refined, it follows that there exists an index j, such that $\mathbf{m}_j$ is subsumed by some $\mathbf{m}_i$ with index $i < j$, which is not possible since $\mathbf{m}_{j+1}$ is a child of $\mathbf{m}_j$. Thus, infinitely many among those nodes are refined. The fact that a node cannot be refined infinitely often implies that there is an infinite sequence $T_{k_0}, T_{k_1}, \ldots$ of trees and a corresponding subsequence $\mathbf{n}_0, \mathbf{n}_1, \ldots$ of $\mathbf{m}_0, \mathbf{m}_1, \ldots$ such that each node $\mathbf{n}_i$ is refined in the tree T_{k_i} and for each index k strictly greater than k_i, $\mathbf{n}_i$ is not deleted from or refined in T_k. This concludes the proof. □

What remains now is to show the second property of the refinement, which is stated below.

Proposition 2. *The procedure LA[BF] refines only finitely many pivot nodes.*

Proof. Assume that the procedure refines infinitely many pivot nodes and consider an infinite sequence $\mathbf{n}_0, \mathbf{n}_1, \ldots$ of different nodes and an infinite sequence $T_{k_0}, T_{k_1}, \ldots$ of trees that satisfy the conditions stated in Lemma 4. Let σ_i be the trace, with respect to which the node $\mathbf{n}_i$ is refined in the tree T_{k_i}. As every node $\mathbf{n}_i$ in the sequence is not deleted in any tree T_k with index k greater than k_i, by Lemma 3 the traces $\sigma_0, \sigma_1, \ldots$ are pairwise different. As the set of labels C is finite, we can assume w.l.o.g. that we have chosen the sequences in a way that each trace has length strictly less than the length of the next. For each trace σ_i, we denote with τ_i the trace obtained from σ_i by removing its first element. Let the sequence of nodes $\mathbf{m}_0, \mathbf{m}_1, \ldots$ be such that each node $\mathbf{m}_i$ is the child of the node $\mathbf{n}_i$ in the tree T_{k_i} with the edge between them labeled with the first element of σ_i. Let the formulas φ_i and ψ_i be the reachable regions in the tree T_{k_i} of the nodes $\mathbf{n}_i$ and $\mathbf{m}_i$ respectively. The intersection of ψ_i and $\mathsf{pre}(\tau_i, \mathsf{unsafe})$ is not empty since the node $\mathbf{n}_i$ is refined in the tree T_{k_i} w.r.t. σ_i. Therefore, there exists a sequence of states $s_0, s_1, \ldots$ such that each state s_i is an element of the corresponding intersection $\psi_i \wedge \mathsf{pre}(\tau_i, \mathsf{unsafe})$. Since $\preceq$ is a well-quasi order, there exist indices i and j such that $i < j$ and $s_i \preceq s_j$. The set of states $\mathsf{pre}(\tau_i, \mathsf{unsafe})$ is upward-closed. Therefore, as the state s_i is an element of this set and $s_i \preceq s_j$, s_j is also an element of $\mathsf{pre}(\tau_i, \mathsf{unsafe})$. The node $\mathbf{n}_j$ is refined in the tree T_{k_j} w.r.t. the trace σ_j. Hence, a node $\mathbf{n}$ with depth equal to the sum of the depth of $\mathbf{m}_j$ and the length of τ_j is processed in this tree. We can apply Lemma 1 to the node $\mathbf{n}$, the node $\mathbf{m}_j$ and the trace τ_i, because the length of the trace τ_i is strictly less than the length of the trace τ_j. Thus, for the reachable region of the node $\mathbf{m}_j$ it holds that the intersection of ψ_j and $\mathsf{pre}(\tau_i, \mathsf{unsafe})$ is empty. This contradicts to the fact that the state s_j is an element of both these sets. This completes the proof by contradiction. □

Finally, the two propositions yield our main result.

Theorem 1. *The procedure LA[BF] is a decision procedure for the coverability problem for WSS.*

5 LA[$\star$] is Not a Decision Procedure

We use LA[$\star$] to refer to lazy abstraction with completely non-deterministic control for building up the the abstract reachability tree. In this section we give an example of a system and a sequence of non-deterministic choices that results in non-termination.

Consider the program given below that has three variables x, y and z, each of which ranges over $\mathbb{N}$. The guarded commands are given in Table 1 (we use "syntactic sugar" and list only the "true" updates). The set of initial states is given by $x = 0 \wedge y = 0 \wedge z = 0$ and the set of error states is denoted by $z \geq 2$. The order $\preceq$ between the states of the corresponding transition system is the pointwise ordering between the elements of $\mathbb{N}^3$ defined by $\leq$. It is a well-quasi order according to Dickson's lemma [14]. The resulting transition system $\mathcal{S}$ equipped with the order $\preceq$ is a WSS and the set of error states is upward-closed w.r.t. this order. The system $\mathcal{S}$ is safe.

If we execute LA[$\star$] with a sequence of non-deterministic choices that never refines the root node as pivot node, then it creates longer and longer counterexamples (and refines pivot nodes deeper and deeper in the abstract reachability tree). It adds predicates of the form $x \geq 2,\ x \geq 3, \ldots$ and $y \geq 2,\ y \geq 3, \ldots$.

Table 1. Guarded commands

Label	**Guard**	**Update**
c_1	true	$y := 1$
c_2	$y > 1$	$x := 1 \wedge y := 0$
c_3	$x > 0$	$x := x + 1$
c_4	$x > 0$	$x := x - 1 \wedge y := y + 1$
c_5	true	$z := x$
c_6	$x > 0$	$y := y + 1$
c_7	$y > 1$	$y := y - 1 \wedge x := x + 1$
c_8	true	$z := y$

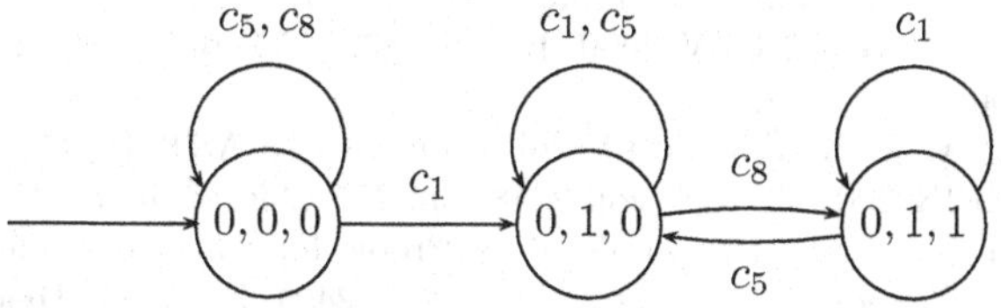

Fig. 1. Transition system $\mathcal{S}$

Thus, at each iteration it generates more and more non-subsumed regions. Since it never refines the root, the initial overapproximation that occurs by approximating $y = 1$ with $y \neq 0$ in the abstract execution of c_1 is never eliminated. Thus, the sequence of non-deterministic choices results in a non-terminating run of the iterative refinement.

It is instructive to follow the execution of LA[BF] on this example. The initial set of abstract predicates is $P_0 = \{z \geq 2, x = 0, y = 0, z = 0\}$. After a few iterations the procedure LA[BF] refines the root node as pivot node w.r.t. the trace $c_1c_2c_3c_5$ and adds the atoms $y > 1$ and $x \geq 2$ to the set of predicates for the root. After that there are no more abstract counterexamples and the procedure LA[BF] terminates.

6 Conclusion

An abstraction-based algorithm trades higher efficiency with the loss of definiteness. It may return "Don't Know" answers in some cases; it implements only a semi-test. A procedure based on counterexample-guided abstraction refinement trades a higher degree of automation with the loss of the termination guarantee. It may iterate forever without hitting a ("non-spurious") counterexample nor proving its absence; it implements only a semi-algorithm. Lazy abstraction goes one step further towards trading a potential practical gain with the risk of theoretical deficiencies (since it avoids redundant computations of abstract subtrees by localizing refinements, with the risk of having to generate the same predicate infinitely often). It is thus perhaps surprising that, as stated by our result, lazy abstraction with deterministic control is a decision procedure for the coverability problem for well-structured system.

It is not the point of this paper to advocate lazy abstraction as a promising practical alternative to existing decision algorithms for well-structured systems, including the other algorithms based on abstraction refinement. It is, however, an outcome of the work presented in this paper that a thorough experimental comparison on the wide range of well-structured systems (see, e.g., `http://www.ulb.ac.be/di/ssd/lvbegin/CST/#examples`) has come to make sense.

References

1. Henzinger, T.A., et al.: Lazy abstraction. In: POPL, pp. 58–70 (2002)
2. Clarke, E.M., et al.: Counterexample-guided abstraction refinement. In: Emerson, E.A., Sistla, A.P. (eds.) CAV 2000. LNCS, vol. 1855, pp. 154–169. Springer, Heidelberg (2000)
3. Henzinger, T.A., et al.: Software Verification with BLAST. In: Ball, T., Rajamani, S.K. (eds.) SPIN 2003. LNCS, vol. 2648, pp. 235–239. Springer, Heidelberg (2003)
4. Henzinger, T.A., et al.: Temporal-Safety Proofs for Systems Code. In: Brinksma, E., Larsen, K.G. (eds.) CAV 2002. LNCS, vol. 2404, Springer, Heidelberg (2002)
5. Finkel, A., Schnoebelen, P.: Well-structured transition systems everywhere! Theor. Comput. Sci. 256(1-2), 63–92 (2001)

6. Ganty, P., Raskin, J.F., Van Begin, L.: A complete abstract interpretation framework for coverability properties of wsts. In: Emerson, E.A., Namjoshi, K.S. (eds.) VMCAI 2006. LNCS, vol. 3855, pp. 49–64. Springer, Heidelberg (2005)
7. Geeraerts, G., Raskin, J.F., Begin, L.V.: Expand, Enlarge, and Check: New algorithms for the coverability problem of wsts. In: Lodaya, K., Mahajan, M. (eds.) FSTTCS 2004. LNCS, vol. 3328, pp. 287–298. Springer, Heidelberg (2004)
8. Raskin, J.-F., Van Begin, L., Geeraerts, G.: Expand, enlarge and check.. made efficient. In: Etessami, K., Rajamani, S.K. (eds.) CAV 2005. LNCS, vol. 3576, pp. 394–404. Springer, Heidelberg (to appear, 2005)
9. Delzanno, G., Esparza, J., Podelski, A.: Constraint-Based Analysis of Broadcast Protocols. In: Flum, J., Rodríguez-Artalejo, M. (eds.) CSL 1999. LNCS, vol. 1683, pp. 50–66. Springer, Heidelberg (1999)
10. Abdulla, P.A., et al.: General decidability theorems for infinite-state systems. In: LICS, pp. 313–321 (1996)
11. Bouajjani, A., Fernandez, J.C., Halbwachs, N., Raymond, P.: Minimal state graph generation. Sci. Comput. Program. 18(3), 247–269 (1992)
12. Ball, T., Podelski, A., Rajamani, S.K.: Relative Completeness of Abstraction Refinement for Software Model Checking. In: Katoen, J.-P., Stevens, P. (eds.) ETAPS 2002 and TACAS 2002. LNCS, vol. 2280, Springer, Heidelberg (2002)
13. McMillan, K.L.: Lazy Abstraction with Interpolants. In: Ball, T., Jones, R.B. (eds.) CAV 2006. LNCS, vol. 4144, pp. 123–136. Springer, Heidelberg (2006)
14. Dickson, L.: Finiteness of the odd perfect and primitive abundant numbers with n prime factors. Amer. J. Math. 35, 413–422 (1913)

Model Checking for Action Abstraction*

Harald Fecher and Michael Huth

Imperial College London, United Kingdom
{hfecher, M.Huth}@doc.ic.ac.uk

Abstract. We endow action sets of transition systems with a partial order that expresses the degree of specialization of actions, and with an intuitive but flexible consistency predicate that constrains the extension of such orders with more specialized actions. We develop a satisfaction relation for such models and the μ-calculus. We prove that this satisfaction relation is sound for Thomsen's extended bisimulation as our refinement notion for models, even for consistent extensions of ordered action sets. We then demonstrate how this satisfaction relation can be reduced, fairly efficiently, to classical μ-calculus model checking. These results provide formal support for change management of models and their validation (e.g. in model-centric software development), and enable verification of concrete systems with respect to properties specified for abstract actions.

1 Introduction

Transition systems and their variants are popular models of state and behavior for programs and reactive systems alike. Transitions are triples (s, a, s') specifying that action a may cause the system to change from state s to state s'. Whenever transition systems function as models we can validate these models, e.g. through property verification in the form of model checking formulas of the μ-calculus [13] over the action set pertinent to the model and property. Most popular and tool-supported branching-time temporal logics embed into the μ-calculus so the latter is an ideal target for foundational studies.

Often one wishes to specify and verify properties that are more abstract than the model itself. Consider a model for a stack-like data structure. An input action $put(n)$ puts value $n \in \mathbb{N}$ on top of the stack; output action $get(m)$ reads $m \in \mathbb{N}$ as the top value of the stack and then pops the top of the stack. A property that this model should enjoy is that, at all states, there is a finite sequence of output actions whose execution in sequence results in a state where no output actions are possible: the stack can always be emptied completely. For the above infinite action set, this property can be expressed in the μ-calculus if we extend it with infinite conjunctions and disjunctions:

$$\nu X.((\bigwedge_{n\in\mathbb{N}} [put(n)]X \wedge [get(n)]X) \wedge \mu Y.((\bigvee_{m\in\mathbb{N}} \langle get(m)\rangle Y) \vee (\bigwedge_{n\in\mathbb{N}} [get(n)]\mathsf{ff}))) \quad (1)$$

where ff denotes falsity. The formula in (1) is a greatest fixed point (νX) whose body is a conjunction. The first conjunct is a recursion and ensures that the second conjunct is

* This work is in part financially supported by the DFG project (FE 942/2-1) and by the UK EPSRC project *Complete and Efficient Checks for Branching-Time Abstractions* EP/E028985/1.

F. Logozzo et al. (Eds.): VMCAI 2008, LNCS 4905, pp. 112–126, 2008.

true at all reachable states. The second conjunct states that, at the present state, there is a finite (least fixed point μY) sequence of transitions, labeled with possibly different output actions $get(m)$, to a state at which no such output actions are possible. Representing this property in an idiom such as (1) has a number of disadvantages:

- The infinite conjunctions and disjunctions in (1) appeal to an infinite state space, making model checking hard or undecidable.
- The encoding in (1) cannot be model checked on more abstract models, e.g. for one in which get abstracts all instances of $get(n)$, we cannot verify the subformula $\langle get(0)\rangle \dots$ as any transition labeled with get could be refined to $get(1)$ instead.
- The encoding in (1) lacks flexibility and support for top down development; e.g. if we extend the stack data type with a non-destructive output action $read(n)$ for all $n \in \mathbb{N}$, the formula in (1) has to be extended to

$$\nu X.((\bigwedge_{n\in\mathbb{N}} \cdots \wedge [read(n)]X) \wedge \mu Y.((\bigvee_{m\in\mathbb{N}} \cdots \vee \langle read(m)\rangle Y) \vee (\bigwedge_{n\in\mathbb{N}} \cdots \wedge [read(n)]\mathsf{ff})))$$

The last two points state that property specifications have to change each time a model changes its level of abstraction. This need for change management of property specifications increases even more if a model has components expressed at different levels of abstraction.

We address all these disadvantages by using an order on the set of actions. Consider the action order in Fig. 1. It has a most abstract action $anyAction$, abstracts all finite or infinite action sets of the same kind with an action for that kind (e.g. put abstracts all $put(n)$), and introduces a new action out that is a common abstraction of the already abstract output actions get and $read$. For this action order we can rewrite (1) in the ordinary μ-calculus as

$$\nu X.([anyAction]X \wedge \mu Y.(\langle out\rangle Y \vee [out]\mathsf{ff})) \tag{2}$$

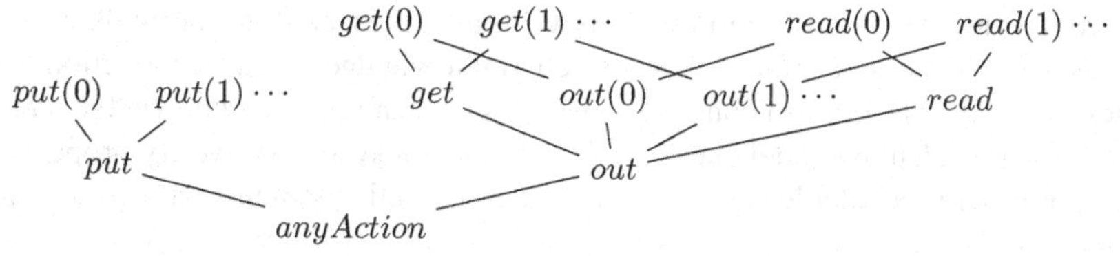

Fig. 1. An infinite partial order of actions, depicted in a Hasse diagram. Action abstraction (resp. specialization) is modeled by a decrease (resp. increase) in the order .

With a compact and abstract property such as (2) at hand, we now want to be able to verify it for models that may express these actions at more concrete levels of abstraction, without having to change the formula in (2). Moreover, we want such verification to be sound for refinements of the model we check, even though the respective models and their actions may be at different levels of abstraction. In particular more concrete models may introduce new actions that are common specializations of actions. For example, *put* and *out* of Fig. 1 may obtain a common specialization *swap* that replaces the top of the stack with another item but also outputs the value of the item at the top of the stack as it was prior to that swap. This use of common specializations is familiar from multiple inheritance if we dare to think for a moment of actions as objects.

The ability to specify abstract properties that capture potentially evolving action structure then fits well with model-centric software development where models may predate executable code, and so we can validate models with the same abstract property without knowing the actual action structure of the source code.

In developing this approach, we employ two orthogonal ways of model refinement – which can be applied in any order in a refinement process:

- the extension of ordered actions sets, similar in spirit to the introduction of (more) multiple inheritance; and
- a co-inductive refinement, the extended bisimulation of Thomsen in [23] for transition systems with ordered action sets.

Our contributions. In this paper we make the following contributions:

1. Develop a satisfaction relation for action-ordered transition systems and formulas of the μ-calculus. We show that this satisfaction relation is sound with respect to Thomsen's refinement of action-ordered transition systems.
2. Show that any sensible satisfaction relation is unsound for the unconstrained extension of pairs of actions with new common specialized actions.
3. Extend partial orders of actions with a *consistency* predicate, stating which pairs of actions may obtain common specialized action, and adapt our satisfaction to ensure its soundness for new common specializations of consistent pairs of actions.
4. Give a fairly efficient reduction of this satisfaction relation to the standard one over transition systems with unordered actions and formulas of the ordinary μ-calculus, in which actions are also interpreted without any appeal to an order.

The combination of the first and third contribution above guarantees that, once a property has been verified for a model, its validity is preserved if that model then undergoes a sequence of changes, where each single change extends the action set or refines the model. The fourth contribution means we can reuse the knowledge and tool support for $\mu-$calculus model checking over transition systems to verify properties of the action-ordered μ-calculus over action-ordered transition systems with consistency.

Outline. In Section 2 we show that extensions of ordered action sets with new action specializations poses a problem for sound model checking of abstract models. In Section 3 we present our models, their refinement, and consistent extensions of ordered action sets. A satisfaction relation for the μ-calculus over transition systems that have partial orders with consistency as action sets is motivated, defined, and proved to be sound in Section 4. A reduction of that satisfaction relation to classical μ-calculus model checking is given in Section 5. Related work is discussed in Section 6 and we conclude in Section 7.

2 Naive Extension of Ordered Action Sets is Unsound

The stack-like data structure discussed in the introduction may be modeled with more abstract labels as a state machine in Fig. 2. Transitions are triples of synchronization event, guard, and side effects. For example, in states on the right hand side in Fig. 2 transition $put(m)$ [tt] $i := i + 1$ specifies that any synchronization with a $put(m)$ action will increment the counter of the stack size as a side effect since the guard is true.

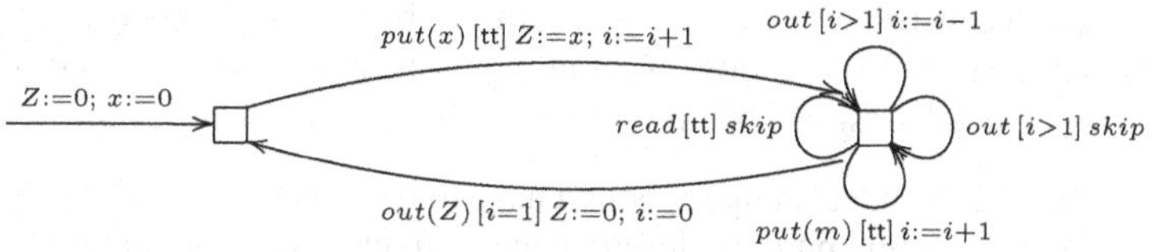

Fig. 2. Abstract model for the implementation of a stack-like data structure. Variable $i \in \mathbb{N}$ counts the stack size, and variable $Z \in \mathbb{N}$ records the value found at the bottom of the stack. The values of output actions *read* and *out* are unspecified. In particular, in an implementation *read* could return the sum of all values stored in such a non-standard stack .

Example 1. 1. For the action order given in Fig. 3, the abstract model from Figure 2 is expected to satisfy $\langle put \rangle [out(0)]$ff, stating that it is possible to input a value such that 0 cannot be output immediately thereafter. We expect this since $out(0)$ has no further specialization in its action set, the state on the right state side with $i = 1$ and $Z = 1$ is reached after the $put(1)$-action, and there is no transition from that state that can be specialized to $out(0)$.
2. But the same abstract model does not satisfy $\langle put \rangle [out(0)]$ff for the order given in Fig. 1, since in a left hand state with $i = 1$ and any Z there is a transition with label *read* that can be specialized to an action $read(0)$ that also specializes $out(0)$.

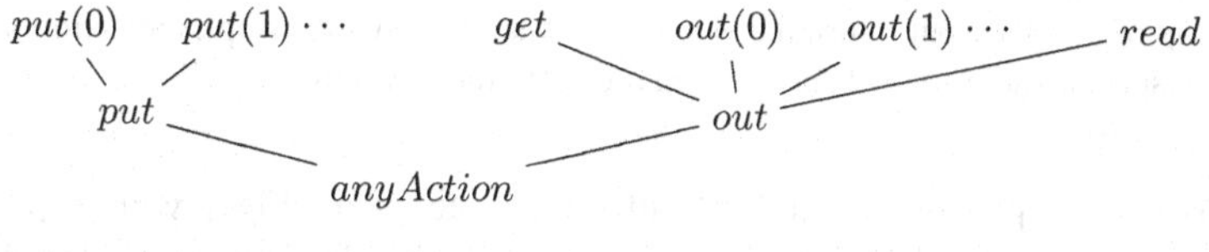

Fig. 3. Possible partial order of the set of abstract actions for the system in Fig. 2

Since the partial order in Fig. 1 is intuitively an extension of the one in Fig. 3, Example 1 suggests that soundness of satisfaction is not preserved if two actions can always obtain a common specialized action. To remedy this, we need to constrain such extensions. If we ban the introduction of new upper bounds for pairs of actions in extensions, this is simply too restrictive for modeling, validation, and code development. Yet, Example 1 mandates constraints on the introduction of new common upper bounds.

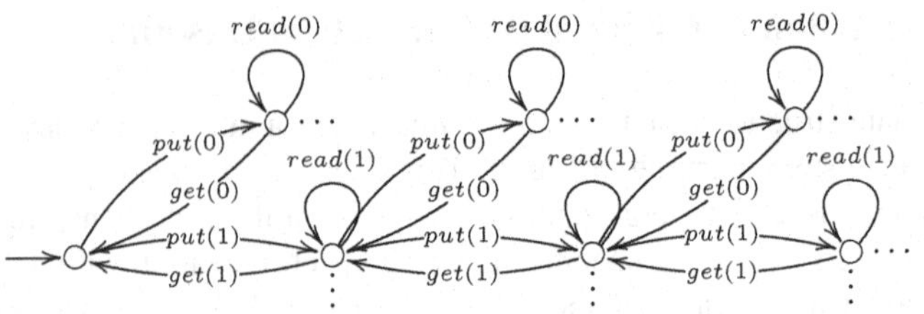

Fig. 4. A transition system realizing a full implementation of the abstract model in Fig. 2

We suggest a consistency predicate – determined by the modeler – as a flexible policy for introducing specialized actions, saying which pairs of actions a and a' can have common specialized versions. Natural requirements for such a policy are:

- pairs that already have an upper bound have to be consistent, and
- consistency of action pairs is closed under abstraction of either action.

The most restrictive change policy, for a given partial order, is to stipulate that pairs are consistent iff they have an upper bound in that partial order. We use this policy for the partial orders in Fig. 1 and 3. The partial order with consistency, depicted in Fig. 5 employs a more liberal change policy. That partial order is extended by both partial orders in Fig. 1 and 3 and the term "extension" will be formalized in Definition 2.3. Satisfaction of properties now needs to take this consistency predicate into account.

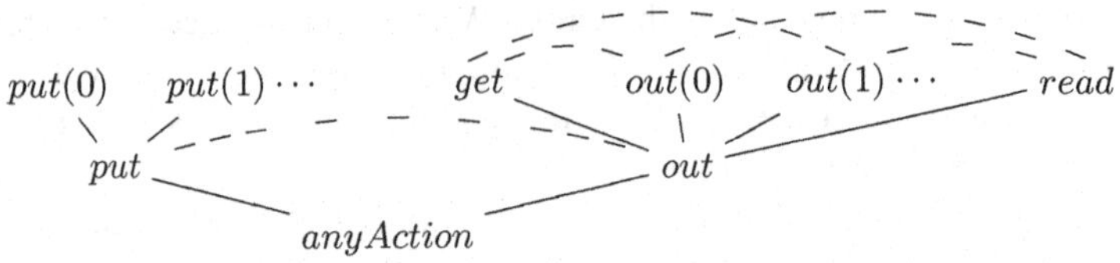

Fig. 5. A partial order of actions with a consistency predicate. Dashed bows connect pairs of actions a and a' that are consistent but have no common upper bound in this partial order already. For example, the consistency of *put* and *out* allows an extension with an action $swap$ (which may swap the top of the stack but return the value of the top prior to that swap), but action $swap$ then cannot be a specialization of *get* since *put* and *get* are inconsistent .

Example 2. We expect property (2) not to hold in the system from Fig. 2 with respect to the order with consistency of Fig. 5: On a state on the right hand side with $i = 1$ and any Z there is a transition with label $read$ but actions $read$ and $out(0)$ could have a common specialization, since $out(0)$ and $read$ are specified to be consistent. This expectation on a satisfaction relation will be fulfilled with our formal satisfaction relation developed in Section 4.

3 Ordered Actions, Transition Systems, and Refinement

Preliminaries. $|M|$ denotes the cardinality of a set M. For a ternary relation $\rightsquigarrow \subseteq M_1 \times \mathrm{Act} \times M_2$ we write $m_1 \overset{a}{\rightsquigarrow} m_2$ for $(m_1, a, m_2) \in \rightsquigarrow$. For $m_1 \in M_1$ the expression $m_1.\overset{a}{\rightsquigarrow}$ denotes $\{m_2 \in M_2 \mid m_1 \overset{a}{\rightsquigarrow} m_2\}$. Let $\sqsubseteq\ \subseteq M \times M$ be a partial order, i.e., a reflexive, antisymmetric, and transitive relation. The upper set of $X \subseteq M$ with respect to $\sqsubseteq$ is $\uparrow_{\sqsubseteq} X = \{m \in M \mid \exists m' \in X\colon m' \sqsubseteq m\}$ and the lower set of X with respect to $\sqsubseteq$ is $\downarrow_{\sqsubseteq} X = \{m \in M \mid \exists m' \in X\colon m \sqsubseteq m'\}$. If $X = \{m\}$, we write $\uparrow_{\sqsubseteq} m$ (resp. $\downarrow_{\sqsubseteq} m$) for $\uparrow_{\sqsubseteq} X$ (resp. $\downarrow_{\sqsubseteq} X$). For $x, y \in M$ we write $x \Uparrow_{\sqsubseteq} y$ to denote that x and y have an upper bound in M: $\uparrow_{\sqsubseteq} x \cap \uparrow_{\sqsubseteq} y \neq \{\}$. The inverse relation of a binary relation $R \subseteq M \times M$ is $R^{-1} = \{(m_1, m_2) \mid (m_2, m_1) \in R\}$. For $R_1 \subseteq M_1 \times M_2$ and $R_2 \subseteq M_2 \times M_3$ let $R_1 \circ R_2$ be the relational composition $\{(m_1, m_3) \mid \exists m_2\colon m_1 R_1 m_2, m_2 R_2 m_3\}$.

We formalize ordered action sets and their consistency predicate.

Definition 1. *A* partial order with consistency *is a partial order $(M, \sqsubseteq)$ with a symmetric consistency predicate $\frown\ \subseteq M \times M$ that contains $\Uparrow_{\sqsubseteq}$ and is preserved by downward closure: $\frown\ =\ \frown^{-1}$, $\Uparrow_{\sqsubseteq}\ \subseteq\ \frown$, and $\sqsubseteq \circ \frown\ \subseteq\ \frown$.*

A partial order with consistency is illustrated in Fig. 5, where elements of $\frown \setminus \Uparrow$ (consistent pairs that are not deemed consistent by $\Uparrow$ alone) are drawn as dashed bows.

Definition 2. *Let $((M_i, \sqsubseteq_i), \frown_i)$, $i = 1, 2$, be partial orders with consistency. Then*

1. $((M_1, \sqsubseteq_1), \frown_1)$ *is* finite *if M_1 is finite.*
2. $((M_1, \sqsubseteq_1), \frown_1)$ *is* discrete *if* $\sqsubseteq_1\ = \{(m, m) \mid m \in M_1\} =\ \frown_1$.
3. $((M_1, \sqsubseteq_1, \frown_1))$ *is an* extension *of $((M_2, \sqsubseteq_2), \frown_2)$ iff $M_2 \subseteq M_1$, $\sqsubseteq_2\ =\ \sqsubseteq_1 \cap (M_2 \times M_2)$, and $\frown_1 \cap (M_2 \times M_2) \subseteq\ \frown_2$.*

Example 3. The partial order with consistency of Fig. 1 is an extension of the one of Fig. 5 (where new actions are added and a consistency dependency is removed), but not of the one of Fig. 3.

We define transition systems as usual, but their set of actions may then be endowed with any partial order and consistency predicate.

Definition 3 (Transition system).

1. *A* transition system *T over a (possibly infinite) set of transition labels* Act *is a tuple $(S, s^{\mathrm{i}}, \longrightarrow)$ such that $(s \in) S$ is its set of states, $s^{\mathrm{i}} \in S$ its initial state, and $\longrightarrow\ \subseteq S \times \mathrm{Act} \times S$ its transition relation.*
2. *We call T* concrete *with respect to a partial order with consistency $((\mathrm{Act}, \sqsubseteq), \frown)$ if only maximal elements of* Act *with respect to $\sqsubseteq$ occur in $\longrightarrow$ and these occurring elements are consistent with their abstractions only, i.e., $(s, a, s') \in\ \longrightarrow$ implies $a \in \max(\mathrm{Act}, \sqsubseteq)$ and $\{a\}.\frown\ = \downarrow a$ (which equals $\{a\}.\Uparrow$ as a is maximal).*

Example 4. Fig. 6 depicts a transition system which is not concrete for the action order from Fig. 5. This is so since, e.g., the non-maximal action *out* occurs or since, e.g., action *read* (which is consistent with another maximal element) occurs. The transition system of Fig. 4 is concrete for the order from Fig. 1.

A transition system may be concrete for one action order but not for another one.

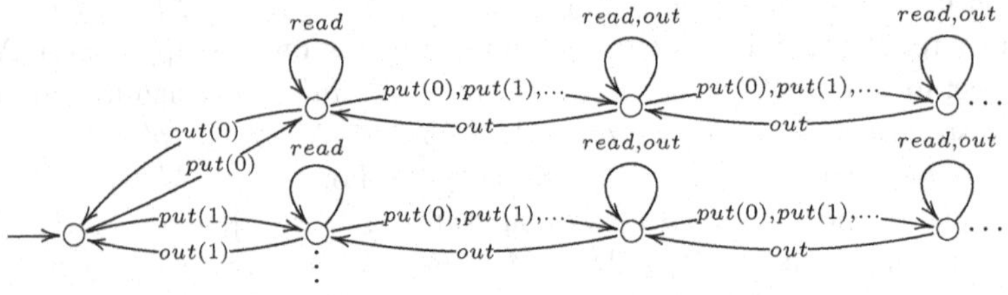

Fig. 6. The transition system corresponding to the state machine of Fig. 2

Table 1. Moves of $\sqsubseteq$-refinement game at configuration $(s_1, s_2) \in S_1 \times S_2$. The $\sqsubseteq$-refinement plays are sequences of configurations generated thus.

$\longrightarrow_1$: The Refuter chooses $a_1 \in$ Act and $s_1' \in s_1.\xrightarrow{a_1}_1$; Verifier responds with $a_2 \in \downarrow_{\sqsubseteq} a_1$ and with $s_2' \in s_2.\xrightarrow{a_2}_2$; the next configuration is (s_1', s_2').

$\longrightarrow_2$: Refuter chooses $a_2 \in$ Act and $s_2' \in s_2.\xrightarrow{a_2}_2$; Verifier responds with $a_1 \in \uparrow_{\sqsubseteq} a_2$ and with $s_1' \in s_1.\xrightarrow{a_1}_1$; the next configuration is (s_1', s_2').

Refinement for transition systems based on ordered actions were introduced by Thomsen under the name "extended bisimulation" in [23]: To show that s refines t, one keeps the "zig-zag" nature of the bisimulation game [16] but relaxes the burden on Verifier: if Refuter moves with $(s, a, s') \in \longrightarrow$, then Verifier only has to find an abstract version a' of a and then reply with $(t, a', t') \in \longrightarrow$. Dually, if Refuter moves with some $(t, a, t') \in \longrightarrow$, Verifier needs only reply with $(s, a'', s') \in \longrightarrow$ for an action a'' that is more specialized than a, where $a' = a$ and $a'' = a$ are legal replies.

This refinement notion does not appeal to any consistency predicates and assumes that models have the same partial order of actions. This won't constrain our approach.

Definition 4 (Refinement). *Let* (Act, $\sqsubseteq$) *be a partial order.*

- $\sqsubseteq$*-refinement plays between a Refuter and a Verifier, for transition systems* T_1 *and* T_2 *over* Act, *proceed as stated in Table 1. All infinite plays are* won by *Verifier.*
- T_1 $\sqsubseteq$-refines T_2, *written* $T_1 \sqsubseteq_{\text{ref}} T_2$, *iff Verifier has a strategy for the corresponding* $\sqsubseteq$*-refinement game between* T_1 *and* T_2 *such that Verifier wins all refinement plays started at* $(s_1^{\mathrm{i}}, s_2^{\mathrm{i}})$ *with her strategy.*

We note that $\sqsubseteq$-refinement corresponds to bisimulation between transition systems whenever $\sqsubseteq$ is discrete. The complexity of deciding refinement is bounded by the product of the respective sizes of the transition relation, assuming that there are at least as many transitions as states in models.

Example 5. The transition system in Fig. 4 is a refinement of the one in Fig. 6 with respect to the order from Fig. 1.

If the partial order (Act, $\sqsubseteq$) is an extension of (Act$'$, $\sqsubseteq'$), then $\sqsubseteq'_{\text{ref}}$ equals $\sqsubseteq_{\text{ref}}$ restricted to transition systems over Act$'$. This is vital for our approach since it implies that refinement checks won't render conflicting results if such checks are conducted for different extensions of the systems under check.

4 Satisfaction

We present our action-ordered μ-calculus and its semantics through tree automata and games, respectively. This presentational choice simplifies proofs and anticipates future extensions of this work to fairness constraints in refinements as seen, e.g., in [6,7].

Definition 5 (Tree automata). *An* alternating tree automaton A *with respect to a set of actions* Act *is a tuple* $(Q, q^{\mathrm{i}}, \delta, \Theta)$ *such that*

- $(q \in)Q$ *is a finite, nonempty set of states with initial element* $q^{\mathrm{i}} \in Q$,
- δ *is a transition relation mapping automaton states to one of the following forms, where* $q \in Q$, $\tilde{Q} \subseteq Q$, *and* $a \in \mathrm{Act}$*:* $\tilde{\vee}\tilde{Q} \mid \tilde{\wedge}\tilde{Q} \mid [a]q \mid \langle a \rangle q$ *and*
- $\Theta\colon Q \to \mathbb{N}$ *is an acceptance condition whose finite image has non-empty intersection with* $\{0, 1\}$. *An infinite sequence of automaton states is accepted iff the maximal acceptance number occurring infinitely often in that sequence is even.*

The formulas tt and ff are expressible as empty conjunctions and disjunctions in our setting (resp.) and will be used subsequently whenever convenient.

An intuitive semantics for the diamond ($\langle a \rangle$) and box ($[a]$) modalities, where labels are ordered by a partial order with consistency $((\mathrm{Act}, \sqsubseteq), \frown)$, is a possibly infinite disjunction and conjunction (resp.):

$$\langle a \rangle q' \equiv \bigvee\{\langle\!|\, a' \,|\!\rangle\, q' \mid a \sqsubseteq a'\} \qquad\qquad [a]q' \equiv \bigwedge\{[\![\, a' \,]\!]\, q \mid a \frown a'\} \tag{3}$$

where $\langle\!|\, a' \,|\!\rangle$ and $[\![\, a' \,]\!]$ are the diamond and box modalities defined in the classical, unordered, setting for a' (resp.). Quantification over actions is implicit within actions. Consequently, properties such as $\forall n \in \mathbb{N}\colon \mathsf{AG}(put(n) \to \mathsf{AF}get(n))$ have no finite representation in our approach to action abstraction.

These intuitive equations would indeed be formal equivalences if we were to extend the μ-calculus with infinite conjunctions and disjunctions. Note that $a \sqsubseteq a'$ implies $a' \frown a$ and so the box modality $[a]\phi$ will imply the diamond modality $\langle a \rangle \phi$ on transition systems that are serial for each action a. We emphasize that formulas $[a]\phi$ and $\neg\langle a \rangle \neg \phi$ are *not* equivalent for our satisfaction relation over action-ordered transition systems in general. However, for any partial order with consistency that contains a these formulas turn out to be equivalent if the transition system is *concrete*.

The constraint that the image of Θ contains 0 or 1 is a convenience so that the dual of the dual automaton of A is A again.

Definition 6 (Dual automaton). *The dual automaton of an automaton A, written* A^{d}, *is* $(Q, q^{\mathrm{i}}, \delta^{\mathrm{d}}, \Theta^{\mathrm{d}})$, *where*

$$\forall q\colon \Theta^{\mathrm{d}}(q) = \begin{cases} \Theta(q) + 1 & \textit{if } 0 \in \Theta(Q) \\ \Theta(q) - 1 & \textit{otherwise} \end{cases}$$

and δ^{d} *swaps* $\tilde{\wedge}$ *with* $\tilde{\vee}$, *and swaps* $\langle a \rangle$ *with* $[a]$.

An alternating tree automaton and its dual one are depicted in Fig. 7. Next we introduce some technical notation needed for defining our satisfaction relation. For any bounded

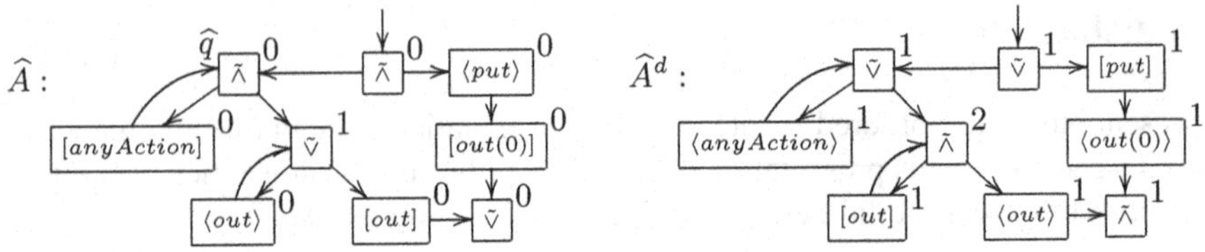

Fig. 7. Left: alternating tree automaton for the conjunction of the formula in (2) and $\langle put\rangle[out(0)]\mathsf{ff}$. Right: its dual automaton. Accepting values and some state names are depicted to the right (resp. left) of states.

Table 2. Moves of $(\sqsubseteq, \frown)$-satisfaction game at configuration $(s, q) \in S \times Q$, by a case analysis on $\delta(q)$. The $(\sqsubseteq, \frown)$-satisfaction plays are sequences of configurations generated thus .

$\tilde{\vee}\tilde{Q}$: Verifier picks a q' from $\tilde{Q}$; the next configuration is (s, q').
$\tilde{\wedge}\tilde{Q}$: Refuter picks a q' from $\tilde{Q}$; the next configuration is (s, q').
$\langle a\rangle q'$: Verifier picks $a' \in \uparrow_{\sqsubseteq} a$ and $s' \in s.\xrightarrow{a'}$; the next configuration is (s', q').
$[a]q'$: Refuter picks $a' \in \mathrm{Act}$ with $a' \frown a$ and picks $s' \in s.\xrightarrow{a'}$; the next configuration is (s', q').

sequence $\boldsymbol{n}$ of elements in $\mathbb{N}$ we write $\sup(\boldsymbol{n})$ for the largest m that occurs in $\boldsymbol{n}$ infinitely often. Let $\mathrm{map}(f, \Phi)$ be the sequence obtained from the sequence Φ by applying function f to all elements of Φ in situ. We write $\Phi[2]$ for the sequence obtained from Φ by projecting to the second coordinate of each configuration.

We can now define satisfaction formally.

Definition 7. *Let* $((\mathrm{Act}, \sqsubseteq), \frown)$ *be a partial order with consistency.*

- *Finite* $(\sqsubseteq, \frown)$*-satisfaction plays for transition system* T *over* Act *and alternating tree automaton* A *over* Act *have the rules as stated in Table 2. An infinite play* Φ *is a* win *for Verifier iff* $\sup(\mathrm{map}(\Theta, \Phi[2]))$ *is even; otherwise it is won by Refuter.*
- T $(\sqsubseteq, \frown)$-satisfies A*, written* $T \models_{\sqsubseteq}^{\frown} A$*, iff Verifier has a strategy for the corresponding satisfaction game between* T *and* A *such that Verifier wins all satisfaction plays started at* $(s^{\mathrm{i}}, q^{\mathrm{i}})$ *with her strategy.*

The decision problem of whether T $(\sqsubseteq, \frown)$-satisfies A is in UP$\cap$coUP [12], as the rules for the $(\sqsubseteq, \frown)$-satisfaction game specify a parity game. If $((\mathrm{Act}, \sqsubseteq), \frown)$ is discrete, $(\sqsubseteq, \frown)$-satisfaction corresponds to the classical μ-calculus satisfaction [13]. Note that at a state $\langle a\rangle q'$ Verifier has to pick a more or equally specialized action, whereas at a $[a]q'$ state Refuter may pick any action that is consistent to a with respect to $\frown$, i.e., Refuter may pick any action a' that may have a common specialization with a. This semantics of the box modality is reasonable and even necessary since such labels a' may be subsequently specialized to some a'' with $a \sqsubseteq a''$ and so need to be under the scope of $[a]q'$.

A transition system may satisfy neither an alternating tree automaton nor its dual:

Example 6. The transition system in Fig. 6 satisfies the automaton $\widehat{A}_{\widehat{q}}$, which is $\widehat{A}$ but with initial state $\widehat{q}$. But it does not satisfies the automata $\widehat{A}$ from Fig. 7 nor its dual for the order of Fig. 5. For the disjunct $\langle put \rangle [out(0)]$ff we saw in Section 2 that this is false. The disjunct $[put]\langle out(0)\rangle$tt is not satisfied since, after $put(1)$ no out(0) is guaranteed, the transition labeled with $read$ can be specialized to $read(0)$ only.

Satisfaction checks are inherently three-valued. A fourth truth value for "inconsistency", as found in Belnap's four-valued bilattice [2], is not required.

Proposition 1. *For any transition system T and alternating tree automata A over the partial order with consistency $((\mathrm{Act}, \sqsubseteq), \frown)$ as actions, T cannot $(\sqsubseteq, \frown)$-satisfy A as well as its dual: never do $T \models^{\frown}_{\sqsubseteq} A$ and $T \models^{\frown}_{\sqsubseteq} A^{\mathrm{d}}$ hold at the same time.*

We prove that order extensions provide sound extensions of satisfaction and that our notion of satisfaction is closed under all ordered refinements. Both are essential meta-properties for our modeling and validation framework for systems at varying abstraction levels. In particular, we secure soundness for any finite sequence of refinement steps where each refinement step extends the action order or refines the transition system.

Theorem 1. *1. If T_1, T_2 are transition systems over* Act*, and A an automaton over* Act *such that T_1 $(\sqsubseteq, \frown)$-refines T_2, and T_2 $(\sqsubseteq, \frown)$-satisfies A, then transition system T_1 $(\sqsubseteq, \frown)$-satisfies A.*

2. Let $((\mathrm{Act}, \sqsubseteq), \frown)$ be an extension of $((\mathrm{Act}', \sqsubseteq'), \frown')$. Then
   (a) $\models^{\frown'}_{\sqsubseteq'}$ implies (i.e. is contained in) $\models^{\frown}_{\sqsubseteq}$ for all transition systems over Act'.
   (b) if T_1 is a transition system over Act*, T_2 a transition system over Act', and A an automaton over Act' such that T_1 $\sqsubseteq$-refines T_2 and T_2 $(\sqsubseteq', \frown')$-satisfies A, then T_1 $(\sqsubseteq, \frown)$-satisfies A.*

We next illustrate this soundness of order extensions and model refinement.

Example 7. Let $((\mathrm{Act}, \sqsubseteq), \frown)$ be the partial order with (most restrictive) consistency from Fig. 1. Let $((\mathrm{Act}', \sqsubseteq'), \frown')$ be the partial order with consistency from Fig. 5. The former is an extension of the latter as seen in Example 3. Let T_1 be the transition system over Act given in Fig. 4. Let T_2 be the transition system over Act', and therefore also over Act, given in Figure 6. Let A be the automaton on the left in Fig. 7, except that the initial state is $\widehat{q}$. Then T_1 $\sqsubseteq$-refines T_2 by Example 5. Also, T_2 $(\sqsubseteq', \frown')$-satisfies A by Example 6. So by Theorem 1(2) we know that T_1 $(\sqsubseteq, \frown)$-satisfies A.

The usage of a consistency predicate, operative in Theorem 1(2), is not only sufficient but also necessary as already illustrated in Section 2.

5 Reduction

In this section we show that our satisfaction relation for ordered actions reduces to the usual one for transition systems and the μ-calculus. This enables the reuse of existing theory, algorithms, and tool support. Let T be a transitions system and A an automata over the same partial order with consistency $((\mathrm{Act}, \sqsubseteq), \frown)$. The reduction of their satisfaction check will be done in several stages, each illustrated with the transition system from Fig. 6, the automata $\widehat{A}$ from Fig. 7, and the action order with consistency of Fig. 5.

Restriction to relevant actions. This is an optimization and does not affect the correctness of the reduction. We therefore defer its description to a full version of this paper.

Derived order. Let Act_A be the set of actions occurring in A. We built a finite quotient of $((\mathrm{Act}, \sqsubseteq), \frown)$: each $a \in \mathrm{Act}$ determines an equivalence class that identifies actions with a if they behave in the same manner with respect to the ordering and consistency for elements of Act_A. Formally, we define an equivalence relation $\equiv\ \subseteq \mathrm{Act} \times \mathrm{Act}$ by

$$a_1 \equiv a_2 \quad \text{iff} \quad \forall a \in \mathrm{Act}_A \colon \forall R \in \{\sqsubseteq, \sqsubseteq^{-1}, \frown\} \colon a_1 R a \Leftrightarrow a_2 R a \tag{4}$$

and define the quotient order with consistency $((\mathrm{Act}', \sqsubseteq'), \frown')$ of $((\mathrm{Act}, \sqsubseteq), \frown)$ by

$$\begin{aligned} \mathrm{Act}' &= \{[a]_\equiv \mid a \in \mathrm{Act}\} \text{ with } [a]_\equiv = \{a' \in \mathrm{Act} \mid a \equiv a'\} \\ \Lambda_1 &\sqsubseteq' \Lambda_2 \text{ iff } \forall a_2 \in \Lambda_2 \colon \exists a_1 \in \Lambda_1 \colon a_1 \sqsubseteq a_2 \\ \Lambda_1 &\frown' \Lambda_2 \text{ iff } \exists a_1 \in \Lambda_1 \colon \exists a_2 \in \Lambda_2 \colon a_1 \frown a_2 \end{aligned}$$

The derived order of our running example is illustrated in Fig. 8.

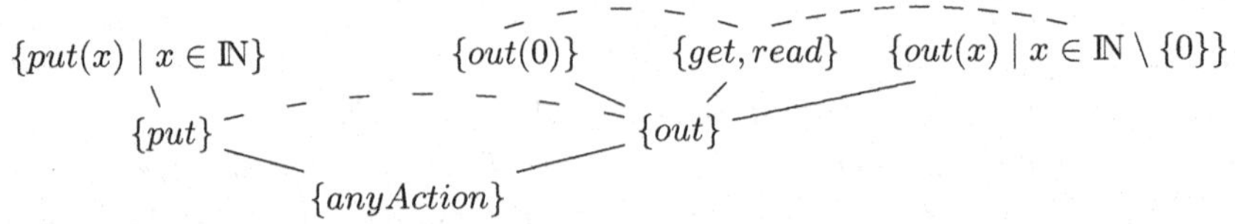

Fig. 8. The derived order of the one of Fig. 5 with respect to the automata $\widehat{A}$ from Fig. 7

Derived transition system. Next, transition system T is transformed such that it has only elements from the action set Act' of the derived order: replace any transition (s, a, s') with $(s, [a]_\equiv, s')$. This transformation won't lose any precision. The derived transition system of our running example is illustrated in Fig. 9.

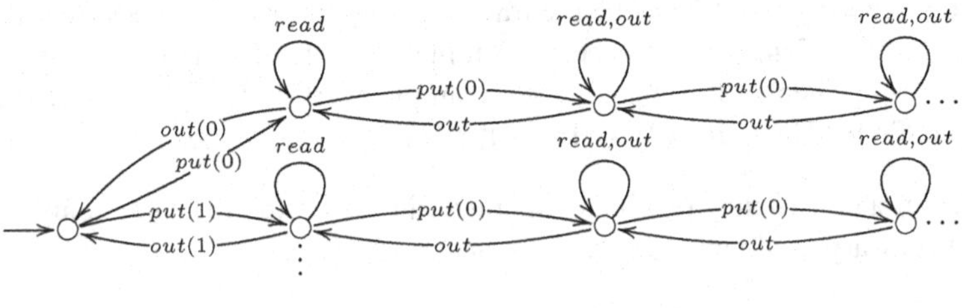

Fig. 9. The derived transition system T' of the one of Fig. 6 with respect to Act', where a set of representatives of the partition is $\{anyAction, put, put(0), out, out(0), read, out(1)\}$

To state the correctness of this reduction step, we have to rename actions in the automata A so that they are interpretable with respect to T': let A' be obtained from A be replacing each action a occurring in A with $[a]_\equiv$, which is $\{a\}$. Then we have

$$T' \models^{\frown'}_{\sqsubseteq'} A' \iff T \models^{\frown}_{\sqsubseteq} A \tag{5}$$

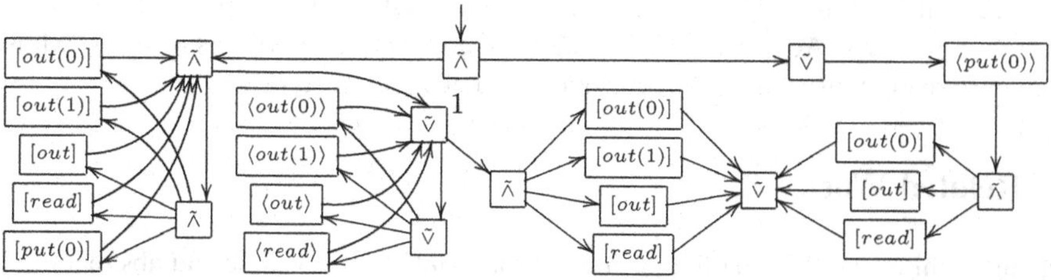

Fig. 10. The discretization of the automata $\widehat{A}$ from Fig. 7 with respect to the transition system of Fig. 9 and the order of Fig. 8. All acceptance values 0 are omitted.

Derived automaton. The model check $T' \models_{\widehat{\sqsubseteq}'} A'$ is now over a *finite* partial order with consistency. Guided by (3) we exploit this finiteness to convert A' into a discrete automaton A'' such that the classical model check $T' \models A''$ captures the ordered model check $T' \models_{\widehat{\sqsubseteq}'} A'$. In doing so, we optimize this discretization of A' by slicing it with respect to the subset $\mathrm{Act}_{T'}$ of Act' of those actions that occur in T'. This is done by letting any quantifier automata state $\langle \Lambda \rangle q$ (resp. $[\Lambda]q$) become a $\tilde{\vee}$-state (resp. $\tilde{\wedge}$-state) that then points to newly added states $(\Lambda', q, \Diamond)$ (resp. $(\Lambda', q, \Box)$), where Λ' ranges over all states from $\mathrm{Act}_{T'}$ that are $\sqsubseteq'$-above (resp. $\frown'$-consistent with) Λ. Such newly added states $(\Lambda', q, \Diamond)$ (resp. $(\Lambda', q, \Box)$) in turn point to q via $\langle \Lambda' \rangle$ (resp. via $[\Lambda']$). Acceptance values remain unaffected by this optimization. New states get acceptance value 0.

Formally, the $\mathrm{Act}_{T'}$*-discretization* of A' with respect to $((\mathrm{Act}', \sqsubseteq'), \frown')$ is the alternating tree automaton $A'' = (Q' \cup Q^{dis}, q^{\mathrm{i}'}, \delta'', \Theta'')$ where

- $Q^{dis} = \{(\Lambda', q, \Diamond) \mid \Lambda' \in \mathrm{Act}_{T'} \;\&\; \exists \Lambda \in {\downarrow_{\sqsubseteq'}} \Lambda', \tilde{q} \in Q' \colon \delta'(\tilde{q}) = \langle \Lambda \rangle q\} \cup \{(\Lambda', q, \Box) \mid \Lambda' \in \mathrm{Act}_{T'} \;\&\; \exists \Lambda \in \mathrm{Act}', \tilde{q} \in Q' \colon \Lambda \frown' \Lambda' \;\&\; \delta'(\tilde{q}) = [\Lambda]q\}$
- $\delta''(\tilde{q}) = \begin{cases} \tilde{\bigvee}\{(\Lambda', q, \Diamond) \mid \Lambda' \in \mathrm{Act}_{T'} \cap {\uparrow_{\sqsubseteq'}} \Lambda\} & \text{if } \tilde{q} \in Q' \;\&\; \delta'(\tilde{q}) = \langle \Lambda \rangle q \\ \tilde{\bigwedge}\{(\Lambda', q, \Box) \mid \Lambda' \in \mathrm{Act}_{T'} \;\&\; \Lambda \frown' \Lambda'\} & \text{if } \tilde{q} \in Q' \;\&\; \delta'(\tilde{q}) = [\Lambda]q \\ \langle \Lambda' \rangle q & \text{if } \tilde{q} = (\Lambda', q, \Diamond) \in Q^{dis} \\ [\Lambda']q & \text{if } \tilde{q} = (\Lambda', q, \Box) \in Q^{dis} \\ \delta'(\tilde{q}) & \text{otherwise} \end{cases}$
- $\Theta''(\tilde{q}) = \begin{cases} \Theta'(\tilde{q}) & \text{if } \tilde{q} \in Q' \\ 0 & \text{otherwise} \end{cases}$

The discretization automata of our running example is illustrated in Fig. 10.

Theorem 2. *For the reduction described in this section we have*

$$T' \models A'' \iff T' \models_{\widehat{\sqsubseteq}'} A' \iff T \models_{\widehat{\sqsubseteq}} A \tag{6}$$

where $\models$ denotes the ordinary satisfaction relation between transition systems and alternating tree automata [24]. Thus, model checking property A on T with respect to the partial order with consistency $((\mathrm{Act}, \sqsubseteq), \frown)$ reduces to classical model checking of property A'' on transition system T'.

The complexity of this reduction is as follows: the size of the derived order is $|\mathrm{Act}'| \leq \min\{4^{|\mathrm{Act}_A|} + |\mathrm{Act}_A|, |\mathrm{Act}|\}$. The size of the transition system does not increase.

The size of the automaton is $O(\max\{m_1, m_2\} \cdot |Q|)$ where m_1 is the size of the largest filter $\uparrow_{\sqsubseteq'} a$ with $a \in \mathrm{Act}_{T'}$, and m_2 the size of the largest set of actions in $\mathrm{Act}_{T'}$ whose elements are all consistent to the same singleton element in $\mathrm{Act}_{T'}$.

6 Related Work

Having a finite and compact (e.g. symbolic) description of concrete and abstract models enables automated abstraction and refinement methods (e.g. predicate abstraction). If our transition systems are represented in such form, e.g. in a kind of state machine, we would like to express the derived transition system defined in Section 5 in the same formalism. For state machines this can be achieved by extending their modeling language with an operator for persistent choice [8].

In our treatment of consistency in action sets pairs with upper bounds *must* be consistent, and pairs that are in the consistency predicate *may* be consistent. This is similar to the interpretation of may- and must-transitions in modal transition systems [17]. It is different to that interpretation, though, it that our box and diamond modalities are not always duals whereas this is the case for modal transition systems. So our setting is similar to that of intuitionistic modal logic [22] where, additionally, propositional logic operators cannot be interdefined.

Lattice automata [14] map propositions and transitions to elements of a lattice, and lattice elements are derived for computation paths through the algebraic operations on the lattice. In our approach, elements of a partial order are annotated with subformulas and no algebraic or lattice structure of elements is present or used. Our consistency predicate ensures that we reason about an entire set of partial orders in a compact and incremental fashion. Our approach is different to that of multi-valued model checking [4] for essentially the same reasons. Latticed simulation [15] can be considered as the simulation version of the refinement [23], presented here. The reduction of multi-valued model checking to the ordinary one [3] exploits the representation theorem for finite distributive lattices, structures we do not have in our approach.

The order on actions sets defined in this paper and our talk of "abstracting" and "specializing" actions suggests an alternative presentation of such orders through the use of abstract interpretation [5]. For any action order, one can obtain a Galois connection between the set of bounded lower sets of that action order and the powerset of maximal actions in that action order. The details of that construction are given in [11], but in a completely different setting.

Let us dare to equate actions with objects and action orders with the transitive subtype relationship between classes in an object-oriented language with inheritance, interfaces and abstract classes. Then common lower bounds of actions are similar to interfaces, and common upper bounds of actions are similar to multiple inheritance. These similarities may be helpful in understanding our approach.

The abstraction of infinitely many actions $a(n)$ to a single abstract action a may suggest that our work has connections to parameterized model checking [25] and data independence techniques [19]. In parameterized systems, parameters represent size instances of finite-state modules (e.g. the number of layers in a bus architecture). Invisible auxiliary assertions and counting abstractions are two methods for addressing the undecidability of model checking that occurs for most of such systems. In our approach actions such as put are like local parameters but they can't function as global ones since their disjunctive interpretation cannot be moved to the front of formulas that contain recursion. As for data independence, this usually requires a polymorphic treatment of data variables whereas actions such as put are evaluated over models that may specialize this action and thereby expose implementation details for that data type.

We note that (weak) bisimulation [21,20] is not a suitable refinement notion for ordered-labeled models, since abstract labels cannot be refined into concrete ones.

Our approach is not connected to action refinement [9,1,10]. In the latter an action is being replaced by a unique process (possibly another action name) whereas, in our setting, an action can be replaced by any number of concrete actions that are not yet specified and where such replacements may differ from instance to instance.

Finally, our approach can be extended or adapted to other abstract models of systems, e.g. to the aforementioned modal transition systems and disjunctive modal transition systems [18]. Such extensions are routine matters and so not discussed here.

7 Conclusion

We considered transition systems as models of implementations and μ-calculus formulas as validation properties of such models (and so of their implementations). We then sought notions of model refinement and a satisfaction relation between models and properties that can, at the same time, accommodate abstraction and the incremental specialization of actions in models. We discovered the extended bisimulation in [23] as a suitable candidate for refinement of models. We then saw that a naive satisfaction relation cannot be sound for extending ordered action sets with novel specialized actions. This led us to endow ordered action sets with a robust consistency predicate that provides sufficient constraints to such extensions so that a satisfaction relation that takes action orders into account is indeed sound for refinement of models *and* for extension of action orders. This consistency notion is flexible enough to be potentially useful for model-driven development and validation. Finally, we demonstrated that this ordered satisfaction problem can be, fairly efficiently, reduced to a standard model checking problem for the μ-calculus and so to the use of standard tools.

Acknowledgments. We thank the anonymous referees and Nir Piterman for their comments which helped with improving the presentation of this paper.

References

1. Aceto, L.: Action refinement in process algebras. Cambridge University Press, Cambridge (1992)
2. Belnap, N.D.: A useful four-valued logic. In: Dunn, J.M., Epstein, G. (eds.) Modern Uses of Multiple-Valued Logic, pp. 8–37. D. Reidel, Dordrecht (1977)
3. Bruns, G., Godefroid, P.: Generalized Model Checking: Reasoning about Partial State Spaces. In: Palamidessi, C. (ed.) CONCUR 2000. LNCS, vol. 1877, Springer, Heidelberg (2000)

4. Chechik, M., et al.: Multi-Valued Symbolic Model-Checking. ACM Transactions on Software Engineering and Methodology 12, 1–38 (2003)
5. Cousot, P., Cousot, R.: Abstract interpretation: a unified lattice model for static analysis of programs by construction or approximation of fixpoints. In: Proc.of POPL 1977, pp. 238–252. ACM Press, New York (1977)
6. Dams, D., Namjoshi, K.S.: The existence of finite abstractions for branching time model checking. In: Proc.of LICS 2004, pp. 335–344. IEEE Computer Society Press, Los Alamitos (2004)
7. Fecher, H., Huth, M.: Ranked Predicate Abstraction for Branching Time: Complete, Incremental, and Precise. In: Graf, S., Zhang, W. (eds.) ATVA 2006. LNCS, vol. 4218, pp. 322–336. Springer, Heidelberg (2006)
8. Fecher, H., et al.: Refinement sensitive formal semantics of state machines with persistent choice. In: Proc. of AVoCS 2007, ENCTS (to appear)
9. Glabbeek, R.v., Goltz, U.: Refinement of actions and equivalence notions for concurrent systems. Acta Informatica 37, 229–327 (2001)
10. Gorrieri, R., Rensink, A.: Action refinement. In: Bergstra, J.A., Ponse, A., Smolka, S.A. (eds.) Handbook of Process Algebra, pp. 1047–1147. North-Holland, Amsterdam (2001)
11. Huth, M.: Labelled transition systems as a Stone space. Logical Methods in Computer Science 1(1), 1–28 (2005)
12. Jurdzinski, M.: Deciding the winner in parity games is in UP $\cap$ co-UP. Inf. Process. Lett. 68(3), 119–124 (1998)
13. Kozen, D.: Results on the propositional μ-calculus. Theor. Comput. Sci. 27, 333–354 (1983)
14. Kupferman, O., Lustig, Y.: Lattice Automata. In: Cook, B., Podelski, A. (eds.) VMCAI 2007. LNCS, vol. 4349, pp. 199–213. Springer, Heidelberg (2007)
15. Kupferman, O., Lustig, Y.: Latticed Simulation Relations and Games. In: Namjoshi, K.S., et al. (eds.) ATVA 2007. LNCS, vol. 4762, pp. 316–330. Springer, Heidelberg (2007)
16. Lange, M., Stirling, C.: Model checking games for branching time logics. J. Log. Comput. 12(4), 623–639 (2002)
17. Larsen, K.G., Thomsen, B.: A modal process logic. In: In Proc.of *LICS 1988*, pp. 203–210. IEEE Computer Society Press, Los Alamitos (1988)
18. Larsen, K.G., Xinxin, L.: Equation solving using modal transition systems. In: Proc. of LICS 1990, pp. 108–117. IEEE Computer Society Press, Los Alamitos (1990)
19. Lazic, R.: A semantic study of Data Independence with Applications to Model Checking, DPhil thesis, Oxford University Computing Laboratory (April 1999)
20. Milner, R.: A Calculus of Communication Systems. LNCS, vol. 92. Springer, Heidelberg (1980)
21. Park, D.: Concurrency and automata on infinite sequences. In: Deussen, P. (ed.) GI-TCS 1981. LNCS, vol. 104, pp. 167–183. Springer, Heidelberg (1981)
22. Plotkin, G., Stirling, C.: A framework for intuitionistic modal logics. In: Theoretical aspects of reasoning about knowledge, Monterey (1986)
23. Thomsen, B.: An extended bisimulation induced by a preorder on actions. Master's thesis, Aalborg University Centre (1987)
24. Wilke, Th.: Alternating tree automata, parity games, and modal μ-calculus. Bull. Soc. Math. Belg. 8, 359–391 (2001)
25. Zuck, L., Pnueli, A.: Model Checking and Abstraction to the Aid of Parameterized Systems (a survey). Computer Languages, Systems, and Structures 30(3-4), 139–169 (2004)

On Bridging Simulation and Formal Verification

Eugene Goldberg

Cadence Research Labs, USA, 2150 Shattuck Ave., 10th floor, Berkeley, California, 94704, Tel.: (510)-647-2825, Fax: (510)-647-2801
egold@cadence.com

Abstract. Simulation and formal verification are two complementary techniques for checking the correctness of hardware and software designs. Formal verification proves that a design property holds for all points of the search space while simulation checks this property by probing the search space at a subset of points. A known fact is that simulation works surprisingly well taking into account the negligible part of the search space covered by test points. We explore this phenomenon by the example of the satisfiability problem (SAT). We believe that the success of simulation can be understood if one interprets a set of test points not as a sample of the search space, but as an "encryption" of a formal proof. We introduce the notion of a *sufficient* test set of a CNF formula as a test set encrypting a formal proof that this formula is unsatisfiable. We show how sufficient test sets can be built. We discuss applications of *tight* sufficient test sets for testing technological faults (manufacturing testing) and design changes (functional verification) and give some experimental results.

1 Introduction

Development of new methods of hardware and software verification is in growing demand due to ever-increasing design complexity. Simulation and formal verification are two complementary verification techniques. Given a design property ξ, formal verification proves that ξ holds for every point of the search space. Simulation verifies ξ by testing a small subset of the search space. The main drawback of formal verification is its unscalability while an obvious flaw of simulation is its inability to prove that ξ holds for every point of the search space. Nevertheless, the main bulk of verification is currently done by simulation: it is scalable and works surprisingly well even though the set of test points (further referred to as the **test set**) comprises a negligible part of the search space.

We study why simulation is so effective on the example of the satisfiability problem (SAT). In terms of SAT, formal verification is to prove that a CNF formula $F(x_1,.., x_n)$ is unsatisfiable at every point $\boldsymbol{p} \in \{0,1\}^n$. On the other hand, simulation is to give some guarantee that F is unsatisfiable by testing it at a (small) set of points from $\{0,1\}^n$. (Local search algorithms pioneered in [5,6] can be viewed as solving SAT by "simulation". While these algorithms target *satisfiable* formulas, in this paper, we are mostly interested in applying simulation to *unsatisfiable* formulas.) We believe that the success of simulation

F. Logozzo et al. (Eds.): VMCAI 2008, LNCS 4905, pp. 127–141, 2008.

can be explained if one interprets a test set not as a sample of the search space but as an *"encryption"* of a formal proof that the CNF formula under test is unsatisfiable.

We introduce procedure $Sat(T,F,L)$ that checks satisfiability of a CNF formula F using a test set T and a set L of lemma clauses (or just lemmas for short). Henceforth we will also refer to a set of lemma clauses L as a **proof.** $Sat(T,F,L)$ is not *a practical procedure* and is introduced just to formally define what it means that a test set T encrypts a proof L . Namely, ***T* encrypts *L*** if $Sat(T,F,L)$ proves F to be unsatisfiable.

The set of lemma clauses $L_1,\ldots,L_k$ is ordered and the last clause L_k is empty. The $Sat(T,F,L)$ procedure is based on the fact that a CNF formula is unsatisfiable iff it has a stable set of points (SSP) [4]. In this paper, we introduce an efficient procedure that, given a CNF formula F' and a set of points T, checks if T contains an SSP of F'. This procedure is used by $Sat(T,F,L)$ to prove that F implies L_i. This is done by checking if the set T contains an SSP for a CNF formula F' equivalent to $F \rightarrow L_i$. If $F \rightarrow L_i$ holds, clause L_i is added to F. Both L and T are crucial for $Sat(T,F,L)$. The set L specifies a "high-level structure" of the proof by indicating the set of lemmas to prove. On the other hand, the set T is necessary for proving the lemmas of L efficiently.

A test set T is called **sufficient** for a CNF formula F, if there is a set of lemma clauses L for which $Sat(T,F,L)$ proves unsatisfiability of F. The fewer lemmas a sufficient test set T needs for proving unsatisfiability of F by $Sat(T,F,L)$, the larger the size and the higher the quality of T is. If the set L of lemma clauses consists only of an empty clause, $Sat(T,F,L)$ succeeds in proving unsatisfiability of F only if T contains an SSP. So an SSP is a test set of the highest quality but it usually contains an exponential number of points [4]. In [3], we introduced the notion of a *point image* of resolution proof R that a CNF formula is unsatisfiable. We show in this paper that if the clauses of L are the resolvents of R, the procedure $Sat(T,F,L)$ succeeds if T is a point image of R. A point image of a resolution proof is a sufficient test set of lower quality but it contains dramatically fewer points than an SSP.

A sufficient test set may occupy a negligible part of the search space. (For example, a point image of a resolution proof is at most two times the size of the proof.) This fact sheds light on why simulation works so well even though it samples only a tiny portion of the search space. A cleverly selected set of tests (e.g. tests exercising various corner cases) may specify a set of points that encrypt a formal proof that the property in question holds (or a "significant part" of such a proof).

Simulation can be used for two kinds of problems. We will refer to the problems of the first kind as *property checking.* In the context of SAT, property checking by simulation is to prove the satisfiability of a CNF formula F by probing the value of F at a (small) set of points or to give some "guarantee" that F is unsatisfiable. The problems of the second kind are referred to as *property preservation.* In the context of SAT, property preservation is as follows. Suppose that F is an unsatisfiable formula and we need to find a (small) set of points T such that a satisfiable formula F' obtained by a (small) variation of F most likely evaluates to 1 for a point $\boldsymbol{p}$ of T. In other words, we want to find a set of points T that will most likely identify satisfiable variations of F. Assuming that F describes a design property, the variation of F may specify a design change (if we deal with a software model of the design) or a technological fault (if F describes a hardware implementation of the design).

Although the theory we develop can be applied to the problems of both kinds, the main focus of this paper is property preservation. (Some insights into how sufficient test sets can be used for property checking are given in [2].) The main idea is as follows. Let R be a proof that F is unsatisfiable. To build a test set that detects satisfiable variations of F we propose to extract tests from a tight sufficient test set T specified by R. Informally, a sufficient test set is **tight** if points of T falsify as few clauses of F as possible. (Since F is unsatisfiable, obviously a point of T has falsify at least one clause of F). "Regular" tests i.e. input assignments are extracted from the points of T. (If F describes a property of a circuit N, then a point $\boldsymbol{p}$ of T is a complete an assignment to the variables of N. By dropping all the assignments of $\boldsymbol{p}$ but the input assignments of N we obtain a regular test vector. In more detail, the relation between regular tests and points is described in Section 5). If R is a resolution proof, then tests are extracted from a tight point image of R.

As a practical application of our theory we study regular tests (i.e. input assignments) extracted from a tight point image T of a resolution proof that two copies of a circuit N are functionally equivalent. We show that such regular tests detect the testable stuck-at faults of N. This result explains why the stuck-at fault model is so successful. Besides, this result suggests that the success of this model may have nothing to do with the assumption made by many practitioners that the stuck-at fault model works so well because it correctly describes the "real" faults. Interestingly, tests extracted from T may detect the same stuck-at fault many times (i.e. for the same stuck-at fault different test vectors may be generated). At the same time, in [8] it was shown experimentally, that test sets where the same stuck-at fault was tested many times had the best performance in identifying faulty chips.

In the experimental part of this paper, we apply tests extracted from a resolution proof that two copies of a circuit are identical to detection of literal appearance faults (such faults are more subtle than stuck-at faults). Our results show that tests extracted from resolution proofs have much higher quality than random tests.

This paper is structured as follows. Section 2 describes a procedure for checking if a set of points contains an SSP of a CNF formula. In Section 3, we describe the procedure $Sat(T,F,L)$ and introduce the notion of a sufficient test set. Generation of tight sufficient test sets is described in Section 4. In Section 5, we discuss the specifics of testing formulas describing circuits. Section 6 describes application of sufficient test sets for testing design changes and manufacturing faults. We give some experimental results in Section 7 and conclude by Section 8.

2 Checking if Test Set Contains SSP

In this section, we give some basic definitions, recall the notion of a stable set of points (SSP) [4] and introduce a procedure that checks if a set of points contains a stable subset.

2.1 Basic Definitions

Let F be a CNF formula (i.e. conjunction of disjunctions of literals) over a set X of Boolean variables. The satisfiability problem (SAT) is to find a complete assignment $\boldsymbol{p}$ (called a **satisfying assignment**) to the variables of X such that $F(\boldsymbol{p}) = 1$ or to prove that such an assignment does not exist. If F has a satisfying assignment, F is called **satisfiable.** Otherwise, F is **unsatisfiable**. A disjunction of literals is further referred to as a **clause.** A complete assignment to variables of X will be also called a **point** of the Boolean space $\{0,1\}^{|X|}$. A point $\boldsymbol{p}$ **satisfies** clause C, if $C(\boldsymbol{p})$=1. If $C(\boldsymbol{p})$=0, $\boldsymbol{p}$ is said to **falsify** C. Denote by $Vars(C)$ and $Vars(F)$ the set of variables of C and F, respectively. We will call a complete assignment $\boldsymbol{p} \in \{0,1\}^{|X|}$ **a test** for F. We will call a set of points $T \subseteq \{0,1\}^{|X|}$ **a test set** for F.

2.2 Stable Set of Points

Let a point $\boldsymbol{p} \in \{0,1\}^{|X|}$ falsify a clause C of k literals. Denote by $Nbhd(\boldsymbol{p},C)$ the set of k points obtained from $\boldsymbol{p}$ by flipping the value of one of k variables of C. For example, let X=$\{x_1,.., x_5\}$ and $C = x_2 \vee x_3 \vee \overline{x_5}$ and $\boldsymbol{p}$=(x_1=0, x_2=0, x_3=0, x_4=1, x_5=1). (Note that $C(\boldsymbol{p})$=0.) Then $Nbhd(\boldsymbol{p},C)$ =$\{\boldsymbol{p}_1, \boldsymbol{p}_2, \boldsymbol{p}_3\}$ where $\boldsymbol{p}_1$ = (.., x_2=1,..), $\boldsymbol{p}_2$=(.., x_3=1,..), $\boldsymbol{p}_3$ = (..., x_5=0). (For each $\boldsymbol{p}_i$, the skipped assignments are the same as in $\boldsymbol{p}$.)

Let a CNF formula F over a set X of Boolean variables consist of clauses $C_1,\ldots,C_s$. Let $T = \{\boldsymbol{p}_1,\ldots,\boldsymbol{p}_m\}$ be a non-empty set of points from $\{0,1\}^{|X|}$ such that $F(\boldsymbol{p}_i)$=0, i=1,..,m. The set T is called a **stable set of points (SSP)** of F if for each $\boldsymbol{p}_i \in T$, there is a clause C_k of F such that $C_k(\boldsymbol{p}_i)$=0 and $Nbhd(\boldsymbol{p}_i,C_k) \subseteq T$. (In [4] we used a slightly different but equivalent definition of SSP.)

Proposition 1. *Let F=$\{C_1,..,C_s\}$ be a CNF formula over a set X of Boolean variables. Formula F is unsatisfiable iff there is a set T of points from $\{0,1\}^{|X|}$ such that T is an SSP of F.*

Proof is given in [4].

2.3 Checking if a Test Set Contains an SSP

Given a set of points T and a CNF formula F, checking if T is an SSP for F is very simple. One just needs to check if for every point $\boldsymbol{p}$ of T there is a clause C of F such that $Nbhd(\boldsymbol{p},C) \subseteq T$. If the check passes, then T is an SSP for F

and hence the latter is unsatisfiable. The complexity of this check is $|T|*|F|*|X|$ where X is the set of variables of F.

It is quite possible that a subset of T is an SSP of F while T itself is not. The procedure of **Figure 1** checks if there is a subset of T that is an SSP of F. For every point $\boldsymbol{p}$ of T it checks if there is a clause C of F such that $Nbhd(\boldsymbol{p},C) \subseteq T$ (the function *no_clause*($\boldsymbol{p}$,F,T)). If such a clause does not exist, $\boldsymbol{p}$ is removed from T and every point of T is checked again. (The reason for starting over again is as follows. Suppose that in the previous iterations a point $\boldsymbol{p}^*$ was not removed from T because for some clause C of F, $Nbhd(\boldsymbol{p}^*,C) \subseteq T$. If $\boldsymbol{p}$ was in $Nbhd(\boldsymbol{p}^*,C)$), then removing $\boldsymbol{p}$ from T would break the relation $Nbhd(\boldsymbol{p}^*,C) \subseteq T$.)

```
Stable_subset_check(T,F)
  {removed=true;
  while (removed)
    {removed=false;
    for (every point p ∈ T)
      if (no_clause(p,F,T))
        {T = T\ {p};
        removed=true;
        break;}}
  if (T ≠ ∅) return (stable)
  else return(unstable);}
```

Fig. 1. Checking if T contains an SSP

This repeats until no point is removed from T, which may happen only in two cases: a) T is empty (and so the original set T did not contain a stable subset); b) The remaining points of T form an SSP. The complexity of this procedure is $|T|^2*|F|*|X|$.

3 Procedure *Sat*(T,F,L) and Sufficient Test Sets

In this section, we describe a procedure *Sat*(T,F,L) that uses a test set T to prove that a CNF formula F is unsatisfiable. *Sat*(T,F,L) is *not a practical procedure.* We introduce it just to formally define what it means that T encrypts a proof L. We also introduce the notion of a sufficient test set and describe how sufficient test sets can be obtained.

3.1 *Sat*(T,F,L) Procedure

The pseudocode of the procedure *Sat*(T,F,L) is shown in **Figure 2**. Here L is a set of lemma clauses L_1,.., L_k where the clause L_k is empty. First, *Sat*(T,F,L) checks if a point $\boldsymbol{p}$ of T satisfies F. If such a point exists, *Sat*(T,F,L) reports that F is satisfiable. Then *Sat*(T,F,L) processes the clauses of L in the order they are numbered. For every lemma clause L_i of L, this procedure checks if F implies L_i, by calling the function *implies*(T,F,L_i). If it succeeds in proving this implication, L_i is *added* to F. To check if F implies L_i, the function *implies*(T,F,L_i) uses the procedure *Stable_subset_check* of **Figure 1** as follows.

```
Sat(T,F,L)
  {if (satisfy(T,F)) return(sat)
  for (i=1,..,k))
    {if (implies(T,F,L_i)==false)
      return(unknown)
    F = F ∪ {L_i} }}
  return(unsat);}
```

Fig. 2. Pseudocode of procedure *SAT* (T,F,L)

First, the subformula F_{L_i} is obtained from F by making the assignments setting all the literals of L_i to 0. Formula F implies L_i iff F_{L_i} is unsatisfiable. To check if F_{L_i} is unsatisfiable, the procedure *Stable_subset_check*(T_{L_i},F_{L_i}) is called by the function *implies*(T,F,L_i) where T_{L_i} is the subset of points of T falsifying L_i. This procedure checks if the set T_{L_i} contains a subset that is an SSP with respect to F_{L_i}. The complexity of *Sat*(T,F,L) is $|T|^2 * |F| * |X| * |L|$ where X is the set of variables of F and $|L|$ is the number of lemma clauses. (In [2], we give a version of *Sat*(T,F,L) that is linear in $|T|$ but needs more information than the procedure of **Figure 2**.)

3.2 Sufficient Test Sets

We will say that a test set T is **sufficient** for F, if there is a set L of lemma clauses such that *Sat*(T,F,L) succeeds in proving the unsatisfiability of F. That is, T is a sufficient test set for F, if it has enough points to show that F is unsatisfiable by proving a sequence of lemmas L.

In general, the fewer lemma clauses are in the set L, the larger test set T is necessary for *Sat*(T,F,L) to succeed. In particular, if L contains only an empty clause, then *Sat*(T,F,L) succeeds only if T contains an SSP. On the other hand, as we show below, if L consists of the resolvents of a resolution proof R that F is unsatisfiable, *Sat*(T, F, L) succeeds even if T is just a point image of R.

A resolution proof is an ordered set of resolution operations that proves unsatisfiability of a CNF formula F by deriving an empty clause [9]. **A resolution operation** is performed over two clauses C' and C'' such that a) they have opposite literals of some variable x_i and b) there is only one such variable for C' and C''. The result of the resolution operation is a clause C called the **resolvent** of C' and C''. The resolvent C consists of all the literals of C' and C'' but the literals of x_i. (C is said to be obtained by resolving C' and C'' in variable x_i.) For example, if $C'=x_2 \vee \overline{x_4} \vee x_{20}$ and $C''=x_4 \vee \overline{x_{31}}$, then by resolving them in variable x_4 we obtain the resolvent $C= x_2 \vee x_{20} \vee \overline{x_{31}}$.

The notion of a point image of a resolution proof R was introduced in [3]. A set of points T is called a **point image of *R*** if for any resolution operation of R over clauses C' and C'', there are points $\boldsymbol{p}'$,$\boldsymbol{p}'' \in T$ satisfying the following two conditions: a) $C'(\mathbf{p'})= C''(\mathbf{p''})=0$; b) $\boldsymbol{p}'$,$\boldsymbol{p}''$ are different only in the variable in which clauses C' and C'' are resolved. Such two points are called **a point image of the resolution operation** over C' and C''.

Now we show that if R is a resolution proof that F is unsatisfiable and T is a point image of R, then $Sat(T, F, L)$ returns *unsat* where L is the set of resolvents of R. Let C be a resolvent of R obtained by resolving C' and C''. Then C is in L. When the $Sat(T,F,L)$ procedure gets to proving that C is implied by the current formula F, clauses C' and C'' are in F. Let F_C be the formula obtained from F (by making the assignments setting the literals of C to 0) for checking if F implies C. In F_C, clauses C' and C'' turn into unit clauses x_i and $\overline{x_i}$ (where x_i is the variable in which C' and C'' are resolved). Then the points $\boldsymbol{p}',\boldsymbol{p}''$ form an SSP with respect to these unit clauses and hence with respect to F_C. So the procedure $Sat(T,F,L)$ succeeds in proving unsatisfiability of F. A point image is a weak sufficient test set, because it can be used only to prove very simple lemmas (that the resolvent of C' and C'' is implied by $C' \wedge C''$).

3.3 Generation of Sufficient Test Sets

Given a CNF formula F, one can build its sufficient test set as a point image T of a resolution proof R that F is unsatisfiable. Building T is very simple. For every pair of clauses C' and C'' whose resolvent is in R one just needs to find a point image of the resolution operation over C' and C''. The union of point images of all resolution operations forms a point image of R (and so a sufficient test set for F). The size of such a point image is twice the size of R at most.

As we mentioned above, a point image of a resolution proof R is a weak sufficient test set. However, one can always get a stronger test set by "rarefying" R. The idea is to remove some resolvents from R (preserving an empty clause) and use the remaining clauses as the set L of lemmas. Then for every clause L_i of L we build an SSP S_i for F_{L_i} thus proving that $F \rightarrow L_i$. (We assume that the lemma clauses L_1,.., L_{i-1} proved before L_i have been added to F.) A procedure for building an SSP is described in [4]. Since some resolvents of R are missing, now one may need more than two points to prove that $F \rightarrow L_i$. The set $T = S_1 \cup .. \cup S_k$ where $k = |L|$ forms a sufficient test set that is stronger than a point image of R (because T can prove more complex lemmas). If one removes from R all the resolvents but an empty clause, T turns into an SSP.

4 Tight Sufficient Test Sets

The fact that a test set T is sufficient for a CNF formula F means that T is complete in the sense that it encrypts a proof that F is unsatisfiable. However, this completeness alone does not make T a high-quality test set for a property preservation problem. Recall that we are interested in finding a test set such that, given an unsatisfiable formula F, it will most likely "detect" satisfiable variations of F. In other words, given a satisfiable formula F' obtained from F by a small change, we want T to contain a point $\boldsymbol{p}$ that satisfies F' and so detects this change. This can be done by making sufficient test sets tight. Informally, a sufficient test set T is **tight** if every point $\boldsymbol{p}$ of T falsifies as few clauses of the *original* formula F as possible. (Ideally, every point $\boldsymbol{p}$ of T should falsify only one original clause). The intuition here is that if $\boldsymbol{p}$ falsifies only clause C_i of F, then $\boldsymbol{p}$ may detect a variation of F that includes disappearance of C_i from F (or adding to C_i a literal satisfied by $\boldsymbol{p}$).

Let us consider building a tight point image T of a resolution proof R. Let C be the resolvent of C' and C''. When looking for two points $\boldsymbol{p}',\boldsymbol{p}''$ forming a point image of the resolution operation over clauses C' and C'' (and so forming an SSP of sub formula F_C) we have freedom in assigning variables of F that are not in C' and C''. To make the test set T tight, these assignments should be chosen to minimize the number of clauses falsified by $\boldsymbol{p}',\boldsymbol{p}''$. Note that since $\boldsymbol{p}',\boldsymbol{p}''$ are different only in one variable (in which C' and C'' are resolved), picking one point, say $\boldsymbol{p}'$, completely determines the point $\boldsymbol{p}''$. This poses the following problem. It is possible that no matter how well one picks the point $\boldsymbol{p}'$ to falsify only one clause of F, the corresponding point $\boldsymbol{p}''$ falsifies many clauses of F.

In [2], we describe a solution to the problem above. Namely we describe a version of the procedure *Sat*(T,F,L) that slightly "relaxes" the definition of a sufficient test set. (By changing procedure *Sat*(T,F,L), we essentially change the definition of proof encryption we use. Obviously, the same proof can be encrypted in many ways.) In this version, in points $\boldsymbol{p}',\boldsymbol{p}''$, only the parts consisting of the assignments of the variables of $Vars(C') \cup Vars(C'')$ have to be at Hamming distance 1 (i.e. one just needs to guarantee that both $\boldsymbol{p}',\boldsymbol{p}''$ falsify the resolvent of C' and C''). Assignments to the variables that are not in C' and C'' can be done *independently* in $\boldsymbol{p}',\boldsymbol{p}''$. (In [2], we also describe how to extract a tight sufficient test set from a "rarefied" resolution proof introduced in subsection 3.3, i.e. how to build tight sufficient tests sets that are *stronger* than those obtained from resolution proofs.)

5 Circuit Testing

So far we have studied the testing of *general* CNF formulas. In this section, we consider the subproblem of SAT called Circuit-SAT. In this subproblem, CNF formulas describe *combinational circuits*. In this section, we discuss some specifics of testing formulas of Circuit-SAT.

5.1 Circuit-SAT

Let N be a single-output combinational circuit. Let F_N be a CNF formula specifying N and obtained from it in a regular way. That is for every gate G_i,i=1,..,k of the circuit N, a CNF formula $F(G_i)$ specifying G_i is formed and $F_N = F(G_1) \wedge \ldots \wedge F(G_k)$. For example, if G_i is an AND gate implementing $v_i = v_m \wedge v_n$ (where v_i, v_m,v_n describe the output and inputs of G_i), $F(G_i)$ is equal to $(\overline{v_m} \vee \overline{v_n} \vee v_i) \wedge (v_m \vee \overline{v_i}) \wedge (v_n \vee \overline{v_i})$. Let variable z describe the output of N. Then the formula $F_N \wedge z$ (where z is just a single-literal clause) is satisfiable iff there is an assignment to input variables of N for which the latter evaluates to 1. We will refer to testing the satisfiability of $F_N \wedge z$ as **Circuit-SAT**.

5.2 Specifics of Testing Circuit-SAT Formulas

Let $N(Y,H,z)$ be a circuit where Y, H are the set of input and internal variables respectively. Let $F_N \wedge z$ be a CNF formula describing the instance of *Circuit-SAT* specified by $N(Y,H,z)$. Let $\boldsymbol{p}$ be a test as we defined it for SAT (i.e. a complete assignment to the variables of $Y \cup H \cup \{z\}$. We will denote by $inp(\boldsymbol{p})$ **the input part** of $\boldsymbol{p}$ that is the part consisting of the assignments of $\boldsymbol{p}$ to the variables of Y.

The main difference between the definition of a test as a complete assignment $\boldsymbol{p}$ that we used so far and the one used in circuit testing is that in circuit testing *the input part* of $\boldsymbol{p}$ is called a test. (We will refer to $inp(\boldsymbol{p})$ as a **circuit test**.) The reason for that is as follows. Let $N(Y,H,z)$ be a circuit and $F_N \wedge z$ be the CNF formula to be tested for satisfiability. A complete assignment $\boldsymbol{p}$ can be represented as $(\boldsymbol{y},\boldsymbol{h},z^*)$ where $\boldsymbol{y}$, $\boldsymbol{h}$ are complete assignments to Y, H respectively and z^* is an assignment to variable z. Denote by F the formula $F_N \wedge z$. If $F(\boldsymbol{p})$=0, then no matter how one changes assignments $\boldsymbol{h}$, z^* in $\boldsymbol{p}$, the latter falsifies a clause of F. (So, in reality, $inp(\boldsymbol{p})$ is a cube specifying a huge number of complete assignments.) Then instead of enumerating the complete assignments to $Vars(F)$ one can enumerate the complete assignments to the set Y of input variables. In our approach, however, using cubes is unacceptable because the complexity of $Sat(T,F,L)$ is proportional to the size of T.

Note that, given a sufficient test set T= $\{\boldsymbol{p}_1,\ldots,\boldsymbol{p}_m\}$, one can always form a circuit test set $inp(T)$= $\{\boldsymbol{y}_1,\ldots,\boldsymbol{y}_k\}$, $k \leq m$, consisting of input parts of the points from T. (Some points of T may have identical input parts, so $inp(T)$ may be smaller than T.) In the case of manufacturing testing, transformation of T into $inp(T)$ is mandatory. In this case, a *hardware* implementation of a circuit N is tested and usually one has access only to the input variables of N. (In the case of functional verification, one deals with a *software model* of N and so any variable of F can be assigned an arbitrary value.)

A point $\boldsymbol{p}_i$ of T has an interesting *interpretation* in Circuit-SAT if the value of z is equal to 1 in $\boldsymbol{p}_i$. Let F' be the subset of clauses of F_N falsified by $\boldsymbol{p}_i$. (For a tight test set, F' consists of a very small number of clauses, most likely one clause.) Suppose N has changed (or has a fault) and this change can be simulated by removing the clauses of F' from F_N or by adding to every clause of F' a literal satisfied by $\boldsymbol{p}_i$. Then $\boldsymbol{p}_i$ satisfies the modified formula F. So the internal part of $\boldsymbol{p}_i$ specifies the change that needs to be brought into circuit N to make $inp(\boldsymbol{p}_i)$ a circuit test that detects the satisfiability of the modified N.

6 Testing Design Changes/Manufacturing Faults

In this section, we consider the problem of property preservation (i.e. the problem of testing design changes and manufacturing faults) in more detail. In terms of SAT, the objective of property preservation is to detect a satisfiable variation (fault) of an unsatisfiable CNF formula F. We assume here that F specifies a property ξ of a circuit N. The idea of our approach is to build a resolution proof R that F is unsatisfiable and then use R (possibly "rarefied") to build a *tight* sufficient test set T. This test set is meant to detect changes/faults that break the property ξ. Every point $\boldsymbol{p}_i$ of T can be trivially transformed to a circuit test by taking the input part of $\boldsymbol{p}_i$. For the sake of clarity, in the following write-up we consider the testing of manufacturing faults (however the same approach can be used for verifying design changes).

Usually, to make manufacturing test generation more efficient, a fault model (e.g. the stuck-at fault model [1]) is considered. Then a set of tests detecting all testable faults of this model is generated. An obvious flaw of this approach is that one has to foresee what kind of faults may occur in the circuit. Nevertheless, some fault models (especially the stuck-at fault model) are widely used in industry. The reason for such popularity is that a set of tests detecting all testable stuck-at faults also detects a great deal of faults of other types. An obvious advantage of our approach is that it is *fault model independent*. So one does not need to guess what may happen with the chip.

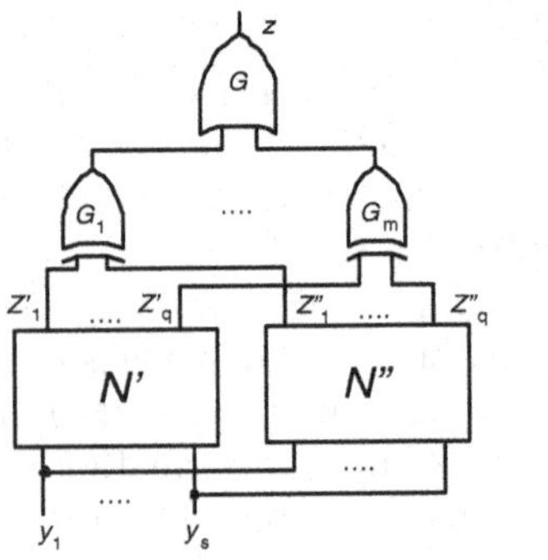

Fig. 3. Miter M of circuits N' and N''

For the case of generality, we consider the situation when one does not know any specific property of the circuit N to be tested. In this case, one can employ the most fundamental property of a circuit which is its self-equivalence. In this section, we show that a tight sufficient test set T for the formula specifying self-equivalence of N contains tests for detecting stuck-at faults. (In [2], we prove that on the one hand, $inp(T)$ contains tests for detecting *all testable stuck-at faults*, on the other hand, $inp(T)$ is *stronger* than a set of tests detecting all testable stuck-at faults.) These results offer a good explanation of why test sets detecting stuck-at faults work so well for other types of faults.

Further exposition is structured as follows. First we describe a circuit (called a miter) that is used for equivalence checking. Then we give the definition of a stuck-at fault in circuit N. After that we show how one can build a test detecting a stuck-at fault using a formula F that describes checking self-equivalence of N. Finally, we show that a tight point image of a "natural" resolution proof that F is unsatisfiable contains such tests.

6.1 Manufacturing Tests and Self-equivalence Check

Fig. 3 shows a circuit M (called **a miter**) composed of two s-input, q-output circuits N' and N''. Here G_i is an XOR gate and G is an OR gate. The circuit M evaluates to 1 iff N' and N'' produce different output assignments for the same input assignment. So N' and N'' are functionally equivalent iff the CNF formula $F_M \wedge z$ is unsatisfiable (here F_M specifies the functionality of M and z is the output variable of M).

Suppose that we want to generate a set of manufacturing tests for a circuit N. We can do this as follows. First we build the miter M of two copies of N. (In this case, N' and N'' of Fig. 3 are just copies of N having the same input variables and separate sets of internal variables.) After that we construct a proof R that the formula $F = F_M \wedge z$ is unsatisfiable and then use R to build a *tight* sufficient test set T. The idea is that being tight, T can be used for detection of variations of F describing appearance of a fault in one of the copies of N.

6.2 Stuck-at Faults

A stuck-at fault in a circuit N, describes the situation when a line in N is stuck at *constant* value 0 or 1. Let $G_i(v_m,v_k)$ be a gate of N. Then appearance of a stuck-at-1 fault ϕ on the input line v_m of G_i, means that for every assignment to the inputs of N the value of v_m remains 1. (Suppose that the output of gate G_m described by variable v_m, in addition to an input of G_i, feeds an input of some other gate G_p. In the *single* stuck-at fault model we use in this paper, only the input v_m of G_i or G_p is assumed to be stuck at a constant value. However, if the *output* line of G_m is stuck at 1, then input lines v_m of both G_i and G_p are stuck at 1.) Let G_i be an AND gate. Then the functionality of G_i can be described by CNF $F(G_i) = (\overline{v_m} \vee \overline{v_k} \vee v_i) \wedge (v_m \vee \overline{v_i}) \wedge (v_k \vee \overline{v_i})$ where v_i describes the output of G_i. The fault ϕ above can be simulated by removing the clause $v_m \vee \overline{v_i}$ from $F(G_i)$ (it is satisfied by v_m=1) and removing the literal $\overline{v_m}$ from the clause $\overline{v_m} \vee \overline{v_k} \vee v_i$ of $F(G_i)$.

6.3 Construction of Tests Detecting Stuck-at Faults

Suppose the stuck-at-1 fault ϕ above occurred in the copy N' of N (i.e. it occurred on the input line v'_m of the AND gate $G_i(v'_m,v'_k)$ of N'). Let us show how this fault can be detected using the formula F=$F_M \wedge z$. Let $\boldsymbol{p}$ be an assignment falsifying the clause $v'_m \vee \overline{v'_i}$ of $F(G'_i)$ and satisfying *every other* clause of F. Then the input assignment $inp(\boldsymbol{p})$ is a circuit test detecting ϕ. Indeed, since $\boldsymbol{p}$ satisfies all the clauses of F but $v'_m \vee \overline{v'_i}$, then N'' (the correct copy of N) and N' (the faulty copy) produce different output assignments. Besides, since $\boldsymbol{p}$ falsifies $v'_m \vee \overline{v'_i}$ and satisfies the clause $v'_k \vee \overline{v'_i}$ the assignments to the variables of G'_i are v'_m=0,v'_k=1, v'_i=1. That is the output of G'_i has exactly the value, that would have been produced if v'_m got stuck at 1. If there is no point $\boldsymbol{p}$ falsifying $v'_m \vee \overline{v'_i}$ and satisfying the rest of the clauses of F, the stuck-at-1 fault ϕ is **untestable** (i.e. the input/output behavior of N does not change in the presence of ϕ).

6.4 Extracting a Tight Sufficient Test Set from a "Natural" Resolution Proof

A "natural" proof R_{nat} that F is unsatisfiable is to derive clauses describing functional equivalence of corresponding internal points of N' and N''. These clauses are derived in topological order. First, the clauses describing the equivalence of outputs of corresponding gates of topological level 1 (whose inputs are inputs of N' and N'') are derived. Then using the equivalence clauses relating outputs of gates of topological level 1, the equivalence clauses relating outputs of corresponding gates of level 2 are derived and so on.

When building R_{nat}, we resolve clauses $F(G'_i(v'_m, v'_k))$ and $F(G''_i(v''_m, v''_k))$ describing corresponding gates G'_i and G''_i of N' and N'' and equivalence clauses $EQ(v'_m,v''_m)$, $EQ(v'_k,v''_k)$ relating inputs of G'_i and G''_i. Here $EQ(v'_m,v''_m)=(v'_m \vee \overline{v''_m}) \wedge (\overline{v'_m} \vee v''_m)$ if v'_m and v''_m are *internal* variables. If v'_m and v''_m are *input* variables of N' and N'', they denote the same input variable and $EQ(v'_m, v''_m) \equiv 1$. By resolving clauses of $F(G'_i(v'_m, v'_k)) \wedge F(G''_i(v''_m, v''_k)) \wedge EQ(v'_m,v''_m) \wedge EQ(v'_k,v''_k)$ we generate new equivalence clauses $EQ(v'_i,v''_i)$ relating the outputs of G'_i and G''_i. Let $\boldsymbol{p}_1$ and $\boldsymbol{p}_2$ be a tight point image of the resolution operation over clauses C_1 and C_2 performed when deriving clauses of $EQ(v'_i,v''_i)$. Let, say C_1, be a clause of $F(G'_i)$, $\boldsymbol{p}_1$ falsify C_1 and satisfy $F \setminus \{C_1\}$. Then, using the reasoning applied in the previous subsection, one can show that $inp(\boldsymbol{p}_1)$ is a circuit test detecting the stuck-at-fault corresponding to disappearance of C_1 from F. More detailed description of building a tight point image of R and its relation to stuck-at fault tests is given in [2]. In particular, we show that the set $inp(T_{nat})$ where T_{nat} is a tight point image of R_{nat} contains tests detecting all testable stuck-at faults. On the other hand, $inp(T_{nat})$ may have to contain tests that detect the same stuck-at-fault in different ways. So, $inp(T_{nat})$ is stronger than a test set detecting testable all stuck-at faults. Interestingly, the high quality of test sets detecting every stuck-at fault *many times* was observed in [8] experimentally.

6.5 Brief Discussion

The size of R_{nat} and hence the size of T_{nat} is linear in the size of N. Moreover, since different points of T_{nat} may have identical input parts, the size of $inp(T_{nat})$ may be considerably smaller than that of T_{nat}. Importantly, T_{nat} is not meant to detect stuck-at or any other type of faults. The fact that T_{nat} does contain such tests suggests that tight test sets extracted from resolution proofs can be successfully used in manufacturing testing.

One can always get a *stronger* test set (that detects more faults of various kinds) by "rarefying" the proof R_{nat}. Suppose, for example, that a single-output subcircuit K of circuit N is particularly prone to faults and requires some extra testing. This can be achieved, for example, by dropping all the resolvents of R_{nat} that were generated from clauses $F_{K'}$ and $F_{K''}$ when obtaining the equivalence clauses $EQ(v'_i,v''_i)$. Here $EQ(v'_i,v''_i)$ relate the outputs of K' and K'' in N' and N'' and F_K are the clauses specifying the functionality of subcircuit K. Let C be a clause of $EQ(v'_i,v''_i)$. Then an SSP S of the subformula F_C (here F_C is the CNF formula built to check if F implies C) will contain more points then the part of a point image of R_{nat} corresponding to resolution operations over clauses of $F_{K'}$ and $F_{K''}$. So a test set containing S will provide better testing of the subcircuit K.

7 Experimental Results

In this section, we describe application of tight sufficient test sets to detect a change in the functionality of a combinational circuit. Such a change may be caused either by a manufacturing fault or by circuit re-synthesis.

In the experiments we compared the quality of circuit tests (i.e. complete assignments to input variables) generated randomly and extracted from tight sufficient test sets. Given a circuit N, a tight sufficient test set T was extracted from a resolution proof R that a CNF formula F describing equivalence checking of two copies of N is unsatisfiable. (The exact procedure for obtaining T from R and many more experimental results are given in [2]. As we mentioned above a resolution proof that two copies of N are functionally equivalent can be easily generated manually. However, for the sake of generality, in experiments we used resolution proofs generated by a SAT-solver, namely by the SAT-solver *FI* [3].) To form a circuit test set from T we randomly picked *a subset* of the set $inp(T)$ (where $inp(T)$ consists of the input parts of the points from T).

Table 1 shows experimental results for four circuits of a MCNC benchmark set. All circuits consist of two-input AND and OR gates inputs of which may be negated. The columns 2-4 give the number of inputs, outputs and gates of a circuit. The fifth column shows the size of the proof R (in the number of resolution operations) that two copies of circuit N are equivalent. The last column gives the size of a tight point image of R (in the number of points).

Table 1. The size of circuits, proofs and point images

Name	#inp	#out	#gates	#proof	#point image T
c432	36	7	215	10,921	5,407
c499	41	32	414	59,582	27,903
cordic	23	2	93	1,443	808
i2	201	1	233	1,777	1,435

Let F be a CNF formula describing equivalence checking of two copies N' and N'' of a circuit N. Here $F = F_M \wedge z$ where z is the variable describing the output of the miter M of N' and N'' (as shown in Fig. 3).

The fault we used in experiments was to add a literal to a clause of F_M. This fault is more subtle than a stuck-at fault in which an entire clause is removed from F_M. In [2] we give the interpretation of the literal appearance fault from a technological point of view. Literal appearance in a clause of F_M can be also used to simulate small design changes that are hard to detect in functional verification.

Let $\boldsymbol{s}$ be a circuit test (i.e. an assignment to the input variables of N). To check if ϕ is detected by $\boldsymbol{s}$ we make the assignments specified by $\boldsymbol{s}$ in F_M and run Boolean Constraint Propagation (BCP) for F_M. If z gets assigned 1 (or 0) during BCP, then $\boldsymbol{s}$ detects (respectively does not detect) ϕ.

In general however, running BCP may not result in deducing the value of z. The reason is that after adding a literal to a clause of F_M, circuit behavior becomes non-deterministic. For example, let $C = \overline{v'_i} \vee \overline{v'_j} \vee v'_k$ be a clause of the CNF $F(G'_k)$ describing the functionality of the AND gate $G'_k(v'_i, v'_j)$. Suppose that ϕ is to add literal v'_m to C. Normally, if v'_i=1,v'_j=1, the value v'_k=1 is derived from the clause C. However, if the value of v'_m becomes equal to 1 during BCP (before the variable v'_k is assigned), then the clause $\overline{v'_i} \vee \overline{v'_j} \vee v'_k \vee v'_m$ is satisfied without assigning 1 to v'_k. So the output of the gate G'_k remains unspecified under the input assignment $\boldsymbol{s}$. In this case, we run a SAT-solver trying to assign values to the unassigned variables to satisfy F (and so set z to 1). If such an assignment exists (does not exist), $\boldsymbol{s}$ is considered to detect (not to detect) ϕ. The reason is that if ϕ simulates a manufacturing fault and we succeed in satisfying the faulty F, then $\boldsymbol{s}$ will detect ϕ in case the output of G'_k is set to the wrong value (i.e. 0).

Table 2. Circuit testing

Name	#tests	SIS #flts	rand #flts	extr. from *inp*(*T*) #flts
c432	58	86	69.7(65)	79.7 (76)
	100	-	77.1 (72)	86.7 (78)
	200	-	88.7(85)	95.5 (90)
c499	93	90	78.7 (70)	85.9(83)
	200	-	86.9 (84)	91.2 (89)
	400	-	91 (88)	95.2 (92)
cordic	43	84	28.5 (23)	81.6 (74)
	100	-	36.6 (29)	94.2 (87)
	200	-	54.8 (36)	99 (98)
i2	221	71	7.8 (3)	66.4 (62)
	400	-	9.2 (6)	74.6 (69)
	600	-	11.6 (10)	82.4 (80)

Table 2 shows the results of fault testing for the circuits of Table 1. In every experiment we generated 100 *testable* faults (i.e. every fault specified a satisfiable variation of F). The second column of Table 2 gives the size of a test set. The third column gives the result for a test set detecting all stuck-at faults in N. This test set was generated by the logic synthesis system SIS [7]. Since we could not vary the size of the test set produced by SIS, only one test set was used per circuit. For example, for the circuit *c432*, a test set of 58 tests was generated by SIS. These tests were able to detect 86 out of 100 faults of literal appearance. The fourth column contains the results of fault detection using circuit tests generated randomly. In every experiment we used 10 test sets and computed the average result.The value in parentheses shows the worst result out of 10. For example, for the circuit *c432*, in the first experiment (first line of Table 2) we generated 10 random test sets, each consisting of 58 tests. On average, 69.7 faults were detected, 65 faults being the worst result out of 10.

The fifth column contains the result of fault detection using circuit tests extracted from the set *inp*(T) where T is a point image of a proof R that F is unsatisfiable. Namely, we *randomly* extracted a particular number of tests from *inp*(T). The corresponding sizes of T are given in Table 1. In every experiment we also generated 10 test sets of a particular size and we give the average value and the worst result out of 10. For example, in the first experiment, for the circuit c432, 10 test sets of 58 tests each were extracted from *inp*(T). The average number of detected faults was 79.7 and the worst result was 76 faults.

Table 2 shows that tests extracted from a point image T of a resolution proof R perform better than random tests. For circuits *c432*, *c499* that are shallow (i.e. have few levels of logic) and have relatively large number of outputs (7 and 32 respectively) tests extracted from resolution proofs performed only slightly better. (Testing shallow circuits with many outputs is easy). However, for circuits *cordic* and *i2* that are also shallow but have only 2 and 1 outputs respectively tests extracted from resolution proofs significantly outperformed random tests.

Table 2 also shows that the quality of a test set extracted from a resolution proof depends on proof quality. As we mentioned above, tests detecting stuck-at faults is a part of $inp(T_{nat})$ where T_{nat} is a point image of a natural resolution proof R_{nat}. Table 2 shows that tests found by SIS performed better than tests extracted from proofs found by *FI* (these proofs are significantly larger than R_{nat}).

8 Conclusion

In this paper, we develop a theory of sufficient test sets. The essence of our approach is to interpret a set of tests not as a sample of the search space but as an encryption of a formal proof. We believe that this theory can have many applications. An obvious application is generation of high-quality tests. We show that such tests can be extracted from resolution proofs (possibly rarefied). One more interesting direction for research is extending the notion of stable sets of points (which is the foundation of our approach) to domains other than propositional logic. This may lead to developing new methods of generating high quality test sets for more complex objects like sequential circuits or even programs.

References

1. Abramovici, M., Breuer, M.A., Friedman, A.D.: Digital Systems Testing and Testable Design, p. 672. Wiley-IEEE Press, Chichester (1994)
2. Goldberg, E.: On bridging simulation and formal verification. Technical Report CDNL-TR-2006-1225 (December 2006), `http://eigold.tripod.com/papers/ssim.pdf`
3. Goldberg, E.: Determinization of Resolution by an Algorithm Operating on Complete Assignments. In: Biere, A., Gomes, C.P. (eds.) SAT 2006. LNCS, vol. 4121, pp. 90–95. Springer, Heidelberg (2006)
4. Goldberg, E.: Testing Satisfiability of CNF Formulas by Computing a Stable Set of Points. In: Voronkov, A. (ed.) CADE 2002. LNCS (LNAI), vol. 2392, pp. 161–180. Springer, Heidelberg (2002)
5. Selman, B., Levesque, H., Mitchell, D.: A New Method for Solving Hard Satisfiability Problems. In: AAAI 1992, pp. 440–446 (1992)
6. Selman, B., Kautz, H.A., Cohen, B.: Noise strategies for improving local search. In: AAAI- 1994, Seattle, pp. 337–343 (1994)
7. Sentovich, E., et al.: SIS: A system for sequential circuit synthesis. Technical report, University of California at Berkeley, Memorandum No. UCB/ERL M92/41 (1992)
8. McCluskey, E., Tseng, C.: Stuck-fault tests vs. actual defects. In: Proc. of Int. Test Conf., pp. 336–343 (2000)
9. Bachmair, L., et al.: The Handbook of Automated Reasoning, ch. 2, vol. 1, pp. 19–99. Elsevier, Amsterdam (2001)

Extending Model Checking with Dynamic Analysis*

Alex Groce and Rajeev Joshi

Laboratory for Reliable Software
Jet Propulsion Laboratory
California Institute of Technology
Pasadena, CA 91109, USA

Abstract. In *model-driven verification* a model checker executes a program by embedding it within a test harness, thus admitting program verification without the need to translate the program, which runs as native code. Model checking techniques in which code is actually executed have recently gained popularity due to their ability to handle the full semantics of actual implementation languages and to support verification of rich properties. In this paper, we show that combination with dynamic analysis can, with relatively low overhead, considerably extend the capabilities of this style of model checking. In particular, we show how to use the CIL framework to instrument code in order to allow the SPIN model checker, when verifying C programs, to check additional properties, simulate system resets, and use local coverage information to guide the model checking search. An additional benefit of our approach is that instrumentations developed for model checking may be used without modification in testing or monitoring code. We are motivated by experience in applying model-driven verification to JPL-developed flight software modules, from which we take our example applications. We believe this is the first investigation in which an independent instrumentation for dynamic analysis has been integrated with model checking.

1 Introduction

Dynamic analysis [1] is *analysis of a running program*, usually performed by the addition of instrumentation code or execution in a virtual environment [2]. Model checking [3] is a technique for exploring all states of a program's execution space, which may be a static analysis of an extracted model, as in CBMC [4] or SLAM [5], or a dynamic analysis in which a program is executed, as in CMC [6] or SPIN's *model-driven verification*. In model-driven verification [7] (our focus in this work) a harness embeds code and the model checker runs the program being verified in order to take a transition in its state space.

* The work described in this paper was carried out at the Jet Propulsion Laboratory, California Institute of Technology, under a contract with the National Aeronautics and Space Administration. Funding was also provided by NASA ESAS 6G.

F. Logozzo et al. (Eds.): VMCAI 2008, LNCS 4905, pp. 142–156, 2008.

In this paper we show that the power and ease of use of model-driven verification can be significantly enhanced using dynamic analysis. Our approach extends the capabilities of the model checker by introducing instrumentation into the executed code — instrumentation which interacts with the model checker to perform property checks, modify control flow of the program, compute coverage metrics, and to guide the state-space search. Our approach is motivated by our experience with model-driven verification. In particular, our frustration when debugging model-driven verification harnesses and our interest in properties requiring fine-grained observation or control of execution suggested the use of automated instrumentation. Our examples are taken from JPL flight software produced or tested by our group: **NVDS**, a module used to store critical spacecraft parameters on flash [8] (5K lines of C for the module, plus 2K lines for a harness/reference), **Launchseq**, a model of the launch sequence for a recent mission (1K lines), and a replacement for `string.h`. Another motivation was our interest in random testing [8]: using independent dynamic analysis (rather than modifying SPIN), we are able to use the *same instrumentation* during a model checking run and a random test execution. We simply instrument and compile the program to be tested, and link to the same instrumented binary.

A further interest in such a combination is based on a common objection to dynamic analysis: it is fundamentally unsound. Model checking offers the possibility of combining a dynamic analysis with a complete exploration of the reachable state space (or an abstraction of that state space). It is true that, for realistic programs, the state space is often too large for an exhaustive search (even after abstraction); it is also often the case that analysis for a particular property adds variables to the program state and increases the state space size. Nonetheless, in some non-trivial cases, model checking offers an easy path to sound dynamic analysis.

Below, we discuss the particular instrumentations we developed. We first present a method for checking modifies clauses, also useful in debugging model-driven verification harnesses (Sections 4.1 and 4.2). We then show how the same framework supports a method for simulating software resets (Section 4.3), better coverage measures during model checking (Section 4.4) and, perhaps most interestingly, a novel search approach based on path coverage information produced by instrumentation (Section 4.5). Experimental results confirm our intuition that overhead will be low for most of these approaches (Section 4.6).

2 Model-Driven Verification

Model-driven verification [7] is a form of software model checking that works by executing code embedded in a model[1]. The SPIN model checker [9] operates by translating a model written in PROMELA into a (C) program to model check that program: in a sense, SPIN is less a model checker than it is a *model*

[1] In the current implementation, the executed code must be C, but this is not a fundamental limitation of the technique; in fact, we occasionally make calls to C++ functions in embedded C code.

```
1  c_decl {
2    extern struct s_t *arr;
3    extern int cnt;
4    extern int new_n(void);
5    int tmp;
6  };
7  c_track "arr"     "sizeof(struct s_t) * 100"     "Matched"
8  c_track "&cnt"    "sizeof(int)"                  "Matched"
9  c_track "&tmp"    "sizeof(int)"                  "UnMatched"
10
11 int r;
12 active proctype harness () {
13   c_code { cnt = 0; };
14   do
15   :: c_expr {cnt < MAX} -> c_code { tmp = cnt; now.r = new_n(); };
16                            assert(r != -1);
17                            assert(c_expr {cnt == tmp+1})
18   :: else -> break
19   od
20 }
```

Fig. 1. PROMELA Model with Embedded C Code

checker generator. Model-driven verification exploits this fact to embed C code within PROMELA models[2]. With model-driven verification, it is possible to check a C program against specifications written in linear temporal logic, using all the features of SPIN, including bitstate hashing, abstraction, and multi-core execution [9,7,10].

Figure 1 illustrates the use of SPIN's primitives for embedding C code. The `c_decl` primitive is used to declare external C types and data objects that are used in the embedded C code. The `c_track` declarations are *tracking* statements, which provide knowledge to SPIN of what state is being manipulated by the C program. We describe `c_track` statements in more detail below. The PROMELA process defined by the `proctype` declaration also uses the `c_expr` construct to embed C expressions that are used as guards and the `c_code` construct to embed blocks of C code within the PROMELA model.

During its depth first search[3], the model checker may reach states with no successors (e.g., the `break` from the `do` loop on line 18, which leads to a final state) or states that have already been visited. In such cases, the model checker backtracks to an earlier state to explore alternative successors. For variables in the SPIN model, such as `r`, restoration of an earlier value when backtracking is automatic. In order to restore data objects of the C program, however, the model checker needs knowledge of the set of memory locations that can be modified by the C code, which we call the *tracked* locations. For each data object modified

[2] This feature was introduced in SPIN version 4.0.

[3] Note that SPIN currently supports embedded C code only with DFS.

by the C program, a `c_track` statement is used (see lines 7-9) to indicate three pieces of information needed by SPIN: the starting address in memory where the data object is stored, the size (in bytes) of the C representation of the data, and whether or not the data should be *matched*, i.e., whether it should be included in the check determining if a state has been seen before.

2.1 Tracking and Matching

It is important to note the distinction between tracking and matching. Tracked data objects are stored as part of the state on the stack used by depth first search (DFS). This allows SPIN to properly restore data values on each backtracking step during the DFS. As a rule, *all* data objects that can be modified by a C program should be tracked (with some exceptions, as discussed below).

Matching, on the other hand, allows SPIN to recognize when a state has been seen before. The set of matched data objects therefore constitutes the state descriptor, which is examined whenever a state is generated, to determine if the state has been seen before. The `''Matched''` and `''UnMatched''` keywords are used in a `c_track` declaration to indicate whether an object is matched or not.

Since the amount of data modified by a C program can be large, declaring all data objects as matched makes the state descriptor very large, and increases the size of the state space to be explored. In such cases, careful distinction between matched and unmatched data allows on-the-fly abstractions to be applied during model checking. A simple example is symmetry reduction: e.g., if program states are equivalent (with respect to verification of a property ϕ) up to any ordering of the items in a linked list, we may track the concrete variable but match only on a sorted version of the list, greatly reducing the size of the state space needed to verify ϕ. This approach to abstraction is discussed at length in the original paper on model-driven verification [7].

Note that not all data needs to be tracked. Data that does not change after a deterministic initialization process, or data that is not relevant to the search, does not require tracking. We refer to such data as *ignored* data.[4] There is no memory overhead for ignored data, but of course such data is not restored when backtracking occurs. Program state that is not modified in a way that is visible to SPIN can be ignored. It is also important to ignore memory that stores cumulative or statistical information over an entire model checking run.

2.2 Limitations of Previous Work

Each fragment of C code embedded in a SPIN model (using either the `c_expr` or `c_decl` constructions) is executed as a (deterministic) atomic step. This leads to several limitations of the SPIN approach to model-driven verification: (a) we cannot check properties (such as program invariants) within embedded C code, (b) we cannot interrupt control flow within a C function (for instance to simulate

[4] There are also situations where it is useful to declare *matched* data that is *untracked*; however, these are beyond the scope of this paper.

an asynchronous interrupt or an unexpected reset), and (c) we cannot interleave different fragments of C code (to check multithreaded C programs).

In this paper, we discuss how to address the first two limitations by using *program instrumentation*. In particular, we describe (i) how we check properties within C code, for instance on every write to global data, (ii) how we check C programs against unexpected events, for instance a *warm reboot* in which the program stack is cleared, but global data and the heap are not affected, (iii) how we can dynamically check *modifies clauses* [11], which constrain what data can be modified by a C function, (iv) how we can compute various *coverage metrics* (such as predicate coverage) of a C program over a model checking run, and (v) how we can dynamically apply various (sound and unsound) abstractions (for instance, a dynamic form of path coverage).

3 Dynamic Analysis Via CIL Instrumentation

We insert instrumentation for dynamic analysis via source-to-source transformation. Our applications do not involve binaries without source, and we enjoy the benefits of adding instrumentation before optimization. Running the model checker itself under instrumentation is too expensive (and in some cases impossible), and it is very easy to instrument only certain compilation units. Our interest is in the use of instrumentation for analysis during model checking, not in the specific method used for inserting instrumentation.

3.1 Instrumentation with CIL

CIL (the C Intermediate Language) is a high-level intermediate language for representing C programs, and includes a set of tools that enable analysis and transformation of C programs [12]. CIL rewrites C programs in a semantically clean subset of C. User-written modules may modify the code as it is rewritten. The CIL distribution includes modules providing points-to analysis, array heapification, and other useful transformers and analyses. We use CIL because we find it to be a robust and easy-to-use tool for C source-to-source transformations.

Most of our analysis tools are adapted from the `logwrites.ml` module provided with CIL. This module "logs" all writes to non-stack-local memory, seen in CIL as `Set` or `Call` instructions. Because CIL analyzes program source, it can conservatively avoid instrumenting writes to stack local variables in a function. Our adaptation is to change `logwrites.ml` to call, in place of a logging function

```
void checkWrite (void *p,          /* Address of the memory */
                 size_t size,      /* Size (in bits) of the write */
                 const char* lv,   /* Pretty-print of source lval */
                 const char* f,    /* Name of the file */
                 unsigned int ln   /* Line number of the write */ );
```

Fig. 2. Prototype for `checkWrite`

```
in_stack(p) = ((p > stack_beg_loc) && (p < &stack_end)) ||
              ((p > &stack_end) && (p < stack_beg_loc))
```

Fig. 3. Definition for `in_stack`

expecting a string, a function `checkWrite` that expects more information. The prototype for `checkWrite` is shown in Figure 2.

3.2 Tracking the Location of the Stack

Our most common instrumentation involves checking writes to global memory. CIL distinguishes between local and global variables when this is possible, but cannot statically determine if certain pointers always target the stack. In order to determine the location of the stack, we add a global variable (`stack_beg_loc`) to the model checker, containing the address of a local variable of the `main` function, and declare another local variable (`stack_end`) in the scope of `checkWrite`. We assume that stack variables lie in the region formed by these boundaries, and define `in_stack (p)` to handle different stack orientations (Figure 3).

3.3 Replacing Memory Modification and Allocation Library Calls

Unfortunately, accesses visible to CIL as `Sets` and `Calls` to lvalues do not capture all memory writes. C programs also modify state by calls to system libraries — in particular, by using `memset`, `memcpy`, `memmove`, and the destructive string library functions (`strncpy`, `strcat`, etc.). We do not wish to recompile these libraries with CIL, but do wish to instrument the writes they produce. We therefore use another CIL module to rewrite these calls, making the memory writes visible.

We use a similar CIL module to replace calls to the `malloc` family with calls to `spin_malloc`, in order to make dynamic allocation visible. The `spin_malloc` functions use a static region that is tracked. This method also optionally provides checks for common memory-safety properties (no use after `free`, etc.) and ensures that tracked and allocated regions are equivalent if they overlap.

4 Applications and Experimental Results

We now present the uses we have made of dynamic analysis during model checking, and present experimental results indicating the utility and efficiency of our approach. Significantly, we show that the *relative* overhead for our instrumentation is quite low: the model checking engine is not instrumented, and tends to consume a large portion of runtime during model-driven verification.

Our applications include novel ideas specific to model checking (Sections 4.2 and 4.5). We also present more common analyses applicable in testing, in order to show the degree of reusability provided by independent analysis and to compare analysis overheads for testing and model checking. The range of possible applications is potentially that of most runtime analyses for C programs.

4.1 Checking Modifies Clauses

Modifies clauses are used in ESC/Java [13], JML [14], Larch [15], and other languages to specify which variables a function may alter. We take a lower level approach and consider a specification of which *memory locations* a C function or block may change. These (named) locations are specified as a set of ranges, which may be dynamically computed during execution. A `checkWrite` function determines the correctness of each memory write:

```
void checkWrite (void* p, ...)
  forall (range ∈ modifiable_ranges)
    if (p ∈ range ∧ allowed(range))
      return;    /* Ok, p is in a modifiable range */
  /* p is not in any modifiable range! */
  ERROR;
```

A range is not statically defined, but is a dynamically evaluated region specified by expressions for starting and ending address. Whether a range can be written to can by dynamically toggled, depending on conditions. E.g., the stack will typically be included in the allowed ranges, but not in all cases. In our test harness for a replacement version of the C string library used in a JPL flight module, the `r_strncat` range is computed based on the arguments to the `n_strncat` function — `r_strncat = (t+strlen(t), t+strlen(t)+n)`. Code that calls `n_strncat` (the module's version of `strncat`) is rewritten with CIL to set up the restrictions:

```
disallow_all_ranges(); /* Clear set of modifiable ranges */
allow_range(r_strncat); /* Allow range for n_strncat */
char *result = n_strncat(t, s, n);
```

An advantage of our approach to combining model checking and dynamic analysis is that the analysis can be used in other kinds of testing or as a runtime monitor in deployment. We used the same instrumentation to check modifies clauses in a randomized differential testing harness [8] for the string library, comparing results of operations on randomly generated strings to those returned by the standard string library. These tests detected a minor error in argument checking in one function.

Extending Modifies Clause Checking to Library Calls. In addition to restrictions on memory writes, we also support limitations on which libraries can be called. The most common application may be to restrict write access to devices (such as flash storage in our case) accessed through driver calls. In addition to device access properties, this also allows us to check performance properties, e.g. that no expensive library calls occur while interrupts are disabled on the flight CPU.

4.2 Debugging SPIN Models with Embedded C Code

One application of modifies clause checking is to assist in developing the harness for model-driven verification. A common error in such cases is to leave an important variable untracked, resulting in spurious counterexamples when the model checker backtracks but only partially restores a previous state. Our approach to debugging memory tracking during model-driven verification is to automatically generate a `checkWrite` function from the `c_track` statements in the SPIN harness. Our tool also supports a `c_ignore` statement, used to indicate modifiable memory that does not require tracking. During model checking, `checkWrite` acts as a modifies clause checker, ensuring that the program being verified does not modify any locations that are not tracked or ignored.

If the model checked program does write to untracked/ignored locations, SPIN will produce a warning for each such write — e.g. in the NVDS example:

```
UNTRACKED WRITE: 0x73b980 (nvds_npart) at nvds_init.c:377
UNTRACKED WRITE: 0x73b9d0 (nvds_ptsem[pt]) at nvds_init.c:258
```

In addition to `c_track` and `c_ignore`, we support a `c_constant` declaration. Unlike the C `const` type attribute, this does not indicate that an address is never assigned to (in which case we could simply leave the value out of our declarations). Instead, it produces a check that the value written to an address is always the same as the previous contents of that address. Because many of our models include simulations of system resets, we often call initialization code (such as would be called when a spacecraft reboots) setting global parameters, such as the size of a file system's memory region. The `c_constant` declaration provides warnings if this initialization code is faulty and changes the previous value of such a parameter, while avoiding spurious warnings about non-modifying assignments. Such declarations incur the additional overhead of a `memcpy`, but only before assignments to these addresses.

We used this approach to detect three untracked writes in a SPIN harness for a critical piece of flight software (the NVDS system), and to confirm that these writes were safe. We also verified the tracking of state for launch sequence modeling code derived from an upcoming mission.

4.3 Simulating Warm Resets

Another application of instrumentation is to return control to the model checker to simulate system resets. This is useful in two cases: simulation of cold resets on systems with a persistent hardware state that survives reboot, and simulation of *warm resets*, used in some experimental flight software at JPL.

In a warm reset, all data on the program stack is cleared and the program is restarted, but global data is *not cleared.* In some applications, this memory may need to be recovered, if possible, even after the software has been terminated in mid-operation and re-started. Because stack memory is lost on a reset we can reduce the state space of possible reset points by only considering resets at global writes. Again, we make use of a `checkWrite` function:

```
if (in_stack(p))
  return;    /* p on stack, no need to consider reset */
if (reset_trap > 0)
  reset_trap--;
else if (reset_trap == 0)  /* Trap goes off, reset */
  reset_trap = -1; /* Clear the trap */
  longjmp (context, code);
```

As with modifies clauses, this `checkWrite` requires the model checker to set certain variables before calling the tested code. In particular, it expects `reset_trap` to indicate if a warm reset is scheduled (-1 indicates no trap, a positive number n indicates that a warm reset is to take place on the nth write). A `setjmp` call to establish the `context` for `longjmp` to control to SPIN is also required. The model checking harness places resets nondeterministically.

We use this module in both model checking and random testing. The method has exposed subtle errors, including a very low probability scenario arising from the precise placement of a reset during a `memcpy` in a spacecraft RAM file system — a checksum used to detect memory corruption was too weak [8]. Detecting the error required a precisely placed reset during a memory copy.

4.4 Granularity of Coverage Measurements

Dynamic analysis also allows us to compute (abstraction) coverage at a finer granularity than atomic step boundaries. In our model checking of flash storage systems we use a number of unsound abstractions, as the state spaces for the rich properties we wish to check (essentially full functional correctness) are not amenable to sound abstraction and are large for even small flash devices. We may abstract the state of the flash device by only considering, e.g., the *state* of each block on the device (used, free, bad) and the number of live, dirty, and free pages on that block [16,8]. When SPIN reaches a state in which the abstract state has previously been visited, it will backtrack. Because it may not be possible, under this abstraction, to reach all abstract states (indeed, certain states are defined as errors), we compute the coverage in cumulative fashion as we model check the file system. Unfortunately, computing coverage after every call to the file system does not measure actual abstraction coverage. Before an operation returns control to the harness, it may perform multiple writes to the flash device. In this case, our coverage is a measure of "stable states" of the flash with respect to the storage API, but is an underestimate of all covered states. We remedy this by instrumenting all driver calls for the flash device to recompute coverage after each modification. Again, this coverage instrumentation is as useful in randomized testing as in model checking.

4.5 Using Local Path Coverage to Guide Exploration

Another useful CIL module instruments every branch choice to update a bit vector representing the program path as shown in Figure 4. Before each entry into the tested program the model checking harness clears `pathBV`. At the end of

```
if (buff == NULL) {
   return;
} else {
   copy(x, buff);
}
```

(a) Before

```
if (buff == NULL) {
  add_to_bv(pathBV, 1);
  return;
} else {
  add_to_bv(pathBV, 0);
  copy(x, buff);
}
```

(b) After

Fig. 4. Before and after insertion of path tracking

each call, `pathBV` contains information sufficient to reproduce the control path taken by the tested function, e.g. [] for branch-free code, and [1] or [0, ...] for our example, (where ... represents any branching taken inside `copy`). We limit the size of `pathBV` in some fashion — in our case, simply by taking only the first k bits of history, though other schemes, such as a sliding window, might also yield useful results.

Making `pathBV` a matched location adds path coverage of tested functions to the state space abstraction used in SPIN. This provides no benefit if we are matching on *all* aspects of the program state, but produces a new exploration strategy when combined with coarse abstractions. Consider the extreme case where we match on *no* program state. Without path information, no path will involve more than one entry-point function from the test-harness loop and will never discover any error requiring more than one function call. However, if we match on `pathBV`, SPIN will explore deeper paths, until such exploration fails to cover new paths in the tested functions. In the extreme case, this is unlikely to provide significantly deeper coverage, but for even very coarse abstractions may reach deeper state without the need to guess what additional program state should be tracked.

We applied this approach to our NVDS example, removing all matched state (other than the SPIN variables controlling inputs to tested functions) from the model, and adding matched path information. We ranged k from 0 to 20 bits (at 20 bits, the state space was large enough to exhaust memory on our 8GB machine). As expected, statement coverage of the module increased monotonically with the number of bits – but only by a few statements. The number of states explored increased dramatically — from 607K states for the 0-bit (no coverage) experiment to 48,100K states with 20 bits of path information. Most interestingly, coverage of the abstraction discussed above, approximating the physical state of the flash device (with respect to storage semantics of live and dirty pages) also increased. This increase was not monotonic, but showed a general upwards trend with k, ranging from 39 states at 0 bits to 53 states at 18 bits (falling back to 52 states at 21 bits). Matching the abstract state itself (and thus preventing backtracking whenever a new abstract state was reached) only improved on this by one state, covering 54 of the 55 reachable abstract states. In other words, considering *only path information* when determining whether

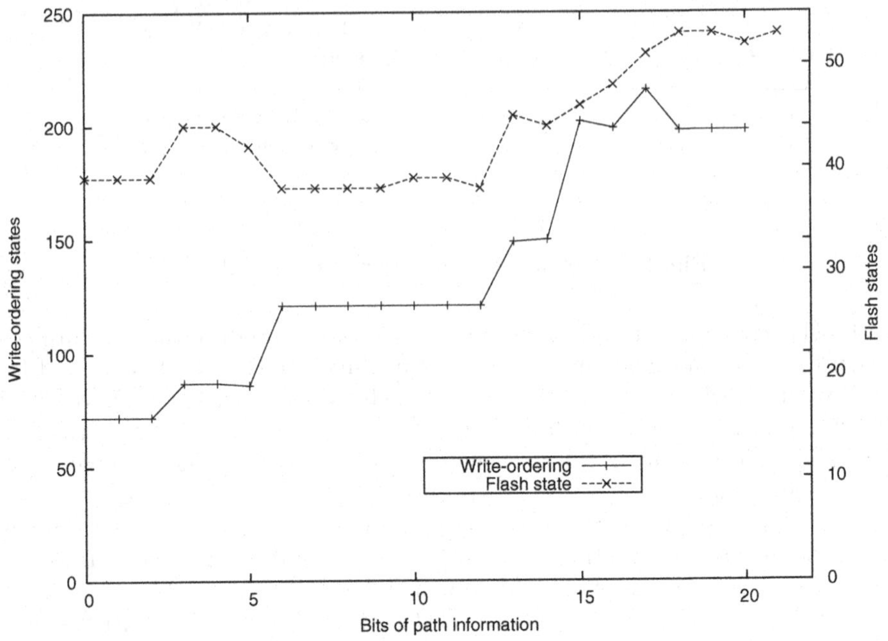

Fig. 5. Preliminary reachability results

to backtrack was almost as effective (in covering the abstract state space) as explicitly basing the search on abstract coverage[5].

Calculating coverage of another coarse abstraction (the ordering of writes to locations) showed even better results — in the two configurations we examined, the path-based approach quickly improved on matching the abstraction in question. With only 3 bits of path information, we were able to cover 87 abstract states, vs. 72 when matching on the abstract state. Figure 5 shows the general trend of increased coverage for both abstractions. Of course, given the high sensitivity of DFS to ordering of transitions [17], these results are at best suggestive. However, given the low overhead of the instrumentation and the difficulty of formulating useful (even unsound) abstractions for rich properties of systems with large state spaces, we believe this strategy merits further investigation.

4.6 Impact of Instrumentation on Model Checking Performance

Table 1 shows the overhead of instrumentation for model checking on our JPL examples. NVDS-1 and NVDS-2 designate different harness configurations. For the string library, two modes of verification were used — exhaustive model checking tests for each function and a random test system for the entire library. We report

[5] Coverage is incomplete in these cases because the abstraction is unsound and does not over-approximate successors.

Table 1. Impact of instrumentation on performance

	Uninstrumented		Instrumented				
Model Checking							
Program	Time	SPIN	Time	SPIN	Check	Slowdown	Type
NVDS-1	123.8	95%	137.1	88%	5.2%	10.5%	track
NVDS-1 (bitstate)	581.9	93%	621.3	86%	3.03%	6.8%	track
NVDS-2	437.4	93%	490.8	89.7%	2.08%	12.2%	pathBV(20)
Launchseq	97.6	99%	98.3	98%	0.06%	0.7%	track
`n_strncpy`	34.6	99.5%	34.9	99.4%	0.22%	0.86%	modifies
`n_strncat`	29.3	99.6%	29.4	99.5%	0.04%	0.34%	modifies
Random Testing							
Program	Time	Test	Time	Test	Check	Slowdown	Type
stringtest	202.9	80%	250.3	41.1%	24.4%	23.4%	modifies

All times in seconds. **SPIN/Test** are % time spent in core SPIN or in generating tests. **Check** is % time spent in `checkWrite` or in the `pathBV` update functions. Experiments performed on dual-core Xeon (3.2 GHz) with 8 GB of RAM, under Red Hat FC 4.

on modifies clause and path coverage instrumentations as representative — reset simulation instruments the same program points as modifies clause checking.

The slowdown for introducing instrumentation in no case exceeded 12.2%, whether instrumenting every global memory write or every branch, during model checking (**stringtest** is a random tester). For some of the programs, the overhead was below 1%. The overhead for modifies clause instrumentation is low enough that it can be used throughout the development of a SPIN harness to refine tracking statements, even when directly model checking flight software modules. The reason for the low (relative) overhead is clear: profiling shows that the time spent running instrumented code is trivial compared to the time spent hashing and storing states in the model checker. The percent of time executing `checkWrite` is typically an order of magnitude or more less than the percent spent executing the SPIN verifier. In unusual cases, it might happen that program execution dominates model checking state storage time, but we have never observed such a profile, even with complex modules such as NVDS. Note that the (relative) overhead for random testing (**stringtest**) of the string library is much higher than the other examples, as the generation of random tests is not computationally intensive. We also note that there was no overhead for checking `n_strlen` and `n_strncmp`, as CIL observes no global writes.

5 Related Work

Musuvathi et al. note that it should be possible to use a dynamic analysis, such as Purify [18] or StackGuard [19], in combination with CMC, a model checker that, like SPIN, executes C code [6]. In their experience, however, the overhead of binary instrumentation is too high to be practical, which supports our decision to rely on source-to-source instrumentation [20].

In a sense, *any* analysis performed in an explicit-state model checker in which code is executed can be considered to be an instance of dynamic analysis during model checking. For example, the Java Pathfinder model checker [21] has been used to generate Daikon [22] traces to detect invariants [23]. Our contribution is to combine model checking with independent dynamic analysis, introduced via traditional source-to-source transformations. Our approach stands in contrast to the more common approach to applying a "dynamic" analysis during model checking, in which the model checker itself is extended to carry out the analysis, as with JPF [23]. We preserve a separation of concerns in which code may be instrumented *just as in testing or regular execution*, without substantial change to the model checker. Any analysis developed for model checking can also be used during normal testing or as a monitor for execution (as well as the reverse — instrumentation developed during testing can be applied while model checking). Perhaps more importantly, instrumented native code executes much faster than code executed in a virtual environment, such as JPF's JVM, and the techniques described in this paper should be applicable (with similar overhead) to any of the numerous model checkers featuring actual execution of C code, including CMC [6], VeriSoft [24], and CRunner [25].

6 Conclusions and Future Work

Applying independent dynamic analysis during model checking enables a large number of useful checks and measurements and saves effort by making it possible to use the same analyses during model checking, testing, and monitoring after deployment. Dynamic analysis can be at least as useful in execution-based model checking as it is in testing, especially given that relative overheads are typically much lower than in testing. We are exploring a number of other applications.

In runtime verification, certain program events are observed by a monitor, and temporal properties of program execution are checked [26]. We hope to reuse monitoring specifications developed for testing or deployed execution. We plan to integrate the RMOR runtime verification system [27] with SPIN to analyze properties of flight software. RMOR's instrumentation is already implemented as a CIL module, and uses only static structures for monitoring, which makes producing `c_track` statements to support monitoring relatively easy.

Another application is the inference, rather than checking, of properties. Daikon [22] infers state invariants of program execution and Perracotta [28,29] infers temporal properties of program *paths*. The information necessary for these tools can be produced using our instrumentation approach. With Perracotta, it is critical to track path information and backtrack it during the search, to avoid inference of spurious properties. This idea also raises a question: when a tool examines traces offline, which traces should we generate during *model checking*? The most conservative approach would only produce traces at final states of the model. Given that an unbounded loop is the most common structure for a verification harness this is not useful. The opposite extreme would be to produce a trace at each state reached. This would produce a very large (and highly redundant) set of traces. We suggest producing a trace every time the model checker backtracks due to reaching a final state or due to reaching an already visited state (but not after exploring all successors): this would produce one trace for each path by which the model checker reached any particular program state, even if that state was produced many times during model checking; no trace which is a prefix of another trace would be generated. Only empirical investigation can determine if such a strategy produces too many traces.

References

1. Ball, T.: The concept of dynamic analysis. In: European Software Engineering Conference/Foundations of Software Engineering, pp. 216–234 (1999)
2. Nethercote, N., Seward, J.: Valgrind: A framework for heavyweight dynamic binary instrumentation. In: Proceedings of the 2007 ACM SIGPLAN Conference on Programming Language Design and Implementation (PLDI) (2007)
3. Clarke, E.M., Grumberg, O., Peled, D.: Model Checking. MIT Press, Cambridge (2000)
4. Kroening, D., Clarke, E.M., Lerda, F.: A tool for checking ANSI-C programs. In: Tools and Algorithms for the Construction and Analysis of Systems, pp. 168–176 (2004)
5. Ball, T., Rajamani, S.: Automatically validating temporal safety properties of interfaces. In: SPIN Workshop on Model Checking of Software, pp. 103–122 (2001)
6. Musuvathi, M., et al.: CMC: A pragmatic approach to model checking real code. In: Symposium on Operating System Design and Implementation (2002)
7. Holzmann, G.J., Joshi, R.: Model-driven software verification. In: SPIN Workshop on Model Checking of Software, pp. 76–91 (2004)
8. Groce, A., Holzmann, G., Joshi, R.: Randomized differential testing as a prelude to formal verification. In: International Conference on Software Engineering (2007)
9. Holzmann, G.J.: The SPIN Model Checker: Primer and Reference Manual. Addison-Wesley, Reading (2003)
10. Holzmann, G.J., Bosnacki, D.: The design of a multi-core extension of the Spin model checker. IEEE Transactions on Software Engineering 33, 659–674 (2007)
11. Leino, K.R.M.: Toward Reliable Modular Programs. PhD thesis, California Institute of Technology (1995)
12. Necula, G., et al.: CIL: Intermediate language and tools for analysis and transformation of C programs. In: International Conference on Compiler Construction, pp. 213–228 (2002)
13. Flanagan, C., et al.: Extended static checking for Java. In: Proceedings of the 2002 ACM SIGPLAN Conference on Programming Language Design and Implementation (PLDI), pp. 234–245 (2002)
14. Burdy, L., et al.: An overview of JML tools and applications. International Journal on Software Tools for Technology Transfer 7, 212–232 (2005)
15. Wing, J.M.: A two-tiered approach to specifying programs (1983)
16. Various: A collection of NAND Flash application notes, whitepapers and articles, `http://www.data-io.com/NAND/NANDApplicationNotes.asp`
17. Dwyer, M., Person, S., Elbaum, S.G.: Controlling factors in evaluating path-sensitive error detection techniques. In: Foundations of Software Engineering, pp. 92–104 (2006)

18. IBM Rational Software: Purify: Advanced runtime error checking for C/C++ developers, http://www-306.ibm.com/software/awdtools/purify/
19. Cowan, C., et al.: StackGuard: Automatic adaptive detection and prevention of buffer-overflow attacks. In: Proc. 7th USENIX Security Conference, pp. 63–78 (1998)
20. Musuvathi, M.: Email communications (2007)
21. Visser, W., et al.: Model checking programs. Automated Software Engineering 10(2), 203–232 (2003)
22. Ernst, M., et al.: Dynamically discovering likely program invariants to support program evolution. In: International Conference on Software Engineering, pp. 213–224 (1999)
23. Groce, A., Visser, W.: What went wrong: Explaining counterexamples. In: SPIN Workshop on Model Checking of Software, pp. 121–135 (2003)
24. Godefroid, P.: Verisoft: A tool for the automatic analysis of concurrent software. In: Computer-Aided Verification, pp. 172–186 (1997)
25. Kroening, D., Groce, A., Clarke, E.M.: Counterexample guided abstraction refinement via program execution. In: International Conference on Formal Engineering Methods, pp. 224–238 (2004)
26. Havelund, K., Goldberg, A.: Verify your runs. In: Verified Software: Theories, Tools, Experiments (2005)
27. Havelund, K.: RMOR Version 2.0 user manual. Kestrel Technology, California, USA (2006)
28. Yang, J., et al.: Perracotta: Mining temporal API rules from imperfect traces. In: International Conference on Software Engineering, pp. 282–291 (2006)
29. Yang, J., Evans, D.: Dynamically inferring temporal properties. In: Workshop on Program Analysis For Software Tools and Engineering, pp. 23–28 (2004)

Deriving Bisimulations by Simplifying Partitions

Isabella Mastroeni

Dipartimento di Informatica - Università di Verona - Verona, Italy
isabella.mastroeni@univr.it

Abstract. In this paper we analyze the problem of transforming partitions in order to satisfy completeness in the standard abstract interpretation framework. In order to obtain this, we exploit the relation existing between completeness and the Paige-Tarjan notion of stability, already detected in the particular context of *refining* partitions for completeness. Here we extend this relation in order to cope not only with the existing notions of completeness, but also with the simplification of domains for completeness (the so called core). Then we show that completeness lies, under the stability form, in two fields of computer science security: abstract non-interference and opacity.

1 Introduction

The notion of bisimilarity [13] has turned out to be one of the most fundamental notions of operational equivalences in the field of process algebra. The widespread study of bisimulation in several fields of computer science is due to the fact that bisimulation is a *behaviour equivalence*, which goes beyond trace equivalence by comparing systems also on their capability of simulating each others. This notion became important also in abstract model checking (AMC for short), where it has been proved that bisimulation corresponds to strong preservation [15], i.e., there are not counterexamples to the model which do not correspond to concrete examples. In other words, a strong preserving model does not contain false negatives. In particular, it turned out that bisimulation precisely models the observational equivalence between a concrete system and a strong preserving abstraction of it. This important connection was discovered through the analysis of the Paige and Tarjan (PT for short) algorithm [14], a well-known partition refinement algorithm. More precisely, this algorithm finds the coarsest partition *refinement* leading to a *stable* partition, i.e., a partition of the system states such that the *post* image of its blocks (i.e., equivalence classes) is still the union of some of its blocks. It corresponds to the closest partition strong preserving for the underlying concrete system [16]. Hence, this algorithm finds a refinement of the original partition, which in AMC [3] means to move towards the risk of state explosion of the model. In fact, in abstract model checking the abstract model usually represents a compromise between *precision* and *simplicity* of the model. Clearly, whenever strong preservation fails, it means that we have to loose one of these constraints. The standard refinement approach weakens simplicity by making more precise the model, but also the other direction could be

F. Logozzo et al. (Eds.): VMCAI 2008, LNCS 4905, pp. 157–171, 2008.

taken into account. If we can simplify partitions for stability, then we can also weaken precision by making simpler the model, and nevertheless reaching strong preservation. The possibility of considering also the simplification direction is made even more intuitive if we consider the strong relation existing between strong preservation and completeness [9], where both the directions, i.e., refinement (shell) and simplification (core), are possible [11]. In particular, it has been proved that a *strong preserving* abstraction, which corresponds to a *stable* partition of states, coincides with a *complete* abstraction of the powerset of concrete states. Abstract domain *completeness* means that no loss of precision is generated by abstracting a concrete computation. Therefore, if we can instantiate the complete core, existing for abstract domains, to partitions then we find a way for simplifying partitions in order to get strong preservation.

Note that this result would not be interesting only in AMC. Indeed, another field of computer science, where abstract domain completeness is important, is abstract non-interference in language based security [8]. In this model the security policy can be characterized by either an abstraction or a partition of program states [12]. The program is secure if there is no release of information, which corresponds to completeness [1]. In this case to refine the abstract domain corresponds to consider more powerful observers, since the more concrete is the model of the observer and the more it can distinguish concrete states, inducing a more precise and therefore dangerous observation of the system to protect. Therefore, if we have a program that doesn't satisfy a given security policy it is clear that a useful thing to do is to characterize how we can weaken the policy in order to make the program secure. In other words, we are interested in looking for the strongest policy that the program, as it is written, is able to satisfy. This clearly provides a security certification of the program wrt a given model of observers/attackers. At this point, if we model attackers as abstract domains, then the abstract domain completeness framework provides all the tools for generating these certifications. The things are slightly different if the policy is modelled by using partitions, since we would need a technique for making partitions complete by simplifying them. As suggested in [12], due to the strong correspondence between abstract domains and partitions, we could complete a partition in the following way: (1) transform the partition in the corresponding abstract domain, (2) complete it, (3) derive the corresponding partition. Clearly this way is writhed and, above all, the completing technique cannot exploit the fact that in practice we are working on partitions and not on domains. In fact, partitions corresponds to particular abstract domains that admit a compressed representation, the partition itself. This clearly implies that, working with the corresponding abstract domain means to deal with a consistent amount of redundant information. For this reason we are interested in studying directly completeness on partitions.

As underlined before, the PT algorithm corresponds to a completeness refinement technique for partitions, hence what is missing is a corresponding simplification technique. Consider the following example. Let $f = \lambda x.\, 2x$ be on natural numbers and $\mathtt{R} = \{\mathit{Odd},\ \mathit{Even}\}$. This partition is not stable/complete since the images of its equivalence classes under f are not unions of blocks in R, for example $f(Odd) \subset Even$. The problem is that there are no simplifications of R which are stable. In particular the only possible partition coarser than R is All (i.e., all the numbers are in the same equivalence class), which again is not stable since $f(All) = Even \subset All$. This simple example shows that the best stable simplification does not always exist. Hence, we are interested in understanding when this completeness core exists. We will show that the core exists for a partition on a concrete system, whenever forward completeness can be rewritten also as a problem in the dual notion of *backward completeness* [11], for which, exactly as it happens for abstract domains, the completeness core always exists. Note that, the difference between these completeness notions depends on how we abstract the computation: either by directly abstracting the result of the concrete computation (backward) or by performing the computation on the abstract values (forward).

In this paper we rewrite completeness for partitions in terms of stability, defining a new notion which corresponds to backward completeness. We show that, while the shell always exists for both the notions of completeness, the core needs some restrictions in the forward case. Then, we recall the PT algorithm for refining partitions and we show how we can dualize it in order to simplify partitions for completeness. Finally, we propose a discussion on the results where we show an example of well-known notion in language based security which is an instantiation of the new notion of stability, and we propose the non-interference example, where the characterization of the most powerful harmless attacker is an instantiation of the simplification algorithm for stability.

2 Domain Completeness

Completeness in abstract interpretation is a property of abstract domains relative to a fixed computation. In particular, an abstract domain is complete for a concrete function f if we do not lose precision by computing the function in the abstract domain. This means that for that particular function the domain is precise enough. Let C be a complete lattice, $f : C \to C$ and $\rho \in uco(C)$ an upper closure operator[1]. Then *backward completeness* ($\mathcal{B}$-completeness for short), formally $\rho \circ f \circ \rho = \rho \circ f$, means that the domain ρ is expressive enough such that no loss of precision is accumulated by abstracting in ρ the arguments of f. Conversely, *forward completeness* ($\mathcal{F}$-completeness) [9], formally $\rho \circ f \circ \rho = f \circ \rho$, means that no loss of precision is accumulated by approximating the result of the function f computed in ρ. While $\mathcal{B}$-completeness corresponds to the standard notion of completeness [11], the notion of $\mathcal{F}$-completeness is less known [9].

The domain of partitions (equivalence relations) on C, $Eq(C)$, is an abstraction of $uco(\wp(C))$ [12]. Namely, with each partition we can associate a

[1] An upper closure operator (uco) ρ is a monotone, extensive, i.e. $\forall x.\, x \leq \rho(x)$, and idempotent function on C. $uco(C)$ denotes the domain of all the ucos on C. An uco is closed by concrete greatest lower bound and contains the concrete top.

set of closures, those that induce the given partition on C. Consider an abstract domain $\eta \in uco(\wp(C))$. We define $Rel^{\eta} \subseteq C \times C$ as follows: $\forall x, y \in C \,.\, x\ Rel^{\eta}\ y \Leftrightarrow \eta(\{x\}) = \eta(\{y\})$. Rel^{η} is an equivalence relation. Consider now an equivalence relation $\mathtt{R} \subseteq C \times C$. We define $Clo^{\mathtt{R}} \in uco(\wp(C))$ as follows: $\forall X \subseteq C. Clo^{\mathtt{R}}(X) = \bigcup_{x \in X} [x]_{\mathtt{R}}$. $Clo^{\mathtt{R}}$ is an upper closure operator, in the following called *partitioning*. Finally, we consider $f : C \longrightarrow C$ and its additive lift, defined as $f(X) = \bigcup_{x \in X} f(x)$. In the following we abuse notation by identifying any function with its additive lift.

At this point, let us define backward completeness of equivalence relations in terms of completeness of the corresponding closure operators. Let $\mathtt{R}, \mathtt{S} \in Eq(C)$ and $f : C \longrightarrow C$, then $\mathtt{S} \circ f \circ \mathtt{R} = \mathtt{S} \circ f$ iff $Clo^{\mathtt{S}} \circ f \circ Clo^{\mathtt{R}} = Clo^{\mathtt{S}} \circ f$ iff

$$[f([x]_{\mathtt{R}})]_{\mathtt{S}} = [f(x)]_{\mathtt{S}} \text{ iff } \forall w \in [x]_{\mathtt{R}}.\, f(w) \in [f(x)]_{\mathtt{S}} \text{ [12]} \tag{1}$$

Analogously, we can define forward completeness in terms of completeness of the corresponding closure operators. Let $\mathtt{R}, \mathtt{S} \in Eq(C)$, and f a map on C, then $\mathtt{S} \circ f \circ \mathtt{R} = f \circ \mathtt{R}$ iff $Clo^{\mathtt{S}} \circ f \circ Clo^{\mathtt{R}} = f \circ Clo^{\mathtt{R}}$ iff $[f([x]_{\mathtt{R}})]_{\mathtt{S}} = f([x]_{\mathtt{R}})$. In the following we denote respectively by $\top$ and id the equivalence relations induced by the corresponding ucos.

A pattern for domain transformation. The problem of making abstract domains $\mathcal{B}$-complete and $\mathcal{F}$-complete has been solved [11,9] constructively for continuous functions. The key point in these constructions is that both $\mathcal{F}$- and $\mathcal{B}$-completeness are properties of the underlying abstract domain A relative to the concrete function f. In a more general setting let $f : C \rightarrow D$ be a function on the complete lattices C and D, and $\rho \in uco(D)$ and $\eta \in uco(C)$ be abstract domains. $\langle \rho, \eta \rangle$ is a pair of $\mathcal{B}[\mathcal{F}]$-complete abstractions for f if $\rho \circ f = \rho \circ f \circ \eta$ $[f \circ \eta = \rho \circ f \circ \eta]$. A pair of domain transformers can be associated with any completeness problem. We define a *domain refinement* [*simplification*] as any monotone function $\tau : uco(L) \rightarrow uco(L)$ such that $X \subseteq \tau(X)$ $[\tau(X) \subseteq X]$ [10]. The *shell* of a domain is the closest complete refinement of the domain, while the *core* is the closest complete simplification. For making a domain $\mathcal{F}$-complete we can refine the domain by adding all the direct images of the concrete function to the output abstract domain (*$\mathcal{F}$-complete shell*) [9], or simplify the domain by removing all the elements whose direct image is outside the output domain (*$\mathcal{F}$-complete core*). On the other hand, for $\mathcal{B}$-completeness we can add all the maximal elements of the inverse images of the function to the input domain (*$\mathcal{B}$-complete shell*), or remove all the elements whose inverse image is outside the input domain (*$\mathcal{B}$-complete core*) [11]. Formally, the constructive characterization of completeness is the following: ρ is $\mathcal{F}$-complete iff $\forall x \in \rho.\, f(x) \in \rho$ [9]; ρ is $\mathcal{B}$-complete iff $\forall x \in \rho \,.\, \bigcup \max(f^{-1}(\downarrow x)) = \bigcup \max\{\, y \,|\, f(y) \leq x \,\} \subseteq \rho$ [11]. If f is additive $\max\{\, x \,|\, f(x) \leq y \,\} = \bigvee\{\, x \,|\, f(x) \leq y \,\} = f^{+}(y)$ is the right adjoint[2], and therefore $\eta \circ f = \eta \circ f \circ \rho \Leftrightarrow f^{+} \circ \eta = \rho \circ f^{+} \circ \eta$.

[2] Let us recall that, if $\alpha : C \longrightarrow A$ is an additive map, then it admits right adjoint $\gamma = \lambda x \in A.\, \bigvee\{\, y \in C \,|\, \alpha(y) \leq_A x \,\}$, i.e, $\langle C, \alpha, \gamma, A \rangle$ is a Galois insertion.

3 Stability vs Completeness

At this point, our aim is to find a characterization of partition completeness that can be exploited in a constructive way. The idea to follow comes from the relation existing between partition stability [14] and $\mathcal{F}$-completeness [15,9]. Namely, the idea is to generalize the notion of stability in order to cope also with $\mathcal{B}$-completeness.

Consider a concrete domain C, a function $f : C \longrightarrow C$, and two partitions of C, induced by the two equivalence relations $\mathtt{R} \subseteq C \times C$ and $\mathtt{S} \subseteq C \times C$. In the following we abuse notation by identifying the equivalence relation with the induced partition.

Let us first consider the notion of stability introduced for the PT algorithm [14] generalized to arbitrary additive functions.

Definition 1 (f-$\mathcal{F}$stability)
$X \in \mathtt{S}$ is f-$\mathcal{F}$stable wrt $Y \in \mathtt{R}$ if $X \cap f(Y) \neq \varnothing \;\Rightarrow\; X \subseteq f(Y)$. $\mathtt{S}$ is f-$\mathcal{F}$stable wrt $Y \in \mathtt{R}$ if $\forall X \in \mathtt{S}$ we have X f-$\mathcal{F}$stable wrt Y. $\mathtt{S}$ is f-$\mathcal{F}$stable wrt $\mathtt{R}$ if $\forall Y \in \mathtt{R}$ we have that $\mathtt{S}$ is f-$\mathcal{F}$stable wrt Y. If $\mathtt{R} = \mathtt{S}$, then we say $\mathtt{S}$ f-$\mathcal{F}$stable.

Namely, if $\mathtt{S}$ is f-$\mathcal{F}$stable wrt $\mathtt{R}$, the image by f of an equivalence class (also referred as *block*) of $\mathtt{R}$ can only be mapped in a block (or union of blocks) in $\mathtt{S}$. Ranzato and Tapparo [15] showed that this notion corresponds to a form of $\mathcal{F}$-completeness for f, for this reason we call it $\mathcal{F}$stability.

Moreover, we prove that transforming partitions for stability corresponds precisely to the $\mathcal{F}$completeness characterization [9] instantiated to partitioning closures. Namely, we show that f-$\mathcal{F}$stable partitions corresponds to partitioning domains closed under direct images of f.

Theorem 2. *Let $f : C \longrightarrow C$, and $\mathtt{S}, \mathtt{R} \subseteq \wp(C)$ be partitions of C. Then the following statements are equivalent*

1. *$\mathtt{S}$ is f-$\mathcal{F}$stable wrt $\mathtt{R}$;*
2. *$[f([x]_{\mathtt{R}})]_{\mathtt{S}} = f([x]_{\mathtt{R}})$;*
3. *$\forall X \in \mathit{Clo}^{\mathtt{R}} \;\Rightarrow\; f(X) \in \mathit{Clo}^{\mathtt{S}}$;*

Note that this theorem holds also for generic functions $f : \wp(C) \longrightarrow \wp(C)$, i.e. not only for additive functions.

At this point, we can think of "reversing" the stability constraint, namely we ask the image of a block to be completely contained in a block. In other words, we require the image of elements, which are in the relation, to be still in the relation. Note that, this corresponds exactly to the $\mathcal{B}$-completeness formalization given in Eq. 1, for this reason we call it $\mathcal{B}$stability. As the previous notion, it is defined parametric on a function f:

Definition 3 (f-$\mathcal{B}$stability)
$X \in \mathtt{S}$ is f-$\mathcal{B}$stable wrt $Y \in \mathtt{R}$ if $X \cap f(Y) \neq \varnothing \;\Rightarrow\; f(Y) \subseteq X$. $\mathtt{S}$ is f-$\mathcal{B}$stable wrt $Y \in \mathtt{R}$ if $\forall X \in \mathtt{S}$ we have X f-$\mathcal{B}$stable wrt Y. $\mathtt{S}$ is f-$\mathcal{B}$stable wrt $\mathtt{R}$ if $\forall Y \in \mathtt{R}$ we have that $\mathtt{S}$ is f-$\mathcal{B}$stable wrt Y. If $\mathtt{R} = \mathtt{S}$, then we say $\mathtt{S}$ is f-$\mathcal{B}$stable.

The next theorem formally relates the new notion of $\mathcal{B}$stability with the notion of $\mathcal{B}$completeness for partitions. Moreover, as for $\mathcal{F}$stability, we also show that we can constructively characterize $\mathcal{B}$stability exactly as $\mathcal{B}$-completeness [11], but clearly restricted to partitioning closures. Namely, $\mathcal{B}$stable partitions correspond to partitioning domains closed under maximal inverse images of f.

Theorem 4. *Let $f : C \longrightarrow C$ (additive), and $\mathtt{S}, \mathtt{R} \subseteq \wp(C)$ be partitions of C. Then the following statements are equivalent*

1. *$\mathtt{S}$ is f-$\mathcal{B}$stable wrt $\mathtt{R}$;*
2. *$[f([x]_{\mathtt{R}})]_{\mathtt{S}} = [f(x)]_{\mathtt{S}}$;*
3. *$\forall X \in Clo^{\mathtt{S}} \Rightarrow \max\{\, Y \mid f(Y) \subseteq X \,\} \in Clo^{\mathtt{R}}$;*

Note that, the theorem above holds only for $f : \wp(C) \longrightarrow \wp(C)$ obtained as additive lifting of $f : C \longrightarrow C$, or in general for additive functions. Indeed, as we can see in the following example, it is sufficient to take $f : C \longrightarrow \wp(C)$ not additive to lose the equivalence.

Example 5. Consider $C = \{a, b, c, x, y\}$, and the partitions $\mathtt{R} = \{\{a, c, x\}, \{b, y\}\}$ and $\mathtt{S} = \{\{a, b\}, \{c, x\}, \{y\}\}$. Consider $f : C \longrightarrow \wp(C)$ such that $f(a) = \{a\}$, $f(b) = \{b\}$, $f(c) = \{c\}$, $f(x) = \{x\}$ and $f(y) = \{a, x\}$. Then

$$[f([y]_{\mathtt{R}})]_{\mathtt{S}} = [f(b, y)]_{\mathtt{S}} = [\{a, b, x\}]_{\mathtt{S}} = \{a, b, c, x\} = [f(y)]_{\mathtt{S}} = [\{a, x\}]_{\mathtt{S}}$$

Hence, it is complete on y. Consider now stability, and in particular consider the blocks $[x]_{\mathtt{S}}$ and $[y]_{\mathtt{R}}$. Note that, $[x]_{\mathtt{S}} \cap f([y]_{\mathtt{R}}) = \{c, x\} \cap \{a, b, x\} = \{x\} \neq \varnothing$, while $f([y]_{\mathtt{R}}) = \{a, b, x\} \nsubseteq \{c, x\} = [x]_{\mathtt{S}}$.

Note that, both these definitions of stability are parametric on a function, explicitly given; in sake of simplicity, in the following, whenever the function is clear from the context or it is not relevant, we omit it.

The parallelism with completeness is clearly quite deep, and in particular, exactly as it happens for completeness, we can note a strong relation between the functions f that make a partition $\mathcal{F}$stable and those making a partition $\mathcal{B}$stable. In the adjoint framework [5], it is well known that $f(Y) \subseteq X$ is equivalent to $X \subseteq f^+(Y)$, where f^+ is the right adjoint of f, which exists since we are considering only additive $f : \wp(C) \longrightarrow \wp(C)$. Hence, it is clear that $\mathtt{R}$ is f-$\mathcal{B}$stable wrt $\mathtt{S}$ iff $\mathtt{S}$ is f^+-$\mathcal{F}$stable wrt $\mathtt{R}$. The problem is that f^+ is co-additive by construction, but in general it is not additive, hence it does not fit in the framework we are considering. For this reason we need to weaken this inversion. In particular we can show that the equivalence between $\mathcal{F}$stability and $\mathcal{B}$stability holds also if we consider the pre-image of f (which is additive by construction) instead of its right adjoint. Consider $f : C \to C$, let us define, $f^{-1} = \lambda X. \{\, y \in C \mid f(y) \in X \,\}$, then we have the following result for all the partitions $\mathtt{R}$ and $\mathtt{S}$ on C.

Proposition 6. *$\mathtt{R}$ is f-$\mathcal{B}$stable wrt $\mathtt{S}$ iff $\mathtt{S}$ is f^{-1}-$\mathcal{F}$stable wrt $\mathtt{R}$.*

Note that the process of transforming a $\mathcal{F}$stability problem in a $\mathcal{B}$stability one, is much more delicate, as the following proposition shows.

Proposition 7. *If* R *is* f^{-1}*-*$\mathcal{B}$*stable wrt* S *then* S *is* f*-*$\mathcal{F}$*stable wrt* R*. If* S *is* f*-*$\mathcal{F}$*stable wrt* R *and* f *injective, then* R *is* f^{-1}*-*$\mathcal{B}$*stable wrt* S*.*

These propositions are important for underlying that the two stability problems are different, in particular any $\mathcal{B}$stability problem can be translated in a $\mathcal{F}$stability one, but the vice versa is not always possible. Formally, the difference between the two propositions is due to the fact that, while $Y \subseteq f^{-1}(X) \Rightarrow f(Y) \subseteq X$ always holds, $X \subseteq f(Y) \Rightarrow f^{-1}(X) \subseteq Y$ requires the injectivity of f.

4 Characterizing Stability Transformations

In the standard abstract interpretation framework, and hence whenever we need to approximate properties, completeness is an important property, since it guarantees that the approximation is precise enough for what we need to observe. Namely, the approximation loses only those aspects which are indeed not useful for the computation of interest. For this reason it is important to have a systematic method for minimally transforming abstract domains in order to make them complete, and hence precise, for the function we have to compute. These kinds of abstract domain transformers are completely characterized, both for refining and simplifying domains, for backward completeness [11] and partially characterized (only in the refinement direction) for forward completeness [9].

On the other hand, partitions form an important abstraction of closure operators, used in many fields of computer science where also completeness has a relevant role, such as abstract model checking or language-based security. Moreover, partitions become quite useful also in practice, for implementations, due to their simplicity. Hence, it becomes interesting to have also a systematic method for transforming partitions in order to make them complete. In the following sections, given a partition, we analyze the existence of the closest stable partition for both $\mathcal{F}$ and $\mathcal{B}$stability. We focus now our attention only on problems of stability where the input relation coincides with the output one, i.e., S = R. Hence, our aim is to characterize given a partition R on C, its *best* approximation, from above or from below, which is stable.

Let us first consider the problem of refining partitions, which corresponds, for $\mathcal{F}$stability, to well known stability refinement [14,15]. The following proposition corresponds to saying that the coarsest $\mathcal{F}$stable refinement of a given partition always exists, exactly as it happens in the context of the PT algorithm [14]. Moreover, we show that the same holds for $\mathcal{B}$stability, meaning that from the refinement point of view the two notions are perfectly equivalent.

Proposition 8. *Given the map* $f : C \longrightarrow C$

- $\left\{ \Pi \in Eq(C) \,\middle|\, \Pi \text{ is } f\text{-}\mathcal{F}\text{stable} \right\} \in lco(Eq(C))$[3]
- $\left\{ \Pi \in Eq(C) \,\middle|\, \Pi \text{ is } f\text{-}\mathcal{B}\text{stable} \right\} \in lco(Eq(C))$.

[3] The domain $lco(D)$ denotes the set of all the lower closure operators on D. An lco η is a monotone, reductive, i.e. $\forall x. x \geq \eta(x)$, and idempotent function on D. An lco is closed by concrete least upper bound and it contains the concrete bottom.

This result is immediate from the well known results on abstract domains [11], and it means exactly that, given a partition R there always exists a unique coarsest $\mathcal{F}$stable [$\mathcal{B}$stable] partition among the partitions more concrete than R.

On the other hand, in order to guarantee the existence of the best approximation by simplifying the partition, we have to prove that $\mathcal{F}$stable and $\mathcal{B}$stable partitions are closed under greatest lower bound. Namely, given a partition R, we have to prove that there always exists a unique most precise $\mathcal{F}$stable [$\mathcal{B}$stable] partition, coarser than R. In this case, while the best $\mathcal{B}$stable simplification always exists, the same does not hold for $\mathcal{F}$stability.

Proposition 9. *Given the map* $f : C \longrightarrow C$

- $\{\, \Pi \in Eq(C) \mid \Pi \text{ is } f\text{-}\mathcal{F}stable \,\} \in uco(Eq(C))$ *if* $f : C \longrightarrow C$ *is both injective and onto, namely if its additive lift is co-additive on* $\wp(C)$ *and* $\top$ *is* $\mathcal{F}$*stable.*
- $\{\, \Pi \in Eq(C) \mid \Pi \text{ is } f\text{-}\mathcal{B}stable \,\} \in uco(Eq(C))$.

This proposition tells us that the conditions that make the simplification for $\mathcal{F}$stability exist are very restrictive. In particular, the $\mathcal{F}$stability "core" exists only for injective functions and only when also the $\top$, i.e., the partition where all the elements are in the same equivalence class, is $\mathcal{F}$stable. In particular, this last condition means that $f(\top) = \top$, being obviously $f(\top) \subseteq \top$. These two conditions correspond exactly to the two conditions that characterize abstract domains, i.e., uco, which always hold for $\mathcal{B}$stability. In fact an abstract domain is an uco if it is closed under concrete greatest lower bound and if it contains the top. It is worth noting that this last condition is implied by injectivity only if the considered concrete domain is *finite*. The next example shows that, in general, injectivity is not sufficient for guaranteeing the existence of the core.

Example 10. Consider the function $f = \lambda x.\, 2x$ defined on natural numbers $\mathbb{N}$. The function is trivially injective, but $f(\mathbb{N}) = 2\mathbb{N} \subset \mathbb{N}$, namely $\top = \mathbb{N}$ is not $\mathcal{F}$stable. Consider now the partition $\mathtt{R} = \{2\mathbb{N}, 2\mathbb{N}+1\}$, of even and odd numbers. Then we have for instance that $2\mathbb{N} \cap f(2\mathbb{N}+1) \neq \varnothing$, since for example $6 = f(3)$ is in both sets, but $2\mathbb{N} \not\subseteq f(2\mathbb{N}+1)$ since 4 is an even number but is not obtained as the f image of an odd number. Clearly, the only possible simplification of R is the $\top$ partition which is not stable, either.

On the other hand, while the condition on the top is necessary by definition of uco, in general it is not sufficient alone in the infinite case, as we can see in the following example.

Example 11. Consider the function f defined as follows:

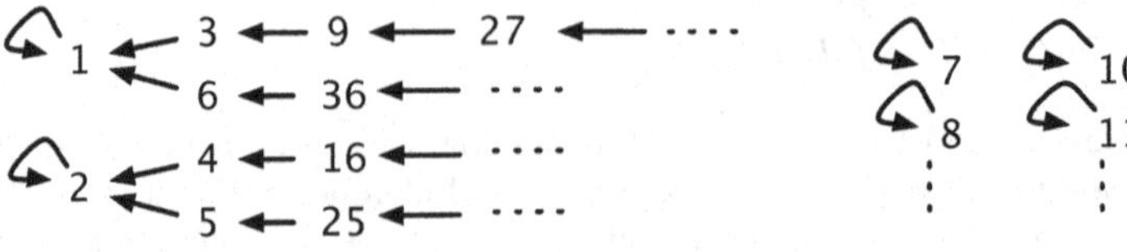

First of all note that f is clearly not injective ($f(3) = f(6)$) while $f(\mathbb{N}) = \mathbb{N}$. Consider the partitions $\Pi_1 = \{\{1,2\},\{3,4\},\mathbb{N} \setminus [1,4]\}$ and $\Pi_2 = \{\{1,2\},\{3,5\},\mathbb{N} \setminus \{1,2,3,5\}\}$. They are both $\mathcal{F}$stable since $f(\{1,2\}) = \{1,2\} = f(\{3,4\})$ and $f(\mathbb{N} \setminus [1,4]) = \mathbb{N}$, and $f(\{3,5\}) = \{1,2\}$ and $f(\mathbb{N} \setminus \{1,2,3,5\}) = \mathbb{N}$. On the other hand, their glb Π contains the blocks $\{1,2\}$ and $\{3\}$ which are such that $f(\{3\}) = \{1\} \cap \{1,2\} \neq \varnothing$ but $\{1,2\} \not\subseteq f(\{3\})$, hence Π is not $\mathcal{F}$stable.

5 Making Partitions Complete

In the previous section, we have seen that it is always possible to refine partitions for making them stable, and that it is always possible to simplify partitions for $\mathcal{B}$stability, whereas the same does not hold for $\mathcal{F}$stability. Due to the strong requirements for the existence of the $\mathcal{F}$-complete core for a given partition, in the following we will focus only on $\mathcal{B}$stability simplifications.

5.1 Refining for Completeness: Generalised PT Algorithm

Ranzato and Tapparo [15] proved that the PT algorithm (`PT-Algorithm`) for characterizing the coarsest bisimilar partition of a given one [14] wrt the pre function of a transition system, corresponds to the forward complete shell of the abstract domain associated to the partition. In particular, the authors prove that the `PT-Algorithm` can be generalized in order to cope with the completeness shell of any abstraction of closure operators (not only the partition abstraction), wrt any function (not only the pre of a transition system). Our idea follows a quite different direction of generalization than [15]. Instead of describing the `PT-Algorithm` in terms of completeness, we are interested in describing completeness "by means of the `PT-Algorithm`" and in terms of a generalized notion of stability.

Let us recall that, the generalized `PT-Algorithm` [15] (Fig. 1) is an efficient algorithm for computing the coarsest bisimulation of a given partition. Consider a function f and a partition $\mathtt{P}$. $\mathtt{PTSplit}_f(S,\mathtt{P})$ splits each unstable block B of a partition $\mathtt{P}$ wrt $f(S)$ into $B \cap f(S)$ and $B \setminus f(S)$, while $\mathtt{PTRefiners}_f(\mathtt{P})$ is the set of all the blocks in $\mathtt{P}$, or obtained as union of blocks in $\mathtt{P}$, which make

$$\mathtt{P} : \text{Partition}$$

$$\mathtt{PTSplit}_f(S,\mathtt{P}) : \begin{cases} \text{Partition obtained from } \mathtt{P} \text{ by replacing} \\ \text{each block } B \in \mathtt{P} \text{ with } B \cap f(S) \text{ and } B \setminus f(S) \end{cases}$$

$$\mathtt{PTRefiners}_f(\mathtt{P}) \stackrel{\text{def}}{=} \left\{ S \,\middle|\, \mathtt{P} \neq \mathtt{PTSplit}_f(S,\mathtt{P}) \ \wedge\ \exists \{B_i\}_i \subseteq \mathtt{P}.\, S = \bigcup_i B_i \right\}$$

$$\mathtt{PT\text{-}Algorithm}_f : \begin{cases} \textbf{while } (\mathtt{P} \text{ is not } f\text{-}\mathcal{F}\text{stable}) \textbf{ do} \\ \qquad \textbf{choose } S \in \mathtt{PTRefiners}_f(\mathtt{P}); \\ \qquad \mathtt{P} := \mathtt{PTSplit}_f(S,\mathtt{P}); \\ \textbf{endwhile} \end{cases}$$

Fig. 1. A generalized version of the PT algorithm

other blocks unstable. The intuition behind the described algorithm is given in the picture (b1). Namely, if the image of a block S does not contain completely one of the blocks X, then we split X in $X \setminus f(S)$ and $X \cap f(S)$. Analogously, we can think of deriving an algorithm for refining partitions for $\mathcal{B}$stability. The idea is given in the picture (a1). In fact, if the image of a block S is not completely contained in one block X, then we split S in order to isolate the elements whose image is completely contained in X. At this point, we could derive directly an algorithm for $\mathcal{B}$stability, but this algorithm is exactly the one given above wrt f^{-1}, by Prop. 6. This means that, whenever we have to refine a partition for f-$\mathcal{B}$stability, since we consider additive maps only, we can solve the problem for f^{-1}-$\mathcal{F}$stability with the algorithm given above.

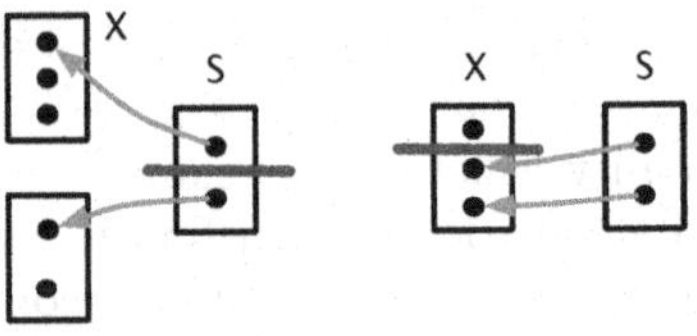

(a1) (b1)

5.2 Simplifying for Completeness: A Dualized PT Algorithm

In the previous subsection, we have seen how the algorithm known for $\mathcal{F}$stability [14] can be used also for refining partitions for $\mathcal{B}$stability, i.e., for $\mathcal{B}$-completeness. At this point we are interested in simplifying domains for making them complete, and therefore in simplifying partitions for making them stable.

In this case the idea is to *merge* blocks. $\mathcal{B}$stability requires that the image by f of any block is completely contained in a block. Hence, as we can see in Fig.(a2), Fig.(b2) for making stability hold we have to merge each block whose image by f is contained in X. This informal

if $f(S) \nsubseteq X$, we merge together all the blocks which have some elements in common with $f(S)$, forcing $f(S)$ to be contained in a block of the new partition so far obtained. On the other hand, $\mathcal{F}$stability requires that the inverse image by f of any block is obtained as union of blocks. Hence, as we can see in

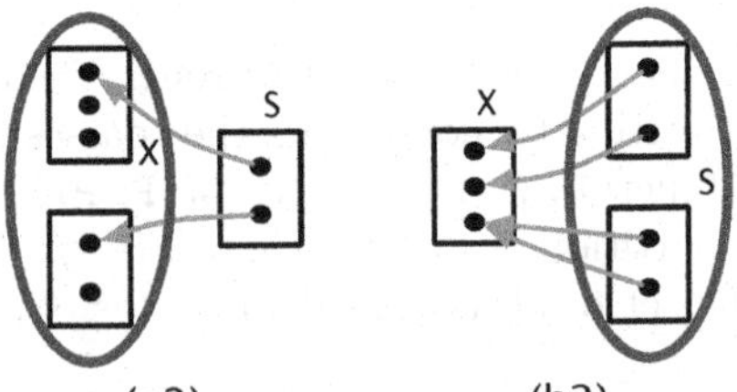

(a2) (b2)

description is sufficient for noting that the simplification for $\mathcal{F}$stability is not so straightforward. Indeed, if there exists one element in X which is not image by f of any other element, then there is no way of inducing $\mathcal{F}$stability by merging blocks. This intuition is exactly a consequence of the conditions required in Prop. 9[4]. On the other hand, the best approximation of a given partition towards $\mathcal{B}$stability always exists. Note that, in this way we solve a $\mathcal{B}$stability problem on f, nevertheless, by Prop. 6, we are also solving a $\mathcal{F}$stability problem, and therefore a *bisimulation* problem for the inverse map f^{-1}.

[4] Note that it is not possible to transform $\mathcal{F}$ problems in $\mathcal{B}$ problems unless the hypotheses of Prop. 7 hold, but this corresponds to the existence of $\mathcal{F}$ simplification.

At this point, the idea is to formalize in an algorithm the intuition given before. In this way, we can generate an algorithm corresponding to the `PT-Algorithm` where $\texttt{PTRefiners}_f(\texttt{P})$ and $\texttt{PTSplit}_f(S, \texttt{P})$ are respectively substituted by the following functions: Let P be a partition and $B \in \texttt{P}$

$$\texttt{PTSimplifiers}_f^{\mathcal{B}}(S) \stackrel{\text{def}}{=} \{\, X \,|\, X \cap f(S) \neq \varnothing \,\}$$

$$\texttt{PTMerge}_f^{\mathcal{B}}(S, \texttt{P}) : \begin{cases} \text{Partition obtained from P by replacing} \\ \text{all the blocks } X \in \texttt{PTSimplifiers}_f^{\mathcal{B}}(S) \text{ with} \\ \bigcup \texttt{PTSimplifiers}_f^{\mathcal{B}}(S) \end{cases}$$

`PTSimplifiers` identifies all the elements that break stability, i.e., those elements intersecting $f(S)$, for any $S \in \texttt{P}$, and `PTMerge` substitutes all these blocks with their union. Exactly as the `PT-Algorithm` [14] does, this algorithm exploits several properties of the `PTmerge` operation and of the $\mathcal{B}$stability notion. In particular, we can note that the effect of the simplification step is to replace a partition, not $\mathcal{B}$stable wrt a block S, by a simplified partition $\mathcal{B}$stable wrt S. Since $\mathcal{B}$stability is inherited by simplification, a given block S can be a simplifier only once. This observation leads us to the following important result.

Theorem 12. *The simplification algorithm is correct and terminating.*

In the following, we have an example of a partition (thin circles) not bisimilar to the underlying system. The dashed lines form an abstract trace which does not correspond to any concrete trace, i.e., a spurious counterexample. Then, on the left the thick line denotes the most precise refinement, of the given partition, bisimilar to the concrete underlying system, on the right the thick lines denote the coarsest simplification.

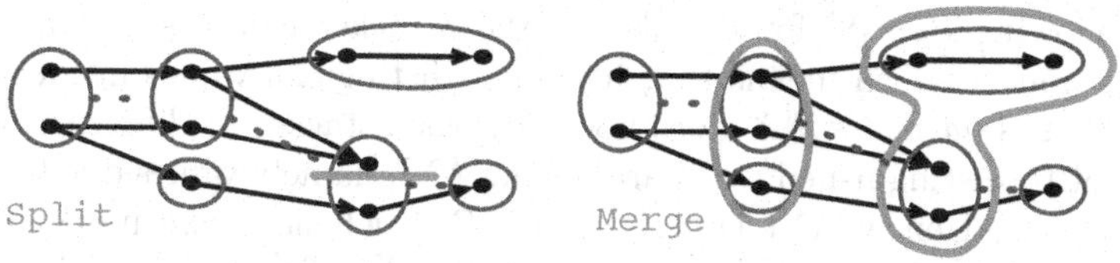

The algorithm given above has the same complexity of the naive refinement one, i.e., the `PT-Algorithm`. Even if this simplifying algorithm seems quite naive, we think that it can be made faster and that an efficient version would be surely interesting in particular for using it for implementations in the contexts described in the following section. Moreover, it could be interesting also to combine this work with the Ranzato and Tapparo work in order to dualize completely their generalized algorithm [15].

6 A Discussion: $\mathcal{B}$stability in SW Security

In this paper, we analyze the problem of making partitions complete, namely stable. In order to characterize completely the framework for completeness, we introduce a new notion of stability, corresponding to $\mathcal{B}$-completeness. Moreover, in order to cope with both the possible ways of transforming partitions (shell and core), we characterize a new algorithm for simplifying partitions for $\mathcal{B}$stability. In the following sections, we provide two examples of $\mathcal{B}$stability problems. These examples are not real applications, but aim to give an idea of two computer science fields where the results we provided can afford new points of view leading to the realization of new links, between also well-known fields, which deserves further research.

6.1 Transforming Partitions for $\mathcal{B}$stability: Non-Interference

Non-interference in language-based security (NI) corresponds to requiring that secret inputs have not to affect public outputs, otherwise it is possible that some secret information is released. Abstract non-interference (ANI) is a weakened NI notion parametric on the public observation [8]. In this model, data are distinguished in public ($\mathbb{V}^{\mathtt{L}}$) and private ($\mathbb{V}^{\mathtt{H}}$), and the attacker is modelled by two abstractions, the observation of the public input η and the observation of the public output ρ. Then, a program P satisfies ANI if: $\forall l_1, l_2\mathbb{V}^{\mathtt{L}}, h_1, h_2 \in \mathbb{V}^{\mathtt{H}}.\eta(l_1) = \eta(l_2) \;\Rightarrow\; \rho(\llbracket P\rrbracket(h_1, l_1)^{\mathtt{L}}) = \rho(\llbracket P\rrbracket(h_2, l_2)^{\mathtt{L}})$. Namely, whenever the attacker can observe η in input and ρ in output, no change of the private input can interfere with the observation of the public output.

The general notion of ANI, modelling input and output observations as abstract domains, allows us not only to model attackers depending on what they are supposed to observe, but provide a framework where, given a program semantics, it is possible to characterize which is the most concrete public output observation unable to disclose secret information.

This characterization is made by means of a predicate *Secr* whose intuition is the following (see [8] for details). If the attacker can observe in output a set X of values (which means that it cannot distinguish values inside X), then the attacker is *harmless* if X does not allow the attacker to discern values that should not be distinguished for guaranteeing ANI, namely values due to different private inputs. Hence, ANI is satisfied by P if, whenever we need to require, for instance, $\llbracket P\rrbracket(2,3)^{\mathtt{L}} = \llbracket P\rrbracket(5,3)^{\mathtt{L}}$, then if $\llbracket P\rrbracket(2,3)^{\mathtt{L}} \in X$, it also must be $\llbracket P\rrbracket(5,3)^{\mathtt{L}} \in X$ and vice versa, otherwise ANI is violated. Therefore, we define $\Upsilon(\eta(l)) \stackrel{\text{def}}{=} \llbracket P\rrbracket(\mathbb{V}^{\mathtt{H}}, \eta(l))^{\mathtt{L}}$, which, for each $l \in \mathbb{V}^{\mathtt{L}}$, consists in all the values that must not be distinguished by an attacker observing η in input. At this point we can say that X satisfies *Secr* if it does not "break" any of these $\Upsilon(\eta(l))$, i.e., $\forall l \in \mathbb{V}^{l}.X \cap \Upsilon(\eta(l)) \neq \varnothing \;\Rightarrow\; \Upsilon(\eta(l)) \subseteq X$. From this last observation it is clear that the predicate *Secr* can be intuitively characterized as a $\mathcal{B}$stability problem. Finally, the most concrete harmless attacker corresponds to the domain obtained by collecting all the sets of values satisfying *Secr* [8], and together with the considerations above we obtain the following result.

Proposition 13. *The domain* $\{\, X \in \wp(\mathbb{V}^{\mathtt{L}}) \,|\, X$ *is* $\mathcal{B}$*stable wrt the function* $\Upsilon \,\}$ *characterizes a possible abstraction of the most concrete harmless attacker. If* P *is deterministic, than this domain precisely characterizes it.*

In this way, the problem of finding the most powerful harmless attacker can be approximated as a problem of simplifying partitions for getting $\mathcal{B}$stability. We would like to underline that this approximation of the strongest harmless attacker by means of $\mathcal{B}$stability becomes important in our task of implementing the certification of program security, since it allows us to use the PTMerge algorithm instead of the theoretical completeness framework.

For instance, consider the program $P \stackrel{\text{def}}{=}$ **while** h **do** $l := l * 2; h := 0;$ **endw**. The maximal harmless observer, obtained as the collection of all the sets X such that $Secr(X)$ holds, is the one unable to distinguish values differing only in the exponent of the factor 2, i.e., $2 * 3 = 6 \equiv 24 = 2^3 * 3$ [8].

This relation between ANI and stability is even stronger if, whenever we model the attacker by means of equivalence relations, we consider the more general case where there is no distinction between private and public data [12]. In this case we can rewrite ANI as $\forall x, y \in \mathbb{V}.\, y \,\mathtt{R}\, x \;\Rightarrow\; f(y) \,\mathtt{S}\, f(x)$. Namely, if the attacker observes R in input, then it cannot observe anything more than S in the output of f [17]. In [12], the authors provide a characterization of this notion of ANI as a $\mathcal{B}$-completeness problem, and hence as a $\mathcal{B}$stability problem.

Proposition 14. *A pair* $\langle \mathtt{R}, \mathtt{S} \rangle$ *of equivalence relations make* f *secure with respect to equivalence relation based ANI, iff* S *is* f*-*$\mathcal{B}$*stable wrt* R.

In particular, the operation of modifying the input observation by fixing the output one [12] corresponds to PTSplit, whereas, the operation of fixing the input by transforming the output observation [12] corresponds to PTMerge.

6.2 A $\mathcal{B}$stability Example: Opacity

Opacity is a well known notion in the context of software security for program obfuscation. In particular, it is usually introduced as a property of predicates whose value is known at "obfuscation time", i.e., *a priori* to the program transformation, but it is "difficult" for an observer to distinguish its real value [4]. It is used for making more difficult the understanding of the control structure of a program, and hence reverse engineering on the program itself. This kind of predicates are usually considered from a very practical point of view, and often they are derived "ad hoc" for a particular problem. The notion of *opacity* has been treated from a more theoretical point of view by Bryans et al. [2] in order to cope with transition systems.

Definition 15 (Opaque predicate [2]). *A predicate* ϕ *over a trace semantics of a transition system is opaque wrt the observation function* obs *if, for every execution* $t_1 \in \phi$ *there is an execution* $t_2 \notin \phi$ *such that* $\text{obs}(t_1) = \text{obs}(t_2)$.

This notion tells us that a predicate is opaque for an observer if the observer cannot distinguish when the predicate holds and when it doesn't. Hence, if we model a predicate as the set of all the computations satisfying the predicate, then it is a partition splitting the domain in two blocks: the set of all the computations satisfying the predicate and those which don't satisfy the predicate. On the other hand, the observation is a function mapping a concrete computation t in the set of those computations that the observer is not able to distinguish from t. In this context we can rewrite the opacity above in the following way.

Proposition 16. *Opacity can be rewritten as* $\forall t. \mathrm{obs}(t) \cap \phi \neq \varnothing \wedge \mathrm{obs}(t) \not\subseteq \phi$*, and hence it corresponds to a* lack of *obs-*$\mathcal{B}$stability/$\mathcal{B}$-completeness.

Dalla Preda et al. [7] characterized the opacity of a particular set of opaque predicates as a lack of completeness, i.e., only attackers whose observation is complete wrt the predicate are able to break the opacity of the predicate. By using the formalization above we can say that this relation between completeness and opacity always holds. In particular, opacity is a lack of $\mathcal{B}$stability, and hence we can exploit the stability framework for analyzing if and how we can transform the predicate for making it opaque wrt the given observation. This formalization of opacity, that we will call *abstract opacity* is, indeed, coherent with the informal definition [4] corresponding to the standard notion of opacity, that we will call *(concrete) opacity*, used in practice. Let us explain this correspondence by means of an example. Consider, for instance, the opaque predicate $3|(x^3 - x)$ (which is always true with $x \in \mathbb{Z}$) and the observation (modelled as an abstract domain) $\alpha = \{\mathbb{Z}, 3\mathbb{Z}, \mathbb{Z} \smallsetminus 3\mathbb{Z}, \varnothing\}$. In this case we don't observe computations but evaluations of the predicate. A possible observation of the predicate on the domain α is $\phi^{\#} = F^{\#}(\alpha(x)) \subseteq 3\mathbb{Z}$, where $F^{\#}(3\mathbb{Z}) = 3\mathbb{Z}$ and $F^{\#}(\mathbb{Z} \smallsetminus 3\mathbb{Z}) = \mathbb{Z}$ is an abstraction of f obtained as the composition of the best correct approximations in α of the functions composing f (see [7] for details). Hence, if this abstract predicate satisfies abstract opacity, then the real predicate satisfies (concrete) opacity. In [7] the authors prove that the observation is incomplete for the abstract predicate which therefore is opaque for the observation. We show here that the partition induced by the abstract predicate is indeed not $\mathcal{B}$stable. Note that the partition induced by the predicate is $\{\, x \mid F^{\#}(\alpha(x)) \subseteq 3\mathbb{Z} \,\} = 3\mathbb{Z}$ and $\{\, x \mid F^{\#}(\alpha(x)) \not\subseteq 3\mathbb{Z} \,\} = \mathbb{Z} \smallsetminus 3\mathbb{Z}$, while the observation of the function involved in the predicate is $obs = F^{\#} \circ \alpha$, hence for example $obs(2) = F^{\#}(\mathbb{Z} \smallsetminus 3\mathbb{Z}) = \mathbb{Z} \cap \phi \neq \varnothing$ and $obs(2) \not\subseteq \phi$. Clearly, depending on how we model the ability of the attacker of analyzing the concrete predicate, we characterize its observation *obs*, characterizing the abstract opacity of the predicate.

This characterization of opacity is important because it allows to stress the strong connection between opacity and the lack of completeness. In this way completeness can be exploited for certifying the resilience of opaque predicate to reverse engineering, whereas opacity can provide new insights and expectations in the seeking for new domain transformers increasing the degree of incompleteness of domains.

Acknowledgments. I would like to thank Roberto Giacobazzi, Anindya Banerjee and Mila Dalla Preda for the useful discussions that led to this work.

References

1. Banerjee, A., Giacobazzi, R., Mastroeni, I.: What you lose is what you leak: Information leakage in declassification policies. In: Proc. of MFPS 2007. ENTCS, vol. 1514, Elsevier, Amsterdam (2007)
2. Bryans, J.W., et al.: Opacity generalized to transition systems. In: Dimitrakos, T., et al. (eds.) FAST 2005. LNCS, vol. 3866, pp. 81–95. Springer, Heidelberg (2006)
3. Clarke, E.M., et al.: Counterexample-guided abstraction refinement. In: Emerson, E.A., Sistla, A.P. (eds.) CAV 2000. LNCS, vol. 1855, pp. 154–169. Springer, Heidelberg (2000)
4. Collberg, C., Thomborson, C., Low, D.: Manufactoring cheap, resilient, and stealthy opaque constructs. In: Proc. of POPL 1998, pp. 184–196. ACM Press, New York (1998)
5. Cousot, P., Cousot, R.: Abstract interpretation: A unified lattice model for static analysis of programs by construction or approximation of fixpoints. In: Proc. of POPL 1977, pp. 238–252. ACM Press, New York (1977)
6. Cousot, P., Cousot, R.: Systematic design of program analysis frameworks. In: Proc. of POPL 1979, pp. 269–282. ACM Press, New York (1979)
7. Dalla Preda, M., et al.: Opaque predicates detection by abstract interpretation. In: Johnson, M., Vene, V. (eds.) AMAST 2006. LNCS, vol. 4019, pp. 81–95. Springer, Heidelberg (2006)
8. Giacobazzi, R., Mastroeni, I.: Abstract non-interference: Parameterizing non-interference by abstract interpretation. In: Proc. of POPL 2004, pp. 186–197. ACM Press, New York (2004)
9. Giacobazzi, R., Quintarelli, E.: Incompleteness, counterexamples and refinements in abstract model-checking. In: Cousot, P. (ed.) SAS 2001. LNCS, vol. 2126, pp. 356–373. Springer, Heidelberg (2001)
10. Giacobazzi, R., Ranzato, F.: Refining and compressing abstract domains. In: Degano, P., Gorrieri, R., Marchetti-Spaccamela, A. (eds.) ICALP 1997. LNCS, vol. 1256, pp. 771–781. Springer, Heidelberg (1997)
11. Giacobazzi, R., Ranzato, F., Scozzari, F.: Making abstract interpretations complete. J. of the ACM 47(2), 361–416 (2000)
12. Hunt, S., Mastroeni, I.: The PER model of abstract non-interference. In: Hankin, C., Siveroni, I. (eds.) SAS 2005. LNCS, vol. 3672, pp. 171–185. Springer, Heidelberg (2005)
13. Milner, R.: Communication and Concurrency. Prentice-Hall, Englewood Cliffs (1989)
14. Paige, R., Tarjan, R.E.: Three partition refinement algorithms. SIAM Journal on Computing 16(6), 977–982 (1987)
15. Ranzato, F., Tapparo, F.: An abstract interpretation-based refinement algorithm for strong preservation. In: Halbwachs, N., Zuck, L.D. (eds.) TACAS 2005. LNCS, vol. 3440, pp. 140–156. Springer, Heidelberg (2005)
16. Ranzato, F., Tapparo, F.: Generalized strong preservation by abstract interpretation. Journal of Logic and Computation 17(1), 157–197 (2007)
17. Sabelfeld, A., Sands, D.: A PER model of secure information flow in sequential programs. Higher-Order and Symbolic Computation 14(1), 59–91 (2001)

Precise Set Sharing Analysis for Java-Style Programs

Mario Méndez-Lojo[1] and Manuel V. Hermenegildo[1,2]

[1] University of New Mexico (USA)
[2] Technical University of Madrid (Spain)

Abstract. Finding useful *sharing* information between instances in object-oriented programs has recently been the focus of much research. The applications of such static analysis are multiple: by knowing which variables definitely do not share in memory we can apply conventional compiler optimizations, find coarse-grained parallelism opportunities, or, more importantly, verify certain correctness aspects of programs even in the absence of annotations. In this paper we introduce a framework for deriving precise sharing information based on abstract interpretation for a Java-like language. Our analysis achieves precision in various ways, including supporting multivariance, which allows separating different contexts. We propose a combined *Set Sharing + Nullity + Classes* domain which captures which instances do not share and which ones are definitively null, and which uses the classes to refine the static information when inheritance is present. The use of a set sharing abstraction allows a more precise representation of the existing sharings and is crucial in achieving precision during interprocedural analysis. Carrying the domains in a combined way facilitates the interaction among them in the presence of multivariance in the analysis. We show through examples and experimentally that both the set sharing part of the domain as well as the combined domain provide more accurate information than previous work based on pair sharing domains, at reasonable cost.

1 Introduction

The technique of Abstract Interpretation [8] has allowed the development of sophisticated program analyses which are at the same time provably correct and practical. The semantic approximations produced by such analyses have been traditionally applied to high- and low-level optimizations during program compilation, including program transformations. More recently, promising applications of such semantic approximations have been demonstrated in the more general context of program development, such as verification and static debugging.

Sharing analysis [14,20,26] aims to detect which variables do not share in memory, i.e., do not point (transitively) to the same location. It can be viewed as an abstraction of the graph-based representations of memory used by certain classes of alias analyses (see, e.g., [31,5,13,15]). Obtaining a safe (over-) approximation of which instances might share allows parallelizing segments of code,

F. Logozzo et al. (Eds.): VMCAI 2008, LNCS 4905, pp. 172–187, 2008.

improving garbage collection, reordering execution, etc. Also, sharing information can improve the precision of other analyses.

Nullity analysis is aimed at keeping track of null variables. This allows for example verifying properties such as the absence of null-pointer exceptions at compile time. In addition, by combining sharing and null information it is possible to obtain more precise descriptions of the state of the heap.

In type-safe, object-oriented languages *class* analysis [1,3,10,22], (sometimes called *type* analysis) focuses on determining, in the presence of polymorphic calls, which particular implementation of a given method will be executed at runtime, i.e., what is the specific class of the called object in the hierarchy. Multiple compilation optimizations benefit from having precise class descriptions: inlining, dead code elimination, etc. In addition, class information may allow analyzing only a subset of the classes in the hierarchy, which may result in additional precision.

We propose a novel analysis which infers in a combined way *set sharing*, *nullity*, and *class* information for a subset of Java that takes into account most of its important features: inheritance, polymorphism, visibility of methods, etc. The analysis is multivariant, based on the algorithm of [21], which allows separating different contexts, thus increasing precision. The additional precision obtained from context sensitivity has been shown to be important in practice in the analysis of object-oriented programs [30].

The objective of using a reduced cardinal product [9] of these three abstract domains is to achieve a good balance between precision and performance, since the information tracked by each component helps refine that of the others. While in principle these three analyses could be run separately, because they interact (we provide some examples of this), this would result in a loss of precision or require an expensive iteration over the different analyses until an overall fixpoint is reached [6,9]. In addition note that since our analysis is multivariant, and given the different nature of the properties being tracked, performing analyses separately may result in different sets of abstract values (contexts) for each analysis for each program point. This makes it difficult to relate which abstract value of a given analysis corresponds to a given abstract value of another analysis at a given point. At the other end of things, we prefer for clarity and simplicity reasons to develop directly this three-component domain and the operations on it, rather than resorting to the development of a more unified domain through (semi-)automatic (but complex) techniques [6,7]. The final objectives of our analysis include verification, static debugging, and optimization.

The closest related work is that of [26] which develops a *pair*-sharing [27] analysis for object-oriented languages and, in particular, Java. Our description of the (set-)sharing part of our domain is in fact based on their elegant formalization. The fundamental difference is that we track *set* sharing instead of *pair* sharing, which provides increased accuracy in many situations and can be more appropriate for certain applications, such as detecting independence for program parallelization. Also, our domain and abstract semantics track additionally nullity and classes in a combined fashion which, as we have argued above, is

$$
\begin{array}{lll}
\mathit{prog} & ::= & \mathit{class\_decl}^* \\
\mathit{class\_decl} & ::= & \texttt{class}\ \mathrm{k}_1\ [\texttt{extends}\ \mathrm{k}_2]\ \mathit{decl}^*\ \mathit{meth\_decl}^* \\
\mathit{meth\_decl} & ::= & \mathit{vbty}\ (\mathrm{t}_{ret}|\texttt{void})\ \mathrm{meth}\ \mathit{decl}^*\ \mathit{com} \\
\mathit{vbty} & ::= & \texttt{public} \mid \texttt{private} \\
\mathit{com} & ::= & \mathrm{v} = \mathit{expr} \quad \mid \mathrm{v}.f = \mathit{expr} \\
 & & \mid \mathit{decl} \quad \mid \texttt{skip} \\
 & & \mid \texttt{return}\ \mathit{expr} \mid \mathit{com}\,\texttt{;}\,\mathit{com} \\
 & & \mid \texttt{if}\ \mathrm{v}\ (== \mid !=)\ (\texttt{null}|\mathrm{w})\ \mathit{com}\ \texttt{else}\ \mathit{com}
\end{array}
$$

$$
\begin{array}{lll}
\mathit{decl} & ::= & \mathrm{v{:}t} \\
\mathit{var\_lit} & ::= & \mathrm{v} \mid \mathrm{a} \\
\mathit{expr} & ::= & \texttt{null} \mid \texttt{new}\ \mathrm{k} \mid \mathrm{v}.f \mid \mathrm{v.m}(\mathrm{v}_1, \ldots \mathrm{v}_n) \mid \mathit{var\_lit}
\end{array}
$$

Fig. 1. Grammar for the language

particularly useful in the presence of multivariance. In addition, we deal directly with a larger set of object features such as inheritance and visibility. Finally, we have implemented our domains (as well as the pair sharing domain of [26]), integrated them in our multivariant analysis and verification framework [17], and benchmarked the system. Our experimental results are encouraging in the sense that they seem to support that our contributions improve the analysis precision at reasonable cost.

In [23,24], the authors use a *distinctness* domain in the context of an abstract interpretation framework that resembles our sharing domain: if two variables point to different abstract locations, they do not share at the concrete level. Their approach is closer to shape analysis [25] than to sharing analysis, which can be inferred from the former. Although information retrieved in this way is generally more precise, it is also more computationally demanding and the abstract operations are more difficult to design. We also support some language constructs (e.g., visibility of methods) and provide detailed experimental results, which are not provided in their work.

Most recent work [28,18,30] has focused on context-sensitive approaches to the points-to problem for Java. These solutions are quite scalable, but flow-insensitive and overly conservative. Therefore, a verification tool based on the results of those algorithms may raise spurious warnings. In our case, we are able to express sharing information in a safe manner, as invariants that all program executions verify at the given program point.

2 Standard Semantics

The source language used is defined as a subset of Java which includes most of its object-oriented (inheritance, polymorphism, object creation) and specific (e.g., access control) features, but at the same time simplifies the syntax, and does not deal with interfaces, concurrency, packages, and static methods or variables. Although we support primitive types in our semantics and implementation, they will be omitted from the paper for simplicity.

```
class Element {
   int value;
   Element next;}

class Vector {
   Element first;

    public void add(Element el) {
        Vector v  = new Vector();
        el.next  = null;
        v.first = el;
        append(v);
    }
}
```

```
public void append(Vector v) {

  if (this != v) {
     Element e = first;
     if (e == null)
        first = v.first;
     else {
        while (e.next != null)
           e = e.next;
        e.next = v.first;
     }
  }
}
```

Fig. 2. Vector example

The rules for the grammar of this language are listed in Fig. 1. The skip statement, not present in the Java standard specification [11], has the expected semantics. Fig. 2 shows an example program in the supported language, an alternative implementation for the `java.util.Vector` class of the JDK in which vectors are represented as linked lists. Space constraints prevent us from showing the full code here,[1] although the figure does include the relevant parts.

2.1 Basic Notation

We first introduce some notation and auxiliary functions used in the rest of the paper. By $\mapsto$ we refer to total functions; for partial ones we use $\rightarrow$. The powerset of a set s is $\mathcal{P}(s)$; $\mathcal{P}^+(s)$ is an abbreviation for $\mathcal{P}(s) \setminus \{\emptyset\}$. The *dom* function returns all the elements for which a function is defined; for the codomain we will use *rng*. A substitution $f[k_1 \mapsto v_1, \ldots, k_n, \mapsto v_n]$ is equivalent to $f(k_1) = v_1, \ldots, f(k_n) = v_n$. We will overload the operator for lists so that $f[K \mapsto V]$ assigns $f(k_i) = v_i$, $i = 1, \ldots, m$, assuming $|K| = |V| = m$. By $f|_{-S}$ we denote removing S from $dom(f)$. Conversely, $f|_S$ restricts $dom(f)$ to S. For tuples $(f_1, \ldots, f_m)|_S = (f_1|_S, \ldots, f_m|_S)$. Renaming in the set s of every variable in S by the one in the same position in T ($|S| = |T|$) is written as $s|_S^T$. This operator can also be applied for renaming single variables. We denote by $\mathcal{B}$ the set of Booleans.

2.2 Program State and Sharing

With $\mathcal{M}$ we designate the set of all method names defined in the program. For the set of distinct identifiers (variables and fields) we use $\mathcal{V}$. We assume that $\mathcal{V}$ also includes the elements *this* (instance where the current method is executed),

[1] Full source code for the example can be found in `http://www.clip.dia.fi.upm.es/~mario`

and *res* (for the return value of the method). In the same way, $\mathcal{K}$ represents the program-defined classes. We do not allow `import` declarations but assume as member of $\mathcal{K}$ the predefined class `Object`.

$\mathcal{K}$ forms a lattice implied by a subclass relation $\downarrow: \mathcal{K} \rightarrow \mathcal{P}(\mathcal{K})$ such that if $t_2 \in \downarrow t_1$ then $t_2 \leq_{\mathcal{K}} t_1$. The semantics of the language implies $\downarrow$`Object` $= \mathcal{K}$. Given $def : \mathcal{K} \times \mathcal{M} \mapsto \mathcal{B}$, that determines whether a particular class provides its own implementation for a method, the Boolean function $redef : \mathcal{K} \times \mathcal{K} \times \mathcal{M} \mapsto \mathcal{B}$ checks if a class k_1 redefines a method existing in the ancestor k_2: $redef(k_1, k_2, \mathrm{m}) = true$ iff $\exists k$ s.t. $def(k, \mathrm{m})$, $k_1 \leq_{\mathcal{K}} k <_{\mathcal{K}} k_2$.

Static types are accessed by means of a function $\pi : \mathcal{V} \mapsto \mathcal{K}$ that maps variables to their declared types. The purpose of an *environment* π is twofold: it indicates the set of variables accessible at a given program point and stores their declared types. Additionally, we will use the auxiliary functions $F(k)$ (which maps the fields of $k \in \mathcal{K}$ to their declared type), and $type_\pi(expr)$, which maps expressions to types, according to π.

The description of the memory state is based on the formalization in [26,12]. We define a frame as any element of $Fr_\pi = \{\phi \mid \phi \in dom(\pi) \mapsto Loc \cup \{\mathrm{null}\}\}$, where $Loc = \mathbb{I}^+$ is the set of memory locations. A frame represents the first level of indirection and maps variable names to locations except if they are null. The set of all objects is $Obj = \{k \star \phi \mid k \in \mathcal{K}, \phi \in Fr_{F(k)}\}$. Locations and objects are linked together through the memory $Mem = \{\mu \mid \mu \in Loc \mapsto Obj\}$. A new object of class k is created as $new(k) = k \star \phi$ where $\phi(f) = null \;\; \forall f \in F(k)$. The object pointed to by v in the frame ϕ and memory μ can be retrieved via the partial function $obj(\phi \star \mu, v) = \mu(\phi(v))$. A valid heap configuration (concrete state $\phi \star \mu$) is any element of $\Sigma_\pi = \{(\phi \star \mu) \mid \phi \in Fr_\pi, \mu \in Mem\}$. We will sometimes refer to a pair $(\phi \star \mu)$ with δ.

The set of locations $R_\pi(\phi \star \mu, v)$ reachable from $v \in dom(\pi)$ in the particular state $\phi \star \mu \in \Sigma_\pi$ is calculated as $R_\pi(\phi \star \mu, v) = \cup\{R^i_\pi(\phi \star \mu, v) \mid i \geq 0\}$, the base case being $R^0_\pi(\phi \star \mu, v) = \{(\phi(v))|_{Loc}\}$ and the inductive one $R^{i+1}_\pi(\phi \star \mu, v) = \cup\{rng(\mu(l).\phi))|_{Loc} \mid l \in R^i_\pi(\phi \star \mu, v)\}$. Reachability is the basis of two fundamental concepts: sharing and nullity. Distinct variables $V = \{v_1, \ldots, v_n\}$ *share* in the actual memory configuration δ if there is at least one common location in their reachability sets, i.e., $share_\pi(\delta, V)$ is true iff $\cap^n_{i=1} R_\pi(\delta, v_i) \neq \emptyset$. A variable $v \in dom(\pi)$ is *null* in state δ if $R_\pi(\delta, v) = \emptyset$. Nullity is checked by means of $nil_\pi : \Sigma_\pi \times dom(\pi) \mapsto \mathcal{B}$, defined as $nil_\pi(\phi \star \mu, v) = true$ iff $\phi(v) = null$.

The *run-time type* of a variable in scope is returned by $\psi_\pi : \Sigma_\pi \times dom(\pi) \mapsto \mathcal{K}$, which associates variables with their dynamic type, based on the information contained in the heap state: $\psi_\pi(\delta, v) = obj(\delta, v).k$ if $\overline{nil_\pi(\delta, v)}$ and $\psi_\pi(\delta, v) = \pi(v)$ otherwise. In a type-safe language like Java runtime types are congruent with declared types, i.e., $\psi_\pi(\delta, v) \leq_{\mathcal{K}} \pi(v) \;\; \forall v \in dom(\pi), \forall \delta \in \Sigma_\pi$. Therefore, a correct approximation of ψ_π can always be derived from π. Note that at the same program point we might have different run-time type states ψ^1_π and ψ^2_π depending on the particular program path executed, but the static type state is unique.

Denotational (compositional) semantics of sequential Java has been the subject of previous work (e.g., [2]). In our case we define a simpler version of that semantics for the subset defined in Sect. 2, described as transformations in the frame-memory state. The descriptions are similar to [26]. Expression functions $\mathcal{E}^I_\pi[\![]\!] : expr \mapsto (\Sigma_\pi \mapsto \Sigma_{\pi'})$ define the meaning of Java expressions, augmenting the actual scope $\pi' = \pi[res \mapsto type_\pi(exp)]$ with the temporal variable res. Command functions $\mathcal{C}^I_\pi[\![]\!] : com \mapsto (\Sigma_\pi \mapsto \Sigma_\pi)$ do the same for commands; semantics of a method `m` defined in class k is returned by the function $I(k.\mathtt{m}) : \Sigma_{input(k.m)} \to \Sigma_{output(k.m)}$. The definition of the respective environments, given a declaration in class k as t_{ret} $\mathtt{m}(this : k, p_1 : t_1 \ldots p_n : t_n)$ `com`, is $input(k.m) = \{this \mapsto k, p_1 \mapsto t_1, \ldots, p_n \mapsto t_n\}$ and $output(k.m) = input(k.m)[out \mapsto t_{ret}]$.

Example 1. Assume that, in Figure 2, after entering in the method `add` of the class `Vector` we have an initial state $(\phi_0 \star \mu_0)$ s.t. $loc_1 = \phi_0(el) \neq null$. After executing `Vector v = new Vector()` the state is $(\phi_1 \star \mu_1)$, with $\phi_1(v) = loc_2$, and $\mu_1(loc_2).\phi(first) = null$. The field assignment `el.next = null` results in $(\phi_2 \star \mu_2)$, verifying $\mu_2(loc_1).\phi(next) = null$. In the third line, `v.first = el` links loc_1 and loc_2 since now $\mu_3(loc_2).\phi(first) = loc_1$. Now v and el share, since their reachability sets intersect *at least* in $\{loc_1\}$. Finally, assume that `append` attaches v to the end of the current instance $this$ resulting in a memory layout $(\phi_4 \star \mu_4)$. Given $loc_3 = obj((\phi_4 \star \mu_4)(this)).\phi(first)$, it should hold that $\mu_4(\ldots \mu_4(loc_3).\phi(next) \ldots).\phi(next) = loc_2$. Now $this$ shares with v and therefore with el, because loc_1 is reachable from loc_2.

3 Abstract Semantics

An abstract state $\sigma \in D_\pi$ in an environment π approximates the sharing, nullity, and run-time type characteristics (as described in Sect. 2.2) of set of concrete states in Σ_π. Every abstract state combines three abstractions: a sharing set $sh \in \mathcal{DS}_\pi$, a nullity set $nl \in \mathcal{DN}_\pi$, and a type member $\tau \in \mathcal{DT}_\pi$, i.e., $D_\pi = \mathcal{DS}_\pi \times \mathcal{DN}_\pi \times \mathcal{DT}_\pi$.

The sharing abstract domain $\mathcal{DS}_\pi = \{\{v_1, \ldots, v_n\} \mid \{v_1, \ldots, v_n\} \in \mathcal{P}(dom(\pi)), \cap_{i=1}^n C_\pi(v_i) \neq \emptyset\}$ is constrained by a class reachability function which retrieves those classes that are reachable from a particular variable: $C_\pi(v) = \cup\{C^i_\pi(v) \mid i \geq 0\}$, given $C^0_\pi(v) = \downarrow\pi(v)$ and $C^{i+1}_\pi(v) = \cup\{rng(F(k)) \mid k \in C^i_\pi(v)\}$. By using class reachability, we avoid including in the sharing domain sets of variables which cannot share in practice because of the language semantics. The partial order $\leq_{\mathcal{DS}_\pi}$ is set inclusion.

We define several operators over sharing sets, standard in the sharing literature [14,19]. The binary union $\uplus : \mathcal{DS}_\pi \times \mathcal{DS}_\pi \mapsto \mathcal{DS}_\pi$, calculated as $S_1 \uplus S_2 = \{Sh_1 \cup Sh_2 \mid Sh_1 \in S_1, Sh_2 \in S_2\}$ and the closure under union $* : \mathcal{DS}_\pi \mapsto \mathcal{DS}_\pi$ operators, defined as $S^* = \{\cup SSh \mid SSh \in \mathcal{P}^+(S)\}$; we later filter their results using class reachability. The relevant sharing with respect to v is $sh_v = \{s \in sh \mid v \in s\}$, which we overloaded for sets. Similarly, $sh_{-v} = \{s \in sh \mid v \notin s\}$. The projection $sh|_V$ is equivalent to $\{S \mid S = S' \cap V, S' \in sh\}$.

$$\mathcal{SE}^I_\pi[\![\texttt{null}]\!](sh,nl,\tau) = (sh,nl',\tau')$$
$$nl' = nl[res \mapsto null]$$
$$\tau' = \tau[res \mapsto \downarrow object]$$

$$\mathcal{SE}^I_\pi[\![\texttt{new}\ k]\!](sh,nl,\tau) = (sh',nl',\tau')$$
$$sh' = sh \cup \{\{res\}\}$$
$$nl' = nl[res \mapsto nnull]$$
$$\tau' = \tau[res \mapsto \{\kappa\}]$$

$$\mathcal{SE}^I_\pi[\![v]\!](sh,nl,\tau) = (sh',nl',\tau')$$
$$sh' = (\{\{res\}\} \uplus sh_v) \cup sh_{-v}$$
$$nl' = nl[res \mapsto nl(v)]$$
$$\tau' = \tau[res \mapsto \tau(v)]$$

$$\mathcal{SE}^I_\pi[\![v\,.\,\texttt{f}]\!](sh,nl,\tau) = \begin{cases} \bot \text{ if } nl(v) = null \\ (sh',nl',\tau') \text{ otherwise} \end{cases}$$
$$sh' = sh_{-v} \cup \bigcup\{\mathcal{P}^+(s|_{-v} \cup \{res\}) \uplus \{\{v\}\} \mid s \in sh_v\}$$
$$nl' = nl[res \mapsto unk, v \mapsto nnull]$$
$$\tau' = \tau[res \mapsto \downarrow F(\pi(v)(\texttt{f}))]$$

$$\mathcal{SE}^I_\pi[\![v\,.\,\texttt{m}(v_1,\ldots,v_n)]\!](sh,nl,\tau) = \begin{cases} \bot \text{ if } nl(v) = null \\ \sigma' \text{ otherwise} \end{cases}$$
$$\sigma' = \mathcal{SE}^I_\pi[\![\texttt{call}(v, m(v_1,\ldots,v_n))]\!](sh,nl',\tau)$$
$$nl' = nl[v \mapsto nnull]$$

Fig. 3. Abstract semantics for the expressions

The nullity domain is $\mathcal{DN}_\pi = \mathcal{P}(dom(\pi) \mapsto \mathcal{NV})$, where $\mathcal{NV} = \{null, nnull, unk\}$. The order $\leq_{\mathcal{NV}}$ of the nullity values ($null \leq_{\mathcal{NV}} unk$, $nnull \leq_{\mathcal{NV}} unk$) induces a partial order in $\mathcal{DN}_\pi$ s.t. $nl_1 \leq_{\mathcal{DN}_\pi} nl_2$ if $nl_1(v) \leq_{\mathcal{NV}} nl_2(v)$ $\forall v \in dom(\pi)$. Finally, the domain of types maps variables to sets of types congruent with π: $\mathcal{DT}_\pi = \{(v, \{t_1,\ldots,t_n\}) \in dom(\pi) \mapsto \mathcal{P}(\mathcal{K}) \mid \{t_1,\ldots,t_n\} \subseteq \downarrow\pi(v)\}$.

We assume the standard framework of abstract interpretation as defined in [8] in terms of Galois insertions. The concretization function $\gamma_\pi : D_\pi \mapsto \mathcal{P}(\Sigma_\pi)$ is $\gamma_\pi(sh,nl,\tau) = \{\delta \in \Sigma_\pi \mid \forall V \subseteq dom(\pi), share_\pi(\delta,V)$ and $\nexists W, V \subset W \subseteq dom(\pi)$ s.t. $share_\pi(\delta,W) \Rightarrow V \in sh$, and $R_\pi(\delta,v) = \emptyset$ if $nl(v) = null$, and $R_\pi(\delta,v) \neq \emptyset$ if $nl(v) = nnull$, and $\psi_\pi(\delta,v) \in \tau(v)$,$\forall v \in dom(\pi)\}$.

The abstract semantics of expressions and commands is listed in Figs. 3 and 4. They correctly approximate the standard semantics, as proved in [16]. As their concrete counterparts, they take an expression or command and map an input state $\sigma \in D_\pi$ to an output state $\sigma' \in D^\sigma_{\pi'}$, where $\pi = \pi'$ in commands and $\pi' = \pi[res \mapsto type_\pi(expr)]$ in expression $expr$. The semantics of a method call is explained in Sect. 3.1. The use of set sharing (rather than pair sharing) in the semantics prevents possible losses of precision, as shown in Example 2.

Example 2. In the `add` method (Fig. 2), assume that $\sigma = (\{\{this, el\}, \{v\}\}, \{this/nnull, el/nnull, v/nnull\})$ right before evaluating `el` in the third line (we skip type information for simplicity). The expression `el` binds to res the location of el, i.e., forces el and res to share. Since $nl(el) \neq null$ the new sharing is $sh' = (\{\{res\}\} \uplus sh_{el}) \cup sh_{-el} = (\{\{res\}\} \uplus \{\{this, el\}\}) \cup \{\{v\}\} = \{\{res, this, el\}, \{v\}\}$.

$$\mathcal{SC}^I_\pi[\![v\texttt{=}expr]\!]\sigma = ((sh'|_{-v})|^v_{res}, nl'|^v_{res}, \tau''|_{-res})$$
$$\tau'' = \tau'[v \mapsto (\tau'(v) \cap \tau'(res))]$$
$$(sh', nl', \tau') = \mathcal{SE}^I_\pi[\![expr]\!]\sigma$$

$$\mathcal{SC}^I_\pi[\![v\texttt{.f=}expr]\!]\sigma = (sh'', nl'', \tau')|_{-res}$$
$$sh'' = \begin{cases} \bot & \text{if } nl'(v) = null \\ sh' & \text{if } nl'(res) = null \\ sh^y \cup sh'_{-\{v,res\}} & \text{otherwise} \end{cases}$$
$$nl'' = nl'[v \mapsto nnull]$$
$$sh^y = (\bigcup\{\mathcal{P}(s|_{-v} \cup \{res\}) \uplus \{\{v\}\} \mid s \in sh'_v\} \cup \bigcup\{\mathcal{P}(s|_{-res} \cup \{v\}) \uplus \{\{res\}\} \mid s \in sh'_{res}\})^*$$
$$(sh', nl', \tau') = \mathcal{SE}^I_\pi[\![expr]\!]\sigma$$

$$\mathcal{SC}^I_\pi[\![\,\texttt{if }\ v\texttt{==null}\ com_1\ \texttt{else}\ com_2\,]\!]\sigma = \begin{cases} \sigma'_1 & \text{if } nl(v) = null \\ \sigma'_2 & \text{if } nl(v) = nnull \\ \sigma_1 \sqcup \sigma_2 & \text{if } nl(v) = unk \end{cases}$$
$$\sigma'_i = \mathcal{SC}^I_\pi[\![com_i]\!]\sigma$$
$$\sigma_1 = \mathcal{SC}^I_\pi[\![com_1]\!](sh|_{-v}, nl[v \mapsto null], \tau[v \mapsto \downarrow\pi(v)])$$
$$\sigma_2 = \mathcal{SC}^I_\pi[\![com_2]\!](sh, nl[v \mapsto nnull], \tau)$$

$$\mathcal{SC}^I_\pi[\![\,\texttt{if }\ v\texttt{==}w\ com_1\ \texttt{else}\ com_2\,]\!](sh, nl, \tau) = \begin{cases} \sigma'_1 & \text{if } nl(v) = nl(w) = null \\ \sigma'_2 & \text{if } sh|_{\{v,w\}} = \emptyset \\ \sigma'_1 \sqcup \sigma'_2 & \text{otherwise} \end{cases}$$
$$\sigma'_i = \mathcal{SC}^I_\pi[\![com_i]\!](sh, nl, \tau)$$

$$\mathcal{SC}^I_\pi[\![com_1\,;com_2]\!]\sigma = \mathcal{SC}^I_\pi[\![com_2]\!](\mathcal{SC}^I_\pi[\![com_1]\!]\sigma)$$

Fig. 4. Abstract semantics for the commands

In the case of pair-sharing, the transfer function [26] for the same initial state $sh = \{\{this, el\}, \{v, v\}\}$ returns $sh'_p = \{\{res, el\}, \{res, this\}, \{this, el\}, \{v, v\}\}$, which translated to set sharing results in $sh'' = \{\{res, el\}, \{res, this\}, \{res, this, el\}, \{this, el\}, \{v\}\}$, a less precise representation (in terms of $\leq_{\mathcal{DS}_\pi}$) than sh'.

Example 3. Our multivariant analysis keeps two different call contexts for the `append` method in the `Vector` class (Fig. 2). Their different sharing information shows how sharing can improve nullity results. The first context corresponds to external calls (invocation from other classes), because of the `public` visibility of the method: $\sigma_1 = (\{\{this\}, \{this, v\}, \{v\}\}, \{this/nnull, v/unk\}, \{this/\{vector\}, v/\{vector\}\})$. The second corresponds to an internal (within the class) call, for which the analysis infers that $this$ and v do not share: $\sigma_2 = (\{\{this\}, \{v\}\}, \{this/nnull, v/unk\}, \{this/\{vector\}, v/\{vector\}\})$. Inside `append`, we avoid creating a circular list by checking that $this \neq v$. Only then is the last element of $this$ linked to the first one of v. We use `com` to represent the series of commands `Element e = first; if (e==null)...else..` and `bdy` for the whole body of the method. Independently of whether the input state is σ_1 or σ_2 our analysis infers that $\mathcal{SC}^I_\pi[\![\texttt{com}]\!]\sigma_1 = \mathcal{SC}^I_\pi[\![\texttt{com}]\!]\sigma_2 = (\{\{this, v\}\}, \{this/nnull, v/nnull\}, \{this/\{vector\}, v/\{vector\}\}) = \sigma_3$. However, the more precise sharing information in σ_2 results in a more precise analysis

Algorithm 1. Extend operation

input : state before the call σ, result of analyzing the call σ_λ and actual parameters A
output: resulting state σ_f

if $\sigma_\lambda = \bot$ **then**
  $\sigma_f = \bot$
else
  let $\sigma = (sh, nl, \tau)$, and $\sigma_\lambda = (sh_\lambda, nl_\lambda, \tau_\lambda)$, and $AR = A \cup \{res\}$

$$\begin{aligned} star &= (sh_A \cup \{\{res\}\})^* \\ sh_{ext} &= \{s \mid s \in star, s|_{AR} \in sh_\lambda\} \\ sh_f &= sh_{ext} \cup sh_{-A} \end{aligned}$$

$$\begin{aligned} nl_f &= nl[res \mapsto nl_\lambda(res)] \\ \tau_f &= \tau[res \mapsto \tau_\lambda(res)] \\ \sigma_f &= (sh_f, nl_f, \tau_f) \end{aligned}$$

end

of `bdy`, because of the guard `(this!=v)`. In the case of the external calls, $\mathcal{SC}^I_\pi[\![\texttt{bdy}]\!]\sigma_1 = \mathcal{SC}^I_\pi[\![\texttt{com}]\!]\sigma_1 \sqcup \mathcal{SC}^I_\pi[\![\texttt{skip}]\!]\sigma_1 = \sigma_1 \sqcup \sigma_3 = \sigma_1$. When the entry state is σ_2, the semantics at the same program point is $\mathcal{SC}^I_\pi[\![\texttt{bdy}]\!]\sigma_2 = \mathcal{SC}^I_\pi[\![\texttt{com}]\!]\sigma_2 = \sigma_3 < \sigma_1$. So while the internal call requires $v \neq null$ to terminate, we cannot infer the final nullity of that parameter in a public invocation, which might finish even if v is null.

3.1 Method Calls

The semantics of the expression $\texttt{call}(v, m(v_1, \ldots, v_n))$ in state $\sigma = (sh, nl, \tau)$ is calculated by implementing the top-down methodology described in [21]. We will assume that the formal parameters follow the naming convention F in all the implementations of the method; let $A = \{v, v_1, \ldots, v_n\}$ and $F = dom(input(k.m))$ be ordered lists. We first calculate the projection $\sigma_p = \sigma|_A$ and an entry state $\sigma_y = \sigma_p|^F_A$. The abstract execution of the call takes place only in the set of classes $K = \tau(v)$, resulting in an exit state $\sigma_x = \bigsqcup\{\mathcal{SC}^I_\pi[\![k'.m]\!]\sigma_y \,|\, k' = lookup(k, m), k \in K\}$, where *lookup* returns the body of k's implementation of m, which can be defined in k or inherited from one of its ancestors. The abstract execution of the method in a subset $K \subseteq \downarrow\pi(v)$ increases analysis precision and is the ultimate purpose of tracking run-time types in our abstraction. We now remove the local variables $\sigma_b = \sigma_x|_{F \cup \{out\}}$ and rename back to the scope of the caller: $\sigma_\lambda = \sigma_b|^{A \cup \{res\}}_{F \cup \{out\}}$; the final state σ_f is calculated as $\sigma_f = extend(\sigma, \sigma_\lambda, A)$. The $extend : D_\pi \times D_\pi \times \mathcal{P}(dom(\pi)) \mapsto D_\pi$ function is described in Algorithm 1.

In Java references to objects are passed by value in a method call. Therefore, they cannot be modified. However, the call might introduce new sharing between actual parameters through assignments to their fields, given that the formal parameters they correspond to have not been reassigned. We keep the original information by copying all the formal parameters at the beginning of each call, as suggested in [23]. Those copies cannot be modified during the execution of the call, so a meaningful correspondence can be established between A and F.

We can do better by realizing that analysis might refine the information about the actual parameters within a method and propagating the new values discovered back to σ_f. For example, in a method `foo(Vector v){if v!=null skip else throw_null}`, it is clear that we can only finish normally if $nl_x(v) = nnull$, but in the actual semantics we do not change the nullity value for the corresponding argument in the call, which can only be more imprecise. Note that the example is different from `foo(Vector v){v = new Vector}`, which also finishes with $nl_x(v) = nnull$. The distinction over whether new attributes are preserved or not relies on keeping track of those variables which have been assigned inside the method, and then applying the propagation only for the unset variables.

Example 4. Assume an extra snippet of code in the `Vector` class of the form `if (v2!=null) v1.append(v2) else com`, which is analyzed in state $\sigma = (\{\{v_1\}, \{v_2\}\}, \{v_1/nnull,\ v_2/nnull\}, \{v_1/\{vector\}, v_2/\{vector\}\})$. Since we have nullity information, it is possible to identify the block `com` as dead code. In contrast, sharing-only analyses can only tell if a variable is definitely null, but never if it is definitely non-null. The call is analyzed as follows. Let $A = \{v_1, v_2\}$ and $F = \{this, v\}$, then $\sigma_p = \sigma|_A = \sigma$ and the entry state σ_y is $\sigma|_A^F = (\{\{this\}, \{v\}\}, \{this/nnull, v/nnull\}, \{this/\{vector\}, v/\{vector\}\})$. The only class where `append` can be executed is `Vector` and results (see Example 3) in an exit state for the formal parameters and the return variable $\sigma_b = (\{\{this, v\}\}, \{this/nnull, v/nnull, out/null\}, \{this/\{vector\}, v/\{vector\}, out/\{void\}\})$, which is further renamed to the scope of the caller obtaining $\sigma_\lambda = (\{\{v_1, v_2\}\}, \{v_1/nnull, v_2/nnull, res/null\}, \{v_1/\{vector\}, v_2/\{vector\}, res/\{void\}\})$. Since the method returns a `void` type we can treat res as a primitive (null) variable so $\sigma_f = extend(\sigma, \sigma_\lambda, \{v_1, v_2\}) = (\{\{v_1, v_2\}\}, \{v_1/nnull, v_2/nnull, res/null\}, \{v_1/\{vector\}, v_2/\{vector\}, res/\{void\}\})$.

Example 5. The *extend* operation used during interprocedural analysis is a point where there can be significant loss of precision and where set sharing shows its strengths. For simplicity, we will describe the example only for the sharing component; nullity and type information updates are trivial. Assume a scenario where a call to `append(v1,v2)` in sharing state $sh = \{\{v_0, v_1\}, \{v_1\}, \{v_2\}\}$ results in $sh_\lambda = \{\{v_1, v_2\}\}$. Let A and AR be the sets $\{v_1, v_2\}$ and $\{v_1, v_2, res\}$ respectively. The *extend* operation proceeds as follows: first we calculate *star* as $(sh_A \cup \{\{res\}\})^* = (sh \cup \{\{res\}\})^* = (\{\{v_0, v_1\}, \{v_1\}, \{v_2\}, \{res\}\})^* = \{\{v_0, v_1\}, \{v_0, v_1, v_2\}, \{v_0, v_1, v_2, res\}, \{v_0, v_1, res\}, \{v_1\}, \{v_1, v_2\}, \{v_1, v_2, res\}, \{v_1, res\}, \{v_2\}, \{v_2, res\}, \{res\}\}$, from which we delete those elements whose projection over AR is not included in sh_λ, obtaining $sh_{ext} = \{\{v_0, v_1, v_2\}, \{v_1, v_2\}\}$. The resulting sharing component is the union of that sh_{ext} with $sh_{-A} = \emptyset$, so $sh_{f1} = sh_{ext} = \{\{v_0, v_1, v_2\}, \{v_1, v_2\}\}$.

When the same sh and sh_λ are represented in their pair sharing versions $sh^p = \{\{v_0, v_1\}, \{v_o, v_0\}, \{v_1, v_1\}, \{v_2, v_2\}\}$ and $sh^p_\lambda = \{\{v_1, v_2\}, \{v_1, v_1\}, \{v_2, v_2\}\}$, the *extend* operation in [26] introduces spurious sharings in sh_f because of the lower precision of the pair-sharing representation. In this case, $sh^p_{f2} = (sh \cup$

$sh^{p}_{\lambda})^{*}_{A} = \{\{v_0, v_1\}, \{v_0, v_2\}, \{v_1, v_2\}, \{v_0, v_0\}, \{v_1, v_1\}, \{v_2, v_1\}\}$. This information, expressed in terms of set sharing, results in $sh_{f2} = \{\{v_0, v_1\}, \{v_0, v_2\}, \{v_0, v_1, v_2\}, \{v_1, v_2\}, \{v_0\}, \{v_1\}, \{v_2\}\}$, which is much less precise that sh_{f1}.

4 Experimental Results

In our analyzer the abstract semantics presented in the previous section is evaluated by a highly optimized fixpoint algorithm, based on that of [21]. The algorithm traverses the program dependency graph, dynamically computing the strongly-connected components and keeping detailed dependencies on which parts of the graph need to be recomputed when some abstract value changes during the analysis of iterative code (loops and recursions). This reduces the number of steps and iterations required to reach the fixpoint, which is specially important since the algorithm implements *multivariance*, i.e., it keeps different abstract values at each program point for every calling context, and it computes (a superset of) all the calling contexts that occur in the program. The dependencies kept also allow relating these values along execution paths (this is particularly useful for example during error diagnosis or for program specialization).

We now provide some precision and cost results obtained from the implementation in the framework described in [17] of our set-sharing, nullity, and class ($SSNlTau$) analysis. In order to be able to provide a comparison with the closest previous work, we also implemented the pair sharing (PS) analysis proposed in [26]. We have extended the operations described in [26], enabling them to handle some additional cases required by our benchmark programs such as primitive variables, visibility of methods, etc. Also, to allow direct comparison, we implemented a version of our $SSNlTau$ analysis, which is referred to simply as SS, that tracks set sharing using only declared type information and does not utilize the (non-)nullity component. In order to study the influence of tracking run-time types we have implemented a version of our analysis with set sharing and (non-)nullity, but again using only the static types, which we will refer to as $SSNl$. In these versions without dynamic type inference only declared types can affect τ and thus the dynamic typing information that can be propagated from initializations, assignments, or correspondence between arguments and formal parameters on method calls is not used. Note however that the version that includes tracking of dynamic typing can of course only improve analysis results in the presence of polymorphism in the program: the results should be identical (except perhaps for the analysis time) in the rest of the cases. The polymorphic programs are marked with an asterisk in the tables.

The benchmarks used have been adapted from previous literature on either abstract interpretation for Java or points-to analysis [26,24,23,29]. We added two different versions of the `Vector` example of Fig. 2. Our experimental results are summarized in Tables 5, 6, and 7.

The first column (*#tp*) in Tables 5 and 6 shows the total number of program points (commands or expressions) for each program. Column *#rp* then provides, for each analysis, the total number of *reachable* program points, i.e., the

		PS				SS				
	#tp	#rp	#up	#σ	t	#rp	#up	#σ	t	%Δt
dyndisp (*)	71	68	3	114	30	68	3	114	29	-2
clone	41	38	3	42	52	38	3	50	81	55
dfs	102	98	4	103	68	98	4	108	68	0
passau (*)	167	164	3	296	97	164	3	304	120	23
qsort	185	142	43	182	125	142	43	204	165	32
integerqsort	191	148	43	159	110	148	43	197	122	10
pollet01 (*)	154	126	28	276	196	126	28	423	256	30
zipvector (*)	272	269	3	513	388	269	3	712	1029	164
cleanness (*)	314	277	37	360	233	277	37	385	504	116
overall	1497	1330	167	2045	1299	1330	167	2497	2374	82.75

Fig. 5. Analysis times, number of program points, and number of abstract states

		SSNl					SSNlTau				
	#tp	#rp	#up	#σ	t	%Δt	#rp	#up	#σ	t	%Δt
dyndisp (*)	71	61	10	103	53	77	61	10	77	20	-33
clone	41	31	10	34	100	92	31	10	34	90	74
dfs	102	91	11	91	129	89	91	11	91	181	166
passau (*)	167	157	10	288	117	18	157	10	270	114	17
qsort	185	142	43	196	283	125	142	43	196	275	119
integerqsort	191	148	43	202	228	107	148	43	202	356	224
pollet01 (*)	154	119	35	364	388	98	98	56	296	264	35
zipvector (*)	272	269	3	791	530	36	245	27	676	921	136
cleanness (*)	314	276	38	383	276	38	266	48	385	413	77
overall	1497	1294	203	2452	2104	61.97	1239	258	2227	2634	102.77

Fig. 6. Analysis times, number of program points, and number of abstract states

number of program points that the analysis explores, while $\#up$ represents the $(\#tp - \#rp)$ points that are not analyzed because the analysis determines that they are unreachable. It can be observed that tracking (non-)nullity (Nl) reduces the number of reachable program points (and increases conversely the number of unreachable points) because certain parts of the code can be discarded as dead code (and not analyzed) when variables are known to be non-null. Tracking dynamic types (Tau) also reduces the number of reachable points, but, as expected, only for (some of) the programs that are polymorphic. This is due to the fact that the class analysis allows considering fewer implementations of methods, but obviously only in the presence of polymorphism.

Since our framework is multivariant and thus tracks many different *contexts* at each program point, at the end of analysis there may be more than one abstract state associated with each program point. Thus, the number of abstract states inferred is typically larger than the number of reachable program points. Column $\#\sigma$ provides the total number of these abstract states inferred by the analysis. The level of multivariance is the ratio $\#\sigma/\#rp$. It can be observed that the simple

	PS		SS	
	#*sh*	%*sh*	#*sh*	%*sh*
dyndisp (*)	640	60.37	435	73.07
clone	174	53.10	151	60.16
dfs	1573	96.46	1109	97.51
passau (*)	5828	94.56	3492	96.74
qsort	1481	67.41	1082	76.34
integerqsort	2413	66.47	1874	75.65
pollet01 (*)	793	89.81	1043	91.81
zipvector (*)	6161	68.71	5064	80.28
cleanness (*)	1300	63.63	1189	70.61
overall	20363	73.39	15439	80.24

Fig. 7. Sharing precision results

set sharing analysis (SS) creates more abstract states for the same number of reachable points. In general, such a larger number for $\#\sigma$ tends to indicate more precise results (as we will see later). On the other hand, the fact that addition of Nl and Tau reduces the number of reachable program points interacts with precision to obtain the final $\#\sigma$ value, so that while there may be an increase in the number of abstract states because of increased precision, on the other hand there may be a decrease because more program points are detected as dead code by the analysis. Thus, the $\#\sigma$ values for $SSNl$ and $SSNlTau$ in some cases actually decrease with respect to those of PS and SS.

The t column in Tables 5 and 6 provides the running times for the different analyses, in milliseconds, on a Pentium M 1.73Ghz, 1Gb of RAM, running Fedora Core 4.0, and averaging several runs after eliminating the best and worst values. The $\%\Delta t$ columns show the percentage variation in the analysis time with respect to the reference pair-sharing (PS) analysis, calculated as $\Delta_{dom}\%t = 100*(t_{dom} - t_{PS})/t_{PS}$. The more complex analyses tend to take longer times, while in any case remaining reasonable. However, sometimes more complex analyses actually take less time, again because the increased precision and the ensuing dead code detection reduces the amount of program that must be analyzed.

Table 7 shows precision results in terms of sharing, concentrating on the SP and SS domains, which allow direct comparison. A more usage-oriented way of measuring precision would be to study the effect of the increased precision in an application that is known to be sensitive to sharing information, such as, for example, program parallelization [4]. On the other hand this also complicates matters in the sense that then many other factors come into play (such as, for example, the level of intrinsic parallelism in the benchmarks and the parallelization algorithms) so that it is then also harder to observe the precision of the analysis itself. Such a client-level comparison is beyond the scope of this paper, and we concentrate here instead on measuring sharing precision directly.

Following [6], and in order to be able to compare precision directly in terms of sharing, column $\#sh$ provides the sum over all abstract states in all reachable program points of the cardinality of the sharing *sets* calculated by the analysis.

For the case of pair sharing, we converted the pairs into their equivalent set representation (as in [6]) for comparison. Since the results are always correct, a smaller number of sharing sets indicates more precision (recall that $\top$ is the power set). This is of course assuming σ is constant, which as we have seen is not the case for all of our analyses. On the other hand, if we compare PS and SS, we see that SS has consistently more abstract states than PS and consistently lower numbers of sharing sets, and the trend is thus clear that it indeed brings in more precision. The only apparent exception is *pollet01* but we can see that the number of sharing sets is similar for a significantly larger number of abstract states.

An arguably better metric for measuring the relative precision of sharing is the ratio $\%_{Max} = 100 * (1 - \#sh/(2^{\#vo} - 1))$ which gives $\#sh$ as a percentage of its maximum possible value, where $\#vo$ is the total number of object variables in all the states. The results are given in column $\%sh$. In this metric 0% means all abstract states are $\top$ (i.e., contain no useful information) and 100% means all variables in all abstract states are detected not to share. Thus, larger values in this column indicate more precision, since analysis has been able to infer smaller sharing sets. This relative measure shows an average improvement of 7% for SS over PS.

5 Conclusions

We have proposed an analysis based on abstract interpretation for deriving precise sharing information for a Java-like language. Our analysis is multivariant, which allows separating different contexts, and combines Set Sharing, Nullity, and Classes: the domain captures which instances definitely do not share or are definitively null, and uses the classes to refine the static information when inheritance is present. We have implemented the analysis, as well as previously proposed analyses based on Pair Sharing, and obtained encouraging results: for all the examples the set sharing domains (even without combining with Nullity or Classes) offer more precision than the pair sharing counterparts while the increase in analysis times appears reasonable. In fact the additional precision (also when combined with nullity and classes) brings in some cases analysis time reductions. This seems to support that our contributions bring more precision at reasonable cost.

Acknowledgments

The authors would like to thank Samir Genaim for many useful comments to previous drafts of this document. Manuel Hermenegildo and Mario Méndez-Lojo are supported in part by the Prince of Asturias Chair in Information Science and Technology at UNM. This work was also funded in part by the Information Society Technologies program of the European Commission, Future and Emerging Technologies under the IST-15905 *MOBIUS* project, by the Spanish Ministry of

Education under the TIN-2005-09207 *MERIT* project, and the Madrid Regional Government under the *PROMESAS* project.

References

1. Agesen, O.: The cartesian product algorithm: Simple and precise type inference of parametric polymorphism. In: Olthoff, W. (ed.) ECOOP 1995. LNCS, vol. 952, pp. 2–26. Springer, Heidelberg (1995)
2. Alves-Foss, J. (ed.): Formal Syntax and Semantics of Java. LNCS, vol. 1523. Springer, Heidelberg (1999)
3. Bacon, D.F., Sweeney, P.F.: Fast static analysis of C++ virtual function calls. In: Proc. of OOPSLA 1996, SIGPLAN Notices, October 1996, vol. 31(10), pp. 324–341 (1996)
4. Bueno, F., García de la Banda, M., Hermenegildo, M.: Effectiveness of Abstract Interpretation in Automatic Parallelization: A Case Study in Logic Programming. ACM Transactions on Programming Languages and Systems 21(2), 189–238 (1999)
5. Burke, M.G., et al.: Carini, Jong-Deok Choi, and Michael Hind. In: Pingali, K.K., et al. (eds.) LCPC 1994. LNCS, vol. 892, pp. 234–250. Springer, Heidelberg (1995)
6. Codish, M., et al.: Improving Abstract Interpretations by Combining Domains. ACM Transactions on Programming Languages and Systems 17(1), 28–44 (1995)
7. Cortesi, A., et al.: Complementation in abstract interpretation. ACM Trans. Program. Lang. Syst. 19(1), 7–47 (1997)
8. Cousot, P., Cousot, R.: Abstract Interpretation: a Unified Lattice Model for Static Analysis of Programs by Construction or Approximation of Fixpoints. In: Proc. of POPL 1977, pp. 238–252 (1977)
9. Cousot, P., Cousot, R.: Systematic Design of Program Analysis Frameworks. In: Sixth ACM Symposium on Principles of Programming Languages, San Antonio, Texas, pp. 269–282 (1979)
10. Dean, J., Grove, D., Chambers, C.: Optimization of object-oriented programs using static class hierarchy analysis. In: Olthoff, W. (ed.) ECOOP 1995. LNCS, vol. 952, pp. 77–101. Springer, Heidelberg (1995)
11. Gosling, J., et al.: Java(TM) Language Specification, 3rd edn. Addison-Wesley Professional, Reading (2005)
12. Hill, P.M., Payet, E., Spoto, F.: Path-length analysis of object-oriented programs. In: Proc. EAAI 2006 (2006)
13. Hind, M., et al.: Interprocedural pointer alias analysis. ACM Trans. Program. Lang. Syst. 21(4), 848–894 (1999)
14. Jacobs, D., Langen, A.: Accurate and Efficient Approximation of Variable Aliasing in Logic Programs. In: 1989 North American Conference on Logic Programming, MIT Press, Cambridge (1989)
15. Landi, W., Ryder, B.G.: A safe approximate algorithm for interprocedural pointer aliasing (with retrospective). In: McKinley, K.S. (ed.) Best of PLDI, pp. 473–489. ACM Press, New York (1992)
16. Méndez-Lojo, M., Hermenegildo, M.: Precise Set Sharing for Java-style Programs (and proofs). Technical Report CLIP2/2007.1, Technical University of Madrid (UPM), School of Computer Science, UPM (November 2007)
17. Méndez-Lojo, M., Navas, J., Hermenegildo, M.: A Flexible (C)LP-Based Approach to the Analysis of Object-Oriented Programs. In: 17th International Symposium on Logic-based Program Synthesis and Transformation (LOPSTR 2007) (August 2007)

18. Milanova, A., Rountev, A., Ryder, B.G.: Parameterized Object Sensitivity for Points-to and Side-effect Analyses for Java. In: ISSTA, pp. 1–11 (2002)
19. Muthukumar, K., Hermenegildo, M.: Determination of Variable Dependence Information at Compile-Time Through Abstract Interpretation. In: 1989 North American Conference on Logic Programming, October 1989, pp. 166–189. MIT Press, Cambridge (1989)
20. Muthukumar, K., Hermenegildo, M.: Combined Determination of Sharing and Freeness of Program Variables Through Abstract Interpretation. In: 1991 International Conference on Logic Programming, June 1991, pp. 49–63. MIT Press, Cambridge (1991)
21. Navas, J., Méndez-Lojo, M., Hermenegildo, M.: An Efficient, Context and Path Sensitive Analysis Framework for Java Programs. In: 9th Workshop on Formal Techniques for Java-like Programs FTfJP 2007 (July 2007)
22. Palsberg, J., Schwartzbach, M.I.: Object-oriented type inference. In: OOPSLA, pp. 146–161 (1991)
23. Pollet, I.: Towards a generic framework for the abstract interpretation of Java. PhD thesis, Catholic University of Louvain, Dept. of Computer Science (2004)
24. Pollet, I., Le Charlier, B., Cortesi, A.: Distinctness and sharing domains for static analysis of java programs. In: Knudsen, J.L. (ed.) ECOOP 2001. LNCS, vol. 2072, Springer, Heidelberg (2001)
25. Sagiv, S., Reps, T.W., Wilhelm, R.: Parametric shape analysis via 3-valued logic. In: POPL 1999 (1999)
26. Secci, S., Spoto, F.: Pair-sharing analysis of object-oriented programs. In: SAS, pp. 320–335 (2005)
27. Søndergaard, H.: An application of abstract interpretation of logic programs: occur check reduction. In: Duijvestijn, A.J.W., Lockemann, P.C. (eds.) Trends in Information Processing Systems. LNCS, vol. 123, pp. 327–338. Springer, Heidelberg (1981)
28. Sridharan, M., Bodík, R.: Refinement-based context-sensitive points-to analysis for Java. In: PLDI, pp. 387–400 (2006)
29. Streckenbach, M., Snelting, G.: Points-to for java: A general framework and an empirical comparison. Technical report, University Passau (November 2000)
30. Whaley, J., Lam, M.S.: Cloning-based context-sensitive pointer alias analysis using binary decision diagrams. In: PLDI, pp. 131–144. ACM Press, New York (2004)
31. Wilson, R.P., Lam, M.S.: Efficient context-sensitive pointer analysis for C programs. In: PLDI, pp. 1–12 (1995)

Sufficient Preconditions for Modular Assertion Checking*

Yannick Moy

France Télécom, Lannion, F-22307
INRIA Futurs, ProVal, 4 rue Jacques Monod, Orsay, F-91893
Lab. de Recherche en Informatique, Univ Paris-Sud, CNRS, Orsay, F-91405

Abstract. Assertion checking is the restriction of program verification to validity of program assertions. It encompasses safety checking, which is program verification of safety properties, like memory safety or absence of overflows. In this paper, we consider assertion checking of program parts instead of whole programs, which we call modular assertion checking. Classically, modular assertion checking is possible only if the context in which a program part is executed is known. By default, the worst-case context must be assumed, which may impair the verification task. It usually takes user effort to detail enough the execution context for the verification task to succeed, by providing strong enough preconditions. We propose a method to automatically infer sufficient preconditions in the context of modular assertion checking of imperative pointer programs. It combines abstract interpretation, weakest precondition calculus and quantifier elimination. We instantiate this method to prove memory safety for C and Java programs, under some memory separation conditions.

1 Introduction

Modular program verification is the application of program verification to a known subset of some unknown larger program, and the composition of such verifications. This issue arises e.g., for the verification of libraries and third-party software components, as well as an easy means to perform program verification on large programs by a divide-and-conquer approach. Safety checking is the restriction of program verification to safety properties, mostly language-bound safety properties, like non-null checking or array bound checking for Java and C programs. Our target is modular safety checking, which is modular program verification of safety properties. Actually, we consider in this paper the problem of modular assertion checking, to which modular safety checking reduces in many cases.

Deductive verification makes program verification possible in an essentially modular way. Indeed, deductive verification builds on annotations provided by a user at procedure boundaries (pre- and postconditions) and loop dominators (loop invariants) to generate verification conditions at the level of a procedure or a loop, computed as weakest preconditions or strongest postconditions. A verification condition (VC) is a

* This research is partly supported by CIFRE contract 2005/973 with France Télécom company, and ANR RNTL 'CAT'.

F. Logozzo et al. (Eds.): VMCAI 2008, LNCS 4905, pp. 188–202, 2008.

formula whose validity, checked by an automatic or interactive theorem prover, implies validity of the desired property at some specific program point. The problem with this approach is that it requires a large amount of work from the user, namely writing all the necessary logical annotations for deductive verification to apply.

In the context of global program analyses, where the whole program is known, it is common to use abstract interpretation techniques (or other dataflow static analyses) as a preliminary step to build invariants at given program points. An invariant is a formula whose validity holds whenever the execution of a program reaches the associated program point. Abstract interpretation is much harder to apply in a modular setting [1]. Without further knowledge of the calling context of procedures, the worst-case context must be assumed, e.g., all reference (resp. pointer) parameters may be null or aliased in Java (resp. in C). Aliasing is particularly problematic, since non-aliasing is usually relied upon implicitly by the programmer where program correctness depends on it, and thus not checked against in the program.

We show in this paper that assertion checking for pointer programs can be reduced to assertion checking for integer programs plus memory separation conditions. Our first result (Theorem 1) is a method that solves the modular assertion checking problem for imperative integer programs. Given some part of a program with assertions and without knowledge of the execution context, our method infers a sufficient precondition for these assertions to hold. Our second result (Theorem 2) shows how to reduce memory safety for an imperative pointer program to assertion checking on an integer program, thus building on our first result. Our third result (Theorem 3) extends applicability of our method to the modular assertion checking problem for imperative pointer programs, under the hypothesis that aliasing is restricted (Rule 1). Conformance to Rule 1 can be translated into additional preconditions on memory separation. All proofs can be found in an extended version of the paper [2].

Although we are only concerned in this paper with the generation of such sufficient preconditions, and not with their use in a particular program verification framework, we present the results of our preliminary experiments in verifying programs with WHY [3], a platform for deductive verification of C and Java programs.

We start with reviewing related work in Section 2. We describe our inference method for imperative integer programs in Section 3. We show how to lift it to pointer programs in Section 4. We report on the results of our experiments in Section 5. We finally conclude and discuss ongoing work in Section 6.

2 Related Work

Array Bound Checking and Loop Invariant Inference. Historically, array bound checking has been one of the first difficult properties about programs that people tried to prove, the hardest part of the verification task being the automatic inference of loop invariants. In 1978, Cousot and Halbwachs [4] applied abstract interpretation over polyhedrons and managed to check memory safety of an implementation of heapsort, using manual preconditions. A year later, Suzuki and Ishihata [5] devised a method based on weakest preconditions to check memory safety of an implementation of tree sort. They used Fourier-Motzkin elimination at loop entrance as a heuristic to make their induction-iteration method converge. More recently, Xu et al. [6,7] have refined with success the induction-iteration method for safety checking of machine code. They rely on user-provided preconditions too. Our method directly builds upon these works.

Modular Program Verification and Precondition Inference. Bourdoncle defines abstract debugging [8] as backward abstract interpretation from assertions. Along the way, he generates loop invariants and preconditions in order to prove these assertions. He focuses on array bound checking too. His backward propagation merges the conditions to reach the program point where the assertion is checked and the conditions to make this assertion valid. The dual approach of propagating backward a superset of the forbidden states is described by Rival [9]. We show in this paper problematic cases in which our approach performs better.

Gulwani and Tiwari [10] consider the problem of assertion checking for the special case of equalities in a restricted language with only non-deterministic branching. Using a method based on unification, they manage to generate necessary and sufficient preconditions for assertions to hold. Unfortunately, unification does not work for the relations that arise most often in practice for safety checking, namely less-than and greater-than relations. Our method only generates sufficient preconditions, but it applies to any kind of assertions.

Memory Separation and Precondition Inference. The necessity for some logical specification of pointer separation in C dates back to the C99 standard [11], with the addition of the *restrict* keyword. Various authors have described annotation-based systems to help programmers specify pointer separation [12,13]. Our treatment of separation with a dedicated first-order predicate is inspired from these works. It is simple enough that inferring sufficient separation preconditions is possible and general-purpose automatic theorem provers correctly handle our separation annotations. It may come to a surprise that we do not need a deeper understanding of the heap to analyze programs with lists, trees, or other pointer-based data structures. This is because we only consider here safety checking, which is not so much concerned with the shape of the heap, contrary to program termination and verification of behavioral properties. In particular, we do not relate to separation logic or shape analysis. Calcagno et al. [14] present an analysis to infer sufficient preconditions for list manipulating programs.

Abstract Interpretation and Deductive Verification Combined. Recent works combine abstract interpretation and deductive verification. Leino and Logozzo [15] build a real feedback loop between a theorem prover and an abstract interpretation module. Although very promising, their method suffers from the high cost of calling the theorem prover repeatedly and it cannot generate preconditions.

In [16], the same authors present an embedding of the abstract interpretation technique of widening inside a theorem prover. The opposite approach of performing abstract interpretation on logic formulas has been presented by Tiwari and Gulwani [17]. Our method is a different way of combining abstract interpretation and deductive verification techniques (weakest precondition, quantifier elimination).

3 Modular Assertion Checking for Integer Programs

In both Section 3 and Section 4, we define an imperative language $\mathcal{L}$ and we assume we are given a program in this language with an assertion A at some program point. A can be seen equivalently as a statement that some boolean side-effect free expression of the language holds or as the corresponding logic formula. Our goal is to infer a sufficient precondition P for the program such that, if P holds when the program starts executing, assertion A holds whenever execution reaches the program point of A.

In the following, program statements make use of the C programming language operators (e.g., <= or &&), while logic statements make use of mathematical operators (e.g., $\leq$ or $\wedge$). We allow chained comparisons in our logic formulas (e.g., $i = 0 < j \leq k$) with the meaning that it is equivalent to the conjunction of the individual comparisons (here, $i = 0 \wedge 0 < j \wedge j \leq k$).

Our simple imperative integer language $\mathcal{L}_i$ is a subset of C, and we borrow C syntax and semantics (note that on the simple subset we present, such semantics are well defined by the C standard). We could have made it an equivalent subset of Java instead, so that the results presented in this paper apply equally to C and Java programs. The only base type is `int`, the type of integers, so that all variables are of integer type. We make the target program part a function that takes integer parameters and returns nothing. For simplicity, function parameters are special local variables that are never assigned to (which can always be obtained with a simple program transformation).

Side-effect free expressions (denoted by `e`) contain integer constants, variables, and basic operations on those, like arithmetic operations and comparison operations.

`e ::= 0, 1, 2, ...`	constant
`| x, y, z, ...`	variable
`| e + e, e - e, e * e, ...`	arithmetic operation
`| e <= e, e == e, e > e, ...`	comparison operation

Statements (denoted by `s`) contain assignments, conditionals, branchings, loops, assertions, and sequences of those.

`s ::= x = e;`	assignment
`| if (e) { s }`	conditional
`| if (e) { s } else { s }`	branching
`| while (e) { s }`	loop
`| assert (e);`	assertion
`| s s`	sequence

3.1 State-of-the-Art Is Not Enough

We consider a very simple program `foo` in this language. We apply state-of-the-art methods to infer a precondition P sufficient to prove an assertion A. As seen from this simplified example, we are not concerned here with program termination.

```
void foo(int s, int n) {
    int i = 0;
    while (1) {
        if (i < n) {
            assert (0 <= i && i < s);
        }
        i = i + 1;
    }
}
```

With a worst-case assumption for the calling context of foo, this assertion is trivially false. Here, the worst-case assumption means that parameters s and n could be any integers in the allowed range for integers. Take for example $s = 1$ and $n = 2$ at function start. When control reaches the assertion for the second time, $i = s = 1$, which violates the assertion. A coarse precondition for function foo that is sufficient to prove the assertion is *false*. We aim at finding a better sufficient precondition, that should be implied by the calling context of foo.

Finding such a precondition is a backward propagation problem. Therefore, we should first expose problems encountered by classical backward propagation methods, namely weakest precondition and backward abstract interpretation. Actually, we consider refinements of these techniques that have been developed in order to generate sufficient loop invariants for checking assertions. These are the induction-iteration method of Suzuki and Ishihata [5,6] and the abstract debugging method of Bourdoncle [8].

Let us start with classical weakest precondition. First of all, one should notice that the assertion we are trying to prove is enclosed in a loop. Then, the problem is that we cannot propagate the necessary condition to the start of the function, as this backward propagation is stopped at loop start: Hoare-style weakest precondition imposes that the invariant, which is *true* here, implies the validity of the propagated formula $i < n \Rightarrow 0 \leq i < s$, which is not the case here. The induction-iteration method requires us to define the formula $W(0) = i < n \Rightarrow 0 \leq i < s$ as a preliminary invariant candidate and propagate it backward through the loop, generating formula $W(1) = i+1 < n \Rightarrow 0 \leq i+1 < s$. After a theorem prover fails to prove that $W(0) \Rightarrow W(1)$, it is possible to either continue propagating backward the candidate invariant $W(0) \wedge W(1)$ or to generalize the formula $W(0) \Rightarrow W(1)$ to eliminate induction variables, i.e. variables modified in the loop body. This generalization proceeds by universally quantifying the variables to eliminate, and then calling a quantifier elimination procedure to produce an equivalent qantifier-free formula. Here, the formula $\forall\ i \in \mathbb{Z}.\ W(0) \Rightarrow W(1)$ is false, therefore the quantifier elimination procedure, e.g., Fourier-Motzkin as in [5,6], gives the result *false*. We get an interesting result only if we consider separately each conjunct $0 \leq i$ and $i < s$ in the original assertion. Then, generalization still produces *false* starting from assertion $0 \leq i$, but it now produces loop invariant candidate $n \leq s$ starting from assertion $i < s$. This formula can then be propagated backward to give the precondition $n \leq s$ which is sufficient to prove the last part of the assertion.

Induction-iteration method cannot generate a precondition for the first part of the assertion because it lacks knowledge of what precedes the loop, as already noted by Xu et al. [6]. To alleviate this problem, they advocate the use of preliminary forward static analyses. It makes it possible to prove both parts of the assertion here under the precondition $n \leq s$. With or without preliminary static analyses, induction-iteration suffers from two crucial problems. First, it repeatedly calls a theorem prover to check tautologies, which is very time-consuming. Secondly, it does not take into account information from outside of the loop, which leads to a precondition too restrictive here.

Let us now turn to backward abstract interpretation. Here, we assume our starting point is the output of a forward abstract interpretation pass, operating on convex abstract domains. Thus we assume that the invariant produced at the point of assertion is $0 \leq i \wedge i < n$. Abstract debugging [8] then proceeds with backward abstract interpretation from the program point of the assertion, with initial invariant $0 \leq i \wedge i < n \wedge i < s$. It already does not look as if we can get to a sufficient precondition for the assertion to hold, as n and s get symmetric roles in this formula, although they have quite opposite responsibilities w.r.t. the assertion holding or not. If we keep working with convex domains, the best we can get at loop beginning is the formula $0 \leq i$, which does not improve on the forward pass. If we relax this requirement, and allow some kind of trace partitioning based on the branching condition $i < n$, we get the formula $(0 \leq i \wedge n \leq i) \vee (0 \leq i \wedge i < n \wedge i < s)$. Any further backward propagation through the loop body does not improve on this formula. Backward propagating this formula out of the loop leads to the formula $(i = 0 \wedge n \leq 0) \vee (i = 0 \wedge 0 < n \wedge 0 < s)$, which yields precondition $(n \leq 0) \vee (0 < n \wedge 0 < s)$ after i has been projected out as the result of backward propagation over i initialization. Backward propagation of forbidden states instead of desired states, as in [9], suffers from the same problem when joining states around the loop. Starting from forbidden states $0 \leq i < n \wedge s \leq i$, it produces states $0 \leq i < n-1 \wedge s-1 \leq i$ after one iteration backward through the loop, and so on. Joining all these states produces the forbidden states $0 \leq i < n$ at loop entry, which result in the overly restrictive precondition $n \leq 0$.

Although the resulting precondition $(n \leq 0) \vee (0 < n \wedge 0 < s)$ is an interesting case distinction (see Section 3.2), it is not sufficient to prove the assertion correct, e.g., it does not rule out the case $s = 1$ and $n = 2$ that we mentioned above. We are going to show that by combining induction-iteration and abstract interpretation, we get a better precondition than the one obtained by weakest precondition and abstract interpretation separately.

3.2 A Solution by Combining Methods

Forward Abstract Interpretation + Quantifier Elimination. In our attempt to provide a better solution to this precondition inference problem, we assume as in the backward abstract interpretation attempt that we can run a forward abstract interpretation pass that provides us with an invariant at each program point. Ideally, we would like that the invariant at an assertion point implies the assertion correctness. In our example, assuming convex abstract domains, the most precise invariant obtained by forward abstract interpretation at the assertion point is $0 \leq i < n$. Therefore, we would like the following formula to be valid (variables are implicitly universally quantified):

$$0 \leq i < n \Rightarrow 0 \leq i < s. \tag{1}$$

Formula (1) is trivially invalid, as a theorem prover would easily show by outputting an assignment of variables that falsifies it, e.g., $s = 1$, $n = 2$ and $i = 1$. But notice all variables do not play the same role in this formula: some variables (n and s) are in fact parameters of function `foo`, which we should keep in the final precondition we seek, while other variables (only i here) are local variables which should not appear in the precondition. Then, we rewrite Formula (1) by quantifying over local variables:

$$\forall\, i \in \mathbb{Z}.\; 0 \leq i < n \Rightarrow 0 \leq i < s. \tag{2}$$

If the first-order logic fragment we are working in has a quantifier elimination procedure, it is possible to get rid of the local variables we do not want to keep in the precondition. Indeed, quantifier elimination procedures take a quantified formula and return an equivalent formula without quantifiers (thus removing the quantified variables). In our case, quantifier elimination over the integers in Presburger arithmetic, using e.g., Cooper's method or Fourier-Motzkin elimination here (as coefficients are all ± 1), results in the following formula which is equivalent to Formula (2):

$$n \leq 0 \vee n \leq s. \tag{3}$$

First, Formula (3) is a valid precondition for function `foo`, as it only mentions parameters and constants. Furthermore, it is by construction a sufficient precondition for assertion A to hold. Indeed, it is equivalent to Formula (2) whose validity implies that the assertion holds. In particular, it rules out the case $s = 1$ and $n = 2$ mentioned above.

Notice that Formula (3) is stronger than the insufficient precondition $(n \leq 0) \vee (0 < n \wedge 0 < s)$ obtained by abstract debugging, and weaker than the overly restrictive precondition $n \leq s$ obtained by induction-iteration. For such a simple example, it is even a necessary and sufficient precondition for the assertion to hold, but in general we can only assure it is a sufficient precondition.

Same + Weakest Precondition. It is not always the case that the method we described in the previous section constructs the desired sufficient precondition. In particular, the invariant at the assertion point obtained by forward abstract interpretation may not be precise enough. This happens frequently due to a merge of paths through the function before control reaches the assertion point. Recovering this path-sensitive information is precisely the purpose of weakest precondition. Therefore, we propose to postpone calling the quantifier elimination procedure on inductive variables until the loop head is reached by weakest precondition. This is similar to performing the generalization of induction-iteration [5,6] at the very first iteration. It is not possible in their setting, as they use the second pass through the loop body to gather information on the code after the assertion point. In our setting, we can rely on the forward abstract interpretation pass to compute this information.

Figure 1 describes our method in details. It consists in two phases. In a first phase, we compute an invariant at each program point using forward abstract interpretation (line 2). In a second phase, we consider each assertion in turn, weaken it by the computed invariant and propagate it backwards in the program using a combination of weakest precondition (*WP*) and quantifier elimination (*QE*) (lines 4-23).

```
1  let a⃗ be the variables local to the function
2  perform forward abstract interpretation
3  P := true
4  for each assertion A do
5      f := A and pp := program point of A
6      while pp enclosed or preceded by a loop L do
7          let I_pp be the forward invariant at pp
8          let I_L be the invariant of loop L
9          let C be the looping condition of loop L
10         if pp is enclosed in L then
11             f_wp := (I_L ∧ C) ⇒ WP_{L,pp}(I_pp ⇒ f)
12         else
13             f_wp := (I_L ∧ ¬ C) ⇒ WP_{L,pp}(I_pp ⇒ f)
14         fi
15         let x⃗ be the variables modified in L
16         f_qe := QE(x⃗, f_wp)
17         I_L := I_L ∧ f_qe
18         f := f_qe and pp := program point before loop L
19     done
20     f_wp := WP_{begin,pp}(I_pp ⇒ f)
21     f_qe := QE(a⃗, f_wp)
22     P := P ∧ f_qe
23 done
24 return P
```

Fig. 1. Precondition Inference Method

During backward propagation, we consider the DAG created by the control-flow graph whose back edges are removed. Our method works by reverse crawling the unique path from the top of the DAG to the assertion point. Each propagation step reaches the next closest loop dominator on this path, which can be defined either as the program point that dominates a loop or the target of the back edge in the control flow that creates the loop. We say that the current program point is enclosed in a loop if the first loop dominator encountered in this reverse crawl is reached from inside the loop. Otherwise, if the first loop dominator is reached from outside the loop, we say that the current program point is preceded by a loop. In the last case, no loop dominator is reached. An invariant at a loop dominator is a loop invariant.

First, we form the implication formula $I_{pp} \Rightarrow f$. It weakens formula f by the computed forward invariant at pp (lines 11 and 13). Then, we compute the weakest precondition at loop entry or loop exit starting from f at pp, that we denote $WP_{L,pp}(I_{pp} \Rightarrow f)$ (lines 11 and 13). We weaken this formula by the conjunction of the loop invariant and the loop entry test C or loop exit test $\neg\, C$, as appropriate (lines 11 and 13). In order to proceed with the next propagation phase, we need to eliminate from f_{wp} the variables modified in the loop. Thus we call QE on f_{wp}, which produces the formula f_{qe} (line 16). This formula is used to strengthen the loop invariant (line 17) and as a starting point for the next propagation step (line 18). Finally, when the current program point is neither enclosed nor preceded by a loop, we compute the weakest precondition of the implication formula $I_{pp} \Rightarrow f$ at function entry, that we denote f_{wp} (line 20). Eliminating from this formula the variables local to the function produces a sufficient precondition formula f_{qe} (line 21) that we add to the function precondition. The process repeats for all assertions.

Applying this method to function `foo` computes the loop invariant and function precondition $n \leq 0 \vee n \leq s$ (i.e. Formula (3)).

Theorem 1. *Given an imperative integer program in $\mathcal{L}_i$, our method produces a sufficient precondition that solves the assertion checking problem for this program.*

Notice that our method also gives valid loop invariants under the same assumption that the sufficient precondition is respected. The proof proceeds by structural induction on the control-flow graph and presents no difficulty.

Our method combines the strengths of induction-iteration and abstract debugging. Like abstract debugging, it builds on invariants known by abstract interpretation. Like induction-iteration, it is path-sensitive and it allows the generation of arbitrary complex formulas, possibly with many disjunctions (that usually correspond to execution paths).

4 Modular Safety and Assertion Checking for Pointer Programs

We now extend our simple language $\mathcal{L}_i$ into $\mathcal{L}_p$, which adds support for pointers to integers. The results presented here extend to multi-level pointers as well. Expressions now contain dereferences. Statements contain allocations, for which we borrow the keyword `new` from Java and C++, to avoid introducing the low-level memory allocation of C. Here are the additional rules in $\mathcal{L}_p$ w.r.t. $\mathcal{L}_i$:

`e ::= *e`	dereference
`e ::= e + e, e - e`	pointer arithmetic
`s ::= x = new int[e];`	allocation

Pointer arithmetic adds or subtracts an integer expression from a pointer expression. Allocation `new int[e]` returns a new uninitialized memory block of size `e`.

4.1 Memory Safety as Assertion Checking for Integer Programs

We show here the reduction of memory safety for pointer programs to assertion checking for integer programs. This makes it possible to use the method developed in Section 3 to solve modular memory safety for pointer programs.

A program in $\mathcal{L}_p$ is memory safe if all pointers that are dereferenced point inside the bounds of a previously allocated memory block. In the simplest case, the size of the memory block pointed-to can be statically known. E.g., it is the case for arrays in C, for which the static type contains the array size. Then, memory safety is easily expressed as assertions in the language of integer linear inequalities. E.g., safety of access $*(arr+i)$ in C, where *arr* is an array of size 10, reduces to validity of assertion $0 \leq i < 10$. This simple approach is used, e.g., in the already mentioned works [4,5,8]. In general, the actual value for the size of an allocated block as well as the precise block pointed-to by a pointer are only known at runtime. Therefore, the best we can do statically is to model this size as a *ghost* or *model* integer variable associated to every pointer. This is the approach taken by various verification tools like BOON [18], CSSV [19] and Overlook [20]. This effectively reduces the problem of checking memory safety for pointer programs to the problem of checking assertions for integer programs.

In practice, one has to choose both a model for pointers and a suitable representation for this model in the verification framework. E.g., a model some authors used in past work on verification of C programs [21] defines, for each allocated pointer, a base address, that points to the beginning of the allocated memory block, a block size, that contains the size of the allocated block, and an integer offset, that corresponds to the difference between the pointer and its base address. In more recent work [22], we describe a different model for pointers better suited to inference of annotations and automatic verification. It defines a left and a right integer bounds for pointers, such that adding an integer between these bounds to the pointer and dereferencing it is safe. This is the model we adopted in our current work. Our representation for this pointer model is different in the inference tool we describe in this paper and in the deductive verification platform WHY which uses the annotations inferred to perform verification. On the inference side, we model left and right integer bounds as meta-variables that abstract interpretation transfer functions and weakest precondition take into account. On the deductive verification side, the same model variables are treated like uninterpreted functions, for which an appropriate axiomatization is given. These functions take two parameters: the pointer for which they provide a bound and the current heap. The heap is modeled by a functional array which is updated at each allocation statement. For the moment, we consider that our inference method deals with dereferenced values like $*p$ by assuming these can be any integer.

Using the above mentioned model and representation for pointers, we can solve the modular memory safety problem for programs in $\mathcal{L}_p$. Associativity of pointer arithmetic allows us to rewrite each memory access in $\mathcal{L}_p$ into a unique normal form $*(p+e)$ where p is a pointer variable and e an integer offset expression. Call *offset_min_p* (resp. *offset_max_p*) the left (resp. right) integer bound variable associated to p. Safety of access $*(p+e)$ reduces to validity of assertion $offset\_min\_p \leq e \leq offset\_max\_p$.

Theorem 2. *Given an imperative pointer program in $\mathcal{L}_p$, our method produces a sufficient precondition that solves the memory safety problem for this program.*

The proof derives from our model and representation of pointers. It basically says that if you check that every pointer dereference is in bounds, then you achieve memory safety. Memory safety for function `bar` below reduces to assertion checking for a function very similar to our running example function `foo`. For this function, our inference method generates the sufficient precondition

$$n \leq 0 \vee (offset\_min\_p \leq 0 \wedge n \leq offset\_max\_p + 1). \qquad (4)$$

```
void bar(int* p, int n) {
    int i = 0;
    while (1) {
        if (i < n) {
            *(p + i) = 0;
        }
        i = i + 1;
    }
}
```

4.2 Modular Assertion Checking for Pointer Programs

We consider now the broader problem of assertion checking for pointer programs. Say we would like to verify the validity of assertion $*p < *q$. The simple solution we adopted in Section 4.1 is not enough.

The problem of *aliasing* arises when applying our method to check memory safety of programs in real languages like C or Java. Aliasing is the possibility that two distinct names in the program refer to the same memory location. At worst, any two names in the program may refer to the same memory location, which makes it impossible to apply our method precisely. This problem appears readily in our toy language $\mathcal{L}_p$: just change the type of n in example `bar` from `int` to `int*` and change the test to $i < *n$. Then, nothing prevents pointer n from being an alias of $p+i$ for some value of i, which makes it possible to change the value pointed-to by n in statement $*(p+i) = 0$;.

Our criterion for separating pointers comes from a simple observation, related to the fact we target the verification of source code programs written, read and maintained by human programmers. The natural idiom we impose on the programs we analyze is the following: if, in a function, a read to some memory location x follows a write to some memory location *with a different name* y, we impose that x and y refer to different memory locations. Similarly, two consecutive writes to memory locations *with different names* x and y without an intermediate read to x should refer to different memory locations. Otherwise, the second write invalidates the first one. To make it more concrete, compare now the programs below.

```
void plusminus(int* x, int* y,
               int* z, int* t) {
    *z = *x + *y;
    *t = *x - *y;
}
```

```
void id(int* p, int* q) {
}
void opp(int* p, int* q) {
    *q = - *q;
}
```

It is not clear to see that functions `id` and `opp` are direct specializations of function `plusminus`, using specific aliasing between parameters x, y, z and t. Indeed, `id` can be defined as `plusminus(p,q,p,p)` and `opp` as `plusminus(p,q,q,q)`, whenever p and q point to different memory locations. Other choices of aliasing lead to many more different functions, which is probably not the intent of the author of function `plusminus`.

To avoid considering all such unintended possible aliasing of the parameters when analyzing a function in isolation, we therefore restrict our attention to the functions that obey the following rule.

Rule 1 ***(write-read-rule).*** *Between a write to memory through pointer variable x (or the beginning of the function if there is no such write) and a read from memory through the same variable x (or the end of the function if there is no such read), and unless x is redefined in-between, all other writes to memory should not write to the location pointed-to by x.*

Function `plusminus` follows Rule 1 if and only if variable z is not aliased to any of the variables x, y and t. Indeed, between the beginning of the function and the last line where x and y are read, the write to z should not modify x and y underlying values. And before the write to z on the first line and the end of the function, the write to t should not modify z just written value. This rules out in particular the odd specializations `id` and `opp` that we considered above.

The immediate consequence of analyzing only programs that follow Rule 1 is that memory locations can be treated almost like normal integer variables by our analyses. Indeed, whenever value $*p$ is read, it can only be a value obtained by previously writing to $*p$ (or the value at function entry), or else by redefining p, in which case all information on $*p$ is lost. Modifying $*p$ by aliasing would break Rule 1. Adapting our abstract interpretation and weakest precondition to these pseudo-variables is quite straightforward. The main difference is that modifying p also destroys the value of $*p$. Another twist is that mentioning the value of $*p$ in an invariant computed by abstract interpretation counts as a read of $*p$ for Rule 1.

Theorem 3. *Given an imperative pointer program in $\mathcal{L}_p$ that follows Rule 1, our method produces a sufficient precondition that solves the assertion checking problem for this program.*

The proof derives from the above remark that $*p$ cannot be modified by aliasing, and from our adjustment of abstract interpretation and weakest precondition.

4.3 Sufficient Separation Preconditions for Pointer Programs

Ideally, we would like to be able to detect that a program does not follow Rule 1. It is easy to see this is undecidable. Therefore, in practice, we settle for a stronger condition than Rule 1. Let *base pointers* be pointer parameters and pointers returned by `new`. Let *cursor pointers* be pointer values syntactically aliased to some offset from a base pointer. First, we rewrite cursor pointers in the program as integer offsets from base pointers. Then, we impose that pointers that are written to in the function must be separated, so that writes cannot interfere. In function `plusminus`, this forbids z and t from being aliased. We also impose that pointers that are only read from must be separated from those that are written to, so that reads and writes cannot interfere. In function `plusminus`, this forbids z from being aliased to x or y.

To express these requirements in the logic, we adopt here a simple binary predicate $separated(p,q)$ which expresses the separation of pointers p and q, i.e. the memory blocks pointed to by p and q do not overlap. In particular, $separated(p,p+1)$ holds. This predicate is a basic predicate in our logic, that is not defined in terms of simpler ones. The postcondition of the allocation operation uses it to express that a newly allocated block does not overlap with previously allocated blocks. In practice, we use predicates derived from the simple *separated* predicate, in order to express, e.g., non-overlapping of arrays.

On function `plusminus`, the over-approximation of Rule 1 gives the same results as strict conformance to Rule 1, which can be expressed as the precondition

$$separated(x,z) \wedge separated(y,z) \wedge separated(z,t). \tag{5}$$

5 Experimental Results

Implementation Details. We have implemented the algorithm of Figure 1 for Jessie programs. Jessie is an internal intermediate language in our platform WHY [3], that is suitable for deductive verification and a target of translation from C and Java. We perform abstract interpretation on the interval, octagon and polyhedral domains from the APRON library [23]. We chose Fourier-Motzkin as quantifier elimination for formulas in Presburger arithmetic. After inferring preconditions, we prove assertions or memory safety in WHY, which generates verification conditions and calls automatic provers on them. On our running example, function `foo`, our implementation infers a precondition equivalent to Formula (3):

$$(1 \leq s \wedge n \leq s) \vee (n \leq 0 \wedge n \leq s) \vee (n \leq 0 \wedge s \leq -1). \tag{6}$$

Indeed, Formula (6) is equivalent to $n \leq 0 \vee n \leq s$ on integers.

Inference in Practice: Calls and Structures. We did not discuss the two main features of structured languages which allow modular development, and thus deserve special attention in modular verification: control-flow modularity through function calls and data-flow modularity through structured types. Although not directly related to modularity, we also support exception handling.

We support calls by extending the algorithm of Figure 1 to propagate assertion formulas beyond function boundaries. When analyzing a module (e.g., a file in C or a class in Java), we distinguish external functions, which can be called from outside the current module, from internal functions. In the first phase of our method, the forward abstract interpretation step, external functions are taken as root whereas internal function calls are analyzed. In particular, recursive internal functions lead to a fixpoint computation. In the second phase of our method, backward propagation of assertions, we begin with assertions in leaf functions of the call-graph and continue with assertions higher in the call-graph. For each such assertion in an internal function, the precondition inferred is further propagated higher in the call-graph, starting from the function call sites. Currently, we do not treat recursion specially in this backward propagation.

We naturally support structures without further modification of our method. The problem of annotating structured types with invariants given some policy to check these invariants is an orthogonal issue [24]. In the WHY platform, the frontends for C and Java programs both allow a user to annotate its structured types with such invariants. WHY then generates verification conditions that take these invariants into account.

Preliminary Experiments. During our experiments, we focused on C programs, especially on string manipulating functions which account for a large number of memory safety vulnerabilities. We successfully generated correct annotations and automatically proved memory safety in WHY for 20 functions of the C standard string library implemented in the Minix 3 operating system [25]. This is to contrast with a previous work on sufficient preconditions inference [22] in which we could only prove 18 of these functions because the preconditions we could infer were not expressive enough. With the method we present in this paper, any kind of formula can be inferred using the appropriate combination of abstract domains and quantifier elimination.

We also analyzed several functions from the Verisec buffer overflow benchmark [26]. This benchmark is issued from real-world vulnerabilities on popular open source applications like `sendmail` or `wu-ftpd`. It provides simplified versions of the real vulnerabilities. Each test consists in a program containing a vulnerability and a patched version of the same program. In order to test our method, we considered each function as external. We successfully generated sufficient preconditions for various patched versions while failing to prove correct the vulnerable versions.

Finally, we generated sufficient preconditions for checking absence of integer overflows when adding or subtracting integers, which can be expressed as linear inequality assertions. We applied it successfully to the well-known binary-search program, which got some more attention recently after a possible overflow was spotted in its Java library implementation [27].

6 Conclusion and Ongoing Work

In this paper, we have described a method to solve the modular assertion checking problem for imperative integer programs. Given a function with assertions, our method infers a sufficient precondition for these assertions to hold. The method consists in a special arrangement of existing well-established techniques in program analysis: abstract interpretation, weakest precondition, quantifier elimination. This plugin architecture allows both reuse of existing building blocks and specialization to specific assertions, programs and languages, which makes our method powerful and customizable.

More importantly, we have shown that the same method can be applied to the modular assertion checking problem for imperative pointer programs that follow a simple aliasing restricting rule. Rule conformance can be expressed as separation preconditions that must be respected too. Finally, we have shown how to reduce memory safety to assertion checking.

We present convincing preliminary results that our method is effective for modular safety checking of C programs. We are currently working on applying our method to larger real-world programs in C and Java.

Acknowledgements. I would like to thank Pierre Crégut and Claude Marché for their advisory work and many others for their comments on this paper or earlier work leading to it: Mathieu Baudet, Dariusz Biernacki, Nicolaj Bjørner, Sylvain Conchon, Jean-François Couchot, Jean-Christophe Filliâtre, Francesco Logozzo, Matteo Slanina, Nicolas Stouls. Finally, many thanks to the anonymous referees for their useful comments.

References

1. Cousot, P., Cousot, R.: Modular static program analysis. In: Horspool, R.N. (ed.) CC 2002 and ETAPS 2002. LNCS, vol. 2304, pp. 159–178. Springer, London (2002)
2. `http://www.lri.fr/~moy/publis/moy08vmcai-ext.pdf`

3. Filliâtre, J.C., Marché, C.: The Why/Krakatoa/Caduceus platform for deductive program verification. In: Damm, W., Hermanns, H. (eds.) CAV 2007. LNCS, vol. 4590, Springer, Heidelberg (2007)
4. Cousot, P., Halbwachs, N.: Automatic discovery of linear restraints among variables of a program. In: Proc. POPL 1978, pp. 84–96. ACM, New York (1978)
5. Suzuki, N., Ishihata, K.: Implementation of an array bound checker. In: Proc. POPL 1977, pp. 132–143. ACM, New York (1977)
6. Xu, Z., Miller, B.P., Reps, T.: Safety checking of machine code. ACM SIGPLAN Notices 35(5), 70–82 (2000)
7. Xu, Z.: Safety checking of machine code. PhD thesis, Univ. of Wisconsin, Madison (2000)
8. Bourdoncle, F.: Assertion-based debugging of imperative programs by abstract interpretation. In: Sommerville, I., Paul, M. (eds.) ESEC 1993. LNCS, vol. 717, pp. 501–516. Springer, London (1993)
9. Rival, X.: Understanding the origin of alarms in ASTRÉE. In: Hankin, C., Siveroni, I. (eds.) SAS 2005. LNCS, vol. 3672, pp. 303–319. Springer, London (2005)
10. Gulwani, S., Tiwari, A.: Assertion checking unified. In: Cook, B., Podelski, A. (eds.) VMCAI 2007. LNCS, vol. 4349, Springer, Heidelberg (2007)
11. International Organization for Standardization (ISO) (The ANSI C standard (C99))
12. Aiken, A., et al.: Checking and inferring local non-aliasing. In: Proc. PLDI 2003, pp. 129–140. ACM, New York (2003)
13. Koes, D., Budiu, M., Venkataramani, G.: Programmer specified pointer independence. In: MSP 2004, pp. 51–59. ACM, New York (2004)
14. Calcagno, C., et al.: Footprint analysis: A shape analysis that discovers preconditions. In: Riis Nielson, H., Filé, G. (eds.) SAS 2007. LNCS, vol. 4634, Springer, Heidelberg (2007)
15. Leino, K.R.M., Logozzo, F.: Loop invariants on demand. In: Yi, K. (ed.) APLAS 2005. LNCS, vol. 3780, pp. 119–134. Springer, Heidelberg (2005)
16. Leino, K.R.M., Logozzo, F.: Using widenings to infer loop invariants inside an SMT solver, or: A theorem prover as abstract domain. Technical Report RISC-Linz Report Series No. 07-07, RISC, Hagenberg, Austria, Proc. WING 2007 (2007)
17. Tiwari, A., Gulwani, S.: Logical interpretation: Static program analysis using theorem proving. In: Pfenning, F. (ed.) CADE 2007. LNCS (LNAI), vol. 4603, pp. 147–166. Springer, Heidelberg (2007)
18. Wagner, D., et al.: A first step towards automated detection of buffer overrun vulnerabilities. In: NDSS Symposium, San Diego, CA, pp. 3–17 (2000)
19. Dor, N., Rodeh, M., Sagiv, M.: CSSV: towards a realistic tool for statically detecting all buffer overflows in C. In: Proc. PLDI 2003, pp. 155–167. ACM Press, New York (2003)
20. Allamigeon, X., Godard, W., Hymans, C.: Static analysis of string manipulations in critical embedded C programs. In: SAS. LNCS, pp. 35–51. Springer, Heidelberg (2006)
21. Filliâtre, J.C., Marché, C.: Multi-prover verification of C programs. In: Davies, J., Schulte, W., Barnett, M. (eds.) ICFEM 2004. LNCS, vol. 3308, pp. 15–29. Springer, Heidelberg (2004)
22. Moy, Y., Marché, C.: Inferring local (non-)aliasing and strings for memory safety. In: Heap Analysis and Verification (HAV 2007), Braga, Portugal (2007)
23. APRON numerical abstract domain library, `http://apron.cri.ensmp.fr/`
24. Barnett, M., et al.: Boogie: A modular reusable verifier for object-oriented programs. In: FMCO, Springer, Heidelberg (2005)
25. MINIX 3 Operating System, `http://www.minix3.org/`
26. Ku, K., et al.: A buffer overflow benchmark for software model checkers. In: Proc. ASE 2007 (2007)
27. Tuch, H., Klein, G., Norrish, M.: Types, bytes, and separation logic. In: Hofmann, M., Felleisen, M. (eds.) Proc. POPL 2007, pp. 97–108. ACM, Nice, France (2007)

Runtime Checking for Separation Logic

Huu Hai Nguyen[1], Viktor Kuncak[2], and Wei-Ngan Chin[1,3]

[1] Computer Science Programme, Singapore-MIT Alliance
[2] Swiss Federal Institute of Technology (EPFL)
[3] Department of Computer Science, National University of Singapore

Abstract. Separation logic is a popular approach for specifying properties of recursive mutable data structures. Several existing systems verify a subclass of separation logic specifications using static analysis techniques. Checking data structure specifications during program execution is an alternative to static verification: it can enforce the sophisticated specifications for which static verification fails, and it can help debug incorrect specifications and code by detecting concrete counterexamples to their validity.

This paper presents Separation Logic Invariant ChecKer (SLICK), a runtime checker for separation logic specifications. We show that, although the recursive style of separation logic predicates is well suited for runtime execution, the implicit footprint and existential quantification make efficient runtime checking challenging. To address these challenges we introduce a coloring technique for efficiently checking method footprints and describe techniques for inferring values of existentially quantified variables. We have implemented our runtime checker in the context of a tool for enforcing specifications of Java programs. Our experience suggests that our runtime checker is a useful companion to a static verifier for separation logic specifications.

1 Introduction

Linked structures are ubiquitous in modern software. Such structures appear both in container implementations of software libraries and in application code as the form of syntax trees, XML data, and other application-specific relationships. The diversity of linked structures implies that there is a wide range of invariants that they satisfy. Automated verification of these invariants is an active area of research and includes verification of shape properties [19, 2, 13] as well as properties that extend shape descriptions with specifications of size, balancing, sortedness, and content change [20,26,30,17,22]. The specification language for expressing these properties has a significant impact on the effectiveness of the analysis and its ability to interact with the developer. Separation logic with inductively defined predicates [27, 3, 22] has emerged as a popular approach to specify properties that involve linked structures. In Hoare logic based on separation logic [16], a precondition specifies not only the condition on the initial heap but also the operation's *footprint* [5]. As a result, a precondition simultaneously plays the role of a 'modifies' clause [14] and leads to a frame rule that enables modular reasoning [16]. The *footprint* of an operation in a program heap is the part of the heap that the operation may access. The *footprint* of a separation logic formula in a program heap is the part of the heap that satisfies the formula.

F. Logozzo et al. (Eds.): VMCAI 2008, LNCS 4905, pp. 203–217, 2008.

Runtime checking as complementary technique. We expect that many operations and properties in practice can be checked statically, but some will remain beyond the reach of current analysis tools. In this paper we describe a system called SLICK which can check properties during program execution and can therefore serve as a fall-back of static analysis. Such runtime checking has long been recognized as useful [7, 1]. Runtime checking detects violations of desired properties in individual runs, and, unlike many static analyses, can identify cases when code or specification definitely contain an error. Other benefits of runtime checking include interfacing to unverified code, automated checking of input data that cannot be trusted, and detecting errors that result from violating design-time assumptions (for example, operating system corruption or hardware malfunction).

Previous work on runtime checking. Despite the long history of runtime assertion checking [10], to the best of our knowledge, our work is the first runtime checker for separation logic specifications. Most existing runtime assertion checkers either check assertions in classical logic [1, 11, 31, 9], weave global checks into code at multiple program points [8, 4], address blame assignment for properties expressed in the programming language [12], or explore incremental checking of assertions [28].

The closest to our system is a checker for heap contracts expressed in linear logic [25], whose authors observe the usefulness of checking contracts in separation logic, but proceed to check assertions in *linear* logic instead. Note that [25] does not deal with the problem of checking that the footprint of the code executed is contained in the footprint of the assertion. The footprint checking is one of the main problems addressed in our paper: it makes precondition checking more than just evaluating formulas in a fixed program state and requires the checking of fine-grained modifies clauses. Another difference with [25] is that, instead of invoking a modified interpreter for a linear logic programming language, our system emits Java code that can be compiled and executed using existing virtual machines. In translation from separation logic into Java our system exploits the deterministic flavor found in most common data structure descriptions. The generated code executes using standard environments and benefits from just-in-time compilation of the Java virtual machine.

Contributions. The paper makes the following contributions:

- **A translation** of declarative predicate definitions, method preconditions and postconditions expressed in separation logic specification language [22] into executable Java code.
- **Efficient runtime mechanism** for checking separation logic assertions based on coloring heap objects and method invocations. Our approach avoids the memory blow up of naïve implementations of separation logic semantics.
- **Mode analysis** for existentially quantified variables. In most specifications we encountered, existentially bound variables are ultimately given as a function of other variables. SLICK includes mode analysis that determines the place where predicate parameters are bound, classifying them into input and output parameters. SLICK also identifies *conditionally bound parameters* for parameters whose binding time depends on the invocation context of the predicate. SLICK uses a boxed representation to instantiate such parameters at runtime at the point of their first use.

– **Integration of static and runtime checking.** SLICK ensures that annotated, but statically unverified, methods conform to their specifications at runtime, providing a fall-back for the static analyzer and enabling the interface to unverified code. Conversely, the static checker can act as an optimizer for the code generated from runtime checks.

2 Example

This section illustrates our run-time checking techniques through an example that manipulates (possibly sorted) doubly-linked lists. A list is created in a region of code that was not annotated or statically verified. Therefore, our system performs a run-time check to ensure that the subsequent code can safely use the created list. Depending on the complexity of subsequent data manipulation, the system ensures invariants in subsequent piece of code either statically, using entailment checker for separation logic [22], or dynamically, using further run-time checks.

class Node { **int** val; Node next, prev; }

root::dll⟨p,n⟩ $\equiv$ (root = null $\wedge$ n=0) $\vee$ (root::Node⟨v,r,p⟩ $*$ r::dll⟨root, m⟩ $\wedge$ n=m+1)
inv n $\geq$ 0;
root::sdll⟨p,n,s⟩ $\equiv$ (root = null $\wedge$ n = 0)$\vee$(root::Node⟨s,r,p⟩ $*$ r::sdll⟨root,m,rs⟩ $\wedge$ n=m+1 $\wedge$ s$\leq$rs)
inv n $\geq$ 0;

Fig. 1. Predicate definitions for unsorted and sorted doubly-linked list

Figure 1 shows predicate definitions used by the example. Predicate `root::dll⟨p,n⟩` means `root` points to a doubly-linked list of length `n`; `root::sdll⟨p,n,s⟩` means `root` points to a *sorted* doubly-linked list of length `n`. `root` is a reserved name which denotes a pointer to the data structure from which all objects of the data structure are reachable. The first nodes of these lists has a `prev` field pointing to `p`. The `sdll` definition ensures that the list is sorted using the `s` parameter to check that values of subsequent list elements are greater than the value of the first element, where `s` is the value of the first element in the list. The specification of the predicate uses the connectives of classical logic such as $\wedge, \vee$ as well as the separating conjunction operator $*$ which requires that its two arguments hold for two disjoint partitions of the heap [27]. In our system, a fresh variable, such as `r` in the definition of `dll` is implicitly existentially quantified. The underscore _ denotes a fresh variable whose name is omitted.

Figure 2 shows the Java code of our example along with specifications of preconditions and postcondition in separation logic with inductive definitions and numerical constraints. The `loadData` method loads a list from a file, sorts it, and returns the sorted list. Its postcondition ensures that the returned value is a sorted doubly-linked list. `loadData` ensures this condition by calling the `sort` procedure that accepts a doubly-linked list and returns a sorted list. The expectation is that `getFromFile` method will produce a doubly-linked list. However, `getFromFile` procedure in our

```
class Process {
  static Node loadData()
    requires emp
    ensures res::sdll⟨_,_,_⟩
  { Node l = getFromFile();
    Node sl = sort(l);
    return sl; }
  static Node sort(Node l)
    requires l::dll⟨_,n⟩
    ensures res::sdll⟨_,n,_⟩
  { if (l != null) {
      Node tmp = sort(l.next);
      tmp = insert(tmp, l);
      return tmp; }
    return l; }
  static Node insert(Node l, Node v)
    requires l::sdll⟨p,n,s⟩ ∗ v::Node⟨vv,_,_⟩
    ensures (res::sdll⟨_,n+1,min(s,vv)⟩ ∧ l!=null)
      or (res::sdll⟨_,1,rs⟩ ∧ rs=vv ∧ l=null)
  { ... } }
```

Fig. 2. Annotated code for loading a list from a file and sorting it

example is not statically verified and we cannot guarantee statically that it will indeed produce a doubly-linked list structure expected by `sort`. In such a situation SLICK performs a runtime check to ensure that the data structure invariant holds. Consequently, we can still assume when reasoning about the body of `sort` that the data structure given is a doubly-linked list; and when reasoning about the body of `loadData` that the result returned by `sort` is a sorted list. When reasoning about callers of `loadData`, we can also make use of its postcondition.

Outline. In the rest of this paper we define our specification language and the desired semantics of runtime checks, we then describe the compile-time and runtime techniques that SLICK uses to generate the checks, discuss the issues in combining static and runtime checking and present preliminary experience with the system.

3 Specification Language

We designed our specification language for preconditions and postconditions to enable simultaneously runtime checking and static analysis [22], so it largely follows the syntax and semantics of languages in previous separation logic system.

Specification language syntax. Figure 3 shows the grammar for our specification language. Shape predicate spred is the main specification construct that provides data structure descriptions. Formulas are canonicalized into an internal representation akin to the superhomogeneous form [29], namely arguments for heap formulas are distinct and fresh. Additional existentially quantified variables are introduced if necessary to obtain the above form. The semantics of our specification language is included in the accompanying technical report [23].

Recursive shape predicate definitions need to satisfy certain syntactic restrictions, namely *well-formed* and *well-founded* conditions, to ensure soundness and termination of static reasoning [22]. *Well-formed* conditions ensure that shape predicates and formulas do not admit garbage (consequently, code generated for runtime checks can traverse the entire footprint of the formula). *Well-founded* conditions disallow `root` to be passed as argument to a recursive predicate invocation. That means `root` either is `null`, dangles, or points to an object. Well-foundedness ensures that the generated runtime checking code terminates when executed on any given heap, since every invocation of the generated code either fails/succeeds or recolors at least one object.

$$
\begin{array}{rcl}
\mathsf{spred} & ::= & [\texttt{root::}]c\langle(v\,[\mu])^*\rangle \equiv \Phi\ [\mathbf{inv}\ \pi_0] \\
\mu & ::= & \mathbf{@in} \mid \mathbf{@out} \\
\Phi & ::= & \bigvee \exists v^* \cdot (\kappa \wedge \pi) \\
\pi & ::= & \gamma \wedge \phi \\
\gamma & ::= & v_1 = v_2 \mid v = \mathbf{null} \mid v_1 \neq v_2 \mid v \neq \mathbf{null} \mid \gamma_1 \wedge \gamma_2 \\
\kappa & ::= & \mathbf{emp} \mid v{::}c\langle v^*\rangle \mid \kappa_1 * \kappa_2 \\
\phi & ::= & \mathsf{arith} \mid \phi_1 \wedge \phi_2 \mid \phi_1 \vee \phi_2 \mid \neg\phi \mid \exists v \cdot \phi \mid \forall v \cdot \phi \\
\mathsf{arith} & ::= & \mathsf{a}_1 = \mathsf{a}_2 \mid \mathsf{a}_1 \neq \mathsf{a}_2 \mid \mathsf{a}_1 < \mathsf{a}_2 \mid \mathsf{a}_1 \leq \mathsf{a}_2 \\
\mathsf{a} & ::= & k \mid v \mid k \times \mathsf{a} \mid \mathsf{a}_1 + \mathsf{a}_2 \mid -\mathsf{a} \mid \mathbf{max}(\mathsf{a}_1, \mathsf{a}_2) \mid \mathbf{min}(\mathsf{a}_1, \mathsf{a}_2) \\
k & \in & \text{Integer constants} \\
v, c & \in & \text{Identifiers}
\end{array}
$$

Fig. 3. Grammar for Shape Predicates

Predicate parameter modes. To make the execution of predicates at runtime more efficient, we assign *modes* to predicate parameters, following the approaches in logic programming [29, 24]. We currently support two modes: **in** and **out**. These modes can be inferred using a constraint-based analysis. In the current paper, we assume that the developer specifies mode annotations (implicitly or explicitly). For example, the parameters of the `dll` predicate can be annotated as `dll`⟨`p`**@out**, `n`**@out**⟩. Both parameters `p` and `n` have **out** mode.

We use several conventions for default modes, which allows developers to omit most mode declarations in practice. Most of the parameters are **out**, so we make **out** the default mode. Next, a data structure is typically given as the set of objects obtained by traversing the data structure starting from the `root` node and terminating at either `null` or at some of the **in** parameters. `root` is therefore always an **in** parameter; the **out** parameters are values computed by traversing the data structures. SLICK considers method parameters as **in** parameters for their preconditions and postconditions. **out** parameters from preconditions are **in** parameters for corresponding postconditions.

4 Semantics of Run-Time Checking

In this section we present the semantics for run-time checking separation logic specifications and outline challenges in implementing this semantics. We then describe how we approach these challenges in our runtime checker.

4.1 Abstract Description of Run-Time Checks

The intended meaning of runtime checking is as follows. Given a stack s, an initial partial map L from logical variable names to values, and a heap h, we define the set of pairs (h_0, L_0) where h_0 is subheap of h and L_0 is partial map extending L such that formula Φ is true for h_0, L_0:

$$\mathsf{submodelsFor}(s, h, L, \Phi) = \{(h_0, L_0) \mid (s \cup L_0), h_0 \models \Phi \ \wedge\ L \subseteq L_0 \wedge\ h_0 \subseteq h\}$$

A procedure with precondition Φ should succeed when $\Phi * \texttt{true}$ holds in the caller, which happens when $\mathsf{submodelsFor}(s, h, \emptyset, \Phi)$ is nonempty. Let h denote the current heap. Consider a procedure call of procedure f with precondition pre_f, body $body_f$, and postcondition $post_f$. Taking into account the usual semantics of logic variables that can relate pre- and postcondition, the execution of a procedure call with runtime checks is the following. Note that $body_f$ may update the current heap h.

```
let M = submodelsFor(s, h, ∅, pre_f);        // subheaps satisfying precondition
if M = ∅ then error "Precondition failed";
let (h_0, L) ∈ M;                            // pick subheap and logic var. bindings
let h_1 = h \ h_0;                           // save context
h := h_0;                                    // narrow heap to footprint
body_f;                                      // actual body of the method
let M' = submodelsFor(s, h, L, post_f);      // check post in current h,L
if M' = ∅ then error "Postcondition failed";
let (h_R, _) ∈ M';                           // pick subheap to return
h := h_R ∪ h_1;                              // restore context
```

4.2 Separation Logic Runtime Checking Challenges

Given the semantics of separation logic formulas and the semantics of checks in Section 4.1, there are two main challenges in making runtime checking feasible. We next discuss the challenges specific to separation logic execution.

Evaluating spatial conjunction inside formulas. Consider first the problem of checking whether a given state satisfies a formula without numerical constraints. This model checking problem has been studied for first-order logic (with or without inductive definitions) [15] and, more recently, for separation logic [6]. Separation connective increases the complexity of the model checking problem because it essentially involves second-order quantification [18]. In general it is not clear how to split a heap into two parts each of which satisfies the corresponding conjunct, so each separation logic formula could in principle admit an exponential number of sets of locations that denote its footprint.

Approach: marking the footprint. Our approach stems from the observation that, in practice, data structure specifications often contain formulas that have a small number of possible footprints that can be computed while evaluating the formula. Moreover, separation logic connective does not appear under a negation in our system. Therefore, instead of maintaining an explicit container containing objects in the footprint, we mark objects that participate in the footprint of the formula. An attempt to mark an object twice makes the entire formula disjunct unsatisfiable.

Representing method footprints. A naïve implementation of the semantics in Section 4.1 would associate with each method invocation a set of references that covers the method's footprint. For a call stack of depth n, it would need n copies of these footprints to maintain the information about all contexts h_1 for procedures on the call stack. In the worst case this would cause an n-fold increase in memory consumption. Next, we need a mechanism to adjust the heap h for each procedure call and check each individual field read or write, to ensure that they perform operations only on the current footprint.

Approach: maintaining marking across procedure calls. When a precondition succeeds, our system retains the marking of nodes, which is unique for a procedure invocation. Reads, writes and procedure calls check the marking and adjust it accordingly. Postcondition check restores the marking.

5 The Runtime Engine

We now present in more detail the runtime mechanisms of our checker. SLICK augments each object with a field named `color`, which indicates the object's availability to different method invocations. The color of an object may change during program execution. Each method invocation is also associated with a unique color, maintained on a global stack. A method invocation can access an object if and only if their colors match. Newly allocated objects belong to the current method invocation's footprint; the objects receive the color of the current invocation via instrumented object constructors. An invocation of method m is permitted if the footprint F of m's precondition is a subset of the caller's footprint at the call site. In that case, the system colors the footprint F to match the color of the invocation of m. A return from invocation of m is permitted if the footprint F' of the postcondition of m is a subset of the current execution footprint at the end of m. The system then recolors the postcondition footprint F' to the color of the caller.

Checking formulas. Runtime checking of formulas consists in verifying the formula footprint and computing **out** parameters. SLICK translates each formula to executable code in the form of a class with a method `traverse` that, when executed, traverses the footprint of the formula in the current heap. `traverse` accepts two input parameters, `curColor` and `newColor` and returns **boolean**. `traverse` recolors each object it visits to `newColor` if the current color of the object is `curColor`. If `traverse` succeeds in recoloring all visited objects and all pure constraints are also satisfied, it sets **out** parameters and returns **true**. Otherwise it fails.

Checking formulas with disjunction. The recursive definition of predicates such as `dll` and `sdll` contain the disjunction operator to differentiate the base case and the recursive case of the definition. When evaluating the truth of a pure classical logic formula $F_1 \vee F_2$ in a given heap, it is possible to simply evaluate F_1 first, and, if it fails, proceed with the evaluation of F_2. In the case of our separation logic formulas, however, evaluation changes the coloring of the heap. Therefore, if the evaluation of F_1 fails, SLICK must undo the coloring performed by F_1. Based on the recursive predicates we have examined, we expect the failure of false disjuncts to occur quickly. SLICK therefore undoes the coloring by re-executing the evaluation of F_1 with opposite color parameters. This approach avoids additional bookkeeping that would be required to maintain the set of marked objects. In our example of `dll` and `sdll`, the footprint of the first disjunct is empty, which means that its execution performs no marking and there is nothing to undo.

Computing bindings for existential quantifiers. Existentially quantified variables in program specifications are often either determined by variables in program state, or they do not affect the truth value of the formula at all. Consider, for example, the precondition of `sort`, given by the formula `l::dll⟨p,n⟩`. The root parameter of `dll` predicate is bound to the value of the local variable `l`. The `n` parameter, on the other hand, is existentially quantified, but is given as the length of the list. The `p` parameter of `dll` is given as the `prev` field of the first node whenever the list is non-empty. When the list is empty, the `p` parameter is left unconstrained, but the truth value of `dll` does not depend on it either. Therefore, the value of `p` is either given by the context where `dll` is called, as in the recursive invocation inside `dll` definition, or it is not used anywhere, as in the precondition of `sort`. SLICK uses mode analysis, described in Section 6, to determine how to compute values of such existentially quantified variables.

Precondition. SLICK invokes precondition checking code in the caller prior to method invocation. If a precondition check succeeds, it also provides values for the **out** parameters of the formula. These values can then be used by the postcondition of the same invocation. Note that pre- and postcondition checks are performed in the caller to facilitate integration with the static verifier. More details are provided in section 7.

As an illustration, consider the `sort` method from Figure 2. Figure 4 shows the runtime checking code that SLICK generates for `sort`. SLICK compiles the precondition to a class with fields to store all free logic variables of the formula (in this case, variables `l` and `n`). In callers of `sort`, SLICK also generates instructions to create an instance of the generated class (the checker object), initialize the **in** parameter (`l`) and then invoke `traverse` on the initialized checker object. `traverse` receives two colors as arguments: the current method invocation's color is passed to `curColor`, a freshly generated color to `newColor`. Upon successful completion of `traverse`, SLICK sets `n` to the length of the list. SLICK stores a reference to the checker object in a local variable that is visible to the code that verifies the postcondition.

```
class sort_pre { Node l; int n;
      boolean traverse(color curColor,
            color newColor) { ... }
}
Node loadData() {
      Node l = getFromFile();
/// generated code
      sort_pre prchk = new sort_pre();
      prchk.l = l;
      SLICK.pushCurrentColor();
      SLICK.setCurrentColor(
            SLICK.freshColor());
      prchk.traverse(SLICK.topColor(),
            SLICK.currentColor());
/// end of generated code
      Node sl = sort(l);
      ...
```

Fig. 4. Compiled precondition of `sort`

```
class sort_post {
      Node res;
      int n;
      boolean traverse(...)
}
Node loadData() {
      ...
      Node sl = sort(l);
/// generated code
      sort_post pockr = new sort_post();
      pockr.res = sl;
      pockr.n = prchk.n;
      color c = SLICK.popColor();
      pockr.traverse(SLICK.currentColor(), c);
      SLICK.setCurrentColor(c);
/// end of generated code
      return sl; }
```

Fig. 5. Compiled postcondition of `sort`

Postcondition. When a method returns, SLICK checks postcondition against the current method's footprint. SLICK then makes the objects covered by the postcondition accessible to the caller. As an example, Figure 5 shows the translation of the postcondition of `sort`, whose internal representation is $\exists \mathtt{r}_1 \cdot \mathtt{res}{::}\mathtt{sdll}\langle \mathtt{r}_1 \rangle \wedge \mathtt{r}_1 = \mathtt{n}$.

Note that it is possible that the postcondition does not cover all objects of the current invocation's footprint. The uncovered objects, even if reachable from the caller, are not accessible under separation logic semantics. The use of coloring in SLICK correctly enforces this semantics. Indeed, observe that any objects in the footprint of the returning method, if not covered by the postcondition thereof, will retain the color of the returning method invocation. This color is unique for the dynamic method invocation, so no current or future method invocations will be able to access these objects.

Unannotated code. When a method has no annotations, as is the case of `getFromFile` in Figure 2, both precondition and postcondition are **true**. This means that the footprint of the precondition is the same as the caller's current footprint and that the entire footprint of the callee is returned to the caller. SLICK thus executes the callee without any recoloring of the heap and with the callee invocation having the same color as the caller invocation.

6 From Separation Logic to Executable Code

We now present our translation from separation logic formula to executable code. The basic idea is to compile a separation logic formula into a function that checks if a given program state (s, h) is a model of the formula. The translation consists of mode analysis and Java code generation. In addition to checking that the formula holds in the current program state, the translated code recolors the formula's footprint and computes the values of **out** parameters. Each formula is translated to a class with a method `traverse` and fields representing the free variables of the formula. The fields have the same names as the free variables they represent. Fields for **in** parameters need to be initialized before each invocation of `traverse`; fields for **out** parameters are set by `traverse` upon successful completion of checking.

Mode analysis. At compile time, variables in a formula are classified into two main groups: bound and unbound. Initially, unbound variables include **out** parameters and existentially quantified variables of the present formula. Bound variables include **in** parameters of the present formula and **out** arguments of recursive predicate invocations. If an **out** argument is not unified with a value in all disjuncts of a predicate definition, we further classify it as *conditionally bound*.

Conditionally bound variables use a boxed representation of their underlying types. Each boxed value has a flag indicating whether the underlying value is bound. The first time when the compiled formula uses a conditionally bound variable v at runtime, it binds v to a concrete value. When v is used in an equality $v = t$ and the value of term t is known, v is bound to t; otherwise both v and t are bound to the same value by instantiating unbound variables in t. If used in a disequality or inequality, v is bound to a random value such that the constraint holds. This treatment is incomplete, but sound.

The translation consists of two passes. The first pass determines subformulas that generate bindings for the unbound variables. The second one compiles the selected subformulas to assignments and the rest of the formulas to tests. To make it easier to read the formalization, the following names have dedicated meanings in our rules. $vmap$ is the binding map of unbound variables. $vmap$ also keeps track of which variables and terms are conditionally bound to help the code generator to invoke correct operations on these values. ins and $outs$ are **in** and **out** parameter sets, respectively. *INS*(c) returns all the **in** parameters of predicate c. $uvars$ is the set of unbound variables. Function *UVAR* returns the set of unbound variables of a term. Note that ins and $outs$ are the same for all disjuncts of a formula, whereas $vmap$ and $uvars$ are computed anew for each disjunct. $||\ C\ ||$ marks C as executable code emitted by the compilation.

The first pass computes a mapping from unbound variables to terms, where a term can be either constant, variable, field access, or combination of terms using arithmetic operations. This pass also produces a partial ordering, which determines the order in which assignments are generated by means of a topological sort. There are three sources of bindings for unbound variables, namely i) **in** parameters of the present formula, ii) **out** parameters of predicate invocations, and iii) object fields. The computation is formalized as the genMap function in the technical report [23]. As genMap generates the bindings, it also removes from the input formula all unifications $v = t$ that it uses in bindings generation.

Translation of disjunction. SLICK compiles a DNF formula $\bigvee F_i$ as follows:

```
boolean traverse(color curColor, color newColor) {
    ...
    boolean r_i = disji(curColor, newColor);
    if (r_i) return true;
    disji(newColor, curColor);
    ...
    return false; }
```

Translation of conjunction. SLICK compiles a formula $F_i = \exists v^* \cdot \kappa \wedge \pi$ into a function **boolean** disji(color curColor, color newColor). Figure 6 formalizes the compilation of the body of disji as a function that takes a formula and emits executable code.

$TR[[p{::}c\langle v^*\rangle]] \mid IsObj(c) \stackrel{\text{def}}{=}$
  $||$ **if** $p \neq$ `null` $\wedge\ curColor = p.color$
  then $p.color = newColor$
  else return false; $||$

$TR[[p{::}c\langle v^*\rangle]] \mid IsPred(c) \stackrel{\text{def}}{=}$
  $||\ p =$ **new** $c\_Checker$; $||$
  genInitialization $p{::}c\langle v_i^*\rangle$;
  $||$ **if not**$(p.traverse(curColor, newColor))$
  then return false; $||$

$TR[[\kappa_1 * \kappa_2]] \stackrel{\text{def}}{=} TR[[\kappa_1]]; TR[[\kappa_2]]$

$TR[[\exists v^* \cdot \kappa \wedge \pi]] \stackrel{\text{def}}{=}$
  let $uvars = v^* \cup outs$ **in**
  let $\pi' =$ genMap $(\kappa \wedge \pi)$ **in**
   $TR[[\kappa]]$;
   $||$ **if** $||\ TR[[\pi']]\ ||$ **then** $||$
    genAssign;
    $||$ **return true**; $||$
   $||$ **else return false**; $||$

$TR[[p = t]] \mid p$ is conditionally bound, t is bound $\stackrel{\text{def}}{=}\ ||\ p.EQ(t)\ ||$

Fig. 6. Translation Rules

The translation also makes use of the following functions. The genInitialization function emits assignments to initialize **in** parameters of the formula, subject to the constraint that all **in** parameters must be initialized.

$$\begin{array}{l}\mathsf{genInitialization}\ p{::}c\langle v_i^*\rangle \stackrel{\text{def}}{=} \\ \quad \textbf{foreach}\ f_i\ \textbf{in}\ \mathit{INS}(c)\ \textbf{do}:\ \ \|\, p.f_i = \|\ \mathsf{genBinding}\ v_i\end{array}$$

The genAssign function emits assignments to **out** parameters of the predicate. If a variable does not have a binding from the formula, it is assigned an unbound boxed value. The genBinding function computes the closure of the bindings to get bound terms.

$$\begin{array}{l}\mathsf{genAssign} \stackrel{\text{def}}{=} \\ \quad \textbf{foreach}\ p\ \textbf{in}\ outs\ \textbf{do}: \\ \quad\quad \|\, p = \|\ \mathsf{genBinding}\ p \\ \quad\quad \textbf{if}\ \mathsf{genBinding}\ failed\ \textbf{then} \\ \quad\quad\quad \|\, p = \textbf{new}\ \texttt{(boxed(p))}\ \|\end{array}
\qquad
\begin{array}{l}\mathsf{genBinding}\ v \stackrel{\text{def}}{=} \\ \quad \textbf{if}\ v \notin uvars\ \textbf{then}\ \ \|\, v\, \| \\ \quad \textbf{else}\ \mathsf{genBinding}\ (\mathsf{lookUp}\ v\ vmap)\end{array}$$

If the first argument is a term, genBindings performs the obvious recursion on the structure of the term and emits a term with identical structure, except for the translated variables. If lookUp fails to find an entry for an unbound variable, genBinding fails.

7 Integrating Static and Runtime Verification

In this section we discuss the integration of static and runtime verification. The general idea is that assertions that can be statically verified need not be checked at runtime. However, such combination is more difficult for analysis domains based on spatial conjunction of facts than for analysis domains based on classical conjunction of facts. Indeed, to ensure that assertion $F_1 \wedge F_2$ holds after a given program point, it is possible to ensure F_1 statically and then check F_2 dynamically. On the other hand, given assertion $F_1 * F_2$, it is necessary to communicate to both the run-time and the static time checker the footprints of individual formulas in order to enable separation of these two checks. In the rest of the paper, we describe optimizations that are nevertheless possible in our runtime checking approach; more fine-grained combinations are possible but beyond the scope of the current paper.

Field access. If the static verifier proves a field access safe, no runtime check is required. This is because field access does not affect the coloring of the objects or method invocations. On the other hand, if the static verifier fails to verify a field read, it emits runtime check for the pointer and continues with a suitably modified symbolic state.

$$\frac{\Delta \nvdash x{::}c\langle f^*\rangle}{\vdash \{\Delta\} v = x.f \{\exists v \cdot \Delta\}}$$

If it fails to verify a field write, it stops static verification and emits runtime check for all subsequent code. As an optimization, once a field access has been issued a runtime check, it needs not be checked again until the pointer itself or its color may have changed. In many cases this information can be obtained statically.

Method contract. Method contract checks, on the contrary, cannot be as readily eliminated since they change the heap coloring. Let us consider a method g that calls another method f with precondition pre_f and postcondition $post_f$:

```
void g()
  { g1; f(); g2; }
```

```
void f()
  requires pre_f ensures post_f { ... }
```

There are the following possibilities:

1. f is statically verified.
   - pre_f is statically proved: if the part g_2 of g following the call to f is statically verified by assuming $post_f$, g need not emit runtime checks for pre_f and $post_f$. Otherwise, as g_2 may attempt to access objects that do not belong to $post_f$'s footprint, runtime checks for pre_f and $post_f$ (and certainly for g_2) are needed.
   - pre_f is not statically proved: g issues runtime checks for pre_f and $post_f$. Static verification of g_2 can assume $post_f$.
2. f is not statically verified: g issues runtime checks for pre_f and $post_f$. Static verification of g_2 can assume $post_f$.

The static verifier can take advantage of the fact that after a method call, the callee's postcondition holds. Even if it cannot verify the callee's precondition, it can still assume the postcondition, and continues static verification after issuing appropriate runtime checks. When the precondition is a pure formula, static verification proceeds as follows:

$$\frac{\Delta \nvdash pre(mn) \qquad IsPure(pre(mn))}{\vdash \{\Delta\} mn(v^*) \{(\Delta \wedge pre(mn)) * post(mn)\}}$$

On the other hand, if the precondition has a nonempty heap component, the static verifier assumes the postcondition as the current program state. Note that we cannot simply $*$-conjoin the postcondition with the current program state, as they may cover overlapping footprints. Replacing the entire program state by the postcondition is sound, but may result in loss of precision if the callee's postcondition covers only parts of data structures.

$$\frac{\Delta \nvdash pre(mn) \qquad HasHeap(pre(mn))}{\vdash \{\Delta\} mn(v^*) \{post(mn)\}}$$

Integration in the example. In the example of section 2, `sort` and `insert` are both statically verifiable. `loadData` fails to verify the precondition of `sort` because the information is simply not available, so it emits runtime check, but by assuming postcondition of `sort`, the postcondition of `loadData` can be statically verified, a fact that callers of `loadData` can exploit. Note that the runtime checking is localized within `loadData` only, so the overhead is small.

8 Implementation

We implemented SLICK in the context of a system for checking data structure properties [22]. We report our experience with the system on several examples.

Memory overhead. Memory overhead consists of one field per object to store the object's color and a single stack of live colors which has the same height as the program call stack. Since the `color` type can be implemented as **long**, memory overhead decreases if the program uses larger objects. `traverse` method also creates a number of intermediate objects, but they exist only during the formula traversal and do not permanently accumulate in the memory overhead of the code instrumented with runtime check. Consequently, we were not able to measure any significant difference in memory consumption for our examples.

Runtime overhead. We evaluate the runtime overhead of our approach by running experiments with different levels of runtime checking: 1) no runtime checking, 2) all operations runtime checked, 3) all field accesses runtime checked, 4) and checking at boundaries of data structure operations. In case 3), the entire program runs with a single color, hence no precondition or postcondition check is performed. This case measures the overhead of checking field accesses. In case 4), SLICK checks only the first precondition and the last postcondition of a data structure operation at runtime since the static verifier can assert that checks for recursive calls and field accesses are statically safe. This case simulates a scenario where these data structures are used in conjunction with unverified or untrusted inputs. In order to minimize the timing effects of class loading and JIT compilation, we repeat the experiments and ignore the timings of the first two runs.

Timings for the experiments, measured with JVM 1.5 on Linux 2.6 running on a PC having a 3GHz CPU and 2GB RAM, are reported in Figure 7. The data structures used in our experiments have sizes ranging from 1000 to 5000 elements. The first experiment sorts a list using insertion sort. The "Full" check for `sort` causes very large increases in running time. However, the "Boundary" version, which we expect to be used in practice, causes insignificant increases since the data structure is traversed only two more times. The second example performs an in-order traversal of a binary search tree to produce a sorted list. The "Full" check incurs large overhead since it forces the entire subtree to be traversed at each recursive invocation. The other two checks are significantly cheaper. The third example performs the following two operations 1000 times: inserting a random element to and deleting the maximum element from a priority queue. The "Native" and "Field" timings reflect the logarithmic complexity of operations on priority queues. The "Full" and "Boundary" timings are linear in data structure size as expected, since every `insert` and `deletemax` operation traverses the entire heap, rather than just a path with logarithmic length from root to leaf. The fourth example is a popular operation in data mining algorithms. It traverses a table containing the iterative patterns used in software specification mining and calculates the support of a mined pattern [?]. The operation is repeated 10 times. Note that the computation of support itself does not need to traverse the entire table, since the table provides caching of most of the subcomputations. Precondition and postcondition checking therefore causes a significantly larger number of objects to be visited, causing the large increase in running time. A common property across all the examples is that "Field" check timings show that the overhead of checking every heap access in SLICK is small.

	Insertion Sort				Binary Search Tree			
Size	Native	Full	Field	Boundary	Native	Full	Field	Boundary
1,000	6	49,235	10	7	0.03	181	0.06	0.93
2,000	28	>50,000	44	31	0.07	866	0.12	4.50
3,000	69	>50,000	108	81	0.11	2,253	0.18	10.45
4,000	127	>50,000	183	135	0.14	4,965	0.24	8.62
5,000	209	>50,000	296	211	0.18	9,360	0.30	9.07

	Priority Queue				Support Calculation			
Size	Native	Full	Field	Boundary	Native	Full	Field	Boundary
1,000	0.93	2,585	1.62	765	0.22	12,205	0.30	25
2,000	0.99	5,171	2.68	1,521	0.45	>50,000	0.63	61
3,000	1.02	7,767	1.79	2,321	0.68	>50,000	0.94	111
4,000	1.01	10,320	2.69	3,032	0.93	>50,000	1.40	169
5,000	1.03	13,070	1.89	3,827	1.18	>50,000	1.73	173

Fig. 7. Performance Measurements (in milliseconds)

9 Conclusion

We presented SLICK, the first runtime checker for separation logic program specifications. We have identified several challenges that make separation logic specification seemingly more difficult to check at run time than for classical logic. The notable features of SLICK include runtime mechanism that avoids memory blow up and a compilation of separation logic specification to executable code that runs natively on the JVM. Overall, the run-time checking cost can be significant for large data structure instances when all intermediate states are checked, but even in those cases the absolute performance is sufficiently good for debugging the code and the specifications. Performing only "boundary checks" is an appealing alternative to all intermediate checks: because specifications capture operation footprint, boundary checks ensure data structure consistency at the end of an operation regardless of the internal behavior of the operation. In some cases (such as the insertion sort example), the overhead when performing only boundary checks appears acceptable even for deployed applications. Preliminary results demonstrate that running time can be significantly reduced using static verification to remove most of the runtime checks.

References

1. Barnett, M., Leino, K.R.M., Schulte, W.: The Spec# programming system: An overview. In: CASSIS 2004 (2004)
2. Berdine, J., et al.: Shape analysis for composite data structures. In: CAV 2007 (2007)
3. Berdine, J., Calcagno, C., O'Hearn, P.W.: Smallfoot: Modular automatic assertion checking with separation logic. In: FMCO, pp. 115–137 (2005)
4. Bodden, E., Hendren, L., Lhoták, O.: A staged static program analysis to improve the performance of runtime monitoring. In: Ernst, E. (ed.) ECOOP 2007. LNCS, vol. 4609, Springer, Heidelberg (2007)

5. Calcagno, C., et al.: Footprint analysis: A shape analysis that discovers preconditions. In: Riis Nielson, H., Filé, G. (eds.) SAS 2007. LNCS, vol. 4634, Springer, Heidelberg (2007)
6. Calcagno, C., Yang, H., O'Hearn, P.: Computability and complexity results for a spatial assertion language for data structures. In: FSTTCS 2001 (2001)
7. Cartwright, R., Fagan, M.: Soft typing. In: PLDI 1991, pp. 278–292 (1991)
8. Chen, F., Roşu, G.: MOP: An Efficient and Generic Runtime Verification Framework. In: OOPSLA 2007 (2007)
9. Cheon, Y.: A Runtime Assertion Checker for the Java Modeling Language. PhD thesis, Iowa State University (April 2003)
10. Clarke, L.A., Rosenblum, D.S.: A historical perspective on runtime assertion checking in software development. SIGSOFT Softw. Eng. Notes 31(3), 25–37 (2006)
11. Demsky, B., et al.: Efficient specification-assisted error localization. In: Second International Workshop on Dynamic Analysis (2004)
12. Findler, R.B., Felleisen, M.: Contracts for higher-order functions. In: ICFP (2002)
13. Guo, B., Vachharajani, N., August, D.I.: Shape analysis with inductive recursion synthesis. In: PLDI 2007 (2007)
14. Guttag, J., Horning, J.: Larch: Languages and Tools for Formal Specification. Springer, Heidelberg (1993)
15. Immerman, N.: Descriptive Complexity. Springer, Heidelberg (1998)
16. Ishtiaq, S., O'Hearn, P.W.: BI as an assertion language for mutable data structures. In: Proc. 28th ACM POPL 2001 (2001)
17. Kuncak, V.: Modular Data Structure Verification. PhD thesis, EECS Department, Massachusetts Institute of Technology (February 2007)
18. Kuncak, V., Rinard, M.: On spatial conjunction as second-order logic. Technical Report 970, MIT CSAIL (October 2004)
19. Lev-Ami, T.: TVLA: A framework for Kleene based logic static analyses. Master's thesis, Tel-Aviv University, Israel (2000)
20. Lev-Ami, T., et al.: Putting static analysis to work for verification: A case study. In: Int. Symp. Software Testing and Analysis (2000)
21. Lo, D., Khoo, S.-C., Liu, C.: Efficient mining of iterative patterns for software specification discovery. In: SIGKDD 2007 (2007)
22. Nguyen, H.H., et al.: Automated verification of shape and size properties via separation logic. In: VMCAI 2007 (2007)
23. Nguyen, H.H., Kuncak, V., Chin, W.-N.: Runtime Checking for Separation Logic. EPFL Technical Report LARA-REPORT-2007-003 (2007)
24. Overton, D., Somogyi, Z., Stuckey, P.J.: Constraint-based mode analysis of mercury. In: PPDP, pp. 109–120. ACM Press, New York (2002)
25. Perry, F., Jia, L., Walker, D.: Expressing heap-shape contracts in linear logic. In: GPCE, pp. 101–110. ACM Press, New York (2006)
26. Reineke, J.: Shape analysis of sets. Master's thesis, Universität des Saarlandes, Germany (June 2005)
27. Reynolds, J.C.: Separation logic: A logic for shared mutable data structures. In: 17th LICS, pp. 55–74 (2002)
28. Shankar, A., Bodik, R.: Ditto: Automatic incrementalization of data structure invariant checks. In: PLDI 2007 (2007)
29. Somogyi, Z.: A system of precise modes for logic programs. In: ICLP 1987 (1987)
30. Wies, T., et al.: Field constraint analysis. In: VMCAI 2006 (2006)
31. Zee, K., et al.: Runtime checking for program verification systems. In: RV (collocated with AOSD) (2007)

Decision Procedures for Multisets with Cardinality Constraints

Ruzica Piskac and Viktor Kuncak

School of Computer and Communication Science
École Polytechnique Fédérale de Lausanne (EPFL), Switzerland

Abstract. Applications in software verification and interactive theorem proving often involve reasoning about sets of objects. Cardinality constraints on such collections also arise in these scenarios. Multisets arise for analogous reasons as sets: abstracting the content of linked data structure with duplicate elements leads to multisets. Interactive theorem provers such as Isabelle specify theories of multisets and prove a number of theorems about them to enable their use in interactive verification. However, the decidability and complexity of constraints on multisets is much less understood than for constraints on sets.

The first contribution of this paper is a polynomial-space algorithm for deciding expressive quantifier-free constraints on multisets with cardinality operators. Our decision procedure reduces in polynomial time constraints on multisets to constraints in an extension of quantifier-free Presburger arithmetic with certain "unbounded sum" expressions. We prove bounds on solutions of resulting constraints and describe a polynomial-space decision procedure for these constraints.

The second contribution of this paper is a proof that adding quantifiers to a constraint language containing subset and cardinality operators yields undecidable constraints. The result follows by reduction from Hilbert's 10th problem.

1 Introduction

Collections of objects are fundamental and ubiquitous concepts in computer science and mathematics. It is therefore not surprising that they often arise in software analysis and verification [1], as well as in interactive theorem proving [19]. Moreover, such constraints often involve cardinality bounds on collections. Recent work describes decision procedures for constraints that involve sets and their cardinalities [10,12], characterizing the complexity of both quantified and quantifier-free constraints.

In many applications it is more appropriate to use multisets (bags) rather than sets as a way of representing collections of objects. It is therefore interesting to consider constraints on multisets along with cardinality bounds. There is a range of useful operations and relations on multisets, beyond the traditional disjoint union and difference. These operations are all definable using quantifier-free Presburger arithmetic (QFPA) formulas on the number of occurrences of

F. Logozzo et al. (Eds.): VMCAI 2008, LNCS 4905, pp. 218–232, 2008.

each element in the multiset. This paper describes such a language that admits reasoning about integers, sets and multisets, supports standard set and multiset operations as well as any QFPA-definable operation on multisets (including the conversion of a multiset into a set), and supports a cardinality operator that counts the total number of elements. We present a decision procedure for this language, provide a PSPACE upper bound on the decision problem, and show that its extension with quantifiers is undecidable.

Our language can express sets as a special kind of multisets, so our new decision procedure is also a decision procedure for constraints in [12]. However, multisets introduce considerable additional difficulty compared to the original problem. For example, while the number of non-equivalent set terms is finite (they are unions of Venn regions), the number of non-equivalent multiset terms is infinite due to non-idempotent operators such as multiset sum $\uplus$. Instead of considering Venn regions, our new algorithm reduces multiset constraints to an extension of Presburger arithmetic with a particular sum expression. To decide this extension, we rely on the fact that solutions of formulas of Presburger arithmetic are semilinear sets [8] and use bounds on generators of such sets [23] to establish small model property for this extension.

Previously, Zarba [25] considered decision procedures for quantifier-free multisets but without the cardinality operator, showing that it reduces to quantifier-free pointwise reasoning. However, the cardinality operator makes that reduction impossible. More recently Lugiez [13] showed (in the context of a more general result on multitree automata) the decidability of quantified constraints with a weaker form of cardinality operator that counts only distinct elements in a multiset, and shows decidability of certain quantifier-free expressible constraints with cardinality operator. Regarding quantified constraints with the general cardinality operator, [13, Section 3.4] states "the status of the complete logic is still an open problem". We resolve this question, showing that the quantified constraints with cardinality are undecidable (Section 6). The decidable quantified constraints in [13] allow quantifiers that can be eliminated to obtain quantifier-free constraints, which can then be expressed using the decidable constraints in the present paper. We analyze the complexity of the decision problem for our quantifier-free constraints, and show that it belongs to PSPACE, which is the first complexity bound for constraints on multisets with a cardinality operator.

Contributions. We summarize our contributions as follows.

1. We show how to decide expressive quantifier-free constraints on multisets and cardinality operators in polynomial space, and
2. We show that adding quantifiers to a constraint language containing subset and cardinality operators yields undecidable constraints.

Overview. We continue by presenting examples that motivate the constraints we consider in this paper. We then outline our decision procedure through an example. The main part of the paper describes the decision procedure and its correctness. We then show that an extension of our constraints with quantifiers is undecidable.

1.1 Multisets in Interactive Verification

As an example of using multisets with cardinalities in interactive verification, consider the Multiset library [20] of the interactive theorem prover Isabelle [19]. This library represents a multiset as a function f from some (parameter) type to the set of natural numbers, such that the set S of elements x with $f(x) > 0$ is finite. It defines the `size` function on multisets as the sum of $f(x)$ over all $x \in S$. Several lemmas proved in the library itself mention both multisets and the `size` function, such as the `size_union` lemma ($\texttt{size}(M + N) = \texttt{size}\ M + \texttt{size}\ N$), where `+` on the left-hand side is resolved as the disjoint multiset union. Other Isabelle theories build on the Multiset library, including the Permutation library for reasoning about permutations, formalization [22] of the UNITY parallel programming approach [17], and example specifications of sorting algorithms.

This paper considers such a theory of multisets with size constraints. For simplicity, we fix the set E from which multiset elements are drawn. We assume E to be finite, but of unknown cardinality. If m is a multiset, we call $\texttt{size}(m)$ the cardinality of m, and denote it $|m|$ in this paper. As an example, the `size_union` lemma in our notation becomes $|M \uplus N| = |M| + |N|$.

1.2 Multisets in Software Analysis and Verification

It is often desirable to abstract the content of mutable and immutable data structures into collections to raise the level of abstraction when reasoning about programs. Abstracting linked structures as sets and relations enables high-level reasoning in verification systems such as Jahob [9]. For collections that may contain duplicates, abstraction using multisets is more precise than abstraction using sets. The decision procedure described in this paper would therefore enable reasoning about such precise abstractions, analogously to the way current decision procedures enable reasoning with set abstraction.

To illustrate the role of the cardinality operator, note that data structure implementations often contains integer size fields. If s is a data structure size field and L an abstract multiset field denoting data structure content, data structure operations need to preserve the invariant $s = |L|$. When verifying an insertion of an element x into a container, we therefore obtain verification conditions such as $|L|{=}s \rightarrow |L \uplus x|{=}s{+}1$. When verifying deletion of an element from a container we obtain verification conditions such as

$$x \subseteq L \wedge |x| = 1 \rightarrow |L \backslash x| = |L| - 1 \qquad (1)$$

The decision procedure described in this paper can prove such verification conditions.

To describe data structure operations it is useful to have not only operations such as disjoint union $\uplus$ and set difference, but also an operation that, given multisets m_1 and m_2 produces a multiset m_0 which is the result of removing from m_1 *all* occurrences of elements that occur in m_2. Let $m_i(e)$ denote the number of occurrences of an element e in multiset m_i. Then we can specify such a removal operation with $\forall e.(m_2(e) = 0 \implies m_0(e) = m_1(e)) \wedge (m_2(e) > 0 \rightarrow m_0(e) = 0)$.

We introduce a shorthand $m_0 = m_1 \setminus\setminus m_2$ for this formula. Our constraints support any such operation definable pointwise by QFPA formula.

Multisets have already been used in the verification system for data structures with bag and size properties [18], which invokes Isabelle to prove the generated multiset constraints. Our paper describes a decision procedure for a language of multisets with cardinalities, which could be used both within program verification systems and within interactive theorem provers, obtaining completeness and improved efficiency for a well-defined class of formulas. In addition to reasoning about abstractions of data structures, our constraints can be used directly to specify properties in programming languages such as SETL [24], which has built in set data type, and in the Gamma parallel programming paradigm [2, Page 103] based on multiset transformations.

2 Decision Procedure Through an Example

We next outline our decision procedure by applying it informally to the constraint (1) from the previous section. This section demonstrates only the main idea of the algorithm; Sections 4 and 5 give the detailed description (the reader may wish to revisit this example after reading those details). To prove validity of (1), we show that its negation,

$$x \subseteq L \wedge |x| = 1 \wedge |L \setminus x| \neq |L| - 1, \tag{2}$$

is unsatisfiable. Our algorithm expresses a given formula through quantifier-free Presburger arithmetic (QFPA) extended with sum expressions $\sum t$ over other QFPA terms t. In such sum expressions, the number of occurrences of an element e in a multiset m is denoted by $m(e)$. Every sum ranges over all elements e of some fixed domain E of unknown size. For example, our algorithm converts $|x| = 1$ into $\sum x(e) = 1$.

We also allow conditional expressions ite in our formulas. If c is a QFPA formula and t_1 and t_2 two QFPA terms, then $\mathsf{ite}(c, t_1, t_2)$ has value t_1 when c holds, and t_2 otherwise. A multiset inclusion $x \subseteq L$ becomes $\forall e.\ x(e) \leq L(e)$ which in turn is transformed into the sum $\sum \mathsf{ite}(x(e) \leq L(e), 0, 1) = 0$. By introducing fresh variables x_1 for $L \setminus x$, we obtain formula $x_1 = L \setminus x$. The formula $x_1 = L \setminus x$ becomes the sum $\sum \mathsf{ite}(x_1(e) = \mathsf{ite}(L(e) \leq x(e), 0, L(e) - x(e)), 0, 1) = 0$. Formula (2) therefore becomes

$$\sum \mathsf{ite}(x(e) \leq L(e), 0, 1) = 0 \ \wedge \ \sum x(e) = 1 \ \wedge \ \sum x_1(e) \neq \sum L(e) - 1 \ \wedge$$
$$\sum \mathsf{ite}(x_1(e) = \mathsf{ite}(L(e) \leq x(e), 0, L(e) - x(e)), 0, 1) = 0 \tag{3}$$

Because every sum ranges over the same set of elements $e \in E$, we can combine all sums into one sum with vector summands. Introducing k_1 for $|x_1|$, and k_2 for $|L|$, we obtain the formula

$$k_1 \neq k_2 - 1 \ \wedge \ (k_1, k_2, 1, 0, 0) = \sum \Big(x_1(e), L(e), x(e),$$
$$\mathsf{ite}(x_1(e) = \mathsf{ite}(L(e) \leq x(e), 0, L(e) - x(e)), 0, 1), \mathsf{ite}(x(e) \leq L(e), 0, 1)\Big) \tag{4}$$

Because the set of index elements E is of arbitrary size and each summand satisfies the same QFPA formula, formula (4) is equisatisfiable with the following formula (5), which uses a different sum operator that computes the set of all sums of solution vectors of the given QFPA formula F:

$$k_1 \neq k_2 - 1 \ \wedge (k_1, k_2, 1, 0, 0) \in \sum_F (x_1, L, x, z_1, z_2), \tag{5}$$

Here F is $z_1 = \mathsf{ite}(x_1 = \mathsf{ite}(L \leq x, 0, L - x), 0, 1) \wedge z_2 = \mathsf{ite}(x \leq L, 0, 1)$. We next show that $(u_1, \ldots, u_n) \in \sum_F (x_1, \ldots, x_c)$ can be replaced with the equisatisfiable QFPA formula. This will reduce the entire problem to QFPA satisfiability.

We first characterize satisfying assignments for F using semilinear sets [8]. This construction is always possible, as described in Section 5. The satisfying assignments for our formula F are given by $\bigcup_{i=1}^{7} (A_i + B_i^*)$ where

$$\begin{aligned}
A_1 &= \{(0,0,0,0,0)\}, B_1 = \{(0,1,1,0,0)\} \\
A_2 &= \{(1,0,0,1,0)\}, B_2 = \{(0,1,1,0,0), (1,0,0,0,0)\} \\
A_3 &= \{(0,0,1,0,1)\}, B_3 = \{(0,1,1,0,0), (0,0,1,0,0)\} \\
A_4 &= \{(1,0,1,1,1)\}, B_4 = \{(0,1,1,0,0), (0,0,1,0,0)\} \\
A_5 &= \{(1,1,0,0,0)\}, B_5 = \{(1,1,0,0,0), (0,1,1,0,0)\} \\
A_6 &= \{(2,1,0,1,0)\}, B_6 = \{(1,1,0,0,0), (0,1,1,0,0), (1,0,0,0,0)\} \\
A_7 &= \{(0,0,1,1,0)\}, B_7 = \{(1,1,0,0,0), (0,1,0,0,0), (0,0,1,1,0)\}
\end{aligned}$$

Here $A + B^*$ denotes the set of sums with exactly one element from A and any number of elements from B.

The meaning of the sum expression then reduces to the condition $(k_1, k_2, 1, 0, 0) \in (\bigcup_{i=1}^{7} (A_i + B_i^*))^*$. In general, this condition is definable using a QFPA formula that uses the finite vectors from A_i and B_i. In our particular case, $(k_1, k_2, 1, 0, 0)$ can only be a linear combination of elements from $A_1 + B_1^*$ and $A_5 + B_5^*$. Such considerations ultimately result in formula $(k_1, k_2) = (\lambda, \lambda + 1)$, so the overall constraint becomes

$$k_1 \neq k_2 - 1 \ \wedge (k_1, k_2) = (\lambda, \lambda + 1) \tag{6}$$

Because (2) and (6) are equisatisfiable and (6) is unsatisfiable, we conclude that (1) is a valid formula.

3 Multiset Constraints

Figure 1 defines constraints whose satisfiability we study in this paper. Our constraints combine multiset expressions and two kinds of QFPA formulas: *outer linear arithmetic formulas*, denoting relationship between top-level integer values in the constraint, and *inner linear arithmetic formulas*, denoting constraints specific to a given index element $e \in E$. Note that the syntax is not minimal; we subsequently show how many of the constructs are reducible to others.

top-level formulas:
$F ::= A \mid F \wedge F \mid \neg F$
$A ::= M{=}M \mid M \subseteq M \mid \forall e.\mathsf{F}^{\mathsf{in}} \mid \mathsf{A}^{\mathsf{out}}$
outer linear arithmetic formulas:
$\mathsf{F}^{\mathsf{out}} ::= \mathsf{A}^{\mathsf{out}} \mid \mathsf{F}^{\mathsf{out}} \wedge \mathsf{F}^{\mathsf{out}} \mid \neg \mathsf{F}^{\mathsf{out}}$
$\mathsf{A}^{\mathsf{out}} ::= \mathsf{t}^{\mathsf{out}} \leq \mathsf{t}^{\mathsf{out}} \mid \mathsf{t}^{\mathsf{out}}{=}\mathsf{t}^{\mathsf{out}} \mid (\mathsf{t}^{\mathsf{out}}, \ldots, \mathsf{t}^{\mathsf{out}}){=}\sum_{\mathsf{F}^{\mathsf{in}}}(\mathsf{t}^{\mathsf{in}}, \ldots, \mathsf{t}^{\mathsf{in}})$
$\mathsf{t}^{\mathsf{out}} ::= k \mid |M| \mid C \mid \mathsf{t}^{\mathsf{out}} + \mathsf{t}^{\mathsf{out}} \mid C \cdot \mathsf{t}^{\mathsf{out}} \mid \mathsf{ite}(\mathsf{F}^{\mathsf{out}}, \mathsf{t}^{\mathsf{out}}, \mathsf{t}^{\mathsf{out}})$
inner linear arithmetic formulas:
$\mathsf{F}^{\mathsf{in}} ::= \mathsf{A}^{\mathsf{in}} \mid \mathsf{F}^{\mathsf{in}} \wedge \mathsf{F}^{\mathsf{in}} \mid \neg \mathsf{F}^{\mathsf{in}}$
$\mathsf{A}^{\mathsf{in}} ::= \mathsf{t}^{\mathsf{in}} \leq \mathsf{t}^{\mathsf{in}} \mid \mathsf{t}^{\mathsf{in}}{=}\mathsf{t}^{\mathsf{in}}$
$\mathsf{t}^{\mathsf{in}} ::= m(e) \mid C \mid \mathsf{t}^{\mathsf{in}} + \mathsf{t}^{\mathsf{in}} \mid C \cdot \mathsf{t}^{\mathsf{in}} \mid \mathsf{ite}(\mathsf{F}^{\mathsf{in}}, \mathsf{t}^{\mathsf{in}}, \mathsf{t}^{\mathsf{in}})$
multiset expressions:
$M ::= m \mid \emptyset \mid M \cap M \mid M \cup M \mid M \uplus M \mid M \setminus M \mid M \setminus\setminus M \mid \mathsf{setof}(M)$
terminals:
m - multiset variables; e - index variable (fixed)
k - integer variable; C - integer constant

Fig. 1. Quantifier-Free Multiset Constraints with Cardinality Operator

Formulas (F) are propositional combinations of atomic formulas (A). Atomic formulas can be multiset equality and subset, pointwise linear arithmetic constraint $\forall e.\mathsf{F}^{\mathsf{in}}$, or atomic outer linear arithmetic formulas ($\mathsf{A}^{\mathsf{out}}$). Outer linear arithmetic formulas are equalities and inequalities between outer linear arithmetic terms ($\mathsf{t}^{\mathsf{out}}$), as well as summation constraints of the form $(u_1, \ldots, u_n) = \sum_F (t_1, \ldots, t_n)$, which compute the sum of the vector expression $(t_1, \ldots, t_n)$ over all indices $e \in E$ that satisfy the formula F. Outer linear arithmetic terms ($\mathsf{t}^{\mathsf{out}}$) are built using standard linear arithmetic operations starting from: 1) integer variables (k), 2) cardinality expressions applied to multisets ($|M|$), and 3) integer constants (C). The $\mathsf{ite}(F, t_1, t_2)$ expression is the standard if-then-else construct, whose value is t_1 when F is true and t_2 otherwise. Inner linear arithmetic formulas are linear arithmetic formulas built starting from constants (C) and values $m(e)$ of multiset variables at the current index e.

Multiset constraints contain some common multiset operations such as disjoint union, intersection, and difference, as well as the setof operation that computes the largest set contained in a given multiset. Additionally, using the constraints $\forall e.\mathsf{F}^{\mathsf{in}}$ it is possible to specify any multiset operation defined pointwise using a QFPA formula. Note also that it is easy to reason about individual elements of sets at the top level by representing them as multisets s such that $|s| = 1$. If s is such a multiset representing an element and m is a multiset, we can count the number of occurrences of s in m with, for example, the expression $\sum \mathsf{ite}(s(e){=}0, 0, m(e))$.

4 Reducing Multiset Operations to Sums

We next show that all operations and relations on multisets as a whole can be eliminated from the language of Figure 1. To treat operations as relations,

INPUT: multiset formula in the syntax of Figure 1
OUTPUT: formula in sum-normal form (Definition 1)

1. Flatten expressions that we wish to eliminate:
   $C[e] \rightsquigarrow (x = e \wedge C[x])$
   where e is one of the expressions $\emptyset$, $m_1 \cup m_2$, $m_1 \cup m_2$, $m_1 \uplus m_2$, $m_1 \setminus m_2$, $\mathsf{setof}(m_1)$, $|m_1|$, and where the occurrence of e is not already in a top-level conjunct of the form $x = e$ or $e = x$ for some variable x.
2. Reduce multiset relations to pointwise linear arithmetic conditions:
   $$\begin{array}{ll} C[m_0 = \emptyset] & \rightsquigarrow C[\forall e.\, m_0(e) = 0] \\ C[m_0 = m_1 \cap m_2] & \rightsquigarrow C[\forall e.\, m_0(e) = \mathsf{ite}(m_1(e) \leq m_2(e), m_1(e), m_2(e))] \\ C[m_0 = m_1 \cup m_2] & \rightsquigarrow C[\forall e.\, m_0(e) = \mathsf{ite}(m_1(e) \leq m_2(e), m_2(e), m_1(e))] \\ C[m_0 = m_1 \uplus m_2] & \rightsquigarrow C[\forall e.\, m_0(e) = m_1(e) + m_2(e)] \\ C[m_0 = m_1 \setminus m_2] & \rightsquigarrow C[\forall e.\, m_0(e) = \mathsf{ite}(m_1(e) \leq m_2(e), 0, m_1(e) - m_2(e))] \\ C[m_0 = m_1 \setminus\setminus m_2] & \rightsquigarrow C[\forall e.\, m_0(e) = \mathsf{ite}(m_2(e) = 0, m_1(e), 0)] \\ C[m_0 = \mathsf{setof}(m_1)] & \rightsquigarrow C[\forall e.\, m_0(e) = \mathsf{ite}(1 \leq m_1(e), 1, 0)] \\ C[m_1 \subseteq m_2] & \rightsquigarrow C[\forall e.\, (m_1(e) \leq m_2(e))] \\ C[m_1 = m_2] & \rightsquigarrow C[\forall e.\, (m_1(e) = m_2(e))] \end{array}$$
3. Express each pointwise constraint using a sum:
   $C[\forall e.F] \rightsquigarrow C[\sum_{\neg F} 1 = 0]$
4. Express each cardinality operator using a sum:
   $C[\,|m|\,] \rightsquigarrow C[\sum_{\mathsf{true}} m(e)]$
5. Flatten any sums that are not already top-level conjuncts:
   $$C[\,(u_1,\ldots,u_n) = \sum_F (t_1,\ldots,t_n)\,] \rightsquigarrow (w_1,\ldots,w_n) = \sum_F (t_1,\ldots,t_n) \wedge C[\,\bigwedge_{i=1}^{n} u_i = w_i\,]$$
6. Eliminate conditions from sums:
   $C[\sum_F (t_1,\ldots,t_n)\,] \rightsquigarrow C[\sum_{\mathsf{true}} (\mathsf{ite}(F, t_1, 0), \ldots, \mathsf{ite}(F, t_n, 0))\,]$
7. Group all sums into one:
   $$P \wedge \bigwedge_{i=1}^{q} (u_1^i,\ldots,u_{n_i}^i) = \sum_{\mathsf{true}} (t_1^i,\ldots,t_{n_i}^i) \rightsquigarrow$$
   $$P \wedge (u_1^1,\ldots,u_{n_1}^1,\ldots,u_1^q,\ldots,u_{n_q}^q) = \sum_{\mathsf{true}} (t_1^1,\ldots,t_{n_1}^1,\ldots,t_1^q,\ldots,t_{n_q}^q)$$

Fig. 2. Algorithm for reducing multiset formulas to sum normal form

we flatten formulas by introducing fresh variables for subterms and using the equality operator. Figure 2 summarizes this process.

Definition 1 (Sum normal form). *A multiset formula is in* sum normal form *iff it is of the form* $P \wedge (u_1,\ldots,u_n) = \sum_{true} (t_1,\ldots,t_n)$*, where P is a quantifier-free Presburger arithmetic formula without any multiset variables, and the variables in $t_1,\ldots,t_n$ occur only as expressions of the form $m(e)$ for m a multiset variable and e the fixed index variable.*

Theorem 1 (Reduction to sum normal form). *Algorithm in Figure 2 reduces in polynomial time any formula in the language of Figure 1 to a formula in sum normal form.*

4.1 From Multisets to Sum Constraints

We next argue that formulas in sum normal form (Definition 1) are equisatisfiable with formulas of linear arithmetic extended with sum constraints (Figure 3). Sum constraints are of the form $(u_1, \ldots, u_n) \in \sum_F (t_1, \ldots, t_n)$ and they test membership in the set of vectors generated using vector addition starting from the set $\{(t_1, \ldots, t_n) \mid \exists k_1, \ldots, k_n . F\}$ where $k_1, \ldots, k_n$ is the set of all variables occurring in F but not occurring in $t_1, \ldots, t_n$.

top-level, outer linear arithmetic formulas:

$\mathsf{F}^{\mathsf{out}} ::= \mathsf{A}^{\mathsf{out}} \mid \mathsf{F}^{\mathsf{out}} \wedge \mathsf{F}^{\mathsf{out}} \mid \neg \mathsf{F}^{\mathsf{out}}$

$\mathsf{A}^{\mathsf{out}} ::= \mathsf{t}^{\mathsf{out}} \leq \mathsf{t}^{\mathsf{out}} \mid \mathsf{t}^{\mathsf{out}} = \mathsf{t}^{\mathsf{out}} \mid (\mathsf{t}^{\mathsf{out}}, \ldots, \mathsf{t}^{\mathsf{out}}) \in \sum_{\mathsf{F}^{\mathsf{in}}} (\mathsf{t}^{\mathsf{in}}, \ldots, \mathsf{t}^{\mathsf{in}})$

$\mathsf{t}^{\mathsf{out}} ::= \mathsf{k}^{\mathsf{out}} \mid C \mid \mathsf{t}^{\mathsf{out}} + \mathsf{t}^{\mathsf{out}} \mid C \cdot \mathsf{t}^{\mathsf{out}} \mid \mathsf{ite}(\mathsf{F}^{\mathsf{out}}, \mathsf{t}^{\mathsf{out}}, \mathsf{t}^{\mathsf{out}})$

inner linear arithmetic formulas:

$\mathsf{F}^{\mathsf{in}} ::= \mathsf{A}^{\mathsf{in}} \mid \mathsf{F}^{\mathsf{in}} \wedge \mathsf{F}^{\mathsf{in}} \mid \neg \mathsf{F}^{\mathsf{in}}$

$\mathsf{A}^{\mathsf{in}} ::= \mathsf{t}^{\mathsf{in}} \leq \mathsf{t}^{\mathsf{in}} \mid \mathsf{t}^{\mathsf{in}} = \mathsf{t}^{\mathsf{in}}$

$\mathsf{t}^{\mathsf{in}} ::= \mathsf{k}^{\mathsf{in}} \mid C \mid \mathsf{t}^{\mathsf{in}} + \mathsf{t}^{\mathsf{in}} \mid C \cdot \mathsf{t}^{\mathsf{in}} \mid \mathsf{ite}(\mathsf{F}^{\mathsf{in}}, \mathsf{t}^{\mathsf{in}}, \mathsf{t}^{\mathsf{in}})$

terminals:

$\mathsf{k}^{\mathsf{in}}, \mathsf{k}^{\mathsf{out}}$ - integer variable (two disjoint sets); C - integer constants

Fig. 3. Syntax of Linear Arithmetic with Sum Constraints

Theorem 2 (Multiset elimination). *Consider a sum normal form formula F of the form*

$$P \ \wedge \ (u_1, \ldots, u_n) = \sum_{\mathsf{true}} (t_1, \ldots, t_n)$$

where free variables of $t_1, \ldots, t_n$ are multiset variables $m_1, \ldots, m_q$. Let $k_1, \ldots, k_q$ be fresh integer variables. Then F is equisatisfiable with the formula

$$P \ \wedge \ (u_1, \ldots, u_n) \in \sum_{\mathsf{true}} (t'_1, \ldots, t'_n) \tag{7}$$

where $t'_i = t_i[m_1(e) := k_1, \ldots, m_q(e) := k_q]$ (t'_i results from t_i by replacing multiset variables with fresh integer variables).

The equisatisfiability follows by bijection between the satisfying assignments where k_i is interpreted as $m_i(e)$ and E has as many elements as there are summands under the sum in (7).

5 Deciding Linear Arithmetic with Sum Constraints

Having reduced in polynomial time multiset constraint satisfiability to satisfiability for linear arithmetic with sum constraints, this section examines the decidability and the complexity of the resulting satisfiability problem.

5.1 Preliminary Transformations

We assume that the constraint whose satisfiability we wish to check is in the form given by Theorem 2. This is sufficient for deciding multiset constraints. We therefore consider a formula of the form

$$P \wedge (u_1, \ldots, u_n) \in \sum_{\mathsf{true}} (m_1, \ldots, m_n) \tag{8}$$

Let $x_1, \ldots, x_q$ be the set of variables in $m_1, \ldots, m_n$ and let $y_1, \ldots, y_q$ and $z_1, \ldots, z_n$ be fresh variables. We then represent (8) as the formula $P \wedge S$ where S is the formula

$$(u_1, \ldots, u_n, y_1, \ldots, y_q) \in \sum_F (z_1, \ldots, z_n, x_1, \ldots, x_q) \tag{9}$$

Here F is the formula $\bigwedge_{i=1}^{q} m_i = z_i$. (The values $y_1, \ldots, y_q$ are not used in P; their purpose is to ensure proper dimensionality of the resulting vector, so that we can assume that all variables of F appear in vector $(z_1, \ldots, z_n, x_1, \ldots, x_q)$.) Note that the formula S says that some number of solutions of QFPA formula F sums up to a given vector. We next show that S is equisatisfiable with a QFPA formula.

5.2 Formula Solutions as Semilinear Sets and Their Bounds

To show that QFPA formulas are closed under unbounded sum constraints, we use representations of solutions of QFPA formulas as semilinear sets. We first review some relevant results from [23]. For an integer vector $x = (x^1, \ldots, x^n)$ let $||x||_1$ denote $\sum_{i=1}^{n} |x_i|$. For a matrix $A = [a_{ij}]$ let $||A||_{1,\infty}$ denote $\sup_i(\sum_j a_{ij})$.

Definition 2 (Sum and Iteration of Sets of Vectors). *Let $C_1, C_2 \subseteq \mathbb{N}^k$ be sets of vectors of non-negative integers. We define*

$$C_1 + C_2 = \{x_1 + x_2 \mid x_1 \in C_1 \wedge x_2 \in C_2\}$$
$$C_1^* = \{0\} \cup \{x_1 + \ldots + x_n \mid x_1, \ldots, x_n \in C_1\}$$

When $x \in \mathbb{N}^n$ and $C_2 \subseteq \mathbb{N}^n$ is finite, we call $\{x\} + C_2^*$ a linear set*. A* semilinear set *is a union of some finite number of linear sets.*

If $C_1, C_2 \subseteq \mathbb{N}^n$ are finite, then $C_1 + C_2^*$ is a particular kind of a semilinear set. Such semilinear sets are solutions of systems of linear equations, which follows from the proof of [23, Corollary 1] and [23, Theorem 1]:

Fact 1 (Pottier 1991). *Consider a system of equations $Ax = b$ where $A \in \mathbb{N}^{m,n}$ and $b \in \mathbb{N}^m$. Let $A_1 = [A; -b]$, let r be the rank of A_1, and let $B_0 = (1 + ||A_1||_{1,\infty})^r$. Then there exist two finite sets $C_1, C_2 \subseteq \mathbb{N}^n$ such that*

1. *for all* $x \in \mathbb{N}^n$, $Ax = b$ *iff* $x \in C_1 + C_2^*$, *and*
2. $\forall h \in C_1 \cup C_2$, $||h||_1 \le B_0$.

Consequently, $|C_1| \le B_0$ *and* $|C_2| \le B_0$. *Moreover, if in* $Ax = b$ *we replace some of the equations with inequations, the statement still holds if* B_0 *is weakened to* $(2 + ||A_1||_{1,\infty})^m$.

Note that each QFPA formula F can be converted into an equivalent disjunction of systems of equations and inequations. The number of such systems is singly exponential in the number of atomic formulas in F. Moreover, the elements of A and b in the resulting systems are polynomially bounded by the coefficients and constants in the original QFPA formula. Consequently, the B_0 bound for each of these systems is at most singly exponential in the size s of the formula F. We denote this bound by $2^{p(s)}$, where p is some polynomial that follows from details of the algorithm for generating all systems of equations and inequations whose disjunction is equivalent to F. We thus obtain the following lemma.

Lemma 1. *Let* F *be a QFPA formula of size* s *with* n *free variables. Then there exist finite sets* $A_i, B_i \subseteq \mathbb{N}^n$ *for* $1 \le i \le d$ *for some* $d \le 2^{p_1(s)}$ *such that the set of satisfying assignments for* F *is given as*

$$\bigcup_{i=1}^{d} (A_i + B_i^*)$$

and such that $||h||_1 \le 2^{p(s)}$ *for each* $h \in \bigcup_{i=1}^{d} (A_i \cup B_i)$.

If $A = \{a_1, \ldots, a_q\}$ and $B = \{b_1, \ldots, b_r\}$ for $a_i, b_j \in \mathbb{N}^n$, then the condition $u \in A + B^*$ is given by the formula $\bigvee_{i=1}^{q}(u = a_i + \sum_{j=1}^{r} \lambda_j b_j)$ where $\lambda_1, \ldots, \lambda_r$ are existentially quantified variables ranging over $\mathbb{N}$. This view leads to the following formulation of Lemma 1.

Lemma 2 (Semilinear normal form for linear arithmetic). *Let* F *be a QFPA formula of size* s *with* n *free variables. Then there exist vectors* a_i *and* b_{ij}, $1 \le j \le q_i$, $1 \le i \le d$ *for* $d \le 2^{p_1(s)}$, *with* $||a_i||_1, ||b_{ij}||_1 \le 2^{p(s)}$ *such that* F *is equivalent to*

$$\exists \lambda_1, \ldots, \lambda_q. \bigvee_{i=1}^{d} (u = a_i + \sum_{j=1}^{q_i} \lambda_j b_{ij}) \tag{10}$$

where $u = (u_1, \ldots, u_n)$ *are the free variables in* F *and* q *is the maximum of all* q_i.

5.3 Formulas Representing Unbounded Sums

Having obtained semilinear normal form for QFPA formulas, we can characterize the set of all sums of solutions of a formula. This corresponds to taking the set of solutions C and computing a representation of C^*. We next give a QFPA formula for C^* (this was also obtained in [14, Section 3.2]).

Lemma 3. *Given a formula F in normal form (10), if x denotes vector of variables $(x_1, \ldots, x_n)$ then the condition $x \in \sum_F(u_1, \ldots, u_n)$ is equivalent to*

$$\exists \mu_i, \lambda_{ij}.\ x = \sum_{i=1}^{d}(\mu_i a_i + \sum_{j=1}^{q_i} \lambda_{ij} b_{ij}) \ \wedge\ \bigwedge_{i=1}^{d}(\mu_i = 0 \implies \sum_{j=1}^{q_i} \lambda_{ij} = 0) \tag{11}$$

The existentially quantified variables μ_i, λ_{ij} become free variables in the satisfiability problem. We have therefore reduced the original formula $P \wedge S$ where S is given by (8) to conjunction of P and (11), which is a QFPA formula. Along with the algorithm in Figure 2, this shows the decidability of the satisfiability problem for multiset constraints in Figure 1.

5.4 Bounds on Solutions for Formulas with Sums

The algorithm described so far produces exponentially large QFPA formulas, so it would only give a non-deterministic exponential bound on the satisfiability problem. To improve this complexity upper bound, we establish bounds on values of variables $(u_1, \ldots, u_n)$ in (8). As the first step, we rewrite (11) by applying case analysis, for each i, on whether $\mu_i = 0$ or $\mu_i \geq 1$. We obtain the formula

$$\exists \mu_i, \lambda_{ij}. \bigvee_{I \subseteq \{1,\ldots,d\}} x = \sum_{i \in I}((1 + \mu_i) a_i + \sum_{j=1}^{q_i} \lambda_{ij} b_{ij}) \tag{12}$$

The key property of (12) is that, although it can still have exponentially large number of variables in the size of the original formula S, each of the disjuncts in disjunctive normal form of (12) has a polynomial number of atomic formulas. In other words, the formula can be represented as a disjunction of systems of equations whose matrices A have polynomially many rows (and potentially exponentially many columns). Consequently, the same property holds for the conjunction $P \wedge$(12). This allows us to proceed similarly as in [15, Section 3]. We apply the well-known bound on integer linear programming problems.

Fact 2 (Papadimitriou [21]). *Let A be an $m \times n$ integer matrix and b an m-vector, both with entries from $[-a..a]$. Then the system $Ax = b$ has a solution in $\mathbb{N}^m$ if and only if it has a solution in $[0..M]^m$ where $M = n(ma)^{2m+1}$.*

Given that all coefficients appearing in (12) are bounded by $2^{p(s)}$ and that m is polynomial in s as well, we obtain the desired bound.

Theorem 3. *There exists a polynomial $p(s)$ such that for every formula F of Figure 3 of the form (8), of size s, F has a solution iff F has a solution in which the number of bits needed to represent the values of outer integer variables is bounded by $p(s)$.*

By Theorem 3 there is a non-deterministic polynomial time algorithm that

1. guesses the values $c_1, \ldots, c_{n+q}$ of variables $u_1, \ldots, u_n, y_1, \ldots, y_q$ in (9) such that P holds, and then

2. checks whether the constraint $(c_1, \ldots, c_{n+q}) \in \sum_F(z_1, \ldots, z_n, x_1, \ldots, x_q)$ has a solution.

We have therefore reduced the satisfiability problem to testing whether a given vector of non-negative integers is a sum of some number of solutions of F. This test is the subject of the next section.

5.5 PSPACE Algorithm for Sum Membership

This section examines the problem of checking for a given constant vector $\boldsymbol{c} \in \mathbb{N}$ and a given QFPA formula F, whether $\boldsymbol{c} \in \{\boldsymbol{v} \mid F(\boldsymbol{v})\}^*$ holds, that is, whether there exists some number $q \geq 0$ of vectors $\boldsymbol{v}_1, \ldots, \boldsymbol{v}_q \in \mathbb{N}^n$ such that $\sum_{i=1}^q \boldsymbol{v}_i = \boldsymbol{c}$ and $F(\boldsymbol{c})$ holds forall $1 \leq i \leq q$. In principle, this problem could be solved by checking the satisfiability of formula (11). However, the number and size of vectors a_i and b_{ij} is exponential. The techniques that we know for constructing them are based on computing Hilbert basis of homogeneous systems of equations over natural numbers ($Ax = 0$) [23,4]. In [5] the authors show that counting the number of solutions of Hilbert basis of a system of equations is complete for the counting class #coNP.

We therefore adopt a more direct approach to checking $\boldsymbol{c} \in \{\boldsymbol{v} \mid F(\boldsymbol{v})\}^*$, which does not attempt to compute semilinear sets for F. A simple non-deterministic polynomial-space algorithm would guess non-zero solutions of the formula F that are bounded by $\boldsymbol{c}$ and subtract them from $\boldsymbol{c}$ until it reaches the zero vector. Figure 4 we presents a refinement of this algorithm that uses divide and conquer approach and can easily be implemented deterministically in polynomial space. Note that in invocations of depth up to t the algorithm will find sums $\boldsymbol{v}_1 + \ldots + \boldsymbol{v}_q = \boldsymbol{c}$ for all $q \leq 2^t$. Because the coordinates of solutions are non-negative integers, it suffices to consider sums of length up to $||c||_1$, which is bounded by $2^{p(s)}$. Therefore, the bound $p(s)$ on the depth of recursion suffices.

The algorithm in Figure 4 also gives a natural encoding of the problem into Presburger arithmetic with bounded quantifiers, which is PSPACE complete. Namely, we can rewrite the two recursive calls in $\mathsf{generated}(\boldsymbol{c}_1, t-1) \wedge \mathsf{generated}(\boldsymbol{c}_2, t-1)$ as

$$\forall \boldsymbol{a}.\ (\boldsymbol{a} = \boldsymbol{c}_1 \vee \boldsymbol{a} = \boldsymbol{c}_2) \implies \mathsf{generated}(\boldsymbol{a}, t-1) \tag{13}$$

Given a formula F of size s, we then unroll the recursion $p(s)$ times, which eliminates all recursive calls and the parameter t. Because (13) contains only one recursive call, the resulting unrolling is polynomially large and it can be encoded as a QFPA formula. This formula contains universal quantification over the $\boldsymbol{a}$ vectors and existential quantifiers over the $\boldsymbol{c}_1, \boldsymbol{c}_2$ vectors in each step of the recursion. It has polynomial size and $p(s)$ quantifier alternations.

Theorem 4 (Membership test). *The algorithm in Figure 4 is correct and runs in polynomial space.*

From Theorem 1, Theorem 2, and Theorem 4, we obtain our main result.

INPUT: A vector $c \in \mathbb{N}^n$, and a QFPA formula F of size s with free variables $k = (k^1, \ldots, k^n)$.
OUTPUT: true iff $c \in \{v \mid F(v)\}^*$
TOP LEVEL: return generated$(c, p(s))$;

proc generated(c, t) :
  if$(c = 0)$ then return true;
  if$(F(c) = \text{true})$ then return true;
  if$(t = 0)$ then return false;
  non-deterministically guess $c_1, c_2 \in \mathbb{N}^n \setminus \{0\}$ such that $c_1 + c_2 = c$;
  return (generated$(c_1, t-1)$ $\wedge$ generated$(c_2, t-1)$);

Fig. 4. PSPACE Algorithm for testing whether a vector is a sum of solutions of a QFPA formula

Corollary 1. *The satisfiability problems for languages in Figure 1 are decidable and belong to PSPACE.*

6 Undecidability of Quantified Constraints

We next show that adding quantifiers to the language of Figure 1 (and to many of its fragments) results in undecidable constraints.

The language in Figure 1 can be seen as a generalization of quantifier-free Boolean algebra with Presburger arithmetic (QFBAPA) [12]. Given that QFBAPA admits quantifier elimination [7,10], it is interesting to ask whether multiset quantifiers can be eliminated from constraints of the present paper. Note that a multiset structure without cardinality operator can be viewed as a product of Presburger arithmetic structures. Therefore, Feferman-Vaught theorem [7] (see also [3], [11, Section 3.3]) gives a way to decide the first-order theory of multiset operations extended with the ability to state cardinality of sets of the form $|\{e \mid F(e)\}|$. This corresponds to multiset theory with counting distinct elements of multisets, which is denoted $FO^{\#D}_{\mathcal{M}}$ in [13]. However, this language is strictly less expressive than a quantified extension of the language in Figure 1 that contains summation expressions $\sum_{F(e)} t(e)$ and that corresponds to $FO^{\#}_{\mathcal{M}}$ in [13]. The decidability of $FO^{\#}_{\mathcal{M}}$ was stated as open in [13]. We next show that this language is undecidable.

The undecidability follows by reduction from Hilbert's 10th problem [16], because quantified multiset constraints can define not only addition (using disjoint union $\uplus$) but also multiplication. To define $x \cdot y = z$, we introduce a new set p that contains x distinct elements, each of which occurs y times. The following formula encodes this property.

$$\begin{aligned} x \cdot y = z \Leftrightarrow \exists p.\ & z = |p| \ \wedge\ x = |\mathsf{setof}(p)| \ \wedge \\ & (\forall m.\ |m| = z \wedge |\mathsf{setof}(m)| = 1 \wedge \mathsf{setof}(m) \subseteq p \implies |m \cap p| = y) \end{aligned}$$

Because we can define multiplication, we can express satisfiability of Diophantine equations, so by [16] we conclude that satisfiability of multiset constraints with quantifiers and cardinality is undecidable. Similarly, we obtain undecidable constraints if in the quantified expressions $\forall e.F$ we admit the use of outer integer variables as parameters. This justifies the current "stratified" syntax that distinguishes inner and outer integer variables.

The reader may wonder whether the presence of the built-in setof operator is needed for undecidability of quantified constraints. However, the setof operator is itself definable using quantifiers. For example, $a = \mathsf{setof}(b)$ iff a is the smallest set that behaves the same as b with respect to simple set membership. Behaving same with respect to simple set membership is given by

$$\mathsf{memSame}(a,b) \iff (\forall x. |x| = 1 \Longrightarrow (x \subseteq a \Longleftrightarrow x \subseteq b))$$

so $a = \mathsf{setof}(b) \iff (\mathsf{memSame}(a,b) \land (\forall a_1.\ \mathsf{memSame}(a_1,b) \implies a \subseteq a_1))$. Moreover, note that, as in any lattice, $\cap$ and $\subseteq$ are inter-expressible using quantifiers. Therefore, adding quantifiers to a multiset language that contains $\subseteq$ and cardinality constructs already gives undecidable constraints. This answers negatively the question on decidability of $FO^{\#D}_{\mathcal{M}}$ posed in [13, Section 3.4].

7 Conclusions

Motivated by applications in verification, we introduced an expressive class of constraints on multisets. Our constraints support arbitrary multiset operations defined pointwise using QFPA as well as the cardinality operator. We presented a decision procedure for the satisfiability of these constraints, showing that they efficiently reduce to an extension of QFPA with unbounded sum expressions. For the later problem we presented a decision procedure based on semilinear set representation of quantifier-free Presburger arithmetic formulas. We established small bounds on solutions of such formulas and then showed that the overall problem can be solved in polynomial space. The satisfiability problem for our constraints is therefore NP-hard and belongs to PSPACE.[1] Finally, we showed that adding quantifiers to these constraints makes them undecidable by defining multiplication in the language.

References

1. Aiken, A.: Introduction to set constraint-based program analysis. Science of Computer Programming 35, 79–111 (1999)
2. Banâtre, J.-P., Le Métayer, D.: Programming by multiset transformation. Commun. ACM 36(1), 98–111 (1993)
3. Bès, A.: Definability and decidability results related to the elementary theory of ordinal multiplication. Fund.Math. 171, 197–211 (2002)
4. Domenjoud, E.: Solving systems of linear diophantine equations: An algebraic approach. In: Tarlecki, A. (ed.) MFCS 1991. LNCS, vol. 520, pp. 141–150. Springer, Heidelberg (1991)

[1] We recently established NP-completeness of these constraints by generalizing [6].

5. Durand, A., Hermann, M., Kolaitis, P.G.: Subtractive reductions and complete problems for counting complexity classes. Theor. Comput. Sci. 340(3), 496–513 (2005)
6. Eisenbrand, F., Shmonin, G.: Carathéodory bounds for integer cones. Operations Research Letters 34(5), 564–568 (2006)
7. Feferman, S., Vaught, R.L.: The first order properties of products of algebraic systems. Fundamenta Mathematicae 47, 57–103 (1959)
8. Ginsburg, S., Spanier, E.: Semigroups, Pressburger formulas and languages. Pacific Journal of Mathematics 16(2), 285–296 (1966)
9. Kuncak, V.: Modular Data Structure Verification. PhD thesis, EECS Department, Massachusetts Institute of Technology (February 2007)
10. Kuncak, V., Nguyen, H.H., Rinard, M.: Deciding Boolean Algebra with Presburger Arithmetic. J. of Automated Reasoning (2006)
11. Kuncak, V., Rinard, M.: On the theory of structural subtyping. Technical Report 879, LCS, Massachusetts Institute of Technology (2003)
12. Kuncak, V., Rinard, M.: Towards efficient satisfiability checking for Boolean Algebra with Presburger Arithmetic. In: Pfenning, F. (ed.) CADE 2007. LNCS (LNAI), vol. 4603, Springer, Heidelberg (2007)
13. Lugiez, D.: Multitree automata that count. Theor. Comput. Sci. 333(1-2), 225–263 (2005)
14. Lugiez, D., Zilio, S.D.: Multitrees Automata, Presburger's Constraints and Tree Logics. Research report 08-2002, LIF, Marseille, France (June 2002), `http://www.lif-sud.univ-mrs.fr/Rapports/08-2002.html`
15. Marnette, B., Kuncak, V., Rinard, M.: On algorithms and complexity for sets with cardinality constraints. Technical report, MIT CSAIL (August 2005)
16. Matiyasevich, Y.V.: Enumerable sets are Diophantine. Soviet Math. Doklady 11(2), 354–357 (1970)
17. Misra, J.: A logic for concurrent programming (in two parts): Safety and progress. Journal of Computer and Software Engineering 3(2), 239–300 (1995)
18. Nguyen, H.H., et al.: Automated verification of shape, size and bag properties via separation logic. In: Cook, B., Podelski, A. (eds.) VMCAI 2007. LNCS, vol. 4349, Springer, Heidelberg (2007)
19. Nipkow, T., Paulson, L.C., Wenzel, M.T. (eds.): Isabelle/HOL. LNCS, vol. 2283. Springer, Heidelberg (2002)
20. Nipkow, T., et al.: Multiset theory version 1.30 (Isabelle distribution) (2005), `http://isabelle.in.tum.de/dist/library/HOL/Library/Multiset.html`
21. Papadimitriou, C.H.: On the complexity of integer programming. J. ACM 28(4), 765–768 (1981)
22. Paulson, L.C.: Mechanizing a theory of program composition for UNITY. ACM Trans. Program. Lang. Syst. 23(5), 626–656 (2001)
23. Pottier, L.: Minimal solutions of linear diophantine systems: Bounds and algorithms. In: Book, R.V. (ed.) RTA 1991. LNCS, vol. 488, Springer, Heidelberg (1991)
24. Schwartz, J.T.: On programming: An interim report on the SETL project. Technical report, Courant Institute, New York (1973)
25. Zarba, C.G.: Combining multisets with integers. In: Voronkov, A. (ed.) CADE 2002. LNCS (LNAI), vol. 2392, Springer, Heidelberg (2002)

All You Need Is Compassion*

Amir Pnueli[1,2] and Yaniv Sa'ar[2]

[1] New York University, New York
amir@cs.nyu.edu
[2] Weizmann Institute of Science
yaniv.saar@weizmann.ac.il

Abstract. The paper presents a new deductive rule for verifying response properties under the assumption of compassion (strong fairness) requirements. It improves on previous rules in that the premises of the new rule are all first order. We prove that the rule is sound, and present a constructive completeness proof for the case of finite-state systems. For the general case, we present a sketch of a relative completeness proof. We report about the implementation of the rule in PVS and illustrate its application on some simple but non-trivial examples.

1 Introduction

An important component of the formal model of reactive systems is a set of *fairness requirements*. As suggested by Lamport [13], these should come in two flavors: *weak fairness* (to which we refer as *justice requirements*) and *strong fairness* (to which we refer as *compassion*). Originally, these two distinct notions of fairness were formulated in terms of enableness and the activation of transitions within a computation, as follows:

- The requirement that transition τ is *just* implies that if τ is continuously enabled from a certain position on, then it is taken (activated) infinitely many times.
  An equivalent formulation is that every computation should contain infinitely many positions at which τ is disabled or has just been taken.
- The requirement that transition τ is *compassionate* implies that if τ is enabled infinitely many times in a computation σ, then it is taken infinitely many times.

Justice requirements are used in order to guarantee that, in a parallel composition of processes, no process is neglected forever from a certain point on. Compassion, which is a more stringent requirement, is often associated with coordination statements such as semaphore *request* y (equivalently *lock* y) operations or message passing instructions. It implies fair arbitration in the allocation of an atomic resource among several competing processes.

In a more abstract setting, a justice requirement is associated with an *assertion* (first-order state formula) J, while a compassion requirement is associated with a pair of assertions $\langle p, q\rangle$. With these identifications, the requirements are:

- A computation σ is just with respect to the requirement J, if σ contains infinitely many occurrences of states that satisfy J.

* This research was supported in part by ONR grant N00014-99-1-0131.

F. Logozzo et al. (Eds.): VMCAI 2008, LNCS 4905, pp. 233–247, 2008.

- A computation σ is compassionate with respect to the requirement $\langle p, q\rangle$, if either σ contains only finitely many p-positions or σ contains infinitely many q-positions.

To see that these definitions are indeed generalizations of the transition-oriented definition, we observe that the requirement that transition τ be just can be expressed by the abstract justice requirement $J_\tau = (\neg En(\tau) \vee \mathit{Taken}(\tau))$, while the requirement that transition τ be compassionate can be expressed by the abstract compassion requirement $C_\tau = \langle En(\tau), \mathit{Taken}(\tau)\rangle$. In these assertions, $En(\tau)$ is true at all states on which τ is enabled. Similarly, $\mathit{Taken}(\tau)$ is true at all states that can result by taking transition τ.

An important observation is that justice is a special case of compassion. This is because the justice requirement J can also be expressed as the degenerate compassion requirement $\langle 1, J\rangle$, where we write 1 to denote the assertion *True* which holds at every state. In view of this observation, one may raise the natural question of the necessity of keeping these two separate notions of fairness.

Several answers can be given to this question. On the modeling level, the argument is that these two notions represent different phenomena. Justice represents the natural independence of parallel processes in a multi-processing system. Compassion is typically used to provide an abstract representation of queues and priorities which are installed by the operating system in order to guarantee fairness in coordination services provided to parallel processes. There is also a different cost associated with the implementation of these two notions. In a multi-processor system, justice comes for free and is a result of the independent progress of parallel processes. In a multi-programming system, where concurrency is simulated by scheduling, justice can be implemented by any scheduling scheme that gives each process a fair chance to progress, such as round-robin scheduling. Compassion, in both types of systems, is usually implemented by maintenance of queues and use of priorities.

There is also a proof-theoretic answer to this question which is based on the fact that, up to now, all the proposed deductive rules for proving properties under the assumption of compassion were significantly more complex than the rule under the assumption of justice alone. The main claim of this paper is this need not necessarily be the case, and there exist deductive rules for verification in which the price of compassion is comparable to that of justice.

1.1 The Legacy Recursive Rule

In the way of a background, we present rule F-WELL which is derived from the proof rule presented in [15] and is representative of the different prices traditionally associated with the distinct notions of fairness. It is modified in order to represent the transition from the computational model of *fair transition systems* (used in [15]) to that of *fair discrete systems* (FDS) which we use here. The rule is presented in Fig. 1.

The FDS $(\mathcal{D}\backslash\{\langle p_i, q_i\rangle\})$ is obtained by removing from $\mathcal{D}$ the compassion requirement $\langle p_i, q_i\rangle$. Thus, $(\mathcal{D}\backslash\{\langle p_i, q_i\rangle\})$ has one compassion requirement less than $\mathcal{D}$.

The rule considers a system (FDS) which has both justice requirements ($\mathcal{J}$) and compassion requirements ($\mathcal{C}$). It establishes for this system the temporal property $p \implies \diamondsuit\, q$ claiming that every p-state is followed by a q-state. The rule relies on "helpful" fairness requirements $F_1, \ldots, F_n$ which may be either justice or compassion

Rule F-WELL

For a well-founded domain $\mathcal{A} : (W, \succ)$,
assertions $p, q, \varphi_1, \ldots, \varphi_n$,
fairness requirements $F_1, \ldots, F_n \in \mathcal{J} \cup \mathcal{C}$,
and ranking functions $\Delta_1, \ldots, \Delta_n$ where each $\Delta_i : \Sigma \mapsto W$

W1. $p \implies q \vee \bigvee_{j=1}^{n} \varphi_j$

For each $i = 1, \ldots, n$,

W2. $\varphi_i \wedge \rho \implies q' \vee (\varphi_i' \wedge \Delta_i = \Delta_i') \vee \left(\bigvee_{j=1}^{n} (\varphi_j' \wedge \Delta_i \succ \Delta_j')\right)$

W3. If $F_i = \langle p_i, q_i \rangle \in \mathcal{C}$ then

C3. $\varphi_i \implies \neg q_i$

C4. $(\mathcal{D} \backslash \{\langle p_i, q_i \rangle\}) \models (\varphi_i \implies \Diamond(p_i \vee \neg\varphi_i))$

Otherwise ($F_i = J_i \in \mathcal{J}$),

J3. $\varphi_i \implies \neg J_i$

$\mathcal{D} \models (p \implies \Diamond q)$

Fig. 1. Legacy (recursive) rule F-WELL

requirements. Premise W3 imposes different conditions on each fairness requirement F_i according to whether F_i is a compassion or a justice requirement.

Consider first the special case in which all the helpful requirements are justice requirements. In this case, we only invoke premise J3 as an instance of W3. For such a case, the rule provides a real reduction by establishing a temporal property, based on premises which are all first-order.

On the other hand, if some of the helpful requirements are compassionate, then some of the premises will include instances of C3 and C4. In this case, some of the premises are temporal and have a syntactic form similar to that of the conclusion. In such a case, one may ask whether this is not a circular rule in which the premises are not necessarily simpler than the conclusion. As observed above, the rule is not really circular because the premise C4 requires the establishment of a similar temporal property but over a system with fewer compassion requirements. So while the methodology is still sound, it appears cumbersome and its application often requires explicit induction on the number of compassion requirements in the analyzed system.

This explanation serves to illustrate that the application of this rule is significantly more complex and cumbersome in the case that we have compassion requirements, and the situation is mush simpler if all the fairness requirements are of the justice type. We refer to this phenomenon by saying that the application of this rule is *recursive* in the presence of compassion requirements.

1.2 A New Flat Rule

The main result of this paper is based on a new deductive rule for response properties which does not need any recursion in order to handle compassion requirements. The rule, called RESPONSE, is presented in Fig. 2.

For simplicity, we presented the rule for the case that the system contains only compassion requirements but no justice requirements. This is not a serious restriction since

Rule RESPONSE
For a well-founded domain $\mathcal{A} : (W, \succ)$,
assertions $p, q, \varphi_1, \ldots, \varphi_n$,
compassion requirements $\langle p_1, q_1 \rangle, \ldots, \langle p_n, q_n \rangle \in \mathcal{C}$,
and ranking functions $\Delta_1, \ldots, \Delta_n$ where each $\Delta_i : \Sigma \mapsto W$

$$
\begin{array}{lll}
\text{R1.} \quad p & \Longrightarrow & q \lor \bigvee_{j=1}^{n} (p_j \land \varphi_j) \\
\multicolumn{3}{l}{\text{For each } i = 1, \ldots, n,} \\
\text{R2.} \; p_i \land \varphi_i \land \rho & \Longrightarrow & q' \lor \bigvee_{j=1}^{n} (p'_j \land \varphi'_j) \\
\text{R3.} \quad \varphi_i \land \rho & \Longrightarrow & q' \lor (\varphi'_i \land \Delta_i = \Delta'_i) \lor \bigvee_{j=1}^{n} (p'_j \land \varphi'_j \land \Delta_i \succ \Delta'_j) \\
\text{R4.} \quad \varphi_i & \Longrightarrow & \neg q_i \\
\hline
\quad p & \Longrightarrow & \diamondsuit\, q
\end{array}
$$

Fig. 2. Deductive rule RESPONSE

any original justice requirement $J \in \mathcal{J}_\mathcal{D}$ can be represented by an equivalent compassion requirement $\langle 1, J \rangle$. Similarly to the previous version of this rule, the rule relies on a set of premises guaranteeing that a computation which contains a p-state that is not followed by a q-state leads to an infinite chain of descending ranks. Since the ranks range over a well-founded domain $\mathcal{A} : (W, \succ)$, this leads to a contradiction.

In view of the simple form of the rule, it appears that, in many cases, the study and analysis of fair discrete systems can concentrate on the treatment of compassion requirements, and deal with justice requirements as a special case of a compassion requirement. This does not imply that we suggest giving up the class of justice requirements altogether. For modeling and implementation of reactive systems, we should keep these two classes of fairness requirements distinct. However, the main message of this paper is that, when verifying temporal properties of FDS's, the treatment of compassion requirements is conceptually not more complex than the treatment of justice requirements. Computationally, though, justice is simpler in the same way that checking emptiness of generalized Büchi automata is simpler than checking emptiness of Street automata.

The new rule has been implemented in the theorem prover PVS [18]. In fact, it has been added as an additional rule (and associated strategy) within the PVS-*based temporal prover* TLPVS [19]. In order to do so, we had to prove the soundness of the RESPONSE rule within PVS.

The rest of the paper is organized as follows. In Section 2 we introduce the computational model of fair discrete systems with its related notions of fairness. We then illustrate the application of the new rule to three examples of increasing complexity in Section 3. The soundness of the rule is stated and proved in Section 4. Section 5 discusses the question of completeness. For finite-state systems, we present a constructive proof of completeness which can be used in order to obtain the auxiliary constructs required for an application of the rule. For infinite-state systems, we sketch a proof of completeness which is based on a reduction to the proof of completeness of rule F-WELL, as presented in [15]. Finally, in Section 6 we discuss some related work.

2 The Computational Model

As a computational model, we take a *fair discrete system* (FDS) $S = \langle V, \Theta, \rho, \mathcal{J}, \mathcal{C} \rangle$, where

- V — A set of *system variables*. A *state* of S provides a type-consistent interpretation of the variables V. For a state s and a system variable $v \in V$, we denote by $s[v]$ the value assigned to v by the state s. Let Σ denote the set of all states over V.
- Θ — The *initial condition*: An assertion (state formula) characterizing the initial states.
- $\rho(V, V')$ — The *transition relation*: An assertion, relating the values V of the variables in state $s \in \Sigma$ to the values V' in an $\mathcal{D}$-successor state $s' \in \Sigma$. For a subset $U \subseteq V$ we define *pres*(U) as $\bigwedge_{v \in U}(v' = v)$. We assume that the system can always *idle*, that is, we assume that ρ has the disjunct *pres*(V).
- $\mathcal{J}$ — A set of *justice* (*weak fairness*) requirements (assertions); A computation must include infinitely many states satisfying each of the justice requirements.
- $\mathcal{C}$ — A set of *compassion (strong fairness)* requirements: Each compassion requirement is a pair $\langle p, q \rangle$ of state assertions; A computation should include either only finitely many p-states, or infinitely many q-states.

For an assertion ψ, we say that $s \in \Sigma$ is a ψ-state if $s \models \psi$. A *computation* of an FDS S is an infinite sequence of states $\sigma : s_0, s_1, s_2, ...$, satisfying the requirements:

- *Initiality*: s_0 is initial, i.e., $s_0 \models \Theta$.
- *Consecution*: For each $\ell = 0, 1, ...$, state $s_{\ell+1}$ is a $\mathcal{D}$-successor of s_ℓ. I.e., $\langle s_\ell, s_{\ell+1} \rangle \models \rho(V, V')$ where, for each $v \in V$, we interpret v as $s_\ell[v]$ and v' as $s_{\ell+1}[v]$.
- *Justice* — for every $J \in \mathcal{J}$, σ contains infinitely many occurrences of J-states.
- *Compassion*: for every $\langle p, q \rangle \in \mathcal{C}$, either σ contains only finitely many occurrences of p-states, or σ contains infinitely many occurrences of q-states.

A state s is called *accessible* if there exists a path of ρ-steps leading from some initial state to s.

A system with no compassion requirements is called a *just discrete system* (JDS). A system with no justice requirements is called a *compassionate discrete system* (CDS). As previously observed, every FDS is equivalent to a CDS. Therefore, we do not lose generality if we present the verification rule RESPONSE for CDS's.

As a specification language specifying properties of systems we use linear temporal logic (LTL) as presented, for example in [16]. In particular, we are interested in response formulas of the form $p \Longrightarrow \diamondsuit q$ (abbreviating $\square(p \rightarrow \diamondsuit q)$). This formula states that every p-state is followed by a q-state. Given an FDS $\mathcal{D}$ and an LTL formula φ, we say that φ is *valid over* $\mathcal{D}$ (is $\mathcal{D}$-valid) if every computation of $\mathcal{D}$ satisfies φ.

Reconsider rule RESPONSE as presented in Fig. 2. The rule assumes a well founded domain $\mathcal{A} : (W, \succ)$. Such a domain consists of a non-empty set W and a partial order $\succ$ over W, such that there does not exists an infinite descending chain $\alpha_0 \succ \alpha_1 \succ a_2 \succ \cdots$, of elements $a_i \in W$. The rule establishes the validity of the response property $p \Longrightarrow \diamondsuit q$ over a CDS $\mathcal{D}$, where p and q are assertions (first-order state formulas). In order to do so, the rule focuses on a list of (not necessarily disjoint) compassion requirements $\langle p_1, q_1\rangle, \ldots \langle p_n, q_n\rangle \in \mathcal{C}$. With each compassion requirement $\langle p_i, q_i\rangle$ we associate a *helpful assertion* φ_i and a *ranking function* $\Delta_i : \Sigma \mapsto W$, mapping states of $\mathcal{D}$ into elements of $\mathcal{A}$.

One of the differences between the application of rule RESPONSE and that of rule F-WELL is that, in applications of F-WELL, the helpful assertions are typically disjoint. That is, every state satisfies at most one helpful assertion. In applications of rule RESPONSE there is typically an overlap among the helpful assertions. Typically, for a compassion requirement $\langle p_i, q_i\rangle$, where p_i is not identically true, every state satisfying $\varphi_i \wedge \neg p_i$ satisfies at least one more helpful assertion φ_j for $j \neq i$.

3 Examples of Verification

In this section we present three examples illustrating the application of rule RESPONSE to proofs of response properties of simple programs. In all cases we assume that the programs are represented as CDS in which we encoded the justice requirements as degenerate compassion requirement of the form $\langle 1, J\rangle$.

Example 1 (Conditional Termination)
Consider program COND-TERM presented in Fig. 3.

$$
\begin{array}{l}
\quad x, y : \textbf{natural init } x = 0 \\
\left[\begin{array}{l}
\ell_1 : \textbf{while } y > 0 \textbf{ do} \\
\qquad \left[\begin{array}{l} \ell_2 : x := \{0, 1\} \\ \ell_3 : y := y + 1 - 2x \end{array}\right] \\
\ell_4 :
\end{array}\right]
\end{array}
$$

Fig. 3. Conditionally Terminating Program COND-TERM

This program has three standard justice requirements $J_1, \ldots, J_3$, associated with the statements $\ell_1, \ldots, \ell_3$. The justice requirement associated with ℓ_i is $J_i : \neg at\_\ell_i$ which requires that the program makes infinitely many visits to a location which is different from ℓ_i, thus guaranteeing that execution does not get stuck at location ℓ_i. Such a requirement is necessary in the context of concurrent programs. In addition to these three justice requirements, we also append to the system the compassion requirement $\langle at\_\ell_3 \wedge x = 0,\ 0\rangle$, requiring that there will be only finitely many states satisfying $at\_\ell_3 \wedge x = 0$. This implies that, from a certain point on, all visits to ℓ_3 must be with a positive value of x. Obviously, under these fairness requirements, program COND-TERM must terminate.

To prove this fact, using rule RESPONSE, we choose the following constructs for $n = 4$, where F_i is the i'th compassion requirement appearing in the list:

i	F_i	φ_i	Δ_i
1	$\langle 1, \neg at\_\ell_1\rangle$	at_ℓ_1	$(y, 2)$
2	$\langle 1, \neg at\_\ell_2\rangle$	$at\_\ell_2 \wedge y > 0$	$(y, 1)$
3	$\langle 1, \neg at\_\ell_3\rangle$	$at\_\ell_3 \wedge y > 0 \wedge x = 1$	$(y, 0)$
4	$\langle at\_\ell_3 \wedge x = 0,\ 0\rangle$	$at\_\ell_{1..3} \wedge y \geq at\_\ell_{2,3} \wedge x \in \{0, 1\}$	$(0, 0)$

As assertions p and q we take at_ℓ_1 and at_ℓ_4, respectively. The well-founded domain is the domain of pairs of natural numbers. The application of this rule already demonstrates the phenomenon of overlap among the helpful assertions. For example, every state satisfying φ_4 satisfies also φ_i for some $i \in [1..3]$.

The validity of the premises of rule RESPONSE for this choice has been verified using the theorem prover PVS [18]. □

Next we consider the example of *mutual exclusion by semaphores*.

Example 2 (Muxsem)
Consider program MUX-SEM presented in Fig. 4.

$$\begin{array}{l} \qquad \textbf{local } y : \textbf{boolean init } y = 1 \\ \overset{n}{\underset{i=1}{\|}} P[i] :: \left[\begin{array}{l}\textbf{loop forever do}\\ \quad \left[\begin{array}{l} \ell_1 : \textbf{NonCritical} \\ \ell_2 : \textbf{request } y \\ \ell_3 : \textbf{Critical} \\ \ell_4 : \textbf{release } y\end{array}\right]\end{array}\right]\end{array}$$

Fig. 4. Mutual Exclusion by Semaphores. Program MUX-SEM.

For this program we wish to prover the response property

$$at\_\ell_2[1] \implies \diamondsuit\, at\_\ell_3[1]$$

To prove this property, using rule RESPONSE, we choose the following constructs:

i	F_i	φ_i	Δ_i
1	$\langle at\_\ell_2[1] \wedge y, at\_\ell_3[1]\rangle$	$at\_\ell_2[1]$	0
$(3, j), j > 1$	$\langle 1, \neg at\_\ell_3[j]\rangle$	$at\_\ell_2[1] \wedge at\_\ell_3[j]$	2
$(4, j), j > 1$	$\langle 1, \neg at\_\ell_4[j]\rangle$	$at\_\ell_2[1] \wedge at\_\ell_4[j]$	1

We also use the following auxiliary invariant:

$$\varphi : \quad y + \sum_{i=1}^{n} at\_\ell_{3,4}[i] \;=\; 1$$

□

Finally, we consider the example of *dining philosophers*.

Example 3 (Dining Philosophers)
Consider program DINE-PHIL presented in Fig. 5.
For this program we wish to prove the response property

$$at\_\ell_1[2] \implies \diamondsuit\, at\_\ell_3[2]$$

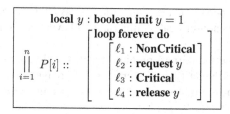

$$
\text{local } f : \text{array } [1..n] \text{ of boolean init } f = 1
$$

$$
\mathop{\Big\|}_{i=1}^{n-1} P[i] :: \left[\begin{array}{l}\textbf{loop forever do} \\ \left[\begin{array}{l} \ell_0 : \textbf{NonCritical} \\ \ell_1 : \textbf{request } f[i] \\ \ell_2 : \textbf{request } f[i+1] \\ \ell_3 : \textbf{Critical} \\ \ell_4 : \textbf{release } f[i] \\ \ell_5 : \textbf{release } f[i+1] \end{array}\right]\end{array}\right] \quad \| \quad P[n] :: \left[\begin{array}{l}\textbf{loop forever do} \\ \left[\begin{array}{l} \ell_0 : \textbf{NonCritical} \\ \ell_1 : \textbf{request } f[1] \\ \ell_2 : \textbf{request } f[n] \\ \ell_3 : \textbf{Critical} \\ \ell_4 : \textbf{release } f[1] \\ \ell_5 : \textbf{release } f[n] \end{array}\right]\end{array}\right]
$$

Fig. 5. Dining Philosophers. Program DINE-PHIL.

which captures the property of *accessibility* for process $P[2]$. According to this property, whenever $P[2]$ exits its non-critical section ℓ_0, it will eventually enter its critical section at location ℓ_3.

In order to enumerate the fairness requirements (as well as transitions) for this system we use the indexing scheme (j, k), where $j : 1..n$ ranges over process indices, and $k : 0..5$ ranges over locations. To prove this property, using rule RESPONSE, we choose the following constructs:

(j,k)	$F_{(j,k)}$	$\varphi_{(j,k)}$	$\Delta_{(j,k)}$
$(2,2)$	$\langle at\_\ell_2[2] \wedge f[3], at\_\ell_3[2]\rangle$	$at\_\ell_2[2]$	0
$(j : [3..n], k : [3..4])$	$\langle 1, \neg at\_\ell_k[j]\rangle$	$at\_\ell_k[j] \wedge \bigwedge_{i=2}^{j-1} at\_\ell_2[i]$	$(0, j, 5-k)$
$(j : [3..n-1], 2)$	$\langle at\_\ell_2[j] \wedge f[j+1], at\_\ell_3[j]\rangle$	$\bigwedge_{i=2}^{j} at\_\ell_2[i]$	$(0, j, 3)$
$(n, 5)$	$\langle 1, \neg at\_\ell_5[n]\rangle$	$at\_\ell_5[n] \wedge \bigwedge_{i=2}^{n-1} at\_\ell_2[i]$	$(0, n, 0)$
$(2,1)$	$\langle at\_\ell_1[2] \wedge f[2], at\_\ell_2[2]\rangle$	$at\_\ell_1[2]$	1
$(1, k : [3..5])$	$\langle 1, \neg at\_\ell_k[1]\rangle$	$at\_\ell_1[2] \wedge at\_\ell_k[1]$	$(1, 1, 5-k)$

We also use the following auxiliary invariant:

$$
\begin{array}{ll}
\bigwedge_{i=1}^{n-2}(at\_\ell_{3..5}[i] + at\_\ell_{2..4}[i+1] + f[i+1] = 1) & \wedge \\
at\_\ell_{3..5}[n-1] + at\_\ell_{3..5}[n] + f[n] = 1 & \wedge \\
at\_\ell_{2..4}[1] + at\_\ell_{2..4}[n] + f[1] = 1 &
\end{array}
$$

The validity of the premises of rule RESPONSE for this choice has been verified using the theorem prover PVS. In Appendix A of [21] we present the program in the format accepted by TLPVS. Appendix B of [21] presents the TLPVS proof of accessibility according to the previously presented constructs. □

It is interesting to compare the proof of accessibility for the Dining Philosophers (program DINE-PHIL) to previous deductive proofs of the same property. Due to the recursiveness of the previous rule, such proofs would necessarily be based on an explicit induction, proceeding from process $P[n]$ down to lower indexed processes. Such a proof is presented, for example, in [17]. In view of this, it is fair to say that the proof presented here is the first mechanically assisted deductive proof of accessibility for program DINE-PHIL for arbitrary $n > 1$ number of processes.

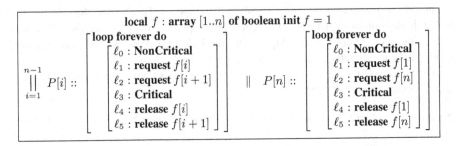

Alternative formal proofs of this property can be given, based on various abstraction methods. For example, the papers [12] and [9] show how to prove this property, using the *network invariant method* of [28].

4 Soundness of the Rule

We will now prove the soundness of rule RESPONSE for proving the response property $p \Longrightarrow \diamondsuit q$.

Claim 1. Rule RESPONSE *is sound. That is, if the premises of the rule are valid over an* CDS $\mathcal{D}$*, then so is the conclusion.*

Proof
Assume, for a proof by contradiction, that the premises of the rule are valid but the conclusion is not. This means that there exists a computation $\sigma : s_0, s_1, \ldots$ and a position $j \geq 0$ such that $s_j \models p$ and no state s_k, for $k \geq j$ satisfies q. With no loss of generality, we can take $j = 0$.

According to premises R1 and R2 and the assumption that no state satisfies q, any state s_r satisfies $p_i \wedge \varphi_i$ for some $i \in [1..n]$. Since there are only finitely many different i's, there exists a cutoff index $t \geq 0$ such that for every i and $r \geq t$, $s_r \models p_i \wedge \varphi_i$ iff σ contains infinitely many $(p_i \wedge \varphi_i)$-positions.

Consider position $r_1 = t$. Choose i_1 to be the index such that $s_{r_1} \models p_{i_1} \wedge \varphi_{i_1}$. According to R3 and the assumption that σ contains no q-position, then either φ_{i_1} holds at all positions $r \geq r_1$, or there exists a position $r_2 \geq r_1$ and an index i_2 such that $s_{r_2} \models p_{i_2} \wedge \varphi_{i_2}$ and $\Delta_{i_1}(s_{r_1}) \succ \Delta_{i_2}(s_{r_2})$. We will show that φ_{i_1} cannot hold at all positions $r \geq r_1$.

If φ_{i_1} holds continuously beyond r_1, then due to premise R4 so does $\neg q_{i_1}$. This violates the requirement of compassion $\langle p_{i_1}, q_{i_1} \rangle$, since $p_{i_1} \wedge \varphi_{i_1}$ holding at $r_1 \geq t$ implies that $p_{i_1} \wedge \varphi_{i_1}$ (and therefore p_{i_1}) holds at infinitely many positions.

We conclude that there exists a position $r_2 \geq r_1$ and an index i_2 such that $s_{r_2} \models p_{i_2} \wedge \varphi_{i_2}$ and $\Delta_{i_1}(s_{r_1}) \succ \Delta_{i_2}(s_{r_2})$.

We now repeat the argument previously applied to i_1 in order to conclude the existence of a position $r_3 \geq r_2$ and an index i_3 such that $s_{r_3} \models p_{i_3} \wedge \varphi_{i_3}$ and $\Delta_{i_2}(s_{r_2}) \succ \Delta_{i_3}(s_{r_3})$.

Continuing in this manner, we derive an infinite sequence such that

$$\Delta_{i_1}(s_{r_1}) \succ \Delta_{i_2}(s_{r_2}) \succ \Delta_{i_3}(s_{r_3}) \succ \cdots$$

which is impossible due to the well-foundedness of $\mathcal{A}$.

We conclude that there cannot exist a computation σ violating the response property $p \Longrightarrow \diamondsuit q$ if the premises of rule RESPONSE are all valid. ┘

This proof of soundness has been formalized and mechanically verified, using PVS. In Appendix C of [21] we present the PVS theory of a variant of the rule. Appendix D presents the proof of soundness of this variant.

5 Completeness of the Rule

In this section we consider the completeness of rule RESPONSE. Completeness means that, whenever a response property $p \Longrightarrow \diamondsuit q$ is valid over a CDS $\mathcal{D}$, there exist auxiliary constructs consisting of a list of compassion requirements $\langle p_1, q_1\rangle, \ldots, \langle p_n, q_n\rangle$ and associated lists of helpful assertions $\varphi_1, \ldots, \varphi_n$ and ranking functions $\Delta_1, \ldots, \Delta_n$ which, together, satisfy the premises of rule RESPONSE.

5.1 Finite-State Systems

We consider first the case of finite-state systems. Here, we actually present an algorithm that produces the auxiliary constructs for the case that the CDS $\mathcal{D}$ satisfies the response property $p \Longrightarrow \diamondsuit q$.

We assume that the reader is familiar with the rudiments of model checking. In particular, we will be using the following formulas as representing elementary model-cheking computations:

- For assertions p and q, the formula $\mathbf{E}(p\mathcal{S}q)$ captures the set of all states that are reachable from a q-state by a (ρ-)path all of whose states, except possibly the first, satisfy q. In this expression we use the *Since* temporal operator $\mathcal{S}$. A special case is $\mathbf{E}\diamondminus q = \mathbf{E}(1\,\mathcal{S}q)$ characterizing all states that are reachable from a q-state.
- The formula $\mathbf{E}(p\mathcal{U}q)$ captures the set of states which originate a path leading to a q-state, such that all the states in the path, except possibly the last, satisfy p.

Model Checking Response Under Compassion. Consider a finite-state CDS $\mathcal{D}$ and a response property $p \Longrightarrow \diamondsuit q$. The following algorithm can be used in order to model check whether the response property is valid over $\mathcal{D}$.

Algorithm $mc\_resp(\mathcal{D}, p, q)$
Let $X := \mathbf{E}((\neg q)\,\mathcal{S}\,(accessible_{\mathcal{D}} \wedge p \wedge \neg q))$
Fix(X)
  Let $X := X \wedge \bigwedge_{i=1}^{n}(\neg p_i \ \vee \ \mathbf{E}(X\,\mathcal{U}(X \wedge q_i)))$
end-Fix(X)
if $(X = 0)$ **then return** 1 **else return** 0

The algorithm contains several expressions using the model-checking formulas introduced above. The expression $accessible_{\mathcal{D}} = \mathbf{E}\diamondminus\Theta$ captures the set of all accessible states within CDS $\mathcal{D}$. The expression $\mathbf{E}((\neg q)\,\mathcal{S}\,(accessible_{\mathcal{D}} \wedge p \wedge \neg q))$ describes all states which are reachable from an accessible p-state by a finite q-free path. Finally, the expression $\mathbf{E}(X\,\mathcal{U}(X \wedge q_i))$ describes all states from which there exists an X-path within $\mathcal{D}$ leading to a q_i-state.

Thus, the algorithm places in X the set of all states which are reachable from an accessible p-state via a q-free path. Then it successively remove from X all p_i-states which do not initiate an X-path leading to a q_i-state.

Finally, the property is $\mathcal{D}$-valid iff the final value of X is empty.

Extracting the Auxiliary Constructs. We will now present an algorithm which extracts a deductive proof according to rule RESPONSE from a successful model checking verification of a response property $p \implies \diamondsuit q$. The algorithm can be viewed as an interleaving of algorithm *mc_resp* interspersed with steps that incrementally construct ranks $\{1, \ldots, f\}$ and, for each rank $i \in [1..f]$, identifies an associated compassion requirement $\langle p_i, q_i \rangle$, and a helpful assertion φ_i.

Algorithm *Extract_constructs*

0 : **Let** $X := \mathbf{E}((\neg q)\,\mathcal{S}\,(\mathit{accessible}_{\mathcal{D}} \wedge p \wedge \neg q))$
1 : **Let** $d := 0$
2 : $\mathbf{fix}(X)$
  3 : **For** $i \in [1...n]$ **do**
    4 : **Let** $\psi := X \;\wedge\; \neg\mathbf{E}(X\,\mathcal{U}(X \wedge q_i))$
    5 : **If** $\psi \wedge p_i \neq 0$ **then**
      6 : **Let** $d := d + 1$
      7 : **Let** $K_d := \psi \wedge p_i$
      8 : **Let** $\varphi_d := \mathbf{E}(\psi\,\mathcal{S}(\psi \wedge p_i))$
      9 : **Let** $F_d := (p_i, q_i)$
      10 : **Let** $\Delta_d := d$
      11 : **Let** $X := X \;\wedge\; \neg K_d$

In line 4 we compute in ψ the set of all X-states from which there exists no X-path leading to a q_i-state. In line 5 we check whether there exists a p_i-state belonging to ψ. If we find at least one such state then we have discovered a new assertion φ_d. In line 7 we place in K_d the set of states which form the kernel of the newly discovered assertion. In line 8 we define φ_d to consist of all the states reachable from a p_i-state by a ψ-path. In lines 9 and 10 we define F_d and Δ_d to be (p_i, q_i) and d, respectively. Finally, in line 11 we remove from X all states satisfying $\psi \wedge p_i = p_d \wedge \varphi_d = K_d$.

The following claim states the correctness of this extraction algorithm.

Claim 2. If the response property $p \implies \diamondsuit q$ is valid over CDS $\mathcal{D}$*, then Algorithm* Extract_constructs *produces auxiliary constructs which satisfy the premises of rule* RESPONSE.

Proof
Assume that the response property $p \implies \diamondsuit q$ is valid over CDS $\mathcal{D}$, and we successfully apply Algorithm *Extract_constructs*. Let us denote by $X_0 \supset X_1 \supset \cdots \supset X_{f-1} \supset X_f = 0$ the successive values assumed by variable X in the application of the algorithm. Note that we view the values of the variables appearing in the program as assertions (represented as BDD's) as well as the sets of state defined by these assertions. For example, $X_f = 0$ means that this assertion is equivalent to *false* and also that it denotes the empty set.

Note that X_0 denotes the set of *pending states*. These are the states that can be reached from an accessible p-state by a q-free path. Observe that the successor of an X_0-state is either another X_0-state, or is a state satisfying q. Also note that, for each $r = 1, \ldots, f$, $X_r = X_{r-1} - K_r = X_{r-1} - (p_r \wedge \varphi_r)$. We will consider in turn each of the premises and show that it holds for the extracted constructs.

Premise R1 claims that every (accessible) p-state s satisfies q or $p_j \wedge \varphi_j$, for some $j \in [1..f]$. Indeed, if s does not satisfy q, it belongs to X_0, and since all X_0-states are eliminated by the algorithm, s must belong to some $K_j = (p_j \wedge \varphi_j)$.

Premise R2 requires that every successor of an (accessible) state s that satisfies $p_i \wedge \varphi_i$ must satisfy q or $p_j \wedge \varphi_j$ for some $j \in [1..f]$. Obviously state s belongs to X_0. Let s_b be any successor of s. As previously observed, s_b must satisfy q or belong to X_0. In the latter case, by an argument similar to the one presented for premise R1, s_b must belong to $K_j = (p_j \wedge \varphi_j)$, for some $j \in [1..f]$.

Premise R3 considers an (accessible) state s_a that satisfies φ_i and its successor s_b. It requires showing that s_b satisfies q, or satisfies φ_i and has the same rank as s_a, or satisfies $p_j \wedge \varphi_j$ for some j and has a rank lower than that of s_a. Since, in our construction, every state that satisfies φ_r has a rank $\Delta_r = r$, this is equivalent to requiring that s_b must satisfy q or φ_i or $p_j \wedge \varphi_j$ for some $j < i$. The fact that s belongs to φ_i implies that s can be reached from a p_i-state by a X_{i-1}-path π such that no state in π initiates an X_{i-1}-path leading to a q_i-state. Consider s_b the successor of s_a. If s_b belongs to X_{i-1}, then it satisfies φ_i. Otherwise, s_b may satisfy q which is also acceptable by R3. The remaining option is that s_b belongs to $X_0 - X_{i-1}$. In this case, s_b must have been removed from X in some earlier stage and, therefore must satisfy $p_j \wedge \varphi_j$ for some $j < i$.

Finally, we consider premise R4 which requires showing that every accessible φ_i-state s cannot satisfy q_i. By the definition of φ_i, s can be reached from a p_i-state by a X_{i-1}-path π such that no state in π initiates an X_{i-1}-path leading to a q_i-state. Since s itself is a member of π, it cannot satisfy q_i. ■

5.2 The General Case

Next, we consider the general case of systems with potentially infinitely many states. Here, we can only claim relative completeness. Completeness is relative to assertional validity. That is, we prove that if the temporal conclusion is valid over a CDS, then there exist appropriate constructs expressible in an assertional language $\mathcal{L}$ such that the premises of the rule are assertionally valid ,i.e. state valid. Furthermore, as shown in [26], the language $\mathcal{L}$ should contain the expressive power of the μ-calculus over the underlying domain.

The approach we present here for establishing this relative completeness is based on a reduction of rule RESPONSE to the legacy rule F-WELL which, as shown in [15], is complete relative to assertional validity.

Claim 3. Rule RESPONSE *is complete relative to assertional validity for proving response properties of arbitrary* CDS*'s.*

Proof Sketch

Assume that the response property $p \Longrightarrow \Diamond q$ is valid over the CDS $\mathcal{D}$. We prove that there exist constructs satisfying the premises of rule RESPONSE. The proof is by induction on the number of compassion requirements in CDS $\mathcal{D}$. Let $\mathcal{D}$ contain C compassion requirements. Assume by induction that the theorem is correct for all systems with a number of compassion requirements that is smaller than C. We invoke the completeness theorem for rule F-WELL which has been established in [15]. This yields constructs which satisfy the premises of rule F-WELL. In particular, for each $i \in [1..n]$, premise C4 guarantees the validity of the entailment $\mathcal{D}^i \models (\varphi_i \implies \diamondsuit(p_i \vee \neg\varphi_i))$, where CDS $\mathcal{D}^i$ stands for $\mathcal{D}\setminus\{\langle p_i, q_i\rangle\}$, and is obtained by removing the compassion requirement $\langle p_i, q_i\rangle$ from $\mathcal{D}$.

Since each $\mathcal{D}^i$ has fewer compassion requirements than C, we apply the completeness claim of rule RESPONSE assumed by induction. This yields the identification of compassion requirements $F^i_1, \ldots, F^i_{n^i}$ and their associated helpful assertions φ^i_1, $\ldots, \varphi^i_{n^i}$ and ranking functions $\Delta^i_1, \ldots, \Delta^i_{n^i}$. We are now ready to identify the constructs necessary for the proof for CDS $\mathcal{D}$.

These consist of the compassion requirements $F_1, \ldots, F_n$ associated with the helpful assertions $\varphi_1, \ldots, \varphi_n$, and the ranking functions $(\Delta_1, 0), \ldots, (\Delta_n, 0)$. The ranking functions are obtained by lexicographic tuples formed by padding the rankings Δ_i on the right by zeros.

In addition, for each $i = 1, \ldots, n$, we add the compassion requirements $F^i_1, \ldots, F^i_{n^i}$ and their associated helpful assertions $\varphi_i \wedge \varphi^i_1, \ldots, \varphi_i \wedge \varphi^i_{n^i}$ and ranking functions $(\Delta_i, \Delta^i_1), \ldots, (\Delta_i, \Delta^i_{n^i})$. Note that the helpful assertions are obtained by conjuncting the original helpful assertions with φ_i, and the ranking functions are obtaining by a lexicographic tuple that prefixes the original ranking with Δ_i. ▪

The entire treatment in this paper focused on the special progress property of response. However, as shown in [11], once we know how to verify response properties, we can use the same methodology for proving an arbitrary LTL property. Let φ be an arbitrary LTL formula. In order to verify $\mathcal{D} \models \varphi$, it is sufficient to verify the response property $(\mathcal{D} \,|||\, T[\neg\varphi]) \models (\Theta \implies \diamondsuit\, 0)$, where $T[\neg\varphi]$ is a *temporal tester* whose computations are all state sequences that satisfy $\neg\varphi$. This tester is composed in parallel with $\mathcal{D}$ to form a CDS whose computations are all computations of $\mathcal{D}$ which violate φ.

6 Related Work

There has been much work dealing with deductive verification of liveness properties under fairness. However, only a small fraction of this work considered compassion and suggested direct approaches for dealing with this special kind of fairness. In most cases, fairness has been reduced away, often by coupling it with the temporal property to be proven. This is the standard treatment of multiple justice requirements, and certainly that of compassion, in model checking, in particular, the automata theoretic approach in which the property is described by a non-deterministic Büchi automata. We refer the reader to [27] and [4] for a description of this reduction method.

The key reference upon which this work improves is [15] which formulated the first complete rule for liveness under compassion. Much work has been done on the deductive verification of liveness properties inspired by the STeP project [14]. Representative contributions of this work is presented in [25] and [3]. However, very little attention has been paid in this work to the special case of compassion, which has always been considered a specially difficult case.

Much work has also been invested in methods for automatically finding ranking functions for proving liveness properties and termination. Representative contributions are

[8], [5], and [2]. Again, the context of this work when addressing systems with fairness has usually been that of justice.

Another approach to the verification of liveness properties can be based on abstraction. In this approach, we abstract a system into a finite-state system and verify the property on the abstract system. As pointed out in [10], the usual state abstraction if often inadequate in order to capture liveness properties. Therefore the paper introduces the notion of *ranking abstraction* which abstracts also changes in ranking. This concept has been further elaborated in [1]. Another solution to the problem has been proposed by Podelski and Rybalchenko who in [23] extend predicate abstraction ([24]) by employing predicates over program transitions, rather than states. In this way, the abstraction preserves the argument for proving termination (general liveness is handled by a reduction to fair termination). An elaboration of this work is [7], where Cook, Podelski, and Rybalchenko present a framework for verifying termination, which formalizes dual refinements – of transition predicate abstraction and of transition invariants [22]. The framework as presented in [7] lacks any notion of fairness. Therefore, [20,6] extend it to allow for fairness requirements.

Acknowledgements. We gratefully acknowledge the extensive and generous help of Tamarah Aarons, the designer of TLPVS who guided us very patiently through the growing pain of extending the system, and teaching PVS more temporal logic. We are very grateful to Lenore Zuck and Ittai Balaban for their continuous support of the development of the ideas that went into this paper. In particular, our joint work on extraction of ranking function has been very instrumental in the completeness proof of Section 5. In fact, the whole idea of the paper came out of a question asked by Dennis Dams at the defense of the thesis of Ittai Balaban. We thank Lenore, Dennis and Ittai for the insights contributed during extended discussions.

References

1. Balaban, I., Pnueli, A., Zuck, L.D.: Modular ranking abstraction. Int. J. Found. Comput. Sci. 18(1), 5–44 (2007)
2. Bradley, A.R., Manna, Z., Sipma, H.B.: Linear ranking with reachability. In: Etessami, K., Rajamani, S.K. (eds.) CAV 2005. LNCS, vol. 3576, pp. 491–504. Springer, Heidelberg (2005)
3. Browne, I., Manna, Z., Sipma, H.: Generalized verification diagrams. In: Thiagarajan, P.S. (ed.) FSTTCS 1995. LNCS, vol. 1026, pp. 484–498. Springer, Heidelberg (1995)
4. Clarke, E., Grumberg, O., Peled, D.: Model Checking. MIT Press, Cambridge (2000)
5. Colon, M., Sipma, H.: Practical methods for proving program termination. In: Brinksma, E., Larsen, K.G. (eds.) CAV 2002. LNCS, vol. 2404, pp. 442–454. Springer, Heidelberg (2002)
6. Cook, B., Gotsman, A., Podelski, A., Rybalchenko, A., Vardi, M.Y.: Proving that programs eventually do something good. In: Proc. 34th ACM Symp. Princ. of Prog. Lang., pp. 265–276 (2007)
7. Cook, B., Podelski, A., Rybalchenko, A.: Abstraction refinement for termination. In: Hankin, C., Siveroni, I. (eds.) SAS 2005. LNCS, vol. 3672, pp. 87–101. Springer, Heidelberg (2005)
8. Dams, D., Gerth, R., Grumberg, O.: A heuristic for the automatic generation of ranking functions. In: Gopalakrishnan, G. (ed.) Workshop on Advances in Verification, pp. 1–8 (2000)

9. Kesten, Y., Piterman, N., Pnueli, A.: Bridging the gap between fair simulation and trace inclusion. Inf. and Comp. 200(1), 35–61 (2005)
10. Kesten, Y., Pnueli, A.: Verification by finitary abstraction. Information and Computation, a special issue on Compositionality 163(1), 203–243 (2000)
11. Kesten, Y., Pnueli, A.: A Compositional Approach to CTL* Verification. Theor. Comp. Sci. 331(2–3), 397–428 (2005)
12. Kesten, Y., Pnueli, A., Shahar, E., Zuck, L.D.: Network invariants in action. In: Brim, L., Jančar, P., Křetínský, M., Kucera, A. (eds.) CONCUR 2002. LNCS, vol. 2421, pp. 101–115. Springer, Heidelberg (2002)
13. Lamport, L.: Proving the correctness of multiprocess programs. Trans. Soft. Eng. 3, 125–143 (1977)
14. Manna, Z., et al.: STeP: The Stanford Temporal Prover. Technical Report STAN-CS-TR-94-1518, Dept. of Comp. Sci., Stanford University, Stanford, California (1994)
15. Manna, Z., Pnueli, A.: Completing the temporal picture. Theor. Comp. Sci. 83(1), 97–130 (1991)
16. Manna, Z., Pnueli, A.: Temporal Verification of Reactive Systems: Safety. Springer, New York (1995)
17. Manna, Z., Pnueli, A.: Temporal verification of reactive systems: Progress. Draft manuscript (1996), http://theory.stanford.edu/~zm/tvors3.html
18. Owre, S., et al.: PVS System Guide. Menlo Park, CA, 2001
19. Pnueli, A., Arons, T.: TLPVS: A PVS-Based LTL Verification System. In: Dershowitz, N. (ed.) Verification: Theory and Practice. LNCS, vol. 2772, pp. 598–625. Springer, Heidelberg (2004)
20. Pnueli, A., Podelski, A., Rybalchenko, A.: Separating fairness and well-foundedness for the analysis of fair discrete systems. In: Halbwachs, N., Zuck, L.D. (eds.) TACAS 2005. LNCS, vol. 3440, pp. 124–139. Springer, Heidelberg (2005)
21. Pnueli, A., Sa'ar, Y.: All you need is compassion. Research Report, Dept. of Computer Science, New York University Technical Report (October 2007), http://www.cs.nyu.edu/acsys/pubs/permanent/all-you-need-is-compassion.pdf
22. Podelski, A., Rybalchenko, A.: Transition invariants. In: LICS 2004, pp. 32–41 (2004)
23. Podelski, A., Rybalchenko, A.: Transition predicate abstraction and fair termination. In: POPL 2005, pp. 132–144 (2005)
24. Graf, S., Saidi, H.: Construction of abstract state graphs with PVS. In: Grumberg, O. (ed.) CAV 1997. LNCS, vol. 1254, pp. 72–83. Springer, Heidelberg (1997)
25. Sipma, H.B., Uribe, T.E., Manna, Z.: Deductive model checking. Formal Methods in System Design 15(1), 49–74 (1999)
26. Stomp, F.A., de Roever, W.-P., Gerth, R.T.: The μ-calculus as an assertion language for fairness arguments. Inf. and Comp. 82, 278–322 (1989)
27. Vardi, M.Y., Wolper, P.: An automata-theoretic approach to automatic program verification. In: LICS 1986, pp. 332–344 (1986)
28. Wolper, P., Lovinfosse, V.: Verifying properties of large sets of processes with network invariants. In: Sifakis, J. (ed.) CAV 1989. LNCS, vol. 407, pp. 68–80. Springer, Heidelberg (1990)

A Forward-Backward Abstraction Refinement Algorithm

Francesco Ranzato, Olivia Rossi Doria, and Francesco Tapparo

Dipartimento di Matematica Pura ed Applicata
Università di Padova, Italy

Abstract. Abstraction refinement-based model checking has become a standard approach for efficiently verifying safety properties of hardware/software systems. Abstraction refinement algorithms can be guided by counterexamples generated from abstract transition systems or by fixpoints computed in abstract domains. Cousot, Ganty and Raskin recently put forward a new fixpoint-guided abstraction refinement algorithm that is based on standard abstract interpretation and improves the state-of-the-art, also for counterexample-driven methods. This work presents a new fixpoint-guided abstraction refinement algorithm that enhances the Cousot-Ganty-Raskin's procedure. Our algorithm is based on three main ideas: (1) within each abstraction refinement step, we perform multiple forward-backward abstract state space traversals; (2) our abstraction is a disjunctive abstract domain that is used both as an overapproximation and an underapproximation; (3) we maintain and iteratively refine an overapproximation M of the set of states that belong to some minimal (i.e. shortest) counterexample to the given safety property so that each abstract state space traversal is limited to the states in M.

1 Introduction

Abstraction techniques are widely used in model checking to blur some properties of the concrete model and then to design a reduced abstract model where to run the verification algorithm [3]. Abstraction provides a successful solution to the state-explosion problem that arises in model checking systems with parallel components [4]. CounterExample-Guided Abstraction Refinement (CEGAR), pionereed by Clarke et al. [5], is become the standard methodology for applying abstraction to model checking. The basic idea of the CEGAR approach is as follows: if the abstract model checker return "YES" then the system satisfies the property; otherwise the abstract model checker returns an abstract counterexample to the property, that is checked to determine whether it corresponds to a real counterexample or not; it it does then return "NO" otherwise refine the abstract model in order to remove that spurious counterexample. Many different algorithms that implement the CEGAR approach have been suggested. Most CEGAR-based model checkers — like BLAST [16,17], MAGIC [5,2] and SLAM [1] — deal with counterexamples that are paths of abstract states, i.e. paths in an abstract transition system defined by an abstract state space and an abstract transition relation. Most often, model checkers aim at verifying so-called safety properties, i.e., states that can be reached from an initial state are always safe. Hence, safety verification consists in automatically proving that systems cannot go wrong.

F. Logozzo et al. (Eds.): VMCAI 2008, LNCS 4905, pp. 248–262, 2008.

Recently, Cousot, Ganty and Raskin [10] (more details are given by the PhD thesis [12]) put forward a new fixpoint-guided abstraction refinement algorithm, here called CGR, for checking safety properties. The CGR algorithm is based on a number of interesting features. (1) CGR maintains and refines generic abstract domains that are defined within the standard abstract interpretation framework, as opposed to most other CEGAR-based algorithms that consider as abstract models a partition of the state space. (2) The refinement of the current abstract domain A is driven by the abstract fixpoint computed within A and not by a path-based counterexample. (3) CGR computes overapproximations of both least and greatest fixpoints, and these two analyses are made iteratively synergic since the current abstract fixpoint computation is limited by the abstract value provided by the previous abstract fixpoint computation.

We isolated a number of examples where the behavior of the CGR algorithm could be improved, in particular where one could abstractly conclude that the system is safe or unsafe without resorting to abstraction refinements. This work puts forward a new fixpoint-guided abstraction refinement algorithm for safety verification, called FBAR (Forward-Backward Abstraction Refinement), that is designed as an enhancement of the CGR procedure that integrates some new ideas.

(i) FBAR maintains and refines a disjunctive abstract domain μ that overapproximates any set S of states by $\mu(S) \supseteq S$. While a generic abstract domain can be viewed as a set of subsets of states that is closed under arbitrary intersections, a disjunctive abstract domain must also be closed under arbitrary unions. The advantage of dealing with a disjunctive abstraction μ is given by the fact that μ can be simultaneously used both as an over- and under-approximating abstraction. As an additional advantage, it turns out that disjunctive abstractions can be efficiently represented and refined, as shown in [20].

(ii) FBAR computes and maintains an overapproximation M of the set of states that occur in some *minimal* safety counterexample. A safety counterexample is simply a path from an initial state to an unsafe state. However, counterexamples may be redundant, namely may contain shorter sub-counterexamples. A counterexample is thus called minimal when it cannot be reduced. It can be therefore helpful to focus on minimal counterexamples rather than on generic counterexamples. In FBAR, abstract fixpoints are always computed within the overapproximation M and other than being used for safety checking they are also used for refining M.

(iii) Each abstraction refinement step in FBAR consists of two loops that check whether the system can be proved safe/unsafe by using the current abstraction. The safety loop is based on a combined forward-backward abstract exploration of the portion of the state space limited by M. This combined forward-backward abstract computation was first introduced by Cousot [6]. The unsafety loop relies on an iterated combination of two abstract fixpoints: the first one is an overapproximation of the states in M that are globally safe and is computed by using the current abstraction μ as an overapproximation; the second one is instead an underapproximation of the states in M that can reach an unsafe state and is computed by viewing μ as an underapproximating abstraction.

We prove that FBAR is a correct algorithm for safety verification and that, analogously to CGR, it terminates when the concrete domain satisfies the descending chain condition. We formally compare FBAR and CGR by showing that FBAR improves CGR in the following sense: if CGR terminates on a given disjunctive abstraction μ with no refinement then FBAR also terminates on μ, while the converse is not true.

Related Work. We discussed above the relationship with the CGR algorithm in [10]. Gulavani and Rajamani [15] also describe a fixpoint-driven abstraction refinement algorithm for safety verification. This algorithm relies on using widening operators during abstract fixpoint computations. When the abstract fixpoint is inconclusive, this algorithm does not refine the abstract domain but determines which iteration of the abstract fixpoint computation was responsible of the loss of precision so that widening is replaced with a concrete union and the abstract computation is re-started from that iteration. Manevich et al. [18] put forward an abstraction refinement algorithm for safety verification that runs over disjunctive abstract domains. However, this algorithm does not compute abstract fixpoints but instead computes paths of abstract values so that the abstraction refinement is based on counterexamples defined as sequences of abstract values.

2 Background

Notation and Orders. Let Σ be any set. If $S \subseteq \Sigma$ then $\neg S$ denotes the complement set $\Sigma \smallsetminus S$ when Σ is clear from the context. A set S of one-digit integers is often written in a compact form without brackets and commas like $S = 1357$ that stands for $\{1, 3, 5, 7\}$. $\mathrm{Part}(\Sigma)$ denotes the set of partitions of Σ. If $R \subseteq \Sigma \times \Sigma$ is any relation then $R^* \subseteq \Sigma \times \Sigma$ denotes the reflexive and transitive closure of R. Posets and complete lattices are denoted by $P_\leq$ where $\leq$ is the partial order. A function f between complete lattices is additive (co-additive) when f preserves least upper (greatest lower) bounds. If $f : P \to P$ then $\mathrm{lfp}(f)$ and $\mathrm{gfp}(f)$ denote, resp., the least and greatest fixpoints of f, when they exist.

Abstract Domains. In standard Cousot and Cousot's abstract interpretation, abstract domains (or abstractions) can be equivalently specified either by Galois connections/insertions through α/γ abstraction/concretization maps or by upper closure operators (uco's) [7]. These two approaches are equivalent, modulo isomorphic representations of domain's objects. The closure operator approach has the advantage of being independent from the representation of domain's objects and is therefore appropriate for reasoning on abstract domains independently from their representation. Given a state space Σ, the complete lattice $\wp(\Sigma)_\subseteq$, i.e. the powerset of Σ ordered by the subset relation, plays the role of concrete domain. Let us recall that an operator $\mu : \wp(\Sigma) \to \wp(\Sigma)$ is a uco on $\wp(\Sigma)$, that is an overapproximating abstract domain of $\wp(\Sigma)$, when μ is monotone, idempotent and extensive (i.e., overapproximating: $X \subseteq \mu(X)$). Each closure μ is uniquely determined by its image $\mathrm{img}(\mu) = \{\mu(X) \in \wp(\Sigma) \mid X \in \wp(\Sigma))\}$ as follows: for any $X \subseteq \Sigma$, $\mu(X) = \cap\{Y \in \mathrm{img}(\mu) \mid X \subseteq Y\}$. On the other hand, a set of subsets $A \subseteq \wp(\Sigma)$ is the image of some closure on $\wp(\Sigma)$ iff A is closed under arbitrary intersections, i.e. $A = \mathrm{Cl}_\cap(A) \stackrel{\mathrm{def}}{=} \{\cap S \mid S \subseteq A\}$ (in particular, note that $\mathrm{Cl}_\cap(A)$ always contains $\Sigma = \cap\varnothing$). This makes clear that an abstract domain μ guarantees that for any concrete set of states X, $\mu(X)$ is the best (i.e., more precise) overapproximation of X

in μ. We denote by $\mathrm{Abs}(\Sigma)$ the set of abstract domains of $\wp(\Sigma)_{\subseteq}$. Capital letters like $A, A' \in \mathrm{Abs}(\Sigma)$ are sometimes used for denoting abstract domains. By a slight abuse of notation, a given abstract domain $A \in \mathrm{Abs}(\Sigma)$ can be viewed and used both as a set of subsets of Σ and as an operator on $\wp(\Sigma)$ when the context allows us to disambiguate this use. If $A_1, A_2 \in \mathrm{Abs}(\Sigma)$ then A_1 is more precise than (or is a refinement of) A_2 when $A_1 \supseteq A_2$. $\mathrm{Abs}(\Sigma)_{\supseteq}$ is called the (complete) lattice of abstract domains of $\wp(\Sigma)$.

Let $f : \wp(\Sigma) \to \wp(\Sigma)$ be a concrete semantic function, like a predicate transformer, and, given an abstraction $\mu \in \mathrm{Abs}(\Sigma)$, let $f^\sharp : \mu \to \mu$ be a corresponding abstract function on μ. Then, $f^\sharp$ is a correct approximation of f in μ when for any $X \in \wp(\Sigma)$, $\mu(f(X)) \subseteq f^\sharp(\mu(X))$. The abstract function $f^\mu : \mu \to \mu$ defined as $f^\mu \stackrel{\text{def}}{=} \mu \circ f$ is called the best correct approximation of f in μ because for any correct approximation $f^\sharp$, for any $X \in \mu$, $f^\mu(X) \subseteq f^\sharp(X)$ always holds.

Disjunctive Abstract Domains. An abstract domain $\mu \in \mathrm{Abs}(\wp(\Sigma))$ is disjunctive (or additive or a powerset abstract domain) when μ is additive, i.e. μ preserves arbitrary unions. This happens exactly when the image $\mathrm{img}(\mu)$ is closed under arbitrary unions, i.e., $\mu = \mathrm{Cl}_{\cup}(\mu) \stackrel{\text{def}}{=} \{\cup S \mid S \subseteq \mu\}$ (in particular, note that $\mathrm{Cl}_{\cup}(\mu)$ always contains $\varnothing = \cup\varnothing$). Hence, a disjunctive abstract domain is a set of subsets of states that is closed under both arbitrary intersections and unions. The intuition is that a disjunctive abstract domain does not loose precision in approximating concrete set unions. We denote by $\mathrm{dAbs}(\wp(\Sigma)) \subseteq \mathrm{Abs}(\wp(\Sigma))$ the set of disjunctive abstract domains. A disjunctive abstraction μ can be specified just by defining how any singleton $\{x\} \subseteq \Sigma$ is approximated by $\mu(\{x\})$, because the approximation of a generic subset $X \subseteq \Sigma$ can be obtained through set unions as $\mu(X) = \cup_{x \in X}\mu(\{x\})$. We exploit this property for representing disjunctive abstractions through diagrams. As an example, the following diagram:

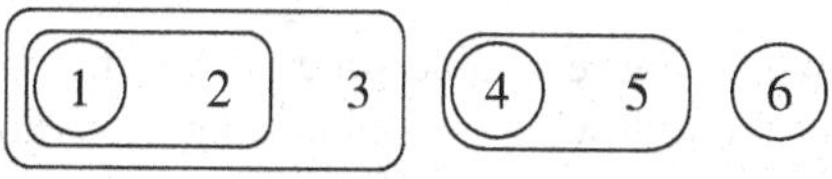

denotes the disjunctive abstract domain μ that is determined by the following behaviour on singletons: $\mu(1) = 1$, $\mu(2) = 12$, $\mu(3) = 123$, $\mu(4) = 4$, $\mu(5) = 45$, $\mu(6) = 6$, so that μ is the closure under unions of the set $\{1, 12, 123, 4, 45, 6\}$.

Underapproximating Abstract Domains. It turns out that a disjunctive abstract domain $\mu \in \mathrm{Abs}(\wp(\Sigma)_{\subseteq})$ can be also viewed as an underapproximating abstract domain, namely an abstraction of the concrete domain $\wp(\Sigma)_{\supseteq}$ where the approximation order is reversed. Formally, this is specified by the closure $\widetilde{\mu} \in \mathrm{Abs}(\wp(\Sigma)_{\supseteq})$ that is defined as the adjoint of μ as follows: for any $X \subseteq \Sigma$, $\widetilde{\mu}(X) \stackrel{\text{def}}{=} \cup\{Y \subseteq \Sigma \mid Y = \mu(Y) \subseteq X\}$. An underapproximating abstraction is thus determined by the behaviour on the sets $\neg x \stackrel{\text{def}}{=} \Sigma \smallsetminus \{x\}$ because, for any $X \subseteq \Sigma$, $\widetilde{\mu}(X) = \cap_{x \notin X}\widetilde{\mu}(\neg x)$. For example, for the above disjunctive abstraction μ, we have that $\widetilde{\mu}(\neg 1) = 456$, $\widetilde{\mu}(\neg 2) = 1456$, $\widetilde{\mu}(\neg 3) = 12456$, $\widetilde{\mu}(\neg 4) = 1236$, $\widetilde{\mu}(\neg 5) = 12346$ and $\widetilde{\mu}(\neg 6) = 12345$.

Transition Systems. A transition system $\mathcal{T} = (\Sigma, R)$ consists of a set Σ of states and a transition relation $R \subseteq \Sigma \times \Sigma$, that is also denoted in infix notation by $\to$. As usual in model checking, we assume that the relation R is total, i.e., for any $s \in \Sigma$ there exists some $t \in \Sigma$ such that $s \rightarrow t$. The set of finite and infinite paths in $\mathcal{T}$ is denoted by $\mathrm{Path}(\mathcal{T})$. For any $\Pi \subseteq \mathrm{Path}(\mathcal{T})$, $\mathrm{states}(\Pi) \subseteq \Sigma$ denotes the set of states that occur in some path $\pi \in \Pi$. If $\pi \in \mathrm{Path}(\mathcal{T})$ is finite then $\mathrm{first}(\pi), \mathrm{last}(\pi) \in \Sigma$ denote, resp., the first and last states of π.

Standard predicate transformers $\mathrm{pre}, \widetilde{\mathrm{pre}}, \mathrm{post}, \widetilde{\mathrm{post}} : \wp(\Sigma) \rightarrow \wp(\Sigma)$ are defined as usual:

- $\mathrm{pre}(X) \stackrel{\text{def}}{=} \{a \in \Sigma \mid \exists b \in X.\ a \rightarrow b\}$;
- $\mathrm{post}(X) \stackrel{\text{def}}{=} \{b \in \Sigma \mid \exists a \in X.\ a \rightarrow b\}$;
- $\widetilde{\mathrm{pre}}(X) \stackrel{\text{def}}{=} \neg\,\mathrm{pre}(\neg X) = \{a \in \Sigma \mid \forall b.\ a \rightarrow b \;\Rightarrow\; b \in X\}$;
- $\widetilde{\mathrm{post}}(X) \stackrel{\text{def}}{=} \neg\,\mathrm{post}(\neg X) = \{b \in \Sigma \mid \forall a.\ a \rightarrow b \;\Rightarrow\; a \in X\}$.

Let us remark that pre and post are additive while $\widetilde{\mathrm{pre}}$ and $\widetilde{\mathrm{post}}$ are co-additive. We use the notation $\mathrm{pre}^*, \widetilde{\mathrm{pre}}^*, \mathrm{post}^*, \widetilde{\mathrm{post}}^*$ when the reflexive-transitive closure R^* is considered instead of R. Let us recall the following standard fixpoint characterizations:

$$\mathrm{pre}^*(X) = \mathrm{lfp}(\lambda Z.X \cup \mathrm{pre}(Z)); \qquad \mathrm{post}^*(X) = \mathrm{lfp}(\lambda Z.X \cup \mathrm{post}(Z));$$
$$\widetilde{\mathrm{pre}}^*(X) = \mathrm{gfp}(\lambda Z.X \cap \widetilde{\mathrm{pre}}(Z)); \qquad \widetilde{\mathrm{post}}^*(X) = \mathrm{gfp}(\lambda Z.X \cap \widetilde{\mathrm{post}}(Z)).$$

Safety Verification Problems. Let $\mathit{Init} \subseteq \Sigma$ be a set of initial states and $\mathit{Safe} \subseteq \Sigma$ a set of safe states. We denote by $\mathit{NInit} \stackrel{\text{def}}{=} \neg\mathit{Init}$ the set of noninitial states and by $\mathit{Bad} = \neg\mathit{Safe}$ the set of bad (i.e. unsafe) states. The set of reachable states is $\mathrm{post}^*(\mathit{Init})$. The set of states that are globally safe is $\widetilde{\mathrm{pre}}^*(\mathit{Safe})$. The set of states that can reach a bad state is $\mathrm{pre}^*(\mathit{Bad})$. The set of states that can be reached only from noninitial states is $\widetilde{\mathrm{post}}^*(\mathit{NInit})$. Note that $\mathrm{pre}^*(\mathit{Bad}) = \neg\widetilde{\mathrm{pre}}^*(\mathit{Safe})$ and $\widetilde{\mathrm{post}}^*(\mathit{NInit}) = \neg\,\mathrm{post}^*(\mathit{Init})$.

A system $\mathcal{T}$ is safe when any reachable state is safe, i.e. $\mathrm{post}^*(\mathit{Init}) \subseteq \mathit{Safe}$, or, equivalently, when one of the following equivalent conditions holds: $\mathit{Init} \subseteq \widetilde{\mathrm{pre}}^*(\mathit{Safe})$ $\Leftrightarrow \mathrm{pre}^*(\mathit{Bad}) \subseteq \mathit{NInit} \Leftrightarrow \mathit{Bad} \subseteq \widetilde{\mathrm{post}}^*(\mathit{NInit})$. A safety verification problem is then specified by a transition system $\mathcal{T} = \langle \Sigma, R, \mathit{Init}, \mathit{Safe} \rangle$ that also defines initial and safe states and consists in checking whether $\mathcal{T}$ is safe (OK) or not (KO).

3 Cousot-Ganty-Raskin's Algorithm

The Cousot-Ganty-Raskin's algorithm, here denoted by CGR, is recalled in Fig. 1. In each abstraction refinement step $i \geq 0$, CGR abstractly computes two overapproximations R_i and S_i of least/greatest fixpoints and a concrete value Z_{i+1} that is added to the current abstract domain μ_i for the purpose of refining it. The correctness of CGR follows from the following three main invariants: for all $i \geq 0$: (1) $Z_{i+1} \subseteq S_i \subseteq R_i \subseteq Z_i$; (2) if the system is safe then $\mathrm{post}^*(\mathit{Init}) \subseteq R_i$, i.e. R_i overapproximates the reachable states; (3) $R_i \subseteq \widetilde{\mathrm{pre}}^i(\mathit{Safe})$, i.e. R_i underapproximates the states that remain inside Safe along paths of length $\leq i$.

CGR admits a dual version, denoted by $\mathrm{CGR}^{\leftarrow}$, where the transition relation is reversed, namely where R is replaced by R^{-1}, Init by Bad and Safe by NInit (so that

Data: *Init* initial states, *Safe* safe states such that $\mathit{Init} \subseteq \mathit{Safe}$
Data: $\mu_0 \in \mathrm{uco}(\wp(\Sigma))$ initial abstract domain such that $\mathit{Safe} \in \mu_0$
begin
  $Z_0 := \mathit{Safe}$;
  for $i := 0, 1, 2, \ldots$ **do**
    $R_i := \mathrm{lfp}(\lambda X.\mu_i(Z_i \cap (\mathit{Init} \cup \mathrm{post}(X))))$;
    if $\mu_i(\mathit{Init} \cup \mathrm{post}(R_i)) \subseteq Z_i$ **then return** OK;
    else
      $S_i := \mathrm{gfp}(\lambda X.\mu_i(R_i \cap \widetilde{\mathrm{pre}}(X)))$;
      if $\mu_i(\mathit{Init}) \not\subseteq S_i$ **then return** KO;
      else
        $Z_{i+1} := S_i \cap \widetilde{\mathrm{pre}}(S_i)$;
        $\mu_{i+1} := \mathrm{Cl}_{\cap}(\mu_i \cup \{Z_{i+1}\})$;
end

Fig. 1. CGR Algorithm

post and $\widetilde{\mathrm{pre}}$ become, respectively, pre and $\widetilde{\mathrm{post}}$). Thus, while CGR performs a forward abstract exploration of the state space through post, $\mathrm{CGR}^{\leftarrow}$ proceeds instead backward through pre.

3.1 Where CGR Could Be Improved

We isolated a number of examples where the CGR algorithm could be improved.

Example 3.1. Let us consider the safety problem represented by the following diagram that also specifies a disjunctive abstract domain $\mu_0 \in \mathrm{Abs}(\wp(\Sigma))$.

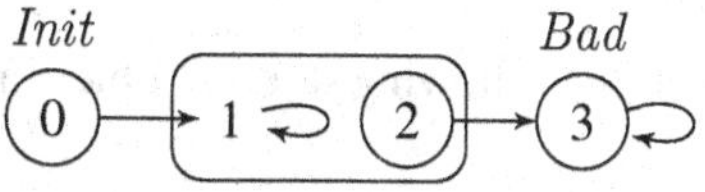

CGR computes the following sequence: $Z_0 = 012$, $R_0 = 012$, $S_0 = 012$, $Z_1 = 01$, $R_1 = 01$ and then outputs OK. Let us observe that $S_0 = 012$ because $\mu_0(R_0 \cap \widetilde{\mathrm{pre}}(R_0)) = \mu_0(01) = 012$. Thus, CGR needs to refine the abstraction μ_0 by adding the singleton $\{1\}$ to μ_0. However, one could abstractly conclude that the system is safe already through the abstraction μ_0. In fact, one could abstractly explore backward the state space by computing the following fixpoint: $T_0 = \mathrm{lfp}(\lambda X.\mu_0(\mathit{NInit} \cap (\mathit{Bad} \cup \mathrm{pre}(X))))$. Thus, $T_0 = 23$ and since $\mu_0(\mathit{Bad} \cup \mathrm{pre}(T_0)) \subseteq T_0$ one can conclude that the system is safe. Thus, the dual algorithm $\mathrm{CGR}^{\leftarrow}$ is able to conclude that the system is safe with no abstraction refinement.

Along the same lines, it turns out that CGR even does not terminate when applied to the following infinite state system, although the abstraction is finite, while a backward abstract exploration would allow to conclude that the system is safe.

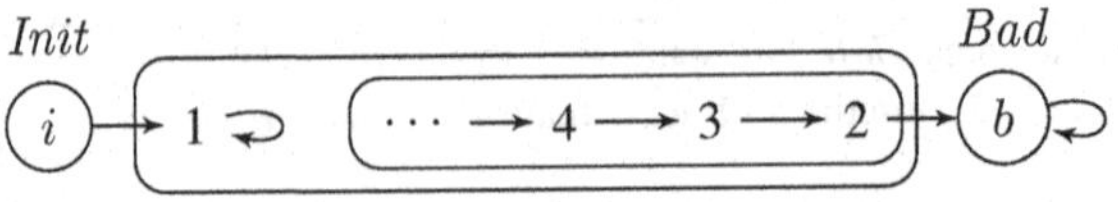

In fact, CGR does not terminate because it would compute the following infinite sequence: $Z_0 = i \cup 12345...$, $R_0 = i \cup 12345...$, $S_0 = i \cup 12345...$, $Z_1 = i \cup 1345...$, $R_1 = i \cup 1345...$, $S_1 = i \cup 1345...$, $Z_2 = i \cup 145....$ Instead, one could proceed backward by computing the following abstract fixpoint: $T_0 = \mathrm{lfp}(\lambda X.\mu_0(\mathit{NInit} \cap (\mathit{Bad} \cup \mathrm{pre}(X)))) = b \cup 2345....$ Hence, since $\mu_0(\mathit{Bad} \cup \mathrm{pre}(T_0)) \subseteq T_0$ we can conclude that the system is safe. Thus, here again, $\mathrm{CGR}^{\leftarrow}$ is able to infer that the system is safe with no abstraction refinement.

Let us consider now the following infinite state system.

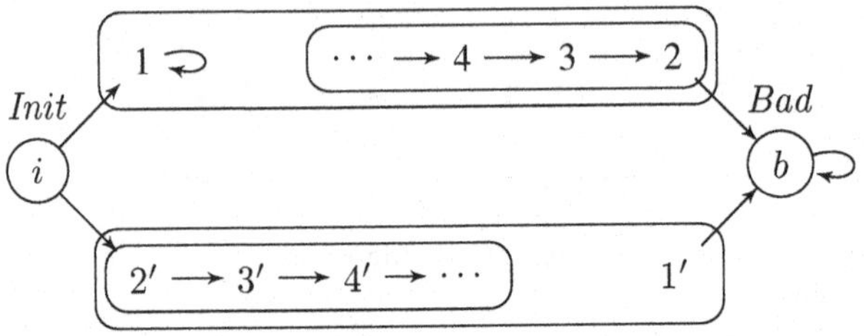

In this case, it turns out that neither CGR nor $\mathrm{CGR}^{\leftarrow}$ terminate. In fact, similarly to the above examples, it is simple to check that both CGR and $\mathrm{CGR}^{\leftarrow}$ would compute infinite sequences of abstract values. However, it is still possible to derive that the system is safe with no abstraction refinement. In fact, we can first compute the following forward abstract fixpoint $U_0 = \mathrm{lfp}(\lambda X.\mu_0(\mathit{Safe} \cap (\mathit{Init} \cup \mathrm{post}(X)))) = i \cup 1234... \cup 2'3'4'....$ Then, we can explore backward starting from Bad but remaining inside $U_0 \cup \mathit{Bad}$, namely we compute the following backward abstract fixpoint $V_0 = \mathrm{lfp}(\lambda X.\mu_0((U_0 \cup \mathit{Bad}) \cap (\mathit{Bad} \cup \mathrm{pre}(X)))) = b \cup 234....$ We can now conclude that the system is safe because $\mu_0(\mathit{Bad} \cup \mathrm{pre}(V_0)) \subseteq V_0$. □

Example 3.2. Let us consider the following safety problem and disjunctive abstract domain $\mu_0 \in \mathrm{Abs}(\wp(\Sigma))$.

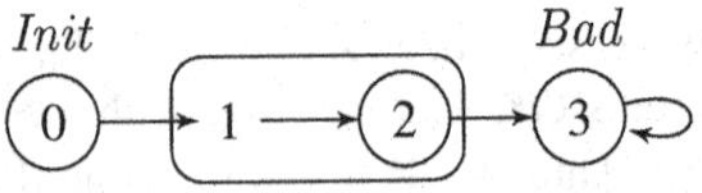

In this case, CGR computes the following sequence: $Z_0 = 012$, $R_0 = 012$, $S_0 = 012$, $Z_1 = 01$, $R_1 = 01$, $S_1 = \varnothing$ and then outputs KO. Thus, CGR needs to refine the abstraction μ_0 by adding the singleton $\{1\}$ to μ_0. However, one could abstractly conclude that the system is not safe already through the abstraction μ_0 by viewing μ_0 as an underapproximating abstraction, i.e. by considering the underapproximating abstraction $\widetilde{\mu}_0$. In fact, one could abstractly explore the state space backward by computing the following abstract fixpoint: $T_0 = \mathrm{lfp}(\lambda X.\widetilde{\mu}_0(\mathit{Bad} \cup \mathrm{pre}(X))) = 0123$. Since T_0 is an underapproximation of the set of states that can reach a bad state and T_0 contains some initial state we can conclude that the system is unsafe. □

These examples suggested us to design an abstraction refinement algorithm that improves the CGR algorithm by integrating a combined forward-backward abstract exploration of the state space and by using disjunctive abstract domains that can be exploited both as overapproximating and underapproximating abstractions.

4 Restricted Predicate Transformers

Let $M \subseteq \Sigma$ be a fixed set of states of interest. In our context, M will play the role of a portion of the state space that limits the abstract search space of our abstraction refinement algorithm. Let us define the following *restricted* (to the states in M) predicate transformers $\mathrm{pre}_M, \mathrm{post}_M, \widetilde{\mathrm{pre}}_M, \widetilde{\mathrm{post}}_M : \wp(\Sigma) \to \wp(\Sigma)$ as follows:

- $\mathrm{pre}_M(X) \stackrel{\text{def}}{=} M \cap \mathrm{pre}(M \cap X)$;
- $\mathrm{post}_M(X) \stackrel{\text{def}}{=} M \cap \mathrm{post}(M \cap X)$;
- $\widetilde{\mathrm{pre}}_M(X) \stackrel{\text{def}}{=} \neg\,\mathrm{pre}_M(\neg X) = \neg M \cup \widetilde{\mathrm{pre}}(\neg M \cup X)$ $= \{a \in \Sigma \mid \forall b.\, (a \to b \;\&\; a, b \in M) \Rightarrow b \in X\}$;
- $\widetilde{\mathrm{post}}_M(X) \stackrel{\text{def}}{=} \neg\,\mathrm{post}_M(\neg X) = \neg M \cup \widetilde{\mathrm{post}}(\neg M \cup X)$ $= \{b \in \Sigma \mid \forall a.\, (a \to b \;\&\; a, b \in M) \Rightarrow a \in X\}$.

Thus, M-restricted predicate transformers only consider states that belong to M. In fact, if $\mathrm{pre}_M, \mathrm{post}_M, \widetilde{\mathrm{pre}}_M, \widetilde{\mathrm{post}}_M$ are viewed as mappings $\wp(M) \to \wp(M)$ — i.e., both the argument and the image of the M-restricted transformers are taken as subsets of M — then they coincide with the corresponding standard predicate transformers on the M-restricted transition system $\mathcal{T}_{/M} = \langle M, R_{/M}\rangle$. Let us remark that, analogously to the unrestricted case, pre_M, post_M are additive functions and $\widetilde{\mathrm{pre}}_M$, $\widetilde{\mathrm{post}}_M$ are co-additive functions. We also consider the following fixpoint definitions:

- $\mathrm{pre}^*_M(X) \stackrel{\text{def}}{=} \mathrm{lfp}(\lambda Z.\, (X \cap M) \cup \mathrm{pre}_M(Z))$ $= \{x \in \Sigma \mid \exists y \in X.\, x \to^* y \;\&\; \mathrm{states}(x \to^* y) \subseteq M\}$;
- $\mathrm{post}^*_M(X) \stackrel{\text{def}}{=} \mathrm{lfp}(\lambda Z.\, (X \cap M) \cup \mathrm{post}_M(Z))$ $= \{y \in \Sigma \mid \exists x \in X.\, x \to^* y \;\&\; \mathrm{states}(x \to^* y) \subseteq M\}$;
- $\widetilde{\mathrm{pre}}^*_M(X) \stackrel{\text{def}}{=} \mathrm{gfp}(\lambda Z.\, (X \cup \neg M) \cap \widetilde{\mathrm{pre}}_M(Z))$ $= \{x \in \Sigma \mid \forall y.\, (x \to^* y \;\&\; \mathrm{states}(x \to^* y) \subseteq M) \Rightarrow y \in X\}$;
- $\widetilde{\mathrm{post}}^*_M(X) \stackrel{\text{def}}{=} \mathrm{gfp}(\lambda Z.\, (X \cup \neg M) \cap \widetilde{\mathrm{post}}_M(Z))$ $= \{y \in \Sigma \mid \forall x.\, (x \to^* y \;\&\; \mathrm{states}(x \to^* y) \subseteq M) \Rightarrow x \in X\}$.

Hence, we have that $x \in \mathrm{pre}^*_M(X)$ iff x may reach X through a path inside M, while $x \in \widetilde{\mathrm{pre}}^*_M(X)$ iff x inside M can only reach states in X. Let us note that, analogously to the unrestricted case, $\widetilde{\mathrm{pre}}^*_M(\neg X) = \neg\,\mathrm{pre}^*_M(X)$ and $\widetilde{\mathrm{post}}^*_M(\neg X) = \neg\,\mathrm{post}^*_M(X)$. Moreover, $\mathrm{pre}^*_M(X) \subseteq \mathrm{pre}^*(X)$ and $\mathrm{post}^*_M(X) \subseteq \mathrm{post}^*(X)$ while $\widetilde{\mathrm{pre}}^*(X) \subseteq \widetilde{\mathrm{pre}}^*_M(X)$ and $\widetilde{\mathrm{post}}^*(X) \subseteq \widetilde{\mathrm{post}}^*_M(X)$.

Example 4.1. Consider the safety verification problem depicted in Fig. 2 where the gray states determine the restricted space $M = 0134568$. It turns out that $\mathrm{post}^*_M(\mathit{Init}) = 013468$, $\mathrm{pre}^*_M(\mathit{Bad}) = 01368$, $\widetilde{\mathrm{post}}^*_M(\mathit{NInit}) = 2579$ and $\widetilde{\mathrm{pre}}^*_M(\mathit{Safe}) = 24579$.

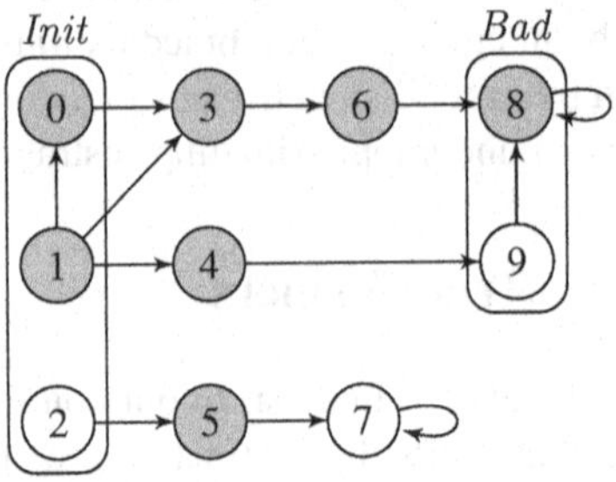

Fig. 2. Restricted predicated transformers

Note, for example, that $9 \in \text{post}^*(\mathit{Init}) = 0134689$ but $9 \notin \text{post}^*_M(\mathit{Init})$. Also, $4 \in \widetilde{\text{pre}}^*_M(\mathit{Safe})$ but $4 \notin \widetilde{\text{pre}}^*(\mathit{Safe}) = 257$ because there is no path that begins with 4 and remains inside M. □

Thus, when using a M-restricted predicate transformer instead of a standard (i.e. unrestricted) predicate transformer it is enough to consider only the states belonging to M. It should be clear that when M is much smaller than the whole state space Σ such a restriction to states in M may induce space and time savings.

5 Minimal Counterexamples

One main idea of our abstraction refinement algorithm consists in overapproximating the set of states that belong to some safety counterexample, i.e. a finite path from an initial state to a bad state. However, a counterexample π may be redundant, namely π might contain a shorther sub-path that still is a safety counterexample. For example, in the transition system in Fig. 2, the path $\pi = 103688$ is a safety counterexample because it begins with an initial state and ends with a bad state although π is redundant because it contains a sub-path $\pi' = 0368$ that is a counterexample. Our algorithm will compute and maintain an overapproximation of the states that belong to counterexamples that are not reducible. Such counterexamples are called minimal counterexamples.

Let us formalize the above notions. Let $\mathcal{T} = \langle \Sigma, R, \mathit{Init}, \mathit{Safe} \rangle$ specify a safety problem. A (safety) counterexample is a finite path $\pi \in \text{Path}(\mathcal{T})$ such that $\text{first}(\pi) \in \mathit{Init}$ and $\text{last}(\pi) \in \mathit{Bad}$. A *minimal counterexample* is a counterexample $\pi \in \text{Path}(\mathcal{T})$ such that $\text{states}(\pi) \smallsetminus \{\text{first}(\pi), \text{last}(\pi)\} \subseteq \mathit{Safe} \cap \mathit{NInit}$. We define $\text{MinCex} \stackrel{\text{def}}{=} \{\pi \in \text{Path}(\mathcal{T}) \mid \pi \text{ is a minimal counterexample}\}$.

Assume that M is an overapproximation of the states that occur in some minimal counterexample, i.e. $\text{states}(\text{MinCex}) \subseteq M$. Then, we provide a characterization of safe systems that only considers states in M: it turns out that a system is safe iff any state that is reachable from an initial state through a path inside M is safe.

Lemma 5.1. *If* $\text{states}(\text{MinCex}) \subseteq M$ *and* $\mathit{Init} \subseteq \mathit{Safe}$ *then the system* $\mathcal{T}$ *is safe iff* $\text{post}^*_M(\mathit{Init}) \subseteq M \cap \mathit{Safe}$ *iff* $\text{pre}^*_M(\mathit{Bad}) \subseteq M \cap \mathit{NInit}$.

6 A Forward-Backward Abstraction Refinement Algorithm

The Forward-Backward Abstraction Refinement algorithm FBAR is defined in Fig. 3. FBAR takes as input a safety verification problem $\mathcal{T} = \langle \Sigma, R, \mathit{Init}, \mathit{Safe} \rangle$ and a disjunctive abstraction $\mu_0 \in \mathrm{dAbs}(\wp(\Sigma))$. The main ideas and features of FBAR are summarized in the following list.

Data: *Init* initial states, *Safe* safe states such that $\mathit{Init} \subseteq \mathit{Safe}$
Data: $\mathit{Bad} = \Sigma \smallsetminus \mathit{Safe}$ bad states, $\mathit{NInit} = \Sigma \smallsetminus \mathit{Init}$ noninitial states
Data: $\mu_0 \in \mathrm{dAbs}(\wp(\Sigma))$ initial disjunctive abstract domain such that $\mathit{Safe}, \mathit{Bad}, \mathit{Init}, \mathit{NInit} \in \mu_0$

1 **begin**
2 $M := \Sigma; U := \mathit{Safe}; V := \mathit{NInit}; X := \mathit{Safe}; Y := \mathit{Bad};$
3 **for** $i := 0, 1, 2, \ldots$ **do**
4 **while** *true* **do**
5 $U' := \mathrm{lfp}(\lambda Z.\mu_i(M \cap U \cap (\mathit{Init} \cup \mathrm{post}(Z))));$
6 **if** $\mu_i(M \cap (\mathit{Init} \cup \mathrm{post}(U'))) \subseteq U$ **then return** OK;
7 $M := U' \cup \mu_i(V \cap \mathit{Bad} \cap \mathrm{post}(U'));$
8 $V' := \mathrm{lfp}(\lambda Z.\mu_i(M \cap V \cap (\mathit{Bad} \cup \mathrm{pre}(Z))));$
9 **if** $\mu_i(M \cap (\mathit{Bad} \cup \mathrm{pre}(V'))) \subseteq V$ **then return** OK;
10 $M := V' \cup \mu_i(U' \cap \mathit{Init} \cap \mathrm{pre}(V'));$
11 **if** $(U' = U$ **and** $V' = V)$ **then break**;
12 $U, V := U', V';$
13 $X := M \cap X; Y := M \cap Y;$
14 **while** *true* **do**
15 $X := X \cap \mu_i(M \smallsetminus Y);$
16 $X' := \mathrm{gfp}(\lambda Z.\mu_i(X \cap \widetilde{\mathrm{pre}}_M(Z)));$
17 **if** $\mathit{Init} \cap M \not\subseteq X'$ **then return** KO;
18 $Y := Y \cup \widetilde{\mu}_i(M \smallsetminus X');$
19 $Y' := \mathrm{lfp}(\lambda Z.\widetilde{\mu}_i(Y \cup \mathrm{pre}_M(Z)));$
20 **if** $Y' \not\subseteq \mathit{NInit}$ **then return** KO;
21 **if** $(X' = X$ **and** $Y' = Y)$ **then break**;
22 $X, Y := X', Y';$
23 $X := X \cap \widetilde{\mathrm{pre}}_M(X);$
24 **if** $X = X'$ **then return** OK;
25 $\mu_{i+1} := \mathrm{Cl}_{\cap,\cup}(\mu_i \cup \{X\});$
26 **end**

Fig. 3. FBAR Algorithm

(A) The loop at lines 4-12 computes and maintains an overapproximation M of the states that occur in some minimal counterexample by relying on a combined forward-backward abstract exploration of the state space. Such a combined forward-backward abstract computation was first described by Cousot [6] and further investigated and applied in [8,9,19]. The following procedure is iterated: we start from $M \cap \mathit{Init}$ and abstractly go forward within M through post_M (line 5); then, we come back by starting from $M \cap \mathit{Bad}$ and abstractly going backward within M through pre_M (line 8). The abstract sets U and V are the results of these, resp., forward and backward abstract fixpoint computations. The following invariant properties hold (cf. Lemma 6.2 (1)): U is an overapproximation of the safe states that can be reached through a path within M, while V is an overapproximation of the noninitial states that can reach a bad state through a path within M. The combined forward-backward computation of U and V allows us to iteratively refine the overapproximation M of states(MinCex) (lines 7 and 10).

(B) The OK condition at line 6 implies that $\mathrm{post}_M^*(\mathit{Init}) \subseteq U$, so that $\mathrm{post}_M^*(\mathit{Init}) \subseteq M \cap \mathit{Safe}$, and therefore, by Lemma 5.1, the system is safe. Analogously, for the "backward" OK condition at line 9.

(C) The loop at lines 14-22 computes iteratively the abstract sets X and Y as follows. X is an overapproximation of the states in M that are globally safe and is computed at line 16 as a greatest fixpoint of the best correct approximation in μ_i of $\widetilde{\mathrm{pre}}_M$. On the other hand, Y is an underapproximation of the states in M that can reach a bad state and is computed at line 19 as a least fixpoint of the best correct approximation of pre_M w.r.t. the underapproximating abstraction $\widetilde{\mu}_i$. This is formally stated by Lemma 6.2 (3). While the sequence of computed X's forms a descending chain of abstract sets, the Y's give rise to an ascending chain of abstract sets. These abstract computations are iterated because the abstract set Y may help in refining X and, vice versa, X may help in refining Y. In fact, observe that the states in $M \smallsetminus Y$ form a superset of the states in M that are globally safe, so that the overapproximation X can be refined by intersection with the abstract set $\mu_i(M \smallsetminus Y)$. A dual reasoning holds for Y, where we exploit the fact that μ_i is a disjunctive abstraction and therefore $\widetilde{\mu}_i$ is an underapproximating abstraction.

(D) Since $X' \supseteq M \cap \widetilde{\mathrm{pre}}^*(\mathit{Safe})$, the KO condition at line 17 implies that $\mathit{Init} \cap M \not\subseteq M \cap \widetilde{\mathrm{pre}}^*(\mathit{Safe})$, namely that $\mathit{Init} \not\subseteq \widetilde{\mathrm{pre}}^*(\mathit{Safe})$, so that the system is unsafe. Analogously, for the "underapproximating" KO condition at line 20.

(E) At the exit of the loop at lines 14-22, we perform a concrete step of computation at line 23 by calculating a refiner set $\mathit{Ref} = X \cap \widetilde{\mathrm{pre}}_M(X)$. In contrast to the algorithm CGR where the refiner Z_{i+1} cannot already be in the abstraction μ_i, here it may happen that $X = \mathit{Ref}$. In this case (line 24), we obtain that $\mathrm{post}_M^*(\mathit{Init}) \subseteq X$ and this allows us to conclude that the system is safe. Otherwise, $\mathit{Ref} \subsetneq X$ is used to refine μ_i to μ_{i+1} that is obtained by closing $\mu_i \cup \{\mathit{Ref}\}$ both under intersections — in order to have an abstraction — and unions — in order to have a disjunctive abstraction.

Let us now illustrate how FBAR works on a simple finite example.

Example 6.1. Let us consider the safety verification problem represented by the following diagram, where $\mu_0 = \mathrm{Cl}_\cup(\{1, 12, 3, 35, 3456, 6, 7\})$.

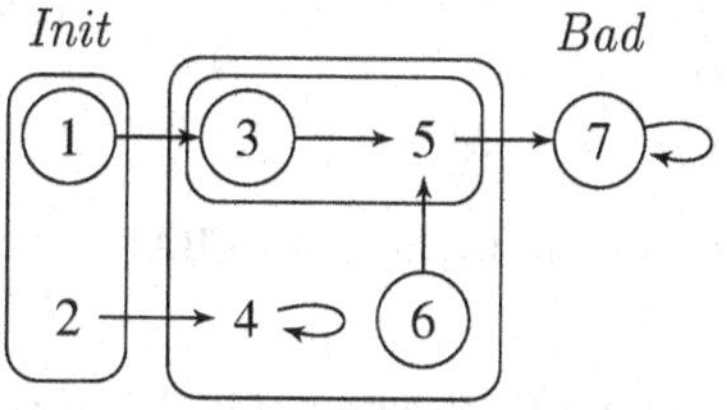

Then, FBAR allows to derive that the system is unsafe with no refinement. In fact, FBAR gives rise to the following "execution trace":

[line 2]:	$M = 1234567;\ U = 123456;\ V = 34567;\ X = 123456;\ Y = 7;$
[line 5]:	$U' = 123456;$
[line 6]:	$1234567 = \mu_{\mathcal{O}}(M \cap (Init \cup \text{post}(U'))) \not\subseteq U = 123456;$
[line 7]:	$M = 1234567;$
[line 8]:	$V' = 3567;$
[line 9]:	$13567 = \mu_{\mathcal{O}}(M \cap (Bad \cup \text{pre}(V'))) \not\subseteq V = 34567;$
[line 10]:	$M = 13567;$
[line 11]:	$U' = U\ \&\ V' \neq V;$
[line 12]:	$U = 123456;\ V = 3567;$
[line 5]:	$U' = 135;$
[line 6]:	$1357 = \mu_{\mathcal{O}}(M \cap (Init \cup \text{post}(U'))) \not\subseteq U = 123456;$
[line 7]:	$M = 1357;$
[line 8]:	$V' = 357;$
[line 9]:	$1357 = \mu_{\mathcal{O}}(M \cap (Bad \cup \text{pre}(V'))) \not\subseteq V = 3567;$
[line 10]:	$M = 1357;$
[line 11]:	$U' \neq U\ \&\ V' \neq V;$
[line 12]:	$U = 135;\ V = 357;$
[lines 5-10]:	a further iteration that does not change U', V' and M
[line 11]:	$U' = U\ \&\ V' = V;$
[line 13]:	$X = 135;\ Y = 7;$
[line 15]:	$X = 135;$
[line 16]:	$X' = \varnothing;$
[line 16]:	$Init \cap M \not\subseteq X' \quad \Rightarrow$ KO

Thus, FBAR needs no abstraction refinement and seven abstract fixpoint computations. On the other hand, CGR needs three abstraction refinements and eight abstract fixpoint computations in order to conclude that the system is unsafe. In fact, it computes the following sequence: $Z_0 = 123456$, $R_0 = 123456$, $S_0 = 123456$, $Z_1 = 12346$, $R_1 = 12346$, $S_1 = 12346$, $Z_2 = 124$, $R_2 = 124$, $S_2 = 124$, $Z_3 = 24$, $R_3 = 24$, $S_3 = 24$ and then concludes KO.

It can be also checked that the dual algorithm CGR$^{\leftarrow}$ needs one abstraction refinement in order to conclude that the system is unsafe while in this case CGR$^{\leftarrow}$ performs just four abstract fixpoint computations. □

The above described properties of the FBAR procedure are stated precisely as follows.

Lemma 6.2. *The following properties are invariant in the algorithm* FBAR *in Fig. 3:*

(1) $\text{post}^*_{M \cap \mathit{Safe}}(\mathit{Init}) \subseteq U' \subseteq U \subseteq M$ & $\text{pre}^*_{M \cap \mathit{NInit}}(\mathit{Bad}) \subseteq V' \subseteq V \subseteq M$.
(2) $\text{states(MinCex)} \subseteq M$.
(3) $M \cap \widetilde{\text{pre}}^*(\mathit{Safe}) \subseteq X' \subseteq X \subseteq M$ & $Y \subseteq Y' \subseteq M \cap \text{pre}^*(\mathit{Bad})$.

These invariant properties allows us to show that FBAR is a correct algorithm for safety checking.

Theorem 6.3 (Correctness). *If* FBAR *outputs* OK/KO *then $\mathcal{T}$ is safe/unsafe.*

6.1 Termination

Termination of FBAR is similar to that of CGR.

Theorem 6.4 (Termination)

(1) *If μ_0 is finite and there exists $\mathcal{X} \subseteq \wp(\Sigma)$ such that for all $i \geq 0$, $X_i \in \mathcal{X}$ and $\langle \mathcal{X}, \subseteq \rangle$ satisfies the descending chain condition then* FBAR *terminates.*
(2) *If $\mathcal{T}$ is unsafe then* FBAR *terminates.*

Hence, if the refiner sets X_i's at line 23 all belong to a subset of the state space that satisfies the descending chain condition then FBAR terminates. This obviously implies termination when the state space Σ is finite. Ganty et al. [13,14] show that this descending chain condition allows to show that the instantiation of the CGR algorithm to the class of well-structured transition systems (WSTSs) always terminates. This is an important result because WSTSs are a broad and relevant class of infinite-state transition systems that include, among others, Petri Nets, broadcast protocols and lossy-channel systems [11]. Since this termination condition works for FBAR exactly in the same way as for CGR, we conjecture that the descending chain condition should allow to show that FBAR terminates on WSTSs.

6.2 Relationship with CGR

We made a formal comparison between the FBAR and CGR algorithms and showed that when no abstraction refinement is needed, FBAR is better than CGR, i.e., if CGR terminates with a given abstraction μ with no abstraction refinement then this also happens for FBAR. As shown by the examples in Section 3, the converse is not true.

Theorem 6.5. *If* CGR *for some disjunctive abstract domain μ outputs* OK/KO *with no abstraction refinement then* FBAR *for μ outputs* OK/KO *with no abstraction refinement.*

We did not succeed in comparing formally FBAR and CGR when abstraction refinements indeed happen. This does not appear to be an easy task mainly because FBAR and CGR use both different refiners — FBAR refines using $\widetilde{\text{pre}}_M$ while CGR uses $\widetilde{\text{pre}}$ — and different ways of refining the abstraction — FBAR needs a refined disjunctive abstraction while CGR needs a mere abstraction. We can only report that we were not able to find an example where CGR terminates while FBAR does not.

Let us also remark that Cousot-Ganty-Raskin [10] described how some acceleration techniques that compute underapproximations of the reflexive-transitive closure R^* of the transition relation R can be integrated into CGR. The correctness of this technique basically depends on the fact that replacing the transition relation R with a relation T such that $R \subseteq T \subseteq R^*$ is still correct in CGR. This also holds for FBAR so that these same techniques can be applied.

6.3 Implementation of Disjunctive Abstractions

An implementation of FBAR is subject for future work. However, let us mention that disjunctive abstractions can indeed be efficiently implemented through a state partition and a relation defined over it.

Let us recall from [20] the details of such a representation. Let $\mu \in dAbs(\wp(\Sigma))$. The partition $par(\mu) \in Part(\Sigma)$ induced by μ is defined by the following equivalence relation $\sim_\mu \subseteq \Sigma \times \Sigma$: $x \sim_\mu y$ iff $\mu(\{x\}) = \mu(\{y\})$. Moreover, let us define the following relation $\unlhd_\mu$ on $par(\mu)$: $\forall B_1, B_2 \in par(\mu)$, $B_1 \unlhd_\mu B_2$ iff $\mu(B_1) \subseteq \mu(B_2)$. It turns out that $\langle par(\mu), \unlhd_\mu \rangle$ is a poset. For example, consider the disjunctive abstraction μ depicted in Section 2, where $\mu = Cl_\cup(\{1, 12, 123, 4, 45, 6\})$. The poset $\langle par(\mu), \unlhd_\mu \rangle$ is then as follows:

$$
\begin{array}{ccc}
3 & & \\
| & & \\
2 & 5 & \\
| & | & \\
1 & 4 & 6
\end{array}
$$

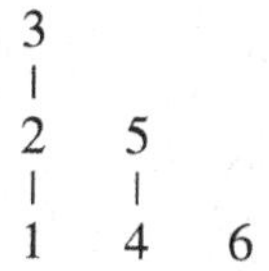

This allows us to represent the abstraction μ as follows: for any $S \subseteq \Sigma$, $\mu(S) = \cup\{B \in par(\mu) \mid \exists C \in par(\mu). C \cap S \neq \varnothing$ & $B \unlhd_\mu C\}$.

As shown in [20], it turns out that this partition/relation-based representation provides an efficient way for representing and maintaining disjunctive abstractions. Moreover, [20] also shows that the abstraction refinement step $\mu_{i+1} = Cl_{\cap,\cup}(\mu_i \cup \{X\})$ at line 25 can be efficiently implemented by a procedure that is based on partition splitting and runs in $O(|par(\mu_i)|^2 + |X|)$-time.

7 Future Work

A number of tasks are left for future research. Firstly, it would be interesting to complete the formal comparison between FBAR and CGR by investigating whether and how their refinements and final outputs can be related in the general case when the abstraction is refined. We also left open our conjecture that, analogously to CGR, the FBAR algorithm terminates when applied to well-structured transition systems. After the completion of such a comparison with CGR, it would be worth to develop a prototype of FBAR that can reuse the implementation of disjunctive abstraction refinements already available from [20].

Acknowledgments. This manuscript has been completed after the death of Olivia Rossi Doria on June 13th, 2006. Francesco Ranzato and Francesco Tapparo take this opportunity to acknowledge Olivia's contribution to this paper as well as her personal friendship and professional skills.

References

1. Ball, T., Rajamani, S.K.: The SLAM Project: Debugging system software via static analysis. In: Proc. 29th ACM POPL, pp. 1–3 (2002)
2. Chaki, S., et al.: Modular verification of software components in C. IEEE Transactions on Software Engineering 30(6), 388–402 (2004)
3. Clarke, E.M., Grumberg, O., Peled, D.A.: Model checking. The MIT Press, Cambridge (1999)
4. Clarke, E., et al.: Progress on the State Explosion Problem in Model Checking. In: Wilhelm, R. (ed.) Dagstuhl Seminar 2000. LNCS, vol. 2000, pp. 176–194. Springer, Heidelberg (2001)
5. Clarke, E.M., et al.: Counterexample-guided abstraction refinement for symbolic model checking. J. ACM 50(5), 752–794 (2003)
6. Cousot, P.: Mèthodes itèratives de construction et d'approximation de points fixes d'opèrateurs monotones sur un treillis, analyse sèmantique de programmes. PhD Thesis, Univ. de Grenoble, France (1978)
7. Cousot, P., Cousot, R.: Systematic design of program analysis frameworks. In: Proc. 6th ACM POPL, pp. 269–282 (1979)
8. Cousot, P., Cousot, R.: Abstract interpretation and application to logic programs. J. Logic Programming 13(2-3), 103–179 (1992)
9. Cousot, P., Cousot, R.: Refining model checking by abstract interpretation. Automated Software Engineering 6(1), 69–95 (1999)
10. Cousot, P., Ganty, P., Raskin, J.-F.: Fixpoint-Guided Abstraction Refinements. In: Riis Nielson, H., Filé, G. (eds.) SAS 2007. LNCS, vol. 4634, pp. 333–348. Springer, Heidelberg (2007)
11. Finkel, A., Schnoebelen, P.: Well-structured transition systems everywhere! Theoretical Computer Science 256(1-2), 63–92 (2001)
12. Ganty, P.: The Fixpoint Checking Problem: An Abstraction Refinement Perspective. PhD Thesis, Université Libre de Bruxelles (2007)
13. Ganty, P., Raskin, J.F., Van Begin, L.: A Complete Abstract Interpretation Framework for Coverability Properties of WSTS. In: Emerson, E.A., Namjoshi, K.S. (eds.) VMCAI 2006. LNCS, vol. 3855, pp. 49–64. Springer, Heidelberg (2005)
14. Ganty, P., Raskin, J.F., Van Begin, L.: From Many Places to Few: Automatic Abstraction Refinement for Petri Nets. In: Kleijn, J., Yakovlev, A. (eds.) ICATPN 2007. LNCS, vol. 4546, pp. 124–143. Springer, Heidelberg (2007)
15. Gulavani, B.S., Rajamani, S.K.: Counterexample Driven Refinement for Abstract Interpretation. In: Hermanns, H., Palsberg, J. (eds.) TACAS 2006 and ETAPS 2006. LNCS, vol. 3920, pp. 474–488. Springer, Heidelberg (2006)
16. Henzinger, T.A., et al.: Lazy abstraction. In: Proc. 29th ACM POPL, pp. 58–70 (2002)
17. Henzinger, T.A., et al.: Software Verification with BLAST. In: Ball, T., Rajamani, S.K. (eds.) SPIN 2003. LNCS, vol. 2648, pp. 235–239. Springer, Heidelberg (2003)
18. Manevich, R., et al.: Abstract Counterexample-Based Refinement for Powerset Domains. In: Reps, T., Sagiv, M., Bauer, J. (eds.) Wilhelm Festschrift. LNCS, vol. 4444, pp. 273–292. Springer, Heidelberg (2007)
19. Massé, D.: Combining Forward and Backward Analyses of Temporal Properties. In: Danvy, O., Filinski, A. (eds.) PADO 2001. LNCS, vol. 2053, Springer, Heidelberg (2001)
20. Ranzato, F., Tapparo, F.: An Abstract Interpretation-Based Refinement Algorithm for Strong Preservation. In: Halbwachs, N., Zuck, L.D. (eds.) TACAS 2005. LNCS, vol. 3440, pp. 140–156. Springer, Heidelberg (2005)

Internal and External Logics of Abstract Interpretations*

David A. Schmidt

Kansas State University, Manhattan, Kansas, USA
schmidt@cis.ksu.edu

Abstract. We show that every abstract interpretation possesses an *internal logic*, whose proof theory is defined by the partial ordering on the abstract domain's elements and whose model theory is defined by the domain's concretization function. We explain how program validation and transformation depend on this logic.

Next, when a logic *external* to the abstract interpretation is imposed, we show how to synthesize a sound, underapproximating, set-based variant of the external logic and give conditions when the underapproximating logic can be embedded within the original abstract domain, *inverted*. We show how model-checking logics depend on this construction.

The intent of this paper is tutorial, to integrate little-publicized results into a standard framework that can be used by practitioners of static analysis.

Perhaps the central issue in program validation and transformation is how to apply the results of a static program analysis to prove that a desired validation/transformation property holds true: How does the domain of logical properties "connect" to the domain of values used in the static analysis?

Here are three examples: *(i)* we use data-flow analysis to compute sets of available expressions and use the sets to decide properties of register allocation [20]; *(ii)* we complete a state-space exploration and use it to model check a temporal-logic formula that defines a safety property [4] or program-transformation criterion [15]; *(iii)* we apply predicate abstraction with counter-example-guided refinement (CEGAR) to generate an assertion set that proves a safety property [1,2,19,28].

This paper asserts that the value domain used by a static analysis and the logic used for validation and transformation should be *one and the same* — the logic should be *internal* to the value domain. If the values and logical properties differ, then the logic must be defined *externally*, and this paper shows how.

Let Σ be the states/stores generated by a program; let A be an abstract domain for static analysis (e.g., sign values or sets of available expressions or names of state partitions); and let $\gamma : A \to \mathcal{P}(\Sigma)$ be the *concretization function* that maps each $a \in A$ to the values it models in Σ.

* Supported by NSF ITR-0326577.

F. Logozzo et al. (Eds.): VMCAI 2008, LNCS 4905, pp. 263–278, 2008.

In this paper, we demonstate that

- γ defines a logic *internal* to A for Σ. The elements of A act *both* as computational values and as logical assertions. (Data-flow analysis, predicate abstraction, and CEGAR-based model checking exploit this coincidence.)
- The internal logic's model theory, $\models$, is defined by γ; its proof theory, $\vdash$, is defined by A's partial ordering, $\sqsubseteq$. (This is the beauty of partial-order-based static analysis — a computable $\sqsubseteq$ defines the deduction system.)
- The notion of (forwards) completeness from abstract interpretation theory [17,25,29] *characterizes* A's internal logic — it tells us from the start what we can express and prove.
- When a logic for Σ is proposed independently from A and γ, then an *external logic* must be fashioned, using a powerset completion. *But,* when γ preserves *both* meets and joins, the external logic can be embedded *within* A by *inverting* A's partial ordering!

We conclude, in the last case, that every abstract domain A with such a γ has *two* interpretations: an overapproximating, *computational* interpretation, used to compute the results of a static analysis, and an underapproximating, *logical* interpretation, used to prove logical properties of the results. In this formal sense, we "overapproximate the model and underapproximate the logic."

These developments are implicit in virtually all applications of static analysis to program validation and transformation, and this paper aims to present the principles as directly as possible.

1 Abstract Interpretation

A program is a discrete dynamic system [6]: there is a domain of possible program states, Σ, and one or more *transition functions*, $f : \Sigma \to \Sigma$, that are repeatedly applied to an initial state selected from Σ.

For a program written in declarative notation the state might be the program's source text, and the transition function is a rewriting engine. For "flowchart programs," there is a control-flow graph, whose nodes are program points, and a transition function is attached to each arc in the graph; the transition function updates the state that traverses the arc. (See Figure 1 for such an example.) Or, there is a single, global transition function, written as a "case" command, that updates the state that is depicted as a program-point, storage pair.

A static analysis is a finitely computed estimate of the states generated by the transition functions. The estimate is typically phrased as a superset of the actual, concrete states that are reached. Based on the estimate, a program validation or transformation might be undertaken.

To compute finitely these state-set estimates, we define a set, A, of abstract representations of those subsets of Σ of interest.

To relate A to Σ, we define a *concretization function*, $\gamma : A \to \mathcal{P}(\Sigma)$, such that for $S \subseteq \Sigma$ and $a \in A$, S *is approximated by* a if $S \subseteq \gamma(a)$.

For a variety of implementational reasons [7,20,22], we partially order the abstract values as $(A, \sqsubseteq)$ such that *(i)* $\sqsubseteq$ is finitely computable and *(ii)* γ is monotone. (For some applications, a discrete ordering on A works fine.)

Example program and its flowgraph annotated by transition functions:

```
p0 : readInt(x)
p1 : if x>0 :
p2 :     x:= pred(x)
p3 : x:= succ(x)
p4 : writeInt(x)
```

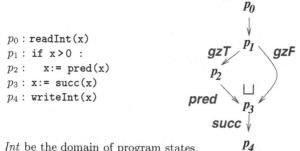

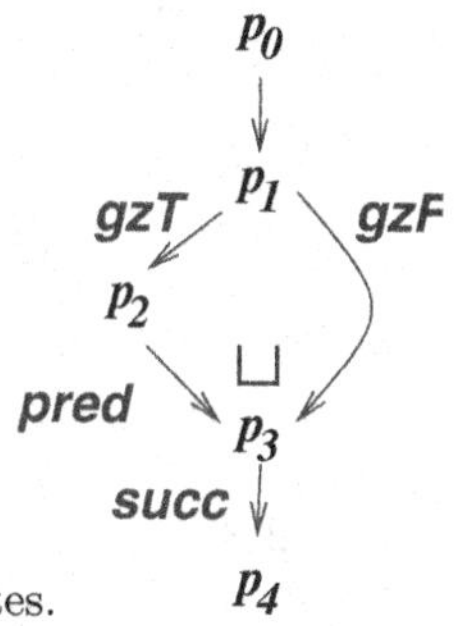

Let $\Sigma = Int$ be the domain of program states.
(Here, the state remembers x's value.)

The transition functions (*standard semantics*) for pred, succ, and >0 have arity, $\Sigma \to \Sigma_\perp$:

$$
\begin{array}{lll}
pred(n) = n - 1 & gzT(n) = n, \text{ if } n > 0 & gzF(n) = n, \text{ if } n \leq 0 \\
succ(n) = n + 1 & gzT(n) = \perp, \text{ if } n \leq 0 & gzF(n) = \perp, \text{ if } n > 0
\end{array}
$$

(Note: gzT and gzF act as "filter functions"; all transition functions are $\perp$-strict — $\perp$ is *not* propagated in a concrete execution trace.)

The *collecting semantics* transition functions have arity, $\mathcal{P}(\Sigma) \to \mathcal{P}(\Sigma)$; let $S \subseteq \Sigma$:

$$
\begin{array}{ll}
pred(S) = \{n - 1 \mid n \in S\} & gzT(S) = \{n \in S \mid n > 0\} \\
succ(S) = \{n + 1 \mid n \in S\} & gzF(S) = \{n \in S \mid n \leq 0\}
\end{array}
$$

Fig. 1. Sample program and its transition functions

Figure 1 introduces an example program that uses transition functions *succ* and *pred* to manipulate integer input. Perhaps we wish to estimate the output sets from this program for the cases when the input sets are all the negatives, or all the positives, or just the integer, 0 — the information might enable useful validations or transformations.

To do this, we define an abstract domain, *Sign*, with representatives for the previously mentioned data sets, along with representatives for the empty set and *Int*, partially ordered (so that $\sqcup$ is defined). γ maps the representations to the sets they represent. See Figure 2.

We might ask if γ has an inverse, which maps a state set, $S \subseteq \Sigma$, to the A-value that most precisely approximates S. If so, a *Galois connection* results:

Definition 1. *For partially ordered sets, $(\mathcal{P}(\Sigma), \subseteq)$ and $(A, \sqsubseteq)$, a pair of monotone functions, $\alpha : \mathcal{P}(\Sigma) \to A$ and $\gamma : A \to \mathcal{P}(\Sigma)$, form a* Galois connection *iff* (i) *for all $S \in \mathcal{P}(\Sigma)$, $S \subseteq \gamma(\alpha(S))$, and* (ii) *for all $a \in A$, $\alpha(\gamma(a)) \sqsubseteq a$.*

Equivalently, there is a Galois connection when $S \subseteq \gamma(a)$ iff *$\alpha(S) \sqsubseteq a$, for all $S \in \mathcal{P}(\Sigma)$ and $a \in A$.*

γ is called the *upper adjoint* and α is the *lower adjoint* of the Galois connection.

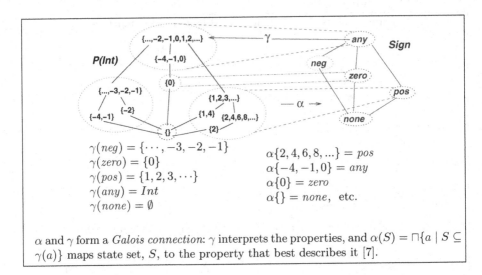

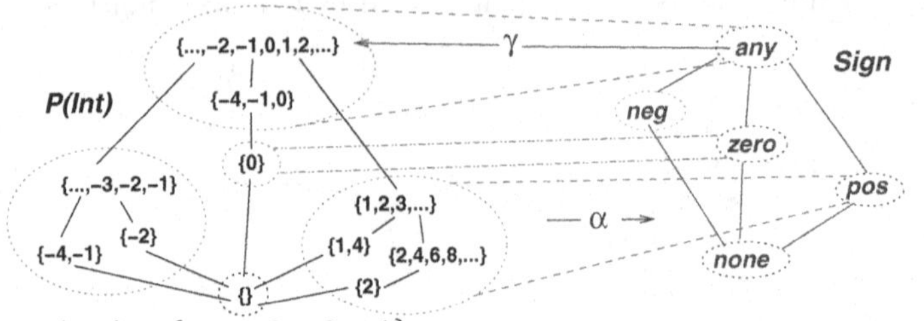

$\gamma(neg) = \{\cdots, -3, -2, -1\}$
$\gamma(zero) = \{0\}$
$\gamma(pos) = \{1, 2, 3, \cdots\}$
$\gamma(any) = Int$
$\gamma(none) = \emptyset$

$\alpha\{2, 4, 6, 8, ...\} = pos$
$\alpha\{-4, -1, 0\} = any$
$\alpha\{0\} = zero$
$\alpha\{\} = none$, etc.

α and γ form a *Galois connection*: γ interprets the properties, and $\alpha(S) = \sqcap\{a \mid S \subseteq \gamma(a)\}$ maps state set, S, to the property that best describes it [7].

Fig. 2. Abstract domain of signed values, placed within a Galois connection

Galois connections enjoy many properties [12,16]; here are a key few. First, α and γ are inverses on each other's ranges: for all $S \in \gamma[A]$, $\gamma(\alpha(S)) = S$, and for all $a \in \alpha[\Sigma]$, $\alpha(\gamma(a)) = a$. Next, every upper (lower) adjoint has a unique lower (upper) adjoint mate, and when we say that γ "is an upper adjoint," we imply the existence of the uniquely defined α. Third, γ preserves meets: for all $T \subseteq A$, $\gamma(\sqcap T) = \cap_{a \in T}\gamma(a)$ (similar for α and joins). Conversely, when A is a complete lattice and function γ preserves meets, then γ is an upper adjoint. In Figure 2, γ is an upper adjoint.

1.1 Abstracting State Transition Functions

Now that concrete state sets are approximated by elements of A, we can approximate the transition functions. For generality, say that each transition function has arity, $f : \mathcal{P}(\Sigma) \to \mathcal{P}(\Sigma)$, so that f can express nondeterminism as well as pre- and post-images of state sets ("collecting semantics" [21] — cf. Figure 1).

For each f, the corresponding *abstract transition function*, $f^\sharp : A \to A$, must soundly overestimate f's post-images:

Definition 2. *$f^\sharp : A \to A$ is* sound *for $f : \mathcal{P}(\Sigma) \to \mathcal{P}(\Sigma)$, if for all $a \in A$, $f(\gamma(a)) \subseteq \gamma(f^\sharp(a))$, that is, $f \circ \gamma \sqsubseteq_{A \to \mathcal{P}(\Sigma)} \gamma \circ f^\sharp$.*

When γ is an upper adjoint, the above is equivalent to $\alpha(f(S)) \sqsubseteq f^\sharp(\alpha(S))$, for all $S \in \mathcal{P}(\Sigma)$. The *most precise* ("best") sound $f^\sharp$ for f is $f^\sharp_{best} = \alpha \circ f \circ \gamma$. See Figure 3 for $succ^\sharp$ and $pred^\sharp$ and an example static analysis.

When the inequalities that define soundness are strengthened to equalities, we have:

Definition 3. *$f^\sharp$ is* γ-complete (forwards complete) *for f iff $f \circ \gamma = \gamma \circ f^\sharp$ [17,29]. $f^\sharp$ is* α-complete (backwards complete) *for f iff $\alpha \circ f = f^\sharp \circ \alpha$ [11,18]*

Abstractly interpret $\mathcal{P}(Int)$ by $Sign = \{neg, zero, pos, any, none\}$; the abstracted program and flowgraph are

```
p0 : readSign(x)
p1 : if gzT♯(x):
p2 :     x:= pred♯(x)
p3 : x:= succ♯(x)
p4 : writeSign(x)
```

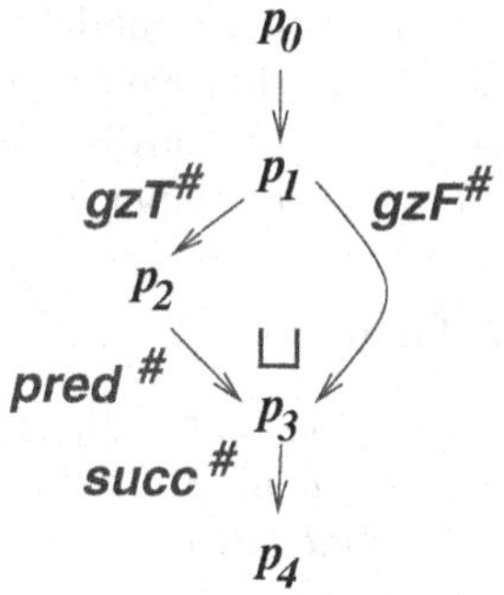

The abstract transition functions are

$succ^\sharp(pos) = pos$ $\quad pred^\sharp(neg) = neg$
$succ^\sharp(zero) = pos$ $\quad pred^\sharp(zero) = neg$
$succ^\sharp(neg) = any$ $\quad pred^\sharp(pos) = any$
$succ^\sharp(any) = any$ $\quad pred^\sharp(any) = any$

$gzT^\sharp(neg) = none$ $\quad gzF^\sharp(neg) = neg$
$gzT^\sharp(zero) = none$ $\quad gzF^\sharp(zero) = zero$
$gzT^\sharp(pos) = pos$ $\quad gzF^\sharp(pos) = none$
$gzT^\sharp(any) = pos$ $\quad gzF^\sharp(any) = any$ (!)

(All functions, $f^\sharp$, are *strict*: $f^\sharp(none) = none$.)

We now calculate a static analysis, *which applies the abstracted transition functions to the abstracted inputs (at* p_0*), computing the abstracted outputs (at* p_4*):*

$$\{zero \mapsto pos,\ neg \mapsto any,\ pos \mapsto any, \}$$

Fig. 3. Static analysis that calculates sign properties of example program

These notions will be explained, developed, and shown useful in Section 3, where we see the relation between logic and the transition functions.

2 Elements of A are Logical Properties

In Figure 2, note how *neg* and *pos* are both names of state sets as well as logical assertions (*"isNeg,"* *"isPos"*). In data-flow analysis, this "pun" — state-set approximations are logical properties — is critical to program transformation, because an estimated state set, $S \subseteq \Sigma$, has *property* $S' \subseteq \Sigma$ if $S \subseteq S'$ holds.

In an analysis like the one in Figure 3, we say that an output, $a \in Sign$, has *property* $a' \in Sign$ if $a \sqsubseteq a'$. (For example, *zero* has properties *zero* and *any*.) Thus, all the concrete states modelled by a have property a', too.

In predicate-abstraction-based static analysis, the abstract data values are sets of primitive propositions (e.g., $\{\mathtt{x} > 0, \mathtt{x} \leq \mathtt{y}\}$), which can also be read as propositions ($\mathtt{x} > 0 \wedge \mathtt{x} \leq \mathtt{y}$) that denote concrete-state sets ($\{(x, y) \in \Sigma \mid x > 0 \text{ and } x \leq y\}$).

This idea is exploited in counter-example-guided refinement [1,2,19,28], which enriches the abstract domain with additional primitive propositions as needed to validate a logical property. This idea also underlies the definition of Kripke structure, used in abstract model checking [4], where each state partition is married to the set of primitive propositions that hold true for the partition.

These observations are hardly novel — they harken back to Cousot's Ph.D. thesis [5] and his tutorial paper [6]. Now we develop the consequences.

2.1 Model Theory of A

Treat A as a set of logical propositions. Define the entailment relation, $\models \subseteq \mathcal{P}(\Sigma) \times A$, as $S \models a$ iff $S \subseteq \gamma(a)$. (When γ is an upper adjoint, $S \models a$ iff $\alpha(S) \sqsubseteq a$ as well.) One key consequence is that $S' \subseteq S$ and $S \models a$ imply $S' \models a$.

An abstract transition function is exposed as a *postcondition transformer*: $S \models a$ implies $f(S) \models f^\sharp(a)$, and this makes $f^\sharp_{best}$ the *strongest* postcondition transformer for f in the language of propositions expressible in A.

2.2 Proof Theory of A

For $a, a' \in A$, define $a \vdash a'$ iff $a \sqsubseteq a'$. (Recall that we require that $\sqsubseteq$ be finitely computable, and the "proof" that $a \vdash a'$ is the computation that affirms $a \sqsubseteq a'$.)

As is standard [14], assert $a \models a'$ iff for all $S \subseteq \Sigma$, $S \models a$ implies $S \models a'$. Evidently, $a \models a'$ iff $\gamma(a) \subseteq \gamma(a')$.

Proposition 4. (soundness) *For all $a, a' \in A$, $a \vdash a'$ implies $a \models a'$ (which implies $S \models a'$, for all $S \subseteq \gamma(a)$).*

Proof. Immediate from γ's monotonicity. □

Soundness justifies validations and transformations based on a static analyis.

Proposition 5. (completeness) *When γ is an upper adjoint and an injective (1-1) function, then $a \models a'$ implies $a \vdash a'$ for all $a, a' \in A$.*

Proof. Assume $\gamma(a) \subseteq \gamma(a')$. By the definition of Galois connection, this gives $\alpha(\gamma(a))) \sqsubseteq a'$. Since γ is injective, $\alpha(\gamma(a))) = a$. □

The best abstract transition function computes post-images that are complete:

Theorem 6. (image completeness) *When γ is an upper adjoint, then $f^\sharp_{best} = \alpha \circ f \circ \gamma$ is* image complete *in the sense that, for all $a, a' \in A$,*

1. $f^\sharp_{best}(a) \models a'$ *iff* $f^\sharp_{best}(a) \vdash a'$
2. $f(\gamma(a)) \models a'$ *iff* $f^\sharp_{best}(a) \vdash a'$

Proof. For 1., we need to prove the only-if part: Assume $\gamma(f^\sharp_{best}(a)) \subseteq \gamma(a')$. By the definition of $f^\sharp_{best}$ and the Galois connection, we have $f \circ \gamma(a) \subseteq \gamma \circ \alpha \circ f \circ \gamma(a) \subseteq \gamma(a')$. By applying monotone α to the previous inclusions and appealing to the definition of Galois connection, we get $f^\sharp_{best}(a) = \alpha \circ f \circ \gamma(a) \sqsubseteq \alpha \circ \gamma(a') \sqsubseteq a'$. The proof of 2. is similar. □

Image completeness does *not* ensure completeness upon *multiple* applications of transition functions, which static analysis must do in practice. In Figure 2, note that $pred(succ\{0\}) \models zero$, yet $pred^\sharp(succ^\sharp(zero)) \not\models zero$ — the problem is that, although $\{0\} = \gamma(zero)$ falls in the range of γ, $succ(\gamma(zero)) = \{1\}$ does *not* and cannot be expressed precisely within *Sign*.

For the remainder of this subsection, assume that γ is an upper adjoint. First, say that $f : \mathcal{P}(\Sigma) \to \mathcal{P}(\Sigma)$ *is* γ*-complete* if there exists some $f^\sharp : A \to A$ that is γ-complete for f (cf. Defn. 3): evidently, $f \circ \gamma = \gamma \circ f^\sharp_{best}$. It is well known that f is γ-complete iff for all $a \in A$, $f(\gamma(a)) \in \gamma[A]$, that is, f stays in γ's range [17].

When f is γ-complete, then its repeated application to an initial argument in γ's range can be precisely approximated by $f^\sharp_{best}$.[1]

An inappropriate choice of A can prevent a transition function from γ-completeness, e.g., $succ : \mathcal{P}(Int) \to \mathcal{P}(Int)$ is not γ-complete for *Sign*. The repeated applications of *succ* to $\{0\} = \gamma(zero)$ require that we add to *Sign* new elements, I, for each $\{i\}$, $i > 0$, so that $\gamma(I) = \{i\}$ and *succ* is γ-complete. This is too expensive of a price to pay, but we see in the next section that γ-completeness plays a critical role in determining a domain's *internal logic.*

3 Internal Logic of A

We understand a *logic* as an inductively defined assertion set, an inductively defined interpretation, and (an inductively defined) proof theory, typically presented as a set of deduction rules. We now explore the logic that is internal to domain A and concretization map γ.

First, we treat the elements of A as primitive propositions and we use ϕ and ψ to represent elements from A. $\gamma : A \to \mathcal{P}(\Sigma)$ interprets the primitive propositions.

Definition 7. *Abstract domain A's internal logic* has conjunction *when*

$$S \models \phi_1 \sqcap \phi_2 \text{ iff } S \models \phi_1 \text{ and } S \models \phi_2, \text{ for all } S \subseteq \Sigma.$$

Proposition 8. *When γ preserves binary meet as set intersection — $\gamma(\phi \sqcap \psi) = \gamma(\phi) \cap \gamma(\psi)$, for all $\phi, \psi \in A$ — then A's internal logic has conjunction.*

Recall that when γ is an upper adjoint, it preserves meets; this is a major benefit of structuring A so that it admits a Galois connection.

Now, we have this inductively defined assertion set, the *internal logic* of A:

$$\phi ::= a \mid \phi_1 \sqcap \phi_2$$

γ interprets the logic, and it satisfies these inductively defined laws:

---

[1] It is also true that precise approximation of multiple applications of f will be maintained if some $f^\sharp$ is α*-complete for* f. (f is α-complete iff for all $S, S' \in \mathcal{P}(S)$, $\alpha(S) = \alpha(S')$ implies $\alpha(f(S)) = \alpha(f(S'))$ — f maps α-related arguments to α-related answers. Alas, when a function is not α-complete, the cost of adding extra elements to A can be just as expensive as when γ-completeness is desired.

$$\gamma(a) = \text{given}$$
$$\gamma(\phi \sqcap \psi) = \gamma(\phi) \cap \gamma(\psi)$$

This logic of primitives and conjunction is already strong enough to express most predicate abstractions and CEGAR structures. The internal logic for *Sign* in Figure 2 possesses conjunction.

Sign's proof theory is defined by the finitely computable $\sqsubseteq$, which obviates the usual set of deduction rules. A static analysis proves its facts, $\phi \vdash \psi$, using $\sqsubseteq$, and this is one of the beauties of the subject.

Now that conjunction exists, we can read the earlier definition of $\models \subseteq A \times A$ in the classical way: For $\Delta \subseteq A$, define $\Delta \models \psi$ iff for all $S \subseteq \Sigma$, if (for all $\psi \in \Delta$, $S \models \psi$) then ($S \models \phi$) as well. Evidently, $\Delta \models \psi$ iff $\gamma(\sqcap \Delta) \subseteq \gamma(\psi)$.

We can explore for other propositional connectives:

Proposition 9. *If γ preserves binary join as set union, then A's internal logic has* disjunction*: $S \models \phi \sqcup \psi$ iff $S \models \phi$ or $S \models \psi$, where $\gamma(\phi \sqcup \psi) = \gamma(\phi) \cup \gamma(\psi)$.*

The *Sign* domain in Figure 2 lacks disjunction: $zero \models neg \sqcup pos$ (because $neg \sqcup pos = any$ but $zero \not\models neg$ and $zero \not\models pos$). If we add new elements to *Sign*, namely, $\leq 0, \neq 0$, and ≥ 0, we have disjunction for the expanded domain.[2]

We can search for intuitionistic (Heyting) implication: Complete lattice A is *distributive* if $a \sqcap (b \sqcup c) = (a \sqcap b) \sqcup (a \sqcap c)$, for all $a, b, c \in A$; this makes the set, $\{a \in A \mid a \sqcap \phi \sqsubseteq \psi\}$, directed, and when $\sqcap$ is Scott-continuous, then

$$\phi \Rightarrow \psi \;\equiv\; \sqcup \{a \in A \mid a \sqcap \phi \sqsubseteq \psi\}$$

defines *implication* in A, where $a \vdash \phi \Rightarrow \psi$ iff $a \sqcap \phi \vdash \psi$ [13].

Proposition 10. *If A is a complete distributive lattice where $\sqcap$ is Scott-continuous and upper adjoint γ is injective, then A's internal logic has* Heyting implication*: $S \models \phi \Rightarrow \psi$ iff $\gamma(\alpha(S)) \cap \gamma(\phi) \subseteq \gamma(\psi)$, where*

$$\gamma(\phi \Rightarrow \psi) = \bigcup \{S \in \gamma[A] \mid S \cap \gamma(\phi) \subseteq \gamma(\psi)\}.$$

Proof. Let $T = \{a \mid a \sqcap \phi \sqsubseteq \psi\}$. First, by [13], $\sqcup T \in T$; This implies $\gamma(\sqcup T) = \cup_{a \in T} \gamma(a) = \cup\{\gamma(a) \mid a \sqcap \phi \sqsubseteq \psi\}$. Consider the predicate, $a \sqcap \phi \sqsubseteq \psi$; since γ is injective, the predicate is equivalent to $\gamma(a \sqcap \phi) \subseteq \gamma(\psi)$ (cf. Proposition 5), which is equivalent to $\gamma(a) \cap \gamma(\phi) \subseteq \gamma(\psi)$, because γ preserves meets. So we have $\gamma(\phi \Rightarrow \psi) = \cup\{\gamma(a) \mid \gamma(a) \cap \gamma(\phi) \subseteq \gamma(\psi)\} = \cup\{S \in \gamma[A] \mid S \cap \gamma(\phi) \subseteq \gamma(\psi)\} \in \gamma[A]$.

Next, $S \models \phi \Rightarrow \psi$ iff $S \subseteq \gamma(\sqcup T)$, implying $S \subseteq \gamma(\alpha(S)) \subseteq \gamma(\alpha(\gamma(\sqcup T))) = \gamma(\sqcup T)$. So, $S \models \phi \Rightarrow \psi$ iff $\gamma(\alpha(S)) \models \phi \Rightarrow \psi$. Finally, because $\gamma(\alpha(S)) \in \gamma[A]$ and pointwise reasoning on set union, $\gamma(\alpha(S)) \models \phi \Rightarrow \psi$ iff $\gamma(\alpha(S)) \cap \gamma(\phi) \subseteq \gamma(\psi)$. □

Heyting implication is weaker than classical implication (where $S \models \phi \Rightarrow \psi$ iff $S \cap \gamma(\phi) \subseteq \gamma(\psi)$ iff for all $c \in S$, if $\{c\} \models \phi$, then $\{c\} \models \psi$).

[2] By adding these elements, we computed the *disjunctive completion* of *Sign* [10].

As an immediate consequence, we have a Deduction Theorem: $\Delta, \psi \vdash \phi$ iff $\Delta \vdash \psi \Rightarrow \phi$. And if $\gamma(\bot_A) = \emptyset \in \mathcal{P}(\Sigma)$, we have falsity ($\bot$); this gives us

$$\phi ::= a \mid \phi_1 \sqcap \phi_2 \mid \phi_1 \sqcup \phi_2 \mid \phi_1 \Rightarrow \phi_2 \mid \bot$$

In particular, $\neg\phi$ abbreviates $\phi \Rightarrow \bot$ and defines the *refutation* of ϕ within A, such as is done with a three-valued static analyzer such as TVLA [27]. In practice, most static analyses do *not* require all this structure — conjunction alone (cf. Figure 2) often suffices.

3.1 The General Principle is γ-Completeness

There is a general principle for determining when an operation is "logical" and is present in A's internal logic as a connective. To expose this principle, consider again the interpretation of conjunction, where both the connective ($\sqcap$) and its concrete interpretation ($\cap$) are stated as binary functions:

$$\gamma(\sqcap(\phi, \psi)) = \cap(\gamma(\phi), \gamma(\psi))$$

γ-completeness is *exactly* the criterion for determining which connectives are embedded in A:

Corollary 11. *For $f : \mathcal{P}(\Sigma) \times \mathcal{P}(\Sigma) \times \cdots \to \mathcal{P}(\Sigma)$, A's internal logic has connective $f^\sharp$ iff f is γ-complete: For all $\phi \in A$, $\gamma(f^\sharp(\phi_1, \phi_2, \cdots)) = f(\gamma(\phi_1), \gamma(\phi_2), \cdots)$.*

Example: reconsider *Sign* in Figure 2, and note that $negate : \mathcal{P}(Int) \to \mathcal{P}(Int)$, where $negate(S) = \{-n \mid n \in S\}$, is γ-complete. We have that $negate^\sharp : A \to A$ (where $negate^\sharp(pos) = neg$, $negate^\sharp(neg) = pos$, etc.) exists in *Sign*'s logic:

$$\phi ::= a \mid \phi_1 \sqcap \phi_2 \mid negate^\sharp(\phi)$$

We can state "negate" assertions, e.g., $pos \vdash negate^\sharp(neg \sqcap any)$. $negate^\sharp$ is a connective, a modality, a *predicate transformer*.

3.2 Predicate Transformers in the Internal Logic

We saw from the example for *Sign* that the absence of γ-completeness for transition functions *succ* (and *pred*) made it impossible to prove $pred^\sharp(succ^\sharp(zero)) \vdash zero$ — the two transition functions *cannot* be connectives in *Sign*'s logic.

But even when a transition function, $f : \mathcal{P}(\Sigma) \to \mathcal{P}(\Sigma)$, is γ-complete, it is *not* used as a connective — for program analysis and transformation, it is not useful to know $a \vdash f^\sharp(\phi)$, that is, state set $\gamma(a)$ falls in f's postimage of $\gamma(\phi)$. It is more useful to know $f^\sharp(a) \vdash \phi$, that is, f's postimage of $\gamma(a)$ lies within $\gamma(\phi)$.

In programming logic, $f^\sharp(a) \vdash \phi$ is written $a \vdash [f^\sharp]\phi$, using a precondition *predicate transformer*. To formalize, for $S \subseteq \mathcal{P}(\Sigma)$, define

$$[f](S) = \widetilde{pre}_f(S) = \bigcup\{S' \in \Sigma \mid f(S') \subseteq S\}$$

We wish to add $[f]$ to the internal logic, so we must show it is γ-complete:

Theorem 12. *Assume that γ is an upper adjoint and preserves joins. Then, $\widetilde{pre}_f$ is γ-complete iff f is α-complete.*

Proof. To prove the if part, we show that $\widetilde{pre}_f(\gamma(a)) = \cup\{S \mid f(S) \subseteq \gamma(a)\}$ is in $\gamma[A]$. By definition of Galois connection, $f(S) \subseteq \gamma(a)$ iff $\alpha \circ f(S) \sqsubseteq a$, and because f is α-complete, this is equivalent to $\alpha \circ f \circ \gamma \circ \alpha(S) \sqsubseteq a$. Again, by the Galois connection, we have the equivalent $f \circ \gamma \circ \alpha(S) \sqsubseteq \gamma(a)$. Thus, $\widetilde{pre}_f(\gamma(a)) = \cup\{S \mid f \circ \gamma \circ \alpha(S) \sqsubseteq \gamma(a)\}$. Now, when some $S \in \mathcal{P}(\Sigma)$ belongs to the set, then so must $\gamma \circ \alpha(S)$ (which is a superset of S): we have $\widetilde{pre}_f(\gamma(a)) = \cup\{S \in \gamma[A] \mid f(S) \subseteq \gamma(a)\}$. Finally, because γ preserves joins, the union of the set must be itself be in $\gamma[A]$.

For the only-if part, assume that $\widetilde{pre}_f$ is γ-complete, that is, for all $a \in A$, $\cup\{S \mid \alpha(f(S)) \sqsubseteq a\} \in \gamma[A]$. To show f is α-complete, we must prove that if $\alpha(S_0) = \alpha(S_1)$, then $\alpha(f(S_0)) = \alpha(f(S_1))$. Assume $\alpha(S_0) = \alpha(S_1)$; we first show $\alpha(f(S_0)) \sqsubseteq \alpha(f(S_1))$. Consider the set, $T_1 = \{S \mid \alpha(f(S)) \sqsubseteq \alpha(f(S_1))\}$. First, note that $S_1 \subseteq \cup T_1$, implying that $\alpha(S_1) \sqsubseteq \alpha(\cup T_1)$. Since $\alpha(S_0) = \alpha(S_1)$, we have $\alpha(S_0) \sqsubseteq \alpha(\cup T_1)$ as well, and this implies $S_0 \subseteq \gamma(\alpha(S_0)) \subseteq \gamma(\alpha(\cup T_1)) = \cup T_1$, since $\cup T_1 \in \gamma[A]$. Within $\mathcal{P}(\Sigma)$, it must be that $S_0 \in T_1$, implying $\alpha(f(S_0)) \sqsubseteq \alpha(f(S_1))$. Identical reasoning with $T_0 = \{S \mid \alpha(f(S)) \sqsubseteq \alpha(f(S_0))\}$ yields the other inclusion, meaning that f is α-complete. □

Similar developments are possible with the other common variants of predicate transformers, but the technicalities increase [30].

Because of their dependence on α-γ-completeness, predicate transformers might not appear in an internal logic. In this case, we must *underapproximate* the transformers with a logic that is *external* to the abstract domain.

4 External Logic

This paper argues that the logical reasoning one uses with a static analysis should be based on the abstract domain's internal logic. Yet, transition functions that lack α- and γ-completeness can make such reasoning hugely imprecise, and adding additional elements to make the abstract domain complete can be too expensive or destroy finite computability — One might be forced to work with a less-precise logic that lives "outside" the internal logic.

Also, it is not uncommon to be presented with a set of assertions, $\mathcal{L}$, and an interpretation, $[\![\cdot]\!] : \mathcal{L} \to \mathcal{P}(\Sigma)$, already fixed for the concrete domain, $\mathcal{P}(\Sigma)$, prior to the selection of A. For Figure 3, *Sign* lacks disjunction and both $succ^\sharp$ and $pred^\sharp$ and neither α- nor γ-complete, but perhaps the logic in Figure 4 is demanded, nonetheless. *How do we deal with this?*

Common sense suggests, for each assertion form, ϕ, that we collect all the $a \in A$ that satisfy ϕ and define an abstract interpretation of $[\![\phi]\!]$ as follows:

$$[\![\phi]\!]^\sharp = \{a \mid \gamma(a) \subseteq [\![\phi]\!]\}$$

Then, we can use the results of a static analysis based on A to prove properties: assert $a \vdash \phi$ iff $a \in [\![\phi]\!]^\sharp$. This defines a logic that is *external* to A.

$$\phi ::= a \mid \phi_1 \wedge \phi_2 \mid \phi_1 \vee \phi_2 \mid [f]\phi \qquad \text{for } a \in Sign \text{ and } f \in \{succ, pred\}$$

$$[\![\cdot]\!] : \mathcal{L} \to \mathcal{P}(\Sigma)$$

$$\begin{aligned}
[\![a]\!] &= \gamma(a)\\
[\![\phi_1 \wedge \phi_2]\!] &= [\![\phi_1]\!] \cap [\![\phi_2]\!]\\
[\![\phi_1 \vee \phi_2]\!] &= [\![\phi_1]\!] \cup [\![\phi_2]\!]\\
[\![[f]\phi]\!] &= \widetilde{pre}_f[\![\phi]\!] = \cup\{S \mid f(S) \subseteq [\![\phi]\!]\}
\end{aligned}$$

Fig. 4. Sample logic for sign properties

Underlying this informal development is a Galois connection whose abstract domain is $\mathcal{P}_\downarrow(A)^{op}$ — downclosed subsets of A, ordered by superset:

$$\mathcal{P}_\downarrow(A)^{op} = (\{T \subseteq A \mid T \text{ is downclosed}\}, \supseteq)$$
$$\text{where } T \text{ is } \textit{downclosed} \text{ iff } T = \{a \in A \mid \exists b \in T, a \sqsubseteq b\}$$

Elements of $\mathcal{P}_\downarrow(A)^{op}$ serve as denotations of $[\![\phi]\!]^\sharp \in \mathcal{P}_\downarrow(A)^{op}$.[3]

Here is the Galois connection: Let A be a partially ordered set and $\mathcal{P}(\Sigma)^{op} = (\mathcal{P}(\Sigma), \supseteq)$. Then, for any monotone $\gamma : A \to \mathcal{P}(\Sigma)$, the functions $\overline{\alpha} : \mathcal{P}(\Sigma)^{op} \to \mathcal{P}_\downarrow(A)^{op}$ and $\overline{\gamma} : \mathcal{P}_\downarrow(A)^{op} \to \mathcal{P}(\Sigma)^{op}$ form a Galois connection, where

$$\begin{aligned}
\overline{\gamma}(T) &= \bigcup\{\gamma(a) \mid a \in T\}\\
\overline{\alpha}(S) &= \bigcup\{T \mid S \supseteq \overline{\gamma}(T)\} = \{a \mid \gamma(a) \subseteq S\}
\end{aligned}$$

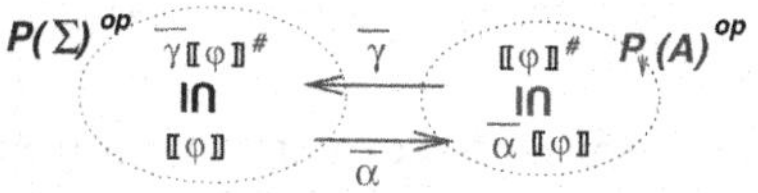

Upper adjoint $\overline{\gamma}$ "lifts" from γ and preserves unions; when γ is an upper adjoint, then $\overline{\gamma}$ preserves intersections, too [30]. $\overline{\alpha}$ is exactly the approximation we guessed earlier: $[\![\phi]\!]^\sharp = \overline{\alpha}[\![\phi]\!]$. The inverted ordering gives *underapproximation:* $[\![\phi]\!] \supseteq \overline{\gamma}[\![\phi]\!]^\sharp$. We have soundness — $a \in [\![\phi]\!]^\sharp$ implies $\gamma(a) \subseteq [\![\phi]\!]$ — because we used the adjoint to define the abstract interpretation of the logic.[4]

$\mathcal{P}_\downarrow(A)^{op}$ is itself an abstract domain, a complete lattice, and *its* internal logic contains disjunction (set union) and conjunction (set intersection) when γ is an upper adjoint. The domain is distributive, but $\overline{\gamma}$ might not be injective, so Heyting implication is not ensured (cf. Proposition 10). But it is the existence of disjunction that is the key to defining a sound $[\![\cdot]\!]^\sharp$. To summarize,

Proposition 13. *For* all *choices of partially ordered set, A, monotone $\gamma : A \to \mathcal{P}(\Sigma)$, and $[\![\cdot]\!] : \mathcal{L} \to \mathcal{P}(\Sigma)$, there is a sound external logic, $[\![\cdot]\!]^\sharp : \mathcal{L} \to \mathcal{P}_\downarrow(A)$, in the sense that, for all $a \in A$, $a \in [\![\phi]\!]^\sharp$ implies $\gamma(a) \subseteq [\![\phi]\!]$, for all $\phi \in \mathcal{L}$. (Indeed, the most precise such logic is $\overline{\alpha} \circ [\![\cdot]\!]$.)*

This proposition underlies "abstract model checking" [3], where A holds the names of partitions of Σ and γ maps each state-partition name to its members.

But we are not finished — we want an *inductively defined* abstract interpretation. This is readily obtained from the inductively defined concrete interpretation, whose equations take the form,

[3] Clearly, all $[\![\phi]\!]^\sharp$ are downclosed sets.

[4] Precisely stated, the best approximation of $[\![\cdot]\!] : \mathcal{L} \to \mathcal{P}_\downarrow(A)$ is $\overline{\alpha} \circ [\![\cdot]\!] \circ id_{\mathcal{L}}$.

$$
\begin{aligned}
&[\![a]\!]^\sharp_{best} = \overline{\alpha}(\gamma(a))\\
&[\![\phi_1 \wedge \phi_2]\!]^\sharp_{best} = \overline{\alpha}\,(\overline{\gamma}[\![\phi_1]\!]^\sharp_{best} \cap \overline{\gamma}[\![\phi_2]\!]^\sharp_{best})\\
&[\![\phi_1 \vee \phi_2]\!]^\sharp_{best} = \overline{\alpha}\,(\overline{\gamma}[\![\phi_1]\!]^\sharp_{best} \cup \overline{\gamma}[\![\phi_2]\!]^\sharp_{best})\\
&[\![[f]\phi]\!]^\sharp_{best} = \overline{\alpha}\,(\widetilde{pre}_f(\overline{\gamma}[\![\phi]\!]^\sharp_{best})) \;=\; \{a \mid f(\gamma(a)) \subseteq \overline{\gamma}[\![\phi]\!]^\sharp_{best}\}\\
\\
&[\![a]\!]^\sharp_{fin} = \overline{\alpha}(\gamma(a))\\
&[\![\phi_1 \wedge \phi_2]\!]^\sharp_{fin} = [\![\phi_1]\!]^\sharp_{fin} \cap [\![\phi_2]\!]^\sharp_{fin}\\
&[\![\phi_1 \vee \phi_2]\!]^\sharp_{fin} = [\![\phi_1]\!]^\sharp_{fin} \cup [\![\phi_2]\!]^\sharp_{fin}\\
&[\![[f]\phi]\!]^\sharp_{fin} = \widetilde{pre}_{f^\sharp}[\![\phi]\!]^\sharp_{fin} = \{a \in A \mid f^\sharp(a) \in [\![\phi]\!]^\sharp_{fin}\}, \text{ where } f^\sharp \text{ is sound for } f
\end{aligned}
$$

Fig. 5. Inductively defined logics for *Sign*: best and finitely computable

$$[\![\mathtt{f}(\phi_1, \phi_2, \cdots)]\!] = f([\![\phi_1]\!], [\![\phi_2]\!], \cdots)$$

We use the adjoints to abstract each logical operation, $f : \mathcal{P}(\Sigma) \times \mathcal{P}(\Sigma) \times \cdots \to \mathcal{P}(\Sigma)$, by $f^\sharp_{best} = \overline{\alpha} \circ f \circ (\overline{\gamma} \times \overline{\gamma} \times \cdots)$. The most precise, inductively defined, abstract logic is therefore

$$[\![\mathtt{f}(\phi_1, \phi_2, \cdots)]\!]^\sharp_{best} = f^\sharp_{best}([\![\phi_1]\!]^\sharp_{best}, [\![\phi_2]\!]^\sharp_{best}, \cdots)$$

Because the fixed-point operators are well behaved, we can also define abstract recursion operators [11,26].

An issue that arises with sets of abstract values is that the synthesized $f^\sharp_{best} : \mathcal{P}_\downarrow(A) \times \mathcal{P}_\downarrow(A) \times \cdots \to \mathcal{P}_\downarrow(A)$ might not be finitely computable — we must locate a computable approximation of it. Consider again $[\![\cdot]\!]$ in Figure 4; its most precise inductively defined logic, $[\![\cdot]\!]^\sharp_{best}$, and a finitely computable approximation, $[\![\cdot]\!]^\sharp_{fin}$, are stated in Figure 5. We see that $\cap = (\overline{\alpha} \circ \cap \circ (\overline{\gamma} \times \overline{\gamma}))$ — precision is preserved — but this is not true for $\cup$: For example, $any \in [\![neg \vee zero \vee pos]\!]^\sharp_{best} = Sign$ but $any \notin [\![neg]\!]^\sharp_{fin} \cup [\![zero]\!]^\sharp_{fin} \cup [\![pos]\!]^\sharp_{fin} = \{neg, zero, pos, none\}$.[5]

For predicate transformers, it is well known that $\widetilde{pre}_{f^\sharp}$ is sound for $\widetilde{pre}_f$, for any $f^\sharp$ sound for f. But it is grossly imprecise. We can improve it by replacing $f^\sharp : A \to A$ by $f^\sharp_\vee : A \to \mathcal{P}_\downarrow(A)$, where $f^\sharp_\vee(a) = \downarrow\{\alpha\{c\} \mid c \in f(\gamma(a))\}$.[6] For example, from Figure 3, $succ^\sharp(neg) = any$, but $succ^\sharp_\vee(neg) = \{neg, zero, none\}$, which gives the more precise $\widetilde{pre}_{succ^\sharp_\vee}$.[7]

These technicalities let us prove that $\widetilde{pre}_{f^\sharp_\vee} = (\overline{\alpha} \circ \widetilde{pre}_f \circ \overline{\gamma})$ [30].

5 The problem is that $\{none, neg, zero, pos\}$ and *Sign* both concretize to $neg \vee zero \vee pos$ and are candidates to represent it in $\mathcal{P}_\downarrow(Sign)$. We must eliminate one of the sets.

6 where $\downarrow S = \{s \mid \exists s' \in S, s \sqsubseteq s'\}$

7 Underlying $f^\sharp_\vee$'s definition is yet another Galois connection, between complete lattices $(\mathcal{P}(\Sigma), \subseteq)$ and $(\mathcal{P}_\downarrow(A), \subseteq)$, where the upper adjoint is $\overline{\gamma}$ and the lower adjoint is $\overline{\alpha_o}(S) = \cap\{T \mid S \subseteq \overline{\gamma}(T)\} = \downarrow\{\alpha\{c\} \mid c \in S\}$. Then, $f^\sharp_\vee = \overline{\alpha_o} \circ f \circ \overline{\gamma}$. This Galois connection is possible when γ is an upper adjoint.

4.1 Provability, Soundness, Completeness

Entailment and provability for an inductively defined external logic is defined as expected: $a \models \phi$ iff $\gamma(a) \subseteq [\![\phi]\!]$, and $a \vdash \phi$ iff $a \in [\![\phi]\!]^\sharp_{fin}$.[8]

Soundness (that is, $\vdash$ implies $\models$) is immediate, and completeness ($\models$ implies $\vdash$) follows when $\overline{\alpha} \circ [\![\cdot]\!] = [\![\cdot]\!]^\sharp_{fin}$. This is called *logical best preservation* or logical $\overline{\alpha}$-completeness [11,29].

There is another, independent, form of completeness, *logical strong preservation* or logical γ-completeness: $\overline{\gamma} \circ [\![\cdot]\!]^\sharp_{fin} = [\![\cdot]\!]$ [17,26,29].[9] For inductively defined $[\![\cdot]\!]^\sharp_{fin}$, if all the mentioned abstract logical operations are α-complete, then $[\![\cdot]\!]^\sharp_{fin}$ has best preservation; when all abstract logical operators are γ-complete, then $[\![\cdot]\!]^\sharp_{fin}$ has strong preservation. (The converses might not hold [26].)

5 When the Upper Adjoint Preserves Joins, the External Logic Lies Within the Inverted Abstract Domain

The "lift" of abstract domain A to $\mathcal{P}_\downarrow(A)$ is a *disjunctive completion* [10], where an element, $\{a_0, a_1, a_2, \cdots\} \in \mathcal{P}_\downarrow(A)$ is meant to be read as the disjunction, $a_0 \vee a_1 \vee a_2 \vee \cdots$, and this is confirmed by the definition, $\overline{\gamma}\{a_0, a_1, a_2, \cdots\} = \gamma(a_0) \cup \gamma(a_1) \cup \gamma(a_2) \cup \cdots$.

But say that γ is an upper adjoint and that it *preserves joins*, that is,

$$\overline{\gamma}T = \bigcup_{a \in T} \gamma(a) = \gamma(\bigsqcup_{a \in T} a) = \gamma(\sqcup T)$$

So, $\overline{\gamma}[\mathcal{P}_\downarrow(A)] = \gamma[A]$ — their ranges are equal — and *there is no new expressivity gained by using sets of A-elements to model subsets of Σ*. So, when upper adjoint γ preserves joins, an external logic can be modelled *internally* within A. The key is to *invert* A and define an underapproximating Galois connection:

Proposition 14. *If A is a complete lattice and $\gamma : A \to \mathcal{P}(\Sigma)$ preserves joins (as unions) and meets (as intersections), then*

- *γ is the upper adjoint of a Galois connection between $(\mathcal{P}(\Sigma), \subseteq)$ and $(A, \sqsubseteq)$, where the lower adjoint, α_o, is defined $\alpha_o(S) = \sqcap\{a \mid S \subseteq \gamma(a)\}$.*
- *γ is the upper adjoint of a Galois connection between $(\mathcal{P}(\Sigma), \supseteq)$ and $(A, \sqsupseteq)$, where the lower adjoint, α_u, is defined $\alpha_u(S) = \sqcup\{a \mid S \supseteq \gamma(a)\}$.*

The first Galois connection defines an overapproximation relationship; the second defines an underapproximation relationship.

When we approximate a state-transition function, $f : \mathcal{P}(\Sigma) \to \mathcal{P}(\Sigma)$, we apply the first Galois connection to define $f^\sharp_{best} = \alpha_o \circ f \circ \gamma$. We call this the *computational interpretation* of f.

---

[8] These notions are equivalently stated with sets: for $T \in \mathcal{P}_\downarrow(A)$, $T \models \phi$ iff $\overline{\gamma}(T) \subseteq [\![\phi]\!]$, and $T \vdash \phi$ iff $T \subseteq [\![\phi]\!]^\sharp_{fin}$.

[9] Strong preservation asserts, for all $c \in \Sigma$, that $c \in [\![\phi]\!]$ iff $\alpha\{c\} \vdash \phi$. In contrast, best preservation states, for all $a \in A$, that $\gamma(a) \subseteq [\![\phi]\!]$ iff $a \vdash \phi$. See [29] for criteria when one implies the other.

When we are given a logical interpretation function, $[\![\cdot]\!] : \mathcal{L} \to \mathcal{P}(\Sigma)$, we apply the second Galois connection to define $[\![\cdot]\!]^\sharp_u = \alpha_u \circ [\![\cdot]\!]$. If $[\![\cdot]\!]$ is inductively defined, that is, has form $[\![\mathtt{f}(\phi_1, \phi_2, \cdots)]\!] = f([\![\phi_1]\!], [\![\phi_2]\!], \cdots)$, we apply the second Galois connection to define $f^\flat_{best} = \alpha_u \circ f \circ (\gamma \times \gamma \times ...)$, giving $[\![\mathtt{f}(\phi_1, \phi_2, \cdots)]\!]^\sharp_{best} = f^\flat_{best}([\![\phi_1]\!]^\sharp_{best}, [\![\phi_2]\!]^\sharp_{best}, \cdots))$ We call this the *logical interpretation* of f.

When all the fs are α_u-complete, then $[\![\cdot]\!]^\sharp_u = [\![\cdot]\!]^\sharp_{best}$. We can also show that the logical interpretation proves the *same assertions* as the external logic:

First, for $[\![\phi]\!]^\sharp = \overline{\alpha}[\![\phi]\!] \in \mathcal{P}_\downarrow(A)$, recall that $a \vdash \phi$ iff $a \in [\![\phi]\!]^\sharp$.

Next, for $[\![\phi]\!]^\sharp_u = \alpha_u[\![\phi]\!] \in A$, define $a \vdash \phi$ iff $a \sqsubseteq [\![\phi]\!]^\sharp_u$.

Theorem 15. *For all $a \in A$, $a \sqsubseteq [\![\phi]\!]^\sharp_u$ iff $a \in [\![\phi]\!]^\sharp$.*

Proof. First, note that $a \in [\![\phi]\!]^\sharp$ iff $\gamma(a) \subseteq [\![\phi]\!]$. Next, $a \sqsubseteq [\![\phi]\!]^\sharp_u$ iff $a \sqsubseteq \sqcup P$, where $P = \{a' \mid \gamma(a') \subseteq [\![\phi]\!]\}$.

To prove the if-part, assume $\gamma(a) \subseteq [\![\phi]\!]$. This places $a \in P$, hence $a \sqsubseteq \sqcup P$.

To prove the only-if part, assume $a \sqsubseteq \sqcup P$. Now, for all $a' \in P$, $\gamma(a') \subseteq [\![\phi]\!]$, implying $\cup_{a' \in P} \gamma(a') \subseteq [\![\phi]\!]$. But γ preserves joins, meaning $\gamma(\sqcup P) \subseteq [\![\phi]\!]$, implying that $\sqcup P \in P$ as well. Since $a \sqsubseteq \sqcup P$, we have $\gamma(a) \subseteq \gamma(\sqcup P) \subseteq [\![\phi]\!]$. □

So, when γ preserves meets and also joins, we embed the external logic as an underapproximation in A^{op}, retaining the logic's proof theory and model theory.

6 Conclusion

Abstract interpretations are fundamentally "logical" — as Cousot and Cousot have stated in key papers [5,6,8,9,11] — an abstract interpretation estimates function pre- and post-images, which are represented as finitely-sized assertions. The same idea underlies Kripke structures and abstract model checking [3,4].

In this paper, we showed that the connection between abstract interpretation and symbolic logic is fundamental: A static analysis *computes proofs* (via $\sqsubseteq$) that are *sound* (via $\models$) within the internal/external logic.

Acknowledgements. This paper was inspired by earlier work of Alan Mycroft and Neil Jones [23,24]. I would like to thank Alan for his interest in internal/external logics and his suggestion that I write this paper.

References

1. Ball, T., Podelski, A., Rajamani, S.K.: Boolean and Cartesian Abstraction for Model Checking C Programs. In: Margaria, T., Yi, W. (eds.) ETAPS 2001 and TACAS 2001. LNCS, vol. 2031, Springer, Heidelberg (2001)
2. Clarke, E., et al.: Counterexample-guided abstraction refinement. In: Emerson, E.A., Sistla, A.P. (eds.) CAV 2000. LNCS, vol. 1855, pp. 154–169. Springer, Heidelberg (2000)

3. Clarke, E.M., Grumberg, O., Long, D.E.: Model checking and abstraction. ACM Transactions on Programming Languages and Systems 16(5), 1512–1542 (1994)
4. Clarke, E.M., Grumberg, O., Peled, D.A.: Model Checking. MIT Press, Cambridge (2000)
5. Cousot, P.: Méthodes itératives de construction et d'approximation de points fixes d'opérateurs monotones sur un treillis, analyse sémantique de programmes. PhD thesis, University of Grenoble (1978)
6. Cousot, P.: Semantic foundations of program analysis. In: Muchnick, S., Jones, N. (eds.) Program Flow Analysis, pp. 303–342. Prentice Hall, Englewood Cliffs (1981)
7. Cousot, P., Cousot, R.: Abstract interpretation: a unified lattice model for static analysis of programs. In: Proc. 4th ACM Symp. POPL, pp. 238–252 (1977)
8. Cousot, P., Cousot, R.: Automatic synthesis of optimal invariant assertions: mathematical foundations. In: Symp. Artificial Intelligence and Programming Languages ACM SIGART Newsletter 64 (1977)
9. Cousot, P., Cousot, R.: Systematic design of program analysis frameworks. In: Proc. 6th ACM Symp. POPL, pp. 269–282 (1979)
10. Cousot, P., Cousot, R.: Higher-order abstract interpretation. In: Proceedings IEEE Int. Conf. Computer Lang. pp. 95–112 (1994)
11. Cousot, P., Cousot, R.: Temporal abstract interpretation. In: Proc. 27th ACM Symp. on Principles of Programming Languages, pp. 12–25. ACM Press, New York (2000)
12. Davey, B.A., Priestley, H.A.: Introduction to Lattices and Order, 2nd edn. Cambridge University Press, Cambridge (2002)
13. Dummett, M.: Intuitionism. Oxford University Press, Oxford (1977)
14. Enderton, H.: A Mathematical Introduction to Logic. Academic Press, London (1972)
15. Lacey, D., et al.: Proving correctness of compiler optimizations by temporal logic. In: Proc. 29th ACM POPL (2002)
16. Gierz, G., et al.: Continuous Lattices and Domains. Cambridge University Press, Cambridge (2003)
17. Giacobazzi, R., Quintarelli, E.: Incompleteness, counterexamples, and refinements in abstract model checking. In: Cousot, P. (ed.) SAS 2001. LNCS, vol. 2126, pp. 356–373. Springer, Heidelberg (2001)
18. Giacobazzi, R., Ranzato, F., Scozzari, F.: Making abstract interpretations complete. J. ACM 47, 361–416 (2000)
19. Graf, S., Saidi, H.: Verifying invariants using theorem proving. In: Alur, R., Henzinger, T.A. (eds.) CAV 1996. LNCS, vol. 1102, Springer, Heidelberg (1996)
20. Hecht, M.: Flow Analysis of Computer Programs. Elsevier, Amsterdam (1977)
21. Jones, N., Nielson, F.: Abstract interpretation. In: Abramsky, S., et al. (eds.) Handbook of Logic in Computer Science, vol. 4, Oxford University Press, Oxford (1995)
22. Muchnick, S., Jones, N.D. (eds.): Program Flow Analysis: Theory and Applications. Prentice-Hall, Englewood Cliffs (1981)
23. Mycroft, A.: Completeness and predicate-based abstract interpretation. In: Proc. ACM Symp. Partial Evaluation (PEPM 1993), pp. 179–185 (1993)
24. Mycroft, A., Jones, N.D.: A relational framework for abstract interpretation. In: Ganzinger, H., Jones, N.D. (eds.) Programs as Data Objects. LNCS, vol. 217, pp. 156–171. Springer, Heidelberg (1986)
25. Ranzato, F., Tapparo, F.: Strong Preservation as Completeness in Abstract Interpretation. In: Schmidt, D. (ed.) ESOP 2004. LNCS, vol. 2986, pp. 18–32. Springer, Heidelberg (2004)

26. Ranzato, F., Tapparo, F.: Strong preservation of temporal fixpoint-based operators. In: Emerson, E.A., Namjoshi, K.S. (eds.) VMCAI 2006. LNCS, vol. 3855, pp. 332–347. Springer, Heidelberg (2005)
27. Sagiv, M., Reps, T., Wilhelm, R.: Parametric shape analysis via 3-valued logic. ACM TOPLAS 24, 217–298 (2002)
28. Saïdi, H.: Model Checking Guided Abstraction and Analysis. In: Palsberg, J. (ed.) SAS 2000. LNCS, vol. 1824, pp. 377–396. Springer, Heidelberg (2000)
29. Schmidt, D.A.: Comparing Completeness Properties of Static Analyses and Their Logics. In: Kobayashi, N. (ed.) APLAS 2006. LNCS, vol. 4279, pp. 183–199. Springer, Heidelberg (2006)
30. Schmidt, D.A.: Underapproximating Predicate Transformers. In: Yi, K. (ed.) SAS 2006. LNCS, vol. 4134, pp. 127–143. Springer, Heidelberg (2006)

From LTL to Symbolically Represented Deterministic Automata

Andreas Morgenstern and Klaus Schneider

University of Kaiserslautern
P.O. Box 3049
67653 Kaiserslautern, Germany
{morgenstern,schneider}@informatik.uni-kl.de

Abstract. Temporal logics like LTL are frequently used for the specification and verification of reactive systems. For verification, LTL formulas are typically translated to generalized *nondeterministic* Büchi automata so that the verification problem is reduced to checking the emptiness of automata. While this can be done symbolically for nondeterministic automata, other applications require deterministic automata, so that a subsequent determinization step is required. Unfortunately, currently known determinization procedures for Büchi automata like Safra's procedure are not amenable to a symbolic implementation.

It is well-known that ω-automata that stem from LTL formulas have special properties. In this paper, we exploit such a property in a new determinization procedure for these automata. Our procedure avoids the use of complicated tree structures as used in Safra's procedure and it generates *symbolic* descriptions of equivalent deterministic parity automata which was so far not possible for full LTL.

1 Introduction

Finite automata on infinite words (called ω-automata) [27] are nowadays used for the specification and verification of all kinds of reactive systems [31,25]. In particular, model checking of the temporal logic LTL [21,7] became one of the most popular verification techniques. To check whether a system $\mathcal{M}$ satisfies a LTL property φ, the negation $\neg\varphi$ is usually first translated to an equivalent *nondeterministic* ω-automaton $\mathfrak{A}_{\neg\varphi}$ so that the emptiness of the product $\mathcal{M} \times \mathfrak{A}_{\neg\varphi}$ can be checked in a second step. Algorithms that translate the LTL formulas to *symbolically*[1] *represented nondeterministic* ω-automata have been developed [29,6,12,24,25,3] to benefit from symbolic set representations [4]. As the use of symbolic methods in verification was the major breakthrough to handle real-world problems, the computation of symbolic descriptions of the automata is,

[1] For an LTL formula φ, these procedures compute in time $O(|\varphi|)$ a symbolic description of a nondeterministic ω-automaton $\mathfrak{A}_\varphi$. The symbolic description of the automaton $\mathfrak{A}_\varphi$ has size $O(|\varphi|)$ and encodes $O(2^{|\varphi|})$ states. Symbolically represented nondeterministic ω-automata are related to alternating ω-automata [28] (but are not the same).

F. Logozzo et al. (Eds.): VMCAI 2008, LNCS 4905, pp. 279–293, 2008.

from a practical point of view, very important to deal with large automata. To summarize, symbolic descriptions are already successfully used for implementations of algorithms on nondeterministic automata.

In contrast, many algorithms like the synthesis of winning strategies that are formulated in LTL [22,14,11] or the analysis of Markov decision processes [30] are based on *deterministic* automata. Many of these algorithms have not yet made their way to industrial practice, although they would solve important problems in the design of reactive systems. We believe that one reason for this situation is the lack of efficient algorithms to compute deterministic automata: Determinization procedures are usually based on data structures that do not make use of symbolic set representations.

In particular, the linear time temporal logic LTL is still one of the most convenient specification logic, and essentially all state-of-the-art translations of LTL formulas to ω-automata yield *nondeterministic* Büchi automata. If deterministic automata are required, Safra's well-known determinization procedure [23] is usually employed to compute a deterministic (Rabin) automaton. Unfortunately, Safra's algorithm is difficult to implement [10,26,13], and the underlying data structures (trees of subsets of states) do not allow the use of symbolic set representations. As a consequence, the related tools are limited to small LTL formulas. We believe that an efficient algorithm to compute deterministic automata for given LTL formulas is the key to push several other algorithms towards industrial use.

In this paper, we therefore present a new determinization procedure for (generalized) Büchi automata that stem from the translation of LTL formulas by the 'standard' translation. To this end, we make use of the fact that these automata have a special property that we call non-confluence (see Definition 1 for a precise definition):

An automaton is non-confluent if whenever two runs of the same infinite word meet at a state q, then they must share the entire finite prefix up to state q.

It is well-known that the ω-automata that stem from LTL formulas are a special class that has already found several characterizations. Due to results of [16], the automata can be characterized as *non-counting* automata, and in terms of alternating automata, the class of *linear weak* or *very weak* automata has been defined [17,9,19,18]. Moreover, many translation procedures from LTL generate *unambiguous automata* [5] where every accepted word has a unique accepting run [25,1] (although there may be additional non-accepting runs for the same word). Without useless states, unambiguity implies the above non-confluence property, but not vice versa; and non-confluence has nothing to do with the non-counting property.

The above non-confluence property allows us to develop a determinization procedure that exploits symbolic set representations. In particular, it does not rely on Safra trees as used by Safra's original procedure [23] or by the improved version of Piterman [20]. The states of the deterministic automata obtained by these procedures are trees of subsets of states of the original automaton. In contrast, our procedure generates deterministic automata whose states consist of n-tuples of subsets of states, where n is the number of states of the nondeterministic automaton.

The non-confluence property has already been used in [8] to obtain a deterministic (Rabin) automaton from a nondeterministic Büchi automaton. However, the algorithm of [8] still uses a tree structure and is therefore not well suited for a symbolic implementation. In contrast, our automata are amenable to a symbolic implementation and are additionally defined with the simpler parity acceptance condition which further reduces the complexities for game solving and emptiness checks.

The outline of the paper is as follows: In the next section, we list basic definitions on ω-automata and we describe the 'standard' translation from LTL to generalized nondeterministic Büchi automata. The core of the paper is the determinization procedure described in Section 3 that is a specialization of Safra's procedure for non-confluent automata. In Section 4, we discuss a symbolic implementation of our algorithm.

2 Preliminaries

2.1 Non-confluent ω-Automata

A *nondeterministic ω-automaton* is a tuple $\mathfrak{A} = (\Sigma, \mathcal{Q}, \delta, \mathcal{I}, \mathcal{F})$, where Σ is a finite alphabet, $\mathcal{Q}$ is a finite set of states, $\delta : \mathcal{Q} \times \Sigma \to 2^{\mathcal{Q}}$ is the transition function, $\mathcal{I} \subseteq \mathcal{Q}$ is the set of initial states, and $\mathcal{F} \subseteq \mathcal{Q}$ is the acceptance condition of the ω-automaton. A *run* ξ of $\mathfrak{A}$ on an infinite word $\alpha = \alpha^{(0)}\alpha^{(1)}\ldots \in \Sigma^\omega$ is an infinite sequence of states $\xi = \xi^{(0)}\xi^{(1)}\ldots \in \mathcal{Q}^\omega$ such that $\xi^{(0)} \in \mathcal{I}$ and for all $i \geq 0$, we have $\xi^{(i+1)} \in \delta(\xi^{(i)}, \alpha^{(i)})$. For a run $\xi = \xi^{(0)}\xi^{(1)}\ldots$, let $\inf \xi := \{q \in \mathcal{Q} \mid |\{i \in \mathbb{N} \mid q = \xi^{(i)}\}| = \infty\}$ be the set of all states that occur infinitely often on the run. In the following, we consider different kinds of acceptance conditions [27,25] that are defined as follows:

- A *Büchi condition* is specified by a set of accepting (marked) states $\mathcal{F} \subseteq \mathcal{Q}$. A run ξ is *accepting* according to the Büchi condition if $\inf \xi \cap \mathcal{F} \neq \emptyset$. That is, the run visits at least one state of $\mathcal{F}$ infinitely often.
- A *generalized Büchi condition* is defined by a set of sets of accepting (marked) states $\{\mathcal{F}_0, \ldots, \mathcal{F}_n\}$ where $\mathcal{F}_i \subseteq \mathcal{Q}$. A run ξ is *accepting* according to the Büchi condition if $\inf \xi \cap \mathcal{F}_i \neq \emptyset$ holds for all $i \in \{0, \ldots, n\}$. That is, the run visits at least one state of each $\mathcal{F}_i$ infinitely often.
- A *parity condition* is specified by a coloring function $c : \mathcal{Q} \to \{0, \ldots k\}$ that assigns a color $\lambda(c) \in \mathbb{N}$ to each state $q \in \mathcal{Q}$ of the automaton. The coloring function induces a partition $\{F_0, F_1, \ldots F_k\}$ of $\mathcal{Q}$ where $F_i := \{q \in \mathcal{Q} \mid \lambda(q) = i\}$. The number of colors k is called the *index* of the parity condition. A run is *accepting* according to the parity condition if for some even number i, we have $\inf \xi \cap F_i \neq \emptyset$ and for all $i' < i$, we have $\inf \xi \cap F_i' = \emptyset$. That is, the minimal color i whose set F_i is infinitely often visited is even.

A word α is *accepted* by $\mathfrak{A}$ if there exists an accepting run of $\mathfrak{A}$ over α. The *language* $\mathsf{Lang}(\mathfrak{A})$ of $\mathfrak{A}$ is the set of words accepted by $\mathfrak{A}$. Two automata are *equivalent* if they accept the same language. An automaton is *deterministic* if for every state $q \in \mathcal{Q}$ and input $\sigma \in \Sigma$, we have $|\delta(q,\sigma)| = 1$ and $|\mathcal{I}| = 1$. In the definition of the determinization construction, we will need the existential successors of a state set. For every $S \subseteq \mathcal{Q}$ define $\mathsf{suc}_{\exists}^{\delta,\sigma}(S) := \{q' \in \mathcal{Q} \mid \exists q \in S.\, q' \in \delta(q,\sigma)\}$

The following property is the basis of our determinization procedure:

Definition 1 (Non-Confluent Automata)
An ω-automaton $\mathfrak{A} = (\Sigma, \mathcal{Q}, \delta, \mathcal{I}, \mathcal{F})$ is called non-confluent if for every word α the following holds: if ξ_1 and ξ_2 are two runs of $\mathfrak{A}$ on α that intersect at a position t_0 (i.e. $\xi_1^{(t_0)} = \xi_2^{(t_0)}$ holds), then we have $\xi_1^{(t)} = \xi_2^{(t)}$ for every $t \leq t_0$.

Note that deterministic automata are trivially non-confluent, since the run is uniquely determined. *Moreover, the product of a non-confluent automaton with another automaton is non-confluent.*

In Section 2.2 and Section 4 we will additionally need symbolic representations of ω-automata. Since both the alphabet Σ and the state set $\mathcal{Q}$ are finite sets, we can encode them by boolean variables V_Σ and use variables $V_\mathcal{Q}$. Introducing new variables v' for each variable $v \in V_\mathcal{Q} \cup V_\Sigma$, we can moreover also encode the transition relation:

Definition 2 (Symbolic Representation of ω-Automata). *Given a finite set of variables $V_\mathcal{Q}$ with $V_\mathcal{Q} \cap V_\Sigma = \{\}$, a propositional formula $\mathcal{I}$ over $V_\mathcal{Q} \cup V_\Sigma$, a propositional formula $\mathcal{R}$ over $V_\mathcal{Q} \cup V_\Sigma \cup \{v' \mid v \in V_\mathcal{Q} \cup V_\Sigma\}$, and formulas $\mathcal{F}_0, \ldots, \mathcal{F}_k$ over $V_\mathcal{Q} \cup V_\Sigma$, then $\mathcal{A}_\exists(V_\mathcal{Q}, \mathcal{I}, \mathcal{R}, \mathcal{F}_0, \ldots \mathcal{F}_k)$ is an (existential) automaton formula.*

It is easily seen [25] that for automaton formulas $\mathcal{A}_\exists(V_\mathcal{Q}, \mathcal{I}, \mathcal{R}, \mathcal{F}_0, \ldots, \mathcal{F}_k)$, we can demand that the formulas $\mathcal{I}$ and $\mathcal{F}_i$ contain only state variables $V_\mathcal{Q}$ (yielding state-based instead of edge-based automata). In these cases, it is clear that an automaton formula describes a nondeterministic ω-automaton in a symbolic way: We identify any set $\vartheta \subseteq V_\mathcal{Q} \cup V_\Sigma \cup \{v' \mid v \in V_\mathcal{Q} \cup V_\Sigma\}$ with a propositional interpretation that exactly assigns the variables of ϑ to true. Having this view, the formula $\mathcal{I}$ describes the set of the initial states $\vartheta \subseteq V_\mathcal{Q}$ that satisfy $\mathcal{I}$. Similarly, $\mathcal{R}$ describes the set of transitions. Finally, the tuple $\mathcal{F}_0, \ldots, \mathcal{F}_k$ represents the acceptance condition (either generalized Büchi or parity).

2.2 From LTL to Non-confluent Bühi Automata

A construction from LTL to non-confluent Büchi automata has already been presented in [8]. Moreover, recent algorithms for the translation of LTL to Büchi automata like the symbolic constructions of [29,6,12,24,25] also yield non-confluent automata. In this section, we briefly review these procedures and prove that their results are non-confluent automata. To this end, we consider LTL with the temporal operators X (next), U (weak until), and $\underline{\mathsf{U}}$ (strong until). Notice that in this section we use the symbolic representation of ω-automata.

As explained in [24,25], the 'standard' translation procedure from LTL to ω-automata traverses the syntax tree of the LTL formula in a bottom-up manner and abbreviates each subformula that starts with a temporal operator. The subformula $[\varphi\ \underline{\mathsf{U}}\ \psi]$ is thereby abbreviated by a new state variable q, and the preliminary transition relation $\mathcal{R}$ is replaced with $\mathcal{R} \wedge (q \leftrightarrow \psi \vee \varphi \wedge q')$. Moreover, we have to add the fairness constraint $\mathcal{F}_i :\equiv (q \rightarrow \psi)$ as a new set of accepting states. The subformula $[\varphi\ \mathsf{U}\ \psi]$ is also abbreviated by a new state variable q with the same update of the transition relation. However, we add the fairness constraint $\mathcal{F}_i :\equiv (\varphi \rightarrow q)$. Finally, a subformula $\mathsf{X}\varphi$ introduces two new state variables q_1 and q_2. The subformula $\mathsf{X}\varphi$ is replaced by q_2, the transition relation $\mathcal{R}$ is updated to $\mathcal{R} \wedge (q_1 \leftrightarrow \varphi) \wedge (q_1' \leftrightarrow q_2)$ and no fairness constraint is generated. For more information, see the detailed explanations in Chapter 5.4.1 of [25].

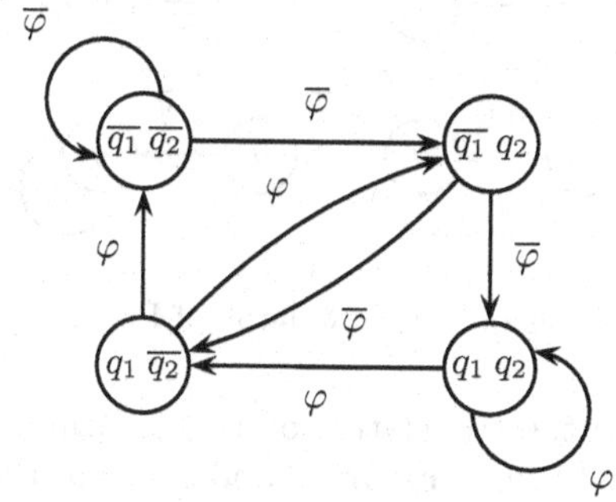

φ	$(q_1 \leftrightarrow \varphi) \wedge (q_1' \leftrightarrow q_2)$
0	$(q_1 \leftrightarrow 0) \wedge (q_1' \leftrightarrow q_2)$
1	$(q_1 \leftrightarrow 1) \wedge (q_1' \leftrightarrow q_2)$

Fig. 1. ω-Automaton with Transition Relation $(q_1 \leftrightarrow \varphi) \wedge (q_1' \leftrightarrow q_2)$

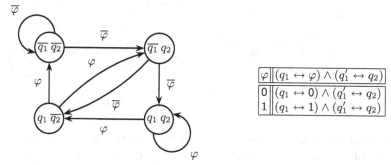

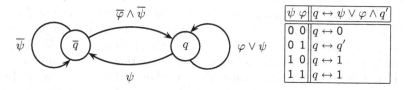

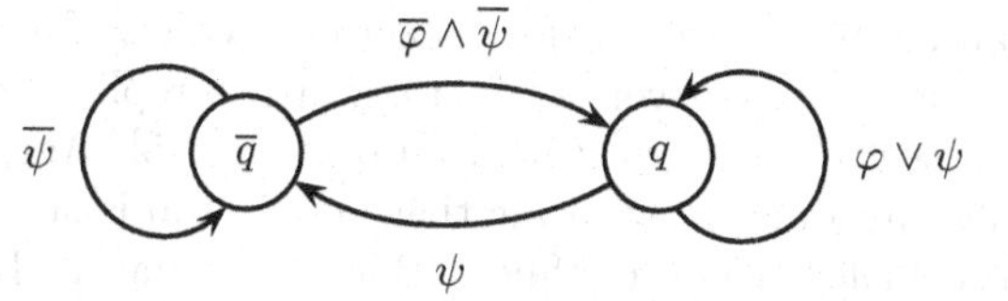

ψ φ	$q \leftrightarrow \psi \vee \varphi \wedge q'$
0 0	$q \leftrightarrow 0$
0 1	$q \leftrightarrow q'$
1 0	$q \leftrightarrow 1$
1 1	$q \leftrightarrow 1$

Fig. 2. ω-Automaton with Transition Relation $q \leftrightarrow \psi \vee \varphi \wedge q'$

Hence, the transition relation of the ω-automaton obtained by this translation is a conjunction of equations $q \leftrightarrow \psi \vee \varphi \wedge q'$ and $(q_1 \leftrightarrow \varphi) \wedge (q_1' \leftrightarrow q_2)$. We only consider the first equation in more detail: As can be seen by Figure 2, the input $\varphi \wedge \neg\psi$ demands that the current state is maintained, but allows the automaton to be in any of the two states. The other three classes of inputs uniquely determine the current state, but leave the successor state completely unspecified. As a consequence, input words that infinitely often satisfy $\neg(\varphi \wedge \neg\psi)$, i.e., $\neg\varphi \vee \psi$, do only have one (infinite) run, while the remaining input words that satisfy $\varphi \wedge \neg\psi$ from a certain point of time on do have two runs that are of the form ξq^ω and $\xi \overline{q}^\omega$ with the same finite prefix ξ. Hence, the automaton is non-confluent. A similar consideration shows that the automaton of Figure 1 is also non-confluent.

An example run tree (that encodes all the runs of a given word) is shown in Fig. 3. It is seen that there is a uniquely determined run, since all other nondeterministic choices lead to finite paths. Another example run tree that contains two infinite runs is shown in Fig. 4.

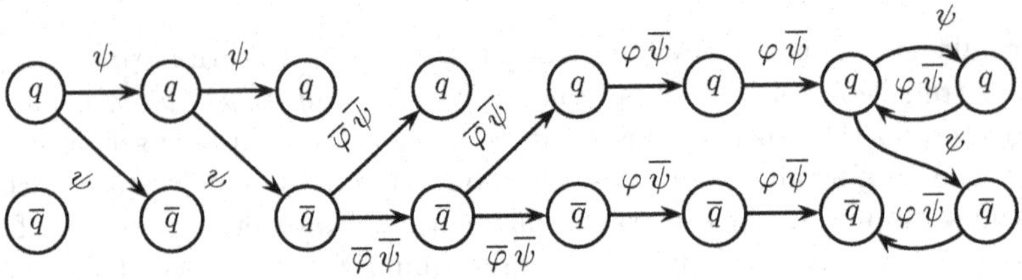

Fig. 3. Run Tree with a Uniquely Determined Run of the Automaton of Fig. 2

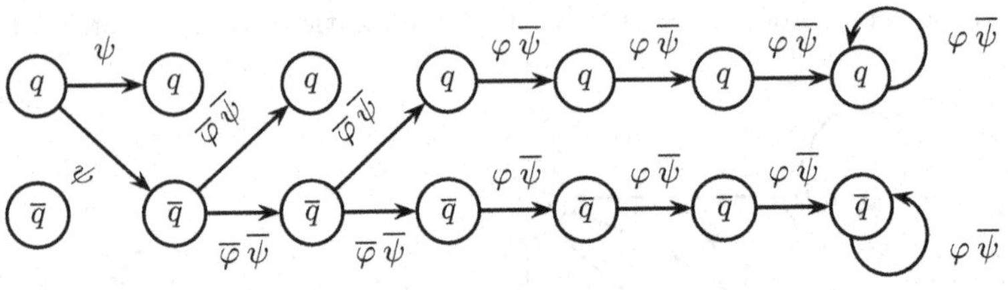

Fig. 4. Run Tree with a Two Runs of the Automaton of Fig. 2

As every automaton $\mathfrak{A}_\varphi$ obtained by the translation of a LTL formula φ is a product of the non-confluent automata shown in Figures 1 and 2, and as the product automaton of non-confluent automata is also non-confluent, it follows that the automata $\mathfrak{A}_\varphi$ obtained by the above 'standard' translation are non-confluent.

The resulting automaton of the above translation is a generalized Büchi automaton, since we obtain an accepting set of states (actually edges) for every occurrence of an until-operator. It is however straightforward to replace a conjunction of fairness constraints with a single Büchi automaton [25]. Again, as the product of a non-confluent automaton with another automaton is still non-confluent, this reduction also yields a non-confluent Büchi automaton. In the following section, we will show how this non-confluent Büchi automaton can be determinized.

3 The Determinization Procedure

The well-known subset construction collects the sets of states that the nondeterministic automaton $\mathfrak{A} = (\Sigma, \mathcal{Q}, \mathcal{I}, \delta, \mathcal{F})$ can reach after having read a finite input word from one of its initial states $\mathcal{I}$. Thus, every state $\tilde{s} \subseteq \mathcal{Q}$ of the deterministic automaton $\tilde{\mathfrak{A}}$ is a set of states of $\mathcal{Q}$. The final states $\tilde{\mathcal{F}}$ are those states $\tilde{s} \subseteq \mathcal{Q}$ that contain an accepting state of $\mathfrak{A}$, i.e. where $\tilde{s} \cap \mathcal{F} \neq \emptyset$ holds.

The acceptance condition of a Büchi automaton $\mathfrak{A} = (\Sigma, \mathcal{Q}, \mathcal{I}, \delta, \mathcal{F})$ is also specified with a set of accepting states $\mathcal{F}$. However, the subset construction is not sufficient to handle the Büchi acceptance, so that the more complex construction of Safra [23] is often used instead. The idea of Safra's construction is to define so-called breakpoints on the path $\tilde{\xi}$ of a word α through $\tilde{\mathfrak{A}}$ so that all paths ξ contained in $\tilde{\xi}$ must visit at least once the accepting states $\mathcal{F}$ in between two subsequent breakpoints. A path $\tilde{\xi}$ is then accepting iff it visits infinitely often breakpoints with non-empty state sets. To this end, the states of the automaton obtained by Safra's construction are trees of subsets of states.

Our determinization procedure is a specialization of Safra's procedure for non-confluent automata. The states of the constructed automaton are n-tuples of pairs (S_i, m_i) where $S_i \subseteq \mathcal{Q}$ and $m_i \in \{\mathsf{false}, \mathsf{true}\}$ holds. We start with the initial state $((\mathcal{I}, \mathsf{false}), (\emptyset, \mathsf{false}), \ldots, (\emptyset, \mathsf{false}))$. To compute the successor of a state $((S_0, m_0), \ldots, (S_{n-1}, m_{n-1}))$, we compute the existential successors $S_i' := \mathsf{suc}_{\exists}^{\delta,\sigma}(S_i)$ for the subsets of states. Hence, the first state set S_0 of a tuple state is the result of the subset construction, i.e., it contains the sets of states that $\mathfrak{A}$ can reach after having read a finite input word from one of its initial states $\mathcal{I}$. The other sets S_i with $i > 0$ are subsets of S_0 that are generated as follows: Whenever we generate a new tuple where $S_0' := \mathsf{suc}_{\exists}^{\delta,\sigma}(S_0)$ contains accepting states, we add the new state set $S_{\mathtt{M}+1}' := S_0' \cap \mathcal{F}$ at the 'rightmost free' entry in the tuple to remember that those paths that lead to states $S_0' \cap \mathcal{F}$ already visited $\mathcal{F}$.

We can however cleanup the states $S_1, \ldots, S_{n-1}$, so that not all combinations of state sets can occur: Whenever we find that a state set S_i with $i > 0$ contains only states that also occur in sets S_j with $j > i$, we mark S_i as accepting by setting its mark $m_i := \mathsf{true}$ and remove the states S_i from the state sets S_j. As a consequence, for every state set S_i with $i > 0$, there must be at least one state that does not occur in the sets S_j with $i < j$, and therefore n-tuples are sufficient for the construction (we use empty sets $\emptyset$ for currently unused entries). Moreover, we can delete empty State sets by simply moving each entry that is on the right of the first empty set one index to the left.

As $\mathfrak{A}$ is non-confluent, we know that a finite run is uniquely characterized by its final state. Hence, if a state occurs in two sets S_i and S_j, then we know that both sets follow the same run. New state sets are only introduced on the 'right' of the tuple, i.e., at position $\mathtt{M}+1$ where $\mathtt{M}$ is the maximal entry with $S_i \neq \emptyset$. Hence, we know that all runs that end in $S_{\mathtt{M}+1}$ now visit an accepting state. If an entry S_i never becomes empty after a certain position on a path $\tilde{\xi}$ and is marked infinitely often, then we know that $\tilde{\xi}$ is introduce infinitely often on the right of S_i, nameley in set $S_{\mathtt{M}+1}$ and hence $\tilde{\xi}$ contains an accepting run of $\mathfrak{A}$.

Definition 3 (Determinization of Non-Confluent Automata). *Given a nondeterministic Büchi automaton $\mathfrak{A} = (\Sigma, \mathcal{Q}, \mathcal{I}, \delta, \mathcal{F})$ with $|\mathcal{Q}| = n$, we construct a deterministic parity automaton $\mathfrak{P} = (\Sigma, \mathcal{S}, s_{\mathcal{I}}, \rho, \lambda)$ as follows:*

- *The states of the parity automaton are n-tuples of subsets of $\mathcal{Q}$ augmented with a boolean flag: $\mathcal{S} = \{((S_0, m_0), \ldots, (S_{n-1}, m_{n-1})) \mid S_i \subseteq \mathcal{Q} \wedge m_i \in \{\mathsf{false}, \mathsf{true}\}\}$.*
- *The initial state is $s_{\mathcal{I}} = ((\mathcal{I}, \mathsf{false}), (\emptyset, \mathsf{false}), \ldots, (\emptyset, \mathsf{false}))$.*
- *The successor state of a state $s = ((S_0, m_0), \ldots, (S_{n-1}, m_{n-1}))$ of automaton $\mathfrak{P}$ when reading input σ is determined by the function* `Successor` *given in Figure 5* [2].

[2] Notice that if $M = n - 1$, each entry is filled with exactly one state. This can be deduced from property 2 of lemma 1. Thus each final state leads to the marking of its corresponding state set, which means that the set S[M+1] would be removed anyway. Thus we skip the introduction of S[M+1] at that point.

```
fun Successor(stateset S[n],bool m[n],input σ) {
  int m,M; stateset P;
  // compute minimal m with S[m]==∅
  m = 0;
  while((S[m]!=∅)&(m<n-1)) m = m+1;
  // compute maximal M with S[M]!=∅
  M = n-1;
  while((S[M]==∅)&(M>0)) M = M-1;
  // compute existential successors and skip the empty set S[m]
  for i=0 to m-1 do S[i] = suc_∃^{δ,σ}(S[i]);
  for i=m to M do S[i] = suc_∃^{δ,σ}(S[i+1]);
  // add new set of states S[M+1] that reached F
  if (M<(n-1)) {
    S[M+1] = S[0]∩F;
  }
  // clean up sets S_1,...,S_{n-1} and compute marking of new state sets
  for i=0 to n-1 do {
    P = ∅;
    for j=i+1 to M do P = P∪S[j];
    if((S[i]\F ⊆ P) & S[i]!=∅) {
      m[i] = true;
      for j=i+1 to M do S[j]=(S[j] \ S[i]);
    }
  }
}
```

Fig. 5. Computation of the Successor State for Input σ

```
fun Color(stateset S[n],bool m[n]) {
  int c;
  if(S[0]==∅) return 1;
  c=2*n+1;
  for i=0 to n-1 do {
    if(S[i]==∅) c=min(c,2*i-1);
    if(m[i]) c=min(c,2*i);
  }
  return c;
}
```

Fig. 6. Computing the Color of a State

- *The color of a state* $s = ((S_0, m_0), \ldots, (S_{n-1}, m_{n-1}))$ *of automaton* $\mathfrak{P}$ *is determined by function* `Color` *given in Figure 6*[3].

As an example of the construction, consider the non-confluent Büchi automaton given in Figure 7 (accepting states have double lines) together with its equivalent

[3] If $S_0 = \emptyset$, we have a rejecting sink state, since this state can never be left. This state corresponds to a situation in the nondeterministic automaton where all runs lead to a dead end.

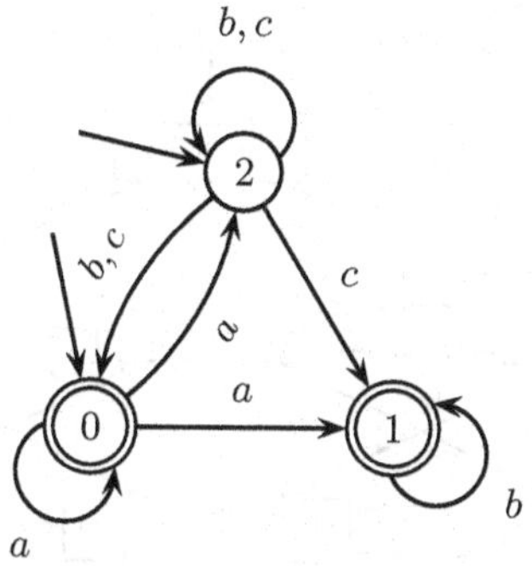

Fig. 7. Nondeterministic non-confluent automaton that accepts every word that either ends with suffix ab^ω or cb^ω or that contains infinitely many occurrences of a

deterministic parity automaton in Figure 8. To improve readability, we omitted the boolean flags, and instead overlined those state sets S_i in the tuples that are marked, i.e., whose flags m_i are true.

Lemma 1. *Given a non-confluent Büchi automaton* $\mathfrak{A} = (\Sigma, \mathcal{Q}, \mathcal{I}, \delta, \mathcal{F})$*, and the corresponding deterministic automaton* $\mathfrak{P} = (\Sigma, \mathcal{S}, s_{\mathcal{I}}, \rho, \lambda)$ *as given in Definition 3. Then, for every infinite word* $\alpha : \mathbb{N} \to \Sigma$*, and the corresponding run* $(S_0^{(0)}, \ldots, S_{n-1}^{(0)}), \ldots$ *of* $\mathfrak{P}$ *on* α*, the following holds:*

1. *For all* $i > 0$ *and* $t \in \mathbb{N}$*, we have* $S_i^{(t)} \subseteq S_0^{(t)}$.
2. *For all* i *and* $t \in \mathbb{N}$ *with* $S_i^{(t)} \neq \emptyset$*, there exists a* $q \in S_i^{(t)}$ *such that* $q \notin S_j^{(t)}$ *for all* $i < j < n$*. This property implies that* n *subsets are sufficient.*
3. *For every* $t_0 \in \mathbb{N}$ *and for every* $0 \leq i < n$*, we have:*

$$q \in S_i^{(t_0)} \Rightarrow \left(\begin{array}{l} \exists \xi : \mathbb{N} \to \mathcal{Q}.\ \left[\xi^{(0)} \in \mathcal{I}\right] \wedge \left[\xi^{(t_0)} = q\right] \wedge \\ \qquad\qquad\qquad \left[\forall t < t_0 . \xi^{(t+1)} \in \delta(\xi^{(t)}, \alpha^{(t)})\right] \end{array} \right)$$

4. *Let* $t_0 < t_1$ *be positions such that*
   - $S_i^{(t_0)}$ *and* $S_i^{(t_1)}$ *are marked, i.e.* $m_i^{(t_0)} = \mathsf{true}$ *and* $m_i^{(t_1)} = \mathsf{true}$
   - $S_i^{(t)} \neq \emptyset$ *for* $t_0 \leq t \leq t_1$
   - $S_j^{(t)}$ *is not marked and* $S_j^{(t)} \neq \emptyset$ *for* $i > j$ *and* $t_0 \leq t \leq t_1$

   Then, each finite run ξ *of* $\mathfrak{A}$ *with* $\xi^{(t_0)} \in S_i^{(t_0)}$ *and* $\xi^{(t_1)} \in S_i^{(t_1)}$ *must have visited* $\mathcal{F}$ *at least once between* t_0 *and* t_1.

Proof. Properties 1 and 2 follow directly from the definition of the transition function of $\mathfrak{P}$. Property 3 holds trivially for S_0: as long as the run continues (i.e. it does not end in a deadend state), we have $S_0 \neq \emptyset$ according to the definition of ρ. Thus $S_0^{(t+1)} = \mathsf{suc}_{\exists}^{\delta,\alpha^{(t)}}(S_0^{(t)})$ for every $t \in \mathbb{N}$. For $i > 0$ the result follows from property 1.

To prove property 4, consider a run ξ of $\mathfrak{A}$ with $\xi^{(t_0)} \in S_i^{(t_0)}$ and $\xi^{(t_1)} \in S_i^{(t_1)}$. For every position t between t_0 and t_1 we have (1) $S_i^{(t)} \neq \emptyset$, (2) $S_j^{(t)} \neq \emptyset$ for every $j < i$, and (3) $m_j^{(t)} = \mathsf{false}$ for every $j < i$.

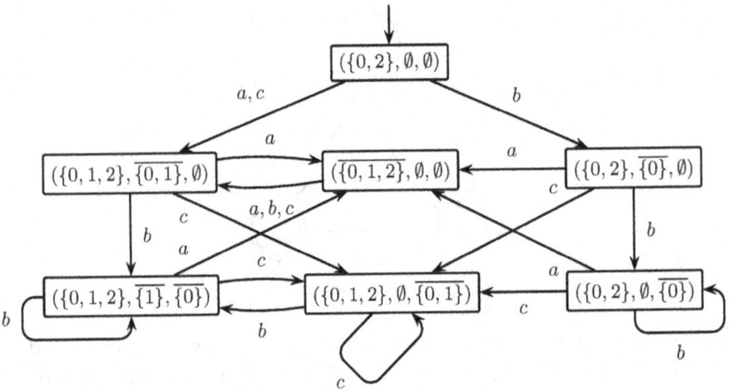

Fig. 8. Deterministic Parity Automaton obtained from the Automaton of Figure 7

We thus have $S_i^{(t+1)} = \mathsf{suc}_\exists^{\delta,\alpha^{(t)}}(S_i^{(t)})$ for every $t \in \{t_0,\dots,t_1-1\}$. Thus, we have $\xi^{(t)} \in S_i^{(t)}$ for every $t \in \{t_0,\dots,t_1\}$. Since $m_i^{(t_0)} = \mathsf{true}$, we have $\xi^{(t_0)} \notin S_j^{(t_0)}$ for every $j > i$ according to the definition of m. Let $t' > t_0$ be the first position after t_0 where $\xi^{(t'+1)} \in \bigcup_{j=i+1}^{n-1} S_j^{(t')}$. Such a position t' must exist in the run of $\mathfrak{P}$, since S_i is marked at position t_1. There must either exist an index $j > i$ such that $\xi^{(t'+1)} \in \delta(S_j^{(t')},\alpha^{(t')})$ or $\xi^{(t'+1)} \in \mathcal{F} \cap \mathsf{suc}_\exists^{\delta,\alpha^{(t')}}(S_0^{(t')})$. We will now show that the first case is impossible, leading to our desired result that ξ visits $\mathcal{F}$ at least once between t_0 and t_1. Assume by contradiction that $\xi^{(t'+1)} \in \mathsf{suc}_\exists^{\delta,\alpha^{(t')}}(S_j^{(t')})$. Then there must exist a state $q \in S_j^{(t')}$ such that $\xi^{(t'+1)} \in \delta(q,\alpha^{(t')})$. Thus according to property 3 there does exist a run ξ' that leads to q, i.e. $\xi'^{(t')} = q$. However, continuing this run with $\delta(q,\alpha^{(t')})$ leads to $\xi'^{(t'+1)}$. Either ξ' and ξ coincide which leads to a contradition to $t'+1$ being the first position where $\xi^{(t'+1)}$ is introduced in some $S_j, j > i$ or they do not coincide which is a contradiction to $\mathfrak{A}$ being non-confluent. □

With the help of this lemma we are prepared to show correctness of our determinization procedure:

Theorem 1. *The deterministic parity automaton $\mathfrak{P}$ constructed for an arbitrary non-confluent Büchi automaton $\mathfrak{A}$ as described in Definition 3 is equivalent to $\mathfrak{A}$.*

Proof.

$\mathsf{Lang}(\mathfrak{P}) \subseteq \mathsf{Lang}(\mathfrak{A})$: Let $\alpha \in \mathsf{Lang}(\mathfrak{P})$ and $\pi = (S_0^{(0)},\dots S_{n-1}^{(0)}), (S_1^{(1)},\dots S_{n-1}^{(1)}), \dots$ be the corresponding run of $\mathfrak{P}$. Since α is accepted, there does exist t_0 such that $\lambda(\pi^{(t)}) = 2i$ for infinitely many t and $\lambda(\pi^{(t)}) \geq 2i$ for every $t > t_0$. Thus we have that $S_j^{(t)} \neq \emptyset$ and $m_j^{(t)} = \mathsf{false}$ for every $j < i$ and every $t > t_0$. Let $t_1 < t_2 < \cdots$ be the i-breakpoints, i.e. positions where $S_i^{(t_j)}$ is marked. Define $Q^{(0)} = \mathcal{I} = S_0^{(0)}$ and for each $t > 1$ define $Q^{(j)} = S_i^{(t_j)}$. For each initial state, we construct a tree as follows: the vertices are taken from the set $\{(q,t) \mid q \in Q^{(t)}\}$. As the parent of $(q, t+1)$ (with $q \in Q^{(t+1)}$) we pick one of the pairs (p,t) such that $p \in Q^{(t)}$ holds and that there is a run ξ of $\mathfrak{A}$ on $\alpha[t, t+1]$ between p and q according to property 3 of lemma 1. Clearly, these trees are finitely branching, since each S_i is finite. Moreover, for at least one initial state q_0 the corresponding tree must have an infinite number of vertices, because we have an infinite sequence of breakpoints and $S_j^{(t)} \neq \emptyset$ for every $j \leq i$. Therefore, we conclude by Königs lemma that there is an initial state such that there is an infinite path $(q_0, 0), (q_1, 1), \cdots$ through the tree we have constructed for q_0. This infinite path corresponds to an infinite run of $\mathfrak{A}$ on α. Recall now that according to the construction of the tree the finite pieces of the run that connect q_i to q_{i+1} while consuming the word $\alpha^{(t_i)}, \cdots \alpha^{(t_{i+1}-1)}$ visit, at least once, the set of accepting states between t_i and t_{i+1} due to property 4. Since we have an infinite number of breakpoints, we have constructed an accepting run of $\mathfrak{A}$.

$\mathsf{Lang}(\mathfrak{A}) \subseteq \mathsf{Lang}(\mathfrak{P})$: Given a word $\alpha \in \mathsf{Lang}(\mathfrak{A})$ with an accepting run ξ. We must prove that the corresponding run π of $\mathfrak{P}$ is also accepting, i.e. there does exist an index i such that for all $j \leq i$ S_i is empty only finitely many times and S_i is marked infinitely many times. Since ξ is an accepting run of α we have $S_0^{(t)} \neq \emptyset$ for every t. If S_0 is marked infinitely often, we are done. Otherwise, let t_0 be the first visit of ξ of a marked state after the last time where S_0 is marked. According to the definition of the transition relation, there must exist a minimal index $j > 0$ such that $\xi^{(t_0)} \in S_j^{(t_0)}$. Let $i^{(t)}$ be the minimal index $i > 0$ such that $\xi^{(t)} \in S_i^{(t)}$ for every $t > t_0$. We first show that such an index must exist for all positions $t > t_0$: since ξ is introduced in a set $S_{j'}^{(t_0)}$ with minimal index, ξ can only be removed from $S_{j'}$ iff either the state set moves to the left (in case a set on the left is empty) or it is removed due to the fact that some S_i is marked for $i < j$. However, both cases do not apply to $S_0^{(t)}$ after position t_0. Thus after finitely many steps the i gets constant and $i > 0$. Let i_1 be the smallest index $i_1 > 0$ to which the $i^{(t)}$ converges and t_1' be the position after which $i^{(t)} = i_1^{(t)}$ for every $t > t_1'$. Then necessarily, we have $S_j^{(t)} \neq \emptyset$ for every $j < i_1$ and every $t > t_0'$. We apply the same argument on S_{i_1}. We again distinguish two cases: either infinitely often S_{i_1} is marked (so that we have constructed an accepting run), or there exists a position t_1 after which $S_{i_1}^{(t)}$ is not marked for every $t > t_1$. But then there must exist another index $i_2 > i_1$ which does (after finitely many steps) contain run ξ and never gets empty. Repeating this argumentation $n = |S|$ times means that all S_i, $i \in \{0, \ldots, n-1\}$ follow run ξ and never get empty according to our assumption. According to lemma 1 every state set contains at least one unique state. Thus $S_n^{(t)}$ can possess no more than one state in every position $t > t_n'$. But then $S_n^{(t)}$ is marked in those positions where this uniquely defined state $q \in S_n^{(t)}$ is a marked state of the nondeterministic automaton. □

Concerning the complexity, we have the following result:

Theorem 2. *Given a non-confluent Büchi automaton with n states, the construction given in Definition 3 yields a deterministic parity automaton with at most $2^{(n+n^2)}$ states and index $2n$.*

Proof. There are 2^n possibilities for the marking variables m_i. Moreover, the membership of a state q in one of the n state sets of a tuple can be represented with n boolean variables, which requires n^2 variables for the n states. All in all, this yields the upper bound $2^{(n+n^2)}$ for the possible states of $\mathfrak{P}$. □

The above upper bound is worse that the best known complexity results for determinization, which is typical for algorithms that allow symbolic set representations: For example, the best known (explicit) algorithm to solve parity games is much better than the best known symbolic algorithm. In our case, we have an additional blowup compared to Piterman's (explicit) determinization procedure that only needs n^{2n} states and index $2n$. However, it is nearly impossible to store such a huge state space explicitely.

The same blowup also occurs when using the approach of [15] for the solution of LTL games or decision procedures: the constructed nondeterministic Büchi tree automaton (that may also be implemented symbolically) has $O(2^{n^2})$ states. In the context of LTL synthesis, the approach of [11] can also be applied that yields parity automata with $2^n \cdot n^{2n}$ states and index $2n$. Their automata can also be represented symbolically. However, they also need n state sets and thus an efficient symbolic implementation will need n^2 state variables as well. The drawback of the approach of [11] is that it can not be used for decision problems as already mentioned there. Moreover, it is unclear wether one of the two approaches can be used for the verification of Markov decision processes.

4 Symbolic Implementation

For the symbolic implementation of our algorithm, we introduce n state variables $q_0, \ldots .q_{n-1}$ together with their next version $q'_0, \ldots, q'_{n-1}$ for each state $q \in \mathcal{Q}$ of $\mathfrak{A}$ to encode the n state sets of the deterministic automaton $\mathfrak{P}$. Thus, the interpretation of $q_i = \mathsf{true}$ is that q is contained in S_i. Additionally, we have to introduce variables m_i to calculate the coloring function. The initial condition is specified by the following equation:

$$\Phi_{\mathcal{I}} = \bigvee_{q\in\mathcal{I}} q_0 \wedge \bigwedge_{q\notin\mathcal{I}} \neg q_0 \wedge \bigwedge_{q\in\mathcal{S}} \bigwedge_{i=1}^{n-1} \neg q_i \wedge \bigwedge_{i=0}^{n-1} \neg m_i$$

To define the transition relation, we assume that we have already calculated a equation for the set S_0. Such an equation can be obtained for example by techniques presented in [2] where it is shown how to represent the Rabin-Scott subset construction symbolically. We thus assume that we have an equation $\Delta_0 = \bigwedge_{q\in\mathcal{Q}} \mathsf{X}q \leftrightarrow \varphi_0^q$ that determines for each q whether q is present in the next step in state set S_0. In the following, we write φ_j^q to denote the formula that is obtained from φ_0^q by replacing each state variable p_0 with p_j. Notice that in φ_0^q only variables of the current step appear, and no next-variables appear in that formula. To define the transition relation, we need some definitions in advance: we will first need a formula that checks wether i is smaller than $\mathtt{M}$ as well as a formula that determines whether or not the current index is bigger than $\mathtt{m}$. Remember that M is the maximal index that represents a nonempty set and m is the minimal index with an empty set. Both formulas that check the position of i between M and m can be defined as follows:

$$\begin{aligned}\Gamma_{(i=\mathtt{M})} &= \left(\bigvee_{p\in\mathcal{Q}} p_i\right) \wedge \left(\neg \bigvee_{j>i} \bigvee_{p\in\mathcal{Q}} p_j\right)\\ \Gamma_{(i\geq\mathtt{m})} &= \bigvee_{j\leq i} \neg \bigvee_{p\in\mathcal{Q}} p_j\end{aligned}$$

We will start by introducing the equations for the variables m_i: a state set S_i is marked, iff every non-marked state $q \notin \mathcal{F}$ would appear in a state set S_j for $j > i$. Thus, we get the following equation:

$$\Xi_i = m_i' \leftrightarrow \bigwedge_{q\in\mathcal{Q}\setminus\mathcal{F}} \left(q_i' \rightarrow \bigvee_{j=i+1}^{n-1} \varphi_j^q \right)$$

To define the equations for the state variables, we have to distinguish the case that S_i moves to the left because of an empty state set on the left of the current index, or it stays at its position. For $q \in \mathcal{Q} \setminus \mathcal{F}$, we obtain:

$$\Phi_i^q = q_i' \leftrightarrow \left(\neg\Gamma_{(i\geq\mathtt{m})} \wedge \varphi_i^q \vee \Gamma_{(i\geq\mathtt{m})} \wedge \varphi_{i+1}^q\right) \wedge \neg \bigvee_{j=0}^{i-1} (q_j' \wedge m_j')$$

If $i \geq \mathtt{m}$, then S_i contains the successors of S_{i+1}, i.e. $\mathsf{suc}_\exists^{\delta,\sigma}(S_{i+1})$ which is reflected by the different φ_{i+1}^q. Otherwise, the presence depends on the successor obtained from S_i which is represented by the different φ_i^q. Notice that the term $\neg \bigvee_{j=0}^{i-1} (q_j' \wedge m_j')$ removes those states that are contained in a marked state set on the left of the current index.

For marked states $p \in \mathcal{F}$, we have to handle the case when the state is introduced at position $\mathtt{M}+1$ because it appears in S_0'.

$$\Psi_i^p = p_i' \leftrightarrow \left(\neg\Gamma_{(i\geq\mathtt{m})} \wedge \varphi_i^p \vee \Gamma_{(i\geq\mathtt{m})} \wedge \varphi_{i+1}^p \vee \Gamma_{(i-1=\mathtt{M})} \wedge \varphi_0^p\right) \wedge \neg \bigvee_{j=0}^{i-1} (q_j' \wedge m_j')$$

The overall transition relation is now given by:

$$\rho = \Delta_0 \wedge \bigwedge_{i=1}^{n-1} \left(\Xi_i \wedge \bigwedge_{q\in\mathcal{Q}\setminus\mathcal{F}} \Phi_i^q \wedge \bigwedge_{p\in\mathcal{F}} \Psi_i^p \right)$$

5 Conclusions

In this paper, we presented a translation of non-confluent nondeterministic Büchi automata to equivalent deterministic parity automata. As non-confluent Büchi automata are obtained by the 'standard' translation from LTL formulas, we obtain an efficient translation from LTL to deterministic parity automata. The outstanding feature of our determinization procedure is that it can be implemented with symbolic set representations and that it directly yields a symbolic description of the generated deterministic parity automaton, which is not possible using previously published procedures.

References

1. Allauzen, C., Mohri, M.: An efficient pre-determinization algorithm. In: H. Ibarra, O., Dang, Z. (eds.) CIAA 2003. LNCS, vol. 2759, pp. 83–95. Springer, Heidelberg (2003)
2. Armoni, R., et al.: Efficient LTL compilation for SAT-based model checking. In: Conference on Computer Aided Design (ICCAD), pp. 877–884. IEEE Computer Society, Los Alamitos (2005)
3. Bloem, R., et al.: Symbolic implementation of alternating automata. In: H. Ibarra, O., Yen, H.-C. (eds.) CIAA 2006. LNCS, vol. 4094, pp. 208–218. Springer, Heidelberg (2006)
4. Burch, J., et al.: Symbolic model checking: 10^{20} states and beyond. In: Logic in Computer Science (LICS), Washington, DC, USA, 1990, pp. 1–33. IEEE Computer Society, Los Alamitos (1990)
5. Carton, O., Michel, M.: Unambiguous Büchi automata. Theoretical Computer Science 297(1-3), 37–81 (2003)
6. Clarke, E., Grumberg, O., Hamaguchi, K.: Another look at LTL model checking. Formal Methods in System Design (FMSD) 10(1), 47–71 (1997)
7. Emerson, E.: Temporal and modal logic. In: van Leeuwen, J. (ed.) Handbook of Theoretical Computer Science. Formal Models and Semantics, ch.16, vol. B, pp. 995–1072. Elsevier, Amsterdam (1990)
8. Emerson, E., Sistla, A.: Deciding branching time logic. In: Symposium on Theory of Computing (STOC), pp. 14–24 (1984)
9. Gastin, P., Oddoux, D.: Fast LTL to Büchi Automata Translation. In: Berry, G., Comon, H., Finkel, A. (eds.) CAV 2001. LNCS, vol. 2102, Springer, Heidelberg (2001)
10. Gurumurthy, S., et al.: On Complementing Nondeterministic Büchi Automata. In: Geist, D., Tronci, E. (eds.) CHARME 2003. LNCS, vol. 2860, pp. 96–110. Springer, Heidelberg (2003)
11. Henzinger, T., Piterman, N.: Solving games without determinization. In: Ésik, Z. (ed.) CSL 2006. LNCS, vol. 4207, pp. 394–409. Springer, Heidelberg (2006)
12. Kesten, Y., Pnueli, A., Raviv, L.: Algorithmic Verification of Linear Temporal Logic Specifications. In: Larsen, K.G., Skyum, S., Winskel, G. (eds.) ICALP 1998. LNCS, vol. 1443, Springer, Heidelberg (1998)
13. Klein, J., Baier, C.: Experiments with deterministic ω-automata for formulas of temporal logic. Theoretical Computer Science 363(2), 182–195 (2006)
14. Kupferman, O., Piterman, N., Vardi, M.: Safraless Compositional Synthesis. In: Ball, T., Jones, R.B. (eds.) CAV 2006. LNCS, vol. 4144, pp. 31–44. Springer, Heidelberg (2006)
15. Kupferman, O., Vardi, M.: Safraless decision procedures. In: Symposium on Foundations of Computer Science, pp. 531–540. IEEE Computer Society, Los Alamitos (2005)

16. McNaughton, R., Papert, S.: Counter-free Automata. MIT Press, Cambridge (1971)
17. Merz, S., Sezgin, A.: Emptiness of linear weak alternating automata. Technical report, LORIA (2003)
18. Muller, D., Saoudi, A., Schupp, P.: Alternating automata, the weak monadic theory of the tree, and its complexity. In: Kott, L. (ed.) ICALP 1986. LNCS, vol. 226, pp. 275–283. Springer, Heidelberg (1986)
19. Pelánek, R., Strejcek, J.: Deeper connections between LTL and alternating automata. In: Farré, J., Litovsky, I., Schmitz, S. (eds.) CIAA 2005. LNCS, vol. 3845, pp. 238–249. Springer, Heidelberg (2006)
20. Piterman, N.: From nondeterministic Büchi and Streett automata to deterministic parity automata. In: Symp. on Logic in Computer Science, IEEE Comp. Soc, Los Alamitos (2006)
21. Pnueli, A.: The temporal logic of programs. In: Foundations of Computer Science (FOCS), Providence, RI, USA, 1977, pp. 46–57. IEEE Computer Society, Los Alamitos (1977)
22. Pnueli, A., Rosner, R.: On the synthesis of a reactive module. In: Symposium on Principles of Programming Languages, Austin, Texas, pp. 179–190. ACM, New York (1989)
23. Safra, S.: On the complexity of ω-automata. In: Symposium on Foundations of Computer Science (FOCS), pp. 319–327 (1988)
24. Schneider, K.: Improving automata generation for linear temporal logic by considering the automata hierarchy. In: Nieuwenhuis, R., Voronkov, A. (eds.) LPAR 2001. LNCS (LNAI), vol. 2250, pp. 39–54. Springer, Heidelberg (2001)
25. Schneider, K.: Verification of Reactive Systems – Formal Methods and Algorithms. In: Texts in Theoretical Computer Science (EATCS Series), Springer, Heidelberg (2003)
26. Schulte Althoff, C., Thomas, W., Wallmeier, N.: Observations on determinization of Büchi automata. In: Farré, J., Litovsky, I., Schmitz, S. (eds.) CIAA 2005. LNCS, vol. 3845, pp. 262–272. Springer, Heidelberg (2006)
27. Thomas, W.: Automata on infinite objects. In: van Leeuwen, J. (ed.) Handbook of Theoretical Computer Science. Formal Models and Semantics, ch. 4, vol. B, pp. 133–191. Elsevier, Amsterdam (1990)
28. Tuerk, T., Schneider, K.: Relationship between alternating omega-automata and symbolically represented nondeterministic omega-automata. Technical Report 340, Dep. of Computer Science, University of Kaiserslautern, Germany (2005)
29. Vardi, M.: An automata-theoretic approach to linear temporal logic. In: Moller, F., Birtwistle, G. (eds.) Logics for Concurrency. LNCS, vol. 1043, pp. 238–266. Springer, Heidelberg (1996)
30. Vardi, M.: Probabilistic linear-time model checking: An overview of the automata-theoretic approach. In: Katoen, J.-P. (ed.) AMAST-ARTS 1999, ARTS 1999, and AMAST-WS 1999. LNCS, vol. 1601, pp. 265–276. Springer, Heidelberg (1999)
31. Vardi, M., Wolper, P.: An automata-theoretic approach to automatic program verification. In: Symposium on Logic in Computer Science (LICS), pp. 332–344. IEEE Computer Society, Los Alamitos (1986)

Monitoring Temporal Properties of Stochastic Systems*

A. Prasad Sistla and Abhigna R. Srinivas

Abstract. We present highly accurate deterministic and randomized methods for monitoring temporal properties of stochastic systems. The deterministic algorithms employ timeouts that are set dynamically to achieve desired accuracy. The randomized algorithms employ coin tossing and can give highly accurate monitors when the system behavior is not known.

1 Introduction

Designing and developing correct concurrent systems is a challenging process. An alternative to developing such components is to use an existing off-the-shelf component even if it does not exactly satisfy the user requirements. In our earlier works [7,8,16], we proposed an approach for customizing such components to user requirements. The approach proposed there uses a run time monitor that continuously monitors the executions of the component and reports any violations of the desired property. In this paper, we develop methods that make such monitors highly accurate using the information about the underlying system. We also develop alternate highly accurate randomized algorithms for monitoring such systems.

We assume that the correctness of the system is specified by a LTL formula or by an automaton on infinite strings. The monitoring problem consists of observing the computation of the system in real-time and reporting a violation if it does not satisfy the formula. This is complicated by the fact that the computations are non-terminating, i.e., infinite, and property violation needs to be detected by observing only the prefixes of computations. It is well known that the only properties that can be monitored exactly are the safety properties [1,14,4]. However, an arbitrary property can still be monitored by erring sometimes. That is, not reporting a violation when there is one (called *false acceptances*), or reporting a violation when there is none (*false rejections*).

Two different techniques have been employed, in the literature, to monitor a general property f. In the first approach [2], call it a *liberal* approach, one monitors for the violations of the safety part of the property f (note that any property f is equivalent to the conjunction of a safety and a liveness property [1].). In this case, the monitor exhibits false acceptances, but not false rejections. In the case of false acceptances, the computation violates the liveness part of f.

* This research is partly supported by the NSF grants CCF-0742686 and CCR-0205365.

F. Logozzo et al. (Eds.): VMCAI 2008, LNCS 4905, pp. 294–308, 2008.

An alternate approach, called *conservative* approach [7,8,16], is to take a safety property h that implies f and to monitor for its violations. This method allows false rejections, but not false acceptances. The number of false rejections can be reduced by taking h to be as weak as possible, although in general there is no weakest such property h [7,8,16]. Note that one can also have monitors that exhibit false rejections as well as acceptances.

We model the system being monitored as a stochastic system and define two different accuracy measures for monitors of stochastic systems— *acceptance* accuracy and *rejection* accuracy. The *acceptance accuracy* is defined to be the probability that a good computation of the system ,i.e., one satisfying the formula f, is accepted by the monitoring algorithm. The *rejection accuracy* is defined to be the probability that a bad computation, i.e., one not satisfying the formula f, is rejected by the algorithm. Ideally, both the accuracies should have value 1. Note that the acceptance accuracy of a liberal algorithm is always 1 while the rejection accuracy of a conservative algorithm is always 1.

In this paper, we consider systems modeled by Hidden Markov Chains (HMC) [3], which are Markov chains that have outputs associated with each state; only the outputs are observable but not the states. HMCs are widely used for modeling systems whose states can not be fully observed. We present a conservative monitor for such systems whose acceptance accuracy can be made as close to 1 as possible. This algorithm dynamically resets the timeouts to achieve the desired accuracy. We show that the timeouts can be reset so that their values increase only linearly with each reset and such that the desired accuracy is achieved. Both the accuracies of the monitor have value 1 when the states of the HMC are fully visible.

The above methods for achieving accuracy assume that the underlying Markov Chain defining the system is known. In this paper we propose probabilistic algorithms for monitoring systems when their possible behaviors are not known in advance. Actually, we use the standard automata based approach [14] for monitoring the safety part of the property and the probabilistic approach for monitoring the liveness part. A *probabilistic monitor* for a property is a randomized algorithm (i.e., one that use random choices) that rejects with probability 1 every computation that does not satisfy the property. A *strong* probabilistic monitor for a property is a probabilistic monitor that accepts, with non-zero probability, every computation that satisfies the property. We say that a property is strongly monitorable if there is a strong monitor for it. For example, a strong monitor for the liveness property $\Diamond P$ rejects with some probability p after each input until P is satisfied.

We show that the class of strongly monitorable properties is exactly the class of properties that can be recognized by deterministic, possibly infinite state, Buchi automata. This implies that that the property $\Box\Diamond P$ is not strongly monitorable. Although, $\Box\Diamond P$ is not strongly monitorable, we present a probabilistic monitor for this property that satisfies some nice properties. We present such probabilistic monitors for the LTL formula $\Box\Diamond P \rightarrow \Box\Diamond Q$ and conjunctions of such formulas. These algorithms together with traditional deterministic algorithms for safety properties give us probabilistic monitors for deterministic Buchi automata as well as deterministic Streett automata.

We also give *hybrid* algorithms that combine the probabilistic methods with the conservative approaches of [7,8,16], that employ counters, to obtain highly accurate monitors. For example, the accuracy of a conservative monitor (for $\Diamond P$) employing a counter of size k can be improved by a factor of 2^k by combining with randomized techniques. We present experimental results demonstrating the high accuracy of the hybrid algorithms.

In summary, the following are the main contributions of the paper:

- A conservative deterministic monitor employing counters, for monitoring properties specified by deterministic Buchi automata, for systems modeled as HMCs. These monitors can be designed to achieve a desired accuracy and have accuracy 1 when the HMC is fully visible.
- A number of probabilistic monitoring techniques for liveness properties.
- Introduction of strong monitors and the result showing that the class of languages having strong monitors is exactly the class of languages whose complement is recognized by possibly infinite state Buchi automata.
- Highly accurate hybrid techniques that combine deterministic and probabilistic methods.

The paper is organized as follows. Section 2 contains definitions. Section 3 presents a highly accurate deterministic monitor when system behavior is known. Section 4 describes probabilistic and hybrid methods. Section 5 describes experimental results. Section 6 has concluding remarks and comparison to related work. The proofs of lemmas can be found in the longer version [15] of the paper.

2 Definitions and Notation

Sequences. Let S be a finite set. Let $\sigma = s_0, s_1, \ldots$ be a possibly infinite sequence over S. The length of σ, denoted as $|\sigma|$, is defined to be the number of elements in σ if σ is finite, and ω otherwise. For any $i \geq 0$, $\sigma[0, i]$ denotes the prefix of σ up to s_i. If α_1 is a finite sequence and α_2 is a either a finite or a ω-sequence then $\alpha_1\alpha_2$ denotes the concatenation of the two sequences in that order. We let S^*, S^ω denote the set of finite sequences and the set of infinite sequences over S. If $C \subseteq S^\omega$ and $\alpha \in S^*$ then αC denotes the set $\{\alpha\beta : \beta \in C\}$.

Automata and LTL. A *Büchi automaton* (NBA for short) $\mathcal{A}$ on infinite strings is a quintuple $(Q, \Sigma, \delta, q^0, F)$ where Q is a possibly infinite set of states; Σ is a finite alphabet of symbols; $\delta\colon Q \times \Sigma \to 2^Q$ is a transition function; $q_0 \in Q$ is an initial state; $F \subseteq Q$ is a set of accepting/final automaton states. The *generalized transition function* $\delta^* : Q \times \Sigma^* \to 2^Q$ is defined in the usual way, i.e., for every state q, $\delta^*(q, \epsilon) = \{q\}$, and for any $\sigma \in \Sigma^*$ and $a \in \Sigma$, $\delta^*(q, \sigma a) = \cup_{q' \in \delta^*(q,\sigma)} \delta(q', a)$. If for every $(q, a) \in Q \times \Sigma$, $|\delta(q, a)| = 1$, then $\mathcal{A}$ is called a *deterministic* Büchi automaton (or DBA for short). Let $\sigma :\ a_1, \ldots$ be an infinite sequence over Σ. A *run* r *of* $\mathcal{A}$ on σ is an infinite sequence $r_0, r_1, \ldots$ over Q

such that $r_0 = q_0$ and for every $i > 0$, $r_i \in \delta(r_{i-1}, a_i)$. The run r of a Büchi automaton is *accepting* if there exists an infinite set I of indices such that, for each $i \in I$, $q_i \in F$. The automaton $\mathcal{A}$ *accepts* the ω-string σ if it has an accepting run over σ (for the case of DBAs, the automaton has a single run over σ). The *language accepted by* $\mathcal{A}$, denoted by $L(\mathcal{A})$, is the set of ω-strings that $\mathcal{A}$ accepts. A language L' is called ω*-regular* if it is accepted by some Büchi automaton. A Streett automaton is like a Buchi automaton excepting that its accepting condition is given by a set of pairs of states the form (U, V) where $U, V \subseteq Q$. In this case, a run $r = r_0, ..., r_i, ...$ is accepting if for every pair (U, V) in the accepting condition, if the set $\{i : r_i \in U\}$ is infinite then the set $\{i : r_i \in V\}$ is also infinite. A finite state Buchi or Streett automaton is one that has only a finite number of states. LTL is the standard Propositional Linear Temporal Logic proposed by Pnueli. It uses the temporal operators $\Box$ (always),$\Diamond$ (some time), $\mathcal{U}$ (until), $\bigcirc$ (next-time) together with standard boolean connectives including $\rightarrow$(implication).

Hidden Markov Chains. We assume that the reader is familiar with basic probability theory and random variables and Markov chains. We consider stochastic systems given as Markov Chains [9] and monitor their computations for satisfaction of a given property specified by an automaton or a temporal formula. A Markov chain $G = (S, R, \phi)$ is a triple satisfying the following: S is a set of countable states; $R \subseteq S \times S$ is a total binary relation (i.e., for every $s \in S$, there exists some $t \in S$ such that $(s, t) \in R$); and $\phi : R \rightarrow (0, 1]$ is a probability function such that for each $s \in S$, $\sum_{(s,t)\in R} \phi((s, t)) = 1$. Note that, for every $(s, t) \in R$, $\phi((s, t))$ is non-zero. Intuitively, if at any time the system is in a state $s \in S$, then in one step, it goes to some state t such that $(s, t) \in R$ with probability $\phi((s, t))$. A finite path p of G is a sequence $s_0, s_1, ..., s_n$ of states such that $(s_i, s_{i+1}) \in R$ for $0 \leq i < n$. We extend the probability function to such paths, by defining $\phi(p) = \prod_{0 \leq i < n} \phi((s_i, s_{i+1}))$.

We assume that there is a finite set $\mathcal{P}$ of atomic propositions that represent conditions on system states. Let Σ denote $2^{\mathcal{P}}$, the power set of $\mathcal{P}$. Each member of Σ denotes the set of atomic propositions that are true in a state of the system. From here onwards, we assume that Σ is the input alphabet of the property automata that we consider. If the property is given by a temporal formula then the atomic propositions appearing in the formula are drawn from $\mathcal{P}$. For any $C \subseteq \Sigma^\omega$, let $\bar{C}$ denote the set $\Sigma^\omega - C$. For an atomic proposition $P \in \Sigma$, when used in a sequence, P represents the set of elements of Σ that contain P; similarly $\neg P$ represents the set of elements that do not contain P.

A Hidden Markov Chain (HMC) [3] $H = (G, O, r_0)$ is a triple where $G = (S, R, \phi)$ is a Markov chain, $O : S \rightarrow \Sigma$ is the output function and $r_0 \in S$ is the initial state. Intuitively, for any $s \in S$, $O(s)$ is the output generated in state s and is the set of atomic propositions true in s; this output is generated when ever a transition entering state s is taken. The generated symbols become inputs to the monitor. H is called Hidden Markov chain because, one only observes the outputs generated in each state but not the actual state. We extend the output function O to paths of G as follows. For any finite path $p = s_0, s_1, ..., s_n$ in G,

$O(p) = O(s_0), O(s_1), ..., O(s_n)$. The probability distribution on the single step state transition of G induces a probability distribution on the sets of sequences of outputs generated. To define these distributions formally, let $\mathcal{E}$ be the smallest class of subsets of Σ^ω satisfying the following properties: for every $\alpha \in \Sigma^*$, $\alpha\Sigma^\omega \in \mathcal{E}$; $\mathcal{E}$ is closed under countable union (i.e., if $C_0, ...C_i, ...$ is a finite or infinite sequence of elements in $\mathcal{E}$, then $\bigcup_{i\geq 0} C_i$ is also in $\mathcal{E}$); it is closed under complementation (i.e., for every $C \in \mathcal{E}$, $\bar{C}$ is also in $\mathcal{E}$). The elements of $\mathcal{E}$ are called *measurable* subsets of Σ^ω. It is not difficult to see that $\mathcal{E}$ is also closed under countable intersections. It can be shown that, for any automaton $\mathcal{A}$ with input alphabet Σ, $L(\mathcal{A})$ is measurable.

Now, for any system state $r \in S$, we define a probability function $\mathcal{F}_r$ defined on $\mathcal{E}$ as follows. Intuitively, for any $C \in \mathcal{E}$, $\mathcal{F}_r(C)$ denotes the probability that an output sequence generated from the system state r, is in C. $\mathcal{F}_r$ is the unique probability measure satisfying all the probability axioms [9], such that for every $\alpha \in \Sigma^*$ and $C = \alpha\Sigma^\omega$, $\mathcal{F}_r(C)$ is the sum of $\phi(p)$, for all finite paths p of G starting from the state r such that $O(p) = \alpha$. For the HMC chain given in figure 1 and for $\alpha = (\{Q\}, \{Q\}, \{Q\})$, there are two paths p, i.e., s_0, s_0, s_0 and s_0, s_0, s_2, such that $O(p) = \alpha$ and hence $\mathcal{F}_{s_0}(C) = \frac{2}{9}$.

Let $D \in \mathcal{E}$ be such that $\mathcal{F}_r(D) \neq 0$. We let $\mathcal{F}_{r|D}$ denote the conditional probability function given D; formally, for any $C \in \mathcal{E}$, $\mathcal{F}_{r|D}(C) = \frac{\mathcal{F}_r(C \cap D)}{\mathcal{F}_r(D)}$. For any LTL formula g, we let $\mathcal{F}_{r|g}$ denote the conditional distribution $\mathcal{F}_{r|D}$ where D is the set of input sequences that satisfy g. For any $\alpha \in \Sigma^*$ and $C = \alpha\Sigma^\omega$, we let $\mathcal{F}_r(\alpha)$ denote the probability $\mathcal{F}_r(C)$ and $\mathcal{F}_{r|\alpha}$ denote the conditional probability function $\mathcal{F}_{r|C}$. For a set $C \subseteq \Sigma^*$, we let $\mathcal{F}_r(C)$ denote $\mathcal{F}_r(C\Sigma^\omega)$.

Example 1. Consider the HMC S_1 given in figure 1. Here the set of atomic propositions $\mathcal{P} = \{P, Q\}$. It should be easy to see that $\mathcal{F}_{s_0}(\Diamond P) = \frac{1}{2}$.

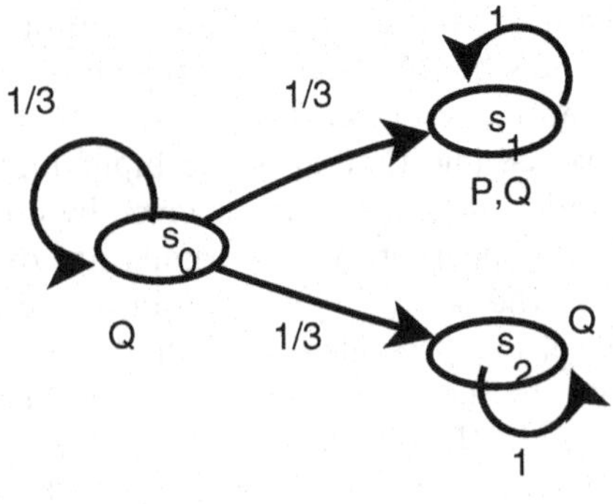

Fig. 1. System S_1

Deterministic Monitors. A monitor $M : \Sigma^* \to \{0, 1\}$ is a computable function with the property that, for any $\alpha \in \Sigma^*$, if $M(\alpha) = 0$ then $M(\alpha\beta) = 0$ for every $\beta \in \Sigma^*$. For an $\alpha \in \Sigma^*$, we say that M rejects α, if $M(\alpha) = 0$, otherwise we say

M accepts α. Thus if M rejects α then it rejects all its extensions. For an infinite sequence $\sigma \in \Sigma^\omega$, we say that M rejects σ iff there exists a prefix α of σ that is rejected by M; we say M accepts σ if it does not reject it. Let $L(M)$ denote the set of infinite sequences accepted by M. It is not difficult to see that $L(M)$ is a safety property and is measurable. The *acceptance accuracy* of M for $\mathcal{A}$ with respect to the HMC H is defined to be the probability $\mathcal{F}_{r_0|L(\mathcal{A})}(L(M))$ where r_0 is the initial state of H. Intuitively, it is the conditional probability that a sequence generated by the system is accepted by M, given that it is in $L(\mathcal{A})$. Roughly speaking, it is the fraction of the sequences in $L(\mathcal{A})$, generated from r_0, that are accepted by M. Let C, D be the complements of $L(\mathcal{A})$ and $L(M)$ respectively, i.e., $C = \Sigma^\omega - L(\mathcal{A})$ and $D = \Sigma^\omega - L(M)$. Then the *rejection accuracy* of M for $\mathcal{A}$ (also for $L(\mathcal{A})$) with respect to H is defined to be the probability $\mathcal{F}_{r_0|C}(D)$. This is the probability that a sequence generated by the system is rejected by M, given that it is not in $L(\mathcal{A})$. It is easy to see that this rejection accuracy is equal to $(1 - \ acceptance\ accuracy\ of\ M\ for\ C\ with\ respect\ to\ H)$.

We say that M is a *conservative monitor* for a language $L' \subseteq \Sigma^\omega$, if $L(M) \subseteq L'$, i.e., it rejects every sequence not in L'. We say that M is a conservative monitor for an automaton $\mathcal{A}$ (resp., for a LTL formula ϕ) if it is a conservative monitor for $L(\mathcal{A})$ (resp., for C where C is the set of sequences that satisfy ϕ). Note that the rejection accuracy of a conservative monitor is 1.

Example 2. Consider the following conservative monitor M_1 for the LTL formula $\Diamond P$. It accepts all finite sequences of length ≤ 2. It accepts a finite sequence of length greater than two only if it has a P in the first three symbols. Clearly, $L(M_1) = \{(\neg P)^i P\beta : i \leq 2, \beta \in \Sigma^\omega\}$. Now consider the system HMC of Example 1. The first input produced by S_1 from state s_0 is $\neg P$, the probability that either the second or the third symbol is a P is $\frac{4}{9}$. From this, it should be easy to see that $F_{s_0|\Diamond P}(L(M_1)) = \frac{8}{9}$. Hence the acceptance accuracy of M_1 for $\Diamond P$ with respect to the system S_1 is $\frac{8}{9}$.

Probabilistic Monitors. We also define probabilistic monitors. A *probabilistic monitor* $M : \Sigma^* \to [0,1]$ is a function that associates a probability $M(\alpha)$ with each $\alpha \in \Sigma^*$ such that for every $\alpha, \beta \in \Sigma^*$, $M(\alpha\beta) \leq M(\alpha)$. Intuitively, $M(\alpha)$ denotes the probability that α is accepted by M. We extend M to infinite sequences as follows. For any $\sigma \in \Sigma^\omega$, $M(\sigma) = \lim_{i\to\infty} M(\sigma[0,\mathtt{i}])$. $M(\sigma)$ represents the probability of acceptance of σ by M. We say that M is a probabilistic monitor for a language L' if $M(\sigma) = 0$ for all $\sigma \in \Sigma^\omega - L'$. That is every sequence not in L' is rejected with probability 1. Although we defined monitors as functions, many times monitors are given by algorithms (deterministic or probabilistic) that take inputs and reject some input sequences. With each such algorithm there is an implicitly defined unique monitor function.

The definition of acceptance accuracy for probabilistic monitors is a little more involved. Let M be a probabilistic monitor for an automaton $\mathcal{A}$ with input alphabet Σ. Let $\mathcal{F}_{r_0|L(\mathcal{A})}$ be the conditional probability distribution function on the set of input sequences generated by the system. For any $n > 0$, let $Y_n = \sum_{\alpha\in\Sigma^n}(\mathcal{F}_{r_0|L(\mathcal{A})}(\alpha)M(\alpha))$; note Σ^n is the set of all sequences of length n.

Because of the monotonicity of the function M, it is easy to see that $Y_n \geq Y_{n+1}$ for all $n > 0$. We define the acceptance accuracy of M for $\mathcal{A}$ with respect to the given system to be $\lim_{n\to\infty} Y_n$. The rejection accuracy of M for $\mathcal{A}$ with respect to the HMC H, is defined to be the $\lim_{n\to\infty} Z_n$ where Z_n is obtained from the expression for Y_n by replacing $L(\mathcal{A})$ by its complement and $M(\alpha)$ by $1 - M(\alpha)$.

Example 3. Consider the following probabilistic monitor M_2 for $\Diamond P$. M_2 looks at the current symbol. If it is a P it accepts and it will accept all subsequent inputs. If the current symbol is $\neg P$ and it has not seen a P since the beginning, then it rejects with probability $\frac{1}{3}$ and accepts with probability $\frac{2}{3}$. Formally, $M_2((\neg P)^{n-1}P\beta) = (\frac{2}{3})^{n-1}$ for all $n \geq 1$ and for all $\beta \in \Sigma^*$. Now consider the HMC S_1 given in Example 1. It can be shown by simple probabilistic analysis that $Y_n = 2\sum_1^{n-1}(\frac{2}{3})^i(\frac{1}{3})^i$. From this, we see that the accuracy of M_2 for $\Diamond P$ with respect to system S_1 , which is $\lim_{n\to\infty} Y_n$, is $\frac{4}{7}$. In general if the rejection probability at each step used is p, it can be shown that the acceptance accuracy of M_2 for $\Diamond P$ with respect to S_1 is $2\frac{1-p}{2+p}$. Thus the acceptance accuracy can be increased arbitrarily close to 1 by decreasing p.

A useful function. Let $\mathbf{Z}_{\geq 2}$ denote the set of integers greater than or equal to two. Let $c \geq 2$ be an integer. Consider a monitor which reads an infinite sequence of inputs. After the ith input, it rejects with probability $\frac{1}{c^i}$ and stops, otherwise it continues. The probability that it never rejects is given by the value $G(c)$ defined as follows. For any integer $c \geq 2$, $G(c) = \prod_{i=1}^{\infty}(1 - \frac{1}{c^i})$. More precisely, $G(c) = \lim_{n\to\infty} \prod_{i=1}^{n}(1 - \frac{1}{c^i})$. Observe that each term in the product increases with i and goes to 1 as $i \to \infty$. Lemma 1 gives bounds on $G(c)$.

Lemma 1. *For every* $c \geq 2$, $\exp\left(\frac{-(2\cdot c^3+3\cdot c^2+c+1)}{2\cdot c^2\cdot(c^2-1)}\right) \leq G(c) \leq (1 - \frac{1}{c})$.

Using the above bound, it can be shown that $G(2) > 0.26$, $G(3) > 0.55$, $G(4) > 0.68$, etc. From the above bound, we see that $\lim_{c\to\infty} G(c) = 1$.

3 Accurate Deterministic Monitors

In this section we give methods for designing highly accurate deterministic monitors that monitor the executions of a system, given as a HMC, against a property specified by a deterministic finite state Buchi automaton. Here we assume that we know the initial system state and the output sequence generated by the system, but we can not observe the system state.

Let $H = (G, O, r_0)$ be a HMC where $G = (S, R, \phi)$ is a finite Markov chain and $\mathcal{A} = (Q, \Sigma, \delta, q_0, F)$ be the given deterministic finite state Buchi automaton. For any $q \in Q$, let $\mathcal{A}_q$ be the automaton obtained by changing the initial state of $\mathcal{A}$ to q. Let $(s, q) \in S \times Q$. We call each such pair as a product state. Note that, for any such (s, q), $\mathcal{F}_s(L(\mathcal{A}_q))$ is the probability that an infinite output sequence generated from the system state s is accepted by the automaton $\mathcal{A}$ when started in the state q. We say that (s, q) is an *accepting* product state if $\mathcal{F}_s(L(\mathcal{A}_q)) = 1$. We say that it is a *rejecting* product state if $\mathcal{F}_s(L(\mathcal{A}_q)) = 0$. Later we show how the accepting and rejecting product states can be determined.

Our monitoring algorithm works as follows. As the monitor gets inputs from the system, it simulates the automaton $\mathcal{A}$ on the input sequence using the variable *a_state*. It also keeps a set *s_states* which is the set of states the system can be in. If at any time all states in $s\_states \times \{a\_state\}$ are accepting product states then it accepts. If all these states are rejecting product states then it rejects. Otherwise, it continues. In addition, it also maintains a counter, denoted by *counter* variable, which is initialized to some value. In each iteration, *counter* is decremented. If *counter* is zero before an accepting automaton state is reached then, it rejects. When ever an accepting automaton state is reached then this counter is reset to a new value using the function f. The algorithm for the monitor is given below. The variable x denotes the current input symbol and the variable i records the number of times the counter has been reset. Here r_0 is the initial state of the system.

$a\_state := q_0;\ s\_states := \{r_0\};$
$i := 1;\ counter := f(s\_states, i, a\_state);$
$x := O(r_0);$
Loop forever
  $a\_state := \delta(a\_state, x);$
  $x := get\_nextinput();$
  $s\_states := \{s' : (s, s') \in R,\ s \in s\_states,\ O(s') = x\};$
  If every state in $s\_states \times \{a\_state\}$ is an accepting product state
    accept();
  If every state in $s\_states \times \{a\_state\}$ is a rejecting product state
    reject();
  $counter := counter - 1;$
  If $counter = 0$ and $a\_state \notin F$ reject();
  If $a\_state \in F$
    $\{i := i + 1;\ counter := f(s\_states, i, a\_state)\}$

When ever the monitor rejects (or accepts) then it immediately stops; in this case, it is assumed that it rejects (or accepts) all future inputs.

It is easy to see that the monitor rejects any input sequence that is not in $L(\mathcal{A})$ since after certain point, *a_state* is never in F. The accuracy of the monitor is highly dependent on the function f used in resetting the counter. One possibility, as indicated in [7,8], is to reset it to a constant k. In this case, it can be shown that the accuracy of the resulting monitor is going to be zero many times. The following theorem shows that by increasing the reset value of *counter* linearly with i, we can achieve a desired accuracy.

Theorem 1. *For any given rational y such that $0 \leq y \leq 1$, there exists a constant a such that if $f(X, i, q) = a \cdot i$, for every $X \subseteq S$ and $q \in Q$, then the accuracy of the above monitor is at least y. Further more such a constant a is computable in time polynomial in the sizes of $H, \mathcal{A}$.*

Proof Sketch: Let y be as given in the statement of the theorem and c be an integer such that $G(c) \geq y$ and $c \geq 2$. We show that there exists an efficiently computable constant a such that by setting $f(X, i, q) = a \cdot i$, the probability that an accepting state of the automaton is not reached with in $f(X, i, q)$ inputs is at most $\frac{1}{c^i}$; that is this probability decreases exponentially with i.

For an automaton state $q \in Q$ and $\alpha \in \Sigma^*$, we say that α is a *minimal acceptable* sequence for q if $|\alpha| > 0$, $\delta^*(q, \alpha) \in F$ and for every proper prefix α' of α, $\delta^*(q, \alpha') \notin F$; that is α is a minimal finite sequence accepted from the automaton state q. For an integer $k > 0$, for any $q \in Q$, let $MINSEQ(q, k)$ denote $\{\alpha : \alpha$ is a minimal acceptable sequence for q and $|\alpha| \leq k\}$. It is easy to see that no sequence in $MINSEQ(q, k)$ is a proper prefix of another sequence in it.

We say that a product state (s, q) is *good* if $\mathcal{F}_s(L(\mathcal{A}_q)) > 0$. For any good product state (s, q), integer $k > 0$, define $h(s, q, k) = \mathcal{F}_{s|L(\mathcal{A}_q)}(MINSEQ(q, k))$. Intuitively, $h(s, q, k)$ is the conditional probability that an infinite output sequence $\beta \in L(\mathcal{A}_q)$ generated from s has a prefix in $MINSEQ(q, k)$; i.e., starting from q an accepting automaton state is reached with in k outputs. Note that for a good product state (s, q), $h(s, q, k)$ monotonically increases with k and goes to 1 in the limit.

Lemma 2. *1. There exists a constant a that is efficiently computable from $G, \mathcal{A}$ and c such that for every good product state (s, q) and every $i > 0$, $h(s, q, a \cdot i) \geq (1 - \frac{1}{c^i})$.*
2. The set of accepting states and rejecting product states can be computed in time linear in the sizes of H and $\mathcal{A}$.

Lemma 3. *For any X, q, if $f(X, i, q) = a \cdot i$ where a is as given in lemma 2, then the accuracy of the above monitor is at least y.*

The complete version of the paper [15] gives an efficient method for computing the value of a of theorem 1. For an interesting subclass of HMCs, called *fully visible* HMCs, we can obtain a much simpler monitoring algorithm. We say that the HMC $H = (G, O, r_0)$ where $G = (S, R, \phi)$, is *fully visible* if O is a one-one function, i.e. for any two distinct $s, s' \in S$, $O(s) \neq O(s')$. This means that one can uniquely determine the current state of the system by its output. In this case, the set *s_states* is always a singleton set. If at any time, s denotes the unique state in the set *s_states*, then from the property of Markov chains, it can be shown that eventually (s, a_state) is either an accepting or a rejecting product state. Thus for fully visible HMCs, we simplify the loop body of the monitoring algorithm by simply checking whether $s\_states \times \{a\_state\}$ contains either an accepting or a rejecting state; thus accepting or rejecting respectively.

Theorem 2. *For a fully visible HMC, the simplified algorithm is correct and its acceptance and rejection accuracies are both equal to one.*

Example 4. Now consider the example of a HMC given in Figure 2. In this example, initially the system is in state s which is non-critical region (labeled by the proposition N). From s, it may loop there or go to s' or go to state t which is the trying region where the user sends a request for the resource. From t, the system may loop, or go to state v denoting that the resource server crashed or go to state w where the resource is granted. Note both states t, v are labeled by T. Thus we can not tell whether the system is in state t or in v. In state s', it can loop or go to u' where it requests for the resource. In u', it may loop or go to w'. In state w' the resource is allocated. Note that the resource server does not crash when requested from u'. This is because, here, a more reliable server is employed. Now our monitoring algorithm can be used to monitor for the desired property $g = \Box(T \rightarrow \Diamond C)$. Using the approach given in the proof of lemma 2, we get $f(X, i, q)$ to be $a \cdot i$ where $a = \max\{2, \lceil \frac{\ln c}{\ln 3} \rceil\}$ and c is an integer such that $G(c) \geq y$.

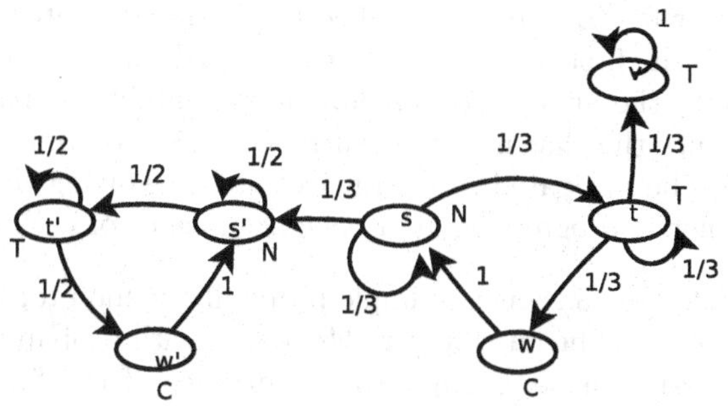

Fig. 2. Resource Acquisition

4 Probabilistic Monitors

In this section we consider probabilistic monitors that can be used to monitor any system for which the underlying HMC is not known.

Recall that if M is a probabilistic monitor for a language L' then for every $\sigma \notin L'$, $M(\sigma) = 0$. (Note that the rejection accuracy of a probabilistic monitor for a property with respect to HMC is one.) We say that M is a *strong monitor* for L' if M is a probabilistic monitor for L', and in addition, for every $\sigma \in L'$, $M(\sigma) > 0$.

Existence of Strong Monitors

Lemma 4. *There is a strong monitor for a language L iff $\bar{L}$ is recognized by a possibly infinite state deterministic Buchi automaton.*

The above lemma has the following implications. Since the sets of sequences satisfying $\neg\Diamond P$, $\neg\Diamond\Box P$ are recognizable by deterministic Buchi automata, it follows that there are strong monitors for $\Diamond P$ and $\Diamond\Box P$. On the contrary, it is well known that the set of sequences satisfying $\neg\Box\Diamond P$ is not recognizable by any finite or infinite state deterministic Buchi automaton. Hence we have the following lemma.

Lemma 5. *There are no strong monitors for the LTL formulas $\Box\Diamond P$ and $\Box\Diamond P \rightarrow \Box\Diamond Q$.*

We have already given in section 2, Example 3, a probabilistic monitor M_3 for $\Diamond P$. This monitor acts as follows. In the beginning, after it sees each input symbol, if the symbol is not P then it rejects with probability p. This behavior continues until the first P is seen. Once it sees a P, it does not reject any more from then onwards. Suppose that the first P occurs as the ith input symbol, then the probability that this sequence is accepted by M is $(1-p)^i$. Clearly, M is a strong monitor for $\Diamond P$.

Monitors with Desirable Properties

The above monitor for $\Diamond P$ can be modified to obtain a monitor for $\Box\Diamond P$ which acts like M_3 until the first P and repeats this algorithm immediately after each subsequent P until the another P is seen. Unfortunately, the resulting monitor rejects any sequence that has infinite occurrences of $\neg P$ even if it satisfies $\Box\Diamond P$. This problem can be mitigated to a large extent by reducing the probability of rejection in geometric progression after each occurrence of a P.

Monitor for $\Box\Diamond P$. We construct a simple probabilistic monitor M_5 for the LTL formula $\Box\Diamond P$. Let $c \geq 2$ be any integer. M_5 rejects with probability $\frac{1}{c}$ after each input until the first P is seen. After the occurrence of the first P and before the occurrence of the second P, it rejects with probability $\frac{1}{c^2}$ after each input symbol. In general, in the period between the occurrence of the ith P and the $(i+1)$st P, after each input symbol, it rejects with probability $\frac{1}{c^{i+1}}$. It is easy to see that M_5 rejects every input sequence that does not satisfy $\Box\Diamond P$ with probability 1 since P never occurs after some point, and after this point, M_5 rejects continuously with the same probability. Now consider any sequence σ that satisfies $\Box\Diamond P$. We say that such a sequence is *well behaving*, if the distance between any two successive Ps is bounded. For such a sequence σ, let $bound(\sigma)$ be the smallest value of m such that the first P occurs with in the first m input symbols and the distance between any successive Ps is bounded by m.

Lemma 6. *The monitor M_5 accepts every well behaving sequence with non-zero probability.*

It is to be noted that no deterministic monitor can accept all well behaving sequences that satisfy $\Box\Diamond P$, even those that use dynamically increasing counters. This is because for any well behaving sequence σ, the value of $bound(\sigma)$ is not known in advance. It is fairly straightforward to obtain a similar monitoring algorithm for any deterministic Buchi automaton.

Monitor for $\Box\Diamond P \rightarrow \Box\Diamond Q$. Now we give the description of probabilistic monitor M_7 for the LTL formula $\Box\Diamond P \rightarrow \Box\Diamond Q$. Let $c \geq 2$ be an integer. M_7 behaves as follows. Through out its operation, whenever it sees a symbol which is a symbol other than P it continues. Whenever it sees a P, M_7 rejects with probability $\frac{1}{c^{i+1}}$ where i is the number of occurrences of Q before the current input. This scheme can be implemented by keeping a variable p initialized to $\frac{1}{c}$. When ever a P

occurs M_7 rejects with probability p. When ever a Q occurs p is set to $\frac{p}{c}$. It is not difficult to see that M_7 is a probabilistic monitor for $\Box\Diamond P \rightarrow \Box\Diamond Q$. A sequence not satisfying the formula, has infinitely many Ps and only finitely many Qs. If the number of Qs is m, then M_7 rejects infinitely often with the same probability which is $\frac{1}{c^{m+1}}$. Hence the input will be rejected with probability 1. Any sequence that has only a finite number of Ps will be accepted with non-zero probability. Consider a sequence that satisfies the formula and that has infinitely many Ps. It also has infinitely many Qs. We say that such a sequence σ is well behaving if the number of Ps between successive Qs is bounded. Using the same reasoning as before, we can conclude that M_7 accepts every well behaving sequence with non-zero probability.

We can extend the above monitor for formulas of the form $\bigwedge_{i=1}^{m}(\Box\Diamond P_i \rightarrow \Box\Diamond Q_i)$. For each $i = 1, ..., m$, we build a monitor $M_7^{(i)}$ that monitors the formula $\Box\Diamond P_i \rightarrow \Box\Diamond Q_i$. They all coordinate so that if any of them rejects then all of them reject and stop. It is easy to see that the resulting monitor is a probabilistic monitor for the main formula. If a sequence satisfying the formula is well behaving with respect to each of the conjuncts of the formula then such a sequence will be accepted with non-zero probability. It is fairly straightforward to see how we can construct monitor for a deterministic Street automaton using the above approach by simulating the automaton on the input string and by monitoring the run of the automaton for the acceptance condition using the above monitor.

Hybrid Algorithms

The accuracy of the monitoring algorithms given earlier for $\Diamond P$, $\Box\Diamond P$ and $\Box\Diamond P \rightarrow \Box\Diamond Q$ can be improved substantially by combining with the deterministic counter based algorithms.

We illustrate this by constructing such a monitor for the formula $\Diamond P$. (The construction can be adopted easily for $\Box\Diamond P$ and $\Box\Diamond P \rightarrow \Box\Diamond Q$.) A deterministic monitor D for $\Diamond P$, uses counter k, and accepts an input if a P occurs in the first k inputs. Otherwise it rejects. We can also combine the above deterministic algorithm with the probabilistic monitor M_3 to get a hybrid algorithm H that works as follows: if a P occurs in the first k inputs then it never rejects; if a P does not occur in the first k symbols then after reading the kth symbol, it rejects with probability p; it repeats this process for ever; that is, if a P occurs in the next k inputs then it does not reject any more, otherwise it rejects with probability p after the second k input symbols, and so on.

We first compare the above three simple algorithms with respect to their acceptance accuracies on uniformly distributed inputs. For $n > 0$, let H_n be a HMC that generates a sequence of outputs such that the first P occurs with equal probability (i.e., with probability $\frac{1}{n}$) in any of the n outputs starting with the second output. The complete version of the paper gives the formal definition of H_n.

Lemma 7. *Let $\rho_{prob,n}$ denote the ratio of the acceptance accuracy of the probabilistic algorithm to that of the deterministic algorithm for the property $\Diamond P$ with* *respect to the HMC* H_n. *Similarly let* $\rho_{hybrid,n}$ *denote the ratio of the acceptance accuracy of the hybrid algorithm to that of the deterministic algorithm. Then, in the limit as* $n \to \infty$, $\rho_{hybrid,n} \to \frac{1}{p}$ *and* $\rho_{prob,n} \to \frac{1-p}{(k-1)p}$.

The above lemma shows that for large values of n, the hybrid algorithm is more accurate than the deterministic algorithm for all values of p, while the probabilistic algorithm is more accurate than the deterministic algorithm for values of $p \leq \frac{1}{k}$.

Generating low probabilities. We see that both the probabilistic and hybrid algorithms can be made more accurate by decreasing p, the probability of rejection. In case of the hybrid algorithm, p can be made as low as $\frac{1}{2^k}$, where k is the counter value, by using a coin tossing scheme as follows. In each step, i.e., after reading each input symbol, the algorithm tosses an unbiased coin. If no P occurs in the first k inputs and all the previous k coin tosses turned "head" then it rejects, otherwise it continues; note that the probability, that all k coin tosses result in "head", is $\frac{1}{2^k}$. (If we take $k = 100$ then this probability is less than 10^{-30}). This process is repeated. In this case, the hybrid algorithm is more accurate than the deterministic one by a factor of 2^k. Note that here k serves a dual purpose— as a counter and also for generating low probabilities.

5 Experimental Results

We conducted some simple experiments to evaluate the acceptance accuracy of the different algorithms. We evaluated the algorithms for monitoring $\Diamond P$ and $\Box\Diamond P$. We generated strings of length 10^6. Each symbol is from $\{P, \neg P\}$. We used two different types of inputs. The first type of inputs is where the distance between successive P symbols is uniformly distributed between 1 and 1000. The second type of input is where this distance is normally distributed with different means (μ) and standard deviations (σ). We considered three different combinations of μ, σ; these are $(200, 20)$, $(300, 30)$ and $(500, 50)$. We evaluated the deterministic, hybrid and probabilistic methods. For deterministic and hybrid algorithms we used counters of length 200,300 and 500. For probabilistic algorithms we used probabilities of $\frac{1}{100}$, $\frac{1}{500}$ and $\frac{1}{1000}$.

For the property $\Box\Diamond P$, for the probabilistic method, we started with an initial probability of rejection and decreased it by a factor of $\frac{1}{2}$ in each successive period. For the hybrid algorithm, we used a biased coin where the probability of getting "heads" is given by this probability. Thus if this probability is $\frac{1}{100}$ then the probability of rejection in the hybrid algorithm is as low as $(\frac{1}{100})^{200}$ if a counter of length 200 is chosen.

For $\Box\Diamond P$, for uniform distribution, all algorithms excepting the hybrid algorithm rejected every input (all false rejections). This is because all of them have some probability of rejection before the next P and this gets amplified with successive Ps. For the hybrid algorithms,the probability of rejection is so low that none of the inputs strings is rejected, i.e., all are accepted.

For normal distribution, the deterministic algorithm with counter 200 rejected all inputs; with counter 300 accepted all inputs where $\mu = 200$ and $\sigma = 20$ but rejected all others and so on. The hybrid algorithm accepted all while the probabilistic algorithm rejected all.

This shows that the hybrid algorithm is best for high acceptance accuracy for $\Box\Diamond P$. We carried out similar experiments for $\Diamond P$ for uniform and normal distributions. As predicted, the hybrid algorithm fared well always and has the best acceptance accuracy. The deterministic algorithm fared well for normal distribution if $\mu + 3\sigma < k$.

6 Conclusion

In this paper, we have proposed algorithms for accurate monitoring of liveness properties. These algorithms combined with traditional algorithms for safety properties can be used for monitoring any ω-regular property. We presented a simple deterministic method that can be tuned to appropriate accuracy for a system given by Hidden Markov Chain. We proposed randomized algorithms when system behavior is not known. Among these algorithms the hybrid algorithms are extremely accurate.

As has been indicated in the introduction, our earlier works [7,8,16] gave different techniques for synthesizing conservative deterministic monitors for monitoring temporal properties. Deterministic liberal monitoring algorithms have been proposed in [2]. Runtime monitoring has also been used for interface synthesis in [10] where the interactions between the module and the interface are considered as a two person game.

In [5,6] Larsen et.al. propose a method which, given a context specification and an overall specification, derive a temporal safety property characterizing the set of all implementations which, together with the given context, satisfy the overall specification. There has been much work in the literature on monitoring violations of safety properties in distributed systems. In these works, the safety property is typically explicitly specified by the user. A method for monitoring and checking quantitative and probabilistic properties of real-time systems has been given in [13]. These works take specifications in a probabilistic temporal logic (called CSL) and monitors for its satisfaction. The probabilities are deduced from the repeated occurrence of events in a computation.

None of the above works employ accuracy measures for monitors and none of them use randomization for monitoring liveness properties as we do. Our techniques are entirely new and have been experimentally validated.

Model checking probabilistic systems models as Markov chains was considered in the works of [17,11,12]. There they also construct a product of the Markov chain and the automata/tableaux associated with the LTL formula. While they concentrate on verification, we concentrate on the corresponding monitoring problem. Further more, we assume that during the computation the state of the system is not fully visible.

Acknowledgments. We are thankful to Amir Pnueli for his insight suggestions and comments, and to Yosef Lischitz for initial help on experiments.

References

1. Alpern, B., Schneider, F.: Defining liveness. Information Processing Letters 21, 181–185 (1985)
2. Amorium, M., Rosu, G.: Efficient monitoring of omega-languages. In: Etessami, K., Rajamani, S.K. (eds.) CAV 2005. LNCS, vol. 3576, pp. 364–378. Springer, Heidelberg (2005)
3. Cappe, O., Moulines, E., Riden, T.: Inferencing in Hidden Markov Models. Springer, Heidelberg (2005)
4. Kupferman, O., Vardi, M.: Model checking safety properties. In: Proceedings of the International Conference on Computer Aided Verification (1999)
5. Larsen, K.: Ideal specification formalisms = expressivity + compositionality + decidability + testability +. In: Baeten, J.C.M., Klop, J.W. (eds.) CONCUR 1990. LNCS, vol. 458, Springer, Heidelberg (1990)
6. Larsen, K.: The expressive power of implicit specifications. In: Leach Albert, J., Monien, B., Rodríguez-Artalejo, M. (eds.) ICALP 1991. LNCS, vol. 510, Springer, Heidelberg (1991)
7. Margaria, T., et al.: Taming Interface Specifications. In: Abadi, M., de Alfaro, L. (eds.) CONCUR 2005. LNCS, vol. 3653, pp. 548–561. Springer, Heidelberg (2005)
8. Margaria, T., et al.: Taming interface specifications (2005), `www.cs.uic.edu/šistla`
9. Papoulis, A., Pillai, S.U.: Probability, Random Variables and Stochastic Processes. McGrawHill, NewYork (2002)
10. Pnueli, A., Zaks, A., Zuck, L.D.: Monitoring interfaces for faults. In: Proceedings of the 5th Workshop on Runtime Verification (RV 2005) (2005), (to appear in a special issue of ENTCS)
11. Pnueli, A., Zuck, L.: Probabilistic verification by tableux. In: Proceedings of First IEEE Symposium on Logic in Computer Science, pp. 322–331 (1986)
12. Pnueli, A., Zuck, L.: Probabilistic verification. Information and Computation 103, 1–29 (1993)
13. Sammapun, U., Lee, I., Sokolsky, O.: Rt-mac:runtime monitoring and checking of quantitative and probabilistic properties. In: Proc. of 11th IEEE International Conference on Embedded and Real-time Computing Systems and Applications (RTCSA 2005), pp. 147–153 (2005)
14. Sistla, A.P.: On characterization of safety and liveness properties in temporal logic. In: Proceedings of the ACM Symposium on Principle of Distributed Computing (1985)
15. Sistla, A.P., Srinivas, A.R.: Monitoring temporal properties of stochastic systems (2007), `www.cs.uic.edu/~{}sistla/pmonitoring.ps`
16. Sistla, A.P., Zhou, M., Zuck, L.: Monitoring off-the-shelf components. In: Proceedings of the International Conference on Verification, Model Checking and Abstract Interpretation (2006)
17. Vardi, M.: Automatic verification of probabilistic concurrent systems. In: 26th annual Symposium on Foundations of Computer Science, pp. 327–338. IEEE Computer Society Press, Los Alamitos (1985)

A Hybrid Algorithm for LTL Games*

Saqib Sohail[1], Fabio Somenzi[1], and Kavita Ravi[2]

[1] University of Colorado at Boulder
{Saqib.Sohail,Fabio}@Colorado.EDU
[2] Cadence Design Systems
kravi@cadence.com

Abstract. In the game theoretic approach to the synthesis of reactive systems, specifications are often given in linear time logic (LTL). Computing a winning strategy to an infinite game whose winning condition is the set of LTL properties is the main step in obtaining an implementation. We present a practical hybrid algorithm—a combination of symbolic and explicit algorithm—for the computation of winning strategies for unrestricted LTL games that we have successfully applied to synthesize reactive systems with up to 10^{11} states.

1 Introduction

Great progress has been made in the verification of reactive systems over the last twenty years. The combination of sophisticated algorithms, powerful abstraction techniques, and rigorous design methodologies has made the verification of large hardware and software systems possible. Synthesis from specifications given as (temporal) logic formulae or automata [7, 11, 39] has proved a more difficult problem and has enjoyed less success in spite of the important applications that depend on efficient solutions of the synthesis problem. In particular, debugging and repair are promising fields in which techniques based on synthesis algorithms have found employment [23, 25].

Recent algorithmic advances in the determinization of Büchi automata and in the solution of parity games have renewed hope that realistic systems may be synthesized from their temporal specifications. In this paper we propose a hybrid approach to this problem that combines symbolic algorithms (operating on the characteristic functions of sets) and explicit algorithms (that manipulate individual set members).

Specifications are often made up of several relatively simple components—for instance, a collection of LTL properties. If that is the case, our approach scales well because it applies the expensive explicit processing steps to the individual components of the specification, and adopts symbolic techniques where they matter most—in the solution of the final generalized parity game. Preliminary experiments demonstrate that the approach is effective in dealing with rather large systems even in its current prototypical form. For instance, we were able to synthesize an optimal Nim player from a description of the game bookkeeping and the property that requires victory from each winning position.

* This work was supported in part by SRC contract 2006-TJ-1365.

F. Logozzo et al. (Eds.): VMCAI 2008, LNCS 4905, pp. 309–323, 2008.

Our approach converts each component of the specification into either a Büchi automaton or a parity automaton of minimum index. The Büchi automaton can be nondeterministic if it fair simulates the deterministic parity automaton obtained from its determinization by Piterman's procedure. We show that in that case the parity automaton must have a parity index less than or equal to two. The reactive system implementing the specification is derived by symbolically computing the winning strategies of a nondeterministic concurrent parity game obtained by composition of the several automata.

The rest of this paper is organized as follows. Section 2 recalls the notions on ω automata and games that are pertinent to this paper. Section 3 summarizes the algorithm. Section 4 discusses algorithmic choices for symbolic implementations. Section 5 discusses related work. Section 6 presents our experiment results and Sect. 7 concludes.

2 Automata and Games

A finite automaton on ω-words $\langle \Sigma, Q, q_{\text{in}}, \delta, \alpha \rangle$ is defined by a finite alphabet Σ, a finite set of states Q, an initial state $q_{\text{in}} \in Q$, a transition function $\delta : Q \times \Sigma \to 2^Q$ that maps a state and an input letter to a set of possible successors, and an acceptance condition α that describes a subset of Q^ω, that is, a set of infinite sequences of states. A run of automaton M on ω-word $w = w_0 w_1 \dots$ is a sequence $q_0, q_1, \dots$ such that $q_0 = q_{\text{in}}$, and for $i \geq 0$, $q_{i+1} \in \delta(q_i, w_i)$. A run is accepting iff (if and only if) it belongs to the set described by α, and a word is accepted iff it has an accepting run in M. The subset of Σ^ω accepted by M is the (ω-regular) language of M. A *deterministic* automaton is such that $\delta(q, \sigma)$ is a singleton for all states $q \in Q$ and all letters $\sigma \in \Sigma$.

Several ways of specifying the acceptance condition α are in use. In this paper we are concerned with Büchi [6], co-Büchi, parity [36, 13], Rabin [40], and Streett [46] acceptance conditions. All these conditions are concerned with the sets of states that occur infinitely often in a run; for run ρ, this set is written $\mathsf{inf}(\rho)$. Büchi and co-Büchi acceptance conditions are both given as a set of states $F \subseteq Q$. A run ρ is accepting for a Büchi (co-Büchi) condition iff $\mathsf{inf}(\rho) \cap F \neq \emptyset$ ($\mathsf{inf}(\rho) \cap F = \emptyset$). A parity acceptance condition is given as a function assigning a *priority* to each state of the automaton. Letting $[k] = \{i \mid 0 \leq i < k\}$, a parity condition of index k is a function $\pi : Q \to [k]$. A run ρ is accepting iff $\max\{\pi(q) \mid q \in \mathsf{inf}(\rho)\}$ is odd; that is, if the highest recurring priority is odd.

Rabin and Streett are given as a set of pairs of sets of states: $\{(U_1, E_1), \dots, (U_k, E_k)\}$; k is called the *index* of the condition. A run ρ is accepted according to a Rabin (Streett) condition iff there exists i such that $\mathsf{inf}(\rho) \cap U_i \neq \emptyset$ and $\mathsf{inf}(\rho) \cap E_i = \emptyset$ (for all i, $\mathsf{inf}(\rho) \cap U_i = \emptyset$ or $\mathsf{inf}(\rho) \cap E_i \neq \emptyset$). Rabin and Streett acceptance conditions are complementary just as Büchi and co-Büchi are. A parity condition $\pi : Q \to [k]$ such that k is even can be easily converted to a Rabin condition with $k/2$ pairs; hence, parity conditions are also known as *Rabin chain* conditions. It is also easy to translate π to a Streett condition. A parity condition π_c complementary to π is obtained by letting $\pi_c(q) = \pi(q) + 1$ for all $q \in Q$.

Büchi, co-Büchi, and parity acceptance conditions may be *generalized*. A generalized Büchi condition consists of a collection $\mathcal{F} \subseteq 2^Q$ of Büchi conditions. A run ρ is accepting for a generalized Büchi (co-Bc̈hi) condition iff it is accepting according to each $F \in \mathcal{F}$ (some $F \in \mathcal{F}$). A generalized parity condition may be either conjunctive or disjunctive and is given as a collection Π of priority functions. A run ρ is accepting according to a conjunctive (disjunctive) condition Π iff it is accepting according to each (some) $\pi \in \Pi$. Disjunctive and conjunctive generalized parity conditions are dual in the same sense in which Rabin and Streett conditions are and extend them just as Rabin and Streett conditions extend generalized co-Büchi and Büchi conditions.[1]

An ω-regular automaton equipped with a Büchi acceptance condition is called a Büchi automaton; likewise for the other acceptance conditions. In this paper, we adopt popular three-letter abbreviations to designate different types of automata. The first letter of each abbreviation distinguishes nondeterministic (N) from deterministic (D) structures. The second letter denotes the type of acceptance condition: Büchi (B), co-Büchi (C), Rabin (R), Streett (S), and parity (P). The final letter indicates that the automata read infinite words (W). As examples, NBW designates a nondeterministic Büchi automaton (on infinite words), while DPW is the acronym for a deterministic parity automaton (also on infinite words).

Despite their similarity to automata on finite words DBWs are less expressive than NBWs and are not closed under complementation; accordingly, determinization is only possible in general by switching to a more powerful acceptance condition and complementation of NBWs cannot be accomplished by determinization followed by complementation of the acceptance condition. Piterman [37] has recently improved Safra's procedure [43] so as to produce a DPW (instead of a DRW) from an NBW. The construction extends the well-known subset construction for automata on finite words. Rather than labeling each state of the deterministic automaton with a subset of states of the NBW, it labels it with a tree of subsets. As a result, the upper bound on the number of states of the DPW derived from an NBW with n states is n^{2n+2}. This fast-growing function discourages determinization of large NBWs. Concerning determinization, it should be noted that generalizing Büchi and co-Büchi conditions provides convenience and conciseness, but does not increase expressiveness. On the other hand, generalized Büchi games, just like Streett games, do not always admit memoryless strategies, to be discussed shortly.

Linear Time Logic (LTL) [49, 31] is a popular temporal logic for the specification of nonterminating reactive systems. LTL formulae are built from a set of atomic propositions, Boolean connectives, and basic temporal operators X (next), U (until), and R (releases). Derived operators G (always) and F (eventually) are usually included for convenience. Procedures exist (e.g., [17]) to translate an LTL formula into an NBW that accepts the language defined by the formula. On the one hand, if not all ω-regular languages can be expressed in LTL, DBWs are not sufficient to translate all of LTL.[2]

Piterman's determinization procedure provides a way to find a DBW equivalent to an NBW whenever it exists. A set of states in an ω-regular automaton M is *essential* if it equals $\mathsf{inf}(\rho)$ for some run ρ of M. A *positive chain* of length m is a sequence of m essential sets $R_1 \subset \cdots \subset R_m$ such that R_i satisfies the acceptance condition of M

[1] Specifically, Rabin and Streett pairs can be seen as parity conditions with three colors, while co-Büchi and Büchi conditions can be seen as parity conditions with two colors.

[2] In fact, LTL formulae exist that describe ω-regular languages with arbitrarily large Rabin indices. [30].

iff i is odd. The *Rabin index* of an ω-regular language L is the minimum k such that there exists a DRW with k pairs recognizing L. The Rabin index $I(L)$ of language L is related to the maximal length $\Xi(M)$ of a positive chain in a deterministic automaton M_L accepting L by the equation $I(L) = \lfloor(\Xi(M_L) + 1)/2\rfloor$ [48]. Carton and Maceiras have devised an algorithm that finds $I(L)$ given a DPW that recognizes L in time $O(|Q|^2|\Sigma|)$ [9]. Moreover, every DPW M that recognizes L can be equipped with a new parity condition $\pi : Q \rightarrow [\Xi(M) + 1]$ without changing the accepted language. The following procedure therefore yields a DBW from an NBW if one exists: Convert NBW N to an equivalent DPW D by Piterman's procedure. Compute $\Xi(D)$ with the algorithm of Carton and Maceiras. If $\Xi(D) \leq 1$ the equivalent parity condition with ≤ 2 priorities computed together with $\Xi(D)$ can be interpreted as a Büchi acceptance condition; otherwise no DBW equivalent to N exists. (If $\Xi(D) = 0$, N accepts the empty language.)

Deterministic ω-regular automata can be used to define infinite games [47] in several ways. Here we consider turn-based and input-based two-player games, in which Player 0 (the *antagonist*) and Player 1 (the *protagonist*) move a token along the transitions of the automaton. If the resulting infinite sequence of states is accepted by the automaton, Player 1 wins, otherwise Player 0 wins. In *turn-based* games the set of states Q is partitioned into Q_0 (antagonist states) and Q_1 (protagonist states). Each player moves the token from its states by choosing a letter from Σ and the corresponding successor according to δ. In *input-based* games, the alphabet Σ is the Cartesian product $\Sigma_0 \times \Sigma_1$ of an antagonist alphabet and a protagonist alphabet. In state q, Player i chooses a letter $\sigma_i \in \Sigma_i$. The token is then moved to $\delta(q, (\sigma_0, \sigma_1))$. Turn-based games are games of perfect information, whereas in input-based games a player may have full, partial, or no advance knowledge of the other player's choices. The amount of information available to one player obviously affects its ability to win the game. If one player has knowledge of the move of the other, then input-based games are easily reduced to turn-based games and are therefore determinate. In our input-based games we assume that Player 1 has no advance knowledge of the other player's choices, while Player 0 sees the opponent's moves.

The existence and computation of winning strategies are central problems in the study of infinite games. A strategy is a function that defines which letter a player should choose at each move. A strategy for Player i in a turn-based game can be defined equivalently as either a function $\tau_i : Q^* \times Q_i \rightarrow \Sigma$, or as a function: $\tau_i : Q_i \times S_i \rightarrow \Sigma \times S_i$. The set S_i is the player's *memory*; according to its cardinality, strategies are classified as *infinite memory*, *finite memory*, and *memoryless* (or *positional*). For input-based games in which Player 1 plays without knowing the opponent's choices but Player 0 knows what Player 1 has chosen, a strategy for Player 1 is defined as either a function $\tau_1 : Q^* \times Q \rightarrow \Sigma_1$ or a function $\tau_1 : Q \times S_1 \rightarrow \Sigma_1 \times S_1$ and a strategy for Player 0 is defined as either a function $\tau_0 : Q^* \times Q \times \Sigma_1 \rightarrow \Sigma_0$ or a function $\tau_0 : Q \times S_0 \times \Sigma_1 \rightarrow \Sigma_0 \times S_0$. A strategy τ_i is *winning* for Player i from a given state of the automaton iff victory is secured from that state regardless of the opponent's choices if Player i plays according to τ_i.

The acceptance condition of the automaton translates into the *winning condition* of the game. We consider Büchi, co-Büchi, and parity games, their counterparts with generalized winning conditions, as well as Rabin and Streett games. All these games are *determinate* [32]; that is, from each state of the automaton if a player has no winning strategy then the opponent has a winning strategy. Büchi, co-Büchi, generalized co-Büchi, Rabin, parity, and disjunctive generalized parity games admit memoryless strategies. The others—generalized Büchi, Streett, and conjunctive generalized parity games—admit finite memory strategies [50].

If the winning condition of an infinite game is given as an LTL formula on the states of the automaton we have an *LTL game*. Such a game can be solved by translating the formula into an equivalent deterministic ω-automaton and composing it with the graph of the given automaton. As recalled above, not all LTL formulae have an equivalent DBW (or DCW for that matter). Therefore, determinization to some more powerful type of automaton is required in general. With Piterman's improvement of Safra's construction [37], the parity condition is the natural choice.

If an NBW derived from the given LTL formula is used in solving an LTL game, there is in general no guarantee that a winning solution will be found if one exists. (See [19] for an example.) Henzinger and Piterman [21, Theorem 4.1] have shown, however, that a nondeterministic automaton may still be used with the guarantee of a winning solution if it fair simulates an equivalent deterministic automaton. (This result subsumes [19, Theorem 1] about *trivially determinizable* NBWs.)

An ω-regular automaton $P = \langle \Sigma, Q_P, q_{P\text{in}}, \delta_P, \alpha_P \rangle$ *fair simulates* [20] another such automaton $A = \langle \Sigma, Q_A, q_{A\text{in}}, \delta_A, \alpha_A \rangle$ with the same alphabet if Player 1 has a winning strategy for the following turn-based game: Initially, the protagonist token is placed on $q_{P\text{in}}$ and the antagonist token is placed on $q_{A\text{in}}$. At each turn, let $p \in Q_P$ be the state with the protagonist token and let $a \in Q_A$ be the state with the antagonist token. Player 0 chooses a letter $\sigma \in \Sigma$ and moves the A token to one of the states in $\delta_A(a, \sigma)$. Player 1 then moves the P token to one of the states in $\delta_P(p, \sigma)$. Player 1 wins if either the run of A is not in α_A or the run of P is in α_P. A winning strategy for Player 1 is a function $\tau : (Q_A \times Q_P \times \Sigma)^+ \to Q_P$ that is consistent with δ_P ($\forall a \in Q_A, p \in Q_P, \sigma \in \Sigma \,.\, \tau(a, p, \sigma) \in \delta_P(p, \sigma)$) and that guarantees victory regardless of the opponent's choices.

When a game played on an ω-regular automaton has nondeterministic transitions one needs to define which player is in charge of resolving nondeterminism. In an input-based game derived from an LTL game, Player 1, whose objective is to force the run of the automaton to satisfy the LTL formula, chooses the next state from $\delta(q, (\sigma_0, \sigma_1))$. A nondeterministic automaton for a given language can be much more compact than a deterministic one. Hence, [21, Theorem 4.1] may lead to considerable savings in the computation of winning strategies. On the negative side, we offer the following theorem, which implies that an NBW can only be used if an equivalent DBW exists.

Theorem 1. *Let N be an NBW and D an equivalent DPW. Let D be of minimum index $k > 2$. Then N does not fair simulate D.*

Proof. We assume that N has a strategy τ to simulate D and show that this leads to a contradiction. Since the winning condition of the simulation game is the disjunction of two parity conditions, we can assume that τ is memoryless. Since $k > 2$ there is a chain of essential sets

$$R_1 \subset R_2 \subset \cdots \subset R_{k-1}$$

with R_{2i+1} accepting and R_{2i} rejecting. Let p be a state of D in R_1. (By the chain property, p is also in R_2.) Let $u \in \Sigma^*$ be a word that takes D from the initial state to p. Let $v \in \Sigma^* \setminus \{\epsilon\}$ be a word that takes D from p back to p while visiting all states of R_1 at least once. Finally, let $w \in \Sigma^* \setminus \{\epsilon\}$ be a word that takes D from p back to p while visiting all states of R_2 at least once. The existence of p, u, v, and w is guaranteed because R_1 and R_2 are essential sets.

We construct an ultimately periodic word x as follows. We initialize x to u and $\Gamma = \emptyset$. Let q_0^1 be the state reached by N when reading x and following τ. Append copies of v to x and extend the run of x in D and N. The run of D will reach p every time a copy of v is added. The run of N will go through states $q_1^1, q_2^1, \ldots$. Stop as soon as, for some $j > 0$ and $i < j$, $q_i^1 = q_j^1$. Call q^1 this repeating state, and add it to Γ. (Repetition is inevitable because N is finite.) Append w to x and call q_0^2 the state reached by N after running over the updated x. (D will be in p.) Now append more copies of v to x until there are j and $i < j$ such that $q_i^2 = q_j^2$. Call q^2 this repeating state. If q^2 is not in Γ add it, append w to x and repeat; otherwise stop.

This process must terminate because $|\Gamma|$ grows at each iteration. At termination, $q_i^n = q^m$ for some $q^m \in \Gamma$ and $m < n$. We let $x = yz^\omega$, with y the prefix of x up to the first occurrence of q^m and z the segment between the first and second occurrence.

D rejects x because its essential set is R_2, but accepts $x' = yv^\omega$ whose essential set is R_1. Consider now N. We know that the run of N on x' according to τ must repeatedly go through q^m. Since x' is accepted by D, the segments of the run in N between occurrences of q^m must visit some accepting state of N. However, this implies that x is also accepted because the run of x also goes through q^m when D is in p, and q^m is in Γ because it was seen twice in conjunction with p while applying v repeatedly. Since D and N are equivalent the assumption that τ exists is contradicted and the theorem is proved. □

For lack of space we do not present the extension of Theorem 1 to simulations between two arbitrary parity automata.

3 Algorithm

We describe an algorithm that takes as input a collection of LTL formulae and NBWs over an alphabet $\Sigma = \Sigma_0 \times \Sigma_1$. The input is converted into a conjunctive generalized parity game with one parity function for each formula and automaton. At each turn, Player 0 chooses a letter from Σ_0 and Player 1 chooses a letter from Σ_1. The objective of Player 1 is to satisfy the conjunctive generalized parity acceptance condition. A winning strategy for Player 1 from the initial state of the parity automaton thus corresponds to an implementation of a reactive system that reads inputs from alphabet Σ_0 and produces outputs from alphabet Σ_1. The reactive system satisfies all the linear-time properties given as LTL formulae or Büchi automata from its initial state. If no such winning strategy exists, there exists no implementation of the given specification.

As an initial step, all LTL formulae are converted to NBWs (using Wring [45]). The objective of the algorithm is to be efficient for practical specifications, which often consist of the conjunction of many simple properties. While in theory one could conjoin all the NBWs to obtain one large NBW and then determinize it, the high complexity of determinization makes this approach infeasible. Instead, each NBW that is not also a DBW is converted to a DPW individually with Piterman's procedure [37]. This keeps the size of the resulting DPWs reasonably small, as discussed in Sect. 6. A parity condition of minimum index is then computed for each DPW by the procedure of [9].

If the parity index is 2, then fair simulation between the NBW and the DPW (which is in fact in this case a DBW), is checked with the algorithm of [26] (implemented as in [14, 18]). If the DPW is simulated by the NBW, the latter replaces the former. (See Theorem 1. From a practical standpoint it should be noted that the NBW is made complete before checking for fair simulation, because otherwise the check is guaranteed to fail.) If there is no fair simulation, the DPW is optionally simplified. (This is done after reducing the index, to increase the chance of simplification.) All the processing up to this point is done by explicit (i.e., non-symbolic) algorithms. At the end of this phase, each specification has been translated into one of the following: a DBW, a DPW, or an NBW that simulates an equivalent DBW.

The next step of processing reduces the collection of automata to a generalized parity game [10]. The transition structures of the automata are converted into one symbolic transition relation—as is customary in symbolic model checking. Effective ways of avoiding blow-up in the composition of the transition relations are well-known [15, 41, 35]. The parity (or Büchi) conditions for all the automata collectively form the generalized parity condition.

We use the "classical" algorithm described in [10] to compute winning strategies for generalized parity conditions. This algorithm is based on [22], which in turn extends Zielonka's algorithm for parity conditions [50].[3] The generalized parity algorithm selects one parity condition and tries to prove all states winning for Player 1, using the maximum color from the selected priority function and recurring on a subgame for the remaining colors and parity conditions.

If Player 1 wins in all the states, the algorithm proceeds to the next parity condition. If, on the other hand, Player 0 has some winning states, the algorithm restarts on a game graph that is pruned of the winning states of Player 0.

At a given recursion level, each parity condition produces a sub-strategy for Player 1. Therefore, Player 1 uses a counter to rotate among these sub-strategies. For a fixed order in the priority conditions, the total memory required is bound by $\prod_{1 \leq i \leq k}(k-i+1)^{d_i}$, where $2d_i + 1$ is the number of colors of the i-th priority condition.

The choice of this algorithm over the dominion-based algorithm in [10, 27] is for two reasons. The first is the unsuitability of the dominion-based algorithm to symbolic implementation as discussed in Sect. 4. The second is that the dominion-based algorithm has better asymptotic bounds only when the number of colors is comparable to the number of states. However, in our application, this is seldom, if ever, the case.

The basic *attractor* computation for each player in the generalized parity algorithm is based on an extension of the MX operator discussed in [23]. Specifically, the set of

[3] The algorithm in [10] contains a bug that is easily fixed by reverting the termination condition of the inner loop to the one given in [22].

states that Player i can control to a target set of states $T \subseteq Q$ (the attractor of T for Player i) is given by:

$$\mathsf{MX}_1 T = \{q \mid \exists \sigma_1 \in \Sigma_1 \,.\, \forall \sigma_0 \in \Sigma_0 \,.\, \exists q' \in \delta(q, (\sigma_0, \sigma_1)) \,.\, q' \in T\}$$
$$\mathsf{MX}_0 T = \{q \mid \forall \sigma_1 \in \Sigma_1 \,.\, \exists \sigma_0 \in \Sigma_0 \,.\, \forall q' \in \delta(q, (\sigma_0, \sigma_1)) \,.\, q' \in T\} \ .$$

This formulation implies that Player 1 chooses σ_1 from Σ_1 first, then Player 0 chooses σ_0 from Σ_0, and finally nondeterminism is resolved in favor of Player 1. (That is, all nondeterminism is due to the NBWs representing the properties.) Since Player 1 has no knowledge of the upcoming opponent's move, it has a winning strategy only if a Moore-style implementation of the specification exists.

4 Practical Symbolic Algorithms

In the context of verification and synthesis of reactive systems, symbolic algorithms are broadly defined as those algorithms that employ characteristic functions to represent sets. The use of Binary Decision Diagrams [5] to manipulate Boolean functions, in particular, is typically associated with the idea of symbolic algorithms. Techniques like the symbolic model checking algorithm of McMillan [33] have significantly contributed to the success of formal verification thanks to their ability to deal—albeit not with uniform efficiency—with sets of size well beyond the capabilities of more conventional, explicit algorithms. While such successes encourage the use of symbolic algorithms, not all algorithms are amenable to symbolic implementation, leading to a conflict between the choice of one with lowest complexity and one that is symbolic-friendly. Our approach is to use the best algorithm in terms of worst-case complexity that is efficiently implementable in a symbolic manner. In this Section, we try to identify some algorithmic features that are best suited to symbolic implementations.

Obviously, algorithms that process the elements of a large set one by one draw only modest benefit from representing such a set symbolically and are limited to manipulating relatively small sets. Some algorithms resort to picking a (hopefully) small number of seed elements from a large set. Examples are provided by the subquadratic symbolic algorithms for Strongly Connected Component (SCC) analysis [2, 16] that grow an SCC with symbolic techniques starting from an individual seed state. (In this context, complexity refers to the number of *images* and *preimages* computed.) While these algorithms are rightfully considered symbolic, it should be noted that for cycle detection in very large graphs they tend to be outperformed by "more symbolic" algorithms based on computing a hull of the SCCs [42] in spite of their better complexity bounds. Closer to the subject of this paper, one can compare two variants of McNaughton's algorithm [34] (adapted to parity automata by Zielonka [50]) that appear in [47] and [27]. The algorithm in [27] is "more symbolic" than the one in [47] because it computes the attractor of all states of maximum priority at once instead of picking one state from that set and computing its attractor. Notice that the computation of the attractor, which is at the heart of the generalized parity algorithm, is very similar to the fixpoint computations performed in symbolic model checking, and therefore eminently suitable for symbolic implementation. Consequently, one can also leverage various techniques to speed up symbolic model checking in the implementation of the algorithms in [50, 22, 10].

Both variants of McNaughton's algorithm, on the other hand, are far more amenable to symbolic implementation than the algorithms that have superseded them in terms of asymptotic performance. Consider the small progress measure algorithm of Jurdziński [26]. If an SCC of the game graph contains a losing position, the number of iterations is bounded from below by the number of states of a certain priority in the SCC. For a large graph that number may be large enough to prevent termination in practice, even with the optimization of [12]. Another problem with the algorithm of [26] is the need to attach and manipulate a vector of integers to every state of the game graph. As the number of distinct measures increases in the course of the computation, the size of the decision diagrams representing the map from states to measures may easily blow up. Similar observations apply to the algorithms of [1] and the small dominion versions of the ones in [10, 27]. Therefore, we use an explicit implementation of the algorithm of [26] to check fair simulations of small automata derived from individual properties, but prefer the algorithm in [10] for the analysis of large games obtained compositionally.

Besides avoiding explicit enumeration of the elements of large sets, successful symbolic algorithms also limit the arity of relations that are represented symbolically. Even ternary relations, as encountered in the computation of the transitive closure of a graph, tend to impact performance significantly. Finally, the need to represent arbitrary subsets of the powerset of a large set puts a very severe limit on the size of the problems that can be handled by a symbolic algorithm. While 10^{20} states have become a rather conservative estimate of what can be done in model checking, algorithms that allocate one BDD variable to each state in a set so as to represent collections of subsets by the characteristic functions of their occurrence vectors (as required by the algorithms of [30, 21]) are limited in most cases to a hundred states or less. For such reasons we prefer an explicit implementation of Piterman's improved determinization procedure [37] to the approach of [21].

5 Related Work

In Sect. 4 we have discussed the relation and indebtedness of our work to [26, 1, 27, 22, 21, 10]. An alternative to our approach is to translate the set of parity conditions arising out of the Piterman's procedure to Streett conditions that are then converted to a single parity condition with the algorithm of [8]. However, the algorithm of [22, 10] has better worst-case complexity.

The approaches of [19] and [38, 3] are symbolic, but are restricted in the class of specifications that can be dealt with. In [38] it is noted that checking the realizability of a formula of the form

$$\bigwedge_{1 \leq i \leq m} (\mathsf{G\,F}\, J_i^1) \rightarrow \bigwedge_{1 \leq i \leq n} (\mathsf{G\,F}\, J_i^2) \ , \tag{1}$$

where each J_i^j is propositional (a generalized Reactivity(1) formula) can be done in time proportional to $(nm|\Sigma|)^3$, where Σ is the set of atomic propositions in (1). Moreover, formulae of the form

$$\bigwedge_{1 \leq i \leq p} \mathsf{G}\, B_i \ , \tag{2}$$

where the only temporal operator allowed in each B_i is the next-time operator X, effectively correspond to the description of transition relations and can be directly regarded as the description of the game graph. This second observation applies also to our approach, while a specification like (1), can be translated into a DPW with $O(mn)$ states, $O(mn|\Sigma|)$ transitions, and 3 colors. Therefore, the class of specifications handled by [38] can be handled efficiently by our algorithm, which on the other hand, can deal with full LTL.

An approach to LTL synthesis that does not require determinization was introduced in [30, 29]. An implementation is described in [24]. From an LTL formula one derives a universal co-Büchi tree automaton (UCT), and transforms it into an NBT. A witness to language nonemptiness, if it exists, corresponds to a winning strategy. While this "Safraless" approach has the same worst-case complexity as the "Safraful" approach based on determinization, its proponents claim three main advantages for it. First, that its implementation is simpler than that of the determinization procedure. Second, that the Safraless approach lends itself to symbolic implementation. Third, that optimizations can be applied at various steps of the Safraless approach to combat the state explosion. Our implementation of Piterman's procedure, however, is only a few hundred lines of code and took only a few days to write and debug. Concerning the symbolic implementation, the Safraless approach requires the manipulation of sets of sets of states. As discussed in Sect. 4, this greatly reduces the effectiveness of a symbolic implementation. The ability to apply intermediate optimizations is beneficial, and the approach is efficient when the UCT is weak. On the other hand, for strong UCT, the approach is practically unable to prove nonrealizability [24]. It appears that only a thorough experimental comparison, beyond the scope of this paper, could ascertain the relative practical strengths of the Safraless and determinization-based approaches.

The work of Jobstmann *et al.* [25] addresses the extraction of efficient implementations from the winning strategies, which is something we do not address in this paper.

Sebastiani and Tonetta [44] present a procedure that strives to produce a deterministic Büchi automaton from an LTL formula. Their approach may improve the performance of our translator by reducing the number of instances in which Piterman's determinization procedure is invoked. The procedure of [44], however, is heuristic. Consider the following LTL formula:

$$\varphi = p \wedge (p \,\mathsf{U}\, \mathsf{G}((\neg p \rightarrow \mathsf{X}\, p) \wedge (p \rightarrow \mathsf{X} \neg p))) \ .$$

Let $\psi = \mathsf{G}((\neg p \rightarrow \mathsf{X}\, p) \wedge (p \rightarrow \mathsf{X} \neg p))$ and $\theta = p \,\mathsf{U}\, \psi$. Expansion yields

$$\begin{aligned} \psi &= (p \wedge \mathsf{X}(\neg p \wedge \psi)) \vee (\neg p \wedge \mathsf{X}(p \wedge \psi)) \\ \varphi &= (p \wedge \mathsf{X}(\neg p \wedge \psi)) \vee (p \wedge \mathsf{X}\,\theta) \\ \neg p \wedge \psi &= \neg p \wedge \mathsf{X}(p \wedge \psi) \\ p \wedge \psi &= p \wedge \mathsf{X}(\neg p \wedge \psi) \\ \theta &= (p \wedge \mathsf{X}(\neg p \wedge \psi)) \vee (\neg p \wedge \mathsf{X}(p \wedge \psi)) \vee (p \wedge \mathsf{X}\,\theta) \ . \end{aligned}$$

This is a set of closed covers. The cover for φ is nondeterministic and branch postponement is not applicable. Hence, the MoDeLLA algorithm would (initially) produce a nondeterministic automaton. However, there exists a deterministic Büchi automaton for

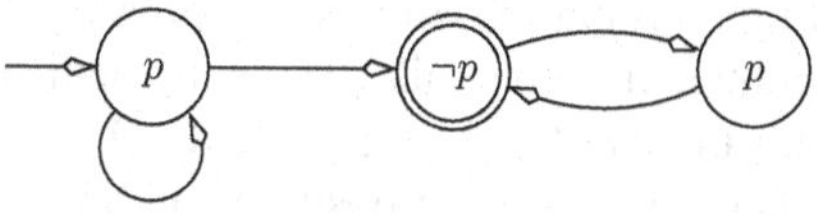

Fig. 1. Deterministic automaton for $\varphi = p \wedge (p \,\mathsf{U}\, \mathsf{G}((\neg p \rightarrow \mathsf{X}\, p) \wedge (p \rightarrow \mathsf{X} \neg p)))$

φ, shown in Fig. 1. Even though the procedure of [44] does not guarantee a deterministic automaton whenever one exists for the given LTL formula, branch postponement tends to increase the chances that the NBW will fair-simulate the DBW produced by determinization.

6 Experiments

The procedure described in Sect. 3 has been implemented as an extension of Wring [45] and Vis [4]. In this section we report on some preliminary experiments intended to test the claim of practicality and scalability of the proposed approach. Each of the following specifications was synthesized, and the the resulting model was verified against the specification. In these experiments we disabled the use of NBWs in the parity game.

Generalized Büchi. In this experiment, Player 1 seeks to satisfy a generalized Büchi condition $(\mathsf{G}\,\mathsf{F}\, b) \wedge (\mathsf{G}\,\mathsf{F}\, c)$ in a simple automaton. The strategy uses one bit of memory.

NBW7. In this experiment the specification is an NBW for $(\mathsf{F}\,\mathsf{G}\, p) \wedge (\mathsf{G}\,\mathsf{F}\, q)$. The language is not in DBW or DCW and as a result the NBW is translated into a DPW of index 3. In the game, Player 1 controls both p and q and wins from all states of the automaton. Since there is only one parity condition, the strategy is memoryless.

Simple Arbiter. Three DBWs specify this simple synchronous arbiter that grants request even if they are not persistent, guarantees fairness, and produces no spontaneous grants. Player 0 chooses the values of the two request signals and Player 1 chooses the values of the grant signals. The specification is symmetric with respect to the two clients, and the strategies computed by the program come in symmetric pairs.

Round Robin Arbiter. This experiment synthesizes an arbiter from a collection of 10 safety properties from [28]. This is a more detailed specification than the one of the simple arbiter, as it prescribes, for example, how ties should be broken. Once again, Player 1 controls the grant signals, while the opponent controls the requests.

Combination Lock. In this experiment the objective is to synthesize the finite state machine controller of a combination lock. Given a counter that can be incremented or decremented by a user and represents the dial of the lock, and a set of seven properties that prescribe that the lock opens iff the correct combination is entered, Player 1 seeks a strategy for the update of the control machine of the lock, while Player 0 operates the counter under a fairness constraint.

Nim Player. The game of Nim is played with several piles of counters. A move consists of taking one or more counters from one pile. The player who removes the last counter wins. The Sprague-Grundy theory of impartial games applies to it and it is known which player has a winning strategy from a given position and how to play according to such strategy. In this experiment, the specification is split between a model that does the game bookkeeping and plays one side of the game, and an LTL property:

$$\mathsf{G}((\neg \mathtt{turn} \wedge \mathtt{winning}) \rightarrow \mathsf{F}\,\mathtt{win}) \ ,$$

which says that when the environment moves from a winning position, it always wins. Satisfying this property entails synthesizing an optimal player. The bookkeeper has a fixed number of piles, but chooses nondeterministically how many counters to place on each pile at the start of a play. This choice is given to Player 0 in the game, while Player 1 plays the environment.

Table 1. Experimental data

name	Spec		Int		colors	bits	σ		σ_o		CPU (s)	
	LTL	NBW	DBW	DPW			edges	nodes	edges	nodes	pp	sol
GB	0	2	2	0	4	1	10	8	8	3	0	0
NBW7	0	1	0	1	3	0	10	7	6	1	0	0
simple	0	3	3	0	6	6	44	53	398	12	0	0.01
rrobin	10	0	10	0	20	17	250	112	16588800	66	13.55	0.1
lock	7	0	5	2	16	13	3196	302	1277280	178	2.71	1.35
nim	0	1	1	0	2	1	8.29e+11	3410	1.87e+11	298	0	22.63

The results of the experiments are summarized in Table 1. For each game the number of LTL formulae and NBWs in the specification are given, followed by two columns that give the statistics of processing each formula or automaton. The remaining columns describe the resulting generalized parity game and its solution by reporting the total number of different priorities (or colors) of the parity acceptance condition, the number of binary state variables of the strategy automaton, the number of edges in the union of all winning strategies computed for Player 1 (σ), the size of the corresponding BDD, the number of edges in an optimized winning strategy (σ_o), and the size of the corresponding BDD. Finally, the time to preprocess (pp) and solve the game and compute the optimized strategy (sol) is given. (The optimization of the strategy [3] never takes more than 0.17 s in the experiments of Table 1.) The number of edges in the optimized strategy may be higher than in the bundle of strategy returned by the algorithm because edges from positions that are losing for Player 1 may be added if they help reduce the size of the BDD. Our algorithm does not yet optimize the number of bits in the strategy automaton, which is therefore far from optimal.

7 Conclusion

We have presented an algorithm for the computation of strategies for LTL games and, in general, for games whose winning conditions are given by a set of LTL formulae and Büchi automata. The solution involves determinization, but only on the individual components of the specification. Since these components are typically small, our approach appears to scale well and is capable of handling games with large numbers of states. To that effect symbolic techniques are applied where it matters most—after the individual automata have been composed. The initial experimental results encourage us to continue in the development of this algorithm so that it may address larger and more realistic problems.

References

[1] Björklund, H., Sandberg, S., Vorobyov, S.: A discrete subexponential algorithm for parity games. In: Alt, H., Habib, M. (eds.) STACS 2003. LNCS, vol. 2607, pp. 663–674. Springer, Heidelberg (2003)

[2] Bloem, R., Gabow, H.N., Somenzi, F.: An algorithm for strongly connected component analysis in $n \log n$ symbolic steps. In: Johnson, S.D., Hunt Jr., W.A. (eds.) FMCAD 2000. LNCS, vol. 1954, pp. 37–54. Springer, Heidelberg (2000)

[3] Bloem, R., et al.: Specify, compile, run: Hardware form PSL. In: 6th International Workshop on Compiler Optimization Meets Compiler Verification. Electronic Notes in Theoretical Computer Science (2007), `http://www.entcs.org/`

[4] Brayton, R.K., et al.: VIS: A system for verification and synthesis. In: Alur, R., Henzinger, T.A. (eds.) CAV 1996. LNCS, vol. 1102, pp. 428–432. Springer, Heidelberg (1996)

[5] Bryant, R.E.: Graph-based algorithms for Boolean function manipulation. IEEE Transactions on Computers C-35(8), 677–691 (1986)

[6] Büchi, J.R.: On a decision method in restricted second order arithmetic. In: Proceedings of the 1960 International Congress on Logic, Methodology, and Philosophy of Science, pp. 1–11. Stanford University Press (1962)

[7] Büchi, J.R., Landweber, L.H.: Solving sequential conditions by finite-state strategies. Trans. Amer. Math. Soc. 138, 295–311 (1969)

[8] Buhrke, N., Lescow, H., Vöge, J.: Strategy construction in infinite games with Streett and Rabin chain winning conditions. In: Margaria, T., Steffen, B. (eds.) TACAS 1996. LNCS, vol. 1055, pp. 207–225. Springer, Heidelberg (1996)

[9] Carton, O., Maceiras, R.: Computing the Rabin index of a parity automaton. Theoretical Informatics and Applications 33, 495–505 (1999)

[10] Chatterjee, K., Henzinger, T.A., Piterman, N.: Generalized Parity Games. In: Seidl, H. (ed.) FOSSACS 2007. LNCS, vol. 4423, pp. 153–167. Springer, Heidelberg (2007)

[11] Clarke, E.M., Emerson, E.A.: Design and synthesis of synchronization skeletons using branching time temporal logic. In: Kozen, D. (ed.) Logic of Programs 1981. LNCS, vol. 131, pp. 52–71. Springer, Heidelberg (1982)

[12] de Alfaro, L., Faella, M.: Accelerated algorithms for 3-color parity games with an application to timed games. In: Damm, W., Hermanns, H. (eds.) CAV 2007. LNCS, vol. 4590, pp. 108–120. Springer, Heidelberg (2007)

[13] Emerson, E.A., Jutla, C.S.: Tree automata, mu-calculus and determinacy. In: Proc. 32nd IEEE Symposium on Foundations of Computer Science. pp. 368–377 (October 1991)

[14] Etessami, K., Wilke, T., Schuller, A.: Fair Simulation Relations, Parity Games, and State Space Reduction for Büchi Automata. In: Orejas, F., Spirakis, P.G., van Leeuwen, J. (eds.) ICALP 2001. LNCS, vol. 2076, Springer, Heidelberg (2001)

[15] Geist, D., Beer, I.: Efficient model checking by automated ordering of transition relation partitions. In: Dill, D.L. (ed.) CAV 1994. LNCS, vol. 818, pp. 299–310. Springer, Heidelberg (1994)

[16] Gentilini, R., Piazza, C., Policriti, A.: Computing strongly connected componenets in a linear number of symbolic steps. In: Symposium on Discrete Algorithms, Baltimore, MD (January 2003)
[17] Gerth, R., et al.: Simple on-the-fly automatic verification of linear temporal logic. In: Protocol Specification, Testing, and Verification, pp. 3–18. Chapman and Hall, Boca Raton (1995)
[18] Gurumurthy, S., Bloem, R., Somenzi, F.: Fair Simulation Minimization. In: Brinksma, E., Larsen, K.G. (eds.) CAV 2002. LNCS, vol. 2404, Springer, Heidelberg (2002)
[19] Harding, A., Ryan, M., Schobbens, P.-Y.: A new algorithm for strategy synthesis in LTL games. In: Halbwachs, N., Zuck, L.D. (eds.) TACAS 2005. LNCS, vol. 3440, pp. 477–492. Springer, Heidelberg (2005)
[20] Henzinger, T., Kupferman, O., Rajamani, S.: Fair simulation. In: Mazurkiewicz, A., Winkowski, J. (eds.) CONCUR 1997. LNCS, vol. 1243, pp. 273–287. Springer, Heidelberg (1997)
[21] Henzinger, T.A., Piterman, N.: Solving games without determinization. In: Ésik, Z. (ed.) CSL 2006. LNCS, vol. 4207, pp. 394–409. Springer, Heidelberg (2006)
[22] Horn, F.: Streett games on finite graphs. In: Workshop on Games in Design and Verification, Edimburgh, UK (July 2005)
[23] Jin, H., Ravi, K., Somenzi, F.: Fate and free will in error traces. Software Tools for Technology Transfer 6(2), 102–116 (2004)
[24] Jobstmann, B., Bloem, R.: Optimizations for LTL synthesis. In: Formal Methods in Computer Aided Design (FMCAD 2006), San Jose, CA, pp. 117–124 (November 2006)
[25] Jobstmann, B., Griesmayer, A., Bloem, R.: Program repair as a game. In: Etessami, K., Rajamani, S.K. (eds.) CAV 2005. LNCS, vol. 3576, pp. 226–238. Springer, Heidelberg (2005)
[26] Jurdziński, M.: Small progress measures for solving parity games. In: Reichel, H., Tison, S. (eds.) STACS 2000. LNCS, vol. 1770, pp. 290–301. Springer, Heidelberg (2000)
[27] Jurdziński, M., Paterson, M., Zwick, U.: A deterministic subexponential algorithm for solving parity games. In: Proceedings of ACM-SIAM Symposium on Discrete Algorithms, SODA 2006, Miami, FL, pp. 117–123 (January 2006)
[28] Katz, S., Grumberg, O., Geist, D.: Have I written enough properties?" — A method of comparison between specification and implementation. In: Pierre, L., Kropf, T. (eds.) CHARME 1999. LNCS, vol. 1703, pp. 280–297. Springer, Heidelberg (1999)
[29] Kupferman, O., Piterman, N., Vardi, M.Y.: Safraless compositional synthesis. In: Ball, T., Jones, R.B. (eds.) CAV 2006. LNCS, vol. 4144, pp. 31–44. Springer, Heidelberg (2006)
[30] Kupferman, O., Vardi, M.Y.: Safraless decision procedures. In: Foundations of Computer Science, Pittsburgh, PA, pp. 531–542 (October 2005)
[31] Lichtenstein, O., Pnueli, A.: Checking that finite state concurrent programs satisfy their linear specification. In: Proceedings of the Twelfth Annual ACM Symposium on Principles of Programming Languages, New Orleans, pp. 97–107 (January 1985)
[32] Martin, D.A.: Borel determinacy. Annals of Mathematics 102, 363–371 (1975)
[33] McMillan, K.L.: Symbolic Model Checking. Kluwer Academic Publishers, Boston (1994)
[34] McNaughton, R.: Infinite games played on finite graphs. Annals of Pure and Applied Logic 65, 149–184 (1993)
[35] Moon, I.-H., Hachtel, G.D., Somenzi, F.: Border-block triangular form and conjunction schedule in image computation. In: Johnson, S.D., Hunt Jr., W.A. (eds.) FMCAD 2000. LNCS, vol. 1954, pp. 73–90. Springer, Heidelberg (2000)
[36] Mostowski, A.W.: Regular expressions for infinite trees and a standard form of automata. In: Skowron, A. (ed.) SCT 1984. LNCS, vol. 208, pp. 157–168. Springer, Heidelberg (1985)

[37] Piterman, N.: From nondeterministic Büchi and Streett automata to deterministic parity automata. In: 21st Symposium on Logic in Computer Science, Seattle, WA, pp. 255–264 (August 2006)

[38] Piterman, N., Pnueli, A., Sa'ar, Y.: Synthesis of reactive(1) designs. In: Emerson, E.A., Namjoshi, K.S. (eds.) VMCAI 2006. LNCS, vol. 3855, pp. 364–380. Springer, Heidelberg (2005)

[39] Pnueli, A., Rosner, R.: On the synthesis of a reactive module. In: Proc. Symposium on Principles of Programming Languages (POPL 1989), pp. 179–190 (1989)

[40] Rabin, M.O.: Automata on Infinite Objects and Church's Problem. In: Regional Conference Series in Mathematics, American Mathematical Society, Providence (1972)

[41] Ranjan, R.K., et al.: Efficient BDD algorithms for FSM synthesis and verification. In: Presented at IWLS 1995, Lake Tahoe, CA (May 1995)

[42] Ravi, K., Bloem, R., Somenzi, F.: A comparative study of symbolic algorithms for the computation of fair cycles. In: Johnson, S.D., Hunt Jr, W.A. (eds.) FMCAD 2000. LNCS, vol. 1954, pp. 143–160. Springer, Heidelberg (2000)

[43] Safra, S.: Complexity of Automata on Infinite Objects. PhD thesis, The Weizmann Institute of Science (March 1989)

[44] Sebastiani, R., Tonetta, S.: More deterministic" vs. "smaller" Büchi automata for efficient LTL model checking. In: Geist, D., Tronci, E. (eds.) CHARME 2003. LNCS, vol. 2860, pp. 126–140. Springer, Heidelberg (2003)

[45] Somenzi, F., Bloem, R.: Efficient Büchi automata from LTL formulae. In: Emerson, E.A., Sistla, A.P. (eds.) CAV 2000. LNCS, vol. 1855, pp. 248–263. Springer, Heidelberg (2000)

[46] Streett, R.S.: Propositional dynamic logic of looping and converse is elementarily decidable. Information and Control 54, 121–141 (1982)

[47] Thomas, W.: On the synthesis of strategies in infinite games. In: Mayr, E.W., Puech, C. (eds.) STACS 1995. LNCS, vol. 900, pp. 1–13. Springer, Heidelberg (1995)

[48] Wagner, K.: On ω-regular sets. Information and Control 43(2), 123–177 (1979)

[49] Wolper, P., Vardi, M.Y., Sistla, A.P.: Reasoning about infinite computation paths. In: Proceedings of the 24th IEEE Symposium on Foundations of Computer Science, pp. 185–194 (1983)

[50] Zielonka, W.: Infinite games on finitely coloured graphs with applications to automata on infinite trees. Theoretical Computer Science 200(1–2), 135–183 (1998)

Author Index

Author Index

Lecture Notes in Computer Science

Sublibrary 1: Theoretical Computer Science and General Issues

For information about Vols. 1–4600
please contact your bookseller or Springer

Vol. 4934: U. Brinkschulte, T. Ungerer, C. Hochberger, R.G. Spallek (Eds.), Architecture of Computing Systems - ARCS 2008. XI, 287 pages. 2008.

Vol. 4927: C. Kaklamanis, M. Skutella (Eds.), Approximation and Online Algorithms. X, 289 pages. 2008.

Vol. 4921: S.-i. Nakano, M.. S. Rahman (Eds.), WALCOM: Algorithms and Computation. XII, 241 pages. 2008.

Vol. 4919: A. Gelbukh (Ed.), Computational Linguistics and Intelligent Text Processing. XVIII, 666 pages. 2008.

Vol. 4917: P. Stenström, M. Dubois, M. Katevenis, R. Gupta, T. Ungerer (Eds.), High Performance Embedded Architectures and Compilers. XIII, 400 pages. 2008.

Vol. 4910: V. Geffert, J. Karhumäki, A. Bertoni, B. Preneel, P. Návrat, M. Bieliková (Eds.), SOFSEM 2008: Theory and Practice of Computer Science. XV, 792 pages. 2008.

Vol. 4905: F. Logozzo, D.A. Peled, L.D. Zuck (Eds.), Verification, Model Checking, and Abstract Interpretation. X, 325 pages. 2008.

Vol. 4904: S. Rao, M. Chatterjee, P. Jayanti, C.S.R. Murthy, S.K. Saha (Eds.), Distributed Computing and Networking. XVIII, 588 pages. 2007.

Vol. 4878: E. Tovar, P. Tsigas, H. Fouchal (Eds.), Principles of Distributed Systems. XIII, 457 pages. 2007.

Vol. 4875: S.-H. Hong, T. Nishizeki, W. Quan (Eds.), Graph Drawing. XIII, 402 pages. 2008.

Vol. 4873: S. Aluru, M. Parashar, R. Badrinath, V.K. Prasanna (Eds.), High Performance Computing – HiPC 2007. XXIV, 663 pages. 2007.

Vol. 4863: A. Bonato, F.R.K. Chung (Eds.), Algorithms and Models for the Web-Graph. X, 217 pages. 2007.

Vol. 4860: G. Eleftherakis, P. Kefalas, G. Păun, G. Rozenberg, A. Salomaa (Eds.), Membrane Computing. IX, 453 pages. 2007.

Vol. 4855: V. Arvind, S. Prasad (Eds.), FSTTCS 2007: Foundations of Software Technology and Theoretical Computer Science. XIV, 558 pages. 2007.

Vol. 4851: S. Boztaş, H.-F.(F.) Lu (Eds.), Applied Algebra, Algebraic Algorithms and Error-Correcting Codes. XII, 368 pages. 2007.

Vol. 4848: M.H. Garzon, H. Yan (Eds.), DNA Computing. XI, 292 pages. 2008.

Vol. 4847: M. Xu, Y. Zhan, J. Cao, Y. Liu (Eds.), Advanced Parallel Processing Technologies. XIX, 767 pages. 2007.

Vol. 4846: I. Cervesato (Ed.), Advances in Computer Science – ASIAN 2007. XI, 313 pages. 2007.

Vol. 4838: T. Masuzawa, S. Tixeuil (Eds.), Stabilization, Safety, and Security of Distributed Systems. XIII, 409 pages. 2007.

Vol. 4835: T. Tokuyama (Ed.), Algorithms and Computation. XVII, 929 pages. 2007.

Vol. 4800: A. Avron, N. Dershowitz, A. Rabinovich (Eds.), Pillars of Computer Science. XXI, 683 pages. 2008.

Vol. 4783: J. Holub, J. Žďárek (Eds.), Implementation and Application of Automata. XIII, 324 pages. 2007.

Vol. 4782: R. Perrott, B.M. Chapman, J. Subhlok, R.F. de Mello, L.T. Yang (Eds.), High Performance Computing and Communications. XIX, 823 pages. 2007.

Vol. 4771: T. Bartz-Beielstein, M.J. Blesa Aguilera, C. Blum, B. Naujoks, A. Roli, G. Rudolph, M. Sampels (Eds.), Hybrid Metaheuristics. X, 202 pages. 2007.

Vol. 4770: V.G. Ganzha, E.W. Mayr, E.V. Vorozhtsov (Eds.), Computer Algebra in Scientific Computing. XIII, 460 pages. 2007.

Vol. 4769: A. Brandstädt, D. Kratsch, H. Müller (Eds.), Graph-Theoretic Concepts in Computer Science. XIII, 341 pages. 2007.

Vol. 4763: J.-F. Raskin, P.S. Thiagarajan (Eds.), Formal Modeling and Analysis of Timed Systems. X, 369 pages. 2007.

Vol. 4759: J. Labarta, K. Joe, T. Sato (Eds.), High-Performance Computing. XV, 524 pages. 2008.

Vol. 4746: A. Bondavalli, F. Brasileiro, S. Rajsbaum (Eds.), Dependable Computing. XV, 239 pages. 2007.

Vol. 4743: P. Thulasiraman, X. He, T.L. Xu, M.K. Denko, R.K. Thulasiram, L.T. Yang (Eds.), Frontiers of High Performance Computing and Networking ISPA 2007 Workshops. XXIX, 536 pages. 2007.

Vol. 4742: I. Stojmenovic, R.K. Thulasiram, L.T. Yang, W. Jia, M. Guo, R.F. de Mello (Eds.), Parallel and Distributed Processing and Applications. XX, 995 pages. 2007.

Vol. 4739: R. Moreno Díaz, F. Pichler, A. Quesada Arencibia (Eds.), Computer Aided Systems Theory – EUROCAST 2007. XIX, 1233 pages. 2007.

Vol. 4736: S. Winter, M. Duckham, L. Kulik, B. Kuipers (Eds.), Spatial Information Theory. XV, 455 pages. 2007.

Vol. 4732: K. Schneider, J. Brandt (Eds.), Theorem Proving in Higher Order Logics. IX, 401 pages. 2007.

Vol. 4731: A. Pelc (Ed.), Distributed Computing. XVI, 510 pages. 2007.

Vol. 4728: S. Bozapalidis, G. Rahonis (Eds.), Algebraic Informatics. VIII, 291 pages. 2007.

Vol. 4726: N. Ziviani, R. Baeza-Yates (Eds.), String Processing and Information Retrieval. XII, 311 pages. 2007.

Vol. 4719: R. Backhouse, J. Gibbons, R. Hinze, J. Jeuring (Eds.), Datatype-Generic Programming. XI, 369 pages. 2007.

Vol. 4711: C.B. Jones, Z. Liu, J. Woodcock (Eds.), Theoretical Aspects of Computing – ICTAC 2007. XI, 483 pages. 2007.

Vol. 4710: C.W. George, Z. Liu, J. Woodcock (Eds.), Domain Modeling and the Duration Calculus. XI, 237 pages. 2007.

Vol. 4708: L. Kučera, A. Kučera (Eds.), Mathematical Foundations of Computer Science 2007. XVIII, 764 pages. 2007.

Vol. 4707: O. Gervasi, M.L. Gavrilova (Eds.), Computational Science and Its Applications – ICCSA 2007, Part III. XXIV, 1205 pages. 2007.

Vol. 4706: O. Gervasi, M.L. Gavrilova (Eds.), Computational Science and Its Applications – ICCSA 2007, Part II. XXIII, 1129 pages. 2007.

Vol. 4705: O. Gervasi, M.L. Gavrilova (Eds.), Computational Science and Its Applications – ICCSA 2007, Part I. XLIV, 1169 pages. 2007.

Vol. 4703: L. Caires, V.T. Vasconcelos (Eds.), CONCUR 2007 – Concurrency Theory. XIII, 507 pages. 2007.

Vol. 4700: C.B. Jones, Z. Liu, J. Woodcock (Eds.), Formal Methods and Hybrid Real-Time Systems. XVI, 539 pages. 2007.

Vol. 4699: B. Kågström, E. Elmroth, J. Dongarra, J. Waśniewski (Eds.), Applied Parallel Computing. XXIX, 1192 pages. 2007.

Vol. 4698: L. Arge, M. Hoffmann, E. Welzl (Eds.), Algorithms – ESA 2007. XV, 769 pages. 2007.

Vol. 4697: L. Choi, Y. Paek, S. Cho (Eds.), Advances in Computer Systems Architecture. XIII, 400 pages. 2007.

Vol. 4688: K. Li, M. Fei, G.W. Irwin, S. Ma (Eds.), Bio-Inspired Computational Intelligence and Applications. XIX, 805 pages. 2007.

Vol. 4684: L. Kang, Y. Liu, S. Zeng (Eds.), Evolvable Systems: From Biology to Hardware. XIV, 446 pages. 2007.

Vol. 4683: L. Kang, Y. Liu, S. Zeng (Eds.), Advances in Computation and Intelligence. XVII, 663 pages. 2007.

Vol. 4681: D.-S. Huang, L. Heutte, M. Loog (Eds.), Advanced Intelligent Computing Theories and Applications. XXVI, 1379 pages. 2007.

Vol. 4672: K. Li, C. Jesshope, H. Jin, J.-L. Gaudiot (Eds.), Network and Parallel Computing. XVIII, 558 pages. 2007.

Vol. 4671: V.E. Malyshkin (Ed.), Parallel Computing Technologies. XIV, 635 pages. 2007.

Vol. 4669: J.M. de Sá, L.A. Alexandre, W. Duch, D.P. Mandic (Eds.), Artificial Neural Networks – ICANN 2007, Part II. XXXI, 990 pages. 2007.

Vol. 4668: J.M. de Sá, L.A. Alexandre, W. Duch, D.P. Mandic (Eds.), Artificial Neural Networks – ICANN 2007, Part I. XXXI, 978 pages. 2007.

Vol. 4666: M.E. Davies, C.J. James, S.A. Abdallah, M.D. Plumbley (Eds.), Independent Component Analysis and Signal Separation. XIX, 847 pages. 2007.

Vol. 4665: J. Hromkovič, R. Královič, M. Nunkesser, P. Widmayer (Eds.), Stochastic Algorithms: Foundations and Applications. X, 167 pages. 2007.

Vol. 4664: J. Durand-Lose, M. Margenstern (Eds.), Machines, Computations, and Universality. X, 325 pages. 2007.

Vol. 4661: U. Montanari, D. Sannella, R. Bruni (Eds.), Trustworthy Global Computing. X, 339 pages. 2007.

Vol. 4649: V. Diekert, M.V. Volkov, A. Voronkov (Eds.), Computer Science – Theory and Applications. XIII, 420 pages. 2007.

Vol. 4647: R. Martin, M.A. Sabin, J.R. Winkler (Eds.), Mathematics of Surfaces XII. IX, 509 pages. 2007.

Vol. 4646: J. Duparc, T.A. Henzinger (Eds.), Computer Science Logic. XIV, 600 pages. 2007.

Vol. 4644: N. Azémard, L. Svensson (Eds.), Integrated Circuit and System Design. XIV, 583 pages. 2007.

Vol. 4641: A.-M. Kermarrec, L. Bougé, T. Priol (Eds.), Euro-Par 2007 Parallel Processing. XXVII, 974 pages. 2007.

Vol. 4639: E. Csuhaj-Varjú, Z. Ésik (Eds.), Fundamentals of Computation Theory. XIV, 508 pages. 2007.

Vol. 4638: T. Stützle, M. Birattari, H. H. Hoos (Eds.), Engineering Stochastic Local Search Algorithms. X, 223 pages. 2007.

Vol. 4630: H.J. van den Herik, P. Ciancarini, H.H.L.M.(J.) Donkers (Eds.), Computers and Games. XII, 283 pages. 2007.

Vol. 4628: L.N. de Castro, F.J. Von Zuben, H. Knidel (Eds.), Artificial Immune Systems. XII, 438 pages. 2007.

Vol. 4627: M. Charikar, K. Jansen, O. Reingold, J.D.P. Rolim (Eds.), Approximation, Randomization, and Combinatorial Optimization. XII, 626 pages. 2007.

Vol. 4624: T. Mossakowski, U. Montanari, M. Haveraaen (Eds.), Algebra and Coalgebra in Computer Science. XI, 463 pages. 2007.

Vol. 4623: M. Collard (Ed.), Ontologies-Based Databases and Information Systems. X, 153 pages. 2007.

Vol. 4621: D. Wagner, R. Wattenhofer (Eds.), Algorithms for Sensor and Ad Hoc Networks. XIII, 415 pages. 2007.

Vol. 4619: F. Dehne, J.-R. Sack, N. Zeh (Eds.), Algorithms and Data Structures. XVI, 662 pages. 2007.

Vol. 4618: S.G. Akl, C.S. Calude, M.J. Dinneen, G. Rozenberg, H.T. Wareham (Eds.), Unconventional Computation. X, 243 pages. 2007.

Vol. 4616: A.W.M. Dress, Y. Xu, B. Zhu (Eds.), Combinatorial Optimization and Applications. XI, 390 pages. 2007.

Vol. 4614: B. Chen, M. Paterson, G. Zhang (Eds.), Combinatorics, Algorithms, Probabilistic and Experimental Methodologies. XII, 530 pages. 2007.

Vol. 4613: F.P. Preparata, Q. Fang (Eds.), Frontiers in Algorithmics. XI, 348 pages. 2007.